# STRATEGIES
## FOR
## ACHIEVING
## COMMUNITY INTEGRATION
## OF
## DEVELOPMENTALLY DISABLED
## CITIZENS

edited by

**K. Charlie Lakin, Ph.D.**
and
**Robert H. Bruininks, Ph.D.**
*Department of Educational Psychology*
*University of Minnesota*

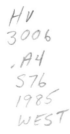
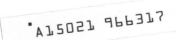

·P A U L·H·
BROOKES
PUBLISHING Cº

Baltimore · London

**Paul H. Brookes Publishing Co.**
Post Office Box 10624
Baltimore, Maryland 21204

Typeset by The Composing Room of Michigan, Inc. (Grand Rapids).
Manufactured in the United States of America by
The Maple Press Company (York, Pennsylvania).

**Library of Congress Cataloging in Publication Data**
Main entry under title:

Strategies for achieving community integration of developmentally disabled citizens.

Bibliography: p.
Includes index.
1. Developmentally disabled—United States—Addresses, essays,
lectures.   2. Developmentally disabled—Services for—United States—Addresses,
essays, lectures.   3. Developmentally disabled—Education—United States—
Addresses, essays, lectures.   4. Social integration—United States—Addresses,
essays, lectures.   5. Community life—Addresses, essays, lectures.   I. Lakin, K.
Charlie.   II. Bruininks, Robert H.
HV3006.A4S76   1985        362.4'048'0973        84–23863
ISBN 0–933716–43–5

# Contents

Contributors . . . . . . . . . . . . . . . . . . . . . . . . . . . . . . . . . . . . . . . . . . . . . . . . . . . . . . . . . . . . . . . . . vii
Preface . . . . . . . . . . . . . . . . . . . . . . . . . . . . . . . . . . . . . . . . . . . . . . . . . . . . . . . . . . . . . . . . . . . . . . xi
Acknowledgments . . . . . . . . . . . . . . . . . . . . . . . . . . . . . . . . . . . . . . . . . . . . . . . . . . . . . . . . . xiii

Part I      **Introduction** . . . . . . . . . . . . . . . . . . . . . . . . . . . . . . . . . . . . . . . . . . . . . . . .      1
   Chapter 1      Social Integration of Developmentally Disabled Persons
                *K. Charlie Lakin and Robert H. Bruininks* . . . . . . . . . . . . . . . . . . . . .      3

Part II      **Assessment and Intervention Strategies** . . . . . . . . . . . . . . . . . . . . . . .     27
   Chapter 2      Enhancing Instruction for Maintenance, Generalization, and
             Adaptation
                *Kathleen A. Liberty* . . . . . . . . . . . . . . . . . . . . . . . . . . . . . . . . . . . . . .     29
   Chapter 3      Assessing and Training Adaptive Behaviors
                *Julie Gorder Holman and Robert H. Bruininks* . . . . . . . . . . . . . . . . .     73
   Chapter 4      Assessing and Managing Problem Behaviors
                *Lanny E. Morreau* . . . . . . . . . . . . . . . . . . . . . . . . . . . . . . . . . . . . . . . .    105
   Chapter 5      Early Education: A Strategy for Producing a Less (Least)
             Restrictive Environment for Young Children with Severe
             Handicaps
                *John E. Rynders and Darlene S. Stealey* . . . . . . . . . . . . . . . . . . . . .    129

Part III      **Vocational Preparation and Employment** . . . . . . . . . . . . . . . . . . . . . . .    159
   Chapter 6      Programming for the Transition to Independent Living for
             Mildly Retarded Persons
                *Daniel W. Close, Jo-Ann Sowers, Andrew S. Halpern, and*
                *Philip E. Bourbeau* . . . . . . . . . . . . . . . . . . . . . . . . . . . . . . . . . . . . . . .    161
   Chapter 7      Competitive Employment Education: A Systems-Analytic
             Approach to Transitional Programming for the Student with
             Severe Handicaps
                *Frank R. Rusch and Dennis E. Mithaug* . . . . . . . . . . . . . . . . . . . . . .    177
   Chapter 8      Impact of Federal Programs on Employment of Mentally
             Retarded Persons
                *Ronald W. Conley* . . . . . . . . . . . . . . . . . . . . . . . . . . . . . . . . . . . . . . . .    193

Part IV      **Managing and Enhancing Integration** . . . . . . . . . . . . . . . . . . . . . . . . . .    217
   Chapter 9      Moving Persons with Developmental Disabilities toward Less
             Restrictive Environments through Case Management
                *Lyle Wray and Colleen Wieck* . . . . . . . . . . . . . . . . . . . . . . . . . . . . . . .    219

Chapter 10   School Integration Strategies
            *Luanna H. Meyer and Gloria Shizue Kishi* . . . . . . . . . . . . . . . . . . . . . . .   231
Chapter 11   Leisure and Recreation Services for Handicapped Persons
            *JoAnne W. Putnam, Judy K. Werder, and Stuart J. Schleien* . . . . . . . .   253

Part V      **Organizational and Fiscal Issues** . . . . . . . . . . . . . . . . . . . . . . . . . . . . . . . .   275
Chapter 12   A Behavior Analytic Approach to Community Integration of
            Persons with Developmental Disabilities
            *Travis Thompson and Lyle Wray* . . . . . . . . . . . . . . . . . . . . . . . . . . . . .   277
Chapter 13   Developing Financial Incentives for Placement in the Least
            Restrictive Alternative
            *William C. Copeland and Iver A. Iversen* . . . . . . . . . . . . . . . . . . . . . . .   291
Chapter 14   Challenges to Advocates of Social Integration of
            Developmentally Disabled Persons
            *K. Charlie Lakin and Robert H. Bruininks* . . . . . . . . . . . . . . . . . . . . . . .   313

Index . . . . . . . . . . . . . . . . . . . . . . . . . . . . . . . . . . . . . . . . . . . . . . . . . . . . . . . . . . . . . .   331

# Contributors

**Philip E. Bourbeau, Ph.D.,** Rehabilitation Research and Training Center in Mental Retardation, University of Oregon, Clinical Services Building, Eugene, Oregon 97403

Philip E. Bourbeau is currently research coordinator of the Administrative Support Functions Project, Direct Instruction Follow-Through Program, University of Oregon. He was formerly a teaching fellow at the Rehabilitation Research and Training Center in Mental Retardation, University of Oregon. He has been involved in the design, management, and evaluation of community-based programs for developmentally disabled persons for many years.

**Robert H. Bruininks, Ph.D.,** Department of Educational Psychology, University of Minnesota, 204 Burton Hall, 178 Pillsbury Drive, Minneapolis, Minnesota 55455

Robert H. Bruininks is Chairman of the Department of Educational Psychology at the University of Minnesota. He has conducted numerous studies and published widely on the impact of public policies in the areas of deinstitutionalization and public education for handicapped children and youth.

**Daniel W. Close, Ph.D.,** Rehabilitation Research and Training Center in Mental Retardation, University of Oregon, Clinical Services Building, Eugene, Oregon 97403

Daniel W. Close is an assistant professor and Director of Clinical Services for the Rehabilitation Research and Training Center in Mental Retardation at the University of Oregon. His research interests include assessment of learning potential, curriculum development in life-styles, program development in postsecondary and independent living areas, and community and semi-independent living arrangements for mentally retarded and other developmentally disabled persons.

**Ronald W. Conley, Ph.D.,** Board and Care Coordinating Unit, Administration on Developmental Disabilities, Office of Human Development Services, U.S. Department of Health and Human Services, Room 339 F.1 Hubert Humphrey Building, 200 Independence Avenue, S.W., Washington, D.C. 20201

Ronald W. Conley is a senior program analyst with the U.S. Department of Health and Human Services. In recent years he has worked primarily in the area of residential housing for disabled and elderly people. He recently prepared a monograph entitled, *Workers' Compensation: Challenge for the 80's* and edited six other research volumes dealing with workers' compensation and the economics of mental retardation.

**William C. Copeland,** Copeland Associates, 1005 W. Franklin Avenue, Minneapolis, Minnesota 55407

William C. Copeland is president of Copeland Associates, Minneapolis, Minnesota. He has consulted with a large number of state governments on human services financing problems, as well as with the Office of Management and Budget, the Department of Justice, and a number of components of the Department of Health and Human Services.

**Julie Gorder Holman, M. A.,** Department of Educational Psychology, University of Minnesota, 206e Burton Hall, 178 Pillsbury Drive, S.E., Minneapolis, Minnesota 55455
Julie Gorder Holman is a Ph.D. candidate in Educational Psychology at the University of Minnesota. She has a program background as a teacher and program director in public schools and in residential settings. The major concentration of her doctoral study is the assessment and training of adaptive behaviors in handicapped individuals.

**Andrew S. Halpern, Ph.D.,** Professor and Center Director, Rehabilitation Research and Training Center in Mental Retardation, College of Education, Clinical Services Building, University of Oregon, Eugene, Oregon 97403
Andrew S. Halpern is a professor of education and director of the Rehabilitation Research and Training Center in Mental Retardation at the University of Oregon. His research interests include the development of functional assessment instruments for use with mentally retarded adolescents and adults, residential programs for mentally retarded adults, and exploration of the learning potential assessment model.

**Iver A. Iversen, M.A.,** Sedna Corporation, 2380 Wycliff Street, St. Paul, Minnesota 55114
Iver A. Iversen is president of Sedna Corporation, St. Paul, Minnesota, a software development company specializing in software packages for manipulating massive information systems. He has been involved for many years in technical assistance to human services agencies in management of information systems and computer aided analysis of public policy.

**Gloria Shizue Kishi, M.Ed.,** Department of Education, State of Hawaii, Windward Oahu District, 45-955 Kamehameha Highway, Kaneohe, Hawaii 96744
Gloria Shizue Kishi is a doctoral student in special education at Syracuse University. She was involved in integrated school programs for students with severe handicaps for several years before taking leave from her Hawaii position to pursue a doctoral degree.

**K. Charlie Lakin, Ph.D.,** Department of Educational Psychology, University of Minnesota, 218 Pattee Hall, 150 Pillsbury Drive, S.E., Minneapolis, Minnesota 55455
K. Charlie Lakin is a research scientist at the University of Minnesota. In recent years, his work has focused on residential services for retarded and other handicapped citizens, and the effects of public policy on them.

**Kathleen A. Liberty, Ph.D.,** Project Coordinator, Research in Education of the Severely Handicapped: Washington Research Organization, 205A Parrington Hall, DC-05, University of Washington, Seattle, Washington 98195
Kathleen A. Liberty is one of the primary researchers at the Washington State Center for the Severely Handicapped. She has been a principal developer of basic knowledge and technology regarding learning hierarchies and has authored numerous articles in the area of learning and instruction.

**Luanna H. Meyer, Ph.D.,** Division of Special Education and Rehabilitation, Syracuse University, 805 S. Crouse Avenue, Syracuse, New York 13210
Luanna H. Meyer is an associate professor of special education at Syracuse University. She is currently editor of *The Journal of the Association for Persons with Severe Handicaps* and chairperson of the executive committee of The Association for Persons with Severe Handicaps. She

has published widely on the education and development of severely and profoundly handicapped children, with particular interest in recent years on strategies for maximizing their integration in regular educational settings.

**Dennis E. Mithaug, Ph.D.,** College of Education, University of Colorado, Austin Bluff Parkway, Colorado Springs, Colorado 80907
Dennis E. Mithaug is the dean of the college of education at the University of Colorado—Colorado Springs. He has published numerous books, chapters, and articles on topics related to vocational training of severely handicapped people.

**Lanny E. Morreau, Ph.D.,** Illinois State University, Department of Special Education, Fairchild Hall, Bloomington-Normal, Illinois 61761
Lanny Morreau is currently professor of special education at Illinois State University. He specializes in the areas of programmed instruction and behavior modification for handicapped people and has published widely on these topics. His experience in these areas ranges from that of a research psychologist to that of a senior planner of a state deinstitutionalization plan.

**JoAnne W. Putnam, Ph.D.,** Department of Special Education, Merrill Hall, 86 Main Street, University of Maine, Farmington, Maine 04938
JoAnne W. Putnam is an assistant professor at the University of Maine. She has experience as a teacher and teacher trainer for moderately and severely mentally handicapped persons. Her research has centered on social integration of moderately handicapped students, and characteristics of developmentally disabled persons who are not in institutions.

**Frank R. Rusch, Ph.D.,** 1310 South Sixth Street, 288 Education Building, Department of Special Education, University of Illinois, Champaign, Illinois 61820
Frank R. Rusch is a professor of special education at the University of Illinois who focuses on vocational training, job development, and career education of handicapped individuals. He has recently organized a major research and development program on vocational training of severely handicapped youth and adults, exploring important aspects of training and management of employment training programs. He has published widely on this topic in the past several years.

**John E. Rynders, Ph.D.,** Department of Educational Psychology, University of Minnesota, 249 Burton Hall, 178 Pillsbury Drive, S.E., Minneapolis, Minnesota 55455
John E. Rynders is a professor of educational psychology at the University of Minnesota. He has published on a wide range of issues concerning the development and education of severely handicapped individuals, but particularly those issues involving early intervention programs and the education of children with Down Syndrome.

**Stuart J. Schleien, Ph.D.,** Physical Education, Recreation and School Health Education, University of Minnesota, 208 Cooke Hall, 1900 University Avenue, S.E., Minneapolis, Minnesota 55455
Stuart J. Schleien is an assistant professor at the University of Minnesota. As a faculty member in the department of physical education, recreation, and school health education, his program development and research work has focused on therapeutic recreation for handicapped persons.

**Jo-Ann Sowers, Ph.D.,** Rehabilitation Research and Training Center in Mental Retardation, University of Oregon, Clinical Services Building, Eugene, Oregon 97403
Jo-Ann Sowers is currently a research scientist at the Oregon Research Institute. She is

presently involved in developing program models and conducting research related to the employment of physically handicapped individuals, with particular focus on transition from school to work and on staff training.

**Darlene S. Stealey, Ph.D.,** Department of Educational Psychology, University of Minnesota, 227 Burton Hall, 178 Pillsbury Drive, S.E., Minneapolis, Minnesota 55455

Darlene S. Stealey completed her Ph.D. in the department of educational psychology at the University of Minnesota where she currently lectures on early childhood special education. Her field experiences include teaching, teacher training, research, and consultation in early education and special education programs.

**Travis Thompson, Ph.D.,** Department of Psychology, University of Minnesota, N241 Elliott Hall, 75 East River Road, Minneapolis, Minnesota 55455

Travis Thompson is a professor of psychology and psychopharmacology at the University of Minnesota. He has been involved in a number of important development and research projects related to deinstitutionalization and has published extensively in this area and in psychopharmacology. He has recently become involved in a number of efforts to provide residential and treatment alternatives for individuals with severe behavior problems entering the community from state hospitals.

**Judy K. Werder, Ph.D.,** Assessment Editor, DLM Teaching Resources, 1 DLM Park, Allen, Texas 75002

Judy K. Werder is assessment editor in the area of assessment for DLM Teaching Resources. She has extensive experience in teaching and consulting with physical education and recreation programs for handicapped children and youth. Her research interest is in the area of motor assessment and intervention techniques.

**Colleen Wieck, Ph.D.,** Minnesota State Planning Agency, 201 Capitol Square Building, 550 Cedar Street, St. Paul, Minnesota 55101

Colleen Wieck is the executive director of the Minnesota Developmental Disabilities Office in the Minnesota Department State Planning Agency. Her research, writing, and planning/advocacy efforts have focused on the impact of public policy on services to handicapped people. Recently, she completed a cost study on public and community residential care for mentally retarded people in the United States. She has continued her interest in cost-related policy issues through a series of studies in Minnesota related to Medicaid financing and other policy problems.

**Lyle D. Wray, Ph.D.,** Director, Quality Assurance, Department of Human Service, Mental Health Office, Centennial Building, 4th Floor, 685 Cedar, St. Paul, Minnesota 55101

Lyle D. Wray serves as monitor for the U.S. District Court on the *Welsch vs. Noot* consent decree. He has extensive experience in Canada and the United States on various aspects of policy research and practice related to deinstitutionalization of developmentally disabled people. He has written and spoken extensively on the many policy, legal, and management problems attendant to deinstitutionalizing developmentally disabled people on a province-wide or statewide basis.

# Preface

This volume was developed as a companion to the recently released *Living and Learning in the Least Restrictive Environment,* edited by Robert H. Bruininks and K. Charlie Lakin (Paul H. Brookes Publishing Company, 1985). In that book, the editors and contributing authors sought to describe the contemporary conceptual, organizational, and programmatic status of service systems for developmentally disabled persons in the United States. Topics covered related to the origins and implications of the significant social changes of the past decade that provided disabled citizens a fuller share of their natural and legal rights to participate in and share the opportunities of society. Critical aspects of and expectations for service provision that derive from contemporary visions of appropriate care and habilitation were outlined in considerable detail in that volume. The current volume expands on the focus of *Living and Learning* by identifying and describing strategies for sustaining the evolution of attitudes, programs, and professional practices that permit fuller integration and opportunity for developmentally disabled individuals in their own communities.

A companion volume to *Living and Learning* was considered valuable for two primary reasons. First, in working with state agencies and provider organizations in various research and dissemination activities, the editors have sensed considerable frustration over the gap between what research and theory suggest contemporary services should be and the character of these services in their everyday implementation. This frustration is noted not only among those who feel service systems are not accomplishing all that they could to reflect the contemporary state-of-the-art in service provision, but it is also expressed by service providers who argue that in many instances the expectations held for them are unrealistic and not always in the best interests of their clients. Therefore, the editors considered it timely to develop a volume that might help bridge the gap between what is and what could be by identifying and describing demonstrably effective means of providing for habilitation and integration of developmentally disabled persons in community settings.

A second impetus for this book grew out of discussions at a working conference on deinstitutionalization and education held in Minneapolis in 1983 (with funding from the U.S. Department of Education). At this conference, a recurring perception of participants was that in the future, services for developmentally disabled persons would be influenced more by the effectiveness of implementing existing programs and policies and of utilizing resources in current allocations than by the creation of new programs or substantially increased funding. Indeed, it was generally agreed that the activities of federal and state courts that were so instrumental in defining rights for developmentally disabled persons in the 1970s and early 1980s would also be considerably diminished. It thus seemed particularly opportune to encourage a knowledgeable and experienced group of scholars to examine ways of further stimulating the physical, social, and economic integration of developmentally disabled persons, ways that did not rely on the standard calls for more money, more legislative and judicial involvement, and more research.

An introductory chapter and four major sections of chapters covering areas of vital importance to integrating developmentally disabled persons comprise this volume. In the introductory chapter, the editors, K. Charlie Lakin and Robert H. Bruininks, describe the social, philosophical, research, and bureaucratic contexts that shape the formal and informal goals that service systems hold for themselves and their clients.

The first principal section, Part II, contains four chapters describing contemporary knowledge and validated professional practices in the areas of assessment and intervention. In Chapter 2, the first chapter of this section, Kathleen A. Liberty thoroughly examines the state-of-the-art in teaching severely handicapped persons, citing methods proven effective in promoting acquisition, maintenance, generalization, and adaptation of skills. In Chapter 3, Julie Gorder Holman and Robert H. Bruininks examine methods of assessing and teaching specific adaptive behavior skills important to the daily lives of developmentally disabled persons. Lanny E. Morreau follows with a chapter that focuses on the efficacy and ethics involved in modifying specific maladaptive behaviors. John E. Rynders and Darlene S. Stealey complete this section with an analysis of the effectiveness of early intervention programs for very young severely handicapped children and their families.

Part III of the volume is devoted to primary issues in the vocational preparation of developmentally disabled youth and adults in and after their transition to adulthood. In Chapter 6, Daniel W. Close, Jo-Ann Sowers, Andrew S. Halpern, and Philip E. Bourbeau examine independent living training for mildly handicapped persons. Frank R. Rusch and Dennis E. Mithaug, in Chapter 7, outline research-based propositions for the future of career planning in programs for severely handicapped persons. In the final chapter in this section, Ronald W. Conley examines the effect of different federal programs on the employment of handicapped persons.

The next section, Part IV, presents strategies for developing and enhancing integrated services and opportunities for developmentally disabled persons. In the first chapter of this section, Lyle Wray and Colleen Wieck examine critical components of community-based, client-centered case management and how these relate to the provision of essential services in community settings. Chapter 10, by Luanna H. Meyer and Gloria Shizue Kishi, discusses strategies for integrating severely handicapped students in regular schools based on a case study in which the authors were participant observers. In Chapter 11, JoAnne W. Putnam, Judy K. Werder, and Stuart J. Schleien outline what has been learned about providing integrated social, leisure, and recreational activities to developmentally disabled persons.

Part V, the final major section of this volume, looks at means of approaching organizational impediments to the integration of developmentally disabled persons. Travis Thompson and Lyle Wray, in Chapter 12, outline a problem-solving approach to addressing impediments to providing integrated community-based services. William C. Copeland and Iver A. Iversen then discuss specific budgetary approaches to eliminating financial disincentives to community-based services. In Chapter 14, the final chapter of the volume, editors K. Charlie Lakin and Robert H. Bruininks review problems currently affecting the capacity of service systems to promote integration, and make a number of specific suggestions about how advocates might approach existing and likely future challenges.

Much has been accomplished in recent years in providing opportunities for developmentally disabled persons to participate in community life. However, much has yet to be done. It is hoped that this volume, in sharing strategies that have strengthened the community-orientation of many programs, may contribute in some way to the eventual community orientation of all.

# Acknowledgments

The initial content of many of the chapters in this volume was first presented in a working conference on deinstitutionalization and education, held in Minneapolis in 1983 and supported in part through a grant from the U.S. Department of Education (Grant No. G008100277). Significant work on this conference was done by Colleen Wieck in preparing the initial grant application and by JoAnne Putnam, who assumed major responsibilities in coordinating the working conference activities.

Valuable assistance in copyediting and checking references in this volume was provided by Elizabeth Balow Laraway and Cheri Gilman. Preparation of the final manuscript was done by Renee Wegwerth, with timely assistance from Steven McGuire and Sharon Olson. The diligent editing of our editor, Melissa Behm, and her patience with missed deadlines, were especially appreciated in the final preparation of the volume. The assistance and support of these people, in addition to the highly valued commitments of time, effort, and spirit by the contributing authors, have made the development of this volume a pleasure. By their dedication to this project, all of these individuals have lent support to this volume's basic premise, that we can accomplish much more in integrating our society's developmentally disabled citizens. The opinions expressed in this volume do not necessarily reflect the views or policies of the U.S. Department of Education, and any errors or omissions are the sole responsibility of the editors.

# Part I

## INTRODUCTION

# Chapter 1

# Social Integration of Developmentally Disabled Persons

*K. Charlie Lakin and Robert H. Bruininks*

In the past two decades, society has increasingly accepted the proposition that severely handicapped persons share with their nonhandicapped and mildly handicapped peers the right to enjoy and benefit from participation in community life (Roth & Smith, 1983; Sandler & Robinson, 1981). Even more important, during the same period tremendous strides have been made in the physical and social integration of handicapped individuals into the society and its institutions. Among numerous statistics, for example, that can be cited as illustrations of these trends, public schools systems expanded special education services from 2.1 million to 3.9 million handicapped children and youth in the 15 years between 1966 and 1981 (Mackie, 1969; U.S. Office of Special Education and Rehabilitative Services, 1982). During essentially the same period, 1967 to 1982, the total population of the traditional, large state institutions for developmentally disabled persons decreased from 194,650 to 119,335 (Lakin, Krantz, Bruininks, Clumpner, & Hill, 1982; Scheerenberger, 1982). Concurrently, the number of developmentally disabled persons in privately operated, generally smaller and more socially integrated placements grew commensurately from 24,355 in

1969 to 115,032 in 1982 (Hill, Lakin, & Bruininks, 1984; Lakin, Bruininks, Doth, Hill, & Hauber, 1982).

Just as crucial as have been the changes in the types of educational and residential care provided to developmentally disabled citizens has been the way in which alternative support and developmental services like day activity, vocational programs, and respite care for parents have affected severely handicapped persons. Indeed, alternative community-based services and the message they convey about the locus of appropriate care for developmentally disabled persons have been arguably responsible for significant changes in the utilization of residential services in recent years. From 1967 to 1982, the total number of developmentally disabled persons in private and state facilities decreased from 130.4 to 106.3 per 100,000 of the U.S. population (Hill et al., 1984; Lakin, 1979; National Institute of Mental Health, 1982). A major factor accounting for this considerable decrease has been that over this period the median age at which developmentally disabled persons were first being admitted to residential placements was rising sharply, from 10.4 years to 16 years between 1967 and 1977 (Lakin, Hill, Hauber, & Bruininks, 1982). Coincidentally, between 1977 and 1982, the total number of children and youth (birth–21 years) in residential care facilities for developmentally disabled persons decreased from 91,000 to 60,500 as a result of both the aging of the current residential population and the reduced rates of their replacement because of the greater tendency to retain developmentally disabled children and youth at home while accessing the community resources available to them (Hill et al., 1984).

Countless other statistics could be cited to suggest that our society has progressed dramatically in making communities accessible to developmentally disabled citizens in recent years. However, such statistics can also be misleading. Although it is appropriate to note the rapid rate of decrease in large state institutions in the past 15 years, it should also be recognized that over 154,000 developmentally disabled individuals are still residing in publicly and privately operated facilities of 64 or more residents (115,300 of these persons are severely/profoundly retarded individuals). It is, indeed, significant that nearly twice as many children and youth have access to special services than did 20 years ago, but it must also be noted that in 1979 over a million school-age children were being educated entirely in segregated special education programs and that another quarter of a million handicapped children were not even attending a neighborhood school. In short, past accomplishments can sometimes mask the even greater tasks that are yet to be accomplished. There is the danger today of losing focus on what is left to be done in self-satisfaction with past achievements. The response to this danger can only be found in enhancing commitments and increasing knowledge so that the benefits that have been provided to many handicapped persons in the recent past can be provided to more, and perhaps eventually all, such persons in the future.

The purpose of this book is to outline specific practicable approaches to achieving fuller social integration of severely handicapped citizens. Yet, although this volume is pragmatic in focus, its content is influenced by clear social goals, comprehensible philosophical and human principles, and a rapidly growing base of research to guide current practices. These factors have been critically important in past efforts to enhance the extent and quality of integration of handicapped persons. They can only increase in value as continuing efforts to provide community-oriented services to persons with special needs lead to enhanced integration and more effective services for increasing numbers of severely and profoundly impaired persons.

This chapter summarizes the social goals, the philosophical principles, and the rapidly growing knowledge base for providing direction to the development of socially integrated residential, habilitation, and support services for developmentally disabled persons. The relationships between these concepts and the specific policies affecting the nature and quality of the services provided are also noted. There is considerable overlap among these concepts, but each is also unique in the perspective it provides on what residential and community services should be accomplishing for developmentally disabled persons. Although contemporary service systems still fall far short of being guided exclusively, or perhaps even primarily, by the goals, principles, and research described in this chapter, clearly these systems have been evolving into greater congruence with them.

## CONTEMPORARY SOCIAL GOALS FOR SERVICES TO DEVELOPMENTALLY DISABLED PERSONS

### Deinstitutionalization

*Deinstitutionalization* is the term that has been used most commonly to describe the recent changes taking place in residential and, to a lesser extent, in other habilitative services for developmentally disabled persons. Although no other general social goal for developmentally disabled persons has enjoyed such widespread advocacy (including support by every president since John F. Kennedy), neither has any other such goal been so susceptible to semantic exploitation and ambiguity. To a certain degree, the problem in establishing a uniform connotation for the term *deinstitutionalization* is that it incorporates a number of legitimate aspects. One of its more obvious aspects is that it is a social policy committed to decreasing the number of developmentally disabled persons living in institutional settings. By virtually all definitions of what constitutes an institution, deinstitutionalization has been an effective social policy. This is demonstrated by the already-mentioned statistics indicating the decrease by approximately 20% in the number of mentally retarded persons in state and county institutions for mentally retarded and mentally ill persons per 100,000 in the general population between 1967 and 1982, or the decrease of mentally retarded persons in public and private facilities of 64 or more residents from 183,500 in 1977 to 154,250 in 1982 (Hauber, Bruininks, Hill, Lakin, Scheerenberger, & White, in press; Hill et al., 1984; Lakin, 1979).

More than just a frequently advocated social goal, deinstitutionalization also encompasses the social, bureaucratic, and fiscal processes for relocating developmentally disabled persons, as well as the redistribution of human and financial resources needed for their programs in "noninstitutional" settings. Again, these processes can be shown to be occurring at a steady, if not spectacular, pace. For example, between 1977 and 1982, the proportion of total federal and state funds spent on residential care for developmentally disabled persons in public facilities of 16 or more residents decreased 10%. However, there is no better demonstration of what is left to accomplish in this regard than the fact that 70% of the state and federal funds expended on residential facilities for developmentally disabled persons is still spent in these same public facilities (Hill et al., 1984). Although efforts to deinstitutionalize developmentally disabled citizens have been accompanied by some transfer of resources to community-based programs, the history of the deinstitutionalization of mentally ill persons is replete with examples of wholesale movement of people out of institutions, with little or no effort to transfer with them the human and

fiscal resources needed for their care. Ironically, it may well be because the deinstitutionalization of developmentally disabled persons has been slower (institutionalized developmentally disabled populations decreased an average of about 4.2% a year between 1967 and 1982, whereas institutionalized mentally ill populations decreased much more rapidly, at about 11%, between 1955 and 1980) and, therefore, has provided opportunities for better planning and coordination, that the problems associated with it have been less pronounced (Lakin, 1979; National Institute of Mental Health, 1956, 1982; Scheerenberger, 1983).

Part of the problem in establishing a uniform connotation for *deinstitutionalization* has been a lack of consensus about what constitutes *institutionalization*. While Clements (1976) defined institutionalization as "placement of the mentally retarded outside their natural homes into any living arrangement not of their own choice," few have accepted this or similar perspectives on the term. On the other hand, less conceptually precise statements that focus on the characteristics of settings (irrespective of the individual's concurrence with the placement) are more universally accepted as defining institutionalization. In general, such definitions depict institutionalization as placement in a relatively large and isolated long-term care facility (an "institution"), even though no uniform standards for differentiating institutions from noninstitutions, either by size or any other characteristic, have yet been accepted.

One of the more commonly cited definitions of an institution is Wolfensberger's (1972):

The term institution refers to a deindividualizing residence in which persons are congregated in numbers distinctly larger than might be found in a large family; in which they are highly regimented; in which the physical and social environment aims at the lowest common denominator; in which all or most of the transactions of daily life are carried on under the roof, on one campus, or in a largely segregated fashion (p. v).

As the foregoing discussion suggests, there has never been complete agreement on what precisely constitutes deinstitutionalization.

However, the term is generally recognized as having two primary aspects: 1) the movement of residents of relatively large (institutional) facilities to smaller ones, and 2) avoidance of initially placing individuals into relatively large (institutional) facilities in preference to placing them in smaller ones or avoiding long-term care altogether. A third aspect has sometimes been ascribed to deinstitutionalization, that of making existing institutions "less institutional" through remodeling the physical plants and/or attempting to improve the quality of their residential and habilitation programs (National Association of Superintendents of Public Residential Facilities for the Mentally Retarded, 1974). Whether this latter aspect is indeed related to the others or actually diverts the commitment to them has been a matter of considerable contention (Taylor, Brown, McCord, Giambetti, Searl, Mlinarcik, Atkinson, & Lichter, 1981).

It is reasonable to hypothesize that the over $1 billion spent by states for capital construction and remodeling of state institutions between 1977 and 1982, primarily to retain Medicaid certification (National Association of State Mental Retardation Program Directors [NASMRPD], 1980; Scheerenberger, 1982, 1983), has resulted in long-term disincentives for maximizing the rates of institution depopulation for the rest of this century, although there is essentially no simple correlation ($r = .04$) between the amounts states invested in physical plants of their state institutions between 1977 and 1980 and the change in the proportion of their residential population in small facilities between 1977 and 1982 (Lakin & Hill, 1984; NASMRPD, 1980). Still, when most states financed these capital improvements they did so with bonds that they expected to be amortized over the remainder of this century through Medicaid reimbursements. Advocates of reducing institutional populations can reasonably contend that by stimulating state fiscal policies that have included long-range plans to maintain a residual population in state institutions, albeit, by improving the institutions where they remain, the federal government has tacitly, but significantly, promoted

institutional care. Indeed, these same improvements have reduced the potential for using courts to move people out of institutional settings that was considerably more easily done before states undertook major capital and staff development projects to correct their most blatant inadequacies. The removal of courts as an efficacious forum for arguing the merits of institution depopulation has helped create a more active and uncompromising advocacy for the elimination of institutional placements, most commonly, in those facilities with 16 or more residents (see, for example, S.2053 [the proposed "Community and Family Living Amendments of 1983"]).

## Noninstitutionalization

Since the meaning of *deinstitutionalization* has been ambiguous, but its social acceptance has been high, groups with varying interests in long-term care have attempted to include their particular vested goals under its rubric. Sociologically, such an occurrence is to be expected. Practically, however, the semantics surrounding the different perceptions of the role of state and other large institutions in the residential care system have increasingly clouded positions that are substantially at variance. Indeed, a significant debate in the field today is not deinstitutionalization versus institutionalization but deinstitutionalization versus noninstitutionalization. If deinstitutionalization is to be semantically coopted to signify a policy of gradual depopulation of state institutions along with continued investment in attempting to improve their internal residential and habilitative conditions, then a growing body of advocates can be said to be calling for a concerted social policy of noninstitutionalization, reflecting a total and uncompromising commitment to systematic and irreversible efforts to discourage institutional placements as much as possible. Such policies that might have once been seen as radical are today being articulated and promoted by mainstream advocacy/consumer organizations such as the Association for Retarded Citizens.

Advocates of noninstitutionalization note that it has been well over a decade since the realities of large institutions were fully documented and made public by researchers, journalists, and concerned others (examples of such documentation include Blatt, 1970, 1973; Goffman, 1961; Rivera, 1972; and most notably, perhaps, Robert F. Kennedy ["Where toys are locked away," 1965]). Furthermore, long-term negative behavioral effects of institutional placements have been empirically established (Kiesler, 1982; Pilewski & Heal, 1980) and, as for general treatment effectiveness, the single best predictor of future institutionalization remains the extent of prior institutionalization (Kiesler, 1982; Rotegard & Bruininks, 1983). Contrasting with the rather discouraging assessments of the benefits of institutional treatment is a wealth of largely encouraging information about the conditions of living and habilitation in smaller, community-based placements (Conroy, Efthimiou, & Lemanowicz, 1982; also chapter by Rotegard, Bruininks, Holman, & Lakin, in Bruininks & Lakin, 1985). The accumulation of this knowledge has led to a growing consensus that the most appropriate care for developmentally disabled persons, regardless of their general levels of impairment or specific presenting conditions, is provided in community-based residential programs that provide for more normal patterns of living, participation in community activities, involvement in socially, economically, or developmentally beneficial activities during daytime hours, and increased use of generic services available to all members of the community.

Advocacy organizations (e.g., Association for Retarded Citizens–United States), professional organizations (The Association for Persons with Severe Handicaps) and, increasingly, state and federal government agencies (Administration on Developmental Disabilities) have cited evidence regarding the effects of different types of residential placements and have argued that what is known about program effects is not in synchrony with contemporary practices of placement. These organizations have, therefore, increased efforts to promote policies that support more desirable practices. A sign of the intensity and

direction of these convictions was demonstrated in the introduction in the U.S. Congress of the Community and Family Living Amendments (to the Social Security Act) of 1983 (S.2053). This legislation, backed by the largest parent/professional advocacy group in the nation, would have entirely phased out Medicaid funding for institutions of more than 75 residents over a 10-year period and of facilities with 16–75 residents over a 15-year period. Although it remains questionable that these amendments can survive the massive resistance that has been organized by state and large private providers through parents, employee groups, and state officials, as well as the ambiguities associated with some of its nonresidential care provisions that have major, but unknown, cost implications, the mere introduction of this legislation in Congress proves the seriousness with which noninstitutionalization is being approached as a policy option.

## Nondiscrimination

One of the increasingly evident negative aspects of service systems for developmentally disabled persons is their discrimination with regard to severity of mental handicap in placement practices. This discrimination has long pervaded decisions about the appropriateness of placements in institutional versus non-institutional settings, in local schools versus special stations, and in work or work training placements versus day activity placements. To a greater degree in recent decades, the most severely impaired persons in the various service systems have become increasingly concentrated within state institutions and other segregated settings. This trend has been noted for nearly 40 years (see Pense, 1946). Indeed, in 1939 about 40% of state institution residents were labeled mildly or borderline-retarded and about 15% profoundly retarded. In 1965 those percentages were 18% for mildly retarded persons and 27% for profoundly retarded persons; in 1982, 6% and 57%, respectively.

The changes in the populations of state institutions have resulted from substantially higher rates of institutional discharge of the more mildly handicapped residents and an implicit acceptance of the appropriateness of large institutional placement of the most severely retarded populations, as reflected in the low discharge rates of these persons. In 1939, despite comprising 15% of the state institutional population, profoundly retarded persons made up less than 4% of all discharges, while mildly and borderline retarded persons (40% of the state institution population) constituted over 75% of all discharges (Lakin, 1979; National Institute of Mental Health, 1956). About 40 years later, 1978 comparative data from a national sample of 75 state institutions showed that profoundly retarded individuals made up 47% of all institutionalized residents but only 19% of all discharges, while mildly and borderline retarded persons made up 9% of state institution residents but 28% of discharges (Sigford, Bruininks, Lakin, Hill, & Heal, 1982). At the same time, profoundly retarded persons comprised only 12% of the persons in long-term care outside of state institutions (Hill, Bruininks, & Lakin, 1983).

There is justifiable concern that these figures represent a systematic discrimination against severely/profoundly retarded persons. Specifically, they raise the question of whether the more severely handicapped persons in the residential care system are deprived of access to community services based on their level of handicap alone. As institutional settings become centers for housing nearly exclusively severely/profoundly retarded citizens, the issue becomes whether a new policy of "separate but equal" is being implicitly implemented. In this regard it is important to note that although the populations of state institutions have decreased from 187,000 in 1965 to 119,000 in 1982 (a 36% decrease), the populations of severely/profoundly retarded persons in those settings decreased only 13% over the same time period, from 112,000 to 97,000, and the population of profoundly retarded persons in state institutions actually increased substantially, from about 51,000 in 1965 to 68,000 in 1982 (Lakin, 1979; Scheerenberger, 1965, 1983). Similar questions can be raised about public schools, public recreation programs, and virtually any other public service. Unfortu-

nately, the data that could respond to questions related to possible discrimination in such programs are not available.

In 1923 a superintendent of a state institution noted that "with a parole and colony system taking our highest grade cases away from institutions, it would appear that the state institution for mental defectives will be largely filled with idiots" (Little, 1923). The gradual coming into being of this prediction substantially altered the focus and goals of institutional programs. Increasingly, the existence of large institutions has been justified on the basis that they provide their severely/profoundly impaired populations with services not otherwise available. This perspective is typified in a recent evaluation of Hawaii's prospects for continued depopulation of its state institution, which recommended "that deinstitutionalization goals should be reevaluated based on a consideration of the characteristics of the clients available for placement and on the capabilities of the community to provide services they need" (Mayeda & Sutter, 1981, pp. 379–380).

In *Garrity v. Galen* (1981), a federal district court noted that such general class treatment in considering the discharge or retention of severely/profoundly retarded persons in institutions may indeed violate Section 504 of the Rehabilitation Act of 1973 (Public Law 93-112), which reads in part that "no otherwise qualified handicapped individual in the United States . . . shall solely by reason of his handicap, be excluded from participation in, be denied the benefits of, or be subjected to discrimination under any program or activity receiving Federal financial assistance" (Sec. 84.4[a]). Specifically, the court found that New Hampshire state institution officials "made placements and disbursed services not in an individual assessment of the abilities and potentials of each resident but on the generalized assumption that certain groups of people (e.g., profoundly retarded or nonambulatory persons) are unable to benefit from certain activities and services. This [is a] kind of blanket discrimination against the handicapped and especially the most severely handicapped . . ."

(522 F. Supp. at 215). In this case, Judge Devine ruled that although this kind of discrimination is "unfortunately rooted in the history of our country" (522 F. Supp. at 215), it violates Section 504, simply because there is nothing per se about being severely or profoundly retarded that makes community placements inappropriate and, indeed, there is evidence that severely and profoundly retarded persons can benefit substantially from such placements and from the community participation and other opportunities that they afford.

The discrimination that is evident today is particularly pernicious because few attempts to justify the continued use of large institutions for residential care base their case on residents' relative opportunity to benefit. Most lists of reasons for maintaining institutions include variations on a general set of factors that include: 1) the large amount of capital invested in institution physical plants and in improvements to them, including recent bonding to bring facilities into compliance with Intermediate Care Facilities for the Mentally Retarded (ICFs/MR) standards; 2) lack of definitive proof demonstrating uniformly superior developmental outcomes in community versus institutional placements (that institutions do not produce superior outcomes has been convincingly demonstrated); 3) lack of clear demonstration that community-based approaches to residential services are less expensive (although most studies conclude that they are); 4) lack of daytime habilitation placements in the community; 5) easier access to federal reimbursements for institutional services; 6) difficulties in obtaining needed health and social services in community settings; 7) difficulties in administering and monitoring decentralized services; 8) difficulties in recruiting and retaining qualified care providers in community settings; 9) need to maintain state commitments to the towns with institution industries; 10) opposition of parents with adult offspring in institutions to their transfer; and 11) lack of community acceptance of severely handicapped persons. It is because these factors provide the primary basis for decisions about retaining severely handicapped persons in institutions (a fact that many state representatives seem to be remarkably open about admitting) that Judge Devine's observations in *Garrity* should have much broader applicability. Similar arguments for segregation in schooling, work, recreation, and other activities of severely handicapped persons reflect the same social toleration for predetermining the nature and quality of an individual's life based solely on his or her level of disability.

## Right to Education

In what today is recognized as one of the most important legal decisions of the 20th century, the U.S. Supreme Court in *Brown v. Board of Education* (1954) unanimously concluded that education

> is required in the performance of our most basic responsibilities [and] . . . is the principle instrument . . . in preparing . . . training and helping [the child] adjust normally to his environment. In these days it is doubtful that any child may reasonably be expected to succeed in life if he is denied the opportunity of an education. Such an opportunity where the state has undertaken to provide it, is a right which must be made available to all on equal terms (p. 483).

Yet while the principles forwarded in the *Brown* decision were universal, their application was largely limited to issues of discrimination on the basis of race. In the years following the *Brown* decision, advocates for handicapped children claimed that the equal-protection doctrine that protected the "class" of children who were black from discrimination based on the uncontrollable fact of their race, also afforded protection against discrimination against children who were handicapped based on the uncontrollable condition of their handicap. Advocates argued that where states chose to provide public education for their school-age residents but failed to permit access to that education to a select few of those students, it denied these few students equal protection (as required by the Fourteenth Amendment to the U.S. Constitution) under that state's school laws. Much of what these advocates argued was heard not in courts but within the school systems themselves. Available statistics indicate that the number of special education recipients grew from 975,000 in the 1957–1958 school year to about 2,850,000 in the 1971–1972 school year (Mackie, 1969; Wilken, 1977).

While schools increasingly recognized the right of handicapped children to a free public education, two major court cases of the early 1970s defined those rights. It was these cases, *Pennsylvania Association for Retarded Citizens (PARC) v. Commonwealth of Pennsylvania* (1971) and *Mills v. Board of Education of the District of Columbia* (1972), that applied the Fourteenth Amendment's equal-protection provisions found applicable to education in *Brown* to establish a right to education for handicapped children and youth. While *PARC* and *Mills* were major steps in the establishment of a right to education for handicapped children and youth, the passage of Public Law 94-142, the Education for All Handicapped Children Act of 1975, codified the major findings of these decisions. Therefore, unlike most of the social and philosophical principles guiding the provision of services to developmentally disabled persons, the right to education has been explicitly recognized in statute and detailed in regulation.

Public Law 94-142 contains four major provisions that outline the extent and nature of the right to education of handicapped children and youth. These stipulate that 1) a free appropriate education be available to every handicapped child regardless of his or her severity of disability or apparent ability to benefit; 2) a formal, public plan be developed that specifies the student's current educational/ developmental performance, goals, and objectives for enhancing that performance, as well as the specific programs and services to be implemented in support of those goals and objectives and the procedures for evaluating their attainment and/or need for modification; 3) due-process procedures be available to parents, surrogate parents, or schools to ensure proper notification about and review of assessment procedures and program provision, and 4) the education provided to handicapped chil-

dren be provided in the least restrictive setting feasible. This last provision, placement in the least restrictive environment, is defined in PL 94-142 to mean:

(1) That to the maximum extent appropriate, handicapped children, including children in public and private institutions or other care facilities, are educated with children who are not handicapped, and

(2) That special classes, separate schooling or other removal of handicapped children from the regular educational environment occurs only when the nature or severity of the handicap is such that education in regular classes with the use of supplementary aids and services cannot be achieved satisfactorily (Sec. 121a.550[b]).

The concept of least restrictive placement is discussed more thoroughly later in this chapter. However, it should be noted that in recognizing a general right to education, Congress specified an obligation of the schools to provide education in the most socially integrated manner feasible. In meeting that obligation, school staff members have responsibility to reflect the best of contemporary practices in providing those supplementary aids and services that have been shown to enhance the degree of integration that can be achieved satisfactorily. In recent years the traditional perceptions of feasible levels of integration of severely/profoundly handicapped students with their peers in local schools have been substantially challenged. Increasingly, research and demonstration are showing that there is no reason, except in cases of extreme health needs, that the right to a free and appropriate education cannot or should not mean, at the minimum, education in one's local school with significant opportunities for physical and social interaction with one's peers.

### Right to Habilitation

Our nation's courts have recognized the right of institutionalized developmentally disabled persons to habilitative services. However, although to a greater and greater extent, in both theory and research, the nature of residential placement and associated activities is being directly related to the outcomes of habilitation, courts recognize a right to habilitation for residents in large institutions without directly linking that right to any particular type of habilitative setting. In large measure the involvement of federal and state courts in assessing the social tolerability of state institutional care systems was stimulated by a desire on the part of advocates to use the judicial system to bring about the kinds of institutional reform that states were otherwise neglecting. A series of cases in the early 1970s focused directly on the existing conditions in state institutions and on the need for their improvement (e.g., *Horachek v. Exon*, 1973; *New York Association for Retarded Citizens [NYARC] and Parisi v. Rockefeller*, 1973; *W lsch v. Likins*, 1974, *Wyatt v. Stickney*, 1972). A general theme of the cases and related cases in mental health institutions (e.g., *O'Conner v. Donaldson*, 1975), was that institutionalization represented a substantial deprivation of liberty and was justifiable only for a legitimate purpose—which was habilitative treatment. The state's obligation to provide habilitation that focuses on improving a client's condition—whatever the conditions that prompted institutional confinement—has been recognized from the initial *Wyatt* case to the recent Supreme Court decision in *Romeo v. Youngberg* (1982), although in the latter case, the Court took a rather restrictive view of "habilitation." The Supreme Court's finding in *Romeo* that the right to habilitation is defined by habilitation that is necessary "to ensure safety and freedom from undue restraint" left more questions unanswered than resolved, since what constitutes a habilitation program sufficient to permit freedom from undue restraint (including unnecessary institutionalization), finds little consensus among program, policy, and research personnel. The Court recognized this current state of affairs and noted specifically that the role of the judiciary is not to pick winners in debates dividing professional communities. This deference to "professional" judgment conflicts, in a major and unflatteringly short-sighted way, with the comments of the federal court in *Society for Good Will to Retarded Children v. Carey* (1979), in which the court warned that this

deference to on-the-scene professionals may present substantial difficulty. . . . Experts charged with administration of the institution may not feel free to exercise untrammeled professional judgment . . . budgetary pressures and statewide standards may cause a yielding of professional judgment. . . . Should these pressures cause a professional in charge to neglect his professional duty to his clients, the court will slip in and provide guidance (p. 2546).

The *Romeo* case and other recent judicial and legislative debates (especially over S.2053) have brought into full view the conflicting purposes, perceptions, and vested interests that still prevail in professional circles, as well as how unconvincing can be any testimony that is contradicted by seemingly equally qualified "experts." Although the present Supreme Court clearly maintains a constitutional requirement for habilitation-oriented activities in institutions, it seems to have established a limited role for federal courts in determining questions of appropriate treatment programs, at least until higher levels of consensus are attained in the professional community. Although there are excellent reasons to question the wisdom of the Court in this matter (including those just cited in *Society for Good Will*), perhaps the most successful approach to broadening the right to habilitation to include the right to habilitation for and by participation in the mainstream culture is to continue to collect and disseminate information that shows the critical importance of the setting in outcomes of habilitation.

How much more data about the varying effects of alternative community-based habilitation models will be required before the Court is willing to make a judgment based on the accumulated evidence rather than on vested professional interests and opinions is not clear. But it would appear that discussions on the right to habilitation may have gone as far toward resolution in the present judicial atmosphere as they will without a preponderance of evidence to indicate that one or more models of treatment fails to provide an adequate opportunity to overcome the personal deficiencies that initially were used to justify institutional confinement. The status of evidence to support community-based placements, which the Supreme Court appears to find inconclusive (although, in fact, it never actually considered), must continue to be enhanced if the right to habilitation as perceived by the courts is to include a right to habilitation that provides the highest probability of socially and developmentally beneficial outcomes. Research considerations also permeate the discussion of philosophical principles guiding the delivery of residential services for developmentally disabled persons. As is noted in the section following, the validity of these principles has been substantiated in considerable research and programmatic experience. Perhaps most validly with respect to the issue of right to habilitation, these principles raise the question of to what end should institutionalized residents be habilitated? If the answer has to do with increasing the clients' abilities to participate in the society from which they were removed, then these philosophical principles become much more than simple value statements about how human agencies should treat their clients; they become powerful definers of adequate habilitation and are highly relevant to deliberations about the specific meaning of right to habilitation.

## PHILOSOPHICAL PRINCIPLES UNDERLYING INTEGRATED SERVICES FOR DEVELOPMENTALLY DISABLED PERSONS

### Normalization

Normalization is a concept that has immeasurably influenced the provision of residential and other services to developmentally disabled persons in recent years and has been the conceptual cornerstone of the changes in the service system for developmentally disabled persons in the United States in the 1970s and 1980s. Whole volumes, perhaps the most complete being Flynn and Nitsch's (1980), have been devoted to this concept, so the brief treatment here will necessarily not fully explicate all that normalization means and implies.

Normalization was largely imported as an egalitarian concept from Scandinavia in the 1960s. It has since been progressively molded into the pragmatic and habilitative perspectives guiding North American developmental disabilities services. However, the concept is not interpreted in the same way by all who have used it. For example, some have implied that it demands that services be provided to make disabled persons more normal, or that the service providers must essentially ignore the abnormalities of disabled persons (Aanes & Haagenson, 1978; Schwartz, 1977; Throne, 1975; Wolfensberger, 1980). However, most interpretations derive essentially from a human and societal value that the "treatment" of developmentally disabled persons should occur within a larger context of recognizing their right to be respected as individuals and their natural membership in their native culture and community. As noted by one of the early and primary exponents of the concept (Nirje, 1976), normalization means that all people, including those with developmental disabilities, should share:

> patterns of life and conditions of everyday living which are as close as possible to the regular circumstances and ways of life of society . . . . a normal rhythm of the day, with privacy, activities and mutual responsibility; a normal rhythm of the week, with a home to live in, a school or work to go to, and leisure time with a modicum of social interaction; a normal rhythm of year . . . opportunity to undergo the normal developmental experiences of the life cycle . . . . respect and understanding given to the silent wishes or expressed self-determination . . . relationships between sexes . . . . [I]f retarded persons cannot or should not live in their family or own home, the homes provided should be of normal size and situated in normal residential areas (pp. 231–232).

Normalization, at its core, does not focus on services provided or on programs of habilitation, although the purpose of these naturally flows from the concept. Instead it describes goals, standards of treatment, and process of integration for a historically devalued group of people, against which the human and, increasingly, professional qualities of services can be judged. The standard is simply whether the treatment of the individual reflects the acceptance of him or her as a member of the culture, allowing that person the opportunity for the maximally normal patterns and experiences of living that his or her disability reasonably allows. Stated in a way that reflects the increasing use of the concept to evaluate the quality of services provided to an individual, the standard might be worded: Can the extent to which and manner in which an individual's life differs from the cultural norm be justified in terms of the individual's disability precluding a more normal life-style?

Normalization as a philosophy and as a guide to professional practices provides a forceful counterpoint to the attitudes and practices that once provided exclusively segregated treatment programs for developmentally disabled persons. Whereas these programs hardly recognized that their clients had justifiable interests in participating in their own culture, the normalization principle contends that these interests are inherent in one's worth as an individual and member of the community, that they are primary interests, and that habilitation must be subjugated to and in service of these greater interests. Substantial analysis and commentary in the literature suggest that total institutions do just the opposite; that is, they subordinate the interests that derive from the residents' humanity and community membership to the institutions' custodial and "habilitative" intentions (Bogdan & Taylor, 1975; Goffman, 1961; Vail, 1967).

Significantly, neither the courts nor Congress has consistently recognized a right to normalized services, but in the long run, this may make relatively little difference. Three seemingly irresistible forces are promoting a gradual reconstruction of long-term care services based on the normalization principle. First is a growing consensus that the fundamental meaning of normalization involves valuing the life, rights, and dignity of citizens with disabilities. Increasingly, the degradation of life, of personal rights, and of dignity in the name of treating disability is seen as intolerable professional arrogance. Second, as was alluded to in the discussion of the right to habilitation, and as will be discussed at greater length in this chapter's review of the knowledge base supporting community services, the development of skills that

most alleviate the effects of disability (i.e., that promote independence, self-care and social participation) is being seen as best conducted in the environments in which those skills must ultimately be demonstrated. Increasingly, failure to reflect this concept will be recognized (on the basis of research and experience) as inadequate professional practice. Third, there is a growing questioning of the validity of arguments for continued institutionalization of developmentally disabled persons, arguments that are based upon strong political, economic, and personal interests (e.g., state legislatures wishing to recoup investments in institution physical plants through long-term Medicaid reimbursements, opposition of state employees unions seeking to retain state employment). Enlightened views dictate that limiting the participation of a minority group in society because of the secondary interests of those who not only see a benefit in maintaining their segregation but who are politically more powerful should be an unacceptable practice, regardless of perceptions of the present Supreme Court.

## Least Restrictive Alternative

If normalization is largely a cultural and moral principle, its programmatic operationalization is most clearly evident in the concept of the *least restrictive alternative*. In a philosophical sense the concept of least restrictive alternative can be seen as a semantic marker for a number of increasingly acknowledged goals for residential, habilitative, and support services including placement at the level of service that permits the maximum feasible social integration. In a habilitative sense the concept reflects the attempt to provide training under the optimal conditions for acquiring, maintaining, and generalizing specific skills of daily living that are part of the expected behavioral repertoire of members of the culture.

As a judicial/constitutional concept, least restrictive alternative has reflected a general recognition that, like their nonhandicapped peers, handicapped persons enjoy constitutional protection from "undue restraint," and that the state may deprive an individual of liberty no more than necessary to provide an effective program of habilitation. As a treatment principle, however, the least restrictive alternative concept is based on an understanding that different placements provide different amounts of restriction on the individual, and that freedom from undue restraint presumes that each individual's placement reflects the appropriate level of freedom/restraint, given his or her needs for protection and habilitation. What is more, as with the right to habilitation, the least restrictive alternative doctrine recognizes that some forms of placement do not allow for effective habilitation to occur.

Because the least restrictive alternative is a somewhat more expansive and subtle concept than the right to habilitation, it is not surprising that courts have been less universal in recognizing the individual's right to habilitative treatment in the least restrictive alternative. Nevertheless, federal courts have extensively supported the view that the right to habilitation includes the expectation that habilitation will be delivered in settings appropriate to the habilitative goal. The most encompassing finding in this regard may be that involving the Pennhurst State School and Hospital in Pennsylvania (*Halderman v. Pennhurst State School and Hospital*, 1977) (henceforth, *Pennhurst*), in which the district court concluded that

> on the basis of the record, we find that minimally adequate habilitation cannot be provided in an institution such as Pennhurst . . . [because] Pennhurst does not provide an atmosphere conductive to normalization which is so vital to the retarded if they are to be given the opportunity to acquire, maintain and improve their life skills. Pennhurst provides confinement and isolation, the antithesis of habilitation (p. 1295).

The support given to the doctrine of the least restrictive alternative in *Pennhurst* reflected the same essential judicial impression of the role of community-based training in imparting skills necessary for community living, first introduced in *Wyatt v. Stickney* (1972):

> Residents shall have a right to the least restrictive conditions necessary to achieve the purposes of habilitation. To this end, the institution shall make every attempt to move residents from (a) more to less structured living; (b) larger to smaller facilities; (c) larger to smaller living units; (d) group to individual residence; (e) segregated from

the community to integrated into the community living; (f) dependent to independent living (p. 396).

The failure of the Supreme Court to recognize the notion of least restrictive placement as critical to the concept of habilitation differs not only from the view of many courts but from the view of Congress. As noted in the discussion of the right to education, Congress made clear in its passage of the Education for All Handicapped Children Act that it perceived the least restrictive environment principle as important in providing equal and appropriate educational opportunities to handicapped children and youth. Congress also recognized this principle in the Developmentally Disabled Assistance and Bill of Rights Act (Public Law 94-103), as follows:

> Congress makes the following findings respecting the rights of persons with developmental disabilities:
> 1) Persons with developmental disabilities have a right to appropriate treatment, services, and habilitation for such disabilities.
> 2) The treatment, services, and habilitation for a person with developmental disabilities should be designed to maximize the developmental potential of the person and should be provided in the setting that is least restrictive of the person's personal liberty (42 U.S.C. Sec. 6010).

However, in *Pennhurst* the Supreme Court not only appeared to differ with Congress on the "right to habilitation in the least restrictive setting," it further ruled that Congress in enacting this legislation created no specific new rights for developmentally disabled persons. Therefore, it would appear that Congress may be required to act on specific legislation if it has intended that treatment in the least restrictive environment should be a right for developmentally disabled persons and/or a means of ensuring environmental support to the purpose of habilitation activities.

## THE KNOWLEDGE BASE REGARDING INTEGRATED SERVICES FOR DEVELOPMENTALLY DISABLED PERSONS

Although the least restrictive alternative has been an important legislative and judicial concept, undoubtedly its major impact has been in influencing the day-to-day decisions made with respect to placement and program design for developmentally disabled people. Increasingly, the concept has helped administrative agencies and service providers to conceptualize programs as a continuum of placement alternatives. These alternatives range in intensity of directed activity and client supervision so that they are able to respond to developmental differences and developmental progress by varying and modifying the personal freedom, opportunities, and expectations afforded individuals. Movement along such continua are accommodated through physical

movement of the individuals to new settings that are more highly physically, socially, and programmatically integrated into the normal cultural life patterns and/or changing relationships between professional, peers, and the disabled clients of the system.

Too often the principles of *normalization* and *least restrictive environment* are affirmed without regard to their logical translation into functional standards and expectations for service programs. These principles form a powerful, integrated basis for organizing and managing service programs for developmentally disabled persons. Without appropriate translations, however, such principles are as often

Table 1.    Categories of service system function, based on principles of normalization and least restrictive environment

### Direct Services

1.  To provide basic maintenance (food, shelter, clothing) as necessary and an *array of residential options* that appropriately serves the varying needs of developmentally disabled persons for different levels of care and different types of programs.

2.  To provide *habilitation activities* that are focused on teaching developmentally disabled persons the skills they need to increase their level of independence, degree of social integration, and ability to fulfill valued social roles (e.g., work); and that promote the health, development, and psychological well-being of developmentally disabled individuals through appropriate, adequate, and timely intervention in response to their needs.

3.  To provide *social, leisure, and recreation activities* that offer frequent and varied opportunities for productive and enjoyable uses of free time by developmentally disabled persons in integrated settings.

4.  To establish *resource allocation*, budgeting, service reimbursements, and income-maintenance policies and practices that are clear, well-publicized, and nonstigmatizing, that provide significant incentives for family and community living, and that ensure continuity of noninstructional alternatives.

5.  To use individualized *assessment, planning, and placement* procedures that gather and utilize information to determine the nature and quality of services needed.

6.  To provide individual case managers to suitably link the individual developmentally disabled person with providers who will deliver appropriate services in the least restrictive, most normalized, appropriate placement.

### Indirect Services

1.  To maintain *information and evaluation systems* that gather, aggregate, and utilize data on individual clients, programs, and systems to establish objectives for services and policies; to assess the effectiveness of services and policies in meeting goals; and to modify services and policies as indicated by evaluation results.

2.  To establish *personnel management* practices that recruit, train, utilize, and retain adequate numbers of skilled professionals and paraprofessionals to provide the services needed by developmentally disabled persons.

3.  To promote *social attitudes*, professional commitments, community experiences, and citizen expectations for public laws, regulations, and policies that increase the acceptance and integration of developmentally disabled persons.

4.  To develop and *share knowledge and experience* among service providers, academic and research institutions, government and private administrative agencies, advocacy/consumer organizations, and natural and surrogate family members about available services, effective practices, new technologies, special opportunities, and useful policies in local, state, and national spheres.

5.  To promote the recognition of *human rights and dignity* for developmentally disabled persons, including maximizing the opportunities for consumer involvement, personal choice, and self-advocacy.

*Source:* Information based on definition contained in Developmentally Disabled Assistance and Bill of Rights Act (42 U.S.C. Sec. 6010).

used to defend discredited practices as they are to promote more widely accepted contemporary standards of practice. Current principles of care and habilitation can be translated into a number of functional requirements for services and communities. One such translation of the principles of normalization and the least restrictive environment as they pertain to the functions of service systems is outlined in Table 1, which is largely based on definitions of direct and indirect services contained in the Developmentally Disabled Assistance and Bill of Rights Act (42 U.S.C. Sec. 6010). *Direct services* provided developmentally disabled persons and their families include education and training, income maintenance, community opportunities, residential living, and other essential assistance. *Indirect services* provide the needed support and management to operate effective service programs of developmentally disabled individuals. One of the greatest shortcomings of current practice is found in the inadequate and/or inappropriate conversion of accepted philosophical premises into operational guidelines and practices in planning and operating service programs. (Many of the program requirements that validly represent contemporary standards and strategies for developing service programs are discussed in detail elsewhere in this volume.)

Although courts have tended to view the least restrictive environment as a static concept—i.e., that one either is or is not in the least restrictive alternative that is appropriate given his or her skills—the concept becomes truly dynamic in service agencies and schools that percieve it as a primary goal of the continally evolving relationship between developmentally disabled persons, service providers, the family, neighbors, and other citizens who respond to disabled persons' changing abilities in the community.

While much of the evolution of the contemporary residential services system has been determined by interpretations of social, philosophical, and constitutional principles, it is important to recognize the substantial and rapidly growing body of literature that has also supported and shaped the system's develop-

ment. Indeed, based on recent court decisions as well as the generally more superficially tolerable conditions in institutions today, it seems inevitable that future decisions about major modifications in service delivery and resource allocation will be based on empirical evidence of treatment effectiveness.

## Standards of Effective Education and Training

Gilhool (1982), citing a federal court decision of over a century ago, recently pointed out that when one accepts professional responsibility for the welfare of other persons, one is accountable for serving those persons with what are demonstrably the highest standards—which are not necessarily the most common standards—of the profession. Therefore, an understanding of contemporary standards of effective training is important and pertinent and is emphasized in this subsection. Note, however, that a discussion of the technology of training is omitted here, owing to its excellent coverage by Liberty in Chapter 2 of this volume. In setting the stage for Liberty's chapter, it is important to respond to two general questions raised about the effectiveness of habilitation programs: 1) What form of habilitation activities represent the most demonstrably effective practices for developmentally disabled persons?, and 2) Can habilitative programs be justified for all developmentally disabled persons?

Today it is generally acknowledged that the teaching-learning paradigm is the only consistently beneficial habilitative approach with developmentally disabled persons, with the exception, of course, of a limited number of treatments for specific disorders associated with developmental disabilities (e.g., phenobarbitol or diphenylhydantoin for grand mal seizure disorders or ventriculo-peritoneal shunts for hydrocephalus). Although there have been claims of success for general nonteaching therapies (e.g. neurodevelopmental patterning, vestibular stimulation or megavitamin treatments as promoting the development of severely impaired persons), none of these claims has been independently substantiated.

Indeed, disorders like autism that were once viewed primarily as emotional disturbances are regarded today as developmental disabilities, largely on the basis of the consistently and often dramatically greater effectiveness of teaching therapies over psychotherapies. What has been learned about teaching that has led to and improved upon the effectiveness of the teaching-learning paradigm is discussed in depth in the chapter by Liberty, this volume.

Discussions of effective habilitative practices for developmentally disabled persons frequently lead to questions about the habilitative potential of the more profoundly impaired persons within that population (Baer, 1981; Bailey, 1981; Burton & Hirshoren, 1979). The issues raised often center on whether there are not persons in this group for whom habilitation is hopeless, purposeless, and/or even cruel. These issues permit considerable opportunity for philosophical and even legal argumentation, but it is also important to approach them from a purely habilitative perspective. From such a viewpoint, experience indicates that at least currently, it must be acknowledged that some developmentally disabled persons do not and perhaps cannot achieve substantially increased levels of self-care, purposeful activity, or social participation despite substantial human and financial resources invested to that end. Admittedly, some habilitation clients have accomplished none of the goals established for them in any given time period, even though the goals for them have been as simple as teaching them to indicate a desire for food.

Research and experience notwithstanding, the crucial point may well be that there is no foolproof way of determining who will or who will not achieve a specific goal if the goal is reasonable and the technology appropriate. Furthermore, if a reasonable goal has been unmet within a particular time period, there has so far been no way of determining whether that goal might be met over a longer time period or by employing a different or modified technology of teaching/conditioning. Nor has it ever been established that failure to meet any particular goal will prevent the attainment of another reasonable goal. Moreover, a decision

by one or more professionals that an individual cannot master a particular skill has been frequently followed by the individual's mastery of the same or a similar goal under the training of other professionals. Therefore, in large measure a right to habilitation remains, even for the most profoundly retarded person, the right to a chance to develop beyond one's present status and perhaps beyond what others think is one's potential. Although such an admission of unreliability in habilitative outcome hardly satisfies more than mechanistic medical perspectives, it is no less real for its unpredictability. Therefore, in the case of profoundly impaired persons, as with other developmentally disabled individuals, the most effective habilitation programs can only be said to be ones that maximize the probability of treatment success by paying careful attention to what has been learned about the practices and conditions under which training has been most successful.

Recent research on habilitation of developmentally disabled persons has highlighted the importance of two aspects of the training situation that are increasingly recognized for their inseparability in maximizing the probability of successful treatment: 1) the content of instruction and 2) the context of instruction. As contemporary research and theory examine the most effective means of imparting skills needed to increase independence, self-care, and social participation of developmentally disabled persons, the context of instruction is increasingly identified as the content, and vice versa. In the following discussion these two salient concepts in the contemporary definition of habilitation activity are treated separately, even though, as will be suggested, the epitome in the application of each would be the same.

## Content of Instruction

The content of instruction can be divided into two subtopics, the technology and the curriculum. The former refers to the state-of-the-art in teaching developmentally disabled persons, irrespective of the relevance of the instruction to their lives; the latter to consideration of what is relevant to their lives, irrespective of how it will be taught. Obviously in application these two aspects of training content should be applied in concert so that habilitative programs are efficacious in input (use of demonstrably effective instructional practices) and outcome (instruction leads to valuable skills).

*Technology*  Behavioral psychology, and specifically the application of behavioral analysis and operant learning principles based on the theoretical work of B. F. Skinner, has had a dramatic effect in the past two decades both on how developmentally disabled persons are taught and on how much they are taught. Behavioral theory is based on a relatively simple notion that learning is an interactive process between the individual and the environment. However, the technology used in its many varied applications is both sophisticated and impressively effective in training people with developmental disabilities (see Liberty, this volume). The applied behavioral paradigm, particularly as it has been expanded in recent years by increased knowledge about "shaping" behaviors that an individual is not currently performing, about observational learning by which an individual learns vicariously from others, and about increasing the individual's ability to discriminate among relevant stimuli that accompany and precede the act being learned, has become increasingly effective for working with behaviors occurring in or desired in natural settings. This specific concern with habilitative therapy in natural settings does not necessarily derive directly from the behavioral technology itself, which is just as applicable to developing the ability to perform a behavior in any setting, but instead derives from the specific questions about what should be taught that have been made possible by improvements in the state-of-the-art technology of teaching.

*Curriculum*  As the technology of teaching developmentally disabled persons has improved, questions about what they should be taught have been determined less by a priori expectations of what is possible to teach an individual and more through analyses of what that individual needs to know to increase his or her level of independence, self-care, and social participation. This new approach to habilitation curricula development represents a clear break with traditional approaches whereby developmentally disabled persons were assessed for their status on a developmental hierarchy (generally a listing of skills in general domains in the order in which those skills tend to be mastered by normally developing children and youth), in which they were provided instruction in the "lowest level" skills in each domain that had not yet been mastered, and in which they were reassessed for progress against the same skill hierarchy. Even though this approach has had an intuitive logic and has frequently led to demonstrable client progress, particularly when coupled with the use of the best contemporary instructional technology, its application has often entailed a number of notable shortcomings. For example, such orientations in isolation tend to produce developmentally disabled adults who exhibit many of the behaviors desired of dependent children, or adults who become fixed at a skill level that even if mastered would have relatively little benefit on their adult lives (e.g., learning letters of the alphabet) or at a level they would never master. In the new approach to habilitation curricula development, the environmental context of learning is viewed as increasingly important in programs for developmentally disabled persons in selecting instructional content, as well as for improving the acquisition, maintenance, and generalization of skills.

One promising alternative to strictly developmentally oriented habilitation practices that has received strong support among professionals involved in the habilitation of developmentally disabled persons has been called by Brown and associates "the criteria of ultimate functioning" (Brown, Nietupski, & Hamre-Nietupski, 1976). According to these criteria, the curriculum for the habilitation of a developmentally disabled person—that is, the objectives for direct instruction—is based on concurrent consideration of the capabilities and characteristics of the individual and the skills required of him or her in the environments of present and probably future daily living. When "ultimate functioning" is used to plan habilitation, objectives are emphasized relating to daily living, such as taking a bus, choosing clothing, crossing streets, performing specific, productive occupational tasks, engaging in accepted forms of social introductions, preparing a bowl of cereal in the morning, recognizing the time to leave the house for work, recognizing restroom signs, using sign language for necessities, or whatever other skills are recognized to be of functional importance to the individual. Many research studies have demonstrated that these and other personally valuable daily living skills can be taught to severely/profoundly retarded persons (see, especially, the chapters by Liberty and Rusch & Mithaug in this volume).

In applying functional criteria to the planning of habilitation programs, it is increasingly accepted that educational and training programs for developmentally disabled persons should ultimately serve the same ends as those for normal people—they should maximize the individual's ability to function independently and productively. Today, the use of applied behavior technologies, observational learning, training in accurate recognition of stimuli, and the use of natural reinforcers in the direct teaching of daily living skills is producing results with developmentally disabled persons that were undreamed of when a more community-centered approach to services for developmentally disabled persons was gathering momentum in the 1960s. The use of this knowledge to continue and expand this effort is increasingly acknowledged as the moral, if not the legal, imperative for the habilitation programs provided in long-term care settings. Furthermore, an awareness of the role that these same approaches to functional habilitation can play in avoiding long-term care placement altogether or in enhancing prospects for living in relatively less restrictive ones is just beginning to surface.

In addition to bringing about the changing focus on "what to teach," recent research, theory, and practice have produced notably new responses to the question of "where to teach."

These components are described here as the "context of instruction."

## Context of Instruction

In recent years, greater emphasis has been placed on instructional designs in which the content of habilitation programs (technology and curriculum) and their context (teaching environment) are seen as a single instructional experience. The importance of the context of instruction—that is, the environment in which it is provided—has been stressed only relatively recently in programs for developmentally disabled persons. Prior to the 1970s, it was generally taken for granted that habilitation would occur in whatever setting was designated for it, whether that be a residential facility, day activity center, special education classroom, work adjustment center, or other setting. In large measure, the settings of habilitation were assumed to be immutable, and programs were expected to adjust their objectives to the setting. Such adjustment was relatively easily done when the program focus was primarily developmental and secondarily functional in orientation. For instance, materials related to color recognition, sorting activities, and picture identification could be used in a classroom setting irrespective of the age of the trainees. Indeed, most curricula for such developmental objectives were expressly designed for "classroom use," and because developmentally disabled persons never progressed beyond "school age " there was never a shortage of curriculum materials designed especially for intramural instruction. However, as the purposes of habilitation of developmentally disabled youth and adults have become increasingly focused on specific skills needed to maximize independence, self-care, and community participation as an adult, the setting or context of habilitation (instruction) has been accorded much greater significance.

A number of considerations have led to a greater reliance on natural community settings as contexts for instruction. Some of these relate simply to a lack of any viable alternative (e.g., in teaching the use of a bus for transportation, a real bus is the only feasible "buslike" setting). At other times, multiple natural settings are used to enhance the generalization of skills (e.g., mastery of public toilet use requires training in the wide range of examples of public toilets available in the community). Natural environments are also used because of the natural reinforcement the community provides when skills are demonstrated (i.e., goods purchased, social contacts, recreational activities, getting to where one wants to be and so forth reward developmentally disabled persons just as they do their nonhandicapped peers). Finally, habilitation in natural environments represents the most valid means of evaluating where a skill has actually been mastered. Purchases at a mock store in a developmental center can serve to prepare an individual for actual store use, but the real test of the acquisition of that skill can only be demonstrated at a real store with a real clerk, and the only test of the generalization of the skill is when other stores are used in ways that are appropriate for the individual.

At present, there is no general consensus about what proportions of training can or should be in simulated versus natural environments, or about how experiences in one should relate to the other. In general, research suggests that both simulated and natural environments can be used effectively in habilitation programs (Kazdin, 1980; Mithaug, 1981). Indeed, there are many advantages to using simulated experiences for part of the training process. For example, teaching someone to tie a shoe only when he or she first puts it on in the morning or when it "naturally" comes untied is not likely to be effective. However, ultimately most skills must be appropriately demonstrated, maintained, and generalized in the environment in which the client lives his or her daily life before a relevant habilitation objective can be said to be attained.

The realization of the vital role that natural environments play in the habilitation of developmentally disabled persons leads to serious questions about the viability of institutional settings to meet the contemporary standards of adequate habilitation. If a meaningful purpose of habilitation is to prepare people to live in normal community settings, then the typical institution or segregated school has no means of providing an adequate context to its training. The observation that institutions are effective at training people in the skills of living in institutions is not new (see Goffman, 1961), but what is more relevant today is how much less effective are institutions than their community-based alternatives at preparing people to live outside institutions.

Contemporary standards of effective training dictate that habilitative programs incorporate the natural community in at least the assessment stage of the skill acquisition process, and, increasingly, in training stages as well. The ability of institutional placements to provide minimally adequate opportunities to meet the individual's right to habilitation is of growing concern, if not to the judiciary, to the professional community. As research and experience continue to show the notable achievement of daily living skills by persons receiving habilitative treatment ("active programming") in natural community contexts, institutional care will be challenged less often on the tolerability of its conditions and more often on the supposition that it simply lacks the environmental potential to provide an adequate program. In these efforts "adequacy" will increasingly be defined by the contemporary knowledge base regarding the development of skills that constitute a culturally meaningful concept of habilitation.

## BUREAUCRATIC CONTEXTS OF INTEGRATED SERVICE DELIVERY

To this point, this chapter has focused primarily on the conceptual and programmatic forces that are of substantial and growing influence in promoting the increased integration of developmentally disabled persons. However, the impetus for desirable social changes often is attended by secondary problems and unintended consequences. Despite considerable progress in the ideas and programs that provide opportunity and acceptance to developmentally disabled citizens, difficult problems are now evident in the capacity of service systems to put that wisdom and knowledge into practice. With the decentralization of services from concentrated institutional service centers to multiple specialized and generic agencies, attempts to increase the social integration of and family support for developmentally disabled persons have often suffered from increasing fragmentation of responsibility. Moreover, the rapid successes of the past few decades, as has been noted, have not occurred without intense conflict over goals, strategies, and the appropriate pace of change. While such antagonisms invariably accompany significant change in largely traditional systems and programs, increasingly the drag caused by seemingly intractable bureaucratic and professionalized modes of operation are having deleterious effects not only on the morale of people working in them but also on the persons those systems and programs were established to serve. A number of chapters in this volume note problems among government and quasi-government agencies in dealing with the strains of altering traditional practices so that developmentally disabled persons can be integrated into the various domains of community living.

Recognition of the need to rededicate and redesign programs for developmentally disabled persons has caused considerable reexamination of care and habilitation systems. The extent to which programmatic and professional structures, and the parallel fiscal structures—all of which were established under quite different and considerably more simplified conceptualizations of appropriate care—can support increasingly integrated and community-oriented service system functions is being questioned to a greater and greater extent. Certainly, among the largest impediments to realizing the principles that were discussed earlier is the organization of service delivery systems and the financing of those systems. Both of these structures have been largely affected by piecemeal and nonintegrated development. These problems and approaches to their resolution are discussed at some length by Conley and by Copeland and Iverson in this volume.

Although often outmoded and dysfunctional, traditional, predominantly state, residential, educational, and habilitation systems for mentally retarded/developmentally disabled persons have survived and have remained largely intact. This is because like most human services organizations that utilize public funds to provide programs to people, these systems have an established base of support committed to maintaining them. In part, this support derives from the historical position of these systems as primary providers of services that might otherwise have been totally unavailable; from their being broker agencies in determining what services would be provided; from the traditional assumption of superior expertise and wisdom imbedded within the agencies; and from the continuing organizational control over the funding that is a prerequisite to any kind of programming. However, since the base of support for these umbrella agencies has derived from persons with a wide variety of vested interests, the foundational beliefs as well as goals of most of these organizations, if articulated at all, are extremely vague. By operating without clear goals, many of these agencies protect themselves from the loss of support and negative criticism of those with differing beliefs.

Human service agencies, by means of their vague objectives, ensure that they do not ''fail'' and, therefore, they seldom run any risk of finding themselves replaced by an agency that will do better, even though in terms of the values and standards discussed in this chapter, success and failure can be established with relative ease. What is more, since the agency is insulated from its own failure, failure can be blamed, instead, on the client or direct service provider (school or teacher; residence or care provider, work activity center or job supervisor). Today, over 100,000 developmentally disabled persons remain in state institutions, and over a quarter of a million handicapped school children, most of whom are severely impaired, receive their education without even being in the same building with nonhandicapped students. However, relatively few persons inside or outside the agencies ostensibly responsible for the services find the agencies to be failing.

It can be argued, and in some states seems obvious, that even if these agencies were willing and able to internally establish strong commitments to integrated, community-based programs, they would not be able to muster the political power or programmatic expertise to achieve them. That possibility notwithstanding, one of the persistent problems in service delivery today is that since systemwide goals and objectives, such as normalization, de-institutionalization, and least restrictive placement, are seldom interpreted or valued in the same way by all members, systems are inclined to develop structures that permit, or even encourage these goals and objectives to be ignored. When this situation is coupled with the fact that most of these organizations permit, or even require, members to become so involved in meeting the obligations of bureaucratic roles that responsibility for the nature of service is effectively alleviated, it becomes clear why service organizations tend to be characterized by inertia. Therefore, organizational changes are often reactive to court decisions, to threats of advocates, and to unignorable shifts in public opinion, rather than being proactive in focus.

Since the activities of human service agencies, including state and local education agencies, are largely structured by their bureaucratic organization, in time the main focus of an increasing number of policies becomes maintaining a need to existing personnel and procedures. Policy decisions become increasingly related to compensating for the lack of clearly formulated goals and objectives with standard operating procedures, finding new bureaucratic and programmatic problems to which old solutions can be applied (e.g., a segregated educational and residential setting no longer seen as appropriate for one target population is made available to a population whose isolation can be presented as acceptable), and generating new interpretations for no longer acceptable practices (e.g., segregated residential settings become interpreted as the new training ground for developing skills needed for integrated living).

Because so many human service agencies have been so eager to abdicate responsibility for shaping the nature and quality of human services in order to preserve organizational safety, there is seldom no alternative but to increase political pressure and expectations that these agencies contribute to improving, not just maintaining, the quality of residential and training services for developmentally disabled persons (see Thompson and Wray in this volume). Hope for future progress in many states, regions, and counties is pegged to an ultimate commitment by society to services that enhance the community integration of developmentally disabled persons that in turn demands leadership at the human service agency level that stimulates the supply of those services.

Ideally the necessary impetus to participate at the forefront of the social integration movement will emanate from the agencies themselves, but change will not happen overnight. There are vested professional and political interests in maintaining the status quo. For example, proponents of the status quo can always argue that the dysjunctions and feudalism that exist among state, regional, and county programs are the fault of the federal government, which, through its various programs and associated funding, is the ultimate dictator of state and local programs (the chapter by Copeland and Iverson in this volume responds well to this notion). But the real issue is that there are too many human service agencies that are not doing their job by even the broadest definitions of contemporary standards of appropriate service provision. Those who are unwilling to attack such political problems with political approaches are not without blame or responsibility for the current status of programs for developmentally disabled persons (see Thompson and Wray, in this volume). Unquestionably, in striving for goals discussed in this chapter, tolerance of complacency of human service agencies by persons professing the associated philosophies rings hollow. Human service agencies are the arm of public concern, and continuing to allow inaction and abrogation of responsibility by those agencies that do not actively support the integration of developmentally disabled persons reflects apathy equal to that of these agencies themselves.

The bureaucratic features of human service agencies cannot alone account for inefficiency and ineffectiveness in achieving the objective of social integration for developmentally disabled citizens. Occasionally, advocates and their legal representatives become too interested in achieving total victory and the submission of public agencies and personnel, rather than seeking accommodation and working with agencies to develop specific plans to implement the principles and goals upon which future improved service provision can be established. Likewise, service providers often place the self-interest of convenience and, occasionally profit, above the needs of clients. The barriers to constructive reform in human services form a complex web, which can only be unraveled by lowering the level of defensiveness and heightening the potential for cooperation among human service agency managers, providers, advocates, and developmentally disabled persons and their families.

But in general, the signs are positive. Perhaps more than ever, it is realized that the problems of providing high-quality social services do not exclusively derive from inadequate resources. It is increasingly recognized that labeling an activity a "social service" does not guarantee that it benefits members of society or is a proper expression of society's values. That many "services" being provided today are based on objectionable assumptions and discredited premises about human rights and potential is obvious. However, within the past few years, such realizations have generated many new service models, much knowledge about strategies for establishing these models, and a truly impressive technology of teaching to assist developmentally disabled persons in acquiring the skills that are common to their culture. This volume describes some of these advances and in the process, it is hoped, contributes to them.

## REFERENCES

Aanes, D., & Haagenson, L. Normalization: Attention to a conceptual disaster. *Mental Retardation*, 1978, *16*(1), 55–56.

Baer, D.M. A hung jury and a Scottish verdict: Not proven. *Analysis and Intervention in Developmental Disabilities*, 1981, *1*, 91–97.

Bailey, J.S. Wanted: A rational search for the limiting conditions of habilitation in the retarded. *Analysis and Intervention in Developmental Disabilities*, 1981, *1*, 45–52.

Blatt, B. *Exodus from pandemonium: Human abuse and reformation of public policy.* Boston: Allyn & Bacon, 1970.

Blatt, B. *Souls in extremis.* Boston: Allyn & Bacon, 1973.

Bogdan, R., & Taylor, S. *Introduction to qualitative research methods.* New York: John Wiley & Sons, 1975.

*Brown v. Board of Education*, 347 U.S. 483 (1954).

Brown, L., Nietupski, J., & Hamre-Nietupski, S. The criterion of ultimate functioning. In: M.A. Thomas (ed.), *Hey, don't forget about me!* Reston, VA: Council for Exceptional Children, 1976.

Bruininks, R.W., & Lakin, K.C. (eds.). *Living and learning in the least restrictive environment.* Baltimore: Paul H. Brookes Publishing Co., 1985.

Burton, J.A., & Hirshoren, A. The education of severely and profoundly retarded children: Are we sacrificing the child to the concept? *Exceptional Children*, 1979, *45*, 598–602.

Clements, J. Appropriateness of nursing home settings. In:

*Nursing homes in the system of residential services: Proceedings of a national symposium.* Arlington, TX: National Association for Retarded Citizens, 1976.

Conroy, J., Efthimiou, J., & Lemanowicz, J. A matched comparison of the developmental growth of institutional and deinstitutionalized mentally retarded clients. *American Journal of Mental Deficiency*, 1982, *86*, 581–587.

*Education for All Handicapped Children Act of 1975.* Federal Register, August 23, 1977, CRF Title 45, Sec. 121a.1–121a.754, pp. 42474–42514.

Flynn, R.J., & Nitsch, K.E. (eds). *Normalization, social integration and community services.* Baltimore: University Park Press, 1980.

*Garrity v. Galen*, 522 F. Supp. 171 (1981).

Gilhool, T.K. The 1980s: Teacher preparation programs, handicapped children, and the courts. In M.C. Reynolds (ed.), *The future of mainstreaming: Next steps in teacher education.* Washington, D.C.: American Association of Colleges of Teacher Education, 1982.

Goffman, E. *Asylums: Essays on the social situation of mental patients and other inmates.* Garden City, NY: Doubleday & Co., 1961.

*Halderman v. Pennhurst State School and Hospital*, 612 F. 2d 84 (3rd Cir. 1979), 100 S. Ct. 3046.

Hauber, F.A., Bruininks, R.H., Hill, B.K., Lakin, K.C., Scheerenberger, R.C., & White, C.C. National census of residential facilities: A 1982 profile of facilities and residents. *American Journal on Mental Deficiency*, in press.

Hill, B.K., Bruininks, R.H., & Lakin, K.C. Physical and behavioral characteristics of mentally retarded people in residential facilities. *Health and Social Work*, 1983, *8*, 85–95.

Hill, B.K., Lakin, K.C., & Bruininks, R.H. *Trends in residential services for mentally retarded people, 1977–1982*. (CRCS Brief #23). Minneapolis: University of Minnesota, Department of Educational Psychology, 1984.

*Horachek v. Exon*, 357 F. Supp. 71 (D. Neb. 1973).

Kazdin, A. *Behavior modification in applied settings*. Homewood, IL: Dorsey Press, 1980.

Kiesler, C.H. Mental hospitals and alternative. *American Psychologist*, 1982, *37*(4), 349–360.

Lakin, K.C. *Demographic studies of residential facilities for mentally retarded*. Minneapolis: University of Minnesota, Department of Educational Psychology, 1979.

Lakin, K.C., Bruininks, R.H., Doth, D., Hill, B.K., & Hauber, F.A. *Sourcebook on long-term care for developmentally disabled people*. Minneapolis: University of Minnesota, Department of Educational Psychology, 1982.

Lakin, K.C., & Hill, B.K. *Expansion of the Medicaid ICF-MR program over a five year period, 1977–1982* (CRCS Brief #25). Minneapolis: University of Minnesota, Department of Educational Psychology, 1984.

Lakin, K.C., Hill, B.K., Hauber, F.A., & Bruininks, R.H. Changes in age at first admission to residential care for mentally retarded people. *Mental Retardation*, 1982, *20*, 216–219.

Lakin, K.C., Krantz, G.C., Bruininks, R.H., Clumpner, J.L., & Hill, B.K. One hundred years of data on public residential facilities for mentally retarded people. *American Journal on Mental Deficiency*, 1982, *87*(1), 1–8.

Little, C.S. Random remarks on state institutions. *Journal of Psychoasthenics*, 1923, *28*, 59–65.

Mackie, R. *Special education in the U.S.: Statistics, 1948–1966*. New York: Teachers College Press, 1969.

Mayeda, T., & Sutter, P. Deinstitutionalization: Phase II. In: R.H. Bruininks, C.E. Meyers, B.B. Sigford, & K.C. Lakin (eds.), *Deinstitutionalization and community adjustment of mentally retarded people*. Washington, DC: American Association on Mental Deficiency, 1981.

*Mills v. Board of Education of the District of Columbia*, 348 F. Supp. 866 (D.D.C., 1972).

Mithaug, D.E. *Prevocational training for retarded students*. Springfield, IL: Charles C Thomas, 1981.

National Association of State Mental Retardation Program Directors [NASMRPD]. *Trends in capital expenditures for mental retardation facilities: A state by state survey*. Arlington, VA: NASMRPD, 1980.

National Association of Superintendents of Public Residential Facilities for the Mentally Retarded. *Contemporary issues in residential programming*. Washington, DC: President's Committee on Mental Retardation, 1974.

National Institute of Mental Health. *Patients in mental hospitals*. Washington, DC: U.S. Government Printing Office, 1956.

National Institute of Mental Health [NIMH]. *Patients in state and county mental hospitals, 1980*. Washington, DC: NIMH, 1982 (microfiche).

*New York Association for Retarded Citizens [NYARC] and Parisi v. Rockefeller*, 357 F. Supp: (E.D.N.Y. 1973).

Nirje, F. The normalization principle. In: R. B. Kugel & A. Shearer (eds.), *Changing patterns in residential services for the mentally retarded* (rev. ed). Washington, DC: U.S. Government Printing Office, 1976.

*O'Conner v. Donaldson*, 422 U.S. 563 (1975).

*Pennsylvania Association for Retarded Citizens v. Commonwealth of Pennsylvania*, 334 F. Supp. 1257 (E.D.Pa. 1971).

Pense, A.W. Trends in institutional care for the mental defective. *American Journal of Mental Deficiency*, 1946, *50*, 453–457.

Pilewski, M.E., & Heal, L.W. Empirical support for deinstitutionalization. In: A.R. Novak & L.W. Heal (eds.), *Integration of developmentally disabled individuals in the community*. Baltimore: Paul H. Brookes Publishing Co., 1980.

Rivera, G. *Willowbrook*. New York: Random House, 1972.

*Romeo v. Youngberg*, 102 S. Ct. 2452 (1982).

Rotegard, L.L., & Bruininks, R.H. *Mentally retarded people in state-operated residential facilities: Years ending June 30, 1981 and 1982*. Minneapolis: University of Minnesota, Department of Educational Psychology, 1983.

Roth, R., & Smith, T.E. A statewide assessment of attitudes toward the handicapped and community living programs. *Education and Training of the Mentally Retarded*, 1983, *18*(3), 164–168.

Sandler, A., & Robinson, R. Public attitudes and community acceptance of mentally retarded persons: A review. *Education and Training of the Mentally Retarded*, 1981, *16*(2), 197–103.

Scheerenberger, R.C. A current census of state institutions for the mentally retarded. *Mental Retardation*, 1965, *3*, 4–6.

Scheerenberger, R.C. *Public residential services for the mentally retarded, 1981*. Minneapolis: University of Minnesota, Department of Educational Psychology, 1982.

Scheerenberger, R.C. *Public residential services for the mentally retarded, 1982*. Minneapolis: University of Minnesota, Department of Educational Psychology, 1983.

Schwartz, C. Normalization and idealism. *Mental Retardation*, 1977, *15*(6), 38–39.

*Section 504 of the Rehabilitation Act of 1973* [P.L. 93-112]. *Federal Register*, May 4, 1977, CFR Title 45, Sec. 84.1–84.61, p. 22676–22702.

Sigford, B.B., Bruininks, R.H., Lakin, K.C., Hill, B.K., & Heal, L.W. Resident release patterns in a national sample of public residential facilities. *American Journal on Mental Deficiency*, 1982, *87*(2), 130–140.

*Society for Good Will to Retarded Children v. Carey*, 47 U.S.L.W. 2546 (E.D.N.Y. 1979).

Taylor, S., Brown, K., McCord, W., Giambetti, A., Searl, S., Mlinarcik, S., Atkinson, T., & Lichter, S. *Title XIX and deinstitutionalization: The issue for the 80's*. Syracuse, NY: Syracuse University, Center on Human Policy, 1981.

Throne, J.M. Normalization through the normalization principle: Right ends, wrong means. *Mental Retardation*, 1975, *13*(5), 23–25.

U.S. Office of Special Education and Rehabilitative Services. *Fourth annual report to Congress on the imple-*

mentation of Public Law 94:142: The Education for All Handicapped Children Act. Washington, DC: U.S. Department of Education, 1982.

Vail, D. Dehumanization and the institutional career. Springfield, IL: Charles C Thomas, 1967.

Welsch v. Likins, 373 F. Supp. 487 (D. Minn. 1974).

Where toys are locked away. Senator R.F. Kennedy's indictment of New York State's institutions for mentally retarded children. Christian Century, September 29, 1965, 1179–1180.

Wilken, W. State aid for special education. Washington,

DC: U.S. Department of Health, Education & Welfare, 1977.

Wolfensberger, W. The principle of normalization in human services. Toronto: National Institute on Mental Retardation, 1972.

Wolfensberger, W. The definition of normalization: Update, problems, disagreements, and misunderstandings. In: R.J. Flynn & K.E. Nitsch (eds.), Normalization, social integration and community services. Baltimore: University Park Press, 1980.

Wyatt v. Stickney, 344 F. Supp. 387 (M.D. Ala. 1972).

# Part II

## ASSESSMENT AND
## INTERVENTION STRATEGIES

The social integration of severely handicapped persons is influenced substantially by the degree to which society and its members tolerate deviance. Studies of children in residential settings outside of the natural family consistently report severity of mental retardation and behavior problems as the primary reasons for initial placements. Severity of mental retardation and related disabilities are the major reasons given for placement of younger children, while problem behaviors in home and community settings are frequently mentioned as the reasons for the placement of older, mildly and moderately retarded persons (Bruininks & Krantz, 1979; Farber, 1968; Saenger, 1960). Consistent with these findings are the reasons cited for the placement failures of individuals in less supervised and less-restrictive settings who are later readmitted to more supervised and more-restrictive institutional settings. Inadequate adaptive behaviors or problem behavior are repeatedly given as the principal reasons for reinstitutionalization (Lakin, Hill, Hauber, Bruininks, & Heal, 1983). Unfortunately, such studies have not included simultaneous analyses of environmental qualities to assess the complex interactions among the individual's behavior, public acceptance of deviation, competence of personnel in training settings, and effectiveness of training programs. When placement failure in less-restrictive settings does occur, it is generally ascribed to the individual's behavioral deficiencies rather than to inadequacies in the environment.

Current theory and research in behavioral science is still too primitive to unravel the complex interactions between behavior and environment for severely handicapped or even nondisabled persons. The importance of behavior in defining publicly acceptable ranges of deviance in Western societies has been documented for centuries, and with particular eloquence by Jean Itard in the 18th century (Itard, 1962, reprint; see also Lane, 1976; Scheerenberger, 1983; Wolfensberger, 1980). Itard, in a classic behavioral intervention study titled *The Wild Boy of Aveyron*, described the deficient adaptive and problem behaviors of Victor, a young boy discovered living in rural forests of France. Seeking to achieve normal functioning for Victor, Itard orchestrated an intensive, sequential program of habilitation that serves as a model even today. A significant application of Itard's work for today's practitioners was his painstaking analysis of behavioral functioning and his carefully prescribed training procedures to improve the adaptation of Victor and thereby enhance his integration into normal community settings. Like effective practitioners today, Itard recognized that assuring fuller social integration and public acceptance of severely handicapped citizens requires both attention to environmental considerations and a focus on the improvement of behavioral functioning.

The chapters in this section address important areas in the assessment and training of handicapped persons. In Chapter 2, Kathleen A. Liberty discusses what research has discovered about learning and teaching as they relate to acquisition, maintenance, generalization, and adaptation of skills among severely handicapped children and youth. Liberty's discussion is a thorough, scholarly, and challenging statement and offers a positive lesson particularly for those who doubt the efficacy of recent policies to provide appropriate education and habilitation to severely/profoundly handicapped persons. The state of the art that she describes is one that schools and other training programs should increasingly be held responsible to implement.

In Chapter 3, Julie Gorder Holman and Robert H. Bruininks discuss the concept of adaptive behavior and its importance in defining retardation and deviance in our society. They further present information on assessment measures of adaptive behavior and trends in research concerned with improvement of adaptive functioning through training. Lanny E. Morreau, in Chapter 4, discusses assessment and intervention issues involved in managing problem behaviors. As he notes, problem behaviors are among the most frequent reasons given for failure in residential, work, and educational placements and are cited as the chief barrier to increased integration of severely handicapped persons.

In Chapter 5, John E. Rynders and Darlene S. Stealey turn to the crucial area of early childhood intervention programs. These programs range from those to train parents to stimulate their own children's development to full-time, special education preschool programs with additional family support. Rynders and Stealey examine carefully the research base related to the efficacy of early education programs for severely handicapped children and interpret the direction of that research as it bears on social policy.

Together these chapters address important issues in assessment, planning of training programs, and strategies for enhancing the adaptation, public acceptance, and social integration of severely handicapped persons. Suggestions for future research in these areas are also made.

## REFERENCES

Bruininks, R.H., & Krantz, G.C. (eds.). *Family care of developmentally disabled members.* Minneapolis: University of Minnesota, Department of Educational Psychology, 1979.

Farber, B. *Mental retardation: Its social context and social consequences.* Boston: Houghton Mifflin Co., 1968.

Itard, J. *The wild boy of Aveyron.* New York: Appleton-Century-Crofts, 1962, reprint.

Lakin, K.C., Hill, B.K., Hauber, F.A., Bruininks, R.H., & Heal, L.W. New admissions and readmissions to a national sample of residential facilities. *American Journal on Mental Deficiency,* 1983, *88,* 13–20.

Lane, H. *The wild boy of Aveyron.* Cambridge: Harvard University Press, 1976.

Saenger, G. *The adjustment of severely retarded adults in the community.* Albany: New York State Interdepartmental Health Resources Board, 1960.

Scheerenberger, R.C. *A history of mental retardation.* Baltimore: Paul H. Brookes Publishing Co., 1983.

Wolfensberger, W. A brief overview of the principle of normalization. In: R.J. Flynn & K.E. Kitsch (eds.), *Normalization, social integration, and community services.* Baltimore: University Park Press, 1980.

# Chapter 2

# Enhancing Instruction for Maintenance, Generalization, and Adaptation

*Kathleen A. Liberty*

E veryone learns. Learning occurs through direct experience with the environment. Learning may be observed by noting changes in the way we behave and in the way we act upon and interact with our environment. Educators attempt to direct learning by controlling and intervening in the environmental interactions of their students. For students with special problems that slow and inhibit learning, it is crucial that instruction not only direct learning but accelerate the learning process.

Researchers can determine how changes in the environment affect learning by measuring observable behavior. The environmental events that accelerate learning are translated into instructional strategies whose effect is verified by further investigations. As a consequence of countless experimental studies in laboratories, in public school classrooms, and in other training settings, powerful instructional techniques that accelerate skill and concept acquisition by students with special difficulties have been identified. Special educators have adopted these practices, and the result has been an explosion in the variety, the quality, and the number of new skills acquired by severely handicapped learners.

Gradually it has become clear, however, that most of the new skills fail to be maintained after instruction ceases. Even if skills maintain, most do not generalize to situations beyond the training situation, nor are they adaptable to differences in application required by different situations. Skills that are not maintained and not generalized and that cannot be adapted are useless to the learner, and the time and effort spent teaching them is a waste. Some have been tempted to attribute the failure to the learner. However, since acquisition can be accelerated with special strategies, it is just as likely that instructional plans can be remediated to produce skills that are maintained, generalized, and adaptable to new situations.

We know that not all instruction teaches. The best teaching not only accelerates acquisition, it produces skills that are maintained, generalized, and adaptable. Acquisition, maintenance, generalization, and adaptation of skills by severely handicapped students cannot be left to chance. Although research is just be-

The activity which is the subject of this report was supported in whole or in part by the U.S. Department of Education, contract 300-82-0364. However, the opinions expressed herein do not necessarily reflect the position or policy of the U.S. Department of Education, and no official endorsement by the department should be inferred.

29

ginning to accumulate that identifies which techniques work best for individual students and specifies exactly when they will be most efficient, information is now available that will increase instructional effectiveness in producing maintenance, generalization, and adaptation—the outcomes of learning. A brief look at the process of learning will provide the basis for a discussion of instruction that enhances maintenance, generalization, and adaptation.[1]

## THE LEARNING PROCESS

Scientists have identified two classes of behavior: respondent and operant. Respondents were originally considered to be unlearned and essentially unmodifiable reflexes, controlled by the "autonomic" nervous system (Butter, 1968). Recent advances in neurology, neurobiology, and neuropsychology, as well as in experimental medicine and psychology, have shown that modern conditioning techniques, such as biofeedback, can result in conscious control of such respondents as tics, seizure disorders, tongue thrust, salivation, spasticity, heart rate, and blood pressure. To date, the equipment currently used for training procedures limits classroom application, although some procedures may eventually affect physical and occupational therapy.

Since most education is directed at enhancing and enlarging the skill repertoire of students, and since skilled behaviors are operant behaviors, this chapter focuses on this class of behavior. The development of operant behaviors is dependent upon active interaction with the environment. A response that brings about a reaction or effect on the environment is called an operant; the reaction or effect produced is called a stimulus. Events, objects, people— indeed, nearly all things in our environment— are considered stimuli for learning. The reaction affects whether or not the response it follows is likely to occur again in the future. The stimulus, in turn, precedes another response in

the chain R---> S---> R---> S---> R---> S--->, and so on. In order to understand learning, one must first consider one unit of the chain—the antecedent stimulus, the response, and the subsequent stimulus—although the principles of learning apply to the entire chain as well as to the discrete unit.

### Subsequent Stimuli

The events that follow an operant may either increase the likelihood that the response will occur again, decrease the likelihood of future occurrence, or have no effect on the response. Events that increase the probability of the behavior recurring are said to be reinforcing stimuli. The response is repeated as the individual learns the relationship between the response and its effect, that is, as he or she learns how to operate on the environment in order to produce a desired effect (reinforcing stimuli).

Since reinforcing events are defined by their impact on responding, reinforcers vary from person to person and from response to response. However, researchers have been able to identify events that almost always reinforce the event they follow, including: attention from another person, proximity to another person, physical contact from another person, social approval, and money. These events have functioned so often to accelerate and/or to maintain behavior that they are referred to as generalized reinforcers (Kazdin & Bootzin, 1972). Although these events are presumed to be reinforcers, individual, social, and even cultural differences make it impossible to predict with perfect accuracy that a specific event will reinforce a specific response at a given time. Individual preferences for events may alter the reinforcing power of that event—for example, coffee may be desired in the morning but not in the evening. Social values and conventions may also affect acceptable reinforcers—for instance, kissing in private versus kissing in public. And cultural values may influence reinforcers—for example, overt praise is an insult in

---

[1]An enormous body of research has accumulated over the past several decades on the principles of learning presented in this chapter. It is not the purpose of this chapter to comprehensively review the experimental literature but to synthesize information important to educators. Readers wishing more information and documentation may begin with the references at the end of this chapter.

some Micronesian cultures. It cannot be assumed that any given event will reinforce a particular operant performed by any specific person.

During acquisition of a response, reinforcement produces an acceleration (increase over time) in the frequency of occurrence of the response. However, the increase is not infinite; other ehaviors are demonstrated, and setting changes or physical limits are reached. Once this happens, the frequency of the behavior is maintained at a level that maximizes reinforcement for the individual. Reinforcement may be inferred from performance graphs that show behavior to be either improving or remaining stable. A response that is decelerating in frequency or that is not occurring is not being reinforced.

An event that follows a response and that results in a decrease in the probability that the response will occur again is a punishing stimulus. The term *punishment* usually connotes physical force, such as a spanking, but in operant terminology, any event is considered punishing if it decelerates the response. As with reinforcers, it cannot be predicted that a particular event will be a punisher. Parents and teachers often react to behaviors they find undesirable with negative statements (e.g., "Don't do that," or "Get back to your seat"). Unfortunately, such statements may have an effect opposite to that intended—the behavior increases in frequency. In such a case the negative statements therefore function as reinforcers.

An event that has no effect on the behavior it follows (a neutral stimulus) can acquire reinforcing or punishing properties if it occurs consistently with a known reinforcer or punisher. Money is an example of a stimulus that does not have intrinsically reinforcing properties; but since money is consistently paired with the opportunity to purchase objects or events of the individual's choice, it quickly acquires reinforcing properties of its own.

Learning occurs most quickly and most often through reinforcement, and, as this chapter will emphasize, effective instruction can be based on the positive properties of reinforcement. Ethical and procedural considerations regarding the use of punishment, coupled with punishment's relative ineffectiveness, limit its use in teaching (see, for example, Morreau in this volume).

## Schedules of Reinforcement

Learning is affected by changes in the density of reinforcement (the number of reinforcing events that occur) and the timing of the reinforcer. The schedule of reinforcement is the quantitative relationship between the response and reinforcement. Reinforcement may occur following each response, or after several responses, or after a period of responding. If a fixed number of responses must occur before reinforcement, the schedule of reinforcement is *fixed ratio* (FR). For example, under a FR5 schedule, the learner would be reinforced following the fifth response, the tenth response, the fifteenth response, and so on. In *variable ratio* (VR) schedules, reinforcement occurs unpredictably, but the total number of reinforcers in relation to the total number of behaviors can be predetermined (e.g., of 25 responses, reinforcing the first, the third, the tenth, the seventeenth, and the twenty-third would produce an average of 1 reinforcer to every 5 responses: VR5). Ratio schedules tend to develop responses that occur with a high frequency, since rapid responding increases the number of reinforcers.

Reinforcement may also be scheduled to follow a time period, or interval, of responding. A response that is reinforced under a *fixed interval* (FI) of 5 minutes (FI5') produces reinforcement after 5 minutes of responding, regardless of the number of responses that have been performed. A *variable interval* (VI) schedule of 5 minutes (VI5') would result in reinforcement, on the average, after 5 minutes of responding. Interval schedules of responding usually produce steady response rates at lower frequencies than those that result from ratio schedules.

The power of a schedule of reinforcement is measured by studying its impact during acquisition and maintenance of the response. Acquisition is the period during which the response first occurs. The more powerful the schedule, the faster the acquisition. Much of instruction currently focuses on acquisition; however, unless that response continues to be performed over time, after instruction ceases, the new response can hardly be considered of value. *Maintenance* is the continued perform-ance of a response after instruction has ceased; presumably, since the response continues, it is being reinforced. Experimenters study the maintenance power of a schedule of reinforce-ment by withdrawing *all* reinforcement from a response. This procedure, called *extinction,* will result in a deceleration (decrease over time) of the response to low or zero levels. The more powerful a schedule of reinforcement, the *longer* the response will be performed (maintained) under extinction conditions.

As might be expected, schedules affect ac-quisition and maintenance differently. Ac-quisition is most rapid when there is consider-able reinforcement (e.g., FR1). But, that same schedule produces the worst maintenance. In general, variable schedules, either ratio or in-terval, produce better maintenance than fixed schedules. Maintenance is further improved by longer intervals and higher ratios (e.g., VI60' produces better maintenance than VI5'). Mixed variable interval and variable ratio schedules at long intervals and high ratios pro-duce the best maintenance.

## Shaping New Behaviors
## and Observational Learning

New responses are shaped by reinforcing dis-crete movements that are already part of the individual's repertoire—either operants, re-spondents, or other movements. By reinforc-ing closer and closer approximations of the de-sired behavior, the "new" response is shaped from "old" responses. The process of shaping a response through reinforcement of successive approximations of the desired behavior is easi-ly observed during the acquisition of language in children. At first any verbalization (crying, gurgling) by the infant is met by attention (rein-forced) by the parent. Later, parents shift rein-forcement to those sounds that more closely resemble verbalizations. Gradually, attention is shifted to those sounds that most resemble

words. Shaping continues until only intelligi-ble responses are reinforced, and then two words are reinforced, and so on. Most operant behaviors are acquired by shaping.

Experimenters have found that successful shaping requires close observation of move-ments and careful attention to appropriate rein-forcement. Reinforcement must be shifted from one movement to another that more close-ly resembles the desired operant. If a move-ment occurs that closely approximates the de-sired response, and if it is not reinforced, it is less likely to occur again, thus delaying learn-ing.

In addition to shaping, responses may be learned by observation. The learner observes another person's behavior and its effect and then imitates the behavior. If the learner is rein-forced for this behavior, it is likely not only that he or she will use that behavior again but that the learner will imitate other behaviors. How-ever, imitative behavior has also been observed to occur even without overt reinforcement of the specific imitative response. Young children who imitate their parents by repeating words they have heard may do so without any obvious reinforcement for that response. Reinforce-ment for a specific imitated response may also result in imitations of other behaviors without specific reinforcement of those behaviors.

Models may provide much information about human behaviors, especially in regard to socially acceptable behaviors. In addition, ob-servational learning may be the quickest meth-od of teaching complex behavior chains and of behaviors where errors must be avoided or in which the consequence for an error will be so punishing that the probability of future re-sponses is likely to be severely curtailed (e.g., as in teaching young children to swim [Bandur-a, 1971, 1973]).

## Antecedent Stimuli

The events that precede the response are also crucial in operant learning. There are two gen-eral levels of antecedent stimuli: the general setting, or disposition, of the environment and the more specific stimuli that precede a particu-lar response. For example, a restaurant consists of an enormous variety of stimuli that dispose us to behave in certain ways (e.g., ordering food, speaking quietly, eating and drinking) that may not be found in other settings (e.g., a synagogue). Specific stimuli within that general setting are associated with more specific responses (e.g., a picture of a hamburger on the menu may precede ordering a hamburger). "Setting events seem to determine which stimulus-response interactions will become functional for the individual" (Wahler & Graves, 1983, p. 27), and this class of stimuli can be thought of as "setting the stage" for a general class of behavior (e.g., a class of specific restaurant-associated behaviors). Unfortunately, little research has been conducted on the influence of setting events during learning on maintenance, generalization, and adaptation. However, interest in this area may be increasing (Wahler & Fox, 1981). Future research on the influence of setting events on learning should help to clarify and strengthen instruction.

Most of the experimental research has been directed at the stimuli that immediately precede a specific response. These stimuli signal whether a particular response from the class of responses available to the learner is likely to be reinforced, punished, or ignored. During the learning process, the antecedent stimuli become associated with the response and, thus, with the consequence of the response. Responding that is followed with reinforcement is not only more likely to occur in the future but is likely to become associated with the stimuli that preceded it.

The process of acquiring a skill not only involves learning the response itself but discriminating when that response is likely to be reinforced. Two important classes of stimuli are associated with a response: stimuli that are associated with response reinforcement (S+) and stimuli that are associated with nonreinforcement (S−). For example, a greeting is likely to be a S+ for the response of "Hi," while "Bye" is an S− for "Hi." A student who consistently responds with "Hi" to a greeting and does not say "Hi" to other stimuli for verbal responding (such as "Bye") has learned an appropriate discrimination. The student who fails to respond or who says "Hi" following other stimuli (such as "Bye") has not learned the discrimination. In order for discrimination learning to occur, both S+ and S− must be presented, but only the response that follows the S+ is reinforced. In general, the more often the S+ and S− are presented, and the more immediate and often the reinforcement, the faster the learning.

In most situations, a response will be appropriate if it follows a range of stimuli that share certain characteristics. For example, the response "Hi" is actually appropriate following a wide variety of different greetings, not just "Hi." Generalized responding is desirable when the response should be associated with a range of stimuli. If generalization is desired, the response must be associated with a range of S+'s that share some characteristic, called a stimulus class. For example, the class of greeting stimuli could contain "Hi," "Hello," "How you doing," "Good Morning," and so on. It is generally impossible to provide instruction in all instances of the S+. When instruction produces responses to untrained S+'s, *generalization* is said to occur. For example, a student who responds with "Hi" to the untrained S+ of "Hey there," has generalized the "Hi" response.

A third class of stimuli, irrelevant stimuli (S$i$), has been identified, and is often associated with the failure to generalize and with problems in accelerating discrimination learning (Becker, Engelmann, & Thomas, 1971). Irrelevant stimuli (S$i$) are those that may occur with the S+ but that are not relevant or required for the response to be reinforced. For example, the facial appearance of the teacher is irrelevant to the response of "Hi." If, following instruction, the student does not respond "Hi" to other greeters, it is possible that irrelevant stimuli, such as differences in facial appearance, have been associated with the behavior.

While a specific response may be associated with a stimulus or a class of stimuli, usually other responses are also appropriate. For example, adding an "s" to form the plural of a word is a specific response that is appropriate for a certain class of stimuli. Other ways of creating plural forms (e.g., as in *foot-feet*) are associated with quite different classes of stimuli. However, many responses are less specific, and a class of responses may be associated with a class of stimuli and with reinforcement. The class of greeting stimuli, for example, can be followed by a wide variety of responses, like "Good to see you," "Hello there," and so on. In addition, the stimuli may induce changes in the topography of the response. *Response adaptation* occurs when the topography of the response is adjusted by the student to meet the requirements of a new, uninstructed situation. Topographical dimensions vary with different behaviors, but most can differ in intensity, in force, in the specific physical movements of which they are constituted, in their locus, and so on. For instance, verbal behavior can vary in tone and inflection (intensity), volume (force), and the person spoken to (locus). The class of responses of "putting on a shoe" will vary in the specific physical topography according to the differences in shoe types (e.g., putting on a tennis shoe requires different physical movements than putting on a loafer). Response adaptation, like generalization, is associated with a class of stimuli. While it is possible to provide instruction in a wide range of behaviors, it is improbable that every response adaptation needed for the possible range of stimuli to be encountered can be included in a curriculum.

Maintenance, generalization, and adaptation are not processes of learning but outcomes of learning. Conditions during instruction, when learning occurs, affect the quality, type, and nature of maintenance, generalization, and adaptation. The principles of learning can be applied to instruction both to speed acquisition and to enhance maintenance, generalization, and adaptation.

## INSTRUCTIONAL PLANNING

Prior to selecting instructional tactics, four important steps must be taken: selecting the behavior that is the target for instruction, selecting instructional aims, sequencing instruction, and determining measures of pupil pro-gress. In the pages following, aspects of each of these steps that relate directly to maintenance, generalization, and adaptation of behaviors are discussed.

## Selecting Behaviors

The probability that a behavior will be maintained, generalized, and adapted can be increased by selecting behaviors that permit the learner to gain access to the natural reinforcers in his or her environment (Stokes & Baer, 1977). For example, teaching the learner to say or sign "want" and then pointing to an object is a functional behavior, since it allows the student to access desirable objects and events in the environment. (For a discussion of the issues of selecting relevant behaviors as targets of instruction, the learner is referred to Brown, Branston, Hamre-Nietupski, Pumpian, Certo, & Gruenewald, 1979; Brown, Nietupski, & Hamre-Nietupski, 1976; Guess, Horner, Utley, Holvoet, Maxon, Tucker, & Warren, 1978; Wilcox & Bellamy, 1982.)

Performing the behavior that accesses reinforcers may be dependent on the actual physical topography (i.e., the muscles, bones, and so forth) involved in a sequence of movements. For example, if the behavior is "writes name," certain physically specific movements are critical. Unfortunately, severe motor problems of some learners may impede acquisition of the skill. Instead of targeting a motorically specific behavior, an analysis of the critical effect of the behavior could lead to adaptations in the selected behavior. For example, if the functional impact of the behavior was to permit the learner to access a variety of experiences and reinforcers (e.g., cashing checks at a bank, labeling personal possessions), then other behaviors could easily be substituted for the specific physical activity of writing (e.g., using a rubber stamp, using a press). Analysis of the critical effect of the behavior may result in selecting instructional targets that will permit learners access to reinforcers that may otherwise be unavailable to them. (An in-depth discussion of this important issue is presented in White [1980].)

For some targets, the form of the behavior may be adapted to specific learner needs. For example, a wide variety of behaviors could be performed by the student that would satisfy the requirements of "responds to name": turning one's head when one's name is called, meeting the eyes of a person who said the name, pointing to a card inscribed with the name, pushing a button when the name is said, saying "What?" when the name is said, touching one's chest when a photograph of one is shown, and so on. Usually the form of behavior selected for instruction will correspond to that of the student's age peers or is the most natural form of the behavior (e.g., saying "What?"). If a student's physical handicaps are likely to severely curtail the probability that the student will acquire the preferred mode of behaving, an alternative form of responding must be designed (see Hopper & Helmick, 1977).

Another method of adapting instructional requirements is to target behaviors that provide the student the opportunity to access reinforcers available to peers of the student's own age in his or her school, neighborhood, community, or eventual workplace through "partial participation" in specific activities. In order to select behaviors for partial participation, the natural events are analyzed (e.g., playing baseball), and the instructor selects those behaviors that he or she estimates the student can acquire most quickly (e.g., keeping score, cleaning baseball bats). Those behaviors are then taught first, permitting access to the reinforcers available to baseball participation (e.g., interpersonal interactions) that may not be otherwise available. The instructor may subsequently design instruction for behaviors that will permit greater participation (e.g., catching the ball) (Baumgart, Brown, Pumpian, Nisbet, Ford, Sweet, Messina, & Schroeder, 1982).

Instruction may also be directed at concepts. A concept is "the set of characteristics shared by a set of instances in a given universe of concepts and not shared by other instances in that universe" (Becker et al., 1971, p. 241). If a concept is the target of instruction, the nature of the response is important only insofar as it is able to identify learning. The specific form of the response is immaterial. For example, in teaching the concept of "more," the physical response could be pointing (to the pile that is "more"), answering a question ("More spoons or more napkins?"), following a direction ("Get some more chairs"), selecting a picture from an assortment ("Which shows more people?"), stacking objects ("Put more cookies on the plate"), and so on.

Flexibility in designing instruction to provide for alternative means of responding will result in increased identification of functional behaviors. Providing instruction in a wide variety of behaviors that permit the learner to access natural reinforcers will facilitate maintenance, generalization, and adaptation.

## Establishing Functional Instructional Aims

The identification and selection of functional instructional aims may enhance the probability of maintenance, generalization, and adaptation. Aims for both *accuracy* and *fluency* of the response should be set. *Accuracy aims* are the ones most often selected by teachers and may be stated as the proportion of the total response opportunities available that are to be performed accurately (e.g., 8 of 10 correct). Accuracy aims also describe the criterion for a correct response when the physical topography of the behavior is of concern (e.g., grasp and pick up object so that it is 2 inches above the table).

Accuracy aims should take into consideration the chance factor, and instruction should be designed to increase levels of confidence in the aim selected. For example, during acquisition of a receptive labeling skill, the instructor presents two objects (e.g., an apple and a truck) to the child and names one of them (e.g., "apple"). As learning occurred, the child would point to the apple (desired S+) with increasing accuracy (accelerating correct behaviors) and the truck or other object (S−) less and less often (decelerating incorrect behaviors). If the child responded randomly, his or her score would average 50% correct over a period of time. However, in any two-choice discrimination, the student could respond at an accuracy level of 100% by chance. Confidence that the discrimination has been actually learned can be increased by reducing the chance factor by increasing the number of objects presented (e.g., from 2 to 10). Learning may also be enhanced if multiple discriminations are required.

In other programs, the chance factor is impossible to calculate. For example, in an instructional program designed to teach the pupil to say "Hi" to the teacher, the probability that the student will say "Hi" as opposed to any one of many other possible responses (e.g., "Bye," turn away, perform a stereotyped behavior, look at someone else, sit down) is impossible to calculate. In such cases, accuracy is assessed over multiple trials.

*Fluency aims* involve the dimension of time. Fluency building aims are less familiar to instructors than accuracy aims, but the former may well be one important key to enhancing maintenance, generalization, and adaptation. For example, researchers provided instruction to students in walking until the students met accuracy criteria (O'Brien, Azrin, & Bugle, 1972). When the researchers returned for a follow-up observation, they found that the students were creeping or crawling instead of walking. The students still walked when requested to do so (walking had been maintained at the level achieved at the end of acquisition training), but walking was not their preferred mode of locomotion when they needed to move to another place. Upon investigation, the researchers found that the students were able to crawl faster than they were able to walk. Walking, because it was less fluent than crawling, could not compete in accessing reinforcers quickly, and was therefore not as functional. The researchers then provided fluency building instruction designed to make crawling less efficient than walking, and when they returned for a second follow-up, they found that walking, not crawling, was the students' preferred locomotion. In this example, the functional level was a fluency aim that permitted the target behavior to be reinforced by the natural consequences (in this case, arriving at the desired location).

The aspect of time that provides the best measure of the behavior is dependent on the type of behavior instructed. Self-care skills, locomotion, and time on task, for example, involve the length of time it takes the learner to perform the desired set of responses (*duration*). The number of behaviors completed within a time period (*rate*) is the important measure of fluency for many tool movement skills, as well as for many vocational production tasks. *Latency,* the time between the end of the stimulus and the beginning of the response, is likely to be the important measure of fluency in receptive communication, as well as in some discrimination tasks, for example.

In some programs, fluency may involve more than one temporal dimension. In some work programs, for instance, both rate of production and duration of production may be accelerated (Bellamy, Inman, & Schwarz, 1978). Sometimes the target behavior is a fluency problem, as when the student speaks too fast or responds before the stimuli are presented. Most often such fluency problems are of concern because the too-fast performance is associated with many errors. In these cases, fluency building aims might involve slowing performance to more natural and functional levels while preserving accuracy. The aspect of fluency most appropriate to the behavior may be determined by an analysis of the type of behavior and the type of performance desired.

Accuracy and fluency aims may be established in several ways. One method is to assess the performance of a competent nonhandicapped peer. For example, the aim for a "grasp, pick up, release" behavior can be set by measuring how accurately (number of objects picked up without dropping) and how fluently (duration to pick up object) peers perform the same behavior. In some instructional programs, a learner's physical handicap may prevent him or her from achieving a fluency aim equivalent to that of a nondisabled person. If such is the case, the other methods of selecting criteria will still permit the achievement of a functional level of performance.

Another method of establishing aims for accuracy and fluency is to assess the standards of the environment where the behavior is expected to be most functional. For instance:

How many minutes are allowed for dressing at home? How long will most people wait for an answer? In terms of the latter example, although educators might be willing to wait 10 or 15 seconds for an answer to a relatively simple yes/no question, rarely will such a long latency be permitted outside of training sessions. Similarly, parents may not be willing to wait for 30 or 40 minutes for their child to get dressed. In such cases, the consequences of disfluent behavior might be removal of the opportunity to behave—i.e., people walk away or the parents dress the child. Removal of an opportunity to behave can hardly be the situation desired at the end of instruction. Of course, combining assessments of both normal performance and standard expectations with the target environment is often important, especially for vocational training. For example, a housekeeping supervisor at a motel may be able to describe certain standards for maids, but it would be best to assess the performance of the maid identified by the supervisor as a good employee and to use those criteria for long-term aims.

Finally, accuracy and fluency aims can be derived by assessing the fluency of the behavior with which the instructed behavior must compete. For example, a "sign 'want' and point" behavior must be more fluent than the "scream" behavior the student uses to obtain objects if it is to replace it; walking must be more fluent than crawling; and so on.

Each of these methods should replace the armchair methods that currently determine most instructional aims. Setting nonfunctional aims or setting instructional aims at lower levels handicaps the learner by ensuring that the behavior will not be functional, will not maintain, and may not generalize or adapt (see Barrett, 1979; Haring, Liberty, & White, 1979, 1980, 1981; Horner, Bellamy, & Colvin, 1983; O'Brien, Azrin, & Bugle, 1972; Stokes & Baer, 1977).

## Sequencing Instruction

Many current methods for sequencing instruction are based on an analysis of the complete temporal sequence of the behavior. For example, the sequence of behaviors that comprise putting on a shoe may be described as:

1. Grasp shoe on sole
2. Open tongue of shoe
3. Insert toes of appropriate foot in shoe
4. Grasp sides of shoe, one hand on each side
5. Pull on shoe at heel of foot
6. Grasp back of heel of shoe
7. Slide heel into shoe

Instruction may be sequenced by beginning with teaching the first behavior and when that is mastered, moving to the second, then the third, and so on. This method of sequencing is called *forward chaining*, because the behaviors are linked one to another in the sequence in which they occur naturally (Figure 1a). In forward chaining, an instructional trial always begins with the first behavior to be performed and continues until the behavior identified as the last for that instructional step has been completed. As a result, the student does not have the opportunity to complete the entire behavior (i.e., the student's shoe will not be on his or her foot at the end of an instructional trial) until he or she reaches the last instructional step. Forward chaining delays the presentation of the natural reinforcer of "finishing a task" until the final instructional step and may, therefore, necessitate the use of more teacher directions or more reinforcers in order to facilitate acquisition. The teacher may choose to finish the entire sequence for the student (e.g., put on his or her shoe) or may physically assist the student to complete the entire sequence after the student responds on the instructed step. Such actions by the teacher *follow* the student's response, and may therefore function as either a reinforcer or a punisher.

Instead of forward chaining, the teacher may choose to *backward chain* (Figure 1b). In backward chaining, the first instructional step is designed to teach the last behavior in the sequence, the second step provides instruction in the final two steps, and so on. Backward chaining allows the student to complete the task and receive both teacher-controlled and natural reinforcers at an appropriate time. In order to provide the opportunity for the student to be-

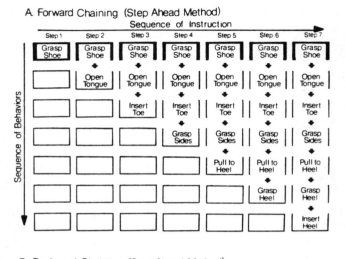

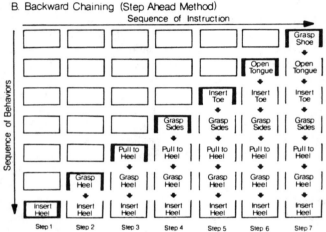

Figure 1.　Methods of sequencing instruction. (See text for discussion.)

have, the teacher may complete the first steps for the student (e.g., for step 1 in Figure 1b, the teacher would grasp the shoe, insert the student's toe, pull the shoe to the heel, and grasp the heel) or may assist the student to complete the sequence himself or herself, prior to the independent response opportunity.

With forward and backward chaining, as each step is acquired, the student moves "ahead" to a more complex behavior. In the examples just described, each step is a part of the whole that has been separated from the natural flow of the entire response. *Step-ahead* methods may be compared with *whole-behavior* approaches to instruction in which, instead of providing instruction on fragments of the desired behavior, instructional trials provide the opportunity to perform the entire sequence (Figure 1c).

The step-ahead method of instruction has also been advocated to teach concepts. However, instead of basing the steps on the temporal sequence of the desired behavior, the steps are based on the manipulation of antecedent stimuli, since

> Concept learning involves a double discrimination: (1) the discrimination of relevant characteristics of instances (S+) from relevant characteristics of not-instances (S−), (2) the discrimination of relevant from irrelevant characteristics (S$i$) within instances or not-instances (Becker et al., 1971, p. 241, italics omitted).

A discussion of sequencing instruction for the concept of "more" further illustrates techniques for accelerating concept learning. However, instruction in concepts should be preceded by a *concept analysis,* as described by Becker et al. (1971, 1975b). They have suggested four strategies for structuring instruction in concepts.

1. When a concept has more than one essential characteristic, begin teaching with the characteristic that leads to the greatest reduction in the alternative possibilities available. . . .
2. To teach a fixed characteristic, the basic strategy is to switch from an instance to a not-instance, changing only the fixed characteristic. . . .
3. To teach a range within S+ or S−, present a series of instances (or not-instances) in

which nothing changes but the range of the characteristics being taught. . . .
4. To teach a range of irrelevant characteristics (S$i$), present a series of instances in which all S$i$ keep changing and S− characteristics stay constant (Becker et al., 1971, p. 278, italics omitted).

The concept "more" has only one essential characteristic, the number of objects. The characteristic has a wide range, since the number in an instance of "more" can vary widely. A series of instances of the S+ and the S− can be arranged to illustrate a part of the range (e.g., the amount in the S+ set varied from two to four, in the S− set from one to three). Individual trials would consist of the presentation of one of the pairs of S+ and S−, with the learner asked to show either the S+ ("more") or the S− ("not more") at each trial.

|   |                      | "More" (S+) | "Not-more" (S−) |
|---|----------------------|-------------|------------------|
| a.| Vary S−              | xxxx        | O                |
|   |                      | xxxx        | OO               |
|   |                      | xxxx        | OOO              |
| b.| Vary S+              | xx          | O                |
|   |                      | xxx         | O                |
|   |                      | xxxx        | O                |
| c.| Vary both<br>S+ and S− | xx        | O                |
|   |                      | xxx         | OO               |
|   |                      | xxxx        | OO               |
|   |                      | xxxx        | OOO              |

The fourth strategy mentioned by Becker et al. (1971), is designed to eliminate irrelevant characteristics that may be associated with the objects used for instruction. For example, if pennies are used for the set of S+ objects and dimes for the S− objects, the student may come to associate the S+ with the physical properties of pennies (S$i$) and the S− with dimes, instead of with the characteristic of relative numbers of objects. Varying S$i$ for both S+ and S− would consist of presenting two sets of objects that consist of identical elements but that differ from instance to instance, as illustrated below.

|   |                         | "More" (S+) | "Not-more" (S−) |
|---|-------------------------|-------------|------------------|
| d.| Vary<br>S+, S−,<br>S$i_{1\text{ objects}}$ . . . | xxxx        | xxx              |
|   |                         | OO          | O                |
|   |                         | qqqq        | qq               |
|   |                         | @@@         | @                |

Other irrelevant characteristics will also have to be varied as well, including: the size of the objects and the constitution of the two sets.

|  | "More" | "Not more" |
|---|---|---|
| e. Vary $S+, S-, Si_{2\ size}$ | XXXX | xxx |
|  | ooo | OO |
|  | QQQQ | qqq |
| f. Vary $S+, S-$, | sev | w |
| $Si_{3\ set\ components}$ | esa | sxi |
|  | aowc | ror |

The instructional sequence can be established as a step-ahead or a *whole-concept* approach, similar in theory to the whole-behavior method. With the step-ahead method, the sequence would be:

1. Vary $S+$
2. Vary $S-$
3. Vary $S+$ and $S-$
4. Vary $S+$, $S-$, and $Si_1$
5. Vary $S+$, $S-$, and $Si_2$
6. Vary $S+$, $S-$, $Si_1$, and $Si_2$
7. Vary $S+$, $S-$, and $Si_3$
8. Vary $S+$, $S-$, and all $Si$

Step 8 includes all of the necessary elements and represents the desired final state of affairs during instruction (except, of course, that the number of elements in the $S+$ and $S-$ instances would be expanded beyond four). However, there are no data to suggest that sequencing steps in the order 1, 2, 3, 4, 5, 6, 7, 8 would result in faster learning than any other sequence that might be derived (e.g., 2, 1, 3, 4, 5, 7, 6, 8).

A step-ahead sequence may also be constructed with fewer steps that might speed learning: (1) Vary $S+$ and $S-$ (incorporates three steps of the previous sequence); (2) Vary $S+$, $S-$, and all $Si$ (incorporates five steps of the previous sequence).

An alternative is to simply present the whole concept at once. Since step 8 represents the final goal, instruction can begin with the conditions of step 8 and then, if learning falters, step back to a specific step identified from an error analysis (discussed later in this chapter), as follows:

| "More" | "Not-more" |
|---|---|
| xT¢d | YT% |
| ce$ | o |
| DrwX | eDr |
| *8s | q$ |
| $$$ | ss |
| #1+ | ½ |
| XXXX | xxx |
| O)1 | O) |

Which approach to sequencing instruction should be used? Before answering this question, it is useful to look at some of the development of the step-ahead approach to special education. The process of task analysis is based on remedial work with mildly handicapped students. Breaking down a complex behavior, like oral reading, for example, was used to define the components (such as pronouncing vowel sounds) that constituted the more complex behavior. Once the components were identified, tests were constructed. A student who demonstrated a learning problem was tested and the specific skill to be remediated identified. This process has proven very effective. Task analysis is extremely useful in identifying the components of a complex task and thus in ensuring that the task to be taught is fully understood by the teacher. However, task analysis was never intended to serve as the sequence for instruction but only to identify the components to be instructed.

Any task can be broken into successively smaller bits of behavior. The minute pieces may be useful for remedial purposes, but they are not necessarily appropriate instructional steps. Instructional technology has provided teachers with the means of effectively speeding learning. The step-ahead approach based on a task analysis may simply negate the effects of the new technology, slowing learning by requiring the student to acquire step 1 before moving to step 2, and then to acquire step 2 before moving to step 3. Oral reading has been broken into over 2,000 steps; if reading were forward chained in a step-ahead approach according to that task analysis, even if the student were able to pass from one step to the next on each school day, and if the student were never absent, it would still take over 10 years of school to teach oral reading.

This problem adversely affects instruction of learners with severe handicaps. The more instructional time required for a particular behavior, the fewer behaviors that can be taught. Many educators seem to assume that a whole-behavior or whole-concept approach to instruction will be too difficult for the learner. Student progress records indicate that instruction is directed at too easy a step over seven times more frequently than it is directed at too difficult a step (Haring et al., 1979, 1981). Instead of assuming before instruction even begins that a whole-behavior/concept approach will be too hard, educators can rely on the student to determine this. Data collected on pupil performance will quickly identify if the whole-behavior/concept approach is too demanding and if it is necessary to step back to a smaller part of the behavior or to a less complicated presentation of antecedent stimuli (this issue is discussed in greater detail later in this chapter). Instead of forcing students to proceed through a sequence of artificially imposed steps, learning may be accelerated by first directing instruction at the whole task.

## Measuring Pupil Performance

Instructional planning is the process of selecting setting events, antecedent events, arrangements, and arranged events from the incredible variety available. Teaching, however, requires that educators evaluate the effectiveness of the instructional plan when it is implemented and that the plan be changed if it is not found to enhance learning.

Procedures for evaluating instructional plans and for remediating ineffective plans are discussed in the final section of this chapter. In order to make good decisions, teachers must have the right information about student progress at the right time, to prevent loss of valuable instructional time on ineffective procedures. Although it is beyond the scope of this chapter to discuss the collection of information on pupil progress required to make accurate, timely, and learning-enhancing decisions, the basic procedures should include steps to:

1. Measure the behavior directly during instruction (do not use inferential or indirect measures such as achievement tests or published behavioral checklists).
2. Measure the behavior often: at least once or twice a week.
3. Measure both accuracy and fluency of the behavior.
4. Assess for generalization and adaptation to untrained conditions during instruction.
5. Probe for maintenance, generalization,

and adaptation following the end of training.

Interested readers are referred to White and Haring (1980) and to Snell (1983) for further information about collecting pupil performance data.

## INSTRUCTIONAL DESIGN FOR MAINTENANCE, GENERALIZATION, AND ADAPTATION

Instructional planning consists of arranging and selecting from a myriad of antecedent and subsequent events. If all goes well, one or more of the antecedent events will become discriminative stimuli; one or more of the subsequent stimuli will become reinforcers; and the combination of events, that is, the instructional plan, will not only speed learning but also produce maintenance, generalization, and adaptation.

Instructional events may be divided into four categories: setting events, antecedent events, arrangements, and subsequent events. *Setting events,* as mentioned earlier, include all of the events and factors in the general instructional situation. Usually these include the days of the week on which instruction occurs, the time of day, the location of instruction, the teacher-pupil ratio during instruction, the position of the teacher in relationship to the pupil, peers present during instruction, the specific teacher conducting the instruction, and other setting characteristics that remain constant during the instructional period. The setting or a particular aspect of the setting may (or may not) dispose the learner to respond with a specific behavior. *Antecedent events* include the curricular or instructional materials, objects that the student is expected to manipulate or use during the opportunity to perform, and any special equipment used for that instructional program. Also included in this category are the directions (verbal, signed, nonverbal, gestural), cues, assistance, or other enhancements the teacher provides *before* the student has the opportunity to respond. Primary antecedent stimuli (S+) will be included in either or both setting and antecedent events. *Arrangements* describe the relationship between the behaviors that occur and the events that follow that behavior. *Subsequent events* are those that are arranged to *follow* behavior: reinforcers, error correction procedures, feedback on performance, grades, points, special privileges, and so on.

There is an incredible variety of events from which to select, as well as innumerable permutations and combinations of setting events, antecedent events, arrangements, and subsequent events. Fortunately, researchers have studied many different instructional events, and their work provides a basis from which to make an initial selection. Instructional strategies that enhance accuracy are different from those that enhance fluent performance. In general, antecedent events and error-correction procedures can be manipulated and enhanced to promote accurate responding, while arrangements and arranged events are used to build fluency. Accuracy building instructional plans are implemented prior to fluency building plans. However, the development of accuracy continues during fluency building, and fluency building also results in improvement in accuracy levels. If the selection is based on an understanding of the learning process and an appreciation of those events that have demonstrated their effectiveness with other learners, it will have a high probability of accelerating learning and of increasing the probability of maintenance, generalization, and adaptation.

## Setting Events

Although most instruction is directed at establishing behaviors that will be useful in a wide diversity of settings (locomotion, object manipulation, expressive communication, receptive communication), some instruction is aimed at behaviors that are specific to certain physical settings (crossing streets, riding buses, performing certain types of work). Many behaviors are specific to a single type of setting, but those settings are many and varied. For example, toileting behaviors occur in bathrooms (and thus teaching toileting on a classroom "potty" is inappropriate), but there are many different types of bathrooms in all kinds of settings (home, schools, parks,

etc.). The setting in which the behavior is to be maintained, generalized, or adapted will influence the selection of the physical location of instruction.

Until recently, few people questioned that the physical setting of instruction would be the school classroom. For millions of children, classrooms are the "natural setting" for formalized instruction. No one has doubted that children learn in other places, but school has been the primary instructional setting for most school-age children, 6 hours a day, 9 months a year. Most children spent more time at school than in any other single setting other than home. Now, however, special educators are advocating that instruction be conducted outside of the school and home, "on location" in the community to increase the probability of maintenance, generalization, and adaptation. One hypothesis for the failure to generalize is that the setting in which instruction occurs (the training setting) is unlike the setting in which generalized responding is desired; either it contains events that are irrelevant but nonetheless come to be associated with responding (S$i$), or it lacks events that are vital in ensuring generalized and adaptive responding (S+). Some educators feel that "on-location" instruction (sometimes referred to as *in vivo*) instruction will provide a solution to some of the problems of generalization, while others advocate modifying the training setting to simulate the setting features they feel are most important. Still others advocate combining typical training settings with simulated settings with on-location instruction.

Unfortunately, evidence to help determine the best settings for instructing different behaviors is insufficient (Kazdin, 1980). Common sense would dictate that if the behavior to be instructed is situation specific, then the natural environment should be the setting of choice, or if that is impossible, then a simulated setting. If a natural or simulated environment is not utilized, the classroom instruction should be supplemented with probes or trials, where the student has the opportunity to perform in the natural environment. Settings that are within the school but outside of the classroom may become instructional sites as well, including bus stops, hallways, offices, gyms, playgrounds, kitchens, cafeterias, janitorial supply closets, auditoriums, bathrooms, and so on (Brown, Ford, Nisbet, Sweet, Donnellan, & Gruenewald, 1983). Continued assessment of the student's behavior in other settings may indicate that changes in the setting of instruction are warranted (Coon, Vogelsberg, & Williams, 1981). Until more research accumulates, we must rely on the trial-and-error method of selecting instructional sites.

The instructor-student ratio is another setting factor to be considered in designing instruction. Typically, instruction is conducted with a ratio of one student to one teacher. An unfortunate side effect of the emphasis on 1:1 instruction is the amount of the available instructional time left unstructured while a student "waits" for his turn at a 1:1 situation. Small-group instruction offers several obvious advantages: it can reduce the periods of "no instruction"; it can increase the opportunities for social behaviors; and it can provide a chance for observational learning to occur. Many behaviors may also be taught more directly, easily, and efficiently in group formats (e.g., social behaviors, expressive and receptive communication behaviors, games, object manipulation), while private behaviors (e.g., toileting, personal care) are taught individually. Group instruction may be as effective in teaching some behaviors as 1:1 instruction. Recent research suggests that learning preacademic and vocational skills may be accelerated equally well in small groups (1:3 or 1:4) as in 1:1, but that small-group instruction may not work as well for some self-help skills like dressing (Alberto, Jobes, Sizemore, & Doran, 1980; Favell, Favell, & McGimsey, 1978; Storm & Willis, 1978; see Brown, Holvoet, Guess, & Mulligan, 1981 for methods of designing small-group instruction.) Although group instruction increases the opportunity for observational learning, a relationship between student-teacher ratio and generalization or adaptation has not been demonstrated to date.

Another important setting event is the scheduling of instruction. Scheduling instruction involves determining the time of day that instruction will occur and the number of response opportunities that will be provided during each instructional session. Time of day is important because the student may learn to associate the target behavior with behaviors that precede or follow it. A hand-washing program scheduled for 10:00 A.M. immediately following a bed-making program may be convenient for the teacher, but it is functionally less relevant than a handwashing program scheduled before lunch and after toileting. Some skills are useful at all times, such as walking, communicating, propelling a wheelchair, holding head in midline, or grasping objects, and instructional trials should be scheduled frequently throughout the day.

In general, the more frequent the instruction, the faster the learning. Opportunities to respond (trials) may be arranged so that many occur together (massed), by distributing trials throughout the day (e.g., waiting for the natural stimuli to appear and then conducting a trial) or by intermixing trials from two or more programs. The desire for large numbers of trials must be tempered by the appropriateness of the response opportunity itself. A pupil repeating "Hi" for 10 consecutive trials is not practicing any particularly useful behavior. On the other hand, natural stimuli may occur so infrequently or inconveniently that learning may be delayed. Research in this area is mixed, with both types effective in some situations for some skills (Mulligan, Guess, Holvoet, & Brown, 1981; Mulligan, Lacy, & Guess, 1982). Generalization and adaptation may be facilitated if instructional trials are designed to occur as they do in the situation in which generalized/adaptive responding is desired.

## Antecedent Events

Antecedent events will most often become the most important stimuli associated with the behavior; selection of inappropriate events may not only delay learning but impede generalization and adaptation. The identification of antecedent events that facilitate learning has dominated research in instruction for the past decade. Information about selecting materials,

Table 1.  Examples of necessary and synthetic antecedent events

| Necessary antecedents | Synthetic antecedents | Behavior |
|---|---|---|
| 1. Sandwich, hunger. | "Take a bite."; physical prompt. | Bites sandwich. |
| 2. Shoes (S+) not on foot (S+), socks on feet (S+ unless sandals), shoes near feet. | "Put your shoes on." | Puts on shoes. |
| 3. Check made out to learner (S+), teller (Si), pen (S+), pencil (S−), or special stamp (S+) and stamp pad (S+). | Teacher (Si). "Sign your name here."; (point); or "Stamp your name here"; (point) (Si). | Picks up pen and writes name, or picks up stamp, inks stamp, stamps name. |
| 4. Acquaintance, friend, or relative (S+) approaches (S+) Sally until within 5 feet (S+--Si), meets her eyes (S+); greets her ("Hi, Sally"; "Hi"; "How you doing?"; "Good morning"; "Morning"; "Evening," etc.) (S+). | "Look at me" (Si). | "Hi"; "Good morning"; "How you doing?"; or "Morning," etc. |
| 5. a. "Point to set with 'more'" (unnatural but necessary to signal a response opportunity). Since it is a Si, vary it with other verbal cues ("Show me more"; "More"; "Which is more"). Also: "Point to set with 'not-more'" (Si but necessary). Vary with "Show me not-more"; or else teach the concept "less" simultaneously. b. Presentation of two sets of objects, one with a larger number (S+) of objects than the other set (S−). | Set with "more" within 2 inches of learner's right hand; set with "not more" 10 inches from hand.<br><br>On S− trials, set with "not-more" close to hand; "more" set farther away. | Draws circle around set with more or not more; points to set; names set; uses head stick to touch set. |
| 6. a. Wide variety of objects (S+) (raisin, dime, vitamin pill, cup, crayon, suitcase). b. Desire to pick up to access reinforcers (S+). | "Pick it up.", "Put it down." | Grasp, pick up, and release object. |

demonstrations, cues, prompts, and the gamut of antecedent events has provided a rich source for the design of instruction.

Antecedents that are necessary to provide instances of S+ may be distinguished from "synthetic" antecedents, which are added to natural antecedents with the intention of enhancing learning. An event may be either synthetic or necessary, depending on the nature of the behavior. (For examples of both types, see Table 1.)

The first step in the selection of antecedent events for instruction is to determine the antecedents that will become the S+ for the behavior (through an analysis of the target behavior) and the type of generalization and adaptation that is desired. If the aim of instruction is a specific physical movement, (e.g., holding up one's head; grasping, picking up, and then releasing an object), the goal of instruction is generalization of the response to other stimulus settings (e.g., holding one's head up at home) and adaptation as needed (e.g., to the movements needed to pick up objects that were not included in the training). When the target of instruction is a concept (e.g., "more") and the specific topography of the response less important, generalization and adaptation must still be of paramount consideration in the selection of instructional events. A survey of the setting in which the response is to be performed and an analysis of the behavior will identify the necessary antecedents. (Procedures for surveying natural settings and determining the necessary antecedents are described in detail by Becker et al., 1971, and by Horner, Sprague, & Wilcox, 1982.)

Objects may or may not be necessary for instruction. Objects that are S+ or that contain S+ characteristics, objects that are S− or that contain S− characteristics, and objects that are S$i$ may all have to be selected, depending on the program. If instruction is designed, for example, to teach walking, or saying ''Hi,'' or toileting, specific objects are not needed (unless a walker, braces, or other objects are required). If a particular object is vital to instruction, it will be identified by the stimulus survey conducted for instructional planning (e.g., dollar bills may be vital to teaching shopping). When a specific object is necessary, it is desirable to use actual objects, rather than simulations (e.g., actual dollar bills versus slips of paper with ''$1'' on them). Simulations may increase instructional time if the relationship between the actual objects and the simulations must be instructed (Giangreco, 1983). If simulations are selected for some noninstructional reason (e.g., cost), then the closer the simulation is to the real object, the easier stimulus generalization is likely to be (e.g., the use of same-size, ''realistic play money'' is preferred to slips of paper).

In other programs, objects may be required, but specific objects may not be associated with the S+, necessitating systematic variation of the objects used—as in the case of teaching the concept ''more'' or teaching the student to grasp, pick up, and release. Blocks, spoons and pennies, for example, can be used for teaching many different operations (e.g., pick up) and concepts (e.g., ''more''). When teaching concepts, three sets of instructional props must be selected, representing the range of S+, S−, and S$i$. An unfortunate stigmatizing effect may be created if teachers select instructional props that are not age appropriate for their students. Observing a program in which an adolescent is instructed with props that are toys used by preschoolers creates the impression that the adolescent is still a child and lessens the dignity that should be accorded individuals. Since the actual object used as a prop is unim-

portant in these cases, educators should always select objects that are age-appropriate. Age-appropriate props may also facilitate generalization and adaptation to objects naturally found in the student's home, neighborhood, or eventual workplace.

It may be necessary to use pictures to expand the set of available S+ and S− and/or to vary the irrelevant stimuli in some programs. In teaching the concept of ''woman,'' for example, women in the teaching setting may be used as natural instances of the S+'s, while men, boys, girls, and objects may serve as S−'s. It may be impractical to bring more S+'s to the situation to extend the available instances. One solution would be to venture outside of the teaching setting to the community; another solution might be to use photographs. In programs where the natural S+ does not occur in the teaching environment (e.g., a ticket window at a movie theatre; a counter, menu, clerk at a fast-food restaurant; a counter, window, and teller at a bank), researchers are experimenting with the effects of arranging the teaching environment to simulate the relevant characteristics, to increase the similarity between the natural S+ and the S+ used for instruction.

In instructional programs where specific objects are not necessary, natural events may be arranged to occur prior to an opportunity to respond, or instruction may be ''scheduled'' to occur whenever the natural S+ occurs. Natural scheduling of instruction refers to the utilization of available S+'s in the learner's environment. For example, if the target of instruction is to teach the student to initiate greetings to peers, instructional trials occur naturally whenever the student first comes into normal greeting proximity to a peer. If the S+ occurs infrequently or if it is impractical to schedule instruction around naturally occurring S+'s, then the teacher must arrange for the S+'s to occur. In this example, the teacher may guide the student from peer to peer, with each new peer initiating a new response opportunity. Care must be taken to avoid irrelevant stimuli inherent in the arranged trial from becoming associated with the behavior (e.g., the sequence of peers greeted) by systematically varying irrelevant stimuli and by associating them with both instances of S+'s, and S-'s as identified by the concept analysis.

How then can educators select appropriate antecedents? *All* of the stimuli that occur in nontraining settings or that exemplify the S+ characteristics could be selected. This is clearly not only impractical but impossible, since one cannot predict all of the future settings or stimuli that might be associated with the behavior unless the behavior has an extremely limited application. Instead of selecting all of the stimuli, one set of stimuli or instance of the S+ may be selected and taught. Unfortunately, however, instruction provided with a single stimulus or stimuli set (the *single-case method*) is most appropriate when generalization is *not* desired.

Neither of these "methods" has shown to be effective, however, there are three approaches to systematically selecting antecedents. First, instruction may include a large number and variety of stimuli. The *multiple-case method* facilitates generalization better than single-case methods, but problems still remain with this approach. Methods for determining the number of stimuli or instances that must be taught to facilitate generalization may be response-learner-, or stimuli-dependent; in any case, empirical and practical methods for determining the number of instances required to produce generalization and/or adaptation remain relatively uninvestigated.

Second, stimuli that are common in training and nontraining environments may be selected. The *common-stimuli method* is designed to facilitate generalization and adaptation by programming stimuli that overlap training and nontraining settings. This method would be combined with the *multiple-case method* in practical classroom application.

A third technique, *general-case methodology,* attempts to reduce the number of examples that are required, while incorporating the common stimuli approach. A set of procedures for identifying stimuli that exemplify the range of S+ characteristics for a particular behavior, based on a systematic setting and response analysis, produces a limited number of exemplary stimuli for instruction. Investigations to date indicate the consistent effectiveness of general-case programming for a number of skills useful in community and vocational settings. Basic steps in general case programming may be found in Horner et al., (1982).

As the body of research expands, technology for selecting representative S+, S-, and S*i* will improve. However, the three methods described can be applied to improve the probability of maintenance, generalization, and adaptation. Methods to date are still at a trial-and-error level, and although refinements and improvements in the original selection of antecedent stimuli will accumulate with additional research, individual learners will continue to modify instructional practices: pupil performance data will determine the modifications in stimuli necessary for the development of accurate and fluent responding and for producing maintenance, generalization, and adaptation.

***Enhancing    Stimulus    Characteristics***
Events that are not a natural part of the S+ may be introduced to accelerate learning. Synthetic antecedents are designed to increase the pupil's opportunity to respond correctly and to thus be reinforced. By maximizing the reinforcers, learning should be accelerated. Two categories of synthetic antecedents are stimulus enhancements and response assistance. Stimulus enhancements are used to shape the association of the correct S+ with the desired response by heightening the differences between S+, S-, and S*i*, increasing the probability of a correct response (and thus reinforcement). Response assistance is designed to prompt the student to respond correctly by directing the response physically or by providing assistance to maximize the probability of a correct response.

Stimulus enhancements function like shaping successive approximations of desired behavior. The probability that a pupil will respond correctly can be enhanced by emphasizing the relevant stimulus characteristics through spatial positioning, voice inflection and intensity, color "cues," size, gestures, and so forth (Gold, 1972; Irvin & Bellamy, 1977; Sidman & Stoddard, 1967; Touchette, 1968). For example, the correct choice in a multiple discrimination task may be enhanced by spatial positioning. It is placed very close to the learner, while the incorrect choice is relatively farther away (e.g., the S+ for "more" could be placed directly in front of the pupil, while the S− is placed out of reach). Voice inflection or volume may also be used to enhance the discriminative characteristic (e.g., "Give me the *DIME*"), or the relevant S+ characteristic may be indicated by a color cue (e.g., a red card may be placed under the set that is "more," while a white card is placed under the set that is "not-more"). Size may be used to enhance the differences as well (e.g., in teaching X and not-X, the instances of X may be represented as twice the size of not-X's).

*Response Prompting* Acquisition may also be enhanced by specific behaviors on the part of the teacher. The teacher may signal when a response opportunity occurs or may use physical and/or verbal assistance, demonstration, or modeling to increase the probability of a correct response. (Literature reviews of research in these procedures may be found in Falvey, Brown, Lyon, Baumgart, & Schroeder, 1980; Haring et al., 1980; Mercer & Snell, 1977; Smith & Snell, 1978a). Since these antecedent events are synthetic and do not represent the natural conditions for maintained, generalized, or adaptive responding, they also must be faded from instruction.

Synthetic antecedent events that signal the beginning of a response opportunity are intended to enhance the initial cuing effects of the S+. For example, a teacher might place an object in front of the student and say, "Pick it up." In the long term, the sight of an interesting object will be associated with the reinforcing properties of picking up the object and will become the natural S+. During acquisition and fluency building, the teacher's signal is designed to clarify this association to speed learning. Since the specific words, gestures, and directions of the signal are irrelevant stimuli,

they should be varied (e.g., "Go on, you can pick it up now"; "O.K., it's your turn"; "You do it"), and then faded.

Physical assistance or manual guidance may be used when the object of instruction is a particular physical movement. Shaping—differentially reinforcing successive approximations of the desired response—is the method of choice; nevertheless, physical assistance or manual guidance in the performance of the response may accelerate learning, especially when a student has a limited repertoire of movements or when movements occur at very low frequencies. First, the student is physically guided through the desired response and then the topography of assistance is gradually reduced as the student demonstrates increasing independence of movement. For example, in teaching grasp, pick up, and release, a considerable amount of guidance may first be used to guide the pupil's hand around a ball. The guidance then may be reduced to see if the pupil moves his or her hand (e.g., tightens fingers). If the student does move his or her hand, that approximation of the response will be reinforced; guidance will then resume to complete the pick up movement. In the next trial, assistance would again be decreased, but at an earlier point, providing the opportunity for a more complete approximation of the entire motor sequence. If no independent movement is observed during the first trial, increased guidance would be resumed and opportunities to demonstrate independent movement provided later in the sequence or in subsequent trials.

The process of guiding, of providing the opportunity to respond, and then of providing further guidance is actually a series of antecedent events followed by responses followed by subsequent events (S→R→S). The initial guidance for grasping is an antecedent for the first opportunity to respond. If small movements do occur independently, the guidance for the movement that follows is both an event subsequent to the first response and an antecedent to the next opportunity to respond. If a movement does not occur independently, guidance is an event subsequent to "no behavior." Since physical assistance may be programmed as both an antecedent and as a subsequent event, methods of fading are discussed in more detail in that subsection later in this chapter.

Physical assistance is appropriate when the target of instruction is a particular motor movement, but at times it may not be appropriate (e.g., in teaching concepts) or possible (e.g., verbal behavior cannot be physically guided). Other forms of teacher assistance may be selected to increase the probability of correct responding, including gestures (e.g., touching the set that has "more"), verbal or signed hints or cues (e.g., "You need more spoons"; "Look for red"), demonstrations (e.g., teacher ties own shoe) or models (e.g., teacher holds up dollar bill when the student has the opportunity to select a dollar from other objects).

As antecedent events, all forms of assistance are provided *before* the student has an opportunity to respond or *during* the response opportunity. For example, a model may be used to prompt a two-word correct answer to a question (e.g., "What's this? A sandwich. What's this?," followed by the student's response). A change in inflection, emphasis, or volume may be used to enhance the difference between the question (S+) and the model. A pointing gesture may be used to indicate the correct choice (e.g., teacher points to correct set and asks "Which one is not-more?").

*Building Fluency* By the time fluency building begins, most of the synthetic antecedents designed to provide information to the student regarding the topography of the movement or the characteristics of the S+ will have been faded, while the necessary antecedents will continue to precede the opportunity to respond. A survey of the setting may identify natural S+'s for fluent behavior that may be introduced during the fluency building stage of instruction (Falvey et al., 1980). However, since fluent behavior is expected in most situations, natural consequences may be directed at nonfluent behavior (e.g., "Hurry up!"), and will be discussed later in the section about subsequent events.

Synthetic antecedent events may be intro-duced during fluency building to provide information on how the student can maximize reinforcement or to announce the reinforcement available for fluent responding (Zimmerman, Overpeck, Eisenberg, & Garlick, 1969). Simple statements of the contingencies involved may be used with some students (e.g., "Go fast!"), either antecedent to the opportunity to respond or during the period that responding is occurring (e.g., "You sure are going fast!"; "You'll make it if you keep it up!").

Other methods of indicating the contingencies may be used. For tasks in which the student must finish a set amount of material, as in some vocational production tasks and academic tasks, the teacher may distribute only the material that is necessary for the student to complete in the specific period, or may mark the material to be completed. The teacher may also tell the student the contingency (e.g., "Finish these"). A kitchen timer with a bell can be set, and the pupil is told that the work must be finished before the bell rings in order to receive the reinforcer. In some situations, the student may work next to a peer model of fluency. All of these procedures would be used in combination with the fluency-building procedures discussed in other sections of this chapter.

When should synthetic S+ enhancers and teacher assistance be used? Stimulus enhancers may be most appropriate when the physical topography of the response has been acquired and is a part of the pupil's behavioral repertoire. Response prompts, on the other hand, may be applied to situations in which the actual physical movement is the target of instruction and when the pupil needs to be directed in how to respond correctly (Billingsley & Romer, 1983; Close, Irvin, Prehm, & Taylor, 1979).

*Fading* The term *fading* applies to the gradual changing of antecedent and/or subsequent stimuli from conditions at the beginning of instruction to conditions at the end of instruction, when stimuli should be identical or as close as possible to those in the settings where maintained, generalized, and adaptive responding are desired. Fading antecedent events eliminates all synthetic S+ enhancements and all response assistance; instruction should not end until the response is associated only with natural S + 's. Two methods of fading are commonly practiced: the time-delay procedure, in which the antecedent assistance becomes an event subsequent to errors (Billingsley & Romer, 1983; Halle, Marshall, & Spradlin, 1979; Snell & Gast, 1981); and a reduction in the topography of assistance, which remains as an antecedent (Billingsley & Romer, 1983; Wilcox & Bellamy, 1982).

Time-delay procedures fade antecedent stimuli by introducing a pause between the necessary S+ and the synthetic S+, which provides an opportunity for the student to respond without the assistance or enhancer. As the delay is gradually increased, reinforcement is shifted to nonassisted/nonenhanced responses only. If the student responds incorrectly or does not respond within the allowable period, assistance is provided immediately before another opportunity to respond to the same S+. Thus the synthetic antecedent event becomes an event subsequent to errors. As error responses decelerate, the synthetic antecedents (now subsequent events) are eliminated. In a slightly different format, trials in which the assistance is provided as an antecedent may be followed by a block of trials in which a constant time period is allotted for pupil responses and in which the assistance is used as an event subsequent to errors (Kleinert & Gast, 1982).

The second method of fading involves changing the topography of the assistance or enhancements. Fading of the examples used in the previous discussion could include: gradually shifting the positions of the S+ set of "more" and the S− set of "not-more" until they are next to each other; gradually reducing the size of the red card until it "disappears"; and gradually increasing the size of not-X until it is equal to X. Verbal assistance could be faded by reducing the number of words and/or the volume of the delivery, and pointing could be faded by increasing the distance between the cue and the S+. The desired discrimination is shaped by slowly fading the enhancements so that correct responding is always maximized while stimuli successively approximate natural stimuli. The definition of "gradually" is not precise, although, ideally, fading can be accomplished without error responses by the student. Errorless learning, as this process has been called, may require more precise definitions of gradients of changes in conditions to facilitate successful application (Horner et al., 1983; Terrace, 1963a, 1963b; Touchette, 1968). Researchers are currently trying to develop methods of ensuring a transition from synthetic to natural conditions that do not interrupt or impede learning.

The fading of synthetic events should begin as soon as accurate and independent responding begins. Differential reinforcement means that successive behaviors must be better (i.e., closer to the desired response; performed with less and less assistance and with fewer and fewer enhancers) in order to be reinforced. Consecutive reinforcement of behavior at identical levels of assistance may impede acquisition, by teaching the pupil that an assisted behavior is all that is necessary in order to be reinforced or that, if the pupil waits, he or she will be given the "answer" and then be reinforced. Quickly shifting the requirements for reinforcement is a vital part of enhancing learning, and immediate fading of assistance and enhancers is an integral part of this process.

Some educators and researchers have recommended that instruction begin with assistance and/or enhancements (Falvey et al., 1980), while others have recommended that these be used as remedial techniques only if acquisition with natural S + 's falters (Etzel & LeBlanc, 1979). The question can best be answered by attempting to estimate the total time required for instruction. The best choice is the one that requires the least time. How many instructional trials will be required for learning if enhancers are first used and then faded? Will learning be slower if enhancers are not used? The rule of parsimony (Etzel & LeBlanc, 1979) would suggest that the stimuli be unenhanced and that only the most simple, natural, and direct procedures be selected for initial instructional designs. As research accumulates, techniques for designing, implementing, and fading appropriate synthetic antecedents will be refined and expanded. Assessment of pupil performance during instruction, coupled with simple decision-rules, will permit quick identification and appropriate remediation of instructional plans that do not result in maintenance, generalization, and adaptation.

## Arrangements

Operant behaviors are controlled by subsequent events. Thus the arrangement between the behavior and the subsequent event may be designed to accelerate learning and to promote maintenance, generalization, and adaptation. There are two parameters to arrangements: the immediacy of the subsequent stimulus and the ratio of subsequent events to the behavior.

The purpose of arrangements during acquisition of behavior is to clarify the relationship between antecedent stimuli, the behavior, and its consequence. Therefore, subsequent events must immediately follow the behavior. Any delay in the delivery of subsequent events may result in inadvertent reinforcement of undesirable behaviors. For example, if the arrangement specifies that each correct response be followed by verbal praise, the praise should be delivered before the student can engage in any other behavior. If the student responds correctly by pointing at the named object and then begins to engage in stereotypic behavior prior to the delivery of praise, the behavior that might be reinforced would be the chain of pointing-stereotyping. Acquisition can be accelerated if subsequent events are delivered immediately after the behavior and if instruction may be arranged so that undesired behaviors do not have the opportunity to occur prior to reinforcement. The arranged ratio is designed to maximize the student's identification of the behavior with its consequence; therefore, FR1 is appropriate during acquisition.

Subsequent events must be arranged not only for correct and incorrect behaviors, where a FR1 arrangement is easy to specify, but also for those occasions when presentation of the antecedent events is not followed by any response (i.e., no-response). The definition of a no-response must depend on the length of time that responding does not occur. Presumably, if

a teacher waited long enough, the student would do something that could be classified as either correct or incorrect. However, the longer a teacher waits, the less likely that the behavior (when it occurs) will be associated with the stimulus characteristics of the antecedent events, and the more likely that the behavior will be associated with other antecedent events that may occur in the setting or with waiting itself—all of which are $Si$'s. In addition, the longer the wait, the more probable that the student will engage in some other behavior that will also interfere with learning.

The subsequent event that follows a no-response is defined by a latency limit, established for the interval between the end of the $S+$ and the beginning of the subsequent event. The latency limit establishes a time that ensures the immediacy of the subsequent event and also provides a definition of no-response. Latency limits that have been arranged during successful instructional programs have generally been equal to or less than 5 seconds. However, recent research indicates that latency limits of 3 seconds or less may better accelerate learning (O. White, personal communication, August 13, 1983). There may be a relationship between the latency limit and the probability that the student will respond correctly, with increasing latencies associated with decreasing correct responses.

The latency limit also means that correct and incorrect behaviors must begin before the time limit expires, providing another criterion for defining correct responses. For example, if the latency limit for a no-response is set for 3 seconds, the criterion for a correct response includes the requirement that responding begin before the 3 seconds have elapsed. Even though it may not be possible to determine if a specific behavior is correct or incorrect until it is completed, one can specify that observable movement will begin before 3 seconds are up (e.g., an accurate response in a "more" concept program may be defined as pointing to the set that has "more" when asked to "Point to more," and beginning to point within 3 seconds of the $S+$). Thus, the establishment of a latency limit for no-responses is the first step in specifying the arrangements that will build fluency during the second stage of learning.

Arrangements during fluency building must be set so that not every response is reinforced; the arrangements describe successive requirements for increasingly fluent responding. Successive requirements for accessing reinforcers improve fluent responding by changing the criterion level of performance needed for reinforcement (Ayllon, Garber, & Pisor, 1976; Hartmann & Hall, 1976; Smith & Snell, 1978b). For example, in a duration-deceleration program, arrangements for a grasp, pick up, and release movement can be gradually decreased from a total duration of 30 seconds to the aim duration of 3 seconds.

Criterion can be changed in increments set by the instructor or can be based on the pupil's performance. For example, set increments of 5 seconds may be used to change the arrangement in the grasp, pick up, and release program. The student would be required to complete the movement in 30 seconds, then in 25 seconds, then in 20 seconds, and so forth. The *set-increments method* is easy to arrange but may not always be successful in facilitating fluency, because the amount of behavior change required is not the same in each of the steps involved. The sequence of 30, 25, 20, 15 provides the learner with four steps to cut duration in half; however, she or he must cut duration in half in a single step in the change from 10 to 5.

A ratio of performance change could be established to correct this problem. For example, if a 10% decrease is set, the sequence would be 30 seconds, 27 seconds, 24.3 seconds, 21.9 seconds, 19.7 seconds, 17.7 seconds, and so forth.[2] *Set-increment methods* are similar to the step-ahead method of sequencing instruction, since the sequence is not based on the pupil's actual performance and carries the same possibility of slowing learning.

Instead of manipulating the arrangement in a preset manner, the student's own performance may be used. This arrangement specifies the student's best performance to date as the criterion arrangement for reinforcement. The previous day's performance is not used, preventing a "one day good, next day not-so-good" sequence, with performance never actually improving (e.g., one day at six per minute [reinforced], next day at five per minute [not reinforced], next day at six per minute [reinforced], next day at four per minute [not reinforced], next day at five per minute [reinforced], and so on). However, problems may still be encountered if the student demonstrates exceptionally fluent performance on one trial or during one session, since any subsequent reinforcement would require that the student surpass his or her previous best performance. For example, if grasp, pick up, and release were performed as in Table 2, the last three responses, which are still more fluent than the first four, would not be reinforced (extinction), and the response may begin to decelerate. This may be avoided by introducing reinforcer bands—arrangements that provide more powerful reinforcers for more fluent responses while also reinforcing responses that are improving. Two or more reinforcers are used. An example of a two-banded arrangement for a changing criterion based on pupil performance is shown in Table 3.

Changing criterion arrangements may also be set by drawing a single line—or more (for bands)—from current performance levels to the aim level on graphs of pupil performance. The pupil is reinforced if performance meets or exceeds the required criterion established by the line on a given day. The rate of change is determined by the steepness of the line. Whichever method is used, changing criterion arrangements function to differentially reinforce increasingly fluent responding and are powerful during the fluency building stage of learning.

Although each response must be reinforced immediately in order to enhance acquisition,

---

[2]The formula for this is current level − (current level × change unit). In this case, 30 seconds − (30 × 10%) = 27. Other examples shown are rounded. As can be seen, this method ensures that the steps in the set increment method are equivalent in the amount of behavior change required, but they are certainly not very easy to use.

Table 2. Performance and reinforcement under a changing criterion arrangement based on "best performance"

| Trial | Grasp, pick up, and release response duration | Subsequent event | Criterion for next reinforced trial |
|---|---|---|---|
| 1 | 30 seconds | Reinforced | Less than 30 seconds |
| 2 | 32 seconds | Not reinforced | |
| 3 | 27 seconds | Reinforced | Less than 27 seconds |
| 4 | 26 seconds | Reinforced | Less than 26 seconds |
| 5 | 13 seconds | Reinforced | Less than 13 seconds |
| 6 | 23 seconds | Not reinforced | |
| 7 | 21 seconds | Not reinforced | |
| 8 | 24 seconds | Not reinforced | |
| 9 | 19 seconds | Not reinforced | |

by the end of fluency building, competent performance should be controlled by the variable arrangements typical of most nontraining settings in order to facilitate maintenance, generalization, and adaptation (Baer & Wolf, 1970; Stokes & Baer, 1977). The setting in which adaptive or generalized responding is desired should be surveyed in order to determine the schedule of reinforcement available. The process of modifying arrangements from very rich schedules like FR1 to natural schedules parallels the process of fading synthetic stimuli. This can be achieved during fluency building or once fluency aims are met by introducing variability into the fixed schedules of reinforcement used during acquisition and by increasing the number of behaviors or interval of responding required before reinforcement is delivered (Schroeder, 1972; Stephens, Pear, Wray, & Jackson, 1977). Schedules may be thinned according to set increments (e.g., from FR1 to FR2 to FR3) or by introducing variability immediately (FR1 to VR2 to VR3). Changing criterion arrangements also introduce variability in reinforcement, since only the most fluent responses are reinforced.

In order to match arrangements in nontraining settings, reinforcement might have to be delayed. For example, most employees are paid on a weekly, biweekly, or monthly arrangement. Reinforcement does not occur immediately after the behavior, but on an FI or FR

Table 3. Performance and reinforcement under a two-banded changing criterion arrangement based on "best performance"

| Trial | Grasp, pick up, and release response duration | Subsequent event | Criterion for next reinforced trial | |
|---|---|---|---|---|
| | | | Band 1 (praise) | Band 2 (praise and money) |
| 1 | 30 seconds | Praised | Less than 30 seconds | |
| 2 | 32 seconds | Not reinforced | | |
| 3 | 26 seconds | Praised and paid | | Less than 26 seconds |
| 4 | 27 seconds | Praised | Less than 27 seconds | |
| 5 | 25 seconds | Praised and paid | | Less than 25 seconds |
| 6 | 26 seconds | Praised | Less than 26 seconds | |
| 7 | 13 seconds | Praised and paid | | Less than 13 seconds |
| 8 | 23 seconds | Praised | Less than 23 seconds | |
| 9 | 21 seconds | Praised | Less than 21 seconds | |
| 10 | 24 seconds | Not reinforced | | |
| 11 | 19 seconds | Praised | Less than 19 seconds | |

schedule of 1 week, 2 weeks, or 4 weeks. If this is the case, then delay in delivery of the reinforcement must be incorporated into the arrangements used during training to enhance adaptation and generalization. Fowler and Baer (1981) found that delayed reinforcement delivered as a student leaves a setting was not as effective in facilitating generalization as reinforcement delayed by several intervening setting changes. Delays may be introduced gradually, in the same fashion as the schedule is thinned.

Arrangements during acquisition are designed to provide information to the student by ensuring that each behavior receives a consequent stimulus immediately after it occurs and by defining the period of time during which a response must begin. During fluency building, arrangements are designed to guarantee that increasingly fluent responding is differentially reinforced, and the rich schedules of reinforcement used to accelerate acquisition are reduced to approximate the schedules available in nontraining settings in order to increase the probability that the instructed behaviors are maintained, generalized, and adapted.

Applied research has not systematically defined how behavior can be maintained if reinforcers in nontraining settings are very scarce or simply not available. It seems that either changing the setting so that reinforcers are available or teaching self-reinforcement procedures to the student are the best available solutions to this problem. In addition, questions about determining the nature of the "gradual" changes involved in changing criterion and thinning reinforcement schedules, as with other questions with fading, are relatively unexplored. However, application of the procedures discussed here can improve instruction, and the student's performance will identify whether or not instruction is successful.

### Subsequent Events

*Reinforcers*   Reinforcement controls responding. If the behavior is not controlled by reinforcers that occur naturally outside of instruction, the behavior will extinguish. The selection of appropriate reinforcers for instruc-

tion, and the introduction and shift to naturally available reinforcers, are primary aspects in designing instruction to promote maintenance, generalization, and adaptation (Stokes & Baer, 1977).

Reinforcers are events that accelerate the probability that the response they follow will occur again. This definition creates an immediate problem in instructional planning, since, at best, one can usually only guess at the potential reinforcement power of a specific event. However, the reinforcing power or value of an event may be assessed prior to instruction. One simple way to do this is to arrange the event in question to follow simple, repetitive motor behavior (e.g., pushing a button). Performance can be measured in short intervals (e.g., 15 seconds) for a few minutes. If the response increases in frequency, the event is a reinforcer for the simple motor behavior and may also function as a reinforcer in other instructional programs (Ferrari & Harris, 1981). Once instruction begins, only the progress of the pupil can confirm or deny the prediction that the event selected will actually reinforce the target behavior. Several methods may be used to increase the probability that the event selected will actually function as a reinforcer. These are outlined in the following paragraphs.

*Survey the events in the nontraining setting that may serve as reinforcers.* Events with a high probability of occurring in nontraining settings that may act as reinforcers include proximity of student to adults or peers, conversation with adults or peers, opportunity to engage in a preferred behavior (e.g., go bowling, go to a movie, go to the race track), and money. Any one or all of the naturally occurring reinforcers should be selected as potential reinforcers. However, special caution should be taken in using the opportunity to engage in a preferred behavior, often characterized as "free time," as a reinforcer. It is certainly appropriate for instruction to be followed by noninstructional time, when the student is "free" to engage in behaviors of his choice. Often a "free-time" area is set aside for students and is filled with toys or games that are supposedly preferred by students. If the student does not know how to access the reinforcers of toys or games, or how to engage in conversation with peers, or how to operate the record player, *or* if those events are not reinforcing, free time becomes time to sit and do nothing or time to engage in stereotypic behaviors. It is unlikely that either "doing nothing" or engaging in stereotypic behaviors will function as reinforcers (Rincover, Cook, Peoples, & Packard, 1979). Free time should not be programmed for students who are unable to choose or perform appropriate behaviors that access reinforcers—instead, teach "free time" skills. Providing instruction in leisure or play skills may introduce students to new communities of reinforcement, may teach them how to use free time, and may identify reinforcers for other skills (see Putnam, Werder, & Schleien, this volume; Wehman, Renzaglia, Berry, Schutz, & Karan, 1978).

*Program the events that are natural consequences for the behavior in other settings.* Some examples of behaviors and natural consequences include:

1. Pick up spoon, spoon to mouth, appropriate table manners, etc. (*behavior*) . . . Food (*natural consequence*).
2. Pick up cup, cup to mouth, drinking without spilling, etc. . . . Drink (coffee, juice, milk).
3. Pick up object, object manipulation . . . Noise made by object.
4. Operate vending machine . . . Object vended.
5. Turn on radio, television, slide projector, other appliance . . . Sound/visual of appliance.
6. Hold head up . . . See people and activities.
7. Answer question . . . Opportunity to ask question.
8. Initiate conversation . . . Conversation.
9. Say, sign, point to subject—e.g., scissors . . . Manipulate object—e.g., cut paper with scissors (Janssen & Guess, 1978).
10. Request item . . . Receive item.

*Select events that most people would consider reinforcing and that are similar to those available to age peers.* Examples of such events include praise, physical contact (e.g., a pat on the back), social approval (e.g., a smile), special classroom privileges (e.g., first in line for lunch, extra recess time, classroom chores such as feeding pets). If praise is selected, the praise should specify the behavior it follows, (e.g. "That's right, you pointed to 'more'!" instead of "Good boy").

*Program an instructional trial in an instructional program in which the student is doing well to follow the desired response in the program being planned.* For example, if the student is doing well in a grasp, pick up, and release program, and you are planning a program to teach pointing to an object, arrange for a correct response to "point to object" to be followed by an opportunity to "pick up" (Dunlap & Koegel, 1980). Or instruction in recreational activity can follow instruction in a less preferred skill.

*If an event has acted as a reinforcer for some other behavior, that same event may be programmed again.* However, caution should be taken not to select a reinforcer from a program that is occurring in the same period of time. If the same reinforcing event is used in two programs, it may quickly lose its reinforcing power in both programs, as satiation will occur.

*Implement a token system. Token* is the name given to the use of a tangible event that can be exchanged for reinforcers. Target behaviors are followed by coins, poker chips, or other tangible items that may be exchanged for toys, activities, special privileges, and so on. Tokens acquire reinforcing power through *pairing* the neutral event (i.e., the token) with a known reinforcer (e.g., listening to music). The purchasing power of the tokens is demonstrated by allowing the student to exchange tokens for reinforcers immediately. Gradually a delay between earning and spending tokens is introduced, until the exchange occurs at special times of the day or week. Tokens may be adjusted up or down in exchange value, and the number of tokens awarded for a particular behavior may also be adjusted, so that the token system can be applied to virtually every behavior. Tokens are, furthermore, amenable to fading procedures, from schedule thinning to delay of reinforcement, and may be easily and efficiently administered by classroom teachers. Token systems provide a means both of using events that are natural without disrupting the instructional flow and of introducing new communities of reinforcement. (For suggestions on implementing a token system, see Alberto & Troutman, 1982; Becker et al., 1971, 1975a; Kazdin, 1982).

*Let the learner select from a variety of available events.* Present objects, or pictures of objects or events, that are potential reinforcers to the student and let him or her indicate by pointing which one is preferred, or ask the student directly about what he or she would like (Alberto & Troutman, 1982; Smith & Snell, 1978b). Self-selection of reinforcers adds another component to the reinforcing potential of an event. In such instances the event should be treated as a potential reinforcer until its effects on the student's behavior are noted.

*If the student engages in stereotypic behavior, consequences that attempt to duplicate the reinforcing stimulation of the behavior may be programmed.* Rincover et al. (1979) used a combination of sensory extinction and sensory reinforcement to accelerate learning and to decelerate stereotypic behavior. For one subject, for example, stereotypic behavior consisted of spinning a plate or other object on a hard surface. The authors identified the auditory stimulation provided by the noise the plate made spinning on the table as a potential reinforcer. They were able to extinguish reinforcement for plate spinning by covering the table with carpet. At the same time, the student was taught to play with a music box, which reinforced appropriate play with auditory stimulation. Following play training, music box play was maintained, and the student continued to play with the music box even when the sensory extinction conditions were removed. In addition, the plate spinning did not recur and was not observed at follow-up observations 6 and then 13 months following training, but music box play was maintained.

*Food and drink can be overused as subsequent events for correct responses.* Since food and drink are natural reinforcers for a limited class of behaviors, and since they are not normally used in school settings or available in nontraining settings, they are appropriate only for a few behaviors. Food and drink may also lose their power quickly if they are the only reinforcers programmed. If the student is not hungry or thirsty, or if the student has a weight problem (overweight or underweight) or if other events may be reinforcing, do not select food and/or drink. If food and/or drink are selected as subsequent events, nutrition must be considered in the selection (Shevin, 1982).

If reinforcers that are unavailable in nontraining settings are selected for use during instruction, instruction may have to be extended to allow for the process of pairing the known reinforcer with the naturally available events until the natural events function as reinforcers. This is accomplished by presenting the event that functions as a reinforcer simultaneously with the event that is supposed to become the reinforcer (the natural event). Eventually, the neutral event is presented before the reinforcer, and the length of time is extended until the old reinforcer is no longer available (it is faded from the instructional setting). Analysis of the data collected on pupil performance will permit teachers to ascertain when the reinforcing function is taken over by natural reinforcers. This process must occur if maintenance, generalization, and adaptation are to be facilitated (Baer & Wolf, 1970; Stokes & Baer, 1977).

It has been noted that it may be difficult to identify reinforcers, and/or that reinforcers seem to lose their power quickly for certain groups of pupils (Spradlin & Spradlin, 1976). The effects of reinforcer satiation can be reduced by selecting events that are unlikely to satiate (e.g., touching, attention), by using a token system with varied choices to back up the tokens, and by saving the reinforcing value of an event by restricting it to contingent use only.

Educators often provide access to potential reinforcers noncontingently. For example, a student who arrives at school early may be allowed to play in the gym or to look at a magazine. Or, the teacher may converse pleasantly with a student even when the student is not behaving appropriately. Educators who give attention to students who are misbehaving not only are likely to reinforce the misbehavior but are diminishing the potential power of that attention in an instructional program. Teachers must be aware that if students are greeted with smiles, hugs, and conversation when they enter the classroom in the morning regardless of how they behave when they enter, the potential reinforcing value of those events is lessened. Instead of giving away reinforcers, educators should hoard and withold potential events, arranging them to follow desirable behavior and making them less readily available at other times. Events such as saying the student's name, standing next to the student, and engaging the student in conversation can be arranged to follow desirable behaviors and should not be available unless and until the student has behaved appropriately. In this fashion, students are not deprived; instead, access to reinforcers is controlled to increase the number of behaviors in the pupil's repertoire.[3] As the student's repertoire expands, he or she has increasing varieties of behaviors that can be chosen in order to access different reinforcers. The first rule in preserving the power of reinforcers or in the identification of potential reinforcers is, therefore, *nothing is for free*. A second procedure that may also be used to retain reinforcer value is to *let different reinforcers follow the same behavior*. For example, 3 seconds of music might follow the first correct response, praise and a hug might follow the second correct response, several seconds with a slide projector might follow the third correct response and so on (Egel, 1981).

A third way to preserve a reinforcer's power is to *distribute instructional trials throughout the school day*. Programs in which opportunities to respond are presented one after the other, and in which correct responses are reinforced with the same event each time, may accelerate satiation.

It is also important to *thin the reinforcement schedule to variable ratio or variable interval as quickly as possible*. During acquisition, praise might be arranged to follow each correct response (FR1), while tokens are arranged to follow every fourth correct response on the average (VR4). Then, in fluency building, the fading process would continue for both praise and tokens. Variable ratio schedules may also accelerate association of the response with the relevant S+ (Koegel, Schreibman, Britten, & Laitinen, 1979).

A reinforcer's value may be improved if the teacher is able to "*hide*" *the reinforcer from the learner*. For example, the teacher may select one of a wide variety of objects and place it in a paper sack prior to the student's arrival at the training setting. The student may then be shown the sack and informed that there is a "prize" inside it. The desired behavior is then followed by giving the student the surprise bag, opening the bag, and then by the instructor exclaiming over the contents, in a way that is potentially more reinforcing than just giving the object. In addition, keeping the object in the bag prevents the student from deciding that he or she does not want it and then not responding. The student may be awarded the sack but may be delayed from opening it as part of the process of teaching natural schedules.

The delivery of reinforcers must be carefully planned. During acquisition, the reinforcer

---

[3]A short discussion of the ethical issues in deprivation may be found in Bragg and Wagner (1970), who argue that if deprivation is used to strengthen reinforcer power, the behaviors learned by institutionalized mental patients can result in extremely positive overall benefits, while the failure to learn such behaviors can have ultimately horrifying effects (i.e., "rejection, increased medication, electroconvulsive therapy, and prolonged hospitalization" [p. 353]). In a recent study, Dougher (1983) found that contingent liquids (e.g., water and coffee) would accelerate socially appropriate behaviors if subjects were deprived of them unless such behaviors were displayed, and would decelerate inappropriate behaviors if subjects were satiated with them when such behaviors were displayed.

should be an event that may be quickly and easily delivered immediately after the behavior. If the event may take a comparatively long time (e.g., if the reinforcer is being allowed to have extra recess time), it may not be appropriate for instructional programs that involve multiple trial presentations unless a token system is used (Kazdin & Bootzin, 1972). If the delivery of the event is unpleasant, the event may not be reinforcing. For instance, it is unlikely that having food shoved into your mouth or juice forced between your lips will be reinforcing. If food and/or drink are used as subsequent events, the student should be able to eat and drink them independently. (If an event is offered to the student and refused by the student, it may be that the opportunity to refuse something is the reinforcing event). Delivery of reinforcers may also be used to enhance S+ characteristics; for example, in teaching the concept "in," the reinforcer could be accessed by having the student find it in a box, in a cupboard, in a book, and so forth (Saunders & Sailor, 1979; Williams, Koegel, & Egel, 1981).

***Consequating Incorrect Behavior*** During acquisition, incorrect behaviors and no-responses may be followed by subsequent events designed to provide information to the learner on how to respond correctly and to obtain reinforcement. Both synthetic S+ enhancers and teacher assistance may be programmed to occur as subsequent events. Procedures may involve using such events first as antecedents and then, via time-delay procedures, shifting them to subsequent events; or assistance and enhancers can be programmed to occur only as subsequent events (Billingsley & Romer, 1983; Csapo, 1981; Falvey et al., 1980).

Presumed levels of assistance or enhancers may be used either in a decreasing or increasing fashion. In *decreasing assistance* (or decreasing enhancement) procedures, the student first has the opportunity to respond to the desired S+, and an error response is followed by a high level of assistance (or enhancement). As correct responses accelerate, error responses are followed by lower and lower levels of assistance. However, if the initial error response is followed with another error response, it is consequated by a repetition of the high level of assistance. Lower levels of assistance are only available after correct responses have intervened (Figure 2a). In this case, the instructor must determine how many correct responses are required before the level of assistance is reduced (e.g., Csapo [1981] required three consecutive correct responses).

The *increasing assistance* method also begins with an opportunity for the student to respond to the S+, but if the first response is incorrect, it is followed by both a low level of assistance and another opportunity to respond. If this results in an error, a higher level of assistance is provided, and another response opportunity is provided. The student must respond correctly in order to have the natural S+ presented again (Figure 2b).

Although these procedures have been reported effective (Billingsley & Romer, 1983), several problems may be directly related to their use. First, when the student has multiple response opportunities on each trial, it is possible that the variation in events will function to reinforce error responses. In addition, instructors often reinforce the pupil's performance after correction with the same reinforcers available for responding correctly in the first place. Correct responses that occur in sequence following the initial error should *not* be reinforced as if they were the equivalent of an initial correct response. Otherwise the student will learn that he or she can eventually be reinforced no matter how poor the performance.

Another problem is caused by the multiple response opportunities for errors (error loops)—the possibility that errors will be reinforced by the increasing attention and proximity that result. More errors lengthen the instructional session; few errors or consecutive corrects may decrease the length of the session. If attention and proximity are reinforcers, the student may access them with increasing frequency simply by responding incorrectly. Such cases have appeared in the literature (Bill-

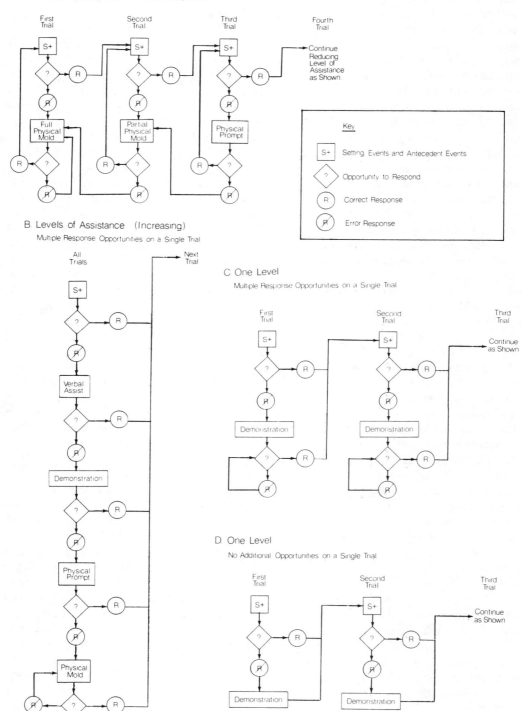

Figure 2.    Error-correction events used subsequent to incorrect or no-responses. (See text for discussion.)

ingsley & Romer, 1983; Csapo, 1981; Gentry, Day, & Nakao, 1979). This problem can be circumvented by allowing the student to access more powerful reinforcers for correct responses.

A further difficulty may be caused because the error-correction procedures intervene between the natural S+ and the opportunity to respond. For example, in Figure 2b, the antecedent event for the third response opportunity is the series: desired S+, error response, verbal assistance, error, demonstration. The total sequence may become an S*i* for responding and may inhibit generalization. Finally, the multiple response opportunities intervene between the natural S+ and the reinforcer for correct behaviors, another probable impediment to acquisition.

As an alternative, one type of assistance may be selected as a subsequent event, so that each error is followed by the same consequence each time. The subsequent event may or may not be followed by additional response opportunities (see Figure 2c and 2d). Although comparative studies on the effects of alternative error-correction procedures are sparse (Billingsley & Romer, 1983), the law of parsimony (Etzel & LeBlanc, 1979) would suggest that the option in Figure 2d, which avoids all of the problems discussed, is the method of first choice.

Despite potential drawbacks, programming assistance and enhancements to occur *after* the behavior has two advantages over using them as antecedent events. First, since assistance and enhancements occur after the behavior, it is unlikely that they will become irrelevant stimuli. Second, the student's correct responses accelerate by reinforcement, error responses should naturally decelerate, and thus the error-correction procedures will be required less and less often. Thus, fading is contingent upon the performance of the pupil, rather than on inferences or guesses made by the teacher as to when fading should begin.

*The events that follow incorrect and no-responses should contrast sharply with the reinforcer that follows correct responses* in order to enhance learning. If teacher attention or proximity is a known reinforcer, it may be difficult to provide error-correction procedures, since the attention and proximity are likely to maintain or accelerate errors at a level that the student desires. If very powerful reinforcers for correct and fluent responding are identified, they may overcome this problem. Or, inaccurate or nonfluent responses may be followed simply by a short period of ignoring (e.g., 5–10 seconds when the opportunity to access any reinforcement is withdrawn), before presenting the next planned antecedent events. The period of ignoring is designed to contrast with the reinforcer that follows accurate/fluent behavior. Of course, ignoring does not provide information to the student on how to respond, and so may be inappropriate during acquisition.

During fluency building, errors are responses that are "too slow." Errors of inaccuracy, if they occur, may be consequated as they were during acquisition. Nonfluency can be most easily responded to by withholding the reinforcer available for fluent behavior. Feedback with respect to the withholding and the cause may be provided (e.g., "Oh, oh, the bell rang and you're not finished. No coffee break for you!").

A *response cost technique* may also be used during fluency building, in which fluent responding is reinforced by objects or tokens, and nonfluent responding results in the removal or loss of the tokens or objects. Events that occur in nontraining settings are often directed at nonfluent behavior. For example, a person who is judged to be "taking too long" to purchase items in a store may be told by the checker or by persons waiting behind him to "hurry up." These natural events may be arranged to occur during instruction.

In summary, reinforcers must be selected and programmed during all stages of instruction in order to ensure learning. Subsequent events programmed to follow inaccurate and no-responses during acquisition should be designed to provide information on how to perform accurately and thus access reinforcement. During fluency building, nonfluent responses should be consequated by not earning reinforcement or by losing items previously earned during fluent responding. *At the end of instruction, the behavior should be controlled only by the reinforcers available in nontraining settings,* to increase the probability of maintenance, generalization, and adaptation.

## OBSERVATIONAL LEARNING AND SELF-CONTROL TECHNIQUES

Two related applications of the procedures discussed show promise in facilitating desired instructional outcomes. However, only a few investigations have systematically studied the procedures' effects with severely handicapped students in producing maintenance, generalization, and adaptation. Because of the procedures' potential, they are included in this chapter.

### Facilitating Observational Learning

Observational learning is a process less well understood than operant learning, although much information about enhancing observational learning is available (a review of the literature is presented in Mercer & Snell, 1977). Observational learning may begin when models demonstrate behavior to students. Competent peers, films, and audiovisual presentations may serve as models. The probability that the student will imitate the model (learn from observation) is increased if the student observes that the model is reinforced for the behavior and if the model verbally describes the actions being demonstrated. Observational learning is enhanced if the demonstration immediately precedes an opportunity for the student to perform and if the model himself or herself reinforces correct imitation by the student.

The lack of observational learning by severely handicapped persons is an often-reported problem. If observational learning is not occurring, imitation training may be incorporated into the curriculum. Imitation can be trained using the principles and procedures discussed in this chapter. In a classic study, Baer, Peterson, and Sherman (1967) used intensive differential reinforcement of responses topographically similar to the model, along with manual guidance following the S+ modeled by

the experimenter. Correct responses were reinforced with food and praise. Four significant findings of the study have been supported by additional research. First, training produced spontaneous generalization to new behaviors that were imitated immediately, without requiring manual guidance or shaping. Second, there was generalized imitation of single motor behaviors, chains, and verbal behaviors. Third, imitative behavior generalized to other models. Fourth, if certain imitative behaviors were reinforced, the students also imitated other behaviors that were not reinforced; however, if reinforcement of all imitation was discontinued (extinction), both previously reinforced and never-reinforced imitations decreased.

These results and further studies demonstrate that the procedures can produce maintained, generalized, and adaptive imitative behavior (Garcia, Guess, & Byrnes, 1973). Imitation training may also improve the effects of modeling and demonstration as antecedent events and error-correction procedures (York, Williams, & Brown, 1976). However, a consistent relationship between imitation training and enhanced observational learning in producing maintained, generalized, and adapted responses by severely handicapped learners has not been demonstrated (Egel, Richman, & Koegel, 1981). It is probable, however, that individuals present in the student's nontraining and training environments could become effective models that might prompt the performance of instructed behaviors. However, it is unlikely that increasing observational learning will prove a direct and effective solution by itself. Research on the effectiveness of imitation training in expanding observational learning is very limited, both in number and in application; therefore, it is only probable that imitation training will generalize in this manner. However, the potential—to date almost ignored—is so great that imitation training should be considered in the establishment of curricula.

### Self-Control Techniques

All of the strategies discussed here so far are dependent on an external agent as the locus of control. In almost every research and/or curriculum report, the handicapped person is seen as the one whose behavior is to be changed, rather than as the individual who is to change his or her behavior and who may ensure maintenance, generalization, and adaptation on his or her own. Students have little or no opportunity to select instructional targets, instructional materials, or instructional strategies themselves. If students are taught to control their own behavior directly, maintenance, generalization, and adaptation may be facilitated.

An alternative to external control is self-control. In self-control procedures, the individual is the locus of control. Many different behaviors have been identified as components of self-control: a) self-determination of behaviors for change, b) self-controlled change of stimuli that may affect responding, c) self-observation of behavior, d) self-recording of behavior, e) self-evaluation of accuracy or fluency of behavior, f) self-delivery of behavioral antecedents, g) self-determination of reinforcing or punishing consequences, h) self-determination of the arrangements, and i) self-delivery of the consequences.

Self-control procedures offer a number of advantages of particular importance in the education of handicapped children and youth. When external agents control changes in behavior, both antecedent and subsequent events may be arranged to act contingently upon the occurrence of the behavior. However, in most natural environments, such contingent control operates intermittently. Responses not only evoke consequences that influence the future occurrences of the response but also change the environment itself (Kazdin, 1980). Self-control can mediate the differences between training and nontraining settings. Self-control techniques can also eliminate the effects of the instruction as a potentially irrelevant stimulus associated with responding. Such procedures can furthermore facilitate generalization and maintenance by providing the individual with general coping skills that may be used in a variety of settings, rather than teaching single responses to specific situations (Cole & Kazdin, 1980; Kazdin, 1980).

Most of the research conducted to date on self-control procedures has involved nonhandicapped individuals. This research has demonstrated that the self-controlled procedures can be just as effective as teacher-controlled procedures for changing and maintaining behavior in a wide variety of settings (Brigham, 1978; Kazdin, 1980; O'Leary & Dubey, 1979; Rosenbaum & Drabman, 1979). Studies concerning the application of self-control techniques by severely handicapped students have, to date, focused primarily on the use of self-reinforcement and on comparing effects of self-control with teacher or experimenter control (Shapiro & Klein, 1980). Research indicates that self-reinforcement is generally as effective as externally controlled procedures in building fluency and maintaining performance for some vocational skills, but consistent effects during acquisition have not been reported. Moreover, few consistent effects with self-monitoring and self-instruction have been reported.

Experimental research in self-control techniques with severely handicapped students has not yet resulted in the development of effective and efficient means of teaching individuals to control their own behavior. In general, a particular self-control strategy (e.g., self-reinforcement) may be treated like any other skill to be taught. Unfortunately, strategies with external locus may counter the development of the concept of self-control inherent in the building of maintained, generalized, and adapted self-control skills.

Although the promise of self-control techniques in overcoming problems encountered in maintenance, generalization, and adaptation has provoked growing interest among researchers, empirical evidence of the effects are scanty (Kazdin, 1980). To date few studies have involved teaching severely handicapped individuals to use self-control procedures and then measuring whether those procedures resulted in improved maintenance, generalization, and adaptation. Only a small number of studies have measured if the self-control skills themselves are maintained, generalized to new behaviors, or adapted to different circumstances. However, the potential promise of self-control techniques for improving the functionality and effectiveness of education is great.

## WHEN INSTRUCTION DOES NOT WORK: REMEDIATING INSTRUCTIONAL PLANS

Approximately 50% of instructional plans will be successful, at least for a short time (this and subsequent percentages in this section are derived from Haring et al., [1979, 1980, 1981]). However, despite educators' best-laid plans, learning does not always occur. An instructional plan may prove effective for a period and then may lose its effectiveness, or another plan may not work at all. When student performance falters, the instructional plan is not working, and one or more of the plan components must be remediated. Any number of changes could be made in instruction and thus facilitate learning. Of course, if the first intervention is not successful, another will be implemented. But instructional time is wasted by interventions that are unlikely to accelerate learning. Without guidelines, the interventions that teachers select will be successful only about 33% of the time.

Decisions about when and how to remediate instructional plans are based on analyses of the pupil performance data, collected by the educator. It is easier to make decisions if the data are graphed or charted. Procedures discussed in this section were developed by N. Haring, K. Liberty, and O. White during a 5-year research project that involved over one hundred teachers and their severely or profoundly handicapped students (Haring et al., 1979, 1980, 1981). The procedures are derived by the students, who, via their performance records, indicated when a specific instructional plan was effective and when it was not. Decision-rules improved the probability of selecting an effective intervention on the first try to 86%. The empirically based procedures are presented here as a sequence of questions that may be answered by examining the performance data and the instructional plan in use when learning faltered.

*Is intervention necessary?* The first decision should be to determine if intervention is necessary. If the student is making adequate progress, accuracy and/or fluency will be accelerating or maintaining at desired levels, errors will be decelerating or maintaining at acceptable levels, and no intervention is required. If the student has failed to show progress for three instructional sessions, it is time to change. Instructional plans that are poorly designed may account for 26% of the problems. Therefore, the original plan should be reviewed to determine if it adheres to the learning-enhancing techniques presented in this chapter.

*Is the target behavior too difficult or too easy?* The next step is to determine if instruction is directed at the appropriate instructional step. Instruction may be set at too difficult a level; if so, *no* correct responses will have been recorded. This problem occurs very infrequently, in less than 2% of the cases. However, if no correct responses have been recorded, then instruction should be directed at a less complicated response, stepping back for remediation.

Haring et al. (1979, 1981) found that the "step back" to an easier skill was the remedial technique most often used by teachers, but it is only successful about 5% of the time. This may be because it is used far too frequently; teachers decide to "step back" rather than to alter antecedent and subsequent events. An ineffective instructional plan simply will not work, regardless of the difficulty of the behavior at which it is directed. If even a single correct response has occurred, it is more likely that changing antecedent or subsequent events will accelerate learning rather than an approach involving "stepping back".

Instruction may also be directed at too easy a level. This occurs far more frequently (15% of the time) than does selecting levels that are too advanced. If the student's performance is extremely variable—moving from very accurate and/or fluent performance during one instructional session to very inaccurate and/or nonfluent performance during the next session—it is highly likely that instruction is directed at too easy a level. This problem may also be identified if the student has once reached a performance near the aim but then decelerates. If either of these performance patterns is identified, the intervention technique of choice is to immediately advance the student to a more difficult level of the task or behavior.

Together, these figures provide some evidence to support the notion that learning is slowed not just by the type of instruction provided but by the way in which instruction is sequenced and by the methods used for setting instructional aims. Learning delays occur particularly when artificial aims are specified for moving from one instructional step to another or when the student is required to perform over several consecutive days or sessions at a preset criterion before advancing to more difficult material. This is not encountered, however, if instruction is directed at the whole behavior or at the desired final target behavior or if aims are properly set.

*Is the student in the acquisition or fluency building stage?* If neither of these problems is evident in the pupil's performance, an intervention must be made in one or more of the planned events. A simple and effective method of remediating problems at either stage of learning is to increase response opportunities by increasing the number of instructional trials (Azrin, Schaeffer, & Wesolowski, 1976; Mayhall & Jenkins, 1977; O'Brien, Azrin, & Bugle, 1972; Smith & Snell, 1978a; Westling & Murden, 1978; White & Haring, 1980).

At this decision level the identification of an appropriate intervention is determined by identifying whether the student is in the acquisition or the fluency building stage of learning. Performance during the acquisition stage may be identified by relatively high numbers of inaccurate responses and by accurate responses that may be nonfluent. Fluency building techniques become more appropriate as the student reaches approximately 80% of the aim desired. If the analysis of the student's performance indicates that he or she has "crossed" from acquisition to fluency building, the remediation might be to switch quickly from the original acquisition-enhancing plan to a completely new plan designed to enhance fluency building. If, on the other hand, the original plan is designed for the stage of learning in which the student is performing, interventions are required of a more subtle nature.

Problems during acquisition indicate that the student requires more information on *how* to respond. Approximately 16% of plan-remediation decisions may fall in this category. If learning falters during acquisition, more complex and more supportive information should be provided. Observation of the type of errors the student makes may assist in selecting appropriate intervention techniques. If a student is making consistent errors (errors of the same type), it is likely that additional assistance or S+ enhancements are needed. Different error-correction procedures may also be required. For example, if the student consistently errs when the objects in the "not-more" set are larger in size than the objects in the "more" set, the teacher may decide either to delay presenting such instances or to use a color cue to enhance the S+ characteristic of number. If errors vary in type, and especially if errors are increasing, then they are being reinforced. In such cases, synthetic antecedents can be substituted for the error-correction procedure, and errors, to the extent possible, can be ignored. Or the reinforcing value of the event that follows correct behavior may be stregthened in order to provide a definite contrast with the events that follow incorrect behavior.

Problems during fluency building occur more than twice as often as during acquisition (40% versus 16%). This may be because many teachers are unfamiliar with techniques that enhance fluency or with the selection of powerful arrangements and reinforcers. Observation of the type of nonfluent behavior that is occurring may help identify a remedial intervention. One option is to show the student how to "go fast," by modeling or demonstrating physical movements or techniques that will enhance fluency. For example, in an assembly program, it was noticed that the student spent time arranging the objects into precise lines when it was not necessary. This was remediated by pointing out to the student that such behavior was not

Table 4. Some suggested methods of remediating instructional plans for problems in maintenance, generalization, and adaptation

| Problem | Suggested remediation of instructional plan |
| --- | --- |
| 1. Response decreasing in frequency. | Reestablish fluency aims and build fluency; establish control via longer intervals/higher ratio mixed arrangements; increase delay in reinforcement. |
| 2. Response associated with irrelevant stimuli. | Identify S$i$ in nontraining setting, introduce and vary with S+ and S− in training. |
| 3. Nondesired response occurs. | Increase fluency with which learner is able to access available reinforcers with the desired behavior. |
| 4. Response associated with limited range of stimuli. | Increase range of S+, S− presented. |
| 5. Response does not topographically adapt. | Increase range of S+ and S− to include topographically different responses. |

necessary and by the teacher preventing the student from engaging in such behavior. Another student was observed picking up objects one at a time. Demonstration and practice in picking up many objects at once remediated the nonfluent behavior. However, if observation does not identify precise movements that are slowing performance, modifying the arrangement or increasing the power of the reinforcing event are the tactics most likely to facilitate learning.

If the first intervention does not show enhanced learning within three days, the plan should be altered again. Students that are having difficulty learning can ill afford to waste time with ineffective instruction. If the student is not progressing, teaching is not occurring.

*Are maintenance, generalization, and adaptation occurring?* Probes conducted to determine generalization and adaptation during training may be used to identify when instructional techniques are resulting in the desired outcomes. After training ends, continued probes will identify when maintenance, generalization, and/or adaptive responding are continuing at desired levels. If they are not, training must be reinstated and revised instructional procedures implemented.

Empirically derived decision-rules for remediating plans to produce maintained, generalized, and adaptive responding have not yet been developed. However, information that is available may assist in improving instruction. If a response does not maintain, generalize, or adapt, first examine the instructional plans

used during training to determine likely areas of weakness. Second, the student's performance may provide information on where the training must be remediated (Horner et al., 1983). Table 4 indicates some suggested methods of remediating instructional plans when training is reinstated.

Third, changes in the events in the generalization setting may be required (Kazdin, 1980). Generally, these involve changing the lows, density, or quality of reinforcement or changing the response opportunity. If a competing and undesirable behavior is occurring, it is being reinforced. Individuals providing attention to competing behaviors should be trained to ignore them and to provide attention for the desired behavior. Maintenance, generalization and adaption may also be influenced by the lack of externally delivered reinforcers in nontraining settings. Another change in the setting may be to increase the reinforcement provided, either by teaching self-reinforcement or by training individuals in the generalization setting to dispense reinforcement. Educators may have to assume a more active role in nonschool settings in order to preserve the fruits of instruction. Further research is expected to identify if and when this is necessary. Too few opportunities to perform the behavior may also affect post-training performance. For example, Thompson, Braam, and Fuqua (1982) trained students to launder their own clothes. At a follow-up, one of the students was not able to demonstrate the behavior (failure to maintain); in the intervening 10 months, he had

had no opportunity to wash clothes. In this case, either the setting should be modified to provide the opportunity to perform the behavior, or other behaviors should be initially selected for instruction.

Empirically derived decision-rules for selecting maintenance-generalization-, and adaptation-enhancing strategies based on the learning patterns of individual students are currently being researched (Haring, Liberty, Billingsley, Butterfield, & White, 1983). This research is designed to identify specific strategies

and to time their implementation during acquisition and fluency building instruction so that the probabilities of maintenance, generalization, and adaptation are increased beyond "train and hope" levels. As research continues to focus on these problems, better individualized and more successful instructional techniques will be identified.

## CONCLUSION

Researchers and educators have successfully identified instructional techniques that enhance

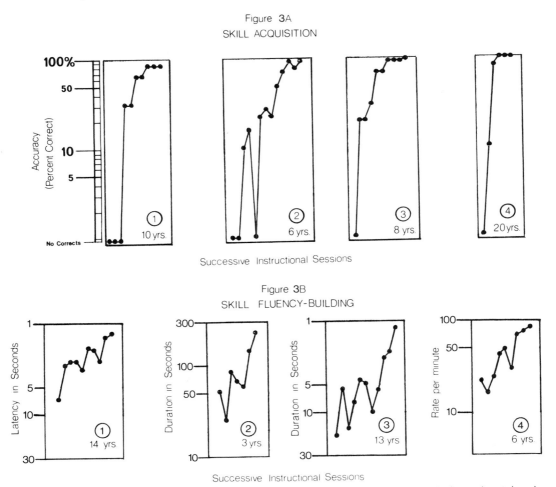

Figure 3.    Illustrations of skill acquisition and fluency building. Part a includes examples of skill acquisition by four students (adapted from published research studies as indicated): 1. "Uses plural form in sentence" (Garcia et al., 1973); 2. "Eats properly with a spoon" (O'Brien, Bugle, & Azrin, 1972); 3. "Says sight words" (Lahey & Drabman, 1974); 4. "Takes photograph with camera" (Giangreco, 1983). (Examples 1 and 4 are severely handicapped students, example 2 is a profoundly handicapped student, and example 3 is a nonhandicapped student.)

Part b includes examples of fluency building by four students (adapted from Haring et al., 1979, 1981): 1. "Answers 'yes'/'no' by pointing"; 2. "Holds head in midline"; 3. "Picks up spoon"; 4. "Discriminates objects by color." (All learners have multiple physical handicaps; all have cerebral palsy; 1 and 4 are severely mentally retarded students; 2 and 3 are profoundly mentally retarded students.)

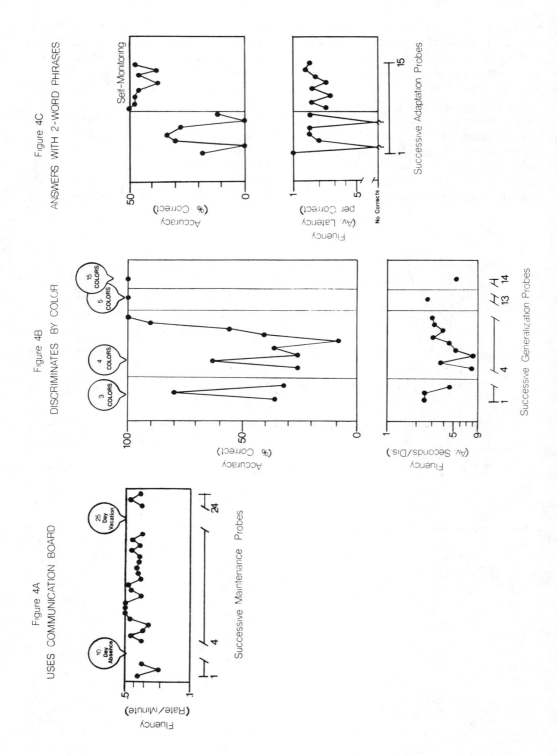

Figure 4A

USES COMMUNICATION BOARD

Figure 4B

DISCRIMINATES BY COLOR

Figure 4C

ANSWERS WITH 2-WORD PHRASES

learning for individuals many thought would never be able to benefit from instruction. Today, empirical evidence attesting to the effectiveness of these strategies is introduced into courtrooms to convince uninformed individuals to provide appropriate services to severely handicapped persons. With learning-accelerating techniques, severely handicapped students can equal or surpass acquisition rates of nonhandicapped students, although differences in the target of instruction may still exist. The power of these techniques during instruction is shown in Figure 3. Figure 3a illustrates the acquisition of accurate performance by four students, two of whom are severely handicapped individuals, one of whom is a profoundly handicapped person, and one of whom is nonhandicapped. (The reader is challenged to identify the students before reading the caption.) The achievement of fluent performance at levels equivalent to nonhandicapped peers by four severely retarded students with cerebral palsy is shown in Figure 3b. Even though concern for performance fluency has

been recognized only in the past decade, powerful techniques for building fluency have been developed.

The strategies discussed in this chapter for producing maintenance, generalization, and adaptation are more than a beginning; applications have been demonstrated that provide solutions. The charts of student performance shown in Figure 4 illustrate the results of instructional plans that incorporated strategies for producing maintenance, generalization, and adaptation outside of instructional settings or after instruction had ceased. Figure 4a illustrates successful maintenance of a communication program following training in accurate and fluent use of the photographs and symbols on the communication board. Although these data are over 3 years old, a follow-up interview with the student's teacher indicates that the student is continuing to use the communication board successfully, and that additional photographs and representative symbols have been added.

Figure 4b illustrates successful generalization of a concept to untrained members of the

Figure 4.    Maintained, generalized, and adapted responding by severely handicapped students.

Part a shows successive *maintenance* probes over an 80-day period in using a communication board by a 16-year old student with cerebral palsy and severe mental retardation. The pupil had the opportunity to use the board to initiate and answer questions, to make requests, and so on with the classroom staff during the school day. Natural reinforcement available included acceding to the student's requests for objects or materials, conversation with the student, and answering the student's questions. Arrangements were mixed interval, since staff were often working with other pupils in the classroom and did not always respond to student initiations. Data show performance after instruction ceased as rate per minute throughout the school day. The student averaged approximately .33 uses per minute, or one "use" every 3 minutes. Rates are maintained across nonschool periods of 10 and then 25 days.

Part b illustrates the performance of a 5-year old severely handicapped student during consecutive *generalization* probes over a 100-day period. The student sorted identical objects by color during the probes. No feedback or reinforcement for accuracy or fluency was available during generalization probes, although the student was thanked for working. The first three probes show performance on 3-color discriminations. During this period, the student was receiving instruction on 2-color discriminations. The generalization probes involved different colors than were used in training. Accuracy was approximately at chance levels, while fluency averaged 2.4 seconds duration per discrimination, above the aim of 3 seconds: fast but inaccurate nongeneralization. When the student met criterion on 2-color discriminations during training, instruction on 3-color discriminations and generalization probes on 4 color discriminations were instituted (phase 2). The student's performance during probe sessions slowed to a low of 8.5 seconds per discrimination, and accuracy was poor; generalization was not occurring. After approximately 15 instructional sessions with 3

colors, the student accurately and fluently generalized to 4-color discriminations. Two consecutive probes of 5-color and 15-color discriminations confirmed successful accurate generalization of color discrimination, although fluency for the 15-color discrimination indicated a slow performance in order to achieve accuracy.

Part c shows the *adaptive* performance of a 10-year old severely handicapped student over a 42-day period. The student was instructed in her classroom to answer questions with intelligible two-word answers, which were reinforced by conversation, while no-responses (within 5 seconds), and one-word responses were ignored. Two-word answers that were unintelligible were followed by an error-correction procedure that allowed one more opportunity to respond (as in Figure 2); a model of an appropriate two-word phrase preceded the opportunity to respond, and a time-delay procedure was used to fade the model in training. Over one hundred different questions and answers were used. Instructional trials occurred throughout the day at natural times for questions. Adaptive performance was probed in another setting where the student attended snack and music two or three times per week. In this setting, unintelligible answers, nonverbal answers (e.g. pointing), one-word answers, and two-word answers were each variably consequated or ignored. The final seven probes of this situation are shown in the first phase of data. Classroom instruction alone produced only very low levels of adaptive responding in the probe setting. Next, instruction in use of a wrist counter was initiated in the classroom. The student was taught how to push the button after each correct two-word answer (although the student did not recognize any numbers and did not count by rote at all). The use of the counter was therefore a subsequent event for a correct response. The student wore the wrist counter to the probe setting, where accuracy levels improved to approximately 50%, as shown in the second phase of "c." (From ongoing research conducted by the author.)

stimulus class, which occurred concurrently with instruction. Additional fluency building techniques may yet be required for adaptative and functional application of the concept (e.g., in using color discrimination to choose attractive clothing).

Figure 4c shows response adaptation; the student was required to answer questions, which differed from those asked in the training setting, with uninstructed two-word answers appropriate to those untrained questions. While initial levels of cross-setting adaptation were very low and probably were not functional, self-monitoring with a wrist counter greatly enhanced the percentage of appropriately adapted responses. Although the 50% accuracy level attained in the probe setting was equivalent to the performance of the other students in that setting, further training or intervention is expected to increase adaptation. In addition, although the student began answering questions with three and four words in the training setting, this type of adaptive responding did not transfer to the probe setting until the student was self-monitoring in that setting. An anecdotal report from the student's mother arrived the morning after the student had inadver-tently worn the wrist counter home. The mother reported that her daughter had never talked so much or for so long before.

Facilitation of maintenance, generalization, and adaptation begins with instructional planning and continues with the selection of setting events, antecedent events, arrangements, and subsequent events. Once instruction begins, appropriate fading of events that are not present outside of instruction will increase the probability that maintained, generalized, and adapted responding will result. Instruction continues until success is achieved.

Continued research will help to resolve questions about selecting the most effective stimuli, methods of fading, methods of thinning reinforcement schedules, and other details that will allow more precise selection and application of strategies. Until data-decision rules are developed, one must apply a trial and error process to determine which procedures have the highest probability of being effective for each student. It is the student, however, who will finally decide how successful a program is in accelerating learning and producing skills that maintain, generalize, and adapt.

## REFERENCES

Alberto, P., Jobes, N., Sizemore, A., & Doran, D. A comparison of individual and group instruction across response tasks. *Journal of the Association for the Severely Handicapped*, 1980, 5(3), 285–293.

Alberto, P., & Troutman, A. *Applied behavior analysis for teachers: Influencing student performance*. Columbus, OH: Charles E. Merrill Publishing Co., 1982.

Ayllon, T., Garber, S., & Pisor, K. Reducing time limits: A means to increase behavior of retardates. *Journal of Applied Behavior Analysis*, 1976, 9, 247–252.

Azrin, N., Schaeffer, R., & Wesolowski, M. A rapid method of teaching profoundly retarded persons to dress by a reinforcement-guidance method. *Mental Retardation*, 1976, 14(6), 29–33.

Baer, D., Peterson, R., & Sherman, J. The development of imitation by reinforcing behavioral similarity to a model. *Journal of the Experimental Analysis of Behavior*, 1967, 10, 405–416.

Baer, D., & Wolf, M. The entry into natural communities of reinforcement. In: R. Ulrich, T. Stachnik, & J. Mabry (eds.), *Control of human behavior, Vol. 2: From cure to prevention*. Glenview, IL: Scott, Foresman, & Co., 1970.

Bandura, A. Analysis of modeling processes. In: A. Bandura (ed.), *Psychological modeling: Conflicting theories*. Chicago: Aldine-Atherton, 1971.

Bandura, A. *Aggression: A social learning analysis*. Englewood Cliffs, NJ: Prentice-Hall, 1973.

Barrett, B. Communitization and the measured message of normal behavior. In: R. York & E. Edgar (eds.), *Teaching the severely handicapped*, Vol. 4. Seattle: American Association for the Education of the Severely/Profoundly Handicapped, 1979.

Baumgart, D., Brown, L., Pumpian, I., Nisbet, J., Ford, A., Sweet, M., Messina, R., & Schroeder, J. Principle of partial participation and individualized adaptations in educational programs for severely handicapped students. *Journal of the Association for the Severely Handicapped*, 1982, 7(2), 17–27.

Becker, W., Engelmann, S., & Thomas, D. *Teaching: A course in applied psychology*. Chicago: Science Research Associates, 1971.

Becker, W., Engelmann, S., & Thomas, D. *Teaching 1: Classroom management*. Chicago: Science Research Associates, 1975a.

Becker, W., Engelmann, S., & Thomas, D. *Teaching 2: Cognitive learning and instruction*. Chicago: Science Research Associates, 1975b.

Bellamy, G., Inman, D., & Schwarz, R. Vocational training and production supervision: A review of habilitation techniques for the severely and profoundly retarded. In: N. Haring & D. Bricker (eds.), *Teaching the severely* handicapped, Vol. 2. Seattle: American Association for the Education of the Severely/Profoundly Handicapped, 1978.

Billingsley, F., & Romer, L. Response prompting and the transfer of stimulus control: Methods, research and a conceptual framework. *Journal of the Association for the Severely Handicapped*, 1983, *8*(2), 3–12.

Bragg, R., & Wagner, M. Issues and implications of operant conditioning: Can deprivation be justified? In: R. Ulrich, T. Stachnik, & J. Mabry (eds.), *Control of human behavior, Vol. 2: From cure to prevention*. Glenview, IL: Scott, Foresman & Co., 1970.

Brigham, T. Self-control. In: C. Cantonia & T. Brigham (eds.), *Handbook of applied behavior analysis*. New York: Irvington Publishers, 1978.

Brown, F., Holvoet, J., Guess, D., & Mulligan, M. The individualized curriculum sequencing model (III): Small group instruction. *Journal of the Association for the Severely Handicapped*, 1981, *5*(4), 352–367.

Brown, L., Branston, M., Hamre-Nietupski, S., Pumpian, I., Certo, N., & Gruenewald, L. A strategy for developing chronological age-appropriate and functional curricular content for severely handicapped adolescents and young adults. *Journal of Special Education*, 1979, *13*, 81–90.

Brown, L., Ford, A., Nisbet, J., Sweet, M., Donnellan, A., & Gruenewald, L. Opportunities available when severely handicapped students attend chronological age-appropriate regular schools. *Journal of the Association for the Severely Handicapped*, 1983, *8*(1), 16–24.

Brown, L., Nietupski, J., & Hamre-Nietupski, S. *The criterion of ultimate functioning and public school services for severely handicapped students*. Madison: University of Wisconsin, Department of Special Education, 1976.

Butter, C. *Neuropsychology: The study of brain and behavior*. Belmont, CA: Brooks/Cole Publishing Company, 1968.

Close, D., Irvin, L., Prehm, H., & Taylor, V. Systematic correction procedures in vocational skill training of severely retarded individuals. *American Journal of Mental Deficiency*, 1979, *83*, 270–275.

Cole, P., & Kazdin, A. Critical issues in self-instruction training with children. *Child Behavior Therapy*, 1980, *2*(2), 1–21.

Coon, M., Vogelsberg, R., & Williams, W. Effects of classroom public transportation instruction on generalization to the natural environment. *Journal of the Association for the Severely Handicapped*, 1981, *6*(2), 46–53.

Csapo, M. Comparison of two prompting procedures to increase response fluency among severely handicapped learners. *Journal of the Association for the Severely Handicapped*, 1981, *6*(1), 39–47.

Dougher, M. Clinical effects of response deprivation and response satiation procedures. *Behavior Therapy*, 1983, *14*, 286–298.

Dunlap, G., & Koegel, R. Motivating autistic children through stimulus variation. *Journal of Applied Behavior Analysis*, 1980, *13*, 619–627.

Egel, A. Reinforcer variation: Implications for motivating developmentally delayed children via an operant shaping procedure. *Journal of Applied Behavior Analysis*, 1981, *14*, 345–350.

Egel, A., Richman, G., & Koegel, R. Normal peer models and autistic children's learning. *Journal of Applied Behavior Analysis*, 1981, *14*, 3–12.

Etzel, B., & LeBlanc, J. The simplest treatment alternative: The law of parsimony applied to choosing appropriate instructional control and errorless learning procedures for the difficult-to-teach child. *Journal of Autism and Developmental Disorders*, 1979, *9*, 361–382.

Falvey, M., Brown, L., Lyon, S., Baumgart, D., & Schroeder, J. Strategies for using cues and correction procedures. In: W. Sailor, B. Wilcox, & L. Brown (eds.), *Methods of instruction for severely handicapped students*. Baltimore: Paul H. Brookes Publishing Co., 1980.

Favell, J., Favell, J., & McGimsey, J. Relative effectiveness and efficiency of group v. individual training of severely retarded persons. *American Journal of Mental Deficiency*, 1978, *83*, 104–109.

Ferrari, M., & Harris, S. The limits and motivating potential of sensory stimuli as reinforcers for autistic children. *Journal of Applied Behavior Analysis*, 1981, *14*, 339–343.

Fowler, S., & Baer, D. "Do I have to be good all day?" The timing of delayed reinforcement as a factor in generalization. *Journal of Applied Behavior Analysis*, 1981, *14*, 13–24.

Garcia, E., Guess, D., & Byrnes, J. Development of syntax in a retarded girl using procedures of imitation, reinforcement and modeling. *Journal of Applied Behavior Analysis*, 1973, *6*, 299–310.

Gentry, D., Day, M., & Nakao, C. *The effectiveness of two-prompt sequencing procedures for discrimination learning with severely handicapped individuals*. Unpublished manuscript, University of Idaho, Moscow, Idaho, 1979.

Giangreco, M. Teaching basic photography skills to a severely retarded young adult using simulated materials. *Journal of the Association for the Severely Handicapped*, 1983, *8*(1), 43–49.

Gold, M. Stimulus factors in skill training of retarded adolescents on a complex assembly task: Acquisition, transfer and retention. *American Journal of Mental Deficiency*, 1972, *76*, 517–526.

Guess, D., Horner, R., Utley, B., Holvoet, J., Maxon, D., Tucker, D., & Warren, S. A functional curriculum sequencing model for teaching the severely handicapped. *AAESPH Review*, 1978, *3*(4), 202–215.

Halle, J., Marshall, A., & Spradlin, J. Time delay: A technique to increase language usage and facilitate generalization in retarded children. *Journal of Applied Behavior Analysis*, 1979, *12*, 341–349.

Haring, N., Liberty, K., Billingsley, F., Butterfield, E., & White, O. *Investigating the problem of skill generalization*. Unpublished manuscript, University of Washington, Research in Education of the Severely Handicapped, Seattle, 1983. (ERIC Document Reproduction Service No. ED234 573.)

Haring, N., Liberty, K., & White, O. *An investigation of phases of learning and facilitating instructional events for the severely handicapped: Fourth annual progress report, 1978–1979*. Seattle: University of Washington, College of Education, September, 1979.

Haring, N., Liberty, K., & White, O. Rules for data-based strategy decisions in instructional programs: Current research and instructional implications. In: W. Sailor, B. Wilcox, & L. Brown (eds.), *Methods of instruction for severely handicapped students*. Baltimore: Paul H. Brookes Publishing Co., 1980.

Haring, N., Liberty K., & White, O. *An investigation of phases of learning and facilitating instructional events for the severely handicapped: Final report 1981.* Seattle: University of Washington, College of Education, January, 1981.

Hartmann, D., & Hall, R.V. The changing criterion design. *Journal of Applied Behavior Analysis,* 1976, *9,* 527–632.

Hopper, C., & Helmick, R. Nonverbal communication and the severely handicapped: Some considerations. *AAESPH Review,* 1977, *2*(2), 47–52.

Horner, R., Bellamy, G.T., & Colvin, G. *Responding in the presence of non-trained stimuli: Implications of generalization error patterns.* Unpublished manuscript, University of Oregon, Research in Education of the Handicapped, Eugene, June, 1983.

Horner, R., Sprague, J., & Wilcox, B. General case programming for community activities. In: B. Wilcox & G. T. Bellamy (eds.), *Design of high school programs for severely handicapped students.* Baltimore: Paul H. Brookes Publishing Co., 1982.

Irvin, L., & Bellamy, G. Manipulation of stimulus features in vocational skill training of the severely retarded: Relative efficacy. *American Journal of Mental Deficiency,* 1977, *81,* 486–491.

Janssen, C., & Guess, D. Use of function as a consequence in training receptive labeling to severely and profoundly retarded individuals. *AAESPH Review,* 1978, *3*(4), 246–258.

Kazdin, A. *Behavior modification in applied settings.* Homewood, IL: Dorsey Press, 1980.

Kazdin, A. The token economy: A decade later. *Journal of Applied Behavior Analysis,* 1982, *15,* 431–445.

Kazdin, A., & Bootzin, R. The token economy: An evaluative review. *Journal of Applied Behavior Analysis,* 1972, *5,* 343–372.

Kleinert, H., & Gast, D. Teaching a multihandicapped adult manual signs using a constant time delay procedure. *Journal of the Association for the Severely Handicapped,* 1982, *6*(4), 25–32.

Koegel, R., Schreibman, L., Britten, K., & Laitinen, R. The effects of schedule of reinforcement on stimulus overselectivity in autistic children. *Journal of Autism and Developmental Disorders,* 1979, *9,* 383–397.

Lahey, B., & Drabman, R. Facilitation of the acquisition and retention of sight word vocabulary through token reinforcement. *Journal of Applied Behavior Analysis,* 1974, *7,* 307–312.

Mayhall, W., & Jenkins, J. Scheduling daily or less-than-daily instruction: Implications for resource programs. *Journal of Learning Disabilities,* 1977, *10*(3), 159–163.

Mercer, C., & Snell, M. *Learning theory research in mental retardation: Implications for teaching.* Columbus, OH: Charles E. Merrill Publishing Co., 1977.

Mulligan, M., Guess, D., Holvoet, J., & Brown, F. The individualized curriculum sequencing model (1): Implications from research on massed, distributed, or spaced trial training. *Journal of the Association for the Severely Handicapped,* 1981, *5,* 325–336.

Mulligan, M., Lacy, L., & Guess, D. Effects of massed, distributed, and spaced trial sequencing on severely handicapped students' performance. *Journal of the Association for the Severely Handicapped,* 1982, *7*(2), 48–61.

O'Brien, F., Azrin, N., & Bugle, C. Training profoundly retarded children to stop crawling. *Journal of Applied Behavior Analysis,* 1972, *5,* 131–137.

O'Brien, F., Bugle, C., & Azrin, N. Training and maintaining a retarded child's proper eating. *Journal of Applied Behavior Analysis,* 1972, *5,* 67–72.

O'Leary, S., & Dubey, D. Applications of self-control procedures by children: A review. *Journal of Applied Behavior Analysis,* 1979, *12,* 449–465.

Rincover, A., Cook, R., Peoples, A., & Packard, D. Sensory extinction and sensory reinforcement principles for programming multiple adaptive behavior changes. *Journal of Applied Behavior Analysis,* 1979, *12,* 221–233.

Rosenbaum, M., & Drabman, R. Self-control training in the classroom: A review and critique. *Journal of Applied Behavior Analysis,* 1979, *12,* 467–485.

Saunders, R., & Sailor, W. A comparison of three strategies of reinforcement of two-choice learning problems with severely retarded children. *AAESPH Review,* 1979, *4*(4), 323–333.

Schroeder, S. Parametric effects of reinforcement frequency, amount of reinforcement, and required response force on sheltered workshop behavior. *Journal of Applied Behavior Analysis,* 1972, *5,* 431–441.

Shapiro, E., & Klein, R. Self-management of classroom behavior with retarded/disturbed children. *Behavior Modification,* 1980, *4*(1), 83–94.

Shevin, M. The use of food and drink in classroom management programs for severely handicapped children. *Journal of the Association for the Severely Handicapped,* 1982, *7*(1), 40–46.

Sidman, M., & Stoddard, L. The effectiveness of fading in programming a simultaneous form discrimination for retarded children. *Journal of the Experimental Analysis of Behavior,* 1967, *10,* 3–15.

Smith, D., & Snell, M. Classroom management and instructional planning. In: M. Snell (ed.), *Systematic instruction of the moderately and severely handicapped.* Columbus, OH: Charles E. Merrill Publishing Co., 1978a.

Smith, D., & Snell, M. Intervention strategies. In: M. Snell (ed.), *Systematic instruction of the moderately and severely handicapped.* Columbus, OH: Charles E. Merrill Publishing Co., 1978b.

Snell, M. (ed.). *Systematic instruction of the moderately and severely handicapped* (2d ed.). Columbus, OH: Charles E. Merrill Publishing Co., 1983.

Snell, M., & Gast, D. Applying time delay procedure to the instruction of the severely handicapped. *Journal of the Association for the Severely Handicapped,* 1981, *6*(3), 3–14.

Spradlin, J., & Spradlin, R. Developing necessary skills for entry into classroom teaching arrangements. In: N. Haring & R. Schiefelbusch (eds.), *Teaching special children.* New York: McGraw-Hill Book Co., 1976.

Stephens, C., Pear, J., Wray, L., & Jackson, G. Some effects of reinforcement in teaching picture names to retarded children. *Journal of Applied Behavior Analysis,* 1977, *10,* 349–367.

Stokes, T., & Baer, D. An implicit technology of generalization. *Journal of Applied Behavior Analysis,* 1977, *10,* 349–367.

Storm, R., & Willis, J. Small-group training as an alternative to individualized programming for profoundly retarded persons. *American Journal of Mental Deficiency,* 1978, *8*(3), 283–288.

Terrace, H. Discrimination learning with and without errors. *Journal of the Experimental Analysis of Behavior,* 1963a, *6,* 1–27.

Terrace, H. Errorless transfer of a discrimination across two continua. *Journal of the Experimental Analysis of Behavior,* 1963b, *6,* 223–232.

Thompson, T., Braam, S., & Fuqua, W. Training and generalization of laundry skills: A multiple probe evaluation with handicapped persons. *Journal of Applied Behavior Analysis,* 1982, *15,* 177–182.

Touchette, P. The effects of graduated stimulus change on the acquisition of a simple discrimination in severely retarded boys. *Journal of the Experimental Analysis of Behavior,* 1968, *8,* 39–48.

Wahler, R., & Fox, J. Setting events in applied behavior analysis: Toward a conceptual and methodological expansion. *Journal of Applied Behavior Analysis,* 1981, *14,* 327–338.

Wahler, R., & Graves, M. Setting events in social networks: Ally or enemy in child behavior therapy?. *Behavior Therapy,* 1983, *14,* 19–36.

Wehman, P., Renzaglia, A., Berry, G., Schutz, R., & Karan, O. Developing a leisure skill repertoire in severely and profoundly handicapped persons. *AAESPH Review,* 1978, *3*(3), 162–171.

Westling, D., & Murden, L. Self-help skills training: A review of operant studies. *Journal of Special Education,* 1978, *12*(3), 253–283.

White, O. Adaptive performance objectives. In: W. Sailor, B. Wilcox, & L. Brown (eds.), *Methods of instruction for severely handicapped students.* Baltimore: Paul H. Brookes Publishing Co., 1980.

White, O., & Haring, N. *Exceptional teaching* (2d ed.). Columbus, OH: Charles E. Merrill Publishing Co., 1980.

Wilcox, B., & Bellamy, G.T. (eds.). *Design of high school programs for severely handicapped students.* Baltimore: Paul H. Brookes Publishing Co., 1982.

Williams, J., Koegel, R., & Egel, A. Response-reinforcer relationships and improved learning in autistic chilren. *Journal of Applied Behavior Analysis,* 1981, *14,* 53–60.

York, R., Williams, W., & Brown, P. Teaching modeling and student imitation: An instructional procedure and teacher competency. *AAESPH Review,* 1976, *1*(8), 11–15.

Zimmerman, J., Overpeck, C., Eisenberg, H., & Garlick, B. Operant conditioning in a sheltered workshop. *Rehabilitation Literature,* 1969, *30,* 326–334.

# Chapter 3

# Assessing and Training Adaptive Behaviors

*Julie Gorder Holman and Robert H. Bruininks*

The concept of adaptive behavior is widely used to define conditions of developmental handicaps. Contemporary definitions of mental retardation, for example, typically contain criteria of social incompetence, inadequate ability to learn and profit from experience, and/or poor adjustment in educational, social, and vocational settings as conditions for the classification. Based upon earlier definitions, the American Association on Mental Deficiency (AAMD) introduced the term *adaptive behavior* to describe a range of age-appropriate maturational, learning, social, and vocational skills, along with subaverage general intellectual functioning, as one important dimension of defining mental retardation (Heber, 1961). Despite some criticism of this concept (Clausen, 1972), adaptive behavior skills continue to represent an important focus of research and practice in programs for handicapped persons.

Adaptive behavior is most commonly defined as "the effectiveness or degree with which individuals meet the standards of personal independence and social responsibility expected for age and cultural group" (Grossman, 1983, p. 1). Adaptive behavior and its two major components, personal independence and social responsibility, involve a variety of skills that are necessary for maximum independence and satisfactory adjustment in society.

The adaptive behavior concept potentially includes all aspects of human behavior (Coulter & Morrow, 1978b); therefore, the specific skills that constitute adaptive behavior have been only partially delineated. Because of the relationship of adaptive behaviors to diagnostic and "common-sense" definitions of handicaps, assessing and training them has been increasingly advanced as a desirable component of educational and habilitation programs for handicapped individuals (Cantrell, 1982; Meyers, Nihira, & Zetlin, 1979).

The subject of adaptive behavior is intricately related to improving the lives of handicapped citizens. The focus of public policy and practice, as noted in earlier chapters and in Bruininks and Lakin (1985), currently stresses maximum integration of handicapped and disabled persons into society. This orientation is reflected most prominently in the policies of *mainstreaming* in education and *deinstitutionalization* in residential services programs. Many of the ideological concepts undergirding our service programs, such as *normalization* and *least restrictive environment,* emphasize the centrality of providing means of improving the adaptation of people in normal environments.

The opportunity to live and learn in the least restrictive environment is limited by three major factors: (1) the adaptive functioning of people, (2) the willingness of social and educational institutions, and of citizens generally, to assimilate people with special learning and adjustment needs, and (3) the extent to which environments provide essential accommodations for persons' handicaps and disabilities. Other authors have discussed important aspects of improving community acceptance (see chapters by Lakin and Bruininks, Bachrach, and Seltzer, in Bruininks & Lakin, 1985,) and environmental modification (see chapters by Wray & Wieck in this volume; and Landesman-Dwyer and Schalock in Bruininks & Lakin, 1985). This chapter discusses the concept of adaptive behavior, reviews literature on assessment of adaptive behavior, and analyzes the research on the training of adaptive behavior skills.

## STRUCTURE OF ADAPTIVE BEHAVIOR

Although the construct of adaptive behavior has been discussed extensively for more than a quarter of a century, there is limited theoretical development and empirically derived information on the structure of adaptive behavior (Mercer, 1978). Without a sound conceptual base, the concept of adaptive behavior is often interpreted in a fragmented, ambiguous manner

by policy makers, planners, researchers, and those concerned with implementing assessment and training programs for handicapped persons.

One contribution to the clarification of the construct of adaptive behavior was recently published by the American Association on Mental Deficiency. The AAMD's publication, *Classification in Mental Retardation* (Grossman, 1983), cites adaptive behavior as one essential condition for the diagnosis of mental retardation. Impairments in adaptive behavior, however, are not limited to mentally retarded individuals and may also be characteristic of persons with other handicapping conditions.

The AAMD (Grossman, 1983) identifies adaptive behavior skill deficits that are likely to be associated with given age levels (see Table 1). Although the skills in Table 1 are listed in terms of deficiencies that are likely to occur for mentally retarded individuals, it is implicitly assumed that these skills should be acquired through normal development by that age level. Successful adaptation during infancy and early childhood necessitates the acquisition of fundamental sensorimotor, communication, selfhelp, and socialization skills. During childhood and early adolescence, adaptive behavior skills that typically develop are social skills, mastery of the environment through reasoning

Table 1.    Deficiencies in adaptive behavior occurring at various age levels

| Age level | Adaptive behavior skills |
| --- | --- |
| Infancy and early childhood | Sensorimotor skills<br>Communication skills (including speech and language)<br>Self-help skills<br>Socialization (development of ability to interact with others) |
| Childhood and early adolescence | Application of basic academic skills to daily life activities<br>Application of appropriate reasoning and judgment in mastery of the environment<br>Social skills (participation in group activities and interpersonal relationships) |
| Late adolescence and adult life | Vocational responsibility<br>Vocational performance<br>Social responsibility<br>Social performance |

*Source:* Adapted from Grossman, H.J. (ed.). *Classification in mental retardation.* Washington, DC: American Association on Mental Deficiency, 1983.

and judgment, and the ability to use basic academic skills in daily life activities. Adaptive behavior skills commonly developed during late adolescence and adult life focus on vocational and social responsibilities and performance.

Despite the continual development and refinement of all facets of adaptive behavior during normal development, specific adaptive behavior skills assume positions of prominence during different developmental periods. Motor skills, for example, continue to expand and to be refined throughout the developmental period, but the major advances, such as sitting unsupported and walking, are made during infancy and early childhood. Although some vocational skills may begin to develop at earlier ages (e.g., attending to tasks, completing school work), they generally do not assume positions of importance until late adolescence and adult life when they are required for successful job performance.

Aside from the notion that different adaptive behaviors assume prominence at particular age levels, the AAMD's description does not provide a comprehensive view of the components of adaptive behavior. The AAMD definition indicates that it is to be evaluated on the basis of the individual's ability to meet the expected standards of personal independence and social responsibility; however, there is no attempt to further define personal independence and social responsibility or to classify behavioral skills according to those factors. Nevertheless, the AAMD description adds to our knowledge of the structure of adaptive behavior by providing information on development of adaptive behavior in handicapped individuals and by stressing the personal independence and social responsibility components of adaptive behavior.

Greenspan's (1979) models of personal competence and social intelligence represent a more comprehensive attempt to define the theoretical structure of adaptive behavior. Greenspan's work focuses primarily on one aspect of adaptive behavior, social intelligence, defined by him as "a person's ability to understand and to deal effectively with social and interpersonal objects and events" (Greenspan, 1979, p.

483). Social intelligence skills are an important determinant of social competence and may be similar to the construct of "social responsibility" included in the AAMD definition of adaptive behavior.

Greenspan's model of social intelligence incorporates three major competencies: (1) social sensitivity, the awareness and understanding of the correct meaning of personal and situational cues; (2) social insight, the ability to think about the meaning of and motivation behind interpersonal processes and institutions; and (3) social communication, the ability to work with others in meeting one's needs. Although it is helpful to be aware of the content and comprehensiveness of Greenspan's model of social intelligence, the primary interest in his theory for the purposes of this chapter is the manner in which he incorporates social intelligence and human abilities into a model of personal competence (see Table 2).

According to Greenspan's model, social intelligence is only one aspect of adaptive intelligence, which in turn, is only one aspect of personal competence. Personal competence refers to all of an individual's abilities, including physical competence (i.e., size, strength, and coordination), adaptive intelligence, and socioemotional adaptation. The adaptive intelligence component of Greenspan's model and adaptive behavior, as defined by the AAMD, appear to be similar. But whereas the AAMD definition incorporates physical competence (in the form of sensorimotor development), Greenspan's model does not deal with physical competence directly but appears to separate it from the concept of adaptive intelligence.

Adaptive intelligence consists of conceptual intelligence (language and thinking ability), social intelligence (ability to deal effectively with social interpersonal events), and practical intelligence (ability to live independently in terms of self-maintenance and vocational activities). Practical intelligence is based on two of the three independent factors identified by Nihira (1978) in his analysis of Part One of the AAMD Adaptive Behavior Scale (Nihira, Foster, Shellhaas, & Leland, 1974). These two factors include maintenance skills—analogous

Table 2.   Greenspan's model of personal competence

I.  Physical competence
II. Adaptive intelligence
   A.  Conceptual intelligence
      1.  Language ability
      2.  Thinking ability
   B.  Practical intelligence
      1.  Maintenance skills (personal self-sufficiency)
      2.  Interchange skills (community self-sufficiency)
   C.  Social intelligence
      1.  Social sensitivity
      2.  Social insight
      3.  Social communication
III. Socioemotional adaptation
   A.  Temperament
      1.  Reflection/impulsivity
      2.  Calmness/emotionality
   B.  Character
      1.  Social activity/inactivity
      2.  Niceness/nastiness

*Source:* Adapted from Greenspan, S. Social intelligence in the retarded. In: N.R. Ellis (ed.), *Handbook of mental deficiency: Psychological theory and research.* Hillsdale, NJ: Lawrence Erlbaum Associates, 1979.

to personal self-sufficiency—and interchange skills—similar to community self-sufficiency.

The third factor identified in the AAMD Adaptive Behavior Scale, personal-social responsibility, seems more closely related to the socioemotional adaptation component of personal competence in Greenspan's model. This component deals with an individual's personality and includes temperament (an individual's biological mode of response to social stimuli) and character (the moral quality of an individual's interactions with others). The inclusion in the model of this aspect of human abilities is interesting, given its presumed importance to personal and social adjustment. The model recognizes these abilities as behaviors that can be altered, rather than simply as innate qualities that an individual possesses with little possibility for growth and change. Greenspan suggests that the social behavior of a retarded person should be viewed as an interaction between social intelligence and socioemotional adaptation.

Although the efforts by Greenspan (1979) and the American Association on Mental Deficiency (Grossman, 1983) are helpful, there remains a need for additional theoretical development directed specifically at defining critical dimensions of the adaptive behavior construct. Unless there is clear and valid information

about the structure of adaptive behavior, problems are likely to arise in determining what adaptive behavior skills are important for successful community integration as well as for training adaptive behavior and developing assessment instruments. Without such information, behaviors are likely to be assessed and trained as narrow, fragmented skills, without a view of the overall adaptive behavior of the individual.

## ASSESSING ADAPTIVE BEHAVIOR

Another avenue for examining the components of adaptive behavior is in the content of adaptive behavior assessment instruments—content that has been developed from conceptual models and analyses of adaptive functioning in various environments. Thus, it is assumed that such skills are salient features of adaptive behavior. This assumption is validated, at least in part, when the adaptive behavior skills being measured are predictive of the ability to meet the expectations of personal independence and social competence necessary for adjustment in community living situations.

### Purpose of Adaptive Behavior Assessment

Adaptive behavior assessment is conducted to measure behaviors believed to be related to personal independence and social competence. Adaptive behavior scales describe an individual's functional abilities in the home, in day programs, in vocational settings, and in the community. The major uses of adaptive behavior assessment results are:

1. To identify and diagnose the existence of a handicap
2. To make placement decisions
3. To provide the basis for the development of individualized educational and training programs
4. To evaluate educational, training, and service programs
5. To describe a given population and estimate service needs
6. To conduct management studies for assessing educational needs of handicapped persons and evaluating effects of human services

***Diagnosis and Placement*** As recommended by the American Association on Mental Deficiency (Grossman, 1983), it is generally acknowledged that assessment of adaptive behavior should be used in conjunction with assessment of intellectual capability in defining the existence of a handicapping condition (Fogelman, 1975; Huberty, Koller, & Ten-Brink, 1980; Spreat, Roszkowski, & Isett, in press). An exception to this position was taken by Futterman and Arndt (1983), who found adaptive behavior to be a better predictor of type of academic program placement than mental age for mentally retarded residents of an institution. They recommended that adaptive behavior be explored as an alternative to mental age in classification and program placement decisions. On the other hand, Clausen (1972) has argued that since adaptive behavior constructs lack validated definitions and reliable means of measurement, intellectual handicap would be best diagnosed by standardized measures of intelligence.

Because of conflicting evidence and points of view, diagnosis and placement decisions for school-age youth must be based on more than one type of assessment (see Public Law 94-142, Section 612C). Nevertheless, it appears that intelligence tests continue to be the most widely used method for diagnosing handicapping conditions (Junkala, 1977; Prillaman, 1975; Roszkowski & Spreat, 1981; Sundberg, Snowden, & Reynolds, 1978). One reason for this practice may be the dearth, until very recently, of adaptive behavior scales that are carefully developed and researched for the purpose of making diagnosis and placement decisions.

***Program Planning*** The stated purpose of many adaptive behavior scales is to identify programming needs (Berkson & Landesman-Dwyer, 1977; Coulter & Morrow, 1978a; Mc-Carthy, Lund, & Bos, 1983; Spreat et al., in press). Adaptive behavior scales developed for programming purposes provide information about the individual's current level of performance and the skills that may require additional instruction. The difficulty with most adaptive behavior instruments is that they rarely provide sufficient detail for program planning purposes (Dubose, Langley, & Stagg, 1977; Meyers et al., 1979; Simeonsson, Huntington, & Parse, 1980). Adaptive behavior scales cannot incorporate all skills that merit training. Since it is impossible in a scale of reasonable length to assess every adaptive behavior skill, developers select items that are representative of the more general domains. Many items must be excluded that may, nevertheless, be important aspects of adaptive behavior. Compromising between reasonable length and comprehensive assessment necessarily delimits the utility of adaptive behavior scales as programming tools. The scales can, however, be linked to a more comprehensive program device, such as a broad-base curriculum, which would include a more complete list of important skills to be targeted for instruction, as well as activities and training suggestions. Such comprehensive programming packages do not now exist across the full range of adaptive behavior skills, but they are available for specific domains of adaptive behavior.

***Program Evaluation and Management*** Adaptive behavior instruments can be used for two types of evaluation procedures: 1) to evaluate the progress of an individual, and 2) to evaluate the effectiveness of programs (McCarthy et al., 1983). An individual's current performance can be compared with previous performance to measure progress over a given period of time. With adequate norms, it is also possible to compare an individual's performance with that of other individuals or groups, either handicapped or nonhandicapped. Adaptive behavior scales can be used at the local program level to describe groups of individuals in programs according to administrative arrangement (Fogelman 1975). Admission and discharge criteria to particular programs or classes, for example, could be specified according to level of adaptive behavior functioning. Moreover, individuals could be assigned to instructional groups on the basis of their adaptive behavior level in that area.

*Population Description and Research*
Adaptive behavior assessment results can be used by policy makers, program administrators, and researchers to describe more fully the functioning level of target groups. Under Public Law 94-142, each state is required to provide to the appropriate committees of Congress the number of children within each disability who are receiving special education and related services (Public Law 94-142, Section 618.1A). Although local education agencies are required to conduct evaluations that draw upon a variety of sources (U.S. Department of Health, Education and Welfare Rules and Regulations for the Implementation of Part B of the Education of the Handicapped Act, Section 121a.533.1), they are not required to provide information to the federal government on the adaptive behavior level of handicapped children and youth. The lack of such functional distinctions within the diagnostic groupings (e.g., mental retardation) renders the data reported by states essentially useless for targeted policy formulation and evaluation. The Developmental Disabilities Amendments of 1978 (Public Law 95-602) incorporate the concept of adaptive behavior into legislation in a more meaningful manner. The intent of the revisions in Public Law 95-602 was to focus on persons with substantial impairments without regard to categorical disabilities (Lubin, Jacobson, & Kiely, 1982). Among other criteria, eligible clients must have substantial functional limita-

tions in three or more of the following life activity areas: mobility, receptive or expressive language, self-care, self-direction, learning, economic self-sufficiency, or ability to live independently. Developing operational definitions for the functional limitations, however, has been problematic (Lubin et al., 1982). Moreover, there is likely to be considerable variation in the approaches agencies use to interpret "substantial" impairment, particularly since no measurement instruments or specific operational criteria were recommended in the legislation. Unlike Public Law 94-142, the diagnosis of a specific handicapping condition under Public Law 95-602 is not sufficient to determine eligibility for services. The Developmental Disabilities Amendments, however, have had a significant impact upon the inclusion of functional aspects of adaptive behavior in establishing eligibility for services.

Adaptive behavior functioning levels can also be used to select and describe the subjects included in research studies. To determine the extent of the use of adaptive behavior levels for such purposes, Smith and Polloway (1979) examined all research using mentally retarded individuals published in the *American Journal of Mental Deficiency* from 1974 through 1978. Of the 374 research projects, only 36(9.6%) included measures of adaptive behavior in subject selection procedures or subject descriptions. Research practices could be improved if investigators placed increased emphasis on adaptive behavior measures in order to better control subject selection, describe participants of studies, and determine the effects of experimental variables on adaptive behavior.

## Review of Selected
## Adaptive Behavior Scales
Numerous adaptive behavior assessment instruments have been developed. The 12 instruments reviewed in this section were selected either on the basis of their common usage or because they were recently published and have not been reviewed elsewhere. In addition, the instruments have undergone at least minimal standardization procedures, and their technical manuals provide some type of validity or relia-

bility data. This brief review concentrates on intended purpose, administration procedures, technical development and norming, and the content of the scales. For more extensive reviews of adaptive behavior scales, see Doucette and Freedman (1980), Halpern, Lehman, Irvin, and Heiry (1982), and Meyers et al. (1979).

1. *Adaptive Behavior Inventory for Children* (Mercer & Lewis, 1977). This scale is designed to be used in conjunction with the System of Multicultural Pluralistic Assessment (Mercer & Lewis, 1978). The Adaptive Behavior Inventory for Children elicits information about the child's performance within the family and within the other social systems in which he or she lives. Information about children ages 5 to 11 is collected from the parents through a structured interview. The instrument consists of 242 questions divided into six subscales: Family, Community, Peer Relations, Nonacademic School Roles, Earner/Consumer, and Self-Maintenance. The norm sample included 2,085 subjects from California, approximately equally divided among blacks, Hispanics, and whites, and with approximately equal numbers of boys and girls at each age level. The manual does not indicate whether the subjects were handicapped or nonhandicapped individuals. Since this scale was standardized on a restricted population (from California only), some caution must be advised in generalizing the norms of this instrument to other populations. Scaled scores are provided by ethnic group and age level for each of the six subscales and for the total scale.

2. *AAMD Adaptive Behavior Scale* (Nihira et al., 1974). The purpose of this assessment is to describe an individual's degree of personal independence in daily living and his or her ability to meet the social demands of the environment (Fogelman, 1975). The scale assesses adaptive behavior (Part One) and maladaptive behavior (Part Two) of mentally retarded, emotionally disturbed, and developmentally disabled individuals ages 3 to 69 years, and is completed by the caregiver who spends the greatest number of hours with the subject. Part One consists of 66 items across 10 domains

considered important for achieving independent living (Independent Functioning, Physical Development, Economic Activity, Language Development, Numbers and Time, Domestic Activity, Vocational Activity, Self-Direction, Responsibility, and Socialization). Part Two focuses on maladaptive social and personal characteristics and contains 44 items in 14 domains. Raw scores from each domain of the scale are converted into percentile ranks and are used to complete a graphic profile of an individual's functioning level in all areas. The standardization group consisted of approximately 4,000 institutionalized residents in 68 public facilities in the United States with an IQ range from 25 to 84. Since standardization was conducted prior to 1968, it is possible that the norms provided are no longer characteristic of the institutionalized population.

3. *AAMD Adaptive Behavior Scale— School Edition* (Lambert & Windmiller, 1981). Based on the AAMD Adaptive Behavior Scale, the AAMD Adaptive Behavior Scale—School Edition is a revised edition of the AAMD Adaptive Behavior Scale—Public School Version (Lambert, Windmiller, & Cole, 1975). Major changes in the revised edition are an expanded age range for reference-group norms and revised procedures for scoring and administration. The AAMD Adaptive Behavior Scale—School Edition was designed to provide an overview of a child's personal independence and social skills and to identify areas where special programming may be required (Lambert, 1981). It consists of two parts: Part One evaluates a person's adaptive skills in 9 behavioral domains (56 items), and Part Two measures behavior related to personality and behavior disorders in 12 domains (39 items). The 9 adaptive behavior domains are Independent Functioning, Physical Development, Economic Activity, Language Development, Numbers and Time, Prevocational Activity, Self-Direction, Responsibility, and Socialization. The targeted populations for the scale include learning disabled, emotionally disturbed, educable mentally retarded, and trainable mentally retarded students ages 3–17 years. Teachers are the

primary respondent for this assessment; items that a teacher would not be able to observe were not included in this scale (Lambert, 1978). The standardization sample for the original public school version and revised edition consisted of a total of 6,523 students, ages 3–17, in regular classes and in special classes for educable and trainable mentally retarded students in California and Florida. The sample was composed of 2,240 regular class students, 3,246 students in classes for educable mentally retarded students, and 1,037 students in classes for trainable mentally retarded persons. Since these students may not be representative of students in the United States as a whole, the normative data must be viewed with the proper skepticism in other areas of the country. Data were analyzed according to class placement, age, sex, ethnic status, socioeconomic status, and population density (urban, suburban, and rural). Results from this scale can be interpreted in three different ways. The Instructional Planning Profile yields percentile scores for each of the 21 domains. The Diagnostic Profile is based on clusters of adaptive behavior identified through factor analysis and provides scaled scores for each of the five factors. Comparison Scores allow the user to compare scores with three classification groups: regular classroom students, educable mentally retarded students, and trainable mentally retarded students.

4. *Balthazar Scales of Adaptive Behavior for the Profoundly and Severely Mentally Retarded* (Balthazar, 1976). These scales contain two parts: 1) Scales of Functional Independence which measure self-help skills and 2) Scales of Social Adaptation, which measure coping behaviors in eight areas. The major domains in Part I are Eating, Dressing, and Toileting. Areas assessed in Part II include Unadaptive Self-Directed Behaviors, Unadaptive Interpersonal Behaviors, Adaptive Self-Directed Behaviors, Adaptive Interpersonal Behaviors, Verbal Communication, Play Activities, and Response to Instructions. The Balthazar Scales are unique in that they are specifically designed to be used as a program-

ming device for severely and profoundly retarded individuals. Moreover, most of the assessment is conducted through direct observation of the student rather than through reliance on information gathered from another individual. The standardization group for Part I consisted of 451 ambulant residents of an institution in Wisconsin and for Part II consisted of 288 residents from the first group plus 100 additional residents from an institution in Illinois. Ages ranged from 5 to 57 years with a median of 17.27 years, and IQs ranged from 20 to 35 (Halpern et al., 1982).

5. *Inventory for Client and Agency Planning* (Bruininks, Hill, Woodcock, & Weatherman, 1985). Designed as a general tool for managing client and program information, this inventory is intended as a brief measure to be used in community-based residential facilities, institutions, nursing homes, various day programs, and work training programs for all types of handicapped and disabled individuals. The assessment scale includes identifying information, diagnostic and health status, service history, current placements, projected service needs, daytime and social-leisure activities, adaptive behavior skills, problem behaviors, and recommendations. The self-report format may be completed by direct caregivers or by anyone familiar with the client. The adaptive behavior portion of the assessment contains approximately 80 items and is organized into four broad clusters of independence: motor skills, social and communication skills, personal living skills, and community living skills. The adaptive and problem behavior sections of this inventory were normed on a representative national sample of approximately 1,600 nonhandicapped persons from infancy to mature adulthood (the latter, 30–40 years old) and include further technical information on large groups of handicapped subjects. The types of scores provided include normative scores for adaptive and problem behaviors and indexes for other areas of the scale.

6. *Scales of Independent Behavior* (Bruininks, Woodcock, Weatherman, & Hill, 1984). The purpose of the Scales of Independent Behavior is to assess behaviors needed to function

independently in home, social, and community settings. The instrument assesses problem behavior in eight areas and adaptive behavior in 14 subscales (226 items) organized into four clusters. The adaptive behavior subscales include: Gross and Fine Motor (Motor Skills Cluster); Social Interaction, Language Comprehension and Language Expression (Social and Communication Skills Cluster); Eating and Meal Preparation, Toileting, Dressing, Personal Self-Care and Domestic Skills (Personal Living Skills Cluster); Time and Punctuality, Money and Value, Work, and Home-Community Orientation (Community Living Skills Cluster). The Short Form of items from all parts of the scales and the Early Development Scales for the developmental range of birth to 3 years provide two additional options for administration of a short survey test and a measure for assessing severely and profoundly handicapped persons. The scale is administered individually through a structured interview, or is self-administered, with a knowledgeable rater. The rater is also asked to provide goals for training in all areas of the test. This assessment was standardized on over 1,700 subjects selected to represent the U.S. population in terms of geography, community size, ethnic status, socioeconomic status, and sex. Cluster scores form the basis for several types of scores and profiles that are available to facilitate interpretation of a subject's behavioral functioning, some of which include: age scores, percentile ranks, standard scores, a relative performance index, expected adaptive behavior scores based upon intellectual functioning, expected range of independence, and the instructional range. Developmental norms are provided for a representative sample from infancy to adult levels, along with detailed technical data on approximately 1,000 handicapped children and adults (Bruininks, Woodcock, Hill, & Weatherman, 1985). The scale is also statistically linked to the Woodcock-Johnson Psycho-Educational Battery (Woodcock & Johnson, 1977), which permits evaluation of adaptive behavior on the same scale with functioning in areas of cognitive development and academic achievement.

7. *Social and Prevocational Information Battery* (Halpern, Raffeld, Irvin, & Link, 1975). This battery consists of nine tests (227 items) designed to measure skills regarded as important for community adjustment of educable mentally retarded adolescents and adults (Purchasing Habits, Budgeting, Banking, Job Related Behavior, Job Search Skills, Home Management, Health Care, Hygiene and Grooming, and Functional Signs). The educable mentally retarded person's knowledge of specific subject matter is assessed directly through the use of an orally administered group test that contains true-false and some multiple choice items. The standardization sample consisted of 453 junior high and 453 senior high educable mentally retarded students from Oregon, Alaska, and Kentucky. The chronological age range was from 14 to 20 years old; the mean IQ was 68; and the majority of the subjects were white. Raw scores from each of the subtests may be converted to percentage correct and reference group percentile ranks.

8. *Social and Prevocational Information Battery, Form T* (Irvin, Halpern, & Reynolds, 1979). The content and format of this assessment (Halpern et al., 1975) were revised and simplified in the *Form T* version to make it applicable to both mildly and moderately retarded individuals in community settings for assessing skills and competencies regarded as important for community adjustment. A total of 291 items are included in nine areas: Hygiene and Grooming, Functional Signs, Job Related Behavior, Home Management, Health Care, Job Search Skills, Budgeting, Banking, and Purchasing Habits. *Form T* of this battery is designed to be administered individually rather than in a group, and it requires that the subject be able to respond appropriately to a paper and pencil test with chiefly yes-no questions. The primary reference group sample consisted of 186 mentally retarded residents of group homes in six western states. Their mean IQ was approximately 60, and the mean chronological age was 27, with an age range of from 15 to 62 years old. In the secondary sample of 128 moderately retarded individuals from schools in Pennsylvania, the mean IQ was ap-

proximately 50, and the mean chronological age was 17. Raw scores from the subtests and total battery may be converted to percentage correct scores and compared with the scores of students similar in terms of age, IQ or grade.

9. *The TARC Assessment System* (Sailor & Mix, 1975). Designed primarily for program planning and evaluation, The TARC Assessment System provides a brief assessment of adaptive skills of mentally retarded or severely handicapped children. Skills are assessed by 194 items in Self-Help, Communication, Motor, and Social Skills domains. The preferred rater of the adaptive behavior skills is not specified in the assessment manual. The TARC Assessment System was standardized in Kansas with 283 severely handicapped individuals ages 3 to 16, most of whom were institutionalized. Raw scores may be entered on individual or group profile sheets, allowing conversion into standard scores.

10. *Tests for Everyday Living* (Halpern, Irvin, & Landman, 1979). This scale measures achievement of life skills in the areas of career education, consumer economics, and health education. Appropriate for junior high and senior high school age students, it is designed for average or low-functioning, but not mentally retarded, students. The seven tests, containing a total of 245 items, are orally administered to individuals or groups of up to 20 students. Purchasing Habits, Banking, Budgeting, Health Care, Home Management, Job Search Skills, and Job Related Behavior are the areas included in the scale. A multiple-choice format is utilized for most of the test, but simulated performance items (i.e., job application form, W-2 form) are also included. Standardization data were obtained from 850 students (525 junior high and 325 senior high) from both large and small communities in Oregon, California, and Alaska during the 1977–1978 academic year. Multiracial students were represented, as well as regular class and remedial class students. Percentage correct scores may be calculated from raw scores for each subtest and for the total battery. Percentage correct scores may also be used to make comparison with reference groups.

11. *Vineland Adaptive Behavior Scales* (Sparrow, Balla, & Cicchetti, 1984). These scales are a revision of the Vineland Social Maturity Scale (Doll, 1935, 1965) and are designed to assess personal and social sufficiency of individuals from birth to 19 years of age and low-functioning adults. Three different editions of the Vineland Adaptive Behavior Scales are available:

1. The Interview Edition, Survey Form is administered through an interview format to parents or primary caregivers and provides a general assessment of adaptive behavior.
2. The Interview Edition, Expanded Form contains about twice as many items as the Survey Form and is used primarily as a basis for the development of individual program plans.
3. The Classroom Edition, completed by teachers, assesses adaptive behavior typically observed in classroom, including basic academic functioning.

Each edition contains four domains that measure adaptive behavior (Communication, Daily Living Skills, Socialization, and Motor Skills), and the Survey Form and Expanded Form include an optional Maladaptive Behavior domain. Derived scores, in the form of standard scores, percentile ranks, stanines, and age equivalents are available. Representative national samples (3,000 individuals for the Survey Form and Expanded Form, 2,984 individuals for the Classroom Edition), stratified according to age, sex, race or ethnic group, community size, region of the country, and parents' educational level, were used in developing norms. Supplementary norms for mentally retarded, emotionally disturbed, hearing impaired, and visually impaired individuals were also developed.

12. *Weller-Strawser Scales of Adaptive Behavior* (Weller & Strawser, 1981). These scales are designed to identify problems of elementary and secondary learning disabled students in the adaptive behavior areas of Social Coping, Relationships, Pragmatic Language, and Production. The scales are intended to be used only with previously diagnosed learning

disabled students (ages 6 through 18 years) as a basis for program planning. Remedial activities based on diagnosed problem areas are also included. The scales are rated according to typical performance of the subject by someone familiar with the person. Ratings can be based on observation of the subject in naturally occurring or simulated situations, or by questioning the parents or the subjects themselves, if necessary. The standardization sample consisted of 236 students (154 elementary and 82 secondary), all previously diagnosed as learning disabled, from six states in the midcentral, midwestern, southern, and western regions of the country. No further information on subject characteristics or on selection procedures is provided. Raw scores from the scales and total battery are recorded on a profile that divides students according to level of adaptive behavior: those with mild to moderate deficits and those with moderate to severe difficulties. Interpretation and recommendations for each possible type of profile are provided.

## Administration Procedures
## for Adaptive Behavior Scales

Adaptive behavior scales most often measure "typical" or "usual" performance of the subject, rather than "optimal" performance. There are several possible methods of collecting information on the subject's typical performance. Ideally, information could be collected by clinicians or observers through observation over extended periods of time (Sundberg et al., 1978). Although this procedure might provide extensive quantitative data, the constraints in terms of time and cost are usually prohibitive (Mercer, 1979; Meyers et al., 1979; Schaefer, 1981). Constraints include the extensive training required for observers to collect data reliably, the need for repeated observations over long time periods to ensure representative recording of low-frequency behaviors, and the necessity of observing the subject throughout the day to collect information on all aspects of adaptive behavior.

To avoid these difficulties, the "third-party informant" technique is usually used, in which someone familiar with the subject is asked to describe the subject's typical performance on various tasks (Meyers et al., 1979). Parents have most often been used as the informant, but primary caregivers and teachers have also been used. Parents or primary caregivers as informants have the advantage of seeing the subject in his or her natural setting during the largest portion of the day, thereby enabling collection of information about the subject's typical performance outside of school and other service settings. They also have the advantage of economy, since extensive training and observation time are not required (Weissman, 1975). However, parents and primary caregivers may lack objectivity and may be less knowledgeable about what constitutes "normal" adaptive behavior (Schaefer, 1981; Meyers et al., 1979), whereas teachers or trainers are likely to have been better trained and to be more experienced in collecting reliable and valid data (Lambert, 1978; Schaefer, 1981). Teachers and trainers, however, are generally familiar with only a small portion of an individual's day, and school settings are not conducive to observing the subject's entire repertoire of adaptive behavior skills. Furthermore, situations that are improvised to test the skill are not likely to yield accurate information about the subject's typical performance in natural settings. In many instances it may be desirable to collect information from a variety of sources.

Although some assessments suggest that the subject himself or herself can be the informant, little information exists as to the accuracy of such ratings. One study (Sigelman, Schoenrock, Winer, Spanhel, Hromas, Martin, Budd, & Bensberg, 1981) concluded that interview information gained from moderately and severely retarded individuals is questionable, although most responses from mildly retarded persons were considered within acceptable ranges of reliability and validity. In another study, a high level of agreement was found between self-ratings, ratings of counselors, and actual behavioral observation of the adaptive behavior skills of mildly retarded adults (Nathan, Millham, Chilcutt, & Atkinson, 1980). Moderately retarded adults, however, tended to rate their behavior very differently from the ratings obtained through behavioral observation. Caution is advised when using the subject as the informant on his or her adaptive behavior, unless he or she is mildly retarded or less handicapped.

Some instruments (e.g., Social and Prevocational Information Battery, and Tests for Everyday Living) have circumvented the problems inherent in the third-party informant method by directly assessing, through a paper and pencil test, the adaptive behavior skills of the person in question. Such direct assessment is economical and relatively easy to administer. However, this method seriously limits the population for whom the instrument is applicable, as well as the type of skills that can be assessed. The functioning of an individual in his or her everyday environment with the natural cues that are available to elicit the behavior is generally thought to be more relevant in many areas than a person's performance in a testing situation (McCarthy et al., 1983; Simeonsson et al., 1980).

Various methods of administering adaptive behavior devices are available, each with their own advantages and disadvantages. The third-party informant method is the most commonly used technique and appears to have the most practical utility in terms of ease of administration, economy, and acquisition of comprehensive information about the subject's functioning level.

## Technical Considerations in Assessing Adaptive Behavior

This section examines the reliability and validity of data provided in the technical manuals accompanying the 12 adaptive behavior assessment instruments described in this chapter.

*Reliability* The reliability of an adaptive behavior scale provides a measure of the degree to which test results are due to systematic sources of error (Salvia & Ysseldyke, 1981). Three methods of estimating reliability are commonly used with adaptive behavior scales: (1) stability, (2) internal consistency, and (3) interrater reliability. Stability, or test-retest, reliability yields an estimate of the degree to

which an individual's score is stable or can be replicated across a brief period of time. Internal consistency reliability is a report of the degree to which items within the scale are measuring essentially the same skills. Interrater agreement/reliability indicates the extent to which two or more independent observers agree on the ratings of a subject. Interrater agreement is generally reported as a proportion of agreement between or among the raters. Interrater reliability, on the other hand, is usually computed as a correlation between the scores of the raters. It is recommended that reliability coefficients be in the 0.80s and 0.90s to enable the instrument to be useful in contributing to decision making about individual students (Meyers et al., 1979; Nunnally, 1967; Salvia & Ysseldyk, 1981). However, interrater reliability is generally lower than that, and coefficients ranging from 0.60 to 0.90 are said to be useful (Isett & Spreat, 1979; Kelley, 1981; Schaefer, 1981). Reliability coefficients vary as a function of many factors, such as content of the test, method of measurement, age and ability range of subjects, conditions of testing, test length, and type of reliability being reported. Unless such factors are considered, it is inaccurate to compare statistics from different tests. One test, for example, could report test-retest reliabilities of .70 to .80, while another might report lower coefficients (e.g., .65 to .75). If the former test reported results on a wider age range, it is quite likely the latter test could produce generally more consistent results even though, in previous studies, lower correlations were produced. Critical evaluation of many factors is essential in evaluating technical information on tests. Nevertheless, if an assessment instrument does not yield consistent results across time or raters, it is generally less valuable for classification, program planning, or evaluation of individuals.

The types of reliability data presented in each of the adaptive behavior scales reviewed in this chapter are shown in Table 3. The Scales of Independent Behavior, the Inventory for Client and Agency Planning, the Vineland Adaptive Behavior Scales, and the Balthazar Scales of Adaptive Behavior are the only instruments that furnish more than two types of reliability estimates.

Across all 12 of the instruments, interrater reliability and internal consistency reliability are the most commonly reported. Given the importance of the stability of scores over time, it is surprising that so few instruments supply test-retest reliability data. When test-retest reliability studies are conducted, two-week intervals are generally recommended as an appropriate amount of time between assessments (Salvia & Ysseldyke, 1981). The greater the amount of time between the two administrations, the more likely that the scores will vary as a result of developmental changes in the individual. The standard error of measurement is reported in relatively few scales, yet it is important since it gives information about the certainty or confidence with which a test score can be interpreted.

Only one scale, the Balthazar Scales of Adaptive Behavior, computes interrater agreement in terms of proportion of agreement. Proportion of agreement indices have several disadvantages: 1) They are often spuriously inflated when the behaviors occur at either a very high or a very low rate; 2) They fail to take into account the percentage of agreement due to chance; and 3) They are restricted to the use of no more than two observers and to tests with categorical rating systems (Berk, 1979). The Adaptive Behavior Inventory for Children presents interobserver agreement in terms of the standard deviations for 322 observers of 10 parent interviews. For this instrument, reliability studies were conducted as a part of interviewer training for instrument standardization, and the number of observers for each interview ranged from 13 to 50 people. The standard deviation agreement index has many of the same disadvantages as interrater agreement measures (Berk, 1979).

Many of the instruments reviewed have adequate to good reliability estimates for their subscales and good to excellent reliability estimates for their total battery scores. Technical research providing several estimates of reliability with different samples is lacking in many instruments. Again, the age ability charac-

teristics of samples and other factors must be considered in evaluating any statistical evidence, and users of tests should critically review technical manuals and research.

*Validity* Validity indicates the extent to which a test measures what it purports to measure. More specifically, it refers to the appropriateness of the inferences that may be drawn from the test results (Salvia & Ysseldyke, 1981). The types of validity commonly reported in adaptive behavior scales are: 1) content validity, 2) construct validity, and 3) criterion-related validity, which may be either concurrent or predictive. Content validity ascertains whether the items included in the assessment are adequate and representative of the total domain of items that could have been used and whether they reflect the intended purpose of the instrument. One way that content validity may be established is by having experts judge the appropriateness of the items. Construct validity examines the manner in which the theoretical idea has been developed to organize and explain the general dimensions or component parts of adaptive behavior. The dimensions may be delineated prior to test development and refined later through statistical techniques such as simplex analysis (Berk, 1980), or the constructs may be determined after test development through the use of methods such as factor analysis (Hill & Bruininks, 1977). Procedures followed in the development of the instrument (i.e., item analysis) may also be used to infer construct validity.

Criterion-related validity refers to the degree to which an individual's score on a criterion measure can be estimated from his or her score on the adaptive behavior scale. A variety of different criterion measures are possible: 1) performance on another instrument measuring the same construct (also called convergent validity [Futterman & Arndt, 1983]); 2) clinical judgment concerning the individual's adaptive behavior level by psychologists, teachers, vocational trainers, or significant others; or 3) placement in particular educational or vocational settings or in diagnostic categories (sometimes called diagnostic validity or discriminant validity [Berk, 1980]). Criterion-re-

Table 3. Reliability data provided in manuals of selected adaptive behavior scales

| Scale | Interrater agreement | Interrater reliability | Stability reliability | Internal consistency | Standard error of measurement |
|---|---|---|---|---|---|
| Adaptive Behavior Inventory for Children (Mercer & Lewis, 1977) | Mean SD 0.9–2.2[a] | | | Total scale 0.96–0.98; subscales 0.76–0.92 | Subscales 3.83–7.05; total scale 1.95–2.59 |
| AAMD Adaptive Behavior Scale (Nihira et al., 1974) | | Domains Part I 0.71–0.93; Part II 0.37–0.77 | | | |
| AAMD Adaptive Behavior Scale–School Edition (Lambert & Windmiller, 1981) | | | | Domains 0.27–0.97 | |
| Balthazar Scales of Adaptive Behavior (Balthazar, 1976) | Domains 0.70–0.97 | Self-care domains 0.57–0.81 | [b] | | |
| Inventory for Client and Agency Planning (Bruininks, Hill, Woodcock, & Weatherman, 1985) | | Domains 0.72–0.94; composite 0.83–0.94 | Domains 0.62–0.98; composite 0.84–0.96 | Reported by age level 0.90–0.97 for handicapped subjects | Reported by age level, domain, and composite scores |
| Scales of Independent Behavior (Bruininks, Woodcock, Weatherman, & Hill, 1984) | | 0.95 and above for separate subscale (correlations between scorers rating the same interview) | Median of cluster scores 0.84–0.93, composite scores 0.87–0.96 | Median of cluster scores 0.83 to 0.93; composite median 0.96 | Reported by age level, subscale, cluster, and composite scores |

| Instrument | | | | |
|---|---|---|---|---|
| Social & Prevocational Information Battery (Halpern et al., 1975) | | Subtests 0.62–0.79 | Total battery 0.94; subtests 0.78–0.82 | |
| Social & Prevocational Information Battery, Form T (Irvin et al., 1979) | | | Total battery 0.95–0.96; subtests 0.68–0.87 | |
| The TARC Assessment System (Sailor & Mix, 1975) | Total inventory 0.85; domains 0.59–0.78 | Total inventory 0.80 or greater | | |
| Tests for Everyday Living (Halpern et al., 1979) | | | Total battery 0.92; subtests 0.68–0.83 | |
| Vineland Adaptive Behavior Scales (Sparrow et al., 1984.) | Survey form domains 0.62–0.78; composite 0.74 | Survey form domains 0.81–0.86; composite 0.88 | Survey form domains 0.70–0.95; composite median 0.94 | Mean SEM survey form 3.6–6.1; expanded form 2.6–4.5; classroom edition 3.4–6.5 |
| Weller-Strawser Scales of Adaptive Behavior (Weller & Strawser, 1981) | Total scale 0.88–0.89 | | Total battery 0.92; subscales 0.94–0.96 | Subtests 0.27–0.47; total scale 1.1–1.6 |

[a]Interrater agreement is presented in terms of standard deviation of all raters observing a parent interview.

[b]Another series of reliability coefficients is presented in the manual, but the type of reliability is not specified.

lated validity is concurrent if the person's score or classification on the criterion measure is obtained at the same time as the score on the adaptive behavior scale. Criterion-related validity is predictive if the score on the adaptive behavior scale is used to predict an individual's performance or classification on the criterion measure at some time in the future. Table 4 presents technical information on validity for several adaptive behavior scales.

Content validity, although often implied, is seldom discussed as a specific aspect of the technical development of adaptive behavior scales. Notable exceptions are the Scales of Independent Behavior, the Inventory for Client and Agency Planning, the Tests for Everyday Living, the Vineland Adaptive Behavior Scales, and the Weller-Strawser Scales of Adaptive Behavior. Perhaps the limited reporting of content validity is due to the difficulties inherent in defining adaptive behavior. Content validity requires a clear definition of what is included in the total domain of adaptive behavior. This same problem may account for the relatively small number of technical manuals that report on construct validity.

Few of the adaptive behavior scales reviewed here have determined construct validity by delineating dimensions of adaptive behavior prior to test development. The Scales of Inde-

Table 4.   Validity information provided in manuals of selected adaptive behavior scales

| Scale | Content validity | Criterion-related validity | | |
|---|---|---|---|---|
| | | Construct validity | Concurrent validity | Predictive validity |
| Adaptive Behavior Inventory for Children (Mercer & Lewis, 1977) | | | | |
| AAMD Adaptive Behavior Scale (Nihira et al., 1974) | | X | X | |
| AAMD Adaptive Behavior Scale—School Edition (Lambert & Windmiller, 1981) | | | X | |
| Balthazar Scales of Adaptive Behavior (Balthazar, 1976) | | | | |
| Inventory for Client and Agency Planning (Bruininks, Hill, Woodcock, & Weatherman, 1985) | X | X | X | X |
| Scales of Independent Behavior (Bruininks, Woodcock, Weatherman, & Hill, 1984) | X | X | X | X |
| Social and Prevocational Information Battery (Halpern et al., 1975) | | | X | X |
| Social and Prevocational Information Battery, Form T (Irvin et al., 1979) | | | X | |
| The TARC Assessment System (Sailor & Mix, 1975) | | | | |
| Tests for Everyday Living (Halpern et al., 1979) | X | | | |
| Vineland Adaptive Behavior Scales (Sparrow et al., 1984) | X | X | X | X |
| Weller-Strawser Scales of Adaptive Behavior (Weller & Strawser, 1981) | X | X | X | |

Note: X = Validity information present.

pendent Behavior and the Client and Program Management Inventory obtained construct validity by building a model of adaptive behavior components prior to test development, by using cluster analysis and factor analysis procedures, and by consulting previous research on adaptive behavior measures. Motor skills, social interaction and communication, personal living skills, and community living skills were identified as the major clusters of adaptive behavior skills. The AAMD Adaptive Behavior Scale utilized factor analysis to identify the major dimensions of adaptive behavior within the scale. Depending upon the population sampled, the dimensions identified in the AAMD Adaptive Behavior Scale have varied (see for example, Guarnaccia, 1976; Nihira, 1969a, 1969b, 1976). The Vineland Adaptive Behavior Scales measure construct validity primarily through factor analysis procedures. Construct validity for the Weller-Strawser Scales of Adaptive Behavior was computed by calculating intercorrelations among subtests and then correlating the subtests with the total scores. Although these data indicate the relationship among the skills assessed in different subscales, they do not reveal any of the general dimensions or theoretical constructs being assessed.

Concurrent criterion-related validity is the type of validity data most frequently reported in technical manuals, while predictive criterion-related validity is seldom conducted as a part of scale development. The Inventory for Client and Agency Planning, the Scales of Independent Behavior, the Social and Prevocational Information Battery, and the Vineland Adaptive Behavior Scales have assessed predictive validity. Criterion measures for concurrent and predictive criterion-related validity have included diagnostic classification (AAMD Adaptive Behavior Scales, Inventory for Client and Agency Planning, Scales of Independent Behavior, and Vineland Adaptive Behavior Scales), school placement (Inventory for Client and Agency Planning, Scales of Independent Behavior and AAMD Adaptive Behavior Scale—School Edition), levels of restrictiveness in residential and work environ-

ments (Inventory for Client and Agency Planning and Scales of Independent Behavior), scores on a behavior rating measure (Social and Prevocational Information Battery and Social and Prevocational Information Battery, Form T), observations of actual performance (Social and Prevocational Information Battery), teacher ratings (Weller-Strawser Scales of Adaptive Behavior), and ratings by vocational rehabilitation counselors (Social and Prevocational Information Battery). The Inventory for Client and Agency Planning, the Scales of Independent Behavior, and the Vineland Adaptive Behavior Scales are the only instruments that utilize convergent validity, comparing its scores to scores on other standardized adaptive behavior scales. The use of convergent validity assumes that the scale to which the test is being compared is itself valid and reliable (American Psychological Association, 1974). At present, many established adaptive behavior instruments may be inadequate to enable a more thorough investigation of the convergent validity of more recently developed instruments.

Some test developers have expressed concern over the practice of validating adaptive behavior assessment instruments. Mercer (1979), for example, believes that validity is inappropriate since a child's adaptive behavior is highly situation-specific, and validation in one situation may not imply generalized validity. Balthazar (1976) utilizes direct behavioral observation in much of the *Balthazar Scales of Adaptive Behavior*. Since the behavior being observed is representative of the criterion itself, he contends that it is meaningless to conduct validity studies. Despite these observations, evidence of validity is reported in nearly all adaptive behavior scales. Reports of evidence for validity of adaptive behavior measures seem highly desirable and appropriate, particularly if such measures are used in important assessment, curriculum planning, and evaluation decisions. Although some adaptive behaviors may be situation-specific, it is quite likely that adaptive behaviors, as defined by most well-standardized measures, provide useful predictions of adjustment in a variety of settings. It is crucial to know whether an instru-

Table 5. Content areas assessed by selected adaptive behavior scales

| Content area | Adaptive Behavior Inventory for Children (Mercer & Lewis, 1977) | AAMD Adaptive Behavior Scale (Nihira et al., 1974) | AAMD Adaptive Behavior Scale—School Edition (Lambert & Windmiller, 1981) | Balthazar Scales of Adaptive Behavior (Balthazar, 1976) | Inventory for Client and Agency Planning (Bruininks, Hill, Woodcock, & Weatherman, 1985) | Scales of Independent Behavior (Bruininks, Woodcock, Weatherman, & Hill, 1984) | Social and Prevocational Information Battery (Halpern et al., 1975) | Social and Prevocational Information Battery, Form T (Irvin et al., 1979) | The TARC Assessment System (Sailor & Mix, 1975) | Tests for Everyday Living (Halpern et al., 1979) | Vineland Adaptive Behavior Scales (Sparrow et al., 1984) | Weller-Strawser Scales of Adaptive Behavior (Weller & Strawser, 1981) | Number of scales, including content area |
|---|---|---|---|---|---|---|---|---|---|---|---|---|---|
| **Self-help, personal appearance** | | | | | | | | | | | | | |
| Feeding, eating, drinking | x | x | x | x | x | x | | | x | | x | | 8 |
| Dressing | x | x | x | x | x | x | x | | x | | x | x | 10 |
| Toileting | | x | x | x | x | x | | | x | | x | | 7 |
| Grooming, hygiene | x | x | x | | x | x | x | x | x | | x | | 9 |
| **Physical development** | | | | | | | | | | | | | |
| Gross motor skills | | x | x | | x | x | | | x | | x | | 6 |
| Fine motor skills | | x | x | | x | x | | | x | | x | | 6 |
| **Communication** | | | | | | | | | | | | | |
| Receptive language | | x | x | x | x | x | | | x | | x | x | 8 |
| Expressive language | x | x | x | x | x | x | | | x | | x | x | 9 |
| **Personal, social skills** | | | | | | | | | | | | | |
| Play skills | x | | | x | x | x | | | x | | x | x | 7 |
| Interaction skills | x | x | x | | x | x | | | x | | x | x | 8 |
| Group participation | x | x | x | | x | x | | | x | | x | x | 8 |
| Social amenities | | x | x | | x | x | | | x | | x | x | 7 |
| Sexual behavior | | | | | | | | | | | x | | 1 |
| **Self-direction, responsibility** | x | x | x | x | | x | | | | | x | x | 7 |
| Leisure activities | x | x | x | x | | x | | | | | x | x | 7 |
| Expression of emotions | | x | | | | | | | | x | x | x | 4 |
| **Cognitive functioning** | | | | | | | | | | | | | |
| Preacademics (e.g., colors) | x | | | | | x | | | | x | x | | 4 |
| Reading | x | x | x | | | x | x | x | | | x | | 7 |
| Writing | x | x | x | | | x | | | | | x | | 5 |
| Numeric functions | | x | x | | x | x | | | | | x | | 5 |
| Time | | x | x | | x | x | | | x | | x | | 6 |
| Money | x | x | x | | x | x | | | | | x | | 6 |
| Measurement | | | | | x | x | | | | x | x | | 4 |

## Table 5.  (continued)

| | Adaptive Behavior Inventory for Children (Mercer & Lewis, 1977) | AAMD Adaptive Behavior Scale (Nihira et al., 1974) | AAMD Adaptive Behavior Scale—School Edition (Lambert & Windmiller, 1981) | Balthazar Scales of Adaptive Behavior (Balthazar, 1976) | Inventory for Client and Agency Planning (Bruininks, Hill, Woodcock, & Weatherman, 1985) | Scales of Independent Behavior (Bruininks, Woodcock, Weatherman, & Hill, 1984) | Social and Prevocational Information Battery (Halpern et al., 1975) | Social and Prevocational Information Battery, Form T (Irvin et al., 1979) | The TARC Assessment System (Sailor & Mix, 1975) | Tests for Everyday Living (Halpern et al., 1979) | Vineland Adaptive Behavior Scales (Sparrow et al., 1984) | Weller-Strawser Scales of Adaptive Behavior (Weller & Strawser, 1981) | Number of scales, including content area |
|---|---|---|---|---|---|---|---|---|---|---|---|---|---|
| **Health care, personal welfare** | | | | | | | | | | | | | |
|   Treatment of injuries, health problems | x | x | x | | | x | x | x | | x | x | | 8 |
|   Prevention of health problems | | x | x | | | x | x | x | | x | x | | 7 |
|   Personal safety | x | | | | | | x | x | | x | x | | 5 |
|   Child-care practices | | | | | | | x | x | | x | | | 3 |
| **Consumer skills** | | | | | | | | | | | | | |
|   Money handling | x | x | x | | x | x | x | x | | x | x | | 9 |
|   Purchasing | x | x | x | | x | | x | x | | x | x | | 8 |
|   Banking | | x | x | | x | x | x | x | | x | x | | 8 |
|   Budgeting | x | x | x | | x | x | x | x | | x | x | | 9 |
| **Domestic skills** | | | | | | | | | | | | | |
|   Household cleaning | x | x | | | x | x | x | x | | x | x | | 8 |
|   Property maintenance, repair | x | | | | | x | x | x | | x | x | | 6 |
|   Clothing care | x | x | x | | x | x | x | x | | x | x | | 9 |
|   Kitchen skills | x | x | | | x | x | x | x | | x | x | | 8 |
|   Household safety | x | | | | | x | x | x | | x | x | | 6 |
| **Community orientation** | | | | | | | | | | | | | |
|   Travel skills | x | x | x | | x | x | | | | | x | x | 7 |
|   Utilization of community resources | x | x | x | | | x | | | | | | | 4 |
|   Telephone usage | x | x | x | | x | x | | | | | x | | 6 |
|   Community safety | x | | | | | x | | | | | x | | 3 |
| **Vocational skills** | | | | | | | | | | | | | |
|   Work habits and attitudes | x | x | x | | x | x | x | x | | x | x | x | 10 |
|   Job search skills | x | | x | | | x | x | x | | x | | | 6 |
|   Work performance | x | x | x | x | x | x | x | x | | x | x | x | 11 |
|   Social vocational behavior | | | | | | x | x | x | | x | x | | 5 |
|   Work safety | | x | x | | | x | x | x | | x | | | 6 |

Note: Many scales also assess problem behaviors.

ment measures what it claims to measure and whether appropriate inferences can be drawn from the results. It is similary important to continue research on adaptive behavior assessment to improve the definition of adaptive behavior and the use of measures for evaluation and planning purposes. Examination of the content, construct, and criterion-related validity of adaptive behavior scales seems essential for responsible utilization of the assessment results.

Most of the adaptive behavior assessment instruments reviewed here are deficient in some aspect of technical development. As noted earlier, few of the instruments have utilized a nationally representative standardization sample. Moreover, few scales have conducted extensive studies examining most or all of the major types of reliability and validity. Recent trends suggest that more emphasis is being placed on the development of technically sound adaptive behavior scales, as can be seen in the Scales of Independent Behavior and the Vineland Adaptive Behavior Scales. Such a trend is encouraging, since it will allow users to place more confidence in the decisions made on the basis of results obtained from adaptive behavior assessment.

## Content of Adaptive Behavior Scales

In their decisions to include particular items or categories of adaptive behavior in their scales, test developers provide information about what they believe to be the salient qualities of adaptive behavior. Table 5 summarizes the content of several adaptive behavior instruments. Selection of content areas for the table was based on examination of the domains and categories commonly occurring in adaptive behavior scales and on several taxonomies of adaptive behavior (Grossman, 1983; Halpern et al., 1982; Hill & Bruininks, 1977; Lubin et al., 1982; Meyers et al., 1979). Table 5 should be interpreted with caution, since the reliability and validity of the classification scheme have not been fully assessed. Although several of the instruments assess both adaptive and maladaptive behavior, only the adaptive behavior

portions of the scales were included in this summary.

To ensure accurate classification by content area, scales were reviewed item by item instead of according to the labels attached to the domains. This was necessary because scales frequently use different names for domains including similar skills. If an assessment instrument contained even one item relating to a content area in the table, it was recorded. Hence, Table 5 does not indicate the extent of coverage of a particular area, only that it was included in the scale. If an item was labeled on the test in a manner that was clearly incompatible with the list in Table 5, the item was recorded according to the topical area in Table 5. For example, item number 10 in the Hygiene and Grooming domain of the Social and Prevocational Information Battery, Form T reads: "Being very fat can be bad for your health." In Table 5, the item was recorded across from "Prevention of health problems" in the "Health care, personal welfare" area rather than across from "Grooming, hygiene" in the "Self-help, personal appearance" area. Although some items required a variety of skills to complete, each item was classified under only one content area. An item such as "Uses a telephone to inquire about a job listed in the want ads of a newspaper," for example, could appropriately be placed under "Job search skills," "Telephone usage," "Reading," or "Expressive language." Since it was included in the vocational area on the test, it was classified only under "Vocational skills" ("Job search skill") in Table 5.

All of the scales reviewed here assess adaptive behavior skills of particular target populations; yet, the actual content areas included in the instruments representing adaptive behavior vary considerably. None of the scales included all aspects of adaptive behavior as identified in Table 5. Moreover, very few of the scales comprehensively evaluate even most of the areas of adaptive behavior. The more limited scope of many instruments appears to be due to self-imposed constraints on the age range or functioning level of the target population. Such is the case with the Tests for Everyday Living (created for average or low-functioning junior and senior high school students), the Social and Prevocational Information Battery (developed for secondary school-age educable mentally retarded individuals), and the Social and Prevocational Information Battery, Form T (intended for moderately retarded junior and senior high school students). Limited age range or target population, however, does not necessarily dictate a limited scope of domain coverage. Although the Adaptive Behavior Inventory for Children was designed for elementary-aged (ages 5 to 11) students only, it includes most major areas of adaptive behavior. Similarly, even though the AAMD Adaptive Behavior Scale was standardized on institutionalized mentally retarded individuals, it, too, provides fairly extensive coverage of most behavioral domains. And the Weller-Strawser Scales of Adaptive Behavior, intended for both elementary and secondary school-age learning disabled students, emphasizes personal and social skills but largely neglect other areas of adaptive behavior. The TARC Assessment System and the Balthazar Scales of Adaptive Behavior are appropriate only for severely and profoundly handicapped persons and, therefore, assess limited areas of adaptive behavior such as self-help and communication skills.

The scales that provide the most extensive coverage of adaptive behavior content areas are the Scales of Independent Behavior, the Vineland Adaptive Behavior Scales, the AAMD Adaptive Behavior Scale, and AAMD Adaptive Behavior Scale—School Edition, the Inventory for Client and Agency Planning, and the Adaptive Behavior Inventory for Children. Within these scales, however, it is important to remember that the extent of coverage in each content area is not apparent in Table 5. The AAMD Adaptive Behavior Scale—School Edition, for example, includes 1 item in toileting, 4 items dealing with money handling, and 5 items in verbal expressive language skills. The Scales of Independent Behavior, on the other hand, have an entire domain in toileting (14 items), 16 items dealing with money han-

dling, and 11 items in verbal expressive language.

Reviewing the content areas assessed in various scales is helpful in determining the skills that are deemed by test developers to be among the most important in measuring adaptive behavior. The overall content areas included most often were: self-help skills and personal appearance, communication, consumer skills, domestic skills, and vocational skills. Some content areas were given more limited coverage in the adaptive behavior scales: community orientation, cognitive functioning, and health care and personal welfare. Community orientation, in this taxonomy, includes travel skills, utilization of community resources, telephone usage, and community safety. These skills may be receiving more emphasis in recent years owing to the movement toward deinstitutionalization and community integration of handicapped persons. Academic, or school-related, skills in the cognitive functioning area are often assessed through achievement and other types of tests rather than through adaptive behavior scales. This practice, and a desire to assess skills related to everyday functioning, may account for the limited emphasis in cognitive functioning. Academic skills, in many scales, were assessed indirectly through other applied areas. Skills such as "arrives at work on time" and "uses money to make purchases" were classified as vocational and consumer skills, rather than as cognitive functioning skills; yet, such items require cognitive and academic skills for satisfactory performance. Health care and personal welfare skills have been assessed in relatively few scales. When handicapped individuals are living in environments with supervision, health care skills may not be a high priority for training. With greater independence being encouraged for handicapped persons, an increase in emphasis on this skill area may become apparent.

The assessment of child-care practices is incorporated into three scales (Tests for Everyday Living, Social and Prevocational Information Battery, and Social and Prevocational

Information Battery, Form T). Sexual behavior, in the form of dating, is assessed in only one scale (Vineland Adaptive Behavior Scales). Expression of emotions is assessed in 4 of the 12 adaptive behavior scales. Although inappropriate expression of emotions may be assessed in the maladaptive sections of other scales, an individual's ability to state his or her desires, needs, and feelings is a very different skill. The development of nurturing and caring relationships and the expression of emotions are two areas that require thorough examination to determine their importance and relevance for the development of adaptive behavior. Relatively few adaptive behavior scales (5) assessed social skills on the job (social vocational behavior). Lack of appropriate social skills in the work setting is one of the major reasons why handicapped individuals lose their jobs (Greenspan & Shoultz, 1981); hence, social vocational behavior appears to be a skill that warrants more emphasis in adaptive behavior scales.

There is apparent consensus among test developers concerning the components of adaptive behavior. The general dimensions addressed most frequently were self-help skills and personal appearance, communication, consumer skills, domestic skills, and vocational skills. Although these results must be regarded circumspectly, due to the limited number of instruments and the constraints of the classification scheme, Table 5 provides some useful information about the content areas assessed in selected adaptive behavior scales. In addition to yielding information about the salient features of adaptive behavior, the content of adaptive behavior scales is important because it frequently serves as the basis for determining both eligibility for services and training needs of handicapped individuals.

## TRAINING ADAPTIVE BEHAVIORS

In the previous section, adaptive behavior instruments were reviewed as one method for gaining insight into the significant components of adaptive behavior. A further indication of

what skills are incorporated as a part of adaptive behavior may be obtained by evaluating the research on the training of adaptive behavior skills. The reader is also directed to Martin, Rusch, and Heal (1982) for a related analysis of studies on community survival skills.

The primary method for reviewing the literature was a computer search; however, the "ancestry" approach (Cooper, 1982) and a manual search were also used. The ancestry approach involves utilizing the studies known to exist (located through the computer or through a manual search) and then tracking citations from one study to another. A manual search of 12 of the more common journals concerned with handicapped individuals was conducted for the year 1982.

Studies were selected for inclusion in this review on the basis of the following criteria:

1. A particular adaptive behavior skill or group of skills was trained.
2. Articles were required to contain some empirical data; however, it was not necessary for training attempts to be successful.
3. Studies were limited to those on mentally retarded subjects. Adaptive behavior skills have more often been trained with retarded persons than with any other group of individuals (handicapped or nonhandicapped); hence, it was believed that the literature on mentally retarded subjects would be most representative of the state of the art in adaptive behavior training.
4. Journal articles were the primary sources included in the review. Books and documents available only on microfiche were not included.
5. The research methodology of the studies was not critically evaluated. Due to inadequate experimental control in many of the studies, it was not always clear that the training procedures were responsible for changes in adaptive behavior skill level. However, the primary purpose was to review what had been researched rather than the soundness of the methodology.
6. With the exception of two areas, the classification scheme used in Table 5 to re-

view content of adaptive behavior scales served as the guide for examining content areas in the training studies. Physical development (gross and fine motor skills) and communication (expressive and receptive language) were not incorporated in this review, since a) given space limitations, it would not have been feasible to comprehensively cover these areas and b) a substantial amount of the training research in these areas involves individuals with developmental delays but whose level of cognitive functioning was undetermined or unreported.

A total of 203 articles were located in the major adaptive behavior content areas of self-help and personal appearance, personal and social skills, cognitive functioning, health care, consumer skills, domestic skills, community orientation, and vocational skills. The following topics are examined in this brief review:

1. The trends over time in the training of adaptive behavior skills
2. The particular types of adaptive behavior skills receiving emphasis in the training literature
3. The characteristics of the subjects involved in the investigations
4. The settings of the research investigations
5. The training techniques used
6. The methods used for determining goal selection and performance criteria
7. The experimental designs used in the studies

**Findings**

Since the earliest studies of adaptive behavior training were conducted in 1964, there has been a steady increase in the number of published training studies. From 1961–1965, only 4 studies were published; 15 studies were published from 1966–1970; 43 studies were published from 1971–1975; 98 studies were published from 1976–1980; and 43 studies were published in the two-year period from 1981–1982. This proliferation of research on the training of adaptive behavior skills reflects the increasing interest in the area of adaptive behavior and a growing commitment to the training of mentally retarded persons to live as independently as possible in the community.

Despite the wide range of adaptive behavior skills selected as training goals in the research studies, nearly all types of adaptive behavior skills were successfully taught to mentally retarded individuals. The adaptive behavior skills trained most frequently were self-help skills and social skills. Specific skills addressed in 10 or more studies include toileting, social interaction, eating, grooming/hygiene, work performance, dressing, money, leisure, and travel skills. Conversely, several adaptive behavior skills received very limited attention in the training literature. Adaptive behavior skills trained in three or fewer studies include banking, budgeting, preacademic skills, linear measurement, time concepts, property maintenance and repair, household safety, community safety, social vocational skills, sexuality, self-direction and management, child care practices, work habits and attitudes, and treatment of injuries and health problems. Yet, many of these skills merit greater consideration since they have been found to be positively related to successful community adjustment (Schalock & Harper, 1978; Schalock, Harper, & Carver, 1981).

Nearly all training studies had a very narrow focus, training fragmented or discrete adaptive behavior skills in isolation. Rarely were specific skills viewed in reference to other related behaviors in the individual's repertoire. Moreover, comprehensive adaptive behavior assessment was rarely indicated to be the basis for the identification and selection of the particular adaptive behavior skills to be trained.

Earlier studies were more likely to emphasize self-help skills that would facilitate the care and maintenance of retarded persons in a custodial setting. Self-help skills, the major type of skill minimizing custodial care, were more often the focus of training studies conducted prior to 1975 than they have been since that time. More recent studies placed greater emphasis on adaptive behavior skills that would prepare mentally retarded individuals to function in the community (e.g., traveling in the community, eating in fast food restaurants). Consumer skills, domestic skills, community orientation, and vocational preparation were rarely, if ever, trained in studies prior to 1977. More emphasis was also placed on training for independent functioning in the recent studies. For example, studies conducted prior to the early 1970s most often had scheduled toileting rather than independent toileting as the goal. Since that time, even the studies employing severely and profoundly mentally retarded subjects trained independent toileting.

Moderately and severely retarded individuals were the subject of the majority of investigations dealing with the training of adaptive behavior skills. Although profoundly handicapped individuals were rarely taught adaptive behavior skills other than self-help skills, it is possible that additional training emphasis for profoundly handicapped persons was placed on motor and communication skills not included in this reveiw. Surprisingly little research focused on training adaptive behavior skills to mildly handicapped individuals, despite the fact that such persons may be prime candidates for independent living in the community. For example, moderately and severely retarded individuals were the subjects in vocational and domestic skill training studies more frequently than were mildly retarded individuals. Perhaps it is assumed that persons with mild handicaps will acquire adaptive behavior skills incidentally or in clusters of discrete behaviors with minimal direct training.

Adaptive behavior skill training was provided to mentally retarded individuals of all ages. Social interaction skills, for example, were trained with individuals ranging from 3 years of age to 69 years of age, and dressing skill training was provided to individuals ranging from 4 years of age to 67 years of age. Although adaptive behavior skill training rarely occurred prior to age 4, there does not appear to be an upper age limit at which training is no longer considered feasible or desirable.

The large majority of training studies were conducted in institutions. As would be expected, the percentage of studies conducted in institutions in each 5-year period since 1961 has declined, but not as dramatically as might be expected. All of the studies conducted from 1961 to 1965 were in institutional settings; approximately half of those conducted from 1971 to 1975 were in institutions; and in 1981 and 1982, over one-fourth of the studies took place in institutions. Despite the social policy of deinstitutionalization, a large number of training studies continue to take place in institutions. Nevertheless, the influence of the social policy on community integration is evidenced in other ways in the training literature. All of the 10 studies conducted in group homes and apartment programs occurred after 1975, as did all of the 22 studies that included some type of *in vivo* training in the community.

A major weakness in the adaptive behavior training literature is the scarcity of studies in which skills were trained cooperatively by both residential and day program staff. In only 13 out of 203 studies did joint programming occur between school and home or between day program and residential program staff. All 13 of these studies trained toileting, weight reduction or self-care skills, skills that readily lend themselves to cooperative programming.

Social skills appear to be very difficult adaptive behavior skills to train. Although the large majority of training attempts for social interaction and assertiveness skills were successful, most training was conducted under simulated conditions in classroom, institution, or workshop settings. When generalization involved a relatively minor change, such as from one setting in an institution to another, generalization was usually effective (e.g., Matson, 1980; Matson & Adkins, 1980; Matson & Andrasik, 1982; Stokes, Baer, & Jackson, 1974). However, when generalization to natural conditions in community settings was assessed, transfer of newly acquired skills did not occur (e.g., Bates, 1980; Fleming & Fleming, 1982).

Approximately one-fourth of the 203 studies assessed the generalization or transfer of newly acquired adaptive behavior skills to novel settings, tasks, materials, or trainers. Considering the increased concern about generalization in recent years (Guess & Noonan, 1982), this represents a relatively small proportion of the studies. The large majority (82%) of the studies examining generalization were conducted after 1976. Because most training and research is conducted under highly structured conditions, it is generally thought that newly acquired skills will not transfer to new situations without the implementation of training programs that systematically introduce planned variations in settings, stimuli, or contingencies (Close, Irvin, Taylor, & Agosta, 1981; Wehman & Hill, 1982). Contrary to this expectation, most (71%) of the studies assessing generalization found that newly acquired adaptive behavior skills did transfer to novel situations without the provision of any additional training. While effective transfer was verified by subjective reports only in some studies, nearly two-thirds of the investigations provided data to support the fact that generalization of training had occurred.

Less than half (44%) of the studies included in this review assessed maintenance of newly acquired adaptive behavior skills over time, after termination of treatment, and a large percentage (81%) of those studies found that skills were maintained. The length of follow-up period varied considerably, however, from as few as 3 days up to 4 years. Twenty percent of the studies assessing maintenance did so within the first month after training ceased; this may not be an adequate duration to ascertain whether skills will continue at the same level of independence over extended periods of time. Most studies examined maintenance from 1 to 6 months after training, and relatively few waited longer than 6 months.

In most studies, the training techniques were not clearly specified, thus making replication difficult or impossible. In studies in which the training techniques were delineated, the most commonly used procedures were task analysis, graduated guidance, and operant conditioning techniques. These techniques, used in combination or individually, were usually effective

in facilitating acquisition of adaptive behavior skills. When more than one technique was used, it was impossible to determine which independent variable or combination of independent variables resulted in the significant improvements in adaptive behavior skills. Moreover, few studies compared one training method with another to examine their relative effectiveness in training particular adaptive behavior skills.

Social validation techniques were utilized in 13 training studies, all of which were conducted after 1975. Social validity refers to judgments made about the social significance of the goals, procedures, and effects of the skill training (Kazdin & Matson, 1981; Wolf, 1978). The social validation of skills to be trained helps to assure that they will be of value to the individual and to society, that they will elicit reinforcement from others in the environment, that they will be socially acceptable, and that they will not result in harm to others (Spence, 1981). Most frequently, social validation in adaptive behavior training studies focused on validating acceptable or "normal" performance. In only two studies was the task analysis for the training sequence socially validated.

Although it was prohibitive to conduct a comprehensive analysis of research design weaknesses with such a vast body of literature, the types of research designs employed in the studies were reviewed. To reduce possible threats to internal validity, appropriate single subject or group designs must be employed. Among the experimental designs identified as being valid (Campbell & Stanley, 1963; Hersen & Barlow, 1976), the multiple baseline and pretest-posttest control group design were the most commonly used in the adaptive behavior training research. The multiple baseline design was used in 31% of the studies, and the pretest-posttest control group design was used in 29% of the studies. Although a single subject reversal design may adequately demonstrate a functional relationship between the independent and dependent variables in most cases, it cannot be assumed in training studies that the adaptive behavior skill level will return to baseline levels during the reversal period (Martin et al., 1982). Hence, such a design may be of limited utility in the adaptive behavior training research. Better-designed experiments appear more common in studies conducted after the mid-1970s.

## Recommendations

The research demonstrates that systematic training has been highly successful in teaching a variety of adaptive behavior skills to mentally retarded individuals; however, much work remains to be done in this area. Following are recommendations for future research and practice in the training of adaptive behavior skills:

1.  More research is needed in the training of some adaptive behavior skills, particularly in areas such as consumer and domestic skills, health, and safety. These and other skills have received limited attention in the training research, despite their importance for successful community adjustment.

2.  Since adaptive behavior skill gains are generally greater for residents of community-based facilities than for residents of institutions, the setting for training studies is important to note. Skills are thought to be acquired more readily when they are practiced in the criterion environment, that is, in the natural environment where the behavior is expected to occur (Liberty, this volume). A more realistic picture of progress toward community integration will be obtained if training research is conducted in settings where the skills are ultimately to be performed.

3.  Adaptive behavior assessment and training should be linked to assure that the selection of skills to be taught is based on assessed needs. Without comprehensive adaptive behavior assessment, skills that do not require training may be selected for instruction; unrelated skills may be selected and trained in isolation; or skills for training may be selected inappropriately when the individual does not possess the prerequisite behaviors, resulting in the acquisition of splinter skills. Use of sound assessment devices and social evaluation procedures would improve the extent to which training programs focus on skills needed for community adjustment.

4.  The training of fragmented splinter skills necessarily delimits the functional utility of those skills in daily living and thus should be avoided. The interdependence of adaptive behavior skills within and across behavioral domains must be recognized and emphasized in instructional programs (Guess & Noonan, 1982).

5.  It is commonly assumed that consistency in programming efforts and increased training time will result in more rapid acquisition of skills (Turnbull, 1978). Proper distribution of practice is also an important aspect in acquisition and generalization of skills. Consistent programming, increased training time, and distributed practice will be achieved more readily if programs are implemented cooperatively by all people involved with the handicapped individual, in both home and school, or in both residential and day programs. More research is needed to determine the feasibility of cooperative programming and to assess its effects on skill acquisition.

6.  Researchers and practitioners need to examine various methods of assessing and assuring generalization of skills to new situations and environments. It is possible that extensive generalization training programs are not necessary in all situations; nevertheless, it is essential to assess transfer to assure its occurrence. *In vivo* probes conducted throughout training have been used effectively to assess transfer to natural environments (e.g., Tofte-Tipps, Mendonca, & Peach, 1982; Van den Pol, Iwata, Ivanic, Page, Neef, & Whitley, 1981). On the other hand, generalization may occur more readily if initial training of critical skills takes place in a variety of contexts under differing stimulus conditions (Guess &

Noonan, 1982). The importance of training for generalization is discussed extensively by Liberty (this volume).

7.  Maintenance of skills over extended time periods must be assessed more frequently in the training research. Moreover, methods to facilitate maintenance must be identified and validated.

8.  Training for independence must be stressed whenever possible, and methods designed to encourage independent functioning must be developed and refined. Unless acquired skills are performed spontaneously in response to naturally occurring stimuli in the environment, independent functioning will not be fully achieved.

9.  Training of the more complex adaptive behavior skills is likely to require the development of innovative training techniques or the adaptation of methods used with other populations. This is particularly true with the training of social interaction skills, since they are very complex and have limited utility when trained in isolation (Bernstein, 1981). Operant conditioning techniques, in and of themselves, may not be sufficient to analyze and train social interaction skills. Modeling and role play with performance feedback offer some promise for successful training of interpersonal skills (e.g., Bates, 1980; Bornstein, Bach, McFall, Friman, & Lyons, 1980). However, further refinement and adaptation of these and other techniques may be necessary to effectively train highly complex adaptive behaviors.

10. Training methods should be more clearly delineated in published research to allow replication and to enable practitioners to use the results of research in their training efforts. Training research is of little value if the findings cannot be applied to the improvement of intervention strategies with handicapped individuals.

11. Additional research is needed that compares various training techniques in an effort to determine the most efficacious procedures for training particular adaptive behavior skills.

12. There is a need for more emphasis on social validation of the adaptive behavior skills chosen for training and of acceptable or ''normal'' performance levels for those skills. Social validation of adaptive behavior skills is usually accomplished through use of one of two methods: 1) social comparison methods that involve collecting data on the performance of normal individuals in the natural environments; or 2) subjective evaluation methods that consist of soliciting the opinions of ''experts'' regarding the appropriateness of the performance (Kazdin & Matson, 1981). Selection of behaviors to be trained and of the acceptable level of performance must be made on the basis of the behaviors' ability to enhance the individual's independent functioning under normalized living conditions.

13. Continued emphasis should be placed on employing experimental designs that allow valid inferences to be drawn about the relationship between the training methods used and the subsequent acquisition, generalization, and maintenance of adaptive behavior skills. Sound methods are also needed to enhance the generalization of research results.

## CONCLUSIONS

This chapter has reviewed the concept of adaptive behavior in terms of its theoretical structure, its inclusion in assessment instruments, and the research on training. Although the state of the art in defining, assessing, and training adaptive behavior skills is far from complete, considerable progress has been made over the past several years.

The construct of adaptive behavior is more clearly defined now than it was when it was first introduced as part of the definition of mental retardation. Still, one of the most crucial needs is the development of a comprehensive model of adaptive behavior—a theoretical foundation to guide future research and development. Improvements in conceptual models are needed that incorporate all aspects of individual adaptation into a meaningful theoretical structure and that focus upon the total growth, development, and functioning of the individual throughout the life cycle. The nature of environmental influences upon the development and expression of adaptive skills is an area that needs significantly more conceptual development and research.

The development and use of theoretically and technically sound assessment instruments has important implications for adaptive behavior training efforts and for the community integration of handicapped individuals. While more than 200 measures of adaptive behavior have been identified (Doucette & Freedman, 1980), only a small number present any normative reference group or technical research. Many scales assess dimensions of adaptive behavior that are implied by definitions of adaptive behavior, but coverage of adaptive behavior skills in available tests is often uneven and quite limited. For scales with a normative reference group and at least some technical characteristics, the scope of the content was often very restricted, and the content areas often contained only a few items.

A number of persistent deficiencies can be found in existing adaptive behavior scales. Achievement on adaptive behavior scales is influenced by environmental circumstance and opportunity. Given the numerous circumstances in which adaptive behaviors are expressed, the manner in which items are worded and scaled is an extremely important consideration. Most scales include vague descriptions of behavior, ambiguous scoring systems, and scoring instructions that vary either from item to item or across different domains of behavior. These technical deficiencies make it difficult to evaluate adaptive behavior skills and to achieve reliable assessments of behavioral functioning.

Of the scales that have been standardized, few have used acceptable standards for establishing normative scores. Most of the norm ref-

erence groups in existing tests are based upon local, state, or regional samples that cannot be considered representative of the U.S. population. Many others use reference groups in special education and other human service programs, assuming that such groups are representative of others in similar programs in other parts of the country. It is widely recognized that standards and practices for determining eligibility for services and placement vary markedly across different service programs and states. Residential placement rates, for example, differ substantially by state and type of setting within states (Bruininks, Hauber, Hill, Lakin, McGuire, Rotegard, Scheerenberger, & White, 1983). Similar differences can be found in school practices (U.S. Department of Education, 1982). Such wide variations in practice make local normative scores of special populations less valuable for many evaluation and planning purposes, since such scores are less liable to represent accurately the developmental characteristics of individuals in other settings. Furthermore, it is highly unlikely that the scores represent persons in the same settings with comparable developmental characteristics who, for reasons of local practice, are not formally included in specially designated groups. Such practices are likely to create serious errors in decisions (e.g., eligibility) and in developmental descriptions of individuals.

The effects of inadequate sampling strategies cannot be eliminated through the use of norm references for groups of handicapped persons. Normative scores on samples of handicapped persons possess a number of conceptual and technical problems. The meaning of development is ambiguous when calibration uses ill-defined, nonrepresentative samples, particularly when the samples are initially selected on the basis of extreme scores. Norms based upon institutional or public school samples, for example, would have changed substantially in the last 10 years, given the major population and service changes accompanying policies of mainstreaming and deinstitutionalization. When normative references are derived, it seems more appropriate to base them upon clearly defined, representative groups. Bruininks, Woodcock, Weatherman, and Hill (1984) and Bruininks, Woodcock, Hill and Weatherman (1985) have addressed this issue in deriving norms and expected adaptive scores based upon levels of intelligence for the Scales of Independent Behavior.

Despite some notable limitations in current assessment devices, substantial development has occurred in the measurement and explication of adaptive behavior. Although it is known that adaptive behavior skills, in general, are important factors in successful community adjustment, scales incorporating representative skills from essential content areas would facilitate the identification of the particular adaptive behavior skills considered most essential for successful adjustment and integration in the community. Knowledge of the individual's needs and of the factors critical to successful adjustment in the community would, in turn, enable the efficient selection and training of meaningful skills required in community and school settings.

Growing interest in assessment of adaptive behavior is paralleled by efforts to enhance skills through structured training. The literature on training in this area has increased phenomenally in recent years, particularly with respect to studies designed to improve skills needed for community adjustment. The literature reflects a growing emphasis upon training skills needed for adjustment in actual living, learning, and work settings. This trend is obviously needed to improve the state-of-the-art in training programs designed to enhance community integration. Increased attention to assessing generalization and maintenance, as well as to acquisition, of skills is increasingly reflected in more recent research studies. Attention to these important issues, however, is still urgently needed in training studies on adaptive behavior. Equally important is the need to focus upon the integration of skills in training efforts in order to avoid focusing on isolating highly specific aspects of performance that are only marginally related to community adjustment. (See chapter by Liberty, in this volume, for an extensive discussion of issues concerning acquisition, learning, and generalization.) Systematic training has repeatedly been shown to be successful in facilitating the acquisition, generalization, and maintenance of adaptive behavior skills. Yet, the acquired skills are merely splinter skills that lack practical utility if they are not selected and trained in relation to the total functioning and needs of the individual in his or her natural environment.

Increasing the adaptive skills of handicapped persons is an essential aspect of promoting opportunities for integration in community living, work, and learning environments. Equally important to successful integration of handicapped citizens is the modification of environments and attitudes to facilitate their social integration. Development of an improved technology of teaching and training is still needed to match advances in the philosophical, social, and organizational strategies on which services for handicapped citizens rely. Through further research and better practices, improvements can occur in the adaptive functioning of handicapped persons, as well as in the expansion of environments to accommodate and respect human diversity.

## REFERENCES

American Psychological Association. *Standards for educational and psychological tests*. Washington, D.C.: American Psychological Association, 1974.

Balthazar, E.E. *Balthazar Scales of Adaptive Behavior for the Profoundly and Severely Mentally Retarded*. Palo Alto, CA: Consulting Psychologists Press, 1976.

Bates, P. The effectiveness of interpersonal skills training on the social skills acquisition of moderately and mildly retarded adults. *Journal of Applied Behavior Analysis*, 1980, *13*(2), 237–248.

Berk, R.A. Generalization of behavioral observations: A clarification of interobserver agreement and interobserver reliability. *American Journal of Mental Deficiency*, 1979, *83*(5), 460–472.

Berk, R.A. Psychometric properties of adaptive behavior scales: Guidelines for producers and consumers. *Mental Retardation*, 1980, *18*, 47–49.

Berkson, G., & Landesman-Dwyer, S. Behavioral research in severe and profound mental retardation (1955–1974). *American Journal of Mental Deficiency*, 1977, *81*(5), 428–454.

Bernstein, G.S. Research issues in training interpersonal

skills for the mentally retarded. *Education and Training of the Mentally Retarded,* 1981, *16*(1), 70–74.

Bornstein, P.H., Bach, P.J., McFall, M.E., Friman, P.C., & Lyons, P.D. Application of a social skills training program in the modification of interpersonal deficits among retarded adults: A clinical replication. *Journal of Applied Behavior Analysis,* 1980, *13*(1), 171–176.

Bruininks, R.H., Hauber, F.A., Hill, B.K., Lakin, K.C., McGuire, S.P., Rotegard, L.L., Scheerenberger, R.C., & White, C.C. *1982 national census of residential facilities: Summary report, Brief #21.* Minneapolis: Center for Residential and Community Services, University of Minnesota at Minneapolis, Fall 1983.

Bruininks, R.H., Hill, B.K., Woodcock, R.W., & Weatherman, R.F. *Inventory for Client and Agency Planning.* Allen, TX: Development Learning Materials/Teaching Resources, 1985.

Bruininks, R.H., & Lakin, K.C. (eds.). *Living and learning in the least restrictive environment.* Baltimore: Paul H. Brookes Publishing Co., 1985.

Bruininks, R.H., Woodcock, R.W., Hill, B.K. & Weatherman, R.F. *Development and standardization of the Scales of Independent Behavior.* Allen, TX: Developmental Learning Materials/Teaching Resources, 1985.

Bruininks, R.H., Woodcock, R.W., Weatherman, R.F., & Hill, B.K. *Scales of Independent Behavior.* Allen, TX: Developmental Learning Materials/Teaching Resources, 1984.

Campbell, D.T., & Stanley, J.C. *Experimental and quasi-experimental designs for research.* Chicago: Rand McNally College Publishing Co., 1963.

Cantrell, J.K. Assessing adaptive behavior: Current practices. *Education and Training of the Mentally Retarded,* 1982, *17*(2), 147–149.

Clausen, J. The continuing problem of defining mental deficiency. *Journal of Special Education,* 1972, *6*(1), 97–106.

Close, D.W., Irvin, L.K., Taylor, V.E., & Agosta, J. Community living skills instruction for mildly retarded persons. *Exceptional Education Quarterly,* 1981, *2*(1), 75–85.

Cooper, H.M. Scientific guidelines for conducting integrative research reviews. *Review of Educational Research,* 1982, *52*(2), 291–302.

Coulter, W.A., & Morrow, H.W. A collection of adaptive behavior measures. In: W.A. Coulter & H.W. Morrow (eds.), *Adaptive behavior: Concepts and measurements.* New York: Grune & Stratton, 1978a.

Coulter, W.A., & Morrow, H.W. A contemporary conception of adaptive behavior within the scope of psychological assessment. In: W.A. Coulter & H.W. Morrow (eds), *Adaptive behavior: Concepts and measurements.* New York: Grune and Stratton, 1978b.

Doll, E.A. *Vineland Social Maturity Scale.* Circle Pines, MN: American Guidance Service, 1935, 1965.

Doucette, J., & Freedman, R. *Progress tests for the developmentally disabled: An evaluation.* Cambridge, MA: Abt Books, 1980.

Dubose, R.F., Langley, M.B., & Stagg, V. Assessing severely handicapped children. *Focus on Exceptional Children,* 1977, *9*(7), 1–13.

Fleming, E.R., & Fleming, D.C. Social skill training for educable mentally retarded children. *Education and Training of the Mentally Retarded,* 1982, *17*(1), 44–50.

Fogelman, C.J. (ed.). *AAMD Adaptive Behavior Scale:*

*Manual.* Washington, DC: American Association on Mental Deficiency, 1975.

Futterman, A.D., & Arndt, S. The construct and predictive validity of adaptive behavior. *American Journal of Mental Deficiency,* 1983, *87*(5), 546–550.

Greenspan, S. Social intelligence in the retarded. In: N.R. Ellis (ed.), *Handbook of mental deficiency: Psychological theory and research.* Hillsdale, NJ: Lawrence Erlbaum Associates, 1979.

Greenspan, S., & Shoultz, B. Why mentally retarded adults lose their jobs: Social competence as a factor in work adjustment. *Applied Research in Mental Retardation,* 1981, *2*(1), 23–38.

Grossman, H.J. (ed.). *Classification in mental retardation.* Washington, D.C.: American Association on Mental Deficiency, 1983.

Guarnaccia, V.J. Factor structure and correlates of adaptive behavior in noninstitutionalized retarded adults. *American Journal of Mental Deficiency,* 1976, *80*, 543–547.

Guess, D., & Noonan, M.J. Curricula and instructional procedures for severely handicapped students. *Focus on Exceptional Children,* 1982, *14*(5), 1–12.

Halpern, A.S., Irvin, L.K., & Landman, J.T. *Tests for Everyday Living.* Monterey, CA: Publishers Test Service, 1979.

Halpern, A.S., Lehman, J.P., Irvin, L.K., & Heiry, T.J. *Contemporary assessment for mentally retarded adolescents and adults.* Baltimore: University Park Press, 1982.

Halpern, A., Raffeld, P., Irvin, L.K., & Link, R. *Social and Prevocational Information Battery.* Monterey, CA: Publishers Test Service, 1975.

Heber, R. A manual on terminology and classification in mental retardation (2nd ed.). *American Journal of Mental Deficiency* (monograph supplement), 1961.

Hersen, M., & Barlow, D.H. *Single case experimental designs: Strategies for studying behavior change.* New York: Pergamon Press, 1976.

Hill, B., & Bruininks, R.H. *Assessment of behavioral characteristics of people who are mentally retarded.* Project Report Number 1. Minneapolis: Developmental Disabilities Project on Residential Services and Community Adjustment, University of Minnesota at Minneapolis, October 1977.

Huberty, T.J., Koller, J.R., & TenBrink, T.D. Adaptive behavior in the definition of mental retardation. *Exceptional Children,* 1980, *46*(4), 256–261.

Irvin, L.K., Halpern, A.S., Reynolds, W.M. *Social and Prevocational Information Battery, Form T.* Monterey, CA: Publishers Test Service, 1979.

Isett, R., & Spreat, S. Test-retest and interrater reliabilities of the AAMD Adaptive Behavior Scale. *American Journal of Mental Deficiency,* 1979, *84*(1), 93–95.

Junkala, J. Teacher assessments and team decisions. *Exceptional Children,* 1977, *44*, 31–32.

Kazdin, A.E., & Matson, J.L. Social validation in mental retardation. *Applied Research in Mental Retardation,* 1981, *2*(1), 39–53.

Kelley, C. Reliability of the behavior problem checklist with institutionalized male delinquents. *Journal of Abnormal Child Psychology,* 1981, *9*, 243–250.

Lambert, N.M. The Adaptive Behavior Scale—Public School Version: An overview. In: W.A. Coulter &

H.W. Morrow (eds.), *Adaptive behavior: Concepts and measurements*. New York: Grune & Stratton, 1978.

Lambert, N.M. *AAMD Adaptive Behavior Scale—School Edition: Diagnostic and technical manual*. Monterey, CA: Publishers Test Service, 1981.

Lambert, N.M., & Windmiller, M. *AAMD Adaptive Behavior Scale—School Edition*. Monterey, CA: Publishers Test Service, 1981.

Lambert, N.M., Windmiller, M., & Cole, L. *AAMD Adaptive Behavior Scale—Public School Version*. Monterey, CA: Publishers Test Service, 1975.

Lubin, R., Jacobson, J.W., and Kiely, M. Projected impact of the functional definition of developmental disabilities: The categorically disabled population and service eligibility. *American Journal of Mental Deficiency*, 1982, 87(1), 73–79.

McCarthy, J.M., Lund, K.A., & Bos, C.S. Assessment of young children with special needs. *Focus on Exceptional Children*, 1983, 15(5), 1–11.

Martin, J.E., Rusch, F..R., & Heal, L.W. Teaching community survival skills to mentally retarded adults: A review and analysis. *Journal of Special Education*, 1982, 16(3), 243–267.

Matson, J.L. Acquisition of social skills by mentally retarded adult training assistants. *Journal of Mental Deficiency Research*, 1980, 24(2), 129–135.

Matson, J.L., & Adkins, J. A self-instructional social skills training program for mentally retarded persons. *Mental Retardation*, 1980, 18, 245–248.

Matson, J.L., & Andrasik, F. Training leisure-time social-interaction skills to mentally retarded adults. *American Journal of Mental Deficiency*, 1982, 86(5), 533–542.

Mercer, J.R. Theoretical constructs of adaptive behavior: Movement from a medical to a social-ecological perspective. In: W.A. Coulter & H.W. Morrow (eds.), *Adaptive behavior: Concepts and measurements*. New York: Grune & Stratton, 1978.

Mercer, J.R. *System of multicultural pluralistic assessment: Technical manual*. New York: Psychological Corporation, 1979.

Mercer, J.R., & Lewis, J.F. *Adaptive Behavior Inventory for Children*. New York: Psychological Corporation, 1977.

Mercer, J.R., & Lewis, J.F. *System of multicultural pluralistic assessment*. New York: Psychological Corporation, 1978.

Meyers, C.E., Nihira, K., & Zetlin, A. The measurement of adaptive behavior. In: N.R. Ellis (ed.), *Handbook of mental deficiency, psychological theory and research*. Hillsdale, NJ: Lawrence Erlbaum Associates, 1979.

Nathan, M., Millham, J., Chilcutt, J., & Atkinson, B. Mentally retarded individuals as informants for the AAMD adaptive behavior scale. *Mental Retardation*, 1980, 18(2), 82–84.

Nihira, K. Factorial dimensions of adaptive behavior in adult retardates. *American Journal of Mental Deficiency*, 1969a, 73(6), 868–878.

Nihira, K. Factorial dimensions of adaptive behavior in mentally retarded children and adolescents. *American Journal of Mental Deficiency*, 1969b, 74(1), 130–141.

Nihira, K. Dimensions of adaptive behavior in institutionalized mentally retarded children and adults: Developmental perspective. *American Journal of Mental Deficiency*, 1976, 81, 215–226.

Nihira, K. Factorial descriptions of the AAMD Adaptive

Behavior Scale. In: W.A. Coulter & H.W. Morrow (eds.), *Adaptive behavior: Concepts and measurements*. New York: Grune & Stratton, 1978.

Nihira, K., Foster, R., Shellhaas, M., & Leland, H. *AAMD Adaptive Behavior Scale*. Washington, DC: American Association on Mental Deficiency, 1974.

Nunnally, J. *Psychometric theory*. New York: McGraw-Hill Book Co., 1967.

Prillaman, D. An analysis of placement factors in classes for the educable mentally retarded. *Exceptional Children*, 1975, 42, 107–108.

Public Law 94-142, Education for all Handicapped Children Act of 1975, November 29, 1975.

Public Law 95-602, Developmental Disabilities Amendments of 1978.

Roszkowski, M., & Spreat, S. A comparison of the psychometric and clinical methods of determining level of mental retardation. *Applied Research in Mental Retardation*, 1981, 2(4), 359–366.

Sailor, W., & Mix, B.J. *The TARC Assessment System*. Lawrence, KS: H & H Enterprises, 1975.

Salvia, J., & Ysseldyke, J. *Assessment in special and remedial education*. Boston: Houghton Mifflin Co., 1981.

Schaefer, E.A. Development of adaptive behavior: Conceptual models and family correlates. In: M.J. Begab, H.C. Haywood, & H.L. Garber (eds.), *Psychosocial influences in retarded performance, Vol. 1: Issues and theories in development*. Baltimore: University Park Press, 1981.

Schalock, R.L., & Harper, R.S. Placement from community-based MR programs: How well do clients do? *American Journal of Mental Deficiency*, 1978, 83(3), 240–247.

Schalock R.L., Harper, R.S., & Carver, G. Independent living placement: Five years later. *American Journal of Mental Deficiency*, 1981, 86(2), 170–177.

Sigelman, C.K., Schoenrock, C.J., Winer, J.L., Spanhel, C.L., Hromas, S.G., Martin, P.W., Budd, E.C., & Bensberg, G.J. Issues in interviewing mentally retarded persons: An empirical study. In: R.H. Bruininks, C.E. Meyers, B.B. Sigford, & K.C. Lakin (eds.), *Deinstitutionalization and community adjustment of mentally retarded people*. Washington, DC: American Association on Mental Deficiency, 1981.

Simeonsson, R.J., Huntington, G.S., & Parse, S.A. Assessment of children with severe handicaps: Multiple problems—Multivariate goals. *Journal of the Association for the Severely Handicapped*, 1980, 5(1), 55–72.

Smith, J.D., & Polloway, E.A. The dimension of adaptive behavior in mental retardation research: An analysis of recent practices. *American Journal of Mental Deficiency*, 1979, 84(2), 203–205.

Sparrow, S.S., Balla, D.A., & Cicchetti, D.V. *Vineland Adaptive Behavior Scales*. Circle Pines, MN: American Guidance Service, 1984.

Spence, S.H. Validation of social skills of adolescent males in an interview conversation with a previously unknown adult. *Journal of Applied Behavior Analysis*, 1981, 14(2), 159–168.

Spreat, S., Roszkowski, M., & Isett, R. Assessment of adaptive behavior of the mentally retarded. In: J. Matson, & S. Breuning (eds.), *Advances in mental retardation and developmental disabilities*, Vol. 1, in press.

Stokes, T.F., Baer, D.M. & Jackson, R.L. Programming the generalization of a greeting response in four retarded children. *Journal of Applied Behavior Analysis, 1974, 7,* 599–610.

Sundberg, N.D., Snowden, L.R., & Reynolds, W.M. Toward assessment of personal competence and incompetence in life situations. *Annual Review of Psychology, 1978, 29,* 179–221.

Tofte-Tipps, S., Mendonca, P., & Peach, R.V. Training and generalization of social skills: A study with two developmentally handicapped, socially isolated children. *Behavior Modification,* 1982, *6*(1), 45–71.

Turnbull, A.P. Parent-professional interactions. In: M.E. Snell (ed.), *Systematic instruction of the moderately and severely handicapped.* Columbus, OH: Charles E. Merrill Publishing Co., 1978.

U.S. Department of Education. *To assure the free appropriate public education of all handicapped children: Fourth annual report to Congress on the implementation of Public Law 94-142: The Education for All Handicapped Children Act.* Washington, DC: U.S. Department of Education, Division of Education Services, Special Education Programs, 1982.

U.S. Department of Health, Education and Welfare. *Federal Register.* Rules and Regulations for the Implementation of Part B of the Education of the Handicapped Act. Washington, DC: U.S. Department of Health, Education, and Welfare, Office of Education, August 23, 1977.

Van den Pol, R.A., Iwata, B.A., Ivanic, M.T., Page, T.J., Neef, N.A., & Whitley, F.P. Teaching the handicapped to eat in public places: Acquisition, generalization and maintenance of restaurant skills. *Journal of Applied Behavior Analysis,* 1981, *14*(1), 61–69.

Wehman, P., & Hill, J.W. Preparing severely handicapped youth for less restrictive environments. *Journal of the Association for the Severely Handicapped,* 1982, *7*(1), 33–39.

Weissman, M.M. The assessment of social adjustment: A review of techniques. *Archives of General Psychiatry, 1975, 32,* 357–365.

Weller, C., & Strawser, S. *Weller-Strawser Scales of Adaptive Behavior.* Novato, CA: Academic Therapy Publications, 1981.

Wolf, M.M. Social validity: The case for subjective measurement of how applied behavior analysis is finding its heart. *Journal of Applied Behavior Analysis,* 1978, *11*(2), 203–214.

Woodcock, R.W., & Johnson, M.B. *Woodcock-Johnson Psycho-Educational Battery.* Hingham, MA: Teaching Resources Corporation, 1977.

# Chapter 4

# Assessing and Managing Problem Behaviors

## Lanny E. Morreau

The concept of normalization has for a decade permeated the literature related to the provision of services to disabled individuals. Applied as a total concept, this principle has considerable potential to affect the development of mentally retarded persons. As defined by Nirje (1969), "normalization means making patterns and conditions of everyday life which are as close as possible to the norms and patterns of the mainstream of society available to the developmentally disabled" (p. 182). Wolfensberger (1972) reformulated the concept, describing normalization as "utilization of means which are as culturally normative as possible, in order to establish and/or maintain personal behavior and characteristics which are as culturally normative as possible" (p. 28).

One key concept implicit in Wolfensberger's definition is often not discussed in relation to the creation of normalized life-styles for developmentally disabled persons: the development of more "normal" environments may be futile if the individuals in them do not acquire the skill/knowledge repertoires needed to interact appropriately with that environment and the people in it. Therefore, if mentally retarded individuals are to achieve the greatest possible level of independence, professionals must identify the specific behavioral needs evidenced by members of the disabled population,

they must isolate variables that interfere with meeting those needs, and they must design strategies by which to respond effectively to client needs. From the perspective of deinstitutionalization, it is imperative that attention be directed specifically toward the needs of developmentally disabled persons who currently reside in public residential facilities and who are potential candidates for placement in less-restrictive residential facilities.

As observed by Lakin (1979), available data support quantitatively the effectiveness of the deinstitutionalization effort. Thousands of developmentally disabled persons who once resided in institutions have been relocated in small community-based facilities, and a concerted effort has been made to avoid initial institutional placements. Unfortunately, data related to placement are frequently cited as the sole evidence of effectiveness in creating more normalized life alternatives for these individuals. However, such transition to community residences does not necessarily assure either society or the individual that the professional and social commitment has been fulfilled. Unless the developmental programs and life options provided in the community consistently surpass those previously provided in institutional environments, deinstitutionalization will have succeeded as a physical process without meeting its primary goal (i.e., increased independence along with the associated skills by which the mentally retarded individual can use the resources of the community advantageously and interact effectively with community members). Program planners and providers must look beyond the bricks-and-mortar definitions of institutions; they must also consider the day-to-day developmental experiences and establish those behaviors that promote living under culturally normative conditions.

## PROBLEMS AFFECTING COMMUNITY INTEGRATION

The determination of client needs and of the sources of interference with those needs can be determined, in part, through an analysis of the reasons for admission and readmission to public facilities. Changes in these data will partially reflect the extent to which persons are not only being placed in community residential facilities but are also adapting to the community. Further, as observed by Smith and Smith (1981), consideration of the events that have been antecedents to institutionalization can serve as the basis for setting goals to expedite client transition from institutions to successful placement in the community.

Behavior problems and the absence of social-personal skills have been identified as major impediments to successful community living and adjustment (Hill, Bruininks, & Lakin, 1983; Sternlicht & Deutsch, 1972; Windle, 1962). In his survey of public facilities, Scheerenberger (1976) found that new admissions equaled nearly 5.5% of the total population residing in these facilities and that the number of readmissions equaled 2% of the total population. While these data reflected a decline in the rates of admissions and readmissions to public facilities, the reasons for clients being admitted at all warrant further analysis. The major causes of unsuccessful placement and of subsequent readmission were cited as the lack of community services (52%) and community rejection of the retarded person (13%). The absence of behavior management

programs accounted for 26% of the cited deficits in community services.

## Initial Placement in Public Residential Facilities

One primary cause of institutionalization is the presence of maladaptive behavior (Eyman & Borthwick, 1980; Eyman, Borthwick, & Miller, 1981; McCarver & Craig, 1974). In their analysis of variables affecting the probability of placement of mentally retarded children in public residential facilities, Eyman, O'Connor, Tarjan, and Justice (1972) found that individuals displaying problem behaviors were more likely to be admitted. Similarly, Hill et al. (1983) found that the prevalence of nearly every type of maladaptive behavior was much higher among both new admissions and readmissions to public residential facilities than among the stable population of either public or community residential facilities. While other factors, including measured intelligence, age, and physical disabilities, affect community placement, the presence of problem behaviors is a major factor in decisions related to the life situation of developmentally disabled persons. In fact, next to the overall severity of mental impairment, problem behavior appears to be the most significant factor influencing initial placements in institutions (Maney, Pace, & Morrison, 1964; Saenger, 1960; Spencer, 1976). This finding becomes increasingly significant when one considers that among institutionalized individuals, maladaptive behavior occurs more frequently among moderately retarded individuals than among severely retarded persons (Pagel & Whitling, 1978). But for evidenced problem behaviors, many retarded individuals would likely not be placed in institutional settings, and many retarded persons who reside in institutions could be successfully placed in less-restrictive community facilities. This conclusion is attested to by a recent investigation conducted at the Minnesota Learning Center, Brainerd, Minnesota, which revealed that, while the center served individuals who functioned on a higher (cognitive) level than clients in most institutions, "virtually every resident is there because of severe personal or socially maladaptive behavior" (Reagan, Murphy, Hill, & Thomas, 1980, p. 140).

Data related to factors influencing initial placement in residential facilities indicate that the impact of behavior problems on community integration of retarded persons is extensive and that, at present, these problems represent a continuing source of interference with community adjustment.

## Readmission to Public Residential Facilities

Consistent with the data related to initial placement is that readmissions are affected by numerous client characteristics. However, behavior problems are also consistently cited as a major factor influencing the readmission of developmentally disabled persons into state institutions (Lakin, Hill, Hauber, Bruininks, Heal, 1983; Landesman-Dwyer & Sulzbacher, 1981). As observed by Pagel and Whitling (1978), maladaptive behavior is the primary cause of failure in community placements across all levels of disability; 45% of the individuals in their study were readmitted to institutions because of maladaptive behavior. Similarly, Keys, Boroskin, and Ross (1973) reported that of 126 readmissions, 35% directly resulted from the presence of behavior problems. These findings were supported by Sutter, Mayeda, Call, Yanagi, and Yee (1980), who reported that mentally retarded clients who were unsuccessfully placed in community programs displayed a variety of maladaptive behaviors significantly more frequently than their successfully placed peers. Of equal importance, the authors reported that it was these kinds of behavior that resulted in requests that clients be removed from the community-based facility.

## Extended Effects of Behavior Problems

The relatively high density of behavior problems among individuals in both public and private residential programs for developmentally disabled persons has been clearly documented (Eyman, et al., 1981; Eyman & Call, 1977; Hill et al., 1983); however, the effects of those problems on planning for individuals has not been clearly established (e.g., Can plans be developed for appropriate, community residential programs for clients who are presently being returned to public facilities because of problem behavior?). Unless public policies change drastically or effective procedures are developed to reduce behavior problems, public residential facilities will likely be the primary residence of and, despite their well-documented shortcomings, the living environment for developmentally disabled individuals exhibiting behavior problems (Landesman-Dwyer & Sulzbacher, 1981). This observation is strongly supported in Minnesota's *Policy Analysis Series: Issues Related to Welsch v. Noot* (Developmental Disabilities Program, 1981, 1982), which has reported that about four out of five admission reports on residents coming from community to public residential facilities specifically mention behavior problems, and that nearly 92% of readmissions to public facilities are behavior related.

The significance of behavior problems and their impact on planning efforts are evidenced by a cooperative study of statewide housing needs conducted by the Illinois Bureau of the Budget and the Illinois Association for Retarded Citizens (McDonald, 1982). One hundred and ten agencies providing services to developmentally disabled persons were asked to specify which of six residential models (described in terms of training provided rather than physical type) would be best suited to their clients' needs. While the data were limited by the number of surveys returned, it was significant that for 4,800 clients, the service providers indicated that nearly 12% would require an intensive behavioral program. If providers are unable to select meaningful target behaviors and to implement effective behavior-change programs that result in generalization of appropriate responding in alternative community settings, such well-intended programs could become permanent living arrangements rather than short-term treatment programs.

In addition to the difficulties in community placement and planning that are created by behavior problems, the negative effects of failure in the community on disabled clients have not been determined. Perceived failure in the community and the return to an institutional environment could result in an increased behavioral disability. Behavior problems are likely to elicit negative reactions from residential staff and community members. Such negative consequences might be presumed to reduce undesirable behavior. However, the total interactions with other people may also decline, and the developmentally disabled individual may establish expectations of failure in future personal/community interactions. Social failure, as evidenced by readmission to a public facility, might well have a permanent negative effect on individual clients and reduce future options to reside in less-restrictive environments. Research should be conducted to determine if such effects occur; the practice of readmission, in itself, may serve to worsen the already maladaptive behaviors of developmentally disabled persons.

## Response to Behavior Problems

Behavior problems are obviously one of the greatest deterrents to the successful community integration of developmentally disabled persons. It is also apparent that existing strategies for reducing such problems are not having a universally positive effect. The questions that must be answered relate to how the interference of behavior problems on community integration of developmentally disabled persons can be resolved and how these behavior problems can be most effectively reduced.

*Environmental Selection* It has been suggested that placement strategies be reconsidered. As indicated by Eyman and Call (1977) and Hill and Bruininks (1981), clients having severe maladaptive behavior problems can be placed in community residential facilities. The potential for community success appears to be far greater if facility staff are more closely matched to client characteristics. That is, clients are more likely to adapt well if facili-

ty staff are more willing and able to deal with specific client needs and problems (Lei, Nihira, Sheehy, & Meyers, 1981; Mayeda & Sutter, 1981; Sutter et al., 1980). However, as observed by Eyman et al. (1981), facility staffs may not have the means to significantly reduce the behavior problems of the residents. The matching of staff characteristics to client needs without consideration of staff skills to alter behavior problems may only enable clients to live in community settings; it does not address the problem of increasing the client's physical and social integration into the community at large. As observed by Schalock and Harper (1978), "without movement or placement, the [community] facilities become reflective of the very institutions we are trying to deinstitutionalize" (p. 240).

Problem behaviors affect the developmentally disabled person's integration into community activities and his or her opportunities to participate in relevant life functions. A survey conducted by Hill and Bruininks (1981) indicated the impact of behavior problems on community integration. When the staffs of facilities for developmentally disabled persons were asked if behavior problems prevented the resident from increasing his or her community experiences, respondents from community residential facilities reported that 47% of their residents would have increased opportunities if their behaviors were better controlled, and respondents from public residential facilities indicated that 53% of all residents were limited in community participation by their problem behaviors (Hill & Bruininks, 1984).

Although all community experiences are likely to be affected by behavior problems, the effects are clearly exemplified in the major life area of employment: the work choices and opportunities of developmentally disabled persons placed in community facilities may be restricted by behavior problems. That behavior problems manifest themselves in the work situation is evidenced by an assessment of training needs of personnel providing prevocational and vocational services to adult developmentally disabled persons (Williams, Friedl, &

Vogelsberg, 1980), which indicated that 66% of the 102 respondents needed improved skills in decreasing inappropriate behaviors. Specific skill in this area was also ranked by the employees as the fourth most important factor related to their current jobs.

Poor interpersonal skills were also reported by Niziol and DeBlassie (1972) as the major source of problems related to developmentally disabled persons' finding and retaining work, and Schalock and Harper (1978) found that inappropriate behavior was one of the major reasons for clients returning to employment training from a job. Foss and Peterson (1981), in their survey of job placement personnel, reported that a great number of respondents indicated that "refraining from exhibiting bizarre or irritating behavior" and "controlling aggressive behavior" were most relevant to job tenure. In general, then, two dimensions of environmental selection are apparent: 1) matching clients with the expectations for them within the environment, and 2) matching clients by their needs with the persons who are qualified to meet those needs. This second dimension raises the issue of staff training.

*Staff Training* Sutter et al. (1980) have suggested that consideration be given to the selection and training of caregivers. They and many others have noted that a need exists for competent primary caregivers, "who carry a major responsibility for the direct care, programming, and supervision of developmentally disabled individuals" (Scheerenberger, 1981, p. 172). As observed by Zaharia and Baumeister (1978), it is this direct-care work force that "is the most critical institutional resource in the pursuit of habilitation for the mentally retarded clients" (p. 131). Similarly, Bergman (1975) contended that "the effectiveness of the housemanagers in a community home is viewed as one of the most important aspects of running a successful community home" (p. 61).

Inadequately trained personnel may, in part, account for the persistence of behavior problems among developmentally disabled persons. As noted by Thormalen (1965), direct-

care paraprofessionals who were not adequately prepared for their job not only failed to enhance the development of the disabled children with whom they worked but actually inhibited individual development by increasing client dependency. In contrast, well-prepared paraprofessionals were able to provide extensive developmental services to disabled individuals (Gartner, 1971; Gartner & Reissman, 1974).

Considering the effects of behavior problems on the community integration of developmentally disabled persons, one would anticipate that personnel would be extensively prepared in the area of behavior management. Schinke and Wong (1977) found that not only did staff instructed in behavioral techniques realize more positive gains from clients, but their job satisfaction and personal interactions with disabled individuals increased as well. Yet, Baldwin (1972) found that additional training was needed in the area of programming for maladaptive behavior, and the need for such training in operant conditioning strategies was also frequently indicated on the survey reported by Dellinger and Shope (1978).

It would appear that caregivers are receiving increased instruction in this area. For example, four of the six instructional programs developed for foster family caregivers reviewed by Intagliata and Willer (1981) contained content in the area of behavior management. Unfortunately, as observed by Intagliata and Willer, wide-scale implementation of such training programs with caregivers has lagged, and there is no systematic review of such training programs.

The need for staff effectiveness to reduce behavior problems is clear, but the efficacy of any particular approach to providing needed skills has been documented only on a situational basis. Furthermore, the effects of behavioral training are usually reported only in terms of improved staff skills. Additional data on the effects of specific skills/training on the environment and the behavior of the clients served by the trainees are needed, particularly in the areas of effective procedures for assessment of problem behavior and strategies for changing behavior.

## ASSESSMENT OF PROBLEM BEHAVIOR

Taylor (1976) indicated the need to find more accurate methods of predicting the adaptation of developmentally disabled individuals to the community. The lack of consistent, precise terminology to describe client behavior and antecedent events (Smith & Smith, 1981) makes such prediction extremely difficult. This problem also hampers the integration of existing studies related to the effects of behavior on community adjustment. Consider, for example, the terminology used in discussing social-interpersonal skill deficits from three articles described by Foss and Peterson (1981): "personality problems and antisocial behavior," "poor social self-esteem," and "social acceptability." These terms may encompass common or totally disparate sets of behaviors. The problem was also raised by Sutter et al. (1980): "Many investigators have produced contradictory results regarding the relationship of client demographic variables to placement failure, while those researchers citing behavior problems as reasons for failure often have not clearly specified the types of behavior involved" (p. 262).

Accurate predictions will, in part, be determined by the precision of available assessment instruments. Yet, much of the discussion surrounding the assessment of problem behavior mirrors observations made by Windle (1962) over 20 years ago. He suggested the need for a more objective definition of personality characteristics and indicated that, "the lack of generally acceptable global measures of personality comparable to the IQ has limited the amount of research into the importance of this factor in mental subnormality" (p. 100). While over 100 adaptive behavior scales have been produced (Meyers, Nihira, & Zetlin, 1979), no one has yet developed a measure of social-personal adaptation that adequately defines degrees of client success or failure or that accurately predicts client success. Therefore, much

of the current literature on client success or failure remains nonspecific. As observed by Hill and Bruininks (1977), no studies of client success in the community indicated that existing measures of adaptive behavior were more effective at predicting community adjustment than were traditional measures of intelligence. If behavior problems are a major source of community rejection, as clearly documented in the literature, adaptive scales should predict success or failure on at least this dimension. However, as suggested by Hill and Bruininks (1977), it is possible that "various adaptive behavior measures do not indeed measure adaptive behavior" (p. 45). In fact, the exact behavior problems that most interfere with community integration have not been identified. In the absence of such knowledge, selecting target behaviors to be changed and designing staff training programs to ensure competency in measuring effects of programs on behaviors most interfering with community adjustment are going to be difficult, if not impossible.

It is noteworthy that while instrumentation for comprehensive, precise assessment of problem behaviors has not been developed for assessing client behavioral needs in the community at large, an assessment instrument specifying exact behavior problems has been developed for vocational settings (La Greca, Stone, & Bell, 1982). Specific interpersonal situations and behaviors that interfered with adjustment to vocational situations were used to establish priorities for development of interpersonal skills. This is the type of assessment needed for meaningful habilitation planning. Yet, most recent studies of clients in community and residential facilities continue to deal with vague specifications of the problem behaviors (e.g., "untrustworthiness," "hyperactive tendencies," "inappropriate personal manners," "rebellious behavior," "psychological disturbances," "acting-out behavior," "self-stimulation," "threatening," "disruptive"). It is instructive to consider how closely these terms match those reported by Windle (1962) more than 20 years ago to describe behavior problems indicative of failure in the community: "acting out," "run away," "quarrelsome," "not obedient/truthful."

While these descriptive terms have provided data to document the general effects of behavior problems on community placement, they have not provided the information needed to arrange behavior-change programs to reduce specific behaviors that most interfere with community adjustment. Taylor (1976), for example, determined that untrustworthy behavior and hyperactive tendencies resulted in the return of individuals to institutions and observed that inappropriate interpersonal manners, psychological disturbances, and rebellious behaviors were tolerated. Similarly, Sutter and her associates (Sutter et al., 1980) found that untrustworthiness (in addition to running away and physical violence) was more prevalent among unsuccessful clients than among their successfully placed peers, but that rebelliousness was also more prevalent. This apparent discrepancy may result from differences in staff tolerance of specific behaviors or from the particular sample of behaviors included under the category of rebelliousness. But again from a client perspective, these data provide no indication of the *exact* behaviors that are reacted to negatively by community staff or of the precise behaviors that need to be altered if unsuccessful clients are to become successful in community settings.

Conversely, studies dealing with discrete behavior-change programs often provide little information on the relationship between the target behaviors and successful community integration. Although exact problem behaviors are specified, the behavior selected for change may be based more on meeting staff or client needs in an institutional setting than on client needs for success in the community. If the goal is client independence in the least restrictive setting, behavior-change programs must be directed toward those specific behaviors that most interfere with community adjustment. Yet, no organizational strategy has been provided to both cluster individual behaviors for purposes of assessment and determine their importance to caregivers or to the community. If the motive for administration of assessment in-

struments were only to describe, in a general way, developmentally disabled individuals, the purpose would be met. However, if the intent of assessment is to prescribe programs to remediate behavior problems of developmentally disabled persons, systematically organized, more precise instrumentation will be requisite.

Concern for the social-emotional problems of developmentally disabled persons is increasing (Meyers et al., 1979). The fact that developmentally disabled individuals are susceptible to the same types of emotional disorders as nondisabled persons (Szymanski & Tanguay, 1980) intensifies the need for precise behavioral assessment. When one considers the four dimensions of emotional disturbance identified by Quay (1979) (i.e., conduct disorder, anxiety withdrawal, immaturity, and socialized aggression), it is clear that manifestations of these behavioral patterns are present among developmentally disabled clients. Unfortunately, appropriate services for the emotional problems of a developmentally disabled person may be "overshadowed" by the focus on mental retardation (Reiss, Levitan, & Szysko, 1982; Reiss & Szysko, 1983). Assessment of problem behaviors in specific terms of frequency, intensity, and setting without primary emphasis on an individual's developmental disability would often prove beneficial.

When considering problem behavior, negative assessment (i.e., observing a developmentally disabled individual in terms of deficits rather than assets) could be detrimental. Emphasis on negative attributes is certainly unnecessary. However, an index of exact behavior problems would be needed to determine the efficacy of behavior-change programs and to determine if a given client would likely be successful in a particular community placement. While concurrent assessment of adaptive social skills would be needed to determine the probability of clients deriving positive social consequences in the community, it is behavior problems primarily that have resulted in both community placement failure and initial placement in public facilities. A comparatively high level of social skills will not necessarily compensate for the presence of problem behaviors (Sutter et al., 1980). The direct measurement of specific behavior problems should not preclude a general focus on those positive client attributes that would be of great significance to client participation in the social community once the client has been accepted into it.

Since the principal objective of most programs is to enhance the life development of clients, developmental/behavioral data provide the bases for planning, modifying, and evaluating the efficacy of the process. Precision assessment will be required to enable planners to estimate the number of community placements needed, to identify the characteristics of needed placements in terms of services required by clients, to promote programs that effectively facilitate client development, and to measure, through the analysis of client progress, the effects of individual programs and the systems as a whole. In addition, only through consistent, precise assessment of the status of clients on selected variables can information on the effects of innovative programs be shared and integrated with data on other programs.

## Focusing Assessment

Problem behaviors must be viewed within the total context of social adjustment and competence. Social adjustment, as broadly defined by Weissman (1975), is the interplay between the individual and the social environment. As defined by Foster and Ritchey (1979), social competence represents "those responses which, within a given situation, prove effective or, in other words, maximize the probability of producing, maintaining or enhancing positive effects for the interactor" (p. 626). A behavior would be considered a problem, therefore, if its presence reduced the probability that an individual would derive positive consequences from it or if it increased the probability that the individual would receive negative consequences from social interactions.

Evaluation scales include problem behaviors that are perceived to be socially negative and, as a consequence, would likely interfere with an individual's adaptation to society and accep-

tance into the community. However, except for defining areas of problem behavior, the scales do not allow for systematic decision making (i.e., they do not include procedures to establish the severity of the problem or to assist in setting goals for changing behavior). A major purpose of assessment should be to establish priorities for training from among numerous behavioral problems. Because the perceived severity of a given behavior is likely to be based on varying standards or assumed norms of behavior, client evaluation must allow for a rater to somehow judge each behavior problem from the perspective of "need for change." Voeltz, Evans, Derer, and Hanashiro (1982) defined three levels of behavior problems which, although not directly incorporated into a formal assessment process, could be considered in assessment and decision making: (1) urgent behaviors requiring immediate attention, (2) serious behaviors requiring immediate attention, and (3) excess behaviors reflecting "normal" deviance. For purposes of assessment and program planning, specific behaviors to be incorporated under each of the three criteria would not need to be delineated in advance. Staff discussion and consequent selection of target behaviors could be based upon collective consideration of each rating and the probable effect of a given behavior on the life adjustment of the individual. Agreement among training staff on a given priority would preclude individual bias becoming the sole criterion for a developmental program.

Behavior problems can be described as falling into two general categories: social-maladaptive and personal-maladaptive (Meyers et al., 1979). These two categories could be further developed to indicate the predictable social/environmental consequences of problem behaviors. Thus, priorities can be established based on probable social consequences or problem behaviors rather than on group or general opinions.

From a behavioral perspective, an individual's actions become a problem when they adversely affect the individual, the physical environment, or others. Further, the type and probable level of environmental effect could provide a gradient for establishing priorities for behavior change (Morreau, 1980). Behaviors that result in damage to the individual, to others, or to the environment would more likely result in negative sanctions than behaviors that disrupt the staff or other clients' activities. At the same time, disruptive behaviors would more likely have negative consequences than behaviors that are only perceived negatively. Based on this premise, a triad for evaluating problem behaviors can be established as follows:

*Maladaptive behaviors* are behaviors that are socially unpleasant to other individuals, that interfere with the individual's coping with environmental demands, or that are repetitious or unusual. Behavior falling within this domain is divided into three subclasses: socially unacceptable, unusual/repetitious, and uncooperative/noncompliant. These behavior problems, although often serious, in themselves may not necessarily prove to be major problems in the person's environment. Clients failing to follow directions, swearing, licking their hand, pacing, flapping their arms, or refusing to engage in a task, for example, would probably not demand as much attention as clients who engage in behaviors that are *destructive* or that *disrupt* the environment.

*Disruptive behaviors* are behaviors that demand inappropriate attention of others, that distract staff from providing developmental programs, or that negatively affect the environment. Clients crying, screaming, stomping their feet, or running in a residence, for example, would ultimately draw negative attention, but such behavior would have less drastic consequences than behaviors that might be classified as destructive. Although disruptive behavior could also be considered maladaptive, it is generally more intrusive. Once the primary implication of the behavior is designated to be in the more serious category, it is not considered in a less severe domain.

*Destructive behaviors* are behaviors that pose a threat to the individual, to those around him or her, or to property. Behavior in this domain is subdivided into three subclasses: self-injurious, other-injurious, and environ-

mentally destructive. Many of these behaviors call for an immediate response to prevent injury (e.g., hitting others, throwing objects, biting others, banging one's head against hard objects). Although a destructive behavior might also be considered maladaptive and disruptive, once the primary implication of a behavior is designated as destructive, it is not considered a problem behavior in the other domains (i.e., maladaptive or disruptive).

In condensed form a behavior classification schema that considers environmental-social impact would appear as follows:

I. Maladaptive behavior
 A. Socially unacceptable behavior
 B. Unusual/repetitious behavior
 C. Uncooperative/noncompliant behavior
II. Disruptive behavior
III. Destructive behavior
 A. Self-injurious behavior
 B. Other-injurious behavior
 C. Environmentally destructive behavior

The efficacy of this classification system is now in the process of being evaluated by Morreau, 1984. A list of behaviors that fall into each class has been obtained by requesting 10 observed problem behaviors from each of over 1,500 teachers and direct-care staff working with nondisabled, mildly disabled, and severely disabled children. Based on their responses, 170 discrete, observable problem behaviors were identified. The resulting inventory of behavior problems was validated using the data base established at the Center for Residential and Community Services, University of Minnesota (Hill & Bruininks, 1981). In this data base, direct-care staff members working with over 2,000 retarded residents of public and private facilities were asked to cite specific behavior problems they observed. Only two of the behaviors cited as significant by the caregivers for the latter data base had not been previously cited by the caregivers for the former data base.

The 11 behaviors cited most frequently by the residential staff members included: hitting others (cited by 16% of respondents), kicking others (11%), yelling/screaming (11%), throwing objects (8%), biting others (8%), biting self (8%), banging head (7%), leaving area unclean (7%), breaking objects (6%), tearing objects (5%), and ignoring directions (5%). It is significant that the majority of problem behaviors cited fell within the destructive category. In conjunction with frequency data and criteria for establishing perceived severity, such analyses conducted across community-based residences and among potential providers could offer direction for organizing behavior-change programs. In additon, staff training on behavior management procedures could be made more behavior specific (i.e., those behaviors that are most likely to be exhibited or that cause the greatest negative reaction could be used as core examples around which specific treatment strategies are taught). The use of this classification of problem behaviors in evaluating clients should provide a needed structure for designing training programs. This strategy is used at a more general level in the Scales of Independent Behavior (Bruininks, Woodcock, Weatherman, & Hill, 1984) and at a detailed level in a criterion-referenced scale (Morreau, 1981) currently being researched.

## MANAGING PROBLEM BEHAVIORS

Marks and Rodd-Marks (1980) have suggested that residential facility staff members should concentrate their efforts on the management of behavior problems. Within the context of the living arrangement, however, it is essential to consider that the ultimate goal is independent functioning in the community and that independent living involves adjustment to a number of social systems having differing norms (Bartnik & Winkler, 1981). What represents appropriate behavior for one environment will not necessarily be appropriate in another. However, it is evident that some behaviors would likely not be tolerated regardless of the environmental context. Program developers must strive to assure that a pattern of appropriate social responding with reduced behavior problems will, in fact, be demonstrated beyond the

training situation. This does not always happen. Keith and Lange (1974), for example, found that up to 42% of the total skills acquired in six areas through training were lost within 3 to 26 months after acquisition: specifically, 30% of skills in controlling problem behaviors and 44% of social skills were not maintained at established criterion levels. Also, actual transition to community living from group homes may, as observed by Crnic and Pym (1979), result in behavioral regression—that is, client behaviors revert to lower skills levels; some residents are unprepared to cope with situations from which they were previously protected in group homes and, consequently, fail to thrive in independent living situations. Along with the management of specific behaviors, new behavior patterns must be established and demonstrated within a variety of contexts. To be considered effective, a training program should lead to the occurrence of desired behavior or to nonoccurrence of undesired behavior, in a variety of settings and with a variety of people over time. The generalization of behavior changes must assume greater priority if clients are to progress toward increased independence in less-restrictive environments. Yet, in the general literature related to single-subject designs, Kendall (1981) found that only one-fifth of randomly selected studies reviewed considered the issue of generalization.

The relatively high recidivism of deinstitutionalized persons—about 25% in the past 2 years (Scheerenberger, 1982, 1983)—would suggest that clients are being placed in the community with placement-threatening behavior problems and/or that programs leading to reduced levels of problem behaviors in institutional settings are not generalizing to community programs. However, along with the possible inadequacy of training programs, the adequacy of institutions as training environments must also be considered. Discrepancies between an institutional environment and the community environment are obviously extensive, and for many clients the environmental shift may be too great to expect generalization to occur routinely. Although it has been suggested that returning clients to community settings might be futile unless presenting problems are first resolved (McCarver & Craig, 1974), generalization of behavior changes are most likely to be facilitated if training occurs in settings that approximate the natural environment in which the resident is expected to live. Training in institutions makes the development and generalization of new behaviors to community settings more difficult.

Along with the failures of behavioral training procedures to generalize to alternative settings, other problems are evident. In spite of the models provided by the numerous reported successes of individual and group programs in reducing problem behaviors, Eyman et al. (1981) found that problem behaviors present at the time of placement tended to persist regardless of the client's age group, level of retardation, or type of residence. This raises questions about the general efficacy of behavioral programming. Perhaps the rigorous application of procedures used in research settings does not extend to the practical day-to-day training situation. The problem may relate to inconsistency in the implementation of developmental programs, a problem evidenced even in the discrepant administration of the independent variable in otherwise tightly controlled studies (Hersen, 1981; Peterson, Homer, & Wonderlich, 1982). If uncertainty exists as to the reliability of a specified treatment in a research study, one must definitely question the degree to which developmental programs are consistently delivered in applied settings. In settings having a large number of caregivers, one staff member may be inadvertently increasing a behavior that other individuals are attempting to reduce, or a program may be implemented in a particular environment by specific personnel for a designated period of time and not be maintained by other staff in other settings at other times, thereby providing a classic opportunity for extinction. These problems demonstrate the need for research that looks at more than the efficacy of existing behavior-management programs. It is becoming evident that sharper focus must be given, in both community and public residential programs, to applications of this technology within the treatment setting, to the identification of problems in behavioral programming, and to the establishment of procedures by which behavioral programs can be made more effective. Consideration must be given to assessment procedures for establishing priorities for behavior programs, to the characteristics of behavior-management strategies, to the generalization of training across settings, and to the environmental context in which behavioral programs are implemented.

## Establishing Priorities for Behavioral Programs

The relative basis by which residential staff and the community determine that behaviors are considered unacceptable makes it difficult to judge the severity of problem behavior among developmentally disabled persons and, consequently, to develop programs that would increase community acceptance. Goroff (1967) used a critical-incident technique to identify specific behavioral events that had precipitated reinstitutionalization of a sample of institutionalized residents. An impressive finding was that the majority of critical incidents that included behavior problems would have been considered inconsequential if they had been performed by a nonretarded person. This is consistent with the conclusion drawn by Hill and Bruininks (1981) that "in non-handicapped populations many maladaptive behaviors are accepted, ignored or tolerated" (p. 64). Establishing priorities for behavior management must therefore consider more than a socially accepted standard of behavior for nondisabled persons.

Neither can priorities be based exclusively upon the logical impact of a particular behavior on others. In their study of 424 retarded residents of community residential facilities, Nihira and Nihira (1975) indicated that of 1,252 incidents of problem behaviors that were considered to be bothersome, unacceptable, or beyond the threshold of community acceptance, only 16% were considered to jeopardize the health, safety, general welfare, or legal status of residents.

In a study of teacher decision making, Voeltz, Evans, Freedland, and Donellon (1982) noted that identifying priorities for behavior change (i.e., selecting target behaviors) may be influenced by attitudes about and personal experiences with individuals exhibiting behavioral excesses. Numerous factors may influence the negative attitude held by others toward specific behaviors exhibited by disabled persons. Caregivers may prefer not to handle behaviors perceived to be very serious—for example, potentially jeopardizing behavior such as running away and self-abuse (Lei et al., 1981). Caregivers' preferences about specific behaviors may be related to their perception of their own skills in managing a behavior or to previous aversive experiences when dealing with a behavior. Moreover, the behaviors considered to be serious would probably not be agreed upon among staff members (Hill & Bruininks, 1981).

Attitudes toward specific behaviors may also be influenced by the caregiver's perception of the disabled person's future. Contrary to the goals of the deinstitutionalization movement, Butterfield (1976) observed that caregivers in a state institution anticipated that 95% of the retarded adults would reside there for the remainder of their lives. Given this perception, behaviors that would be detrimental to ultimate community success might be considered irrelevant. As a result, the priorities for change in behavior might be directed more toward behaviors felt to be aversive to staff or toward behaviors that are most important in adjusting to an institutional environment. Under these conditions, staff might inadvertently reinforce behaviors that increase the likelihood of a client remaining in an institution. Certainly when the probability of greater independence is decreased by a client's learning natural adaptive responses to the physical or human environment of an institution or through modeling of individuals in that environment, environmental alteration rather than behavioral programming might be the best response to the problem.

Based upon the major goal for developmentally disabled persons of achieving as independent a life-style as possible, as well as upon the probable consequences of behavior in particular environments and the developmental goals for clients in selecting behavior-management activities, priority should be placed on eradicating those behaviors that: 1) have the highest probability of increasing negative social consequences to the individual; 2) have the highest probability of increasing negative consequences to significant others; and 3) would most inhibit others from initiating and maintaining social interactions with the developmentally disabled person.

When used in conjunction with criteria that determine the immediate perceived severity of the behavior, such guidelines would enable staff to maintain a developmental perspective while focusing on specific behaviors that have the most immediate impact. At the same time, changes in these behaviors would increase the chances of the retarded person's deriving positive consequences through appropriate social interaction.

## Characteristics of Strategies for Managing Behavior

The fact that particular behavior problems are identified as most detrimental to the present life situation of the individual or as most likely to interfere with the ultimate community adjustment of the disabled person cannot necessarily be interpreted as providing support for designing programs exclusively intended to reduce those behaviors. The selection of strategies for behavior management should be consistent with the overall developmental goals for disabled persons and with the concept of normalization. If the goal is to develop, through the most normal means possible, patterns of behavior that will enable disabled persons to live independently in the community, programs intended to reduce problem behavior should include strategies that: 1) are as nonaversive as possible, 2) facilitate the development of adaptive social skills, and 3) are both efficient and effective.

*Management Through Drugs* Any discussion of strategies used to manage problem behavior would be incomplete without reference to the use of drugs to suppress behavior. As observed by Sprague and Baxley (1978), drugs have been used to treat behavior in four broad categories: 1) acting out, 2) impulse control, 3) self-abuse, and 4) stereotypes. It is highly probable that psychotropic drugs (i.e., drugs that affect mood, cognition, or behavior) are frequently used as a *sole* treatment alternative for changing behaviors of developmentally disabled persons.

Lipman (1970) found that 50% of the residents in state and private facilities had, at some point, been given psychotropic drugs. Consistent with these data, Sprague (1977) found that 66% of the moderately/profoundly retarded residents of a large institution and 65% of the residents of a new, smaller, community-based residence were receiving drug treatment programs. While the use of medication is likely necessary to manage specific conditions (e.g., seizures) and may facilitate the acquisition of desired behavior through temporary suppression of problem behaviors, the prevalence of drug treatment would suggest that the procedure has been and, possibly, continues to be excessive and abused. The issues surrounding the use of drugs as a treatment alternative are extensive (Breuning & Poling, 1982). Yet, no body of research justifies the magnitude of their current use with developmentally disabled persons.

The numerous potential negative physical side effects and the threat of the legal implications (Gadow, 1980; Sprague, 1982a, 1982b) alone should preclude unjustified drug use as a treatment option for remediating problem behavior. One would expect that the potential adverse effects on ongoing behavioral programs would also be a major consideration. In their study of the effects of behavior modification, drugs, and combined programs on self-injurious behavior, Schroeder, Schroeder, Smith, and Dalldorf (1978) found that of residents receiving behavioral programs to reduce self-injurious behavior, 94% exhibited desired changes in behavior, compared to only 21% of the residents not receiving a behavioral program. The staff indicated that most of the time (68%) when neuroleptic drugs were used

alone, they had no positive effect on the behavior.

The potential effects of psychotropic drugs on the acquisition of adaptive behaviors is equally significant. Breuning and Davidson (1981) found that withdrawal of psychotropic drugs resulted in modest gains in IQ and that substantial gains occurred when withdrawal was paired with reinforcement of correct responses. Similarly, Wysocki, Fuqua, Davis, and Breuning (1981) reported major gains on a learning task after drug withdrawal. Without consideration of a resident's drug regimen, the validity of many behavior-management programs could be questioned. Staff must consider the potential effects of drugs on the efficacy of the programs they implement, that is, could a program have been more effective if drugs were removed? Further, the prolific use of drugs and their documented effects have implications for the description in the literature of subjects participating in research studies. Would it not be beneficial to know that drug treatment, a potentially uncontrolled independent variable, may concurrently be affecting subjects' behavior? Finally, once established, drug treatment programs for reducing problem behaviors have the potential for perpetuity. If a resident appeared to be doing well behaviorally, the program could be perceived to be appropriate and would unlikely be changed; if, on the other hand, the problem behaviors were exacerbated, increased amounts or alternative types of drugs could become the logical extension of the program.

Certainly, available data on drug usage and effects dictate that continuous monitoring should occur to ensure that the standards established by the Accreditation Council for Services for Mentally Retarded and Other Developmentally Disabled Persons (1983) are followed. Specifically, two standards would be of paramount importance:

> 1.4.6.8.2 Whenever . . . behavior-modifying drugs . . . are employed to eliminate maladaptive or problem behaviors, the individual's record documents the fact that less restrictive methods of modifying or replacing the behavior have been systematically tried and have been demonstrated to be ineffective (p.32).

1.4.6.10.1 Drugs used for behavior management are utilized only as an integral part of an individual program plan designed by an interdisciplinary team to lead to a less restrictive way of managing, and ultimately to the elimination of, the behaviors for which the drugs are employed (p.33).

The day-to-day reality is that problem behavior must be managed. Like systematic punishment without concurrent reinforcement of adaptive behavior, drug treatment represents an attempt to *control* existing behavior, rather than a process for developing more adaptive responses. Part of the rationale for using drugs for this purpose may rest in the relative density of problem behaviors exhibited by residents, the number of residents exhibiting problem behavior, the perceived inability of staff to handle certain types of behavior, and/or the absence of systematic behavioral programming.

***Behavioral Programming***   Some valuable general impressions regarding the status of current behavior programming can be drawn from the preliminary analysis of the literature reviewed in developing this chapter. Using the key terms, *maladaptive* and *behavior problem*, ERIC and *Psychological Abstracts* were computer searched across mentally retarded, emotionally disturbed, and autistic categories. Another search was conducted across each target population using the following descriptors: *noncompliance, uncooperative, aggressive, self-stimulation, stereotypic, destructive, self-injurious, self-abusive, antisocial, socially inappropriate, withdrawal, hyperactive,* and *sexual misconduct.* The resulting articles were then sorted based on the presence or absence of an intervention strategy. When a clear intervention strategy was present, the article was reviewed and coded to designate the exact population descriptors, target behaviors, and intervention strategies. Finally, those articles describing intervention procedures used with moderately/severely retarded persons were selected for collective analysis. A total of 111 articles describing interventions used with moderately and severely retarded persons were analyzed; of these articles, 84% included severely/profoundly retarded persons as the target population. Several characteristics of the current, applied research were noteworthy:

1.   A majority of interventions intended to reduce behavior problems involved aversive procedures (65% of interventions).
2.   Intervention programs usually specified more than one behavior problem as targets, but most programs were not designed to accelerate specific adaptive social responses. The majority of the studies (77%) were directed toward the reduction of at least one destructive behavior: specifically, 41% of the studies were directed toward alleviation of self-destructive responses. The next most frequently considered problem behaviors fell into the maladaptive category; 70% of the studies considered one or more behaviors in this group. Disruptive behaviors were considered in only 22% of the studies reviewed.
3.   A large number of the interventions included differential reinforcement of other behavior (32% of interventions) or differential reinforcement of incompatible behavior (22% of interventions).

Since interventions reported as successful are likely to be incorporated into training programs and therefore replicated and applied in the field, these results must be further evaluated in terms of both their implications for retarded persons and the programs that are being implemented to reduce problem behavior.

***Punishment Strategies***   The use of punishment may be necessary to immediately affect the probability of a given behavior (Repp & Deitz, 1978), particularly those behaviors that are physically destructive. However, when used as a general strategy for managing behavior, punishment may be counterproductive. If, as observed by Neel (1982), a new set of adaptive, competing behaviors is not concurrently taught, the effects of the strategy will be diminished or will disappear. Punishment will effectively *suppress* behavior, particularly in the presence of the punishing agent or in situations where punishment has previously been administered. But, in novel situations, which can be expected in the community, the behavior may recur. When viewed from a deinstitutionalization and community adjustment perspective, such limitations of effects could be disastrous. Clients must exhibit few problem behaviors in a variety of social and environmental contexts if they are to be successful. Data from at least one study on the use of aversive behavioral programs to suppress self-injurious and life-threatening behavior indicated that such programs may be neither generally effective nor fast-acting (Griffin, Williams, Stark, Altmeyer, & Mason, 1983). In their follow-up of 80 developmentally disabled individuals, these authors found that 60% of the individuals placed on aversive behavioral programs for severe self-injurious/life-threatening behavior and 69% of those placed on aversive programs for moderate self-injurious behaviors in 1976 continued to exhibit the problem behavior 7 years later. In addition, the analysis of the mean number of years that current programs were in effect was 3.4 years for individuals displaying severe self-injurious/life-threatening behavior and 2.8 years for individuals displaying moderate self-injurious behavior.

Along with the possible inefficiency and noneffectiveness of aversive programs, punishment may result in a variety of negative behavioral side effects (Matson & Kazdin, 1981). As a procedure, punishment can produce behaviors that might ultimately be perceived to be client problems—for example, attacking self or others (aggression), running away (escape), and crying (emotional distress)—and can increase behaviors that are counterproductive to living independently in the community, such as soiling, wetting pants, tantrums.

Other practical considerations affect the potential of punishment as a strategy for reducing behavior problems. As observed by Matson and Kazdin (1981), the use of punishment requires a sufficient number of well-trained staff. While extensive training could be provided in nearly all settings, the value of such training, in deference to training in other strategies, would be questionable. There is also the additional problem of preparing persons who are essentially in control of other human beings to use punishment more effectively. Punishment, by

definition, will effectively suppress behavior and, while the initial intent might be to limit punishment's use to specific behaviors requiring immediate, more drastic action, the negative reinforcement provided to staff through the reduction of behaviors aversive to them could result in generalization of punishment to other behaviors as well. Professionals must also consider that the level of aversive control may need to be systematically increased. Although there are many types and degrees of punishment, no matter what form it takes, there is an implied ability to administer it and control the client. When aversive stimuli are presented, some clients are likely to resist or to aggress against staff; what might begin as a mild aversive control procedure could result in the use of highly aversive procedures to control the client.

Although general guidelines have been developed for the use of punishment (American Association on Mental Deficiency, 1975; May, Risley, Twardosz, Friedman, Bijou, & Wexler, 1976), and specific procedures have been established for the use of punishment in many residential facilities, there is no absolute assurance that the guidelines will be followed. Further, most facility guidelines and requirements pertain to formal behavior-change programs and do not account for the moment-to-moment use of incidental punishment.

Most guidelines call for the use of less-restrictive strategies prior to the use of punishment. Unfortunately, both the impediments to consistent implementation across staff and across environments and the fact that the acquisition of adaptive behavior may require a prolonged time period reduce the chances that a less-restrictive strategy will be successful. Punishment strategies, on the other hand, are more likely to have an immediate, apparent effect in suppressing a problem behavior, thereby lending credence to the need for punishment and reinforcing staff in using it. Failure of a nonpunitive approach in reducing problem behavior should not be considered justification for progression to a more punitive procedure. Prior to considering any punishment strategy, personnel should be required to document the conditions under which less-restrictive approaches were used and the consistency with which they were implemented; program planners and evaluators, in turn, should respond to questions regarding whether sufficient data have been presented to document that less-restrictive approaches have failed and whether the failure of the approach is attributable to the approach or to its actual implementation.

Arranged punishment is dehumanizing and often ineffective in the long term. The suppression of a problem behavior in the presence solely of particular staff or in a specific environment only, without concurrent development of desired behavior across environments and staff, is intended to meet immediate needs and, even then, often not those of the client. Punishment may also serve to make presently aversive environments more negative and result in more serious behavior problems. More research should be conducted to identify effective alternatives for remediating problem behaviors, and training programs that are designed for facility staff should increasingly emphasize positive strategies for managing behavior.

*Adaptive Social Development* Although the literature suggests that intervention procedures used with behavior problems are predominantly aversive, it is consistent with effective behavioral programming that other behaviors and incompatible behaviors are concurrently being reinforced or are being strengthened as behavior-change strategies (Deitz, Repp, & Deitz, 1976; Repp & Deitz, 1974; Repp, Deitz, & Deitz, 1976; Repp, Deitz, & Speir, 1975). Unfortunately, because the decision to reinforce other or incompatible behaviors is often directed exclusively toward reduction of the behavior problem, the strengthening of alternative behaviors may serve no other developmental purpose. When such a decision is made, it would seem more effective to target both the behavior problem and a set of desired, relevant social-environmental responses.

Although not frequently discussed in the literature, an alternative programming strategy exists by which problem behaviors might be reduced or extinguished at the same time that specific adaptive social skills are acquired. Gaylord-Ross (1980) and Schroeder, Mulick, and Schroeder (1979), for example, suggested that behavior problems could be reduced through developmental skill training without other formal interventions. This conclusion is supported by studies by Adkins and Matson (1980), in which the investigators found that a reduction in problem behaviors occurred while the client was participating in a leisure development program; by Paloutzian, Hasazi, Streifel, and Edgar (1970), whose study indicated that prompting and associated reinforcement of social-interaction behaviors resulted in increased social responding and reduced levels of "autistic" behavior; and by Burkhart (1981), who found that, for some individuals, self-stimulatory behaviors could be reduced by channeling those behaviors into functional tasks having a similar topography.

Additional consideration should also be given to the possibility of identifying, controlling, and using environmental stimuli that reinforce maladaptive behavior as reinforcers for adaptive behavior. In their study of the effects of sensory reinforcement on stereotypic and play behavior, Rincover, Cook, Peoples, and Packard (1979) found that stereotypic behavior was maintained by sensory reinforcement, that removal of the sensory reinforcers reduced the probability of self-stimulation, and that the sensory stimuli could be used to reinforce new play behaviors. In other words, through environmental analysis, stimuli-reinforcing problem behaviors could be identified and, if arranged contingently, used to strengthen adaptive behavior.

Leon (1982) provided an additional instructional option for systematically strengthening adaptive responses: the contingent arrangement of self-stimulating behavior after a subject displays an adaptive response. Frequently occurring problem behaviors are, by definition, higher probability behaviors than infrequent or nonoccurring adaptive responses (Premack, 1965). By arranging it so that opportunities to engage in the problem behavior are contingent upon the display of an adaptive, preferably incompatible, response, adaptive responding could be systematically increased. The increased probability of desired, adaptive responses would simultaneously reduce the probability of the undesired (less-probable) response occurring. Through the use of these procedures, Leon (1982) increased eye contact, counting responses, and visual tracking by providing opportunities to manipulate a plastic lid, to twirl a piece of cloth, to rub cloth swatches, to tap an object with a spoon, and to observe a flashlight. The use of this strategy would enable program developers to capitalize on some existing problem behaviors by using them as contingent reinforcers for more adaptive ones.

Greater study of skill development approaches is needed to determine the general efficacy of the procedures as well as their effects on specific classes of problem behaviors. However, it is significant that these procedures are consistent with the goal established for developmentally disabled persons and with the need to protect retarded persons from the excessive use of aversive strategies.

## Program Efficiency

As indicated by Voeltz and Evans (1982), "Ultimate treatment validity is affected by the choice of particular behaviors rather than others, and is not simply an issue of demonstrating effective changes in designated targets" (p. 160). If, as suggested by Voeltz and Evans, behaviors are interdependent and generalized behavior patterns could be identified, it might be possible to select target behaviors that would increase the efficiency and effectiveness of behavioral-change efforts. Altering the probability of one behavior problem might also alter the probability of another. Although the direction of change in other problem behaviors would not necessarily be determined in advance, if multiple behavior problems could be affected by a single treatment program, the amount of client programming could possibly be increased. Presuming that programming time is a relevant variable, developmental skills would also be enhanced. The simultaneous alteration of multiple behaviors is evi-

dent in family child-rearing practices. Development of nondisabled persons does not occur through parental selection and systematic reinforcement of single target behaviors. Parents may focus their efforts on specific behaviors at different times, but development is more usually characterized by concurrent reinforcement of a large number of responses. The possibility exists that developers of programs for developmentally disabled persons could systematically decrease the probability of entire classes of behavior, rather than establishing single targets for behavior change. Considering the density of behavior problems exhibited by many developmentally disabled persons, such strategies must be developed if clients are to be successful in the community. Yet, at present, it would appear that programs are being designed to alter the density of single behaviors or combinations of behaviors perceived by experimenters/program-developers to be related. This issue was also noted by Holman and Bruininks in the previous chapter as characteristic of most research studies on training adaptive behavior skills. Increased research must be conducted to provide a basis for the development of procedures whereby response interdependencies and, therefore, response classes, rather than single, isolated behaviors, can be identified and targeted for individual clients.

## Environmental Factors

Many behavior problems manifested by developmentally disabled persons are stimulated and maintained by the environment in which the individual is placed. In addition, many environments are poorly structured to provide sufficient, consistent developmental programming that remediates behavior problems. For example, many programs have extensive amounts of "down time" (i.e., time during which no developmental program is provided and the client behavior is unstructured). Unfortunately, existing standards do not preclude extensive amounts of time engaged in activities that, from a developmental perspective, are nonproductive or counterproductive. The *Standards for Services for Mentally Retarded and*

*Other Developmentally Disabled Individuals* (Accreditation Council for Services for Mentally Retarded and Other Developmentally Disabled Persons, 1983), for example, states that, "Activity schedules do not permit 'dead time' of more than one hour continuous duration" (p. 56).

From a behavioral perspective, the everyday events or characteristics of the environments of many programs for disabled persons would be considered aversive by nondisabled persons. If these events are also aversive to developmentally disabled clients, they could elicit all of the behavioral side effects associated with other forms of punishment. Therefore, settings should be evaluated to assure that the client is not being repetitively punished for merely being present and that observed problem behaviors are not attributable to setting events (e.g., acting out to gain human contact). Simple observation of one institutional environment, for example, yielded the following variables that could be considered potentially aversive: noise; proximity to others; odor; infrequent changes in body position; fixed scheduling events (routine); pain inflicted by others; absence of conversation, attention, and physical contact; negative verbal reactions from staff; inappropriate lighting; or physical discomfort (e.g., being hungry, thirsty, soiled, hot, cold). While setting events could have a major impact on the behavior of clients, it is clear that such associations have not been sufficiently explored (Wahler & Fox, 1981).

Simply removing aversive events/characteristics will not respond to the dictate inherent in the concept of institutional reform that involves "modification or improvement in attitudes, philosophies, policies, effective utilization of all available resources. . . to motivate and assist individuals to reach their maximum level of functioning in the least restrictive environment possible" (President's Committee on Mental Retardation, 1974, p. 4). In addition to removing the inducements to negative behavior, environments should also be designed to effectively assist individuals in developing appropriate social behaviors and, where possible, in managing their own behavior. This can be a particularly effective behavior development and management strategy. Environmental design may include simple manipulation of antecedent events, if a specific event invariably precedes an undesirable behavior.

Environmental design may also include attention to the physical and social environment. As demonstrated by numerous studies on aging, the particular environment arranged for an individual can have a significant effect upon a person and upon his or her behavior (Lawton, 1977). For example, Lawton, Leibowitz, and Charon (1970) found that with no change in staff behavior, senile clients increased their mobility following remodeling of a living area, and Kahana and Kahana (1970) found that, consistent with the normalization principle, elderly clients placed in age-integrated units in a mental hospital were more responsive than clients placed in age-segregated units. If mobility and social responsiveness can be enhanced for the aged citizen through environmental restructuring, planners must consider the potential of similar efforts for accelerating the development of developmentally disabled persons. In conjunction with differential reinforcement of desired behavior, environmental alternatives could significantly affect client development. Spradlin and Girardeau (1966) were among the first to suggest that adaptive behavior of severely retarded persons could be enhanced by arranging environmental conditions to promote the reinforcement of behavior incompatible with problem behaviors. Certainly, many of the behaviors considered to be problems could be functionally related to the environment and, consequently, potentially remediable through environmental alteration (Zentall, 1975, 1979). For example, Zentall (1979) suggests that autism may represent an "attempt to maintain a steady state of sensory deprivation" (p.21) and, therefore, that reductions in auditory and visual stimuli could be evaluated as an approach to reducing the behavior patterns/characteristics of the individual. Similarly, "hyperactivity" could be viewed as increased self-stimulation to compensate for low environmental stimulation. In theory, then, increasing environmental stimulation for some individuals would reduce problem behaviors frequently classed as hyperactive.

Environmental enrichment has also been demonstrated effective in reducing specific behavior problems. Stereotypic body movements have been reduced through the presentation of objects in conjunction with social stimulation (Moseley, Faust, & McGuire-Reardon, 1970) and through the use of sounds and objects (Guess & Rutherford, 1967). Similarly, hyperactive behaviors have been reduced through the use of lights, posters, and music (Evans, 1979). The effectiveness of environmental alteration to reduce behavior problems was further demonstrated by Horner (1980), who found that behavior problems could be reduced through differential reinforcement of object-directed behavior. While most strategies for reducing problem behavior require extensive staff involvement, environmental adaptations to affect behavior are consistent and sometimes permanent positive interventions without the requirements of extensive staff training and utilization.

The relative size and structure of a facility also can influence a client's potential for adapting to community settings. For example, Rotegard, Hill, and Bruininks (1982) found that smaller homes were characterized by increased resident autonomy; the higher level of autonomy might be expected to improve a client's ability to make the personal decisions needed for adaptation to the community. By contrast, as suggested by Bjaanes and Butler (1974), a small group home can interfere with client development of independent functioning if the staff is overprotective; for example, the occurrence of natural consequences to which the client has not been exposed can negatively affect his or her ability to adjust to community living (Crnic & Pym, 1979). Environments should be structured to increase the level of resident autonomy while assuring exposure, with sufficient staff support, to natural consequences likely to occur in the community.

Alteration of the stimulus properties of the environment or within multiple environments is a viable option for managing behavior problems. The density of reinforcement provided within environments can be systematically increased along with desired developmental skills if behaviors are identified for consistent reinforcement when they are observed by any staff member within the faculty. Although any client behavior representing an increase in appropriate independent functioning could be considered for reinforcement, specific universal target behaviors could be designated for direct, immediate attention—for example, spontaneous communication, expressing preferences, arriving at programs by specified times, completing tasks, cleaning up after oneself, sharing, following directions, or helping others.

At the same time, it may be possible to identify and ignore problem behaviors that are likely to be maintained if they are given attention by staff (i.e., nonself-stimulatory and nondestructive behaviors that are unlikely to be imitated by others). Behaviors such as begging, repetitive requesting after denial of an expressed wish, laying down on sidewalks, bizarre comments, and exposing oneself might be systematically reduced through consistent withholding of attention.

Many other behaviors that are systematically reinforced in program environments but that are counter-indicated for successful integration should also be reevaluated as part of a programming procedure. Hugging, kissing, and repetitive handshaking as a form of greeting friends and strangers, or sitting in a chair for prolonged periods of time, for example, may result in a negative reaction from others in a community setting and reduce the likelihood of social interaction. On a larger scale, the strengthening of any behavior that fosters dependence rather than independence must be considered counterproductive to developmental goals for retarded persons. Program and physical environments should be altered to encourage development in two broad areas: independent functioning and decision making. For instance, walking (i.e., marching) in monitored lines, receiving food in prepared compartments, getting assistance on tasks that, if time were allowed, could be completed alone, inhibit the development of independence.

Independent decision making may represent one of the most important goals, in that it is a significant component of development. As indicated by Landesman-Dwyer and Sulzbacher (1981), many severely/profoundly retarded persons have the minimal necessary social repertoire, but they may not use it appropriately. This may be attributable to numerous deficits in the instructional procedure, such as failure to provide clients with the opportunity to make decisions, in conjunction with differential reinforcement for appropriate choices.

With appropriate training, some developmentally disabled persons can be taught to monitor their own performance (Coleman & Blampied, 1977; Mahoney & Mahoney, 1976) and to manage some social and task behaviors (Antonelli & Crowley, 1980). Environments should be developed that include training in decision making and that provide opportunities for acquired responses to occur. For example, choosing what to wear, selecting leisure activities to engage in, and choosing from among foods at mealtime would allow for training in procedures for making decisions. Similarly, clients should, when possible, be actively involved in making program decisions related to their destiny. Arranging for client presence at planning meetings is not sufficient; procedures should be evolved by which clients can participate. As noted by Crnic and Pym (1979), "the most important factor in successful independent living placement was the resident's motivation to work toward independent living as a goal and maintain that functional level once it has been attained" (p. 15). It would likely be easier to motivate clients if, in fact, the value of programs/events were clearly emphasized in conjunction with their participation, even if participation were limited to observed client behavior during the presentation of a sample of available options.

The environment can be a substantial part of the program for managing behavior problems and for developing appropriate social responses. However, expanded information on the effectiveness of environmental manipulation for reducing/eliminating behavior problems and for promoting the acquisition of an adaptive social repertoire that includes independent decision making and involvement in program decisions is needed.

## PRESENT STATUS AND THE FUTURE IMPLICATIONS

Developmental training programs for developmentally disabled persons must be focused directly on enabling clients to live as independently as possible and to effectively manage their physical/social environment. It is apparent from the literature on both admission and readmission of retarded persons to public facilities that behavior problems are a major impediment to the realization of this goal.

Because of the descriptive nature of most measures of behavior problems, a great deal of uncertainty exists as to which behaviors most significantly affect client adjustment and client independence in community settings. There is no agreed upon set of behavior problems that, if modified, would lead to community success. As a result, target behaviors may be selected based on the perceived immediate needs of the client or of the staff without the necessary consideration of a client's total development or future situation. The time spent by professionals in attempting to alter specific client behaviors may well be essentially fruitless if the client is not able to achieve a more independent life as a result.

To reduce behavioral interference with community adjustment of developmentally disabled persons, there is a need for more precise indices to determine those behaviors that interfere with community integration. Precise client data would enable program planners to realistically evaluate the characteristics of behavior from a developmental context (i.e., a given behavior may be appropriate to the person's level of development) and from an environmental context (i.e., a given behavior may represent a natural response to an unnatural or aversive human or physical environment). In fact, such data would enable planners to determine if a perceived problem is in reality a problem at all and to establish tolerance levels for specific behaviors.

The strategies described in the literature for managing problem behavior predominantly involve the use of systematic punishment that is incompatible with the long-range developmental goals for disabled persons and with evolving standards of humane treatment. Punishment places the caregiver in the role of manager for the retarded person, whereas caregivers more appropriately should adopt the role of assistants for self-management. While the immediate concern of staff may be to eliminate disruptive/destructive behavior that affects them or their clients on a day-to-day basis, the primary concern should be the possible failure of clients to acquire an adaptive social repertoire that has long-term implications for the individual, the facility, and society. The development of a repertoire of acceptable social behaviors will require that providers shift not only the reality but also the perception of control over behavior and consequences to the disabled person.

The literature suggests that environmental modification, in conjunction with consistent, differential reinforcement of needed adaptive behavioral skills, can effectively reduce many problem behaviors. Although the need exists for more research into the use of positive strategies and environmental alteration to affect problem behavior, an application of already documented procedures could lead to a more productive independent life for many developmentally disabled persons. A prevailing need, therefore, is to alter practices to match the state of knowledge while continuing to investigate alternatives by which practices can be improved. Only through this course can we humanely assist developmentally disabled persons to achieve a life goal held in esteem by everyone—that is, to live as independently as possible.

## REFERENCES

Accreditation Council for Services for Mentally Retarded and Other Developmentally Disabled Persons. *Standards for services for developmentally disabled individuals.* Washington, DC: Accreditation Council for Services for Mentally Retarded and Other Developmentally Disabled Persons, 1983.

Adkins, J., & Matson, J. Teaching institutionalized mentally retarded adults socially appropriate leisure skills. *Mental Retardation,* 1980, *18,* 249–251.

American Association on Mental Deficiency. *Position papers of the American Association on Mental Deficiency.* Washington, DC: American Association on Mental Deficiency, 1975.

Antonelli, C., & Crowley, R. Facilitating self-management in social interactions among the profoundly developmentally disabled. Unpublished manuscript, 1980 (ERIC Document Service Reproduction No. ED 210 846).

Baldwin, N. *Community living arrangements training needs survey.* Unpublished manuscript, Pennsylvania State University, Department of Special Education, University Park, 1972.

Bartnik, E., & Winkler, R. Discrepant judgments of community adjustment of mentally retarded adults: The contribution of personal responsibility. *American Journal of Mental Deficiency,* 1981, *86,* 260–266.

Bergman, J. *Community homes for the retarded.* Lexington, MA: Lexington Books, 1975.

Bjaanes, A.T., & Butler, E.W. Environmental variation in community care facilities for mentally retarded persons.

*American Journal of Mental Deficiency,* 1974, *78,* 429–439.

Breuning, S.E., & Davidson, N.A. Effects of psychotropic drugs on intelligence test performance of institutionalized mentally retarded adults. *American Journal on Mental Deficiency,* 1981, *85,* 575–579.

Breuning, S.E., & Poling, A. (eds.). *Drugs and mental retardation.* Springfield, IL: Charles C Thomas 1982.

Bruininks, R.H., Woodcock, R., Weatherman, R., & Hill, B.K. *Scales of independent behavior.* Allen, TX: Developmental Learning Materials, 1984.

Burkhart, J. *An investigation in channeling self-stimulatory behavior into functional workshop tasks.* Paper presented at the meeting of the American Association on Mental Deficiency, Detroit, May, 1981.

Butterfield, E. Some basic changes in residential facilities. In: R.B. Kugel & A. Shearer (eds.), *Changing patterns in residential services for the mentally retarded.* Washington, DC: President's Committee on Mental Retardation, 1976.

Coleman, P., & Blampied, N. Effects of self-monitoring, token reinforcement and different back-up reinforcers on the classroom behavior of retardates. *Exceptional Child,* 1977, *24,* 95–107.

Crnic, K., & Pym, H. Training mentally retarded adults in independent living skills. *Mental Retardation,* 1979, *17,* 13–15.

Deitz, S.M., Repp, A.C., & Deitz, D.E. Reducing inappropriate classroom behavior of retarded students through three procedures of differential reinforcement.

*Journal of Mental Deficiency Research*, 1976, *20*, 155–170.

Dellinger, J., & Shope, L. Selected characteristics and working conditions of direct service staff in Pennsylvania CLA's. *Mental Retardation*, 1978, *16*, 19–21.

Developmental Disabilities Program. Admissions/readmissions to state hospitals, September 1, 1980 to May 31, 1981: The behavior problem issues. *Policy analysis series #5: Issues related to Welsch v. Noot*. St. Paul, MN: Developmental Disabilities Program, 1981.

Developmental Disabilities Program. Admissions/readmissions to state hospitals, June 1, 1981 to December 31, 1981: The behavior problem issues. *Policy analysis series #10: Issues related to Welsch v. Noot*. St. Paul, MN: Developmental Disabilities Program, 1982.

Evans, R. The reduction of hyperactive behavior in three profoundly retarded adolescents through increased stimulation. *AAESPH Review*, 1979, *4*, 259–263.

Eyman, R., & Borthwick, S. Patterns of care for mentally retarded persons. *American Journal of Mental Deficiency*, 1980, *18*, 63–66.

Eyman, R., Borthwick, S., & Miller, C. Trends in maladaptive behavior of mentally retarded persons placed in community and institutional settings. *American Journal of Mental Deficiency*, 1981, *85*, 473–477.

Eyman, R., & Call, T. Maladaptive behavior and community placement of mentally retarded persons. *American Journal of Mental Deficiency*, 1977, *82*, 137–144.

Eyman, R., O'Connor, G., Tarjan, G., & Justice, R. Factors determining residential placement of mentally retarded children. *American Journal of Mental Deficiency*, 1972, *76*, 692–698.

Foss, G., & Peterson, S. Social-interpersonal skills relevant to job tenure for mentally retarded adults. *Mental Retardation*, 1981, *19*, 103–106.

Foster, S., & Ritchey, W. Issues in the assessment of social competence in children. *Journal of Applied Behavior Analysis*, 1979, *12*, 625–638.

Gadow, K.D. *Children on medication: A primer for school personnel*. Reston, VA: Council for Exceptional Children, 1980.

Gartner, A. *Paraprofessionals and their performance: A survey of education, health and social service programs*. New York: Praeger Publishers, 1971.

Gartner, A., & Reissman, F. The paraprofessional movement in perspective. *Personnel and Guidance Journal*, 1974, *53*, 253–256.

Gaylord-Ross, R. A decision model for the treatment of aberrant behavior in applied settings. In: W. Sailor, B. Wilcox, & L. Brown (eds.), *Methods of instruction for severely handicapped students*. Baltimore: Paul H. Brookes Publishing Co., 1980.

Goroff, N. Research and community placement—an exploratory approach. *Mental Retardation*, 1967, *5*(4), 17–19.

Griffin, J.C., Williams, D.E., Stark, M.T., Altmeyer, B.K., & Mason, M. *Self-injurious behavior/life threatening behavior: A seven-year statewide follow-up on the effectiveness of aversive behavioral programs*. Richmond, TX: Richmond State School, 1983.

Guess, D., & Rutherford, G. Experimental attempts to reduce stereotyping among blind retardates. *American Journal of Mental Deficiency*, 1967, *71*, 984–986.

Hersen, M. Complex problems require complex solutions. *Behavior Therapy*, 1981, *12*, 15–29.

Hill, B.K., & Bruininks, R.H. *Assessment of behavioral characteristics of people who are mentally retarded*. Minneapolis: University of Minnesota, Department of Educational Psychology, 1977.

Hill, B.K., & Bruininks, R.H. *Physical and behavioral characteristics and maladaptive behavior of mentally retarded people in residential facilities*. Minneapolis: University of Minnesota, Department of Psychoeducational Studies, 1981.

Hill, B.K., & Bruininks, R.H. Maladaptive behavior of mentally retarded people in residential facilities. *American Journal of Mental Deficiency*, 1984, *88*, 380–387.

Hill, B.K., Bruininks, R.H., & Lakin, K.C. Characteristics and maladaptive behavior of mentally retarded people in residential facilities. *Health and Social Work*, 1983, *8*(2), 85–95.

Horner, R. The effects of an environmental "enrichment" program on the behavior of institutionalized profoundly retarded children. *Journal of Applied Behavior Analysis*, 1980, *13*, 473–491.

Intagliata, J., & Willer, B. A review of training programs for providers of foster care to mentally retarded persons. In: R.H. Bruininks, C.E. Meyers, B.B. Sigford, & K.C. Lakin (eds.) *Deinstitutionalization and community adjustment of mentally retarded people*. Washington, DC: American Association on Mental Deficiency, 1981.

Kahana, B., & Kahana, E. Changes in mental status of elderly patients in age-integrated and age-segregated hospital milieus. *Journal of Abnormal Psychology*, 1970, *75*, 177–181.

Keith, K., & Lange B. Maintenance of behavior change in an institution-wide training program. *Mental Retardation*, 1974, *12*(2), 34–37.

Kendall, P.C. Assessing generalization and the single-subject strategies. *Behavior Modification*, 1981, *5*, 307–319.

Keys, V., Boroskin, A., & Ross, R. The revolving door in an MR hospital: A study of returns from leave. *Mental Retardation*, 1973, *11*(1), 55–56.

La Greca, A.M., Stone, W.L., & Bell, C.R. Assessing the problematic interpersonal skills of mentally retarded individuals in a vocational setting. *Applied Research in Mental Retardation*, 1982, *3*, 37–53.

Lakin, K.C. *Demographic studies of residential facilities for the mentally retarded: An historical review of methodologies and findings*. Minneapolis: University of Minnesota, Department of Psychoeducational Studies, 1979.

Lakin, K.C., Hill, B.K., Hauber, F.A., Bruininks, R.H., & Heal, L.W. New admissions and readmissions to a national sample of public residential facilities. *American Journal of Mental Deficiency*, 1983, *88*, 13–20.

Landesman-Dwyer, S., & Sulzbacher, F. Residential placement and adaptation of severely and profoundly retarded individuals. In: R.H. Bruininks, C.E. Meyers, B.B. Sigford, & K.C. Lakin (eds.), *Deinstitutionalization and community adjustment of mentally retarded people*. Washington, DC: American Association on Mental Deficiency, 1981, 182–194.

Lawton, M.P. The impact of the environment on aging and behavior. In: J.E. Burren & K.W. Shail (eds.), *Handbook of the psychology of aging*. New York: Van-Nostrand Reinhold Co., 1977.

Lawton, M.P., Liebowitz, B., & Charon, H. Physical structure and the behavior of senile patients following ward remodeling. *Aging and Human Development*, 1970, *13*, 231–239.

Lei, T., Nihira, L., Sheehy, N., & Meyers, C. A study of small family care for mentally retarded people. In: R.H. Bruininks, C.E. Meyers, B.B. Sigford, & K.C. Lakin (eds.), *Deinstitutionalization and community adjustment of mentally retarded people*. Washington, DC: American Association on Mental Deficiency, 1981.

Leon, J. Stereotypy: An alternative view of self-stimulation. In: R. Rittenhouse (ed.), *Language development in severely disabled children: Theory and pragmatics*. Springfield, IL: Hope School, 1982.

Lipman, R.S. The use of psychopharmacological agents in residential facilities for the retarded. In: F. Menolascino (ed.), *Psychiatric approaches to mental retardation*. New York: Basic Books, 1970.

McCarver, R., & Craig, E. Placement of the retarded in the community: Prognosis and outcome. In: N.R. Ellis (ed.), *International review of research in mental retardation*, Vol. 7. New York: Academic Press, 1974.

McDonald, J. Residential alternatives for the developmentally disabled. Memorandum, Illinois Bureau of the Budget, Springfield, IL, July 28, 1982.

Mahoney, M. & Mahoney, K. Self-control techniques with the mentally retarded. *Exceptional Children*, 1976, *42*, 339–340.

Maney, A., Pace, R., & Morrison, D. A factor analytic study of the need for institutionalization: Problems and populations for program development. *American Journal of Mental Deficiency*, 1964, *69*, 372–384.

Marks, H., & Rodd-Marks, J. On an attempt to assess and predict adaptive behavior of institutionalized mentally retarded clients. *American Journal of Mental Deficiency*, 1980, *85*, 195.

Matson, J., & Kazdin, A. Punishment in behavior modification: Pragmatic, ethical, and legal issues. *Child Psychology Review*, 1981, *1*, 197–210.

May, J.G., Risley, T.R., Twardosz, S., Friedman, P., Bijou, S.W., & Wexler, D. *Guidelines for the use of behavioral procedures in state programs for retarded persons*. Arlington, TX: National Association for Retarded Citizens, 1976.

Mayeda, T., & Sutter, P. Deinstitutionalization: Phase II. In: R.H. Bruininks, C.E. Meyers, B.B. Sigford, & K.C. Lakin (eds.), *Deinstitutionalization and community adjustment of mentally retarded people*. Washington, DC: American Association on Mental Deficiency, 1981.

Meyers, C.E., Nihira, K., & Zetlin, A. The measurement of adaptive behavior. In: N.R. Ellis (ed.), *Handbook of mental deficiency: Psychological theory and research*, (2d ed.) Hillsdale, NJ: Lawrence Erlbaum Associates, 1979.

Morreau, L.E. *Punishment: An educational perspective*. St. Paul, MN: Minnesota Department of Education, 1980.

Morreau, L.E. *Prescriptive inventory of problem behaviors*. Normal, IL: Illinois State University, 1981.

Moseley, A., Faust, M., & McGuire-Reardon, D. Effects of social and nonsocial stimuli on the stereotyped behavior of retarded children. *American Journal of Mental Deficiency*, 1970, *74*, 809–811.

Neel, R. Research findings regarding the use of punishment procedures with severely behavior disordered children. In: F. Wood & K.C. Lakin (eds.), *Punishment and aversive stimulation in special education: Legal, the-*

oretical and practical issues in their use with emotionally disturbed children and youth. Reston, VA: Council for Exceptional Children, 1982.

Nihira, L., & Nihira, K. Jeopardy in community placement. *American Journal of Mental Deficiency*, 1975, *79*, 538–544.

Nirje, B. The normalization principle and its human management implications. In: R. Kugel & W. Wolfensberger (eds.), *Changing patterns in residential services for the mentally retarded*. Washington, DC: President's Committee on Mental Retardation, 1969.

Niziol, O., & DeBlassie, R. Work adjustment and the educable mentally retarded adolescent. *Journal of Employment Counseling*, 1972, *9*, 158–166.

Pagel, S., & Whitling, C. Readmissions to a state hospital for mentally retarded persons: Reasons for community placement failure. *Mental Retardation*, 1978, *16*, 164–166.

Paloutzian, R.F., Hasazi, J., Streifel, J., & Edgar, C.L. Promotion of positive social interaction in severely retarded young children. *American Journal of Mental Deficiency*, 1970, *75*, 519–524.

Peterson, L., Homer, A.L., & Wonderlich, S.A. The integrity of independent variables in behavior analysis. *Journal of Applied Behavior Analysis*, 1982, *15*, 477–492.

Premack, D. Reinforcement theory. In: D. Levine (ed.), *Nebraska Symposium on Motivation*. Lincoln: University of Nebraska Press, 1965, 123–188.

President's Committee on Mental Retardation. *Residential programming*. Washington, D.C.: President's Committee on Mental Retardation, 1974.

Quay, H.C. Classification. In: H.C. Quay & J.W. Werry (eds.), *Psychopathological disorders of childhood*, Vol. 1. New York: John Wiley & Sons, 1979.

Reagan, M., Murphy, R., Hill, Y., & Thomas, D. Community placement stability of behavior problem educable mentally retarded students. *Mental Retardation*, 1980, *18*, 139–142.

Reiss, S., Levitan, G.W., & Szysko, J. Emotional disturbance and mental retardation: Diagnostic overshadowing. *American Journal of Mental Deficiency*, 1982, *86*, 567–574.

Reiss, S., & Szysko, J. Diagnostic overshadowing and professional experience with mentally retarded persons. *American Journal of Mental Deficiency*, 1983, *87*, 396–402.

Repp, A., & Deitz, D.E. On the selective use of punishment-suggested guidelines for administrators. *Mental Retardation*, 1978, *16*, 250–254.

Repp, A., & Deitz, S.M. Reducing aggressive and self-injurious behavior of institutionalized retarded children through reinforcement of other behaviors. *Journal of Applied Behavior Analysis*, 1974, *7*, 313–325.

Repp, A., Deitz, S.M., & Speir, N.C. Reducing stereotypic responding of retarded persons through the differential reinforcement of other behavior. *American Journal of Mental Deficiency*, 1975, *79*, 279–284.

Repp, A., Deitz, S.M., & Deitz, D.E. Reducing inappropriate behaviors in classrooms and in individual sessions through DRO schedules of reinforcement. *Mental Retardation*, 1976, *14*(1), 11–15.

Rincover, A., Cook, R., Peoples, A., & Packard, D. Sensory extinction and sensory reinforcement principles for programming multiple adaptive behavior change. *Jour-*

nal of Applied Behavior Analysis, 1979, 12, 221–233.

Rotegard, L., Hill, B., & Bruininks, R. Environmental characteristics of residential facilities for mentally retarded people in the United States. Minneapolis: University of Minnesota, Department of Psychoeducational Studies, 1982.

Saenger, G. Factors influencing the institutionalization of mentally retarded individuals in New York City. Albany: New York State Interdepartmental Health Resources Board, 1960.

Schalock, R., & Harper, R. Placement from community-based mental retardation programs: How well do clients do? American Journal of Mental Deficiency, 1978, 83, 240–247.

Scheerenberger, R.C. A study of public residential facilities. Mental Retardation, 1976, 14(1), 32–35.

Scheerenberger, R.C. Human services personpower for developmentally disabled people. In: T.C. Muzzio, J.J. Koshel, & V. Bradley (eds.), Alternative community living arrangements and nonvocational social services for developmentally disabled people. Washington, DC: Urban Institute, 1981.

Scheerenberger, R.C. Public residential services for the mentally retarded, 1981. Minneapolis: University of Minnesota, Department of Educational Psychology, 1982.

Scheerenberger, R.C. Public residential services for the mentally retarded, 1982. Minneapolis: University of Minnesota, Department of Educational Psychology, 1983.

Schinke, S., & Wong, S. Evaluation of staff training in group homes for retarded persons. Journal of Mental Deficiency, 1977, 82, 130–136.

Schroeder, S., Mulick, J., & Schroeder, C. Management of severe behavior problems of the retarded. In: N.R. Ellis (ed.), Handbook of mental deficiency, 2d ed.. Hillsdale, NJ: Lawrence Erlbaum, 1979.

Schroeder, S.R., Schroeder, C.S., Smith, B., & Dalldorf, J. Prevalence of self-injurious behaviors in a large state facility for the retarded: A three-year follow-up study. Journal of Autism and Childhood Schizophrenia, 1978, 8, 261–268.

Smith, J.B., & Smith, M.A. Antecedents of the institutionalization of the retarded: A review and critique. Paper presented at the Seventh Annual Convention of the Association for Behavior Analysis, Milwaukee, WI, May, 1981.

Spencer, D. New long-stay patients in a hospital for mental handicap. British Journal of Psychiatry, 1976, 128, 467–470.

Spradlin, J.E., & Girardeau, F.L. The behavior of moderately and severely retarded persons. In: N.R. Ellis (ed.), International review of research in mental retardation, Vol. 1. New York: Academic Press, 1966.

Sprague, R.L. Overview of psychopharmacology for the retarded in the United States. In: P. Mittler (ed.), Research to practice in mental retardation, vol. 3. Baltimore: University Park Press, 1977.

Sprague, R.L. Litigation, laws, and regulations regarding psychoactive drug use. In: S. Breuning & A. Poling (eds.), Drugs and mental retardation. Springfield, IL: Charles C Thomas, 1982a.

Sprague, R.L. Review of tardive dyskinesia malpractice litigation. In: J. Rapoport, Moderator, Pediatric psychopharmacology: New issues and special populations.

Symposium presented at the American Academy of Child Psychiatry Annual Meeting, Washington, DC, October, 1982b.

Sprague, R.L., & Baxley, G.B. Drugs for behavior management. In: J. Wortis (ed.), Mental retardation, Vol. 10. New York: Brunner/Mazel, 1978.

Sternlicht, M., & Deutsch, M. Personality development and social behavior in the mentally retarded. Lexington, MA: D.C. Heath & Co., 1972.

Sutter, P., Mayeda, T., Call, T., Yanagi, G., & Yee, S. Comparison of successful and unsuccessful community placed mentally retarded persons. American Journal of Mental Deficiency, 1980, 85, 262–267.

Szymanski, L.S., & Tanguay, P.E. (eds.) Emotional disorders of mentally retarded persons. Baltimore: University Park Press, 1980.

Taylor, J. Habilitation. Education and Training of the Mentally Retarded, 1976, 7, 57–64.

Thormalen, P. A study of in-the-ward training of trainable mentally retarded children in a state institution: California Mental Health Research Monograph, No. 4. Sacramento: California State Department of Health, 1965.

Voeltz, L., & Evans, I. The assessment of behavioral interrelationships in child behavior therapy. Behavioral Assessment, 1982, 4, 131–165.

Voeltz, L., Evans, I., Derer, K., & Hanashiro, R. Targeting excess behavior for change: A clinical decision model for selecting priority goals in educational contexts. Unpublished manuscript, University of Minnesota, Department of Educational Psychology, Minneapolis, 1982.

Voeltz, L., Evans, I., Freedland, K., & Donellon, S. Teacher decision-making in the selection of educational programming priorities for severely handicapped children. Journal of Special Education, 1982, 16, 179–197.

Wahler, R.G., & Fox, J.J. Setting events in applied behavior analysis: Toward a conceptual and methodological expansion. Journal of Applied Behavior Analysis, 1981, 14, 327–338.

Weissman, M.M. The assessment of social adjustment: A review of techniques. Archives of General Psychiatry, 1975, 32, 357–365.

Williams, W., Friedl, M., & Vogelsberg, T. Training needs of adult developmental disabilities personnel. Career Development for Exceptional Individuals, 1980, 3, 53–60.

Windle, C. Prognosis of mental subnormals. American Journal of Mental Deficiency (monograph suppl.), 1962, 66.

Wolfensberger, W. The principle of normalization in human services. Toronto: National Institute on Mental Retardation, 1972.

Wysocki, T., Fuqua, W.R., Davis, V., & Breuning, S.E. Effects of thioridazine (Mellaril) on titrating delayed matching-to-sample performance of mentally retarded adults. American Journal of Mental Deficiency, 1981, 85, 539–547.

Zaharia, E., & Baumeister, A. Estimated position replacement costs for technician personnel in a state's public facilities. Mental Retardation, 1978, 16, 131–134.

Zentall, S.S. Optimal stimulation as a theoretical basis of hyperactivity. American Journal of Orthopsychiatry, 1975, 45, 549–563.

Zentall, S.S. Effects of environmental stimulation on behavior as a function of type of behavior disorders. Behavioral Disorders, 1979, 5, 19–29.

Chapter 5

# Early Education

## A Strategy for Producing a
## Less (Least) Restrictive
## Environment for Young
## Children with Severe Handicaps

*John E. Rynders and Darlene S. Stealey*

As recently as the mid-1900s, parents of a newborn child with a severe handicap were often advised to seek immediate institutional placement for their baby. That advice was often received with gratitude, since few services were available at that time to assist parents in raising their severely handicapped child at home. Around 1950, however, parents and professionals began to realize that many institutions were highly restrictive living environments with limited opportunities for development or social integration (see, for example, Blatt, 1973). Thereafter, the variety of services to help children with severe handicaps live successfully in the community increased rapidly. One of these services, early education, has been used widely because of its implied promise of maximizing the coping ca-pabilities of severely handicapped children, their parents and siblings, and community agency personnel, while minimizing the need for institutionalization.

This chapter evaluates how well the promise has been fulfilled by addressing two key aspects of the early education movement for children with severe handicaps: 1) the need for early education, and 2) the efficacy of early education programs. Because the deinstitutionalization movement has affected and will continue to affect the lives of severely handicapped persons more than mildly handicapped persons, the present chapter is restricted to early intervention efforts for severely handicapped children. A substantial literature exists regarding early intervention efforts for mildly handicapped and culturally disadvantaged in-

Writing of this paper was supported in part by Contract 300-82-0363, USOE, awarded to the University of Minnesota's Consortium Institute for the Education of Severely Handicapped Learners.

dividuals, much of which has been reviewed by Bronfenbrenner (1974) and Lazar and Darlington (1978).

## ESTABLISHING THE NEED FOR EARLY EDUCATION

Significant socioeducational events such as the deinstitutionalization movement, establishment of the normalization principle (Nirje, 1976), passage of Head Start legislation, and implementation of Public Law 94-142 have stimulated intense interest in early education for children with handicaps, creating a zeitgeist in which it can flourish. Although it is not possible at this time to make an ironclad case for the need for early education (in fact, positive results of early intervention studies provide the best source of evidence with which to make this case), an efficacy-related maxim appears viable for children with severe handicaps: the severely handicapped child, his or her parents, and other family members can derive substantial benefits from sound early education practices, particularly in terms of ensuring and/or improving the quality of early parent-child transactions. Over time, successful early transactions will have a multiplicative effect, creating accelerating opportunities for social integration and development that will have long-term positive consequences for the severely handicapped child, his or her family, and the community. The pages that follow cite evidence from the literature to buttress this maxim.

### Early Caregiver-Child Interactions

Many contemporary researchers in child development stress the theoretical and practical importance of early caregiver[1]-child interactions on the development of the child with handicaps. For example, Sameroff and Chandler (1975), in their transactional view of development, emphasize that caregiver behaviors can either maintain or dissipate the effects on development normally associated with various

disorders, although the process is extremely complex since neither the child nor the environment is constant, and the two sources of variability of outcome are interdependent. Norris (1956), cited in Carolan (1973), reinforces this point when he says of blind children: "we have found that blindness in and of itself is not the determining factor in the child's development. Rather, failure on the part of adults to know what to expect of a blind child or how to encourage his optimal development creates the problem" (p. 263).

Along similar lines, Schoggen and Schoggen (1981) emphasize that not only do caregivers affect the child, but the child also affects caregivers in the myriad of daily events (e.g., nursing, cuddling, attempts at social play), which interact to carry both mother and child as well as members of their social network forward (or backward) developmentally. This set of changing transactions across a number of social networks can be characterized as a trajectory phenomenon (i.e., a situation in which all members of the social network(s) are undergoing change themselves and are causing change in all of the other members). *Trajectory* refers to the developmental paths of the child and caregivers that are influenced continuously by environmental and organismic variables, behaviors, and their interaction. From a dyadic standpoint, Schoggen and Schoggen note that when the young child and his or her mother meet each other's transaction expectations, their individual as well as transactional development advances mutually in an accelerating positive trajectory. But when one member of the mother-child dyad does not meet expectations, a decelerating trajectory occurs, e.g., infants who resist cuddling tend to produce parents who leave their babies alone (Schaeffer & Emerson, 1964), and fussy babies tend to produce frustrated and distraught parents (Denenberg & Thoman, 1976).

When a child has severe handicaps, basic mothering transactions can be at risk almost from birth, as recounted for example, in Taft (1981):

---

[1]The terms *caregiver, mother,* and *parent* are used interchangeably throughout this paper.

The delivery had been complicated, and the child had an Apgar score of only 5 at one minute and 8 at five minutes. A few hours after birth, the child was examined by a pediatrician and thought to be normal.

The nurse gave the swaddled baby to the mother and left the room. The mother immediately unwrapped the baby. Looking pleased with what she saw, she laid the infant against her arm in order to begin breastfeeding. When placed in the supine position, the infant went into slight extension of the truck (probably a sign of cerebral irritability). The mother touched the baby's cheek, using the rooting reflex properly. But when the infant's head turned toward the nipple, this activated a definitely abnormal asymmetrical tonic neck reflex. The baby's arm on the chin side went into extension, as if he were "straight-arming" the mother. By now the mother was exasperated and the child, still hungry, was crying, which intensified the primitive reflexes. . . (p.78).

A number of studies have focused on the importance of early transactions between mothers and their children with Down syndrome. Jones (1977, 1980) sought to examine the nature of vocal transactions in mother-child pairs (in both nonhandicapped babies and babies with Down syndrome) whose developmental ages ranged from 8 months to 19 months. Jones found that babies with Down syndrome, despite being active participants in "turn-taking" communication with their mothers, appeared to be less responsive to or more dissociated from their mothers' behaviors. For example, their vocal behavior was more often relatively inconsiderate of the immediate vocal dialogue; they vocalized relatively longer or with repeated vocalizations within a short period of time; or they vocalized simultaneously with the mother, interrupting her "turn" in the dialogue. These asynchronous interactive behaviors imposed difficulties on the mother's attempts to engage her infant in a smooth-flowing, reciprocal transaction.

Spiker (1982) emphasizes the cumulative effects that asynchrony in the mother-child transaction may have, stressing that an absence in a handicapped child of behaviors thought to reinforce the parent may lead to a parental decrease in playful, enthusiastic stimulation activities. Indeed, according to Spiker, a handicapped child with a lower level and/or unusual pattern of responsiveness might, in some instances, actually contribute to his or her own further delay by helping to create a "deprived" environment. In these instances, one of the most important goals of early intervention should be to reorchestrate an asynchronous mother-child relationship into a synchronous one, from which a developmentally enhancing social network trajectory can emerge and flourish.

The need to accomplish this goal of improving caregiver-child interactions is emphasized when one considers that a substantial number of children who are sensorially impaired, physically handicapped, mentally retarded, severely underdeveloped, or have other handicapping conditions are abused and/or neglected children. After summarizing literature on child abuse, Friedrich and Boriskin (1978) suggested some strategies to prevent child abuse, including assessing mothers' attitudes and interactions with their children and educating and supporting those mothers who appear to be headed for a crisis. Thus, an important goal for early educators is to detect asynchronous caregiver-child transactions, helping the caregiver to change these to synchronous transaction patterns.

One way to approach this goal would be to ask if parents can gain specific insights into their child's handicap and, as a consequence, stimulate their child's development more fully. This was a crucial question in Fraiberg's studies with blind babies and their mothers (Adelson & Fraiberg, 1974; Fraiberg, 1971; Fraiberg, Smith, & Adelson, 1969). Fraiberg observed that parents who had been competent with their sighted children often failed to learn their blind baby's mode of communication. Since a blind baby cannot see someone smiling, Fraiberg advised parents to extend their efforts to talk with their child. When this advice was followed, blind babies began to smile in response to their parents at approximately the same age that sighted babies smiled at their parents.

Infants born prematurely and/or with low birth weights do not match the traditional conceptualization of severe handicap. Nevertheless, the risk of severe handicaps accompanying this condition is serious and, therefore, warrants attention. Moreover, the results of a few of these studies provide additional support for the need to focus on *both* the parents and the child *and* their transactions.

A hypothesis encountered frequently for the generally inferior development of infants born prematurely or with low birth weights is that the hospital intensive care nursery, although highly sophisticated in life-saving technology, is sometimes lacking in the kinds of stimulation (e.g., mothering transactions) provided typically to children who are born at full term and have a normal birth weight. To date, one of the best-designed studies of this hypothesis is that of Scarr-Salapatek and Williams (1973). These investigators assigned 30 consecutively born low-birth-weight infants, born to impoverished mothers (i.e., from the lowest socioeconomic (SES) group in Philadelphia), to either an experimental or control group in order to assess the effects of extra stimulation provided during the hospital stay plus maternal education and support throughout the baby's first year of life. Experimental group babies were talked to, patted, positioned to regard the nurses' faces during feeding, and given mobiles with birds to watch while in the nursery. For the year following discharge from the hospital, their mothers were visited weekly by a social worker who provided information regarding child care and selection of toys. Perhaps most interesting are the 1-year data that showed the experimental group babies had significantly higher (near-normal) scores on the Cattell Infant Intelligence Scale as compared to the control group babies.

Using a sample similar to that of the Scarr-Salapatek and Williams (1973) study, Powell (1974) assessed the effects of extra stimulation and maternal involvement on the development of premature black babies and on the behavior of their mothers. The "maternal" group of babies received contact with mothers during the hospital stay. The "handled" group of babies received extra handling in a nonregimented way for one or two 20-minute periods a day during the hospital stay by an adult other than the mother. The control group received normal hospital care, which excluded maternal contact but included some handling. Babies and their mothers were followed for 6 months. Comparison of the stimulated versus nonstimulated babies revealed significant differences at 4 months on the mental and motor scales of the Bayley Scales of Infant Development, all favoring the stimulated babies.

Unfortunately, attrition may be partially responsible for these differences, since the total number of children was reduced from 36 to 18 by the 6-month follow-up. (The number of children in the maternal contact group was reduced from 11 to 9 by the end of the study. The number of children in the other two groups was reduced from 25 to 9 in the same time period.) Interestingly, the factor of maternal involvement was associated with no significant differences on a later measure of mothers' maternal behavior and emotional attachment to their babies. The fact that Powell found no significant differences on later maternal behavior as a function of maternal involvement in the hospital should not be seen as reason to discourage mothers from being with their babies in the hospital. First, it should be remembered that Powell used only one measure of later maternal involvement. More important, only 4 of the 11 mothers who could have handled their babies did so to any great extent. The heterogeneity of this group may account for the lack of significant differences regarding later maternal behavior, a speculation congruent with Scarr-Salapatek and Williams's (1973) observation that their better-developed babies were played with more often.

Also congruent with Powell's results is Leib, Benfield, and Guidubaldi's (1980) finding that premature babies who received visual, tactile, kinesthetic, and auditory stimulation during their hospital stay scored significantly higher at 6 months on the mental and motor scales of the Bayley Scales of Infant Development than did control babies. Instrumentation may be operating as a threat to the internal validity of this study, however, since one of the authors administered the 6-month Bayley exams.

At least one study, that of Wallick and Thompson (1981), found that amount of maternal contact during the hospital stay following the birth of a baby was related to special class placement and grade retention. However, longitudinal prospective studies will be required to answer the vital question of the extent to which stimulation and maternal contact in the postpartum period influence later development.

This portion of the chapter has been concerned with establishing the need for early education for children with severe handicaps from the standpoint of emphasizing the importance of fostering successful caregiver-child transactions as early as possible. In concluding, it should be noted that the authors' general enthusiasm about early education should not be interpreted as unbridled advocacy for a developmental "quick fix" or a "now or never" critical periods hypothesis. To the contrary, as noted by Clarke and Clarke (1976), the significant malleability of the human development system is not confined solely to the first few years of life. Addressing this issue, Clarke and Clarke reinterpreted the results of some of the classic disadvantagement/deprivation studies, studies that purportedly showed the critical nature of certain deficits in early experience. Clarke and Clarke suggested instead that the unsatisfactory developmental outcome of many of the children was the result of a multi-deficited environment, one that was present not only in infancy but that continued throughout childhood. Thus, although it may not be possible to prove the need for early intervention in the studies reviewed so far, the consequences of not intervening to maximize developmental attributes and to minimize primary and secondary disabling conditions serve as a signal to proceed carefully yet vigorously with early education services. At the same time, however, parents, educators, and legislators increasingly require evidence that early intervention programs are reasonably efficacious for young children with severe handicaps. It is to this issue that we now turn.

## ESTABLISHING THE EFFICACY OF EARLY EDUCATION

Early education programs for children with serious handicaps have been in operation for more than 20 years. Therefore, it should be possible today to provide a definitive answer to the question, "Is early education for children with severe handicaps really effective?" However, the answer to this question is affirmative or negative (or equivocal) depending on one's view of what constitutes efficacy. Therefore, it is important in these times of substantial reductions in educational and social services support to examine studies of program effects, in terms of their methodological sophistication, in as stringent a fashion as possible. Results that have withstood such a review should provide a strengthened knowledge base from which to negotiate for continued and improved services.

A highly useful framework in which to judge efficacy from a methodological standpoint is provided by Dunst and Rheingrover (1981), who contend that of all considerations in evaluating the outcomes of early education programs, control of threats to internal validity is most essential. As they point out, without adequate control of threats to internal validity, the results of an intervention study become for all intents and purposes uninterpretable. An internally valid intervention study permits extraneous variables to be eliminated as primary causative factors of outcomes, permitting, as a result, the interpretation that the intervention is the primary factor responsible for outcomes.

Dunst and Rheingrover (1981) conducted an extensive review of the early education literature, identifying 49 studies involving children with serious organic handicaps. They then scrutinized these studies for threats to internal validity in several sequenced steps. To begin the process, they developed a checklist based on a set of threats to internal validity identified by Campbell and Stanley (1966):

1. *History,* the specific events occurring between the first and second measurement in addition to the experimental variable.
2. *Maturation,* processes within the respondents operating as a function of the passage of time per se (not specific to the particular events), including growing older, growing hungrier, growing more tired, and the like.
3. *Testing,* the effects of taking a test upon the scores of a second testing.
4. *Instrumentation,* in which changes in the

calibration of a measuring instrument or changes in the observers or scorers used may produce changes in the obtained measurements.

5. *Statistical regression*, operating where groups have been selected on the basis of their extreme scores.

6. Biases resulting in differential *selection* of respondents for the comparison groups.

7. *Experimental mortality*, or differential loss of respondents from the comparison groups.

8. *Selection-maturation interaction, etc.*, which in certain of the multiple-group quasi-experimental designs. . . is confounded with, i.e., might be mistaken for, the effect of the experimental variable. (P. 5).

Next, Dunst and Rheingrover (1981) looked at the inherent strengths and weaknesses of various experimental designs, examining each type for possible internal validity flaws as follows:

*Pre-experimental designs* (e.g., a one-group pretest-posttest design, one in which there is no control group or controlling condition and in which *history* and *maturation* are major likely rival explanations for the reported outcomes) have been used fairly often, especially in some of the older studies. A variation of this design is one in which an experimental group outcome is compared, on a posttest-only basis, with an outcome from a group that did not start at the same time and that might have been chosen adventitiously. In nearly all of these studies, *history* is a plausible rival explanation for reported outcome, and *selection* is a particular threat to internal validity. According to Dunst and Rheingrover, since pre-experimental designs do not permit experimental control over important extraneous variables, the use of these designs yields fundamentally uninterpretable results. Therefore, in this chapter's review of early education, efficacy studies with pre-experimental designs have been excluded. However, it should be mentioned that Odom and Fewell (1983) discuss an evaluation procedure that is useful with pre-experimental designs, in which predictions of developmental performance at a posttest data point are made from pretest data. The discrepancy between predicted and actual outcome can be attributed

to the program, if one has documented that development has been linear.

*Quasi-experimental designs using control groups* have been employed frequently in early education studies. The reason that a study design earns the label *quasi* is because groups (sometimes intact groups) rather than individuals are assigned to intervention and nonintervention conditions. Designs may involve pretest-posttest nonequivalent control groups, posttest-only nonequivalent control groups, and variations thereof. Selection is always a possible threat to internal validity in nonequivalent control group designs, since subjects are not randomly assigned to experimental and control conditions. Therefore, the possibility of preexisting differences between the groups contributing to the observed effects cannot be eliminated. This possibility is lessened, however, when it can be demonstrated that the two groups are in fact more similar than dissimilar.

*Quasi-experimental time-series designs* often take one of two forms. The first is an interrupted time-series design, where two groups of subjects are tested repeatedly on several occasions and the intervention is introduced at different points in the time series for each group (this design can afford good control for threats to internal validity). A second form involves using the intervention population as its own control. Most of these studies employ a variation of an across-behavior multiple baseline design (Hersen & Barlow, 1976), in which changes in specific areas of intervention are compared against changes in nonintervention areas. In this type of design the strongest rival explanation for the effects reported is that of regression. Since interventions occur typically in areas in which subjects are most delayed, subsequent testing will amost surely show the average gains to be greater in the intervention areas independent of the treatments, per se. Nevertheless, these designs can be powerful when employed properly.

*True experimental designs* involve a randomization process in assignment of participants to treatment conditions. Studies employing randomization procedures almost always present the fewest threats to interval validity and are recommended by Dunst and Rheingrover (1981) as the design of choice for early intervention programs.

In their review of 49 studies, Dunst and Rheingrover (1981) applied the following general inclusion-exclusion criteria: 1) intervention was begun prior to 3 years of age (the present authors included children up to age 5), 2) the majority of children in the study had one or more serious organic impairment(s), and 3) quantifiable evaluation data were collected. The 49 studies were then divided into the various types of experimental designs and were rated by both Dunst and Rheingrover, working independently, on the basis of whether the outcomes of each study could withstand threats to internal validity.

The availability of the ratings of the 49 studies and the categorization of each according to type of design afford an opportunity to examine efficacy evidence in a reasonably stringent manner. Hence, as a first step, all of the studies from the Dunst and Rheingrover review that were categorized as pre-experimental designs (24 of the 49 studies), were excluded from consideration. Next, for the purposes of examining efficacy studies involving children with Down syndrome—the largest subgroup of studies— any of the remaining 25 studies that were rated by Dunst and Rheingrover in their review with a "minus" in *any* of the eight threats to internal validity categories were excluded. This initial exclusion process left 9 studies from their review involving young children with Down syndrome in which: 1) the designs had no "minus" ratings in terms of internal validity (although many of these had one or more "plus or minus" ratings because of uncertainty in being able to weigh the consequences of a threat adequately or because of lack of information on which to judge threat adequately); and 2) the designs were of a quasi-experimental or true experimental stature. After a careful reading of 7 of 8 of these studies (one was not available), we excluded 4 studies because of threats to internal validity that each of us saw independently as justifying definite "minus" ratings. Thus, 3 studies with a positive rating

and that involved children with Down syndrome emerged from the Dunst and Rheingrover original set of 9. These were: Piper and Pless (1980), Bidder, Bryant, and Gray (1975), and Aronson and Fallstrom (1977). To this group, 5 studies involving children with Down syndrome were added from the authors' own extensive search of the literature. These 5 studies were judged as meeting all of the standards for design adequacy and reasonable protection from threats to internal validity as suggested by Dunst and Rheingrover. The studies were: MacDonald, Blott, Gordon, Spiegel, and Hartmann (1974), Rynders and Horrobin (1980), Jeffree, Wheldall, and Mittler (1973), Harris (1981), and Pothier, Morrison, and Gorman (1974).

All but one of the eight studies (Harris, 1981) have been described and critiqued extensively by Pueschel and Rynders (1982). Thus, only a brief synopsis of these eight studies is provided here. At the outset it should be noted that the majority of these studies do not report data on chromosomal karyotype that can confirm the presence and the form of Down syndrome genotypically. (This problem is returned to at the end of this chapter.)

## Efficacy Findings Involving Children with Down Syndrome

The first five studies presented here emphasize language stimulation. Bidder et al. (1975) taught mothers of children with Down syndrome to use behavior modification techniques to promote their children's verbal expression and comprehension, self-care skills, and motor abilities. Sixteen mothers participated with their Down syndrome children, aged 12 months to 33 months, for a 6-month period. One-half of the mothers (the treatment group) received extensive training in the use of behavior modification techniques and in recordkeeping, while the other half (the control group) only received attention from a health visitor and a general practitioner. After 6 months of treatment, experimental children showed a significant positive difference in language development but not in motor development.

Another study, that by MacDonald et al. (1974), which was conducted at Ohio State's Nisonger Center, has shown positive results in the parent-child language area. MacDonald and colleagues prepared parents of home-reared children with Down syndrome to be language trainers. The subjects were six children, 3 years to 5 years of age. Three children served as experimental subjects, and three served as controls. The major objective of the program was to increase utterance length and grammatical complexity by preparing parents to foster their child's immediate generalization of language changes from imitation to parallel conversation and play activities, and by helping them to effect immediate transfer of training. On the basis of experimental subjects' baseline performance on the Environmental Language Inventory, the "action + object" (e.g., throw ball ) and "X + locative" (e.g., ball there) rules were selected as the major classes for training.

After baseline measurement each language trainer and mother met to interpret the child's baseline in terms of language behaviors and to introduce mothers to the training procedures. A single session consisted of training the "action + object" and "X + locative" rules in imitation, conversation, and play. Once the three procedures had been introduced in separate training sessions, they were combined into a single training model for the duration of the program.

Results of the MacDonald et al. (1974) study revealed statistically significant increases in utterance length and grammatical complexity in imitation and conversation for all experimental subjects when compared with control subjects. Furthermore, an epilogue revealed successful replication of the program with the original control group subjects.

Project EDGE[2] (Rynders & Horrobin, 1980), a family-centered study begun in 1968, was conducted in the homes of infants and toddlers with Down syndrome. A preschool was set up for children as they attained 30 months of age. The chief goal of EDGE was to promote children's communication development through positive, early parent-child (usually mother-child) structured play lessons, making features of the child's environment (e.g., playthings) more engaging, more responsive to the child's activity, and generally more pleasurable for mother and child to use together.

Lessons provided enough structure to help mothers to be goal-directed but allowed considerable freedom so that they could use the materials to suit their style preferences. Materials were chosen for their simplicity, play possibilities, and distinguishing characteristics. Some made a sound, such as a tambourine and a set of animal sound boxes; some fit together in sequence, such as Kitten in a Keg; crayons enabled self-expression through drawing; and a doll and a brush, comb, and mirror set had self-care development value.

Concepts to be developed through activities were introduced so as to compliment Piaget's theory of cognitive development, particularly as interpreted by Sonquist and Kamii (1968). These authors described a symbol-learning framework designed to facilitate the transition from sensorimotor intelligence to conceptual intelligence, building a solid foundation for the child's long-term development. They hypothesized that early educators need to work to effect this transition through two dimensions: symbolization and mastery of elementary types of relations. The former helps a child to move from concrete sensorimotor intelligence to representational intelligence, and the latter enables the child to coordinate the relations among things and events. It was hypothesized that there would be significant differences in the language learning (i.e., concept utilization and/or expressive language scores) of experimental and control children.

An experimental-control research design was employed to compare the performance of

[2]EDGE stands for Expanding Developmental Growth through Education, a former project of the Research, Development and Demonstration Center for the Education of Handicapped Children at the University of Minnesota, funded under Grant No. OEG-0-9-332;89-4533-032.

children in the EDGE program with that of children not in the program. At the end of the 5-year program, there were 35 children enrolled (17 experimental and 18 control). Of the 17 experimental children, 4 were female, and 13 were male; in the group of 18 control children, 8 were female and 10 were male. All had the standard trisomy form of Down syndrome. At the completion of the program, an experimentally blind examiner administered the Boehm Test of Basic Concepts; a language-sampling instrument; a modified version of the Bruininks-Oseretsky Test of Motor Proficiency; and the Stanford-Binet Intelligence Test to children in both groups.

Statistical analyses revealed no significant group differences in specified target variables (concept utilization and/or expressive language), although there were significant differences in IQ favoring the experimental group when adjusted for sex differences.

These results were interpreted as providing general support for early education for young children with Down syndrome, as well as for the EDGE project in many respects, but not for the use of the curriculum materials that were developed.

Jeffree et al. (1973) showed that early two-word utterances of the pivot-open type (e.g., "all gone dinner," where "all gone" is the pivot and "dinner" is an open-class word) could be taught to two preschool children with Down syndrome who were at the one-word utterance stage. After both children had been taught a list of 10 nouns and 1 participle, one child, designated as the experimental subject, was trained to structure pivot-open utterances, with 5 of the 10 nouns ("ball," "bus," "baby," "pin," "car") plus the pivot ("gone") in a play situation. The play situation took the form of directed play using the Pivot-Open Practice Instrument (POP-IN), which consisted of a large posting box into which model objects ("car," "baby," etc.) were dropped and then made to reappear when the child made an appropriate pivot-open utterance. The control subject was given an equal number of nondirective play sessions in which only single-word models and no models

of pivot-open utterances were provided and in which "gone" was taught through modeling.

After 13 sessions of initial training of 15 minutes' duration, the two children were naming and identifying the 10 target words spontaneously and imitating the word "gone." Over a period of 30 sessions the experimental subject progressed from a baseline where he was using no pivot-open utterances to a final stage where he was using appropriate spontaneous utterances. In the control condition, the number of appropriate, spontaneous, single-word utterances rose dramatically to an average of 60 per session, but no pivot-open utterances were elicited. In contrast, the experimental subject structured 90% of the token words into two-word utterances, of which more than 65% were both spontaneous and appropriate. Regarding generalization, in the course of 10 sessions, the experimental subject generated 36 sentences spontaneously for which no model had been given. Following this stage of the experiment, the control subject was successfully taught the spontaneous use of pivot-open construction and its generalization to new words. The Jeffree et al. (1973) results illustrate the value of contingent reinforcement on communication development.

Pothier et al. (1974) investigated the effects of a language-oriented preschool program involving two sequences of language training: reinforcement for imitating a verbal model and reinforcement for a correct response to a verbal request without a model. Sixty percent of the subjects, assigned on a modified randomization basis to either an experimental or control group, were preschool children with Down syndrome.

The language development program took the form of a series of activities involving both receptive and expressive language skills. The first activity established an individual base rate for verbal requests (e.g. "Bounce the ball on the floor,"), then progressed to trials of play-type activities offered with a demonstration of the activity and requiring pairing with a verbal cue, and ended with a verbal cue-only trial.

Results showed that experimental subjects improved significantly, as compared with control subjects, in picture vocabulary items found in the Bayley Scales of Infant Development and the Stanford-Binet Intelligence Test. Differences in receptive language improvement were not significant statistically between groups, although both groups' receptive vocabularies grew dramatically. Findings of the study are intriguing, considering that the training was designed to promote receptive language, yet significant differences turned up in the expressive area only.

Aronson and Fallstrom (1977) emphasized a whole gamut of abilities termed "mental training" in their study. Subjects were 16 children (8 experimentals, 8 controls—4 boys, 12 girls) with Down syndrome between the ages of 21 months and 60 months, living in a small nursing home in Sweden. None of the children had ever lived in his or her own home, and all were between four months and 10 months of age when they first came to the facility. The 16 children whose developmental quotients were, on the average, nearly identical were divided into a training group and a control group, both of which were matched for age and sex.

In order to check the effect of training, children were tested on five occasions with the Griffiths' Mental Development Scales, 0–8 Years. The training period lasted nearly 18 months, and both groups were tested every 6 months. Twelve months after the training had been completed a follow-up testing was done.

Each child in the training group received training, based on developmental norms for nonhandicapped children, twice a week for a period of between 15 minutes to 1 hour, depending on the child's perceived motivation and/or capacity. When children showed little or no developmental progress over a long period, different types of sensorimotor training often had a salutary effect. However, in spite of intensive training, several children reached plateaus in their development. In these cases more emphasis was given to training emotional and social functions in order to give the children a better chance of adjusting to daily life.

Comparing the results from the first and fourth tests for the two groups, trained children showed a statistically greater increase in men-

tal age than those in the control group. The average increase in mental age over the period of almost 18 months was 10.5 months for the trained group and 3.5 months for the controls.

A follow-up study was done 1 year after the training had been completed in order to find out whether the mental training had a long-term effect. No statistically significant differences between the two groups were found in the results of the total test. However, individual differences in the expected direction were found between the trained and the control children on the subscales, especially for speech, and eye-hand coordination. Because of the broad-gauge nature of this intervention, it is unfortunate that formative evaluation data (e.g., teacher reactions to components) were not collected to help identify which elements were most potent.

Harris (1981) examined the effects of a neurodevelopmental treatment approach to physical therapy on minimizing the expected decline in motor and mental development in infants with Down syndrome. Twenty infants with Down syndrome participated (11 females, 9 males), ranging in age from 2.7 months to 21.5 months at the time of pretesting. Eighteen of the infants were enrolled in the Down's Syndrome Infant Learning Program at the Experimental Education Unit at the University of Washington, Seattle. The other two were also from the Down's Syndrome Infant Learning Program and were enrolled in other infant intervention programs, with similar goals and curricula.

Two possible candidates were excluded from the study because cardiac surgery was scheduled during the period of the study. However, at least two of the infants included in the study were known to have serious heart defects but were not excluded because their physicians' referrals did not contraindicate physical therapy. All of the infants had clear signs of varying degrees of hypotonia. Infants were tested before and after the treatment period by means of the Bayley Scales of Infant Development and the Peabody Developmental Motor Scales.

After pretesting and before random assignment to groups, four individual therapy objectives were written for each infant in the study. The objectives were based on the results of individual assessments and were developed with the assumption that each infant would receive neurodevelopmental therapy for a 9-week period. For example, a set of objectives for one infant was:

1. *S* will maintain prone on elbows with head at 45° for 15 seconds.
2. *S* will bring head past midline when tipped laterally to left and to right, two out of three times in each direction.
3. *S* will sit propped with weight on hands for 10 seconds.
4. *S* will demonstrate forward protective extension when rolled forward on therapy ball three out of four times.

During posttesting, an independent therapist evaluated the objectives for each infant, scoring each objective as a pass or fail. Before random assignment to the experimental or control groups, infants were grouped according to age, sex, and pretest Peabody scores, enabling equivalent groups.

All treatment took place at home, except for one infant who received therapy at the Experimental Education Unit. Therapy sessions, each lasting about 40 minutes, were carried out three times weekly for each infant in the experimental group over a 9-week period. Infants in the control group received no additional intervention, other than their weekly involvement in infant learning programs.

Parents were encouraged to observe the therapy sessions but were not instructed in specific techniques, since it was felt that the amount of time the parents would spend on the techniques would vary so greatly that a confounding variable might be introduced. However, if specific advice was requested by parents it was given promptly.

There were three common goals for all the infants receiving therapy: facilitation of normal postural tone; facilitation of righting, equilibrium, and protective responses; and enhancement of normal patterns of movement. Neurodevelopmental techniques used to increase postural tone included joint approxima-

tion through the spine and extremities, bouncing, tapping, and resistance to movement (Semans, 1967). Righting, equilibrium, and protective responses were facilitated in prone and supine positions for the younger infants and in quadruped, sitting, and standing positions for the older ones. Developmentally appropriate movement patterns were shaped and facilitated to increase postural tone and included pivoting in prone, rolling prone to supine and supine to prone, prone progression on abdomen, reciprocal creeping, and moving into and out of the sitting position using trunk rotation.

After the intervention phase of the study, all 20 infants were tested again on the Bayley and Peabody scales. The therapist who did the pretest assessments also did the posttesting and evaluated the attainment of the four individual treatment objectives written for each infant.

Results showed that there was no statistically significant difference between the two groups in either motor or mental performance. In fact, the control group slightly exceeded the treatment group in each of the three dependent measures. However, on the fourth dependent measure, attainment of four individual therapy objectives written for each infant, there were significant differences favoring the experimental group. Harris concluded that this fourth outcome lends substantial support to the main hypothesis. Harris also noted several limitations of her findings, namely, the small sample size and the incongruence of the results of the three dependent measures.

Not all early intervention programs for children with Down syndrome have produced positive treatment outcomes. Piper and Pless (1980) enrolled 37 infants with Down syndrome, all under 24 months of age, in a project in which one group ($n = 21$) received educational treatment and one group ($n = 16$) served as a control. The intervention consisted of center-based biweekly sessions of 1 hour's duration focused on the stimulation of gross motor and speech development. In addition, a set of written instructions was given to parents to follow at home. Results indicated that there were no significant differences between treatment and control group children on the Griffiths' Mental Development Scales after 6 months of intervention.

These findings should be viewed with caution since the intervention period lasted only 6 months, an extremely brief time frame in which to judge the efficacy of an intervention. Furthermore, information about the intervention is scanty and suggests that gross motor activity and general speech stimulation were offered, which might not have had the same impact on the Griffiths' Scales as a more focused, cognitively based program. In addition, center-based sessions were only 1 hour long and were offered biweekly, and the experimental children were stimulated and assessed in Montreal in winter (controls were assessed in summer), so that respiratory and general health problems associated with that season may have diminished children's performance. (Piper and Pless acknowledge most of these problems themselves.) Nevertheless, despite the practical and methodological limitations of this study, the finding of no treatment benefit cannot be brushed aside. In fact, it is rather surprising that the experimental group did not show the fairly common "initial intervention spurt," a spurt that often fades when intervention does not continue over a long period of time.

## Efficacy Findings Involving Children with Severe Handicaps Who Do Not Have Down Syndrome

Each of the studies on the effects of early intervention programs with non–Down syndrome, severely handicapped children, which are reviewed below, met all of the criteria outlined in the previous section. However, in this second body of research, studies have been included if their only "minus" threat to internal validity was "statistical regression." This reduction in inclusion stringency was made primarily because if inclusion criteria as stringent as those applied to studies of programs for children with Down syndrome were used, there would have

been fewer than a handful of studies to review. The continuing requirement that study designs needed to be either true experimental or quasi-experimental, not pre-experimental, lessens (but of course does not eliminate) the importance of this threat to internal validity, but the possibility of a regression artifact should be kept in mind.

Applying these inclusion/exclusion criteria yielded 9 studies from the Dunst and Rheingrover (1981) review. To this set were added 10 studies that were not included in the Dunst and Rheingrover review but that met our criteria, as judged independently by us.[3] These 19 studies were grouped either on the basis of types of children included or the goal of the intervention. Thus, the first eight studies are concerned with children representing a heterogeneous category, developmental delay; the next four studies deal with children with cerebral palsy; following these are three studies dealing with children for whom language is traditionally the greatest area of concern; the final group of four studies is concerned with the impact of group structure as an intervention vehicle for children with severe handicaps.

***Intervention with Children with Severe Developmental Disability***  Brassell and Dunst (1975a, 1975b, 1978), Sandow and Clark (1978), Sandow, Clarke, Cox, and Steward (1981), Revill and Blunden (1979), and Clements, Evans, Jones, Osborne, and Upton (1982) were all interested in the efficacy of having parents present activities designed to enhance particular aspects of their children's cognitive or language development.

Brassell and Dunst (1975a, 1975b) evaluated the effectiveness with which parents could stimulate cognitive changes in their handicapped infants within the context of an ongoing stimulation program. One study involved all infants (6 male, 4 female) who had been observed during a 3- to 4-month baseline and then exposed to cognitive stimulation for the same length of time. Four of the infants had Down syndrome, three had arrested hydro-

---

[3]We regret that we were unable to obtain copies of two studies by Dunst (1974a, 1974b), both of which were judged by Dunst and Rheingrover to be representative of quasi-experimental designs.

cephaly (one of these also had spastic hemi-plegia), and one had cerebral palsy. The mean age of children at the start of baseline was 21 months, while mean mental and psychomotor age equivalents based on the Bayley Scales of Infant Development were 9.7 months and 8.2 months, respectively. Assessment in Infancy: Ordinal Scales of Psychological Development were administered to the infants at program entry and after each of two 3- to 4- month inter-vals. Intervention activities stressed areas of slowest progress and incorporated areas devel-oping most normally. The average number of cognitive intervention programs implemented for each infant was 2 from the first to the sec-ond testing, and 2.6 from the second to the third testing. Although different activities were administered during the two time periods, par-ents tended to continue the activities from the first period. Using a variation of the multiple baseline design, Brassell and Dunst found sta-tistically significant increases in the mean score between the first and second testing times and between the second and third testing times for the areas of intervention, but no significant difference in mean score between the first and second times for the nonintervention area.

Included in a second study were 36 infants (16 females, 20 males) in an intervention pro-gram who had been evaluated at least twice with the Bayley scales. Cognitive, motor, lan-guage, and behavioral intervention were pro-vided by parents in the home. Mental-age equivalents derived from the Bayley scales were used to calculate rate of development pri-or to intervention (base rate) and after a mini-mum of 3 months of intervention (current rate). The mean time period for the base rate encom-passed 19.5 months and for the current rate, 7.5 months. The difference in rate (current rate minus base rate) was the criterion measure of intervention effectiveness. Sixty-one percent of the infants demonstrated at least some in-crease in developmental rate after intervention began.

Brassell and Dunst related rate change to seven child and family variables, in post hoc analyses. ''Parental'' responsiveness (e.g., spontaneous vocalization to or praise of the child) was the variable most clearly related to developmental rate increase.

In these studies, the effect of instrumenta-tion on internal validity is uncertain because it is not clear if the experimenters did the evalua-tions. Testing and statistical regression effects are probably present because evaluation and intervention content came from the same source, and the areas of intervention were those in which children's performance was most delayed.

The development of one particular cognitive concept, object permanence, was the target of another intervention effort by Brassell and Dunst (1978). In this study, concern centered on whether the concept of object permanence could be enhanced within a large-scale, home-based intervention program for handicapped children. The sample of children included 52 males and 39 females. Approximately 50% of all the children were moderately to profoundly retarded, and 35% of the children evidenced moderate to severe motor dysfunction. The children's mean age at program entry was 21 months. The 24 children who received the in-tervention were chosen because their develop-ment of object permanence appeared more de-layed than that of the 67 children designated as controls. Scale I (The Development of Visual Pursuit and the Permanence of Objects) of As-sessment in Infancy: Ordinal Scales of Psycho-logical Development was administered as the pre- and posttest measure by a group of special education teachers. Results of the pretest guided the formulation of intervention ac-tivities designed to enhance the object concept. Home trainers spent 1–1½ hours per week demonstrating activities and monitoring each child's progress. Parents were asked to engage their children in the intervention activities on a daily basis through play and by utilizing mate-rials found commonly in the home. Although there was not a significant difference between the pretest scores of the two groups of children, a significant difference favoring the experi-mental group was found between posttest scores. Thus, the authors concluded that the development of the object concept in handi-capped children appears amenable to training by parents in a home setting once activities have been demonstrated by a home trainer.

Although this study is in some respects a more sophisticated design than is found in Brassell and Dunst's earlier studies (1975a, 1975b), some of the same questions regarding the study's internal validity can be raised. Whenever children are pretested on specific tasks, taught those tasks, and then evaluated on the basis of performance on those same tasks, there is a possibility that testing has compromised the study's internal validity. However, Brassell and Dunst (1978) contend that because toys found in the individual homes were used in a rather informal context for training, while a prespecified set of materials were used in a structured context for testing, this threat to internal validity is minimized.

To bolster the strength of their argument, Brassell and Dunst could have observed whether the children were able to solve problems spontaneously in a free play setting reflecting the different stages of object construct, thereby corroborating their opinion that the significant differences found on posttest reflected genuine intervention effects, not simply testing effects. Because Brassell and Dunst failed to clarify whether the examiners were aware of the goals of the intervention and of group membership of the children, one cannot totally disregard instrumentation as a threat to the internal validity of this study.

Regression poses another potential threat to their study's internal validity, since children were designated for intervention based on having lower pretest scores than the children who served as controls. However, the fact that the difference in the pretest scores of the two groups was not statistically significant diminishes the likelihood of a selection bias affecting the results. Taken together, the three Brassell and Dunst studies reveal that parents can be trained to effectively provide Piagetian-type stimulation to enhance their children's cognitive development.

A study by Revill and Blunden (1979) also examined the efficacy of parent-centered intervention but included a more comprehensive set of behaviors for possible intervention. Using the Portage Curriculum to develop a home-based early intervention program for mentally retarded children, a home adviser visited parents and children each week, charting baseline performance of skills selected from a behavior checklist, helping parents choose several behaviors as targets for the next week's teaching, and modeling and explaining teaching techniques for mastery.

Children in this study ranged in age from 8 months to 4 years when the project began and had initial overall scores on the Griffiths' Mental Developmental Scales ranging from 8 to 89. A time-series design, with subjects as their own controls, was used to evaluate the number and rate of Portage checklist skills acquired.

Collection of baseline measures using the Portage Checklist began with all 19 eligible children at the same time. Home intervention commenced for 9 children and their parents (Group A) following a 2-month baseline and for the other 10 families (Group B) following a 4-month baseline. Intervention was provided for the two groups for 6 or 4 months, respectively. Measures included baseline and post-baseline data collected weekly by the home adviser on each skill taught, daily recordings by the parents of the child's performance on the skills being taught, monthly evaluations of each child using the Portage checklist, and bi-monthly evaluations of each child using the Griffiths' scale.

Ninety-two percent of the 150 tasks established as objectives for the children in Group A and 84.6% of the 156 tasks established as objectives for the children in Group B were learned to criterion, over 67% of these within one week. On the average, the mean number of Portage checklist skills gained per month was considerably greater during intervention than during the baseline period. Interestingly, many more skills were mastered per month than were taught directly. In addition, children gained a greater mean number of points per 2-month period on the test of mental development during the intervention period than during the baseline period.

Because the Portage Curriculum Guide was the source of teaching objectives as well as the basis of evaluation, one cannot disregard a concern that testing is responsible for part of the increase in skills mastered. However, if mere repeated exposure to the test items affected subsequent performance on the test, this effect should be present during the extended baseline. The time-series design allows one to argue against testing having significant effects on the results. In fact, the data obtained by evaluating the checklist skills taught as well as those not taught allow Revill and Blunden (1979) to submit that they were not simply "teaching to the test" to produce changes in the children. Rather, the fact that many more behaviors not taught were mastered than behaviors taught suggests that the general developmental status of the children was being affected. However, one cannot contend that these specific intervention activities were totally responsible for the general improvements in development; that is, had the skills taught been taken from the untaught pool, the same improvements might have been seen. It is also possible that any extra adult attention of a generally nurturing variety might have produced similar results.

Adult nurturing attention was the explanation offered by Clements et al. (1982) to account for the lack of significant differences in their study of parents as the agents of intervention. The intervention program they developed was based on the Portage model and stressed content based on normal child language development and methods of operant technology. The experimental comparison relevant to the present chapter involved six children in the experimental group (with a mean age of 14.25 months) and five in the control group (with a mean age of 6.5 months). Pretesting revealed no significant differences in IQ between the groups. Experimental children were recruited from a waiting list for a home-teaching service in which the control children were already enrolled, and the former were visited once a week for 15 months. Preschool children in the experimental group mastered an average of 58, or roughly one-third, of the skills taught and about 76 nontargeted skills. Comparison of the five subscale scores of the Griffiths' scales (pre- and posttest scores) failed to reveal significantly greater improvement in the experimental children than in control children, although both groups improved over time. However, rather than pronouncing the intervention program ineffective, Clements et al. (1982) suggest that it may be effective—but no more effective than any general effort—at stimulation.

We find the results of this study difficult to interpret for a number of reasons. First, the fact that only one subscale of the Griffiths' scales pertains directly to the intervention activities limits their usefulness as an effective evaluation measure. A more fruitful approach might have been to collect pre- and posttest data, using the checklist of skills with both groups of children, and then to analyze the differences in skills acquired. Parenthetically, it seems likely that the control group, in its home-based intervention program, was receiving stimulation in all five areas of the Griffiths' scales, while the experimental group was stimulated in only one of those areas, creating a possible advantage for the control group.

Second, considering the importance of the age span from 6 months to 14 months in terms of linguistic changes in children, the large disparity in chronological age found between the two groups of children raises the possibility of maturation as a threat to the internal validity of the study. In this case, the age bias would favor the performance of the older experimental children on the Griffiths' scales. A selection bias may also be operating in this study, since the children were not assigned on a random basis and there is at least one variable, preschool attendance, on which there were pre-experimental differences. Moreover, the fact that the older, experimental children were on a waiting list for services that were already being received by the younger control children suggests that the older children were being passed by for services either because they were not in extreme need or because they were so handicapped or difficult to handle that the providers of the service would rather not enroll them.

Setting aside concerns about methodology in the Clements et al. (1982) study, it is important *not* to interpret the nonsignificant results as though a treatment were compared to a non-treatment condition. After all, the control group was receiving home-based intervention. Moreover, because the purpose of the study seemed to be to evaluate a particular basis of curriculum (i.e., normal development) and a particular methodology (i.e., behavior modification), it would have been helpful to provide a detailed description of those elements and to delineate how they overlapped and differed with activities provided to control children.

Participants in a study described by Sandow and Clark (1978) and by Sandow et al. (1981) were 32 mothers, representing the full range of socioeconomic classes, and their severely handicapped preschool children. Children in the study averaged 2½ years of age at the beginning of the 3-year intervention program and represented a variety of diagnoses including Down syndrome and severe cerebral palsy. The 32 mother-child pairs were divided into two groups, which were matched on IQ, social class, and diagnosis. The mean IQs of the two groups of children were 44.5 and 42.5.

One group of 16 mother-child pairs was visited biweekly for 2 to 3 hours, while the other group was visited bimonthly for 2 to 3 hours. A matched group of 15 mother-child pairs was formed in another city to serve as a comparison group. Mothers in the intervention groups, with the aid of an experimenter, designed intervention programs for their children which they then employed. Children's progress was evaluated annually using the Cattell Infant Intelligence Scale, the Vineland Social Maturity Scale, and supplemental criterion-referenced tests.

In terms of changes in children's IQs, although the group visited biweekly made greater progress after 1 year than the group visited bimonthly, the group visited biweekly decelerated in progress in the second year, while the group visited bimonthly accelerated in the second year. By the end of the third year there were no significant differences among the two experimental and one control groups. Whether instrumentation might have affected the results of the study is problematic to determine because one author is mentioned as the initial assessor of the experimental children, a second

author is credited with their subsequent assessments, and a third author is mentioned as the assessor of the contrast group (Sandow et al., 1981, p. 136). Selection also cannot be ruled out as influencing the results, since the method of assigning subjects to groups was not described clearly.

The last study in this category utilized center-based rather than home-based, intervention. Barerra, Routh, Parr, Johnson, Arendshorst, Goolsby, and Schroeder (1976) evaluated the effectiveness of individually tailored intervention programs for children with biologically linked handicaps including congenital blindness, encephalopathy, microcephaly, and severe hypotonia. The 10 children in this study included 6 males and 4 females between the ages of 13 months and 48 months.

Prior to intervention, each child was evaluated using the Memphis Comprehensive Developmental Scale to assess the areas of gross motor, fine motor, language, perceptual-cognitive, and personal-social development. Intervention activities were planned for each child's area of greatest need plus two of the other four areas chosen randomly. Thus each child served as his or her own control. Seven children participated in the minimum number of 15 intervention sessions necessary to qualify for reevaluation. It was hypothesized that developmental progress would be greater in the randomly chosen treatment areas than in the untreated control areas. At the end of the study, which lasted 2 to 3 months, the seven children had progressed an average of 6.43 months in the area of greatest need, 2.43 months in the areas selected randomly for treatment, and 1.68 months in the control areas. The difference between growth in the randomly selected and control areas, although it occurred in the direction predicted, was not statistically significant; but progress in the area of greatest need was significantly greater than progress in either of the other two areas.

Barerra et al. (1976) discuss the difficulty of interpreting the improvement in the area of greatest need in terms of possible regression artifacts. However, test-retest scores on the

Memphis scale were found not to be significantly different, suggesting a negligible regression artifact. Nevertheless, because a staff member evaluated the children and because the evaluation tool was also the source of treatment goals, one cannot dismiss instrumentation and testing as threats to internal validity in this study.

***Intervention with Children with Cerebral Palsy***  Intervention studies for children with cerebral palsy provide examples of three approaches to treatment: 1) visual-motor training, 2) physiotherapy in the form of vestibular stimulation, and 3) neurodevelopmental treatment represented by the Bobath method.

The purpose of a study by Goodman (1973) was to determine if the visual, motor, and integrated visual-motor skills of physically handicapped children could be influenced positively through participation in a visual-motor training program. The 24 girls and 20 boys, ranging in age from 36 months to 81 months, attended classes sponsored by the Easter Seal Society for Crippled Children. Twenty-two of the children had cerebral palsy, while the remaining children exhibited motor impairments due to nine other disorders. Children were assigned randomly to either an experimental or a control group and were pretested by their teachers and therapists using the Preschool Attainment Record (PAR), as well as a motor development checklist designed for this study and three tests of perceptual motor skills. The intervention, which lasted a minimum of 16 hours over 60 days, was a composite of curricula by Kephart and Getman and Kane, and included training in the areas of fine and gross motor skills, eye movement, and form perception and visual memory. Intervention activities were conducted for the experimental group outside of the regular classroom but in the preschool by the teachers and therapists employed there. Control children continued their usual program in their regular classrooms. Posttests included all of the pretest instruments, except the PAR, plus three additional tests from the Merrill-Palmer Scale of Mental Abilities. Statistical analyses of the mean posttest scores for the experimental and control groups failed to reveal any significant differences. The author concluded that the special visual-motor program was no more effective than a regular preschool program in improving the visual, motor, and visual-motor skills of physically handicapped children.

Because Goodman does not specify who performed the posttesting, it is possible that instrumentation is a threat to the internal validity of this study. Although four subjects (three experimental, one control) were excluded from statistical analysis of posttest measures because they failed to participate in the minimum number of hours of training, attrition is probably not a serious problem given the fairly small number of subjects lost and the fact that *t*-tests failed to reveal any significant differences between the original pretest scores and the pretest scores with these four subject's data excluded.

Because pretest data are not presented, one is unable to judge whether there is a trend for the experimental groups to be gaining relatively more than the control group as the intervention progresses. A more straightforward interpretation of Goodman's results would be possible had activities based on one rather than two theories of visual-motor functioning been included in the intervention and had the dependent measures reflected only that approach.

Two groups of authors examined the effects of vestibular stimulation on the motor behavior of children with cerebral palsy: Chee, Kreutzberg, and Clark (1978), and Sellick and Over (1980).

Influenced by previous research findings (e.g., Clark, Kreutzberg, and Chee, 1977), which showed a positive relation between semicircular canal stimulation and motor performance in nonhandicapped infants, Chee et al. (1978) designed a study to examine the effects of semicircular canal stimulation on the gross motor skills of 23 preambulatory cerebral palsied children between the ages of 2 and 6 years. Pretest data, gathered using the Motor Skills Test (which measures gross motor skills while prone and supine, sitting, creeping, standing, and walking) and the Reflex Test (which examines 17 reflexes), were used to assign children to either the treatment group ($n = 12$) or control group ($n = 11$). Intervention consisted of 15 sessions of horizontal and vertical semicircular canal stimulation over a 4-week period. Six of the children in the control group were handled, while the other five were not.

Posttest performance of the treatment group on both the Motor Skills Test and the Reflex Test was significantly better than that of either of the control groups. In addition, each individual in the treatment group showed improvement on both tests. Hence, Chee et al. (1978) concluded that semicircular canal stimulation is an effective therapy to improve the motor behavior of children with cerebral palsy.

With regard to the internal validity of this study, instrumentation is a possible threat because the authors do not describe specifically who assessed the children. Further, because there is no clear statement regarding how the pretest scores were used to assign children to groups, the possibility of statistical regression or a selection bias exists, although the fact that the treatment and control groups appear to have similar pretest scores reduces concern in this area.

Because neither of the previous criticisms represents a clear threat to internal validity, and considering the fact that the positive effects of treatment were found 4 days after treatment, the results of the Chee et al. (1978) study could be considered as sound general support for semicircular canal stimulation as an effective means to enhance the motor behavior of children with cerebral palsy.

This conclusion is not substantiated by Sellick and Over (1980), however, who also examined the effect of vestibular stimulation on the motor behavior of children with cerebral palsy. The 20 children in this study, 10 boys and 10 girls, ranged in age from 8 months to 56 months. Diagnostic categories were not reported, although it was noted that two of the children were blind. Psychomotor development and mental development scores from the Bayley Scales of Infant Development, along with chronological age and diagnostic category, were considered in matching the children into pairs, sometimes creating mixed sex pairs.

The member of each pair to receive vestibular stimulation was determined randomly.

Children in the experimental group participated in two intervention sessions, separated by 30 minutes, on each of 2 days per week for 4 weeks, yielding 16 experimental sessions. A session consisted of 10 spins in a rotating chair located in a dark room. Children in the control group were handled in the treatment room for a period of time equal to the length of treatment. The Bayley scales were readministered by a person who neither participated in the therapy nor had knowledge of the group assignment of the children in the week following treatment or 3 months later.

Items from the Bayley scales were classified into three groupings: gross motor, fine motor, and eye-hand coordination. Mean scores for the control and experimental groups on these three specially derived indices plus the two traditional indices based on the Bayley were used to evaluate the effects of the intervention. No significant differences were found between the two groups of children, although all five indices improved significantly in both groups.

In this review of the Sellick and Over (1980) study, no threats to internal validity were found. As the authors mentioned, one reason for the neutral results could be the relatively short period of intervention. Also, the differences in instruments used to measure change in motor performance could help to explain the discrepant findings between Sellick and Over (1980) and Chee et al. (1978). It would seem that the instruments used by Chee et al. (1978) are more closely related theoretically to the intervention than those used by Sellick and Over (1980). The other factor that may have actually worked against Sellick and Over finding significant differences is that although the conventional indices of the Bayley scales were used as the matching variable, the children's scores on indices (e.g., eye-hand coordination), derived to measure the effects of treatment, were distributed in some unknown fashion (perhaps unequally distributed) throughout the pairs. Indeed, the pretreatment means on all five indices for the control group exceed those of the experimental group, although whether they are greater from a statistical significance standpoint is not addressed.

Wright and Nicholson (1973) assessed the effects of physiotherapy on the functional ability, range of motion, and retention and loss of the primary automatic reflexes of children under the age of 6 with spastic cerebral palsy. Of the 54 children originally identified for inclusion in the study, some of whom were also mentally retarded or had epilepsy, 7 were excluded during the first 6 months of the study for a variety of reasons. Of the remaining 47 subjects, 26 were in the study for 1 year. Nine of these were untreated for 6 months and were then treated for 6 months; 7 were treated for the entire 12 months; and 10 were untreated for the entire 12 months. Another 21 children participated in the study as untreated subjects for the first 6 months.

The results of psychometric, physical, and neurological evaluations prior to intervention were used to place each child into one of four developmental age groups. Children in each age group were allocated randomly to one of the three treatment groups. For each child, an individual treatment plan was designed, based on the Bobath method of treatment. Treatment was provided on an unspecified schedule by two physiotherapists who took no part in the assessments. To evaluate treatment effects, physiotherapists who were not involved in treatment assessed the function, range of motion, and primary automatic reflexes of the children at the beginning of the study, 6 months later, and 1 year after.

Looking only at the data that are congruent with the description of subjects,[4] a comparison of 9 children who were untreated for 6 months, then treated for 6 months reveals no significant difference, owing to treatment in mean change

scores for either function or primary automatic reflex. When the performance of 7 children who were treated for 12 months was compared to the performance of 10 children who were untreated for 12 months, no significant group differences were found in terms of mean change in scores of function or primary automatic reflex. None of the interpretable data addressed range of motion of the children.

It should be emphasized that the total data set reported by Wright and Nicholson corroborates essentially the conclusion based on the subset of data described above of no treatment effect. Wright and Nicholson observed that all of the children, treated or not, made progress both in terms of function and disappearance of the primary automatic reflexes.

Despite the confusion in the data presentation, since the interpretable data are based on subjects used as their own controls and on subjects treated or untreated for an entire year, no threats to internal validity are evident in this study. Thus, it seems that the use of physiotherapy modeled after the Bobath method of treatment to alter function and the presence or absence of primary automatic reflexes in children under the age of 6 with spastic cerebral palsy is not supported in this study.

***Intervention with Children with Severe Language Handicap***    In an address to a group of audiologists, Horton (1973) discussed some of the benefits for young hearing-impaired children associated with an intervention program that stressed the use of binaural hearing aids from as early as the first year of life, to facilitate aural-oral language learning. Of the 94 children between the ages of birth and 3 years treated in this project, only 3 children were believed to have no functional residual hearing. The development of language in a group of children who had participated in the

---

[4]Tables 2, 3, 7, 8, 9, and 10 in the Wright and Nicholson (1973) article contain entries on which we hesitate to comment. Based on the information found on page 147 of their article, one can conclude that 7 children were treated and 40 were untreated in the first 6 months of the study; that during any 6-month period, 16 children were treated and 40 children were untreated, and that 31 children were never treated while 7 children were never untreated. Yet in Tables 2 and 3, which refer to the first 6 months of the study, the figures "16" and "31" are entered, rather than "7" and "40," under columns labeled "Treated" and "Untreated," making the data found in these tables, as well as conclusions based on them, essentially uninterpretable for us. The discrepancy may be due to a minor editorial error in the titling of the tables and, if so, should be corrected.

project for an average of 27.8 months was compared with their development in other areas using the Communicative Evaluation Chart. Language quotients of the children increased markedly compared to their performance quotients, which remained relatively stable. Horton reports that the children gained 21 months in language age during the 28-month period, while their performance age grew only linearly. However, it is not clear whether by "linear" Horton means that no months were gained in performance age, that 1 month was gained for each month passed in time, or that some other pattern occurred. Moreover, a regression artifact is likely to be reflected in these data, since language is undoubtedly the area of greatest delay in the children. Because Horton (1973) does not provide detailed descriptions of the project participants in her paper, it is not possible for us to comment further on the results.

Liff (1976, cited in Horton, 1976) evaluated an intervention program for hearing-impaired children in which parents optimized the auditory environment for their children who were provided with binaural hearing aids prior to age 3. Six hearing-impaired children were in the experimental group. Five hearing-impaired children, who had not been in a parent program and who had been fitted with hearing aids after age 3, served as one contrast group, and six normal-hearing children served as the other contrast group. Median hearing loss scores for the experimental and contrast hearing-impaired groups were 87 dB and 84 dB, respectively. The parent intervention program served children through the first 3 years of life, after which a preschool emphasizing acoustic training was available until the children were 6 years old. (Preschool training had been available for the hearing-impaired children in the contrast group.) At the time of the Liff study, hearing-impaired children who had been in the parent program attended the same public school second-grade class as the normal-hearing children, while the other hearing-impaired children attended a self-contained class for hearing-impaired children.

In order to evaluate the spoken language of the children, Liff (1976) analyzed 50 consecutive utterances produced by each child, using Lee's (1966) Developmental Sentence Types. No significant differences between the types or levels of utterances produced by the early intervention group and the normal-hearing group were observed. Almost all comparisons of the late intervention hearing-impaired children with either of the other two groups revealed significantly poorer performance by the late intervention hearing-impaired children. Liff concluded that the ability of the early intervention group to produce syntax comparable to that of the normal-hearing group was due to the early intervention program, which included parent training plus the early use of hearing aids. Of course, it is not known whether the similarity noted between the spoken language of the experimental group and hearing control group is the result of parent intervention, or of the early use of hearing aids, or of both.

Because 3 or 4 years passed between the end of the parent-focused intervention and Liff's (1976) evaluation, history is a possible threat to the internal validity of this study. Furthermore, because Liff apparently collected and scored the language samples, instrumentation must be a consideration in evaluating her results. Given that so few children who probably participated in the early intervention were evaluated in the study, one must question the extent to which selection and attrition artifacts are reflected in the results. Likewise, if the hearing-impaired children were not assigned randomly to the treatment and control groups, regression may be a factor in the results.

Considering the emotion-laden nature of the debate over methods used to enhance the development of communication skills in hard-ofhearing children, and in light of reservations regarding the internal validity of the Liff study and lack of detail about subjects and treatment in Horton's paper, it seems premature to consider the results of Horton (1973) and Liff (1976) conclusive in making programmatic decisions for hearing-impaired children.

Howlin (1981) was interested in the short- and long-term effects of an 18-month long, home-based training program on the language abilities of a group of 16 autistic boys between the ages of 3 and 11 years. The long-term control group was much older at follow-up than the experimental group. Many of the control group subjects were referred initially in the mid-1960s (possibly before some of the experimental children were even born), so differences could be present, owing to varying historical experiences of the two groups. Therefore, only the data based on the comparison of the experimental group and short-term control group will be discussed here.

The short-term control group, matched to the experimental group on the basis of age, IQ, social class, and general language ability, was employed to assess the efficacy of treatment in the first 6 months. Language samples taken in the home were the basis of language assessment prior to intervention and every 6 months thereafter. For the intervention, parents of children in the experimental group were trained to use behavioral techniques to modify the language, behavioral, play, and social skills deficits of their children.

Using $t$ tests on pre- and posttest gain scores, Howlin found that the experimental group made significantly greater improvements than the short-term control group when language function was assessed. There were less obvious changes in language level, although greater change was associated with the experimental group. Within the experimental group, the greatest changes occurred in the first 6 months for all indices of language improvement. It was concluded that the home training had been effective in improving the language abilities of the 16 autistic boys.

Howlin does not specify who performed the pre- and posttesting; thus instrumentation must be considered as a threat to internal validity. Also, the lack of discussion regarding how children were assigned to the experimental and short-term control groups permits one to suspect a possible selection bias as well as the presence of statistical regression, problematic

factors as one examines the pretest measures of language function and level for the two groups of children. In this regard, in all but one of the eight measures of language function and level, the scores of the experimental group are much lower than those of the control group, a critical fact when one considers that Howlin's results are based primarily on gain scores. (To justify the use of gain scores, one must assume that the rate of growth of the groups being compared are similar. Otherwise it is impossible to attribute changes in subjects' performance solely to the treatment.)

***Intervention Addressing the Effect of Group Structure***   Studies in this section were concerned with the impact of peer influences and grouping arrangements as intervention agents.

Westling, Ferrell, and Swenson (1982) assessed the effect of group versus individual training arrangements on the teaching of four severely and five profoundly retarded children. The children, eight boys and one girl, were between the ages of 3 and 9 years and attended a public school for mentally retarded children. Five of the children had cerebral palsy, two had Down syndrome, and two were undiagnosed as to etiology.

During group instruction, a teacher and two aides were in the classroom, each with a group of three children. During a 45-minute session, every adult would instruct each of the three children for 15 minutes. In two 45-minute sessions per day, each adult taught a different group of children. During individual instruction, the 90 minutes of available time were divided into nine 10-minute sessions during which the teacher saw each of the nine children for one 10-minute session per day. While the teacher instructed one child, aides supervised the remaining eight children without regard to the specific objectives of the teaching sessions. Twenty sessions over an 8-week period were observed, using a reversal design that began with a group session and ended with an individual session. The four dependent variables were number of instructional minutes, number of turnaways from instruction per instructional minute, total number of objectives taught per child, and percentage of trials correct.

Comparison of the total number of instructional minutes and number of turnaways from instruction per minute across adults for each session revealed a definite advantage for the individual instruction arrangement. In anticipation of the obvious criticism that the type of arrangement was confounded with type of adult instructing, Westling et al. (1982) computed the number of instructional minutes and the number of turnaways from instruction per minute across sessions for the teacher only, obtaining corroborating results. No significant differences between the two instructional arrangements were observed for the total number of objectives taught or the percentage of trials correct. Nonetheless, the authors concluded that the individual instruction arrangement was superior to the group instruction arrangement.

Although no definite threats to the internal validity of this study were found, several comments are in order. Because it was not clearly stated that the observer was naive to the biases of the study's authors, one cannot rule out instrumentation as a possible threat to internal validity. Statistical regression and selection are possible similar threats because the description of the study includes neither an explanation of how the subjects were chosen nor a description of the pool from which they were chosen.

Mainstreaming is another perspective for examining group structure. Legal, legislative, social-ethical, and psychological-educational forces have made mainstreaming a reality (Bricker, 1978), despite the limited number both of validated guidelines for its implementation and of appropriate methods for evaluation of the concept (Allen, 1980). Allen contends that social interaction does not just happen when handicapped and nonhandicapped children are in proximity, but that the teacher's attitudes and actions in the classroom are key factors in making it work successfully.

The influence of teacher structure on the social play of seven handicapped preschoolers was investigated by Devoney, Guralnick, and Rubin (1974). Baseline data, which described the social play of the handicapped children on a scale ranging from "1" for autistic play to "6" for cooperative play, stabilized at about "3" for parallel play. Although the introduction of five nonhandicapped children to the play group produced modest improvements in the level of play of the handicapped children, when the teacher structured the play of the combined group, definite improvement was observed, with substantial increases in the percentage of associative and cooperative play engaged in by each handicapped child. These improvements were least noticeable in the behavior of the two nonverbal children.

Because it is not clear whether the seven handicapped children were chosen because they exhibited the most immature levels of play among all of the children in the school, regression and selection factors may influence the results of this study. Despite these relatively minor qualifications, proponents of mainstreaming should be encouraged to recognize the positive effect that the teacher can have on the social play of preschool children at different developmental levels.

Group structure, defined in terms of the developmental level of children in a group, was the variable of interest in two subsequent studies by Guralnick (1980, 1981). In the first study, Guralnick (1980) investigated the influence that developmental level has on the communicative and parallel play interactions of children with mild, moderate, severe, or no handicaps. The 37 children, 4 to 6 years of age, attended an integrated preschool. They included 12 nonhandicapped, 9 mildly handicapped, 5 moderately handicapped, and 11 severely handicapped children, classified on the basis of mean length of utterance plus performance on the Peabody Picture Vocabulary Test.

During integrated free-play periods, teachers encouraged interaction and constructive play, particularly among children of different developmental levels. Children's interactions were observed and recorded by trained raters on a time-sampling basis. Instances of positive and negative motor-gestural communications and vocal-verbal communications were recorded, as were occurrences of parallel play.

In general, it was found that nonhandicapped and mildly handicapped children communicated with each other increasingly as time passed more than would be expected by the criterion of availability, and decreasingly with the other two groups, suggesting that mere contact alone does not facilitate the integration of seriously delayed children with less delayed children. Moderately and severely handicapped children communicated with all groups, as would be predicted by their availability. Although more variability was found on the measures of parallel play, nonhandicapped and mildly handicapped children engaged substantially in parallel play with the moderately handicapped children but engaged in parallel play with the severely handicapped children less than expected by availability.

Having shown that the persons with whom children chose to interact related to the developmental level of the available children, particularly for nonhandicapped and mildly handicapped children, Guralnick (1981) then asked whether particular combinations of developmental levels affect children's behavior. Thirty-seven children were sorted into four developmental levels as described in Guralnick (1980). Homogeneous groupings were nonhandicapped/mildly handicapped, and moderately/severely handicapped, while heterogeneous groupings contained children from all four developmental levels.

Independent observers used time-sampling procedures to record the behavior of the target child, peers, and the teacher. With regard to the target child, three categories of behavior were recorded: level of social participation ranging from unoccupied to cooperative play; constructiveness of play measured on a scale ranging from inappropriate play to pretend play; and frequency and nature of communication directed to peers. The only peer behavior recorded was frequency and nature of communication to target child. The four teacher behaviors of interest were positive reinforcement, negative interaction, presence (i.e., being within 3 feet of the target child), and prompting or initiating and maintaining social interactions between the target child and peers.

These measures were taken at the beginning and end of the school year.

Analysis of the data regarding social participation failed to reveal any important differences during heterogeneous versus homogeneous play. Developmental level was an influential factor, however, with the less-advanced children engaging in more unoccupied play but less onlooker, associative, and cooperative play.

Although homogeneous group composition was significantly associated with an increase in the degree to which the severely delayed children engaged in inappropriate play, communication was not affected significantly by the group composition factor. And, although group composition did not significantly affect teacher behavior either, teachers interacted more positively with the severely handicapped children than with any other group.

Guralnick (1981) concluded that heterogeneous grouping had a positive influence on the severely delayed children by reducing the amount of inappropriate play, and that "*no detrimental* effects" (p. 128) were observed in the nonhandicapped and mildly handicapped children as a result of being integrated with moderately and severely handicapped children.

## SUMMARY AND RECOMMENDATIONS

There were two purposes for this review. The first was to establish that severe handicapping conditions of a primary or secondary nature, if not attended to properly, can have long-term debilitating consequences for the very young child, for his or her caregivers, and for their interpersonal transactions. A second purpose was to critically examine the efficacy findings of early education studies involving young children with severe handicaps, selecting studies for review that appear reasonably able to withstand serious threats to internal validity.

With respect to establishing need, our review showed that when a young child with a handicap and his or her caregiver meet each other's interaction expectations, their individual as well as transactional development advances mutually in an accelerating positive direction. But when one member of the caregiver-child dyad does not perceive an interaction expectation and/or does not meet it in the other dyad member, a decelerating trajectory often occurs. Furthermore, although some handicapping conditions (e.g., congenital blindness) seem to be very amenable to early caregiver stimulation—as reported in Fraiberg (1971), the general issue of need for *specific types* of early intervention remains largely unresolved.

Moving to the second purpose of this chapter, i.e., to critically examine efficacy findings, in the area of Down syndrome, eight studies were reviewed that met both Dunst and Rheingrover's (1981) criteria for adequate design and our criteria. Six of the studies (Bidder et al., 1975; Jeffree et al., 1973; MacDonald et al., 1974; Piper & Pless, 1980; Pothier et al., 1974; Rynders & Horrobin, 1980) gave heavy emphasis to language stimulation. Four of the six studies showed statistically significant improvements in experimental subjects' language; one study (Rynders & Horrobin, 1980) showed significant differences in nonlanguage areas (only language differences were counted as efficacy criteria, since language was the primary target of their curriculum); one study (Piper & Pless, 1980) showed no significant treatment effect whatsoever. A seventh study (Aronson & Fallstrom, 1977) emphasized a broad spectrum of developmental stimulation showing significant differences favoring experimental subjects. The last of the eight studies (Harris, 1981) focused on neurodevelopmental therapy, revealing significant differences in therapy objectives favoring experimental children but not in general motor or mental development scores.

While these eight studies are certainly not perfect from a methodological standpoint, they did meet reasonably stringent standards in terms of experimental control and ability to withstand threats to internal validity. Nevertheless, most of these studies do not report (perhaps do not collect) routine data about subject characteristics that would not be ignored in the child development literature involving non-

handicapped children. For example, more than half of the eight studies reviewed provide no data that can confirm the presence of the genotype, Down syndrome; even fewer indicate the subgroup of the syndrome to which a karyotype belongs. A karyotype is not always needed, of course, depending on the hypotheses to be tested, but in contemporary studies involving young children with Down syndrome, confirming the genotype and collecting basic descriptive data about subjects is very important, not only for research purposes but also for parent counseling purposes. Such reporting is vital because the noncollection of basic descriptive data implies the existence of the unfortunate stereotype that a "Downs is a Downs, is a Downs." Not only is the stereotype of uniform low general development in Down syndrome not accurate but it can lead to the dangerous lowering of child expectations in the eyes of parents, teachers, employers and, eventually, the child himself or herself. If this occurs, a positive trajectory of the entire social network of child and caregivers and others could collapse, with serious negative consequences for all concerned. (See Rynders, Spiker, & Horrobin, 1978, for a fuller description of this problem.)

Regarding early education projects involving young non–Down syndrome severely handicapped children, 5 of the 14 studies across the areas of developmental disabilities, cerebral palsy, and severe language disorders provide reasonably sound evidence regarding the efficacy of early intervention. In the area of developmental disabilities, Brassell and Dunst (1975a, 1975b) found developmental progress during intervention to be statistically significant and nearly twice that observed during baseline, while their 1978 study revealed that the cognitive performance of experimental children was statistically better than that of control children following intervention.

Using subjects as their own control, Revill and Blunden (1979) found the mean number of IQ points gained per 2-month period and the monthly rate of skills acquisition to be greater during intervention than baseline, although there was a 1-month intervention period when one of the groups acquired a smaller mean number of skills than during one of the baseline months.

With regard to hearing-impaired children, Horton (1973) found that the language quotients and language ages of children enrolled in an early intervention program increased more than their performance quotients and ages. Liff (1973) found that the productive language of hearing-impaired children in an early intervention program was not significantly different from that of hearing children, while the productive language of late-intervention hearing-impaired children was significantly inferior to that of both early-intervention hearing-impaired and normal-hearing children.

Three studies provide only partial support for early intervention. In a study by Barrerra et al. (1976), four developmentally delayed subjects' data fell in the predicted direction (i.e., skills targeted in intervention showed more improvement than untreated skills); two subjects showed no difference in improvement between the treated and untreated areas; and one subject's data appeared opposite to the predicted direction of difference.

A second study, Howlin's (1981) assessment of the short-term effects of intervention on the language of autistic children, revealed that experimental children made significantly greater gains than control children on measures of language function. On measures of language level, although the experimental group exhibited greater changes and the one signficant change favored them, control children maintained their pre-intervention advantage.

A third study showing somewhat less support for early intervention for children with cerebral palsy is that by Chee et al. (1978). They found that children in an experimental group performed significantly better than control children on motor measures following intervention. Only the experimental group showed improvement that was statistically significant, although one control group also exhibited improvement. On reflex measures, results were similar, except that both control groups actually decreased in performance, although not significantly so.

Three studies involving developmentally disabled children failed to find significant differences favoring groups in special treatment programs. The study by Sandow and Clarke (1978) and Sandow et al. (1981) found no significant differences in the number of subjects with increasing or decreasing IQ points in the final year of their study, although there were some differences in previous years. No statistically based interpretations were made of the gains in IQ scores, although the months gained over the 3 years of the study of the experimental groups were similar to, but less than, the gains of the control group. Clements et al. (1982) found a near-significant difference among their preschool children, although the experimental group improved no more than the control group.

Two studies (Sellick & Over, 1980; Wright & Nicholson, 1973) involving children with cerebral palsy failed to find significant group differences between experimental and control conditions. In a third study with cerebral palsied children (Goodman, 1973), the means of the experimental children exceeded those of the control children on three measures, with the control children having the advantage on the other seven measures. Only one of these latter differences was statistically significant, attributable to one child's extreme performance.

In summary, results reported in this section concerning non–Down syndrome severely handicapped children lend support to the position that early intervention, either with parents or other professionals interacting directly with children to effect behavioral change, can improve the development (especially in the cognitive domain) of children with severe handicaps. However, support for this position is far from overwhelming, and several questions remain unanswered about the findings and their applications. For example, the need for more study of methods used to treat children with cerebral palsy is apparent, given that four studies reviewed in this chapter yielded no significant effects or conflicting results involving treatment programs.

The studies of group structure reveal that teaching is affected by grouping (Westling et al., 1982) and that although mere contact does not usually lead to a genuine integration of handicapped with nonhandicapped children, teachers can provide structure conducive to such integration (Devoney et al., 1974). Further, although developmental level affects children's communication and play in integrated settings (Guralnick, 1980), grouping children heterogeneously with respect to developmental level is not associated with negative outcomes with regard to communication and play (Guralnick, 1981), so long as the integration is structured carefully.

Guralnick's studies may serve as a model for future research in terms of both the substantive issues they address and their methodology. From them one can generate several suggestions regarding the implementation of mainstreaming. Teachers need to be prepared to structure situations conducive to interaction between handicapped and nonhandicapped children. Heterogeneous groupings should be used properly so that severely handicapped children have an opportunity to observe and imitate more-advanced interactive behaviors without jeopardizing the development of the more advanced children.

Combining the 8 intervention studies on persons with Down syndrome with the 18 intervention studies on non–Down syndrome severely handicapped individuals shows that a total of 16 of the 26 studies (or 62%) manifest clear, significant differences favoring an experimental group or condition; 4 studies show some significant differences and some nonsignificant differences; and 6 studies show nonsignificant differences only. Although this record is encouraging, it should be viewed with some caution, not only because of imperfections in many of the studies but also because of problems inherent in summarizing findings from disparate studies using the inclusion-exclusion criteria that we employed. Furthermore, from the standpoint of external validity, though the summary shows that experimenters in early education can demonstrate a treatment *effect* fairly often, such a demonstration has some distance to go in showing general *effectiveness* for early education. The two concepts, though interrelated, are also quite different.

## Implications for Policy and Research Improvements

This chapter has stressed the importance of aiming the benefits of early education not just at young children with severe handicaps or at their parents but at their siblings and the extended family as well. Emphasis on the home/family milieu as the most desired context for early education is not meant to imply that strong foster home or exemplary group home services for young children with severe handicaps should be abolished; to the contrary, some parents may need these services because of an inability to cope with the problems of raising a child with a severe handicap at home. Nor is such emphasis meant to imply that parents who decide to take on a time-consuming early educator role with their child at home should "martyr" themselves, becoming overly devoted to their handicapped child's educational needs, perhaps sacrificing their own and their spouses' needs and the needs of their other children in the process. Instead, the authors suggest that parents of a young child with a severe handicap deserve to have a reasonable array of excellent educational services available to them. What might some of these services be? Some can be inferred from this review of the literature and include:

1. The need for appropriate education and stimulation begins at birth and is first realized through positive child-caregiver interactions. To promote synchronous parent-child transaction as quickly as possible, in-hospital or at-home *counseling* at the time of a severely handicapped child's birth should be offered routinely to families. The negative effects of asynchrony can multiply rapidly without intervention. Parents of severely handicapped children need to know what to expect of their children developmentally, how to encourage optimal development, and how to cope with uneven (or apparently stagnant) maturation across different areas of cognitive and physical development. To stimulate and maintain attachment, parents of severely handicapped children may need

help in recognizing how the children signal both their needs and their satisfaction with parental interaction. After the newborn period, follow-up counseling can help detect and correct possible asynchrony across the whole social network (family, extended family, neighborhood, etc.). Classes for grandparents, siblings, extended family, and/or friends can further help ensure that the people who potentially have the most contact with the handicapped child and the most influence on the child's parents have accurate information concerning the handicapping condition(s) and its likely ramifications for the growth and development of the child and his or her family. Such a concerted effort would help ensure support for the parents and their decisions with regard to their handicapped child.

2. If parents decide to participate directly in early education, the program provided should offer them a *choice* of roles and instructional modes if possible (e.g., stimulation within prearranged play periods or within normal caretaking activities, unstructured or structured play, data-based or non-data-based instruction, or a combination of these approaches). In other words, it is important to "match" the curricular requirements of a program with parent style and instructional preferences. Early educators developing programs for children whose parents are not, either by choice or necessity, involved directly in the programs, must strive to maintain parents' identity as primary caregivers.

3. Parents who have a young child with a handicap should have a *support group* available to them, composed of parents in similar circumstances. Not only will a support group help parents develop effective lobbying efforts in behalf of their children and help them to stay abreast of best practices in their area, it will provide a new, highly reinforcing, social network for them. The National Down Syndrome Congress, an organization of parents and professionals, is an excellent example of an effective parent support group.

From the standpoint of implications for research, the authors offer five goals:

1. Early education researchers must design their studies so that they meet the basic requirements for verifying *internal validity*. Unless early education research and evaluation findings can withstand scientific scrutiny, arguments for policies favorable to the continuation of early education programs will be severely hampered.

2. Having established internal validity of their work, researchers should establish the *external validity* of their findings, employing multiple indicators of efficacy, both formal and informal, converging on the identification of treatment programs of the highest possible caliber and socioeducational impact.

3. Related to goals 1 and 2 is that only by comprehensively *monitoring* behavioral changes will detection of both the intended and the dispersion effects of intervention be possible. In addition, longitudinal designs are needed to answer the questions of lasting effects as well as the "sleeper" effects of intervention.

4. Researchers must work with practitioners to *evaluate specific intervention practices*. Some data exist to support practices ranging from training parents in behavior modification techniques, to providing individual rather than group instruction, to integrating handicapped and nonhandicapped children, particularly when teachers help structure interactions. However, more research is needed to determine the circumstances under which specific practices are and are not warranted.

5. Assessing the impact of an experimental program on parents, siblings, and the entire social network as well as on the "target" child is of great importance. Not losing the young child in the social network and not losing sight of the network as one strives to help the child pose sizable challenges for researchers. But taking a *holistic* approach to efficacy determination is essential.

When results of early education studies meet the methodological requirements of the scientific community and the practical needs of families and the local community, they become a valuable part of the strategy for producing a truly least restrictive environment for young children with severe handicaps. The research literature on early education for severely handicapped children is limited, but it does provide some promising suggestions for improving the quality of transactions between caregivers and children. And although additional evidence on the effects of treatments is still needed, enough is known now to argue, we think convincingly, that substantial benefits can be realized in promoting the development of children with severe handicaps and in supporting the efforts of parents and other essential caregivers through sound early education programs.

## REFERENCES

Adelson, E., & Fraiberg, S. Gross motor development in infants blind from birth. *Child Development,* 1974, *45,* 114–126.

Allen, K.E. Mainstreaming: What have we learned? *Young Children,* 1980, *35,* 54–63.

Aronson, M., & Fallstrom, K. Immediate and long-term effects of developmental training in children with Down's syndrome. *Developmental (Medicala Medicine) Child Neurology,* 1977, *19,* 489–494.

Barrera, M., Routh, D., Parr, D., Johnson, N., Arendshorst, D., Goolsby, E., & Schroeder, S. Early intervention with biologically handicapped infants and young children: A preliminary study with each child as his own control. In: T. Tjossem (ed.), *Intervention strategies for high risk infants and young children.* Baltimore: University Park Press, 1976.

Bidder, R., Bryant, G., & Gray, O. Benefits to Down's syndrome children through training their mothers. *Archives of Disease in Childhood,* 1975, *50,* 383–386.

Blatt, B. *Souls in extremis: An anthology on victims and victimizers.* Boston: Allyn & Bacon, 1973.

Brassell, W.R., & Dunst, C.J. Cognitive intervention by parents of impaired infants. *Mental Retardation,* 1975a, *13,* 42.

Brassell, W.R., & Dunst, C.J. Facilitating cognitive development in impaired infants. In: C.J. Dunst (ed.), *Trends in early intervention services: Methods, models, and evaluation.* Arlington, VA: Department of Human Resources, 1975b.

Brassell, W.R., & Dunst, C.J. Fostering the object construct: Large-scale intervention with handicapped infants. *American Journal of Mental Deficiency,* 1978, *82,* 507–510.

Bricker, D.D. A rationale for the integration of handicapped and nonhandicapped preschool children. In: M.J. Guralnick (ed.), *Early intervention and the integration of handicapped and nonhandicapped children.* Baltimore: University Park Press, 1978.

Bronfenbrenner, U. *Is early intervention effective? A report on longitudinal evaluation of preschool programs,* Vol. 2. (U.S. Department of Health, Education and Welfare Pub. COHD 76-30025). Washington, DC: U.S. Government Printing Office, 1974.

Campbell, D., & Stanley, J. *Experimental and quasi-experimental designs in research.* Chicago: Rand McNally & Co., 1966.

Carolan, R.H. Sensory stimulation: Two papers. *The New Outlook for the Blind,* 1973, *3,* 119–127.

Chee, F.K.W., Kreutzberg, J.R., & Clark, D.L. Semicircular canal stimulation in cerebral palsied children. *Physical Therapy,* 1978, *58*(a), 1071–1075.

Clark, D.L., Kreutzberg, J.P., & Chee, F.K.W. Vestibular stimulation influence on motor development in infants. *Science,* 1977, *196,* 1228–1229.

Clarke, A.M., & Clarke, A.D.B. (eds.) *Early experience: Myth and evidence.* New York: Free Press, 1976.

Clements, J., Evans, C., Jones, C., Osborne, K., & Upton, G. Evaluation of a home-based language training programme with severely mentally handicapped children. *Behavioral Research and Therapy,* 1982, *20,* 243–249.

Denenberg, V., & Thoman, E. From animal to infant research. In: T. Tjossem (ed.), *Intervention strategies for high-risk infants and young children.* Baltimore: University Park Press, 1976.

Devoney, C., Guralnick, M.J., & Rubin, H. Integrating handicapped and nonhandicapped preschool children: Effects on social play. *Childhood Education,* 1974, *50*(6), 360–364.

Dunst, C.J. *Patterns of cognitive skill acquisition in developmentally delayed infants.* Paper presented at the 98th annual meeting of the American Association on Mental Deficiency, Toronto, Canada, June, 1974a.

Dunst, C.J. The acquisition of sensori-motor skills in a Down's syndrome infant: Training vs. nontraining. *Western Carolina Center Papers and Reports* (Morgantown, NC), 1974b, *4*(11).

Dunst, C.J., & Rheingrover, R.M. An analysis of the efficacy of infant intervention programs with organically handicapped children. *Evaluation and Program Planning,* 1981, *4,* 287–323.

Fraiberg, S. Intervention in infancy: A program for blind infants. *Journal of the American Academy of Child Psychiatry,* 1971, *10*(3), 381–405.

Fraiberg, S., Smith, M., & Adelson, E. An educational program for blind infants. *Journal of Special Education,* 1969, *3*(2), 121–139.

Friedrich, W.N., & Boriskin, J.A. Primary prevention of child abuse: Focus on the special child. *Hospital and Community Psychiatry,* 1978, *29*(4), 248–251.

Goodman, L. The efficacy of visual-motor training for orthopedically handicapped children. *Rehabilitation Literature,* 1973, *34*(10), 299–304.

Guralnick, M.J. Social interactions among preschool children. *Exceptional Children,* 1980, *46*(4), 248–253.

Guralnick, M.J. The social behavior of preschool children

at different developmental levels: Effects of group composition. *Journal of Experimental Child Psychology*, 1981, *31*, 115–130.

Harris, S. Effects of neurodevelopmental therapy on motor performance of infants with Down's syndrome. *Developmental Medicine and Child Neurology*, 1981, *23*, 477–483.

Hersen, M., & Barlow, D. *Single case experimental designs: Strategies for studying behavior change.* New York: Pergamon Press, 1976.

Horton, K. Early amplification and language learning—or sounds should be heard and not seen. *Journal of the Academy of Rehabilitative Audiology*, 1973, *6*, 15–20.

Horton, K. Early intervention for hearing-impaired infants and young children. In: T. Tjossem (ed.), *Intervention strategies for high risk infants and young children.* Baltimore: University Park Press, 1976.

Howlin, P. The results of a home-based language training programme with autistic children. *British Journal of Disorders of Communication*, 1981, *16*(2), 73-88.

Jeffree, D., Wheldall, K., & Mittler, P. Facilitating two-word utterances in two Down's syndrome boys. *American Journal of Mental Deficiency*, 1973, *78*, 117–122.

Jones, O. Mother-child communication with prelinguistic Down's syndrome and normal infants. In: H.R. Schaffer (ed.), *Studies in mother-child interaction*, New York: Academic Press, 1977.

Jones, O. Mother-child communication with very young Down's syndrome and normal children. In: T. Field, S. Goldberg, D. Stern, and A. Sastek (eds.), *Transactions of high-risk infants and children: Disturbances and interventions.* New York: Academic Press, 1980.

Lazar, I., & Darlington, R. *Lasting effects after preschool.* A report of the consortium for longitudinal studies (U.S. Department of Health, Education and Welfare, Office of Human Development Services, Administration for Children, Youth and Families. Pub. # OHDS 79-30178). Washington, DC: U.S. Government Printing Office, 1978.

Lee, L. Developmental sentence types: A method for comparing normal and deviant syntactic development. *Journal of Speech and Hearing Disorders*, 1966, *31*, 311–330.

Leib, S., Benfield, G., & Guidubaldi, J. Effects of early intervention and stimulation on the preterm infant. *Pediatrics*, 1980, *66*(1), 83–90.

Liff, S. *Early intervention and language development in hearing impaired children.* Unpublished master's thesis, Vanderbilt University, Nashville, TN, 1973.

MacDonald, J., Blott, J., Gordon, K., Spiegel, B., & Hartmann, M. An experimental parent-assisted treatment program for preschool language-delayed children. *Journal of Speech and Hearing Disorders*, 1974, *39*, 4, 395–415.

Nirje, B. The normalization principle. In: R.B. Kugel & A. Shearer (eds.), *Changing patterns in residential services for the mentally retarded* (rev. ed.). Washington, DC: President's Committee on Mental Retardation, 1976.

Norris, M. What affects blind children's development. *New Outlook for the Blind*, 1956, *50*, 258–267.

Odom, S.L., & Fewell, R.R. Program evaluation in early childhood special education: A meta-evaluation. *Educational Evaluation and Policy Analysis*, 1983, *5*(4), 445–460.

Piper, M., & Pless, I. Early intervention for infants with Down syndrome: A controlled trial. *Pediatrics*, 1980, *65*, 463–468.

Pothier, P., Morrison, D., & Gorman, F. Effects of receptive language training on receptive and expressive language development. *Journal of Abnormal Child Psychology*, 1974, *2*, 153–164.

Powell, L. The effect of extra stimulation and maternal involvement on the development of low birth-weight infants and on maternal behavior. *Child Development*, 1974, *45*, 106–113.

Pueschel, S., & Rynders, J. *Down syndrome: Advances in biomedicine and the behavioral sciences.* Cambridge, MA: Ware Press, 1982.

Revell, S., & Blunden, R. A home training service for preschool developmentally handicapped children. *Behavioral Research and Therapy*, 1979, *17*, 207–214.

Rynders, J., & Horrobin, J. Educational provisions for young children with Down's syndrome. In: J. Gottlieb (ed.), *Educating mentally retarded persons in the mainstream.* Baltimore: University Park Press, 1980.

Rynders, J., Spiker, D., & Horrobin, J. Underestimating the educability of Down's syndrome children: Examination of methodological problems in recent literature. *American Journal of Mental Deficiency*, 1978, *82*, 440–448.

Sameroff, A.J., & Chandler, M.J. Reproductive risk and the continuum of caretaking casualty. In: F.D. Horowitz (ed.), *Review of child development research*, Vol. 4. Chicago: University of Chicago Press, 1975, pp. 187–244.

Sandow, S., & Clark, A.D. Home intervention with parents of severely subnormal, preschool children: An interim report. *Child: Care, Health, and Development*, 1978, *4*, 29–39.

Sandow, S.A., Clark, A.D.B., Cox, M.V., & Stewart, F.L. Home intervention with parents of severely subnormal pre-school children: A final report. *Child: Care, Health, and Development*, 1981, *7*, 135–144.

Scarr-Salapatek, S., & Williams, M. The effects of early stimulation on low birth-weight infants. *Child Development*, 1973, *44*, 94–101.

Schaeffer, E., & Emerson, P. The development of social attachments in infancy. *Monograph of the Society for Research in Child Development*, 1964, *29*, 1–77.

Schoggen, P., & Schoggen, M. Ecological factors in the prevention of psychosocial mental retardation. In: M.J. Begab, H.C. Haywood, & H. L. Garber (eds.), *Psychosocial influences in retarded performance*, Vol. 1. *Issues and theories in development.* Baltimore: University Park Press, 1981.

Sellick, K.J., & Over, R. Effects of vestibular stimulation on motor development of cerebral-palsied children. *Developmental Medicine and Child Neurology*, 1980, *22*, 476–483.

Semans, S. The Bobath concept in treatment of neurological disorders. *American Journal of Physical Medicine*, 1967, *46*, 732–785.

Sonquist, H., & Kamii, C. Applying some Piagetian concepts in the classroom for the disadvantaged. In: J. Frost (ed.), *Early childhood education rediscovered.* New York: Holt, Rinehart & Winston, 1968.

Spiker, D. Early intervention for young children with Down syndrome: New directions in enhancing parent-child synchrony. In: S. Pueschel & J. Rynders (eds.),

*Down syndrome: Advances in biomedicine and the be-havioral sciences,* Cambridge, MA: Ware Press, 1982.

Taft, T. Intervention programs for infants with cerebral palsy. In: C. Brown (ed.) *Infants at risk: Assessment and intervention. An update for health care professionals and parents.* Palm Beach: Johnson & Johnson Baby Products Co. 1981.

Wallick, M., & Thompson, B. Predicting special needs from information available at birth. *Psychological Reports,* 1981, *48,* 371–375.

Westling, D.L., Ferrell, K., & Swenson, K. Intra-classroom comparison of two arrangements for teaching profoundly mentally retarded children. *American Journal of Mental Deficiency,* 1982, *86*(6), 601–608.

Wright, T., & Nicholson, J. Physiotherapy for the spastic child: An evaluation. *Developmental Medicine and Child Neurology,* 1973, *15,* 146–163.

# Part III

## VOCATIONAL PREPARATION AND EMPLOYMENT

The issues related to the transition of severely handicapped persons from childhood to adulthood are particularly problematic. In large measure the problems are cultural. To most of us adulthood implies independence and productive work. Although the social institutions that provide for nonhandicapped children (such as families, schools, social recreation, and even child protection agencies) can be adapted to severely handicapped children without major organizational change, the same cannot be said for the institutions of adult society. Handicapped children and youth share with their nonhandicapped peers both dependence on adults and the social expectation that productivity will be secondary to personal development. The normal transition to adulthood, however, revises the dominant social expectations of social and economic self-sufficiency.

In a country such as ours that has never adopted formal policies for promoting human independence of its nondisabled population (e.g., through full-employment or guaranteed minimum income policies), it should not be surprising that concern about the importance of meaningful work and personal autonomy for handicapped persons has been slow to develop. As a work-oriented nation, however, our society makes employment and independence central components not only of personal identity but also of perceived worth. One of the primary founding expectations and selling points of American public education was that it would lead to a self-sufficient and readily employable citizenry. Unfortunately, such expectations have rarely been applied to educational programs for severely handicapped youth. Operating from a developmental perspective that viewed severely handicapped persons as remaining at one or another stage of childhood and therefore as never "ready" for the adult tasks of work and autonomy, these programs did little to develop specific adult-living skills for handicapped persons. Moreover, those programs that were created tended almost exclusively to serve mildly handicapped youngsters.

Since the advent and acceptance of normalization and mainstreaming, there has been a growing sense that severely handicapped adults should have the opportunity for adult activities. With increased opportunities have come achievements in the areas of independent and productive living that not long ago would have been believed unattainable. This section of the volume is focused on what has been learned in these efforts to assist handicapped individuals' transition to adulthood. Because the lessons of these programs have varied by the level of handicap of their clients, the chapters herein discuss programs for both mildly and severely handicapped students.

In Chapter 6 Daniel W. Close, Jo-Ann Sowers, Andrew S. Halpern, and Philip E. Bourbeau examine programs providing for the transition to adulthood by mildly handicapped youth. The

159

authors examine specific impediments to a relatively easy transition and describe the content and qualities of programs that make movement from childhood to adulthood more easily accomplished.

In Chapter 7 Frank R. Rusch and Dennis E. Mithaug discuss principles to guide transitional programs for severely handicapped students. They base their discussion on the growing and convincing body of research, much of it conducted by themselves, that has demonstrated powerful techniques for training severely handicapped persons to acquire personally important tasks in the environments in which they are ultimately to function. The authors describe a systems-analytic, ecological view of the requirements of adaptation and of specific programmatic attempts to provide individuals with skills to meet or exceed those requirements.

Continuing the discussion of transition from the world of education to the world of work, Ronald W. Conley, in Chapter 8, examines how federal policies affect the employment and employability of mentally retarded persons. Conley outlines the incentives and disincentives, as well as the direct effects, of federal income support programs, health services, long-term care funding programs, social services, and rehabilitation/reemployment programs on work opportunities for mentally retarded persons. The extent to which such programs foster dependency is discussed and suggestions are included for altering assumptions, programs, and policies that will support mentally retarded persons in obtaining and maintaining socially and personally beneficial levels of employment.

# Chapter 6

# Programming for the Transition to Independent Living for Mildly Retarded Persons

*Daniel W. Close, Jo-Ann Sowers,*
*Andrew S. Halpern, and Philip E. Bourbeau*

The transition from high school to adulthood can be a traumatic event for anyone. The familiarity and security of friends, teachers, school buildings, and traditions often pass away as new challenges and opportunities beckon. For nonhandicapped young high school graduates, the lures of college, work, military service, or marriage frequently dominate their minds, presenting a seemingly endless variety of appealing alternatives.

Unfortunately, this optimistic scenario does not usually apply to students labeled mildly mentally retarded. Their high school experiences have often been characterized by little success and much failure. Although they may have mastered some basic academic tasks, the learning process for them was often frustrating and painful, and skills learned in the classroom were not necessarily remembered and utilized in other environments. Consequently, when mildly retarded persons graduate from high school, they usually experience relatively less success than their nondisabled peers. This tendency toward failure in the transition from high school to adulthood was documented years ago

by Baller, Charles, and Miller (1966), "whose research cohort of mentally retarded young adults was found to be marked by delinquency, dependency on relief, and generally poor adjustment" (p. 87).

This bleak picture of transition is reflected further in research on the post-institutional or postgroup-home experiences of mildly retarded persons. Edgerton's (1967) classic study of the transition from institutional to community-based residence provides insights into the complexities of initial adjustment. He writes, "Earning money, counting it, spending it, banking it, and owing it are all problems of the highest seriousness" (p. 166). Other common problems noted were: poor or nonexistent housekeeping skills, social isolation, and erratic personal behavior. The overall picture Edgerton presents is one of minimal initial adjustment and extensive feelings of personal inadequacy on the part of his subjects.

Recent studies have reported a variety of problems experienced by mildly retarded persons in the transition from group-home living to independent apartment living. McDevitt,

161

Smith, Schmidt, and Rosen (1978) noted that only a few subjects they studied could independently manage money or maintain appropriate social relationships. Crnic and Pym (1979) reported that skills learned in the group-home setting often did not generalize to the apartment setting. Schalock and Harper (1978) suggest that lack of money management, housekeeping, and social skills are characteristics of persons who fail to make successful transitions from group-home to independent apartment settings.

## REASONS FOR
## DIFFICULTY IN TRANSITION

The problems in transition encountered by mildly retarded persons are not surprising when we consider the characteristics of the existing service delivery system. It is certainly no secret that handicapped adolescents and young adults have received less than their fair share of the special education and rehabilitation services to which they are entitled (Halpern, 1979). The mainstreaming movement that has evolved for elementary level students does not provide an adequate model at the secondary level (Clark, 1979). In addition, the academic emphasis within secondary education is inappropriate for many handicapped adolescents and adults (Wimmer, 1981). Graduates of secondary-level programs often have poor basic skills and lack the ability to use cognitive-based strategies that are vital in adult life (Winshel & Ensher, 1978). This lack of a functional-skill orientation often leads to students losing interest in school, which results in impaired functioning in adulthood.

Educational programs for mildly retarded students also rarely *teach* in a manner that facilitates generalization and maintenance. Instead, it is assumed that skills learned in the classroom will *automatically* transfer to other environments. For example, the ability to follow signs and read labels might be viewed as an "extension" of basic reading skills. Children of normal intelligence are often able to make such connections between academic skills taught in isolation and the application of

these skills under different conditions. However, mildly retarded students have difficulty making such generalizations without carefully designed instruction. Furthermore, students often do not have opportunities to practice functional skills in the criterion environment, which enhances the likelihood of impaired performance.

Adult service agencies, such as sheltered workshops or group homes, offer a few opportunities for "graduation" into less restrictive environments (Bellamy, Rhoades, Bourbeau, & Mank, 1982; Sitkei, 1980). Those few opportunities that do arise, however, are increasingly made available to more severely handicapped persons (Haywood, 1979). Furthermore, stigma is often attached to participation in traditional training facilities designed for handicapped adults. Many mildly retarded graduates of special education programs simply want to obtain a job, to live on their own, and to disappear from the social service rolls.

Thus, there is a critical need to plan actively for transition of mildly retarded persons from school or supervised living settings to independent living. Such transition will require the development of service delivery systems that emphasize skill training in functional areas such as vocational adjustment, money management, daily living skills, and social/interpersonal competence. Appropriate functional assessments might be used to guide the selection and monitoring of instructional interventions. Students must be taught how to utilize behavioral and cognitive strategies to perform a variety of skills competently in novel situations. Finally, instruction must take place in integrated, age-appropriate settings to maximize learning and minimize stigma. These desirable characteristics are briefly described next, as an introduction to their more complete exposition in the remainder of this chapter.

## DESIRABLE
## PROGRAM CHARACTERISTICS

### Functional Content

To function competently within community settings of varying complexity, individuals must demonstrate a wide array of skills. These skills range from basic self-care or survival to fairly complex interactions with many different people in varying social and vocational environments. Skills typically included in functionally based instructional programs are: 1) daily living skills; 2) functional academics; 3) personal-social skills; 4) money management and purchasing skills; and 5) vocational guidance and preparation.

A functionally based curriculum differs from an academic approach to curriculum in that skills are taught because of their direct relationship to real life behaviors, rather than as academic building blocks that are *presumed* to be prerequisites for adequate functioning in nonacademic environments. For example, the use of a hand calculator may be taught as an aid to grocery shopping, even though the individual is not very capable at doing basic addition or subtraction. (See Brolin and Kokaska, 1979, for a detailed listing of the specific educational objectives associated with functional skill orientation.)

## Program-Related Assessment

A functional curriculum requires functional assessment as a foundation for planning, monitoring, and evaluating instruction. In this approach to assessment, information is collected with the goal of producing a profile of the examinee's relative strengths and weaknesses. This profile includes not only a catalog of relevant skills that have or have not been mastered but also addresses the process of learning as a variable to be manipulated in response to individualized assessment outcomes. In other words, the assessments are program related, rather than being gathered for the purpose of identifying or confirming a diagnostic label.

## Generalization of Skills

Independent community living requires the individual to function competently in a variety of constantly changing settings. To achieve this goal, the person must respond appropriately on a daily basis to novel situations. For example, an individual may learn to cook on an electric range but then move into an apartment that has only natural gas appliances, or the date for paying one's rent may change from the first to the tenth of each month. As stated earlier, the ability to generalize a learned skill from one setting to another does not occur naturally with mildly retarded persons but must be assiduously taught. This issue is treated extensively by Liberty in this volume.

## Independent Performance

Related to competent performance over a range of related environments is the implied need to function with minimum supervision or assistance. Adjustment in an unsupervised or minimally supervised living setting requires the regular performance of acquired skills when needed. Among mildly retarded persons in less-supervised settings, independent performance of skills is a major problem (Cuvo & Davis, 1981; Schalock & Harper, 1978). This problem can be remediated if the person's instructional program contains a carefully structured component facilitating maintenance of learned skills over time.

## Normalized Service Settings

Educational programs designed to promote the transition to independent living for mildly retarded persons should utilize the same kind of facilities or settings that are designed for nondisabled persons. These facilities or programs should be age-appropriate and integrated into the community. If students are to value and participate in these educational offerings, the offerings must be free of the stigma associated with segregated facilities. Community colleges may provide one of the best administrative structures available for accomplishing this objective with those who are beyond public school age.

Each of these program characteristics is an important component of any service delivery system that purports to address the transitional needs of mildly retarded persons as they move from adolescence into adulthood. Such a system must begin by paying careful attention to functional content and assessment, an approach referred to by the authors as *program-related assessment* (PRA).

## PROGRAM-RELATED ASSESSMENT

In the mental retardation field, assessment information has been used most often simply to confirm a diagnosis of the condition and thereby to document a person's eligibility for services. Typically, the cornerstone of such documentation is an IQ score, although other information may also be provided in the area of adaptive behavior. When assessment data are collected only for this purpose—diagnosis and eligibility determination—the information gathered can rarely be used effectively as a guide to service delivery. IQ scores and global measures of adaptive behavior are not sufficiently fine-grained to produce useful profiles of an individual's strengths and weaknesses, which might then be incorporated into an individual program plan.

We have labeled this second use of assessment information as "program-related assessment." The PRA model assumes that services delivery normally occurs in an orderly, sequential manner and that formal assessment information can and should provide helpful input into the decision making that occurs during each sequential step in the service delivery process. The decision maker, therefore, should understand the principles and practices of assessment well enough to control the information flow and to interpret information properly once received.

In order for PRA to work effectively three considerations must be addressed and understood: 1) the content of assessment; 2) approaches to assessment; and 3) the uses of assessment information. Each of these topics is discussed briefly in the paragraphs following. A more complete presentation of this model can be found in a recent book by Halpern, Lehmann, Irvin, and Heiry (1982).

### Content of Assessment

When one examines the full array of assessment tools that have been developed in the area of mental retardation, it quickly becomes evident that much more attention has been paid to infants and children than to adolescents and adults. Since the content of adaptive behavior is developmental as a function of age, it is not surprising that many measures of adaptive behavior are either weak or totally irrelevant for use with adolescents or adults.

The state of the art, however, is far from hopeless. The earlier-mentioned book by Halpern et al. (1982) reviews 20 readily available instruments that can be used appropriately with mentally retarded adolescents and adults. Four major content dimensions have emerged from a careful analysis of these instruments: 1) foundations of achievement; 2) foundations of adjustment; 3) community adjustment skills; and 4) prevocational and vocational skills. Each of these major dimensions has been further categorized into several clusters of skills or behaviors. This taxonomy is presented in Table 1.

As Table 1 reveals, 15 clusters have been identified that serve to organize a total of 51 discrete skill or behavioral domains. These 51 domains are meant to serve as a primary conceptual link between assessment and service delivery, because the domains represent skills that can both be measured by existing available instruments and taught or modified through service intervention. Assessment of adaptive behavior is discussed extensively in Chapter 3 by Holman and Bruininks.

### Approaches to Assessment

If the results of assessment are to have direct implications for program planning and evaluation, it is usually prudent to employ an "applied performance" approach to measurement. In other words, rather than using a traditional approach of measuring "traits" to predict performance, the actual competencies that will be taught should be directly assessed, with subsequent instructional decisions based on the results of that assessment.

Three general approaches to applied performance assessment are useful and appropriate: 1) direct assessment of criterion behaviors in real or simulated settings; 2) measurement of knowledge about those criterion behaviors; and 3) evaluation of how retarded persons learn new competencies. The first two of these approaches measure the products or outcomes of

Table 1.   Content clusters and domains for assessing adaptive behavior skills

I.   Foundations of Achievement
   A.   Basic development skills
      1.   Sensory development
      2.   Motor development
      3.   Cognitive development
   B.   Survival numerics
      1.   Basic mathematics
      2.   Time management
   C.   Survival reading
      1.   Basic academic skills
      2.   Functional reading
   D.   Communication
      1.   Expressive language
      2.   Receptive language
      3.   Writing and spelling skills

II.  Foundations of Adjustment
   A.   Knowledge of self
      1.   Self-awareness
      2.   Self-concept
   B.   Emotional and personal adjustment
      1.   Acting out or withdrawal
      2.   Self-stimulation
      3.   Coping
   C.   Social and interpersonal skills
      1.   Basic interaction skills
      2.   Group participation
      3.   Play activities
      4.   Social amenities
      5.   Sexual behavior
      6.   Responsibility

III. Community Adjustment Skills
   A.   Self-help skills
      1.   Dressing
      2.   Eating
      3.   Toileting
   B.   Consumer skills
      1.   Money handling
      2.   Banking
      3.   Budgeting
      4.   Purchasing
   C.   Domestic skills
      1.   Kitchen skills
      2.   Household cleaning
      3.   Household management, maintenance, and repair
      4.   Laundering and clothing care
   D.   Health care
      1.   Treatment of various health problems
      2.   Preventive health measures
      3.   Usage of medication
      4.   Corrective devices
   E.   Knowledge of community
      1.   Independent travel skills
      2.   Community expectations
      3.   Community awareness and use
      4.   Telephone use
   E.   Knowledge of community
      1.   Independent travel skills
      2.   Community expectations
      3.   Community awareness and use
      4.   Telephone use

*(continued)*

Table 1.   *(continued)*

IV.  Prevocational and Vocational Skills
   A.   Job readiness
      1.   Job awareness
      2.   Job application and interview skills
      3.   On-the-job information
   B.   Vocational behavior
      1.   Job performance and productivity
      2.   Work habits and work attitudes
      3.   Work-related skills
      4.   Specific job skills
      5.   Learning and transfer of job skills
   C.   Social behavior on the job.

an examinee's previous learning experiences; the third approach provides an estimate of the examinee's learning potential.

Direct assessment of relevant behavior is best accomplished through a ''criterion-referenced, task-analytic'' approach to measurement. In this approach, skills are viewed as sets of specific behaviors that must be broken into sequential component parts for purposes of both assessment and training. The outcome of this type of assessment provides an inventory of skills already mastered, as well as of skills (or parts of skills) still in need of mastery. Such an inventory is especially relevant for decisions concerning the *acquisition* phase of instructional intervention.

Regarding the second general approach to assessment—knowledge measurement—when retarded adolescents and adults fail to maintain performance after training or fail to generalize learned skills from one setting to another, it is often because of the lack of appropriate rule knowledge rather than the lack of skill. This extremely important topic is explored in detail in the next major section of this chapter.

The third recommended approach to assessment involves measurement of an individual's ability to benefit from direct instruction and correction. The purpose of such assessment is to estimate the level of training resources that will be required to achieve training objectives. One diagnoses in order to learn *how* to teach—not *whether* to teach—an individual, making judgments based on the examinee's responses to *standardized* simulated instruction. An example of this approach for use with severely retarded persons is found in a recently completed assessment instrument developed at the Research and Training Center in Mental Retardation at the University of Oregon (Close, Halpern, Slentz & Irvin, 1982).

## Uses of Assessment Information

When assessment is program related, the information generated will be used to guide students or clients through the service delivery system. There are, essentially, four stages of decision making within the PRA model: 1) needs assessment; 2) program planning; 3) program implementation and monitoring; and 4) program evaluation. An elaboration of this model is presented in Figure 1.

Needs-assessment activities and decisions affect service priorities. Information is collected concerning the behavior of handicapped individuals, the goals and priorities that are important for them, and the availability of appropriate services to reduce any gaps between current and desired behavior. Eligibility is a function of the congruence between individual

needs and environmental opportunities. Indeed, the same individual could be "eligible" for a particular service in one community but not in another, the difference lying only in the presence or absence of needed resources.

Once service priorities have been established for a given individual, a specific plan must then be developed for the actual delivery of services. In contemporary programs, this is usually expressed in the form of an individualized program plan (IPP), such as the individualized education program (IEP) in special education or the individualized written rehabilitation program (IWRP) in rehabilitation programs. The development of any form of IPP is greatly enhanced by the integration of assessment information that was gathered and utilized during the needs-assessment process.

Service implementation should logically follow from the prescriptions that are contained within an IPP. Monitoring is required in order to ascertain whether the prescribed services are actually delivered in a timely and appropriate manner. By utilizing the information that is acquired through monitoring, programs that

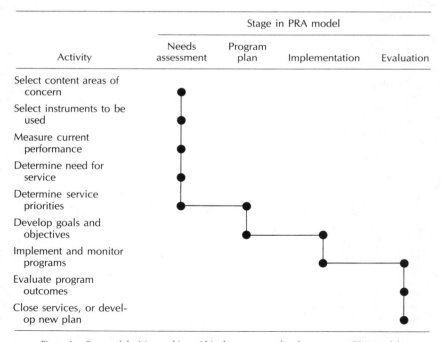

Figure 1.  Stages of decision making within the program-related assessment (PRA) model.

are not achieving their desired effects can be modified.

Program evaluation information serves two purposes: 1) to summarize the extent of IPP accomplishment at the time when a specified set of services is terminated; and 2) to lay a foundation for the development of a new program plan addressing different goals and objectives. In this sense, the PRA model should be regarded as cyclical rather than linear. Several illustrations of the PRA model are provided by Halpern et al. (1982). Utilization of this model can assist in documenting both the successes and failures of instructional interventions.

## EFFECTIVE TEACHING FOR GENERALIZATION AND MAINTENANCE

Contemporary rehabilitation and special education literature is replete with successful demonstrations of teaching strategies to promote skill acquisition. However, the literature remains sparse regarding a methodology that ensures the performance of these skills in nontraining situations and over time (i.e., generalization and maintenance). Given that the goal of education and rehabilitation programs is to prepare individuals for transition to independent adult living, a technology of generalization and maintenance remains one of the most important challenges facing the field today.

The purpose of this section is threefold: 1) to provide definitions of generalization and maintenance; 2) to present a brief historical perspective on these topics; and 3) to describe major current approaches related to programming for generalization and maintenance.

### Generalization and Maintenance Defined

A widely used functional definition of generalization is offered by Stokes and Baer (1977, p. 350) as "the occurrence of relevant behavior under different, non-training conditions (i.e., across subjects, settings, people, behaviors, and/or time) without scheduling of the same events in those conditions as had been scheduled in the training conditions." From the same functional perspective, maintenance is simply a subtype of generalization: namely, the occurrence of behavior over time after training has been discontinued.

A different perspective looks at influencing factors and makes a distinction between generalization and maintenance as two separate phenomena controlled by different events (Koegel & Rincover, 1977). Generalization is primarily affected by the extent to which stimuli present in the training environment are also present in criterion environments. For example, if an individual has been trained in a laboratory setting, the stimuli in the person's home and community will differ greatly from those in the laboratory, and little generalization can be expected. However, if that individual is trained in settings that closely approximate the real world, the likelihood of generalization is greatly enhanced. Thus, generalization is primarily influenced by the similarity of stimuli in both settings. Maintenance is different. When skills are generalized but all programmed consequences cease, the individual may revert to inappropriate behavior. For example, a person who is skilled at washing the kitchen floor using any number of different mops or detergents may still choose not to perform this task regularly. Maintenance, therefore, appears to be influenced more by the presence or absence of consequences in nontraining environments.

### Historical Perspective: Active versus Passive

The phenomenon of generalization was first documented in research related to discrimination and stimulus control. As an organism is brought under the control of a particular stimulus, similar but untrained stimuli will also elicit responding (Skinner, 1953). An analogous phenomenon was found regarding response generalization: similar, but untrained responses will occur after the training of one particular response (Keller & Schoenfeld, 1950).

Important information regarding the effects of reinforcement schedules on response maintenance has also been provided by operant researchers (Ferster & Skinner, 1957; Sidman,

1953). This work was conducted in the context of resistance to extinction. That is, subjects were trained under established schedules of reinforcement, and the degree of continued responding was assessed when all programming was discontinued. It was found that intermittent reinforcement was a more powerful conditioner than continuous reinforcement.

Both approaches to conditioning, classical and operant, have tended to view generalization and maintenance more as phenomena to be observed than to be purposefully manipulated. As a result, many theorists viewed generalization and maintenance as passive phenomena instead of as specific training outcomes.

Stokes and Baer (1977), in their review of the applied behavioral literature, demonstrated the extent to which this "passive" perspective has carried over to teaching practices. The majority of the research reviewed used a "train and hope" method—that is, the target behavior was trained and the occurrence of any generalized effects was assessed but not specifically programmed. Most studies employing this approach failed to achieve expected levels of generalization. These findings substantiated the view expressed by Baer, Wolf, and Risley (1968) that generalization should be programmed rather than expected.

## Current Approaches to Programming for Generalization and Maintenance

At present there are no comprehensive approaches available to train mildly retarded persons to generalize and maintain newly acquired skills. Several techniques, however, provide the foundations upon which such a package might be formulated. Six of these methods appear most promising and are discussed next.

*Select and Teach Functional Skills* The importance of selecting, assessing, and training skills that are *functional* and, thus, have maximum relevance to the daily lives of mentally retarded persons has already been discussed. In the context of generalization and maintenance, training functional skills increases the likelihood that an individual will utilize these skills to obtain reinforcement in the natural environment. For example, an indi-

vidual who is trained to cook a variety of recipes independently will likely utilize these skills, owing to the naturally reinforcing value of being able to choose when and what to eat at meal time. Baer and Wolf (1970) described this technique as "trapping." The success of this approach to programming for generalization and maintenance has been reported by several researchers (Buell, Stoddard, Harris, & Baer, 1963; Hall & Broden, 1967; Seymour & Stokes, 1976).

*Training by Example: Induction* Induction occurs when an individual has been presented with several examples that represent a stimulus or response class (i.e., a concept) and can then identify other members of the same stimulus or response class. In other words, after successfully discriminating the relevant stimuli that define members of a class from those that do not belong, the learner devises a "rule" that can be applied across the entire class (Engelmann & Carnine, 1982). For example, a teacher may want a student to be able to discriminate grocery stores from other types of stores. This concept may be taught by taking the individual to several grocery stores and identifying them as instances, as well as several other stores (e.g., department stores) and identifying them as noninstances. The student will eventually construct a "rule" concerning the essential stimulus characteristics that a store must possess to be classified as a grocery store.

In the Stokes and Baer (1977) review mentioned earlier, three strategies were identified that employed the use of multiple exemplars to obtain generalized performance. However, the most comprehensive application of the inductive approach has been the Direct Instruction model (Engelmann & Carnine, 1982), which provides explicit strategies related to defining an instructional universe, analyzing the content, and designing specific instructional procedures for presenting information to small groups of learners. The Direct Instruction model was originally designed to teach culturally disadvantaged children basic academic skills (reading, language, and arithmetic). Its success has been thoroughly researched and demonstrated (Abt Associates, 1974; Brophy & Evertson, 1976; Soar, 1973) with this population. Recently, the approach has also been applied successfully with severely retarded individuals in facilitating the generalization of skills such as tool use (Colvin, 1981), vending machine operation (Sprague & Horner, 1982), and manual crimping of electronic components (Horner & McDonald, 1982). Both the power and the versatility of the Direct Instruction methodology hold promise for broader applications.

### Training through Rules: Deduction

Skinner defined a rule as a verbal or written description of a contingency (i.e., a response/behavior, the stimulus conditions under which the behavior should occur, and the consequences that will be forthcoming if it occurs or does not occur). Deduction occurs when an individual has been taught a general rule and responds correctly to specific examples of the class described by the rule. For example, an individual who adopts the rule "shop at discount stores for cosmetics, because they are cheaper there," will not need to shop comparatively for such items. Skinner (1953) acknowledged the importance of rules in society and education as an efficient means of instruction. An individual who understands rule statements can use these rules to respond appropriately without the need to be shaped directly by environmental contingencies (i.e., examples).

Instructional strategies leading to the acquisition of rules have been explored extensively in the laboratory. These include utilizing verbal rehearsal, concurrent presentation of stimuli, and methods of rules review (Burger, Blackman, & Clark, 1981; Campione & Brown, 1977). However, the extent to which rule learning actually contributes to generalized or maintained performance in real world settings has not yet been investigated and, thus, remains an empirical question.

In considering the relative applicability of inductive and deductive approaches for teaching generalized skills to mildly handicapped persons, it appears that both offer advantages.

Induction, especially as detailed by the direct instruction model, has clearly been proven to be a powerful means of facilitating generalized performance in many types of learners. However, while this means of instruction may be most efficient for naive or low-performing learners, this may not be the case for more-experienced or more-sophisticated individuals (Becker, Engelmann, & Thomas, 1975). Given the current state of our knowledge, it would appear that a combination of inductive and deductive approaches should be used with older mildly handicapped persons.

### Training in the Criterion Environment

During recent years, teachers of mentally retarded persons have been strongly advised to teach their students in community settings (Belmore & Brown, 1978; Brown, Nietupski & Hamre-Nietupski, 1976; Liberty, this volume). However, this community-based instruction may not always be the most efficient method, especially for mildly retarded individuals (Wilcox & Bellamy, 1982). Classroom instruction provides teachers with the opportunity to present rules and examples clearly, to provide students with practice on the response chains associated with each rule, and to offer students corrective feedback. The provision of such instruction in the community is often limited by staff and resource constraints and by the uncontrolled variability that accompanies real-world settings.

Nevertheless, until an individual can demonstrate skills in the criterion environment, training cannot be considered a success. To ensure generalization of skills learned in the classroom, the individual must ultimately be exposed to the stimuli, variation, and consequences of natural settings. However, students can practice and refine skills in the classroom prior to receiving guidance and feedback on the finer discriminations often required in the community, thereby increasing the overall efficiency of the training program.

*Self-Management Strategies* Historically, mentally retarded individuals have been characterized as very dependent. Even when a mentally retarded person learned a skill, it was assumed that in most cases the individual would not initiate or maintain performance without ongoing supervision. However, a promising approach to maintenance has begun to receive attention in the literature. Skinner (1953) discussed the concept that individuals use strategies to control their own behavior. Thoresen and Mahoney (1974, p. 2) defined self-control as persons "directing, maintaining and coordinating their actions without continuous surveillance." Numerous researchers have demonstrated that individuals can be trained to utilize techniques of self-control that will enable them to manage their own behavior more efficiently. The implications of teaching mentally retarded individuals techniques that will permit them to direct and maintain their own behavior have been elaborated by Mahoney and Mahoney (1976).

Several different self-management strategies have been identified. These include environmental programming and planning, self-monitoring, and self-instructional reinforcement. For example, environmental programming and planning has typically taken the form of training the individual to use written or picture cues as a readily accessible prompt for initiating performance. Such cues have been used to teach mentally retarded subjects independent cooking skills (Bishop, 1981; Robinson-Wilson, 1977) and independent task change in vocational settings (Connis, 1979; Sowers & Verdi, 1983).

Campione and Brown (1977) have advocated the importance of training students to monitor and evaluate their own performance. Self-monitoring provides an individual with a means to track the extent to which critical skills or behaviors are being achieved and is, thus, the basis for self-correction. A large body of research has established that mentally retarded persons can be trained to accurately monitor their own performance (Connis, 1979; Horner & Brigham, 1979; Nelson, Lipinski, & Boykin, 1978).

Self-instruction has been recommended with the rationale that verbal self-instructions are the stimuli most readily available to an individual (Skinner, 1953). Self-instructions may include verbal prompts and feedback to oneself. Meichenbaum (1977) was a pioneer in

this area, working with schizophrenic adults and behavior problem children. A related area of research involves verbal-behavior correspondence (Risley & Hart, 1968; Israel & O'Leary, 1973). The extent to which mentally retarded subjects can be trained to self-instruct or reinforce themselves verbally has yet to be investigated. The absence of literature in this area may be attributed to the poor language skills of many mentally retarded individuals. However, the relatively intact verbal skills of most mildly retarded persons is a factor supporting the use of the technique with this group.

*Long-Term Follow-Up*   A mildly mentally retarded person should be well prepared for independent community living if he or she has learned functionally relevant living skills, a set of rules pertinent to these skills, and has been trained to utilize strategies to manage his or her own performance. The individual should be able to deal adaptively with most new situations and maintain performance over long periods of time. However, when external monitoring and feedback are withdrawn, the deterioration of skills is well documented in the literature. A variety of factors operate to exacerbate this problem. First, a particular skill may not be reinforced by the natural environment and, in fact, competing behaviors may be reinforced. Lack of opportunities to engage in certain low-frequency behaviors— for example, the necessity to respond to emergency situations—may also account for lack of maintenance. Finally, even with a careful analysis of stimulus and response classes that represent the range of stimuli and responses required in the real world, unusual occurrences will undoubtedly arise and cause the individual difficulty in responding. In order to ensure that the skills learned maintain over a long period of time, staff should provide gradually decreasing monitoring checks, feedback for continued performance or lack of it, "booster" sessions on low-frequency behaviors, and assistance related to unusual and novel situations.

No research has been conducted on the topic of postprogram follow-up in community settings. Sowers, Lundervold, Swanson, and

Budd (1980) however, have suggested a useful maintenance checking and programming schedule for staff in competitive employment programs for mentally retarded persons. This schedule advises high levels of in-person checks and feedback during the first few weeks after placement. These are slowly decreased and supplanted by telephone call and work-supervisor-written evaluations. In-person checks are ultimately terminated while telephone call and work supervisor evaluations are maintained but reduced to a minimal level. Through this schedule, any problems in work performance can be pinpointed early and assistance implemented. This approach appears to have direct applicability to the follow-up of mentally retarded graduates of an independent living program.

The next section of this chapter describes an existing curriculum that incorporates the six techniques just described and is focused on teaching independent living skills to mildly retarded persons.

## AVAILABLE CURRICULUM MATERIALS

The principles delineated above have been distilled from the training literature. Individually they offer great potential for teaching a variety of skills in many different contexts. Typically, these techniques are utilized independently or in small combinations for training specific skills or teaching a narrow range of content. The outcome of such applications is generally desirable with regard to attaining a specified objective. Seldom, however, do such restricted approaches result in students acquiring the breadth and depth of knowledge necessary to generalize their performance independently over time. Without such outcomes, the true goal of training has not been realized, and no single technique can guarantee such results.

The Independent Living Skills Curriculum (Taylor, Close, Carlson, & Larrabee, 1981) described here is intended to alleviate those shortcomings by systematically combining the above principles into a comprehensive program package designed to foster efficient learning, generalized performance, and long-term maintenance of independent functioning.

The package employs classroom activities coupled with community-based training and long-term follow-up contact. The program modules include banking, budgeting, bill paying, home maintenance and safety, personal hygiene, meal planning, and cooking.

The power of the program resides in its combining of many successful approaches and techniques into one broad strategy. The variety of methods employed increases the likelihood that the teaching will encompass the learning style of numerous individual students with different needs and will enhance the efficiency of instruction for all. The major steps employed by the Independent Living Skills Curriculum are described in the paragraphs following.

### Analysis

In order for any teaching endeavor to be successful, it is essential that two critical elements be carefully examined prior to initiating instruction. First, the content to be taught must be analyzed with respect to its key features. Second, the learner must be assessed to determine the extent to which the content is appropriate for him or her.

Content analysis for the Independent Living Skills Curriculum follows a somewhat different process than in most curricula. Other programs are typically designed around topics, with information presented to students in a step-by-step fashion within each topic area. Such an organizational scheme, although logically appealing, may actually increase difficulty for the learner by communicating the idea that each topic is a distinct and different entity. By contrast, the Independent Living Skills Curriculum utilizes procedures that analyze instructional content for operational *sameness* across topics. In this manner one can readily identify the range of critical stimulus dimensions and the major response features that are shared by many examples in varied topic areas. These shared characteristics can then be taught as a unit across the entire range of instances to which they apply, thereby inducing generalized performance. Simultaneously, examples that are similar but not the same can be identified and included in the teaching to ensure that discriminations are learned in reference to only those features that are relevant for the operation. For example, while a topical analysis of banking might suggest teaching savings deposits and checking deposits as separate entities, an operational analysis would imply the desirability of teaching all depositing as a unit that presents clearly the sameness as well as the differences between savings and checking operations.

Operational analysis also allows trainers to identify those reinforcers that occur in the natural environment. This encourages trainers to include naturally occurring reinforcers in the training procedures and to utilize them as salient stimuli in fostering independent performance. Finally, a comprehensive analysis of operations facilitates functional assessment of students by specifying the skills required for criterion performance as well as the contexts in which such performance will be expected to occur. With this knowledge it becomes possible to document related skills that are already in the learner's repertoire and thereby to determine the viability of a particular program module and the likelihood of success for any given learner.

## Conversational Method and Rehearsal

The conversational method (Close, Irvin, Taylor, & Agosta, 1981) was designed to strike a balance between the systematic presentation of information and the relaxed, individualized, and creative use of relevant experiences and examples. It is not a free-flowing instructional discussion. Rather, a consistent format is followed to assist students in learning skills and understanding the contexts in which they are to be performed. The method builds upon the instructional design work of Engelmann and Carnine (1982) and is utilized for the initial presentation of both specific discriminations and general rules. Use of this technique permits the linguistic and conceptual abilities of students to contribute to the efficiency of learning.

The conversational method utilizes discussion for the initial presentation of information. In a group format, content is presented that describes the skill to be learned, tells where,

when, and how it is to be used, and why it is important. Students are then asked to generate examples or to respond to questions. In this manner, the conversational method presents information that defines a skill, describes the contexts in which it applies, and delineates the contingencies regarding its utilization.

Following the initial discussion the teacher presents a sequence of positive and negative examples indicating the range of instances and clearly illustrating the essential feature(s) that the student must discriminate among in order to utilize the skill appropriately. The sequence is also designed so that it requires students to overtly perform the critical operation called for by the skill. If the sequence adequately samples the range of instances and juxtaposes positive and negative examples to show sameness and differences, then generalization to other nontrained examples within the set will more readily occur.

After the students have demonstrated criterion performance, they are required to use the skill in rehearsal activities. These behavioral rehearsals allow for practice and feedback, as well as for opportunities to integrate the new skill with other previously learned skills.

In this manner the conversational method and its related classroom activities utilize both inductive and deductive processes in teaching content. Specific motoric and conceptual skills are combined with a sequence of examples that precisely sample the range of application, thereby inducing generalizations to other nontrained examples within that universe. Simultaneously, students are learning and rehearsing general rules and providing relevant examples from their own experiences. Once learned, these rules form the basis for self-instruction in community settings, thereby enhancing generalized performance.

Finally, this phase of the program also incorporates training in self-management techniques that students will later apply to monitor their own performance in the community. Students are provided with either written task lists or picture cue stimuli and are taught to use them to prompt and evaluate their own performance. These self-management skills form the basis for the maintenance of independent living skills after training has been concluded.

## In Vivo Training

The program is not complete until the teacher can *verify* that a student will perform newly acquired skills reliably in the community without prompts. Therefore, the next phase of the program involves training in the criterion environment. Upon completion of the classroom program, students are escorted to community settings in which they apply the rules and perform the skills that have been learned and practiced in the classroom. Assistance is delivered as necessary, but such prompts are faded or dropped as expeditiously as possible in order to encourage independent performance. If the initial teaching and behavioral rehearsal have been properly designed and executed, this segment of the program will be completed quickly and a follow-up phase will commence.

## Follow-Up

During the first phase of follow-up, staff members personally visit the student to ascertain if criterion performance is continuing across all settings. If the data indicate that performance is adequate, these personal contacts are replaced first by weekly telephone calls to the students and then by monthly checkups with either the students themselves or significant others who have knowledge of their performance. If warranted, procedures are reinstated to assure maintenance. The process continues until the data show conclusively that follow-up is no longer needed.

## Summary

The Independent Living Skills Curriculum has been described in terms of its four major components: analysis, the conversational method, in vivo training, and follow-up. Particular emphasis has been placed on illustrating the relationships between these curriculum components and the six techniques described previously for enhancing the generalization and maintenance of skills. The last section of this chapter describes and recommends a service delivery program for instructing mildly retarded adults in a normalized community setting.

## A NORMALIZED INSTRUCTIONAL PROGRAM

Generally speaking, public education facilities are potentially well suited to provide transitional programs for mildly retarded persons. Public Law 94-142 mandates a free and appropriate education for all children up to age 21. The career education movement has legitimized nonacademic alternatives as viable and important components of secondary education. Work-study programs are sometimes available that offer both classroom-based instruction and practicum experience in community-based vocational settings. As a student approaches graduation from high school, concrete planning must promote the transition to adult life in the community. This planning effort should include postsecondary educational opportunities as well as possibilities for work and independent living. The community college is the typical setting available for nondisabled citizens who wish to upgrade skills or learn new information.

As communities continue to provide additional resources to disabled adults, increased emphasis should be placed on utilizing existing facilities and programs. The community college concept fits this criterion nicely in that adult education programs of all kinds are proliferating rapidly throughout the country. A typical community college catalog includes such diverse offerings as associate of arts programs, registered nurse training, welding and diesel mechanics programs, remedial reading, English as a second language, small-business administration, weaving, photography classes, and high school equivalency degrees. The range of course offerings is dictated primarily by the needs of the community and the imagination of college officials.

These varied program offerings of community colleges reflect an underlying instructional philosophy of being responsive to the complete educational needs of the adult community. Many of the program offerings provide a blend of classroom instruction with practicum experiences. For example, students in nursing programs learn basic nursing procedures and practices both in the classroom and in hospital or clinic settings.

Such a model is also ideal for mildly retarded persons learning independent living skills. The classroom setting would include detailed, systematic instruction on functional tasks such as bill paying, banking, meal planning, nutrition, kitchen safety, social/interpersonal competence, and other relevant areas. The practicum component would occur in appropriate natural settings, such as the student's own home or apartment, the bank, grocery store, or job site.

Although community college programs for mildly retarded adults are not widespread at this time, examples are beginning to emerge as the broad mandate grows to encompass disabled persons. One such example can be found in Eugene, Oregon, in the form of a jointly sponsored project involving the Rehabilitation Research and Training Center in Mental Retardation at the University of Oregon and Lane Community College. This project is described next.

### Adult Skills Development Program

The Lane Community College Adult Skills Development Program is designed to provide education and training to mildly retarded young adults in skills that are needed to promote transition to independent living. The service program is located at the downtown branch of the community college. Courses currently include social and interpersonal competence in work and community settings; money management including banking, budgeting, and bill paying; and personal management including health care, home maintenance, food preparation, purchasing, and safety.

Course offerings are organized into 10-week modules, following the regular college schedule. Instruction takes place in both classroom and community settings. Small group and individual instruction is provided to each student. Class size is limited to 10 students per course. Each class is instructed by a lead teacher and part-time instructional aides.

Funds for the program are provided by regular student fees and subsidies from adult service agencies, school districts, and parents. An advisory board comprised of students, parents, school district and adult agency personnel, and representatives from local businesses helps to identify and recruit students, structure the fee system, coordinate individual learner plans where multiple agencies may be involved, guide the content of the educational programs, and help identify job and residential placement opportunities for program graduates.

The program has only been in operation for several months at the time of this writing (January, 1984), and so it is not yet possible to report outcomes. Responsiveness and referrals, however, have been extremely strong and positive, indicating that the need for such a program is great. Extensive information will be gathered on both the process and outcomes of this project, so that its utility as a model program for other community colleges can eventually be evaluated.

### SUMMARY

The trends of the past decade have been a mixed blessing for mildly retarded adults. On the positive side, powerful techniques have evolved in both assessment and instruction, and new legislation has emerged that greatly enhances the opportunities for all disabled persons to live more normal and satisfying lives in their communities. This same legislation, however, has required that resources be first focused on programs for historically ignored, severely disabled persons. As a consequence, many mildly retarded persons have "slipped between the cracks" of programs for disabled persons and generic service programs. This problem has been especially critical for mildly retarded young adults who are in the transitional period of leaving school and assuming adult roles in the community.

The approach described in this chapter would alleviate this problem. Program-related assessment sets the stage for a functional approach to both diagnosis and intervention.

Techniques are available for enhancing the generalization and maintenance of learned skills. These techniques have been incorporated into at least one set of instructional materials known as the *Independent Living Skills Curriculum*. Furthermore, the community college system is emerging as a resource for mildly retarded adults who need additional assistance in assuming adult roles.

These positive trends are not yet firmly entrenched, however, and they will need much nurturance in order to achieve their potential. It is our responsibility to make sure that these opportunities are realized.

## REFERENCES

Abt Associates. *Assessment of selected resources for severely handicapped children and youth*, Vol. 1. Cambridge, MA: Abt Associates, 1974.

Baer, D.M., & Wolf, M.M. The entry into natural communities of reinforcement. In: R. Ulrich, T. Stachnik, & J. Mabry (eds.), *Control of Human Behavior*, 1970, *2*, 319–324.

Baer, D.M., Wolf, M., & Risley, T.R. Some current dimensions of applied behavior analysis. *Journal of Applied Behavior Analysis*, 1968, *1*, 91–97.

Baller, W.R., Charles, D.C., & Miller, E.L. *Mid-Life attainment of the mentally retarded: A longitudinal study*. Lincoln: University of Nebraska, 1966.

Becker, W.C., Engelmann, S.E., & Thomas, P.R. *Teaching 1: Classroom management*. Palo Alto, CA: Science Research Associates, 1975.

Bellamy, G.T., Rhoades, L., Bourbeau, P.E., & Mank, D.M. Mental retardation services in sheltered workshops and day activity programs: Consumer outcomes and policy alternatives. In: W.W. Williams & G.T. Bellamy (eds.), *Appraisal of work opportunities and related services for adults with retardation*. Washington, DC: President's Committee on Mental Deficiency, 1982.

Belmore, K., & Brown, L. A job skill inventory strategy designed for severely handicapped potential workers. In: N. Haring & D. Bricker (eds.), *Teaching the severely handicapped*, Vol. 3. Columbus, OH: Special Press, 1978.

Bishop, K. *Teaching time management to severely handicapped school age children*. Unpublished masters thesis, University of Oregon, Division of Special Education and Rehabilitation, Eugene, 1981.

Brolin, D., & Kokaska, C. *Career education for handicapped children and youth*. Columbus, OH: Charles E. Merrill Publishing Co., 1979.

Brophy, J.E., & Evertson, C.M. *Learning from teaching: A developmental approach*. Boston: Allyn & Bacon, 1976.

Brown, L., Nietupski, J., & Hamre-Nietupski, S. The criterion of ultimate functioning. In: M.A. Thomas (ed.), *Hey, don't forget about me*. Reston, VA: Council for Exceptional Children, 1976.

Buell, S., Stoddard, P., Harris, F.R., & Baer, D.M. Collateral social development accompanying reinforcement of outdoor play in a preschool child. *Journal of Applied Behavior Analysis*, 1963, *1*, 167–173.

Burger, A., Blackman, L.S., & Clark, H.T. Generalization of verbal abstraction strategies by EMR children and adults. *American Journal of Mental Deficiency*, 1981, *85*(6), 611–618.

Campione, J.C., & Brown, A.L. Memory and metamemory development in educable retarded children. In: R.V. Kail, Jr., & J.W. Hagen (eds.), *Perspectives on the development of memory and cognition*. Hillsdale, NJ: Lawrence Erlbaum Associates, 1977.

Clark, G. *Career education for the handicapped child in the elementary classroom*. Denver: Love Publishing Co., 1979.

Close, D.W., Halpern, A.S., Slentz, K.I., & Irvin, L.K. *Community living assessment and teaching system: Assessment manual*. Eugene: University of Oregon, 1982.

Close, D.W., Irvin, L.K., Taylor, V.E., & Agosta, J.M. Community living skills instruction for mildly retarded persons. *Exceptional Education Quarterly*, 1981, *2*(1), 75–85.

Colvin, G.T. *An evaluation of a general case program to teach screwdriver use to severely handicapped learners*. Unpublished doctoral dissertation, University of Oregon, Eugene, 1981.

Connis, R.T. The effects of sequential picture cues, self-recording and praise on the job task sequencing of retarded adults. *Journal of Applied Behavior Analysis*, 1979, *12*, 355–362.

Crnic, K., & Pym, H. Training mentally retarded adults in independent living skills. *Mental Retardation*, 1979, *17*(1), 1316.

Cuvo, A.J., & Davis, P.K. Home living for developmentally disabled persons: Instructional design and evaluation. *Exceptional Education Quarterly*, 1981, *2*(1), 87–98.

Edgerton, R.B. *The cloak of competence*. Berkeley, CA: University of California Press, 1967.

Engelmann, S., & Carnine, D. *Theory of instruction: Principles and applications*. New York: Irvington Publishers, 1982.

Ferster, C.B., & Skinner, B.F. *Schedules of reinforcement*. New York: Appleton-Century-Crofts, 1957.

Hall, R.V., & Broden, M. Behavior changes in brain-injured children through social reinforcement. *Journal of Experimental Child Psychology*, 1967, *5*, 139–149.

Halpern, A. Adolescents and young adults. *Exceptional Children*, 1979, *45*, 518–523.

Halpern, A.S., Lehmann, J.P., Irvin, L.K., & Heiry, T.J. *Contemporary assessment for mentally retarded adolescents and adults*. Baltimore: University Park Press, 1982.

Haywood, H.C. What happened to mild and moderate retardation? *American Journal of Mental Deficiency*, 1979, *83*(5), 429–431.

Horner, R.D., & McDonald, R. Comparison of single instance and general case instruction in teaching a generalized vocational skill. *Journal of the Association of the Severely Handicapped*, 1982, *7*, 7–20.

Horner, R.H., & Brigham, T.A. Self-management of on-task behavior in two retarded children. *Education and Training of the Mentally Retarded*, 1979, *14*, 18–24.

Israel, A.C., & O'Leary, K.D. Developing correspondence between children's words and deeds. *Child Development*, 1973, *44*, 575–581.

Keller, F.S., & Schoenfeld, W.N. *Principles of psychology*. New York: Appleton-Century-Crofts, 1950.

Koegel, R.L., & Rincover, A. Research on the difference between generalization and maintenance in extra-therapy responding. *Journal of Applied Behavior Analysis*, 1977, *10*, 1–12.

Lovitt, T.C. Self-management projects with children with behavioral disabilities. *Journal of Learning Disabilities*, 1973, *6*, 15–28.

McDevitt, S., Smith, P., Schmidt, D., & Rosen, M. The deinstitutionalized citizen: Adjustment and quality of life. *Mental Retardation*, 1978, *16*, 22–28.

Mahoney, M.J., & Mahoney, K. Self-control techniques with the mentally retarded. *Exceptional Children*, 1976, *42*, 338–339.

Meichenbaum, D. *Cognitive-behavior modification: An integrative approach*. New York: Plenum Press, 1977.

Nelson, R.O., Lipinski, D., & Boykin, R.A. The effects of self-recorders training and the obstrusiveness of the self-recording device on the accuracy and reactivity of self-monitoring. *Behavior Therapy*, 1978, *9*, 200–208.

Risley, T., & Hart, B. Developing correspondence between verbal and nonverbal behavior of preschool children. *Journal of Applied Behavior Analysis*, 1968, *1*, 267–281.

Robinson-Wilson, M.A. Picture recipe cards as an approach to teaching severely and profoundly retarded adults to cook. *Education and Training of the Mentally Retarded*, 1977, *12*, 69.

Schalock, R.L., & Harper, R.S. Placement from community-based mental retardation programs: How well do clients do? *American Journal of Mental Deficiency*, 1978, *83*, 240–247.

Seymour, F.W., & Stokes, T.F. Self-recording in training girls to increase work and evoke staff praise in an institution for offenders. *Journal of Applied Behavior Analysis*, 1976, *9*, 41–54.

Sidman, M. Two temporal parameters of the maintenance of avoidance by the white rat. *Journal of Comparative Physiological Psychology*, 1953, 253–261.

Sitkei, E.G. After group home living—what alternatives? *Mental Retardation*, 1980, *18*, 9–13.

Skinner, B.F. *Science and human behavior*. New York: MacMillan Co., 1953.

Soar, R.S. *Follow-through classroom process measurement and pupil growth (1970-71): Final report*. Gainesville, FL: University of Florida, College of Education, 1973.

Sowers, J., Lundervold, D., Swanson, M., & Budd, C. *Competitive employment training for mentally retarded adults: A systematic approach*. Eugene: University of Oregon, Specialized Training Program, 1980.

Sowers, J., Rusch, F.R., Connis, R.T., & Cummings, L.T. Teaching mentally retarded adults to time-manage in a vocational setting. *Journal of Applied Behavior Analysis*, 1980, *13*, 119–128.

Sowers, J., & Verdi, M. *Training moderately retarded secondary school students job flexibility through the use of picture cues*. Unpublished masters thesis, University of Oregon, Division of Special Education and Rehabilitation, Eugene, 1983.

Sprague, J.R., & Horner, R.H. The effects of single-instance, multiple-instance and general case training on generalized vending machine use by moderately and severely handicapped students. *Journal of the Association for the Severely Handicapped*, 1982.

Stokes, T.F., & Baer, D.M. An implicit technology of generalization. *Journal of Applied Behavior Analysis*, 1977, *10*, 349–367.

Taylor, V.E., Close, D.W., Carlson, C., & Larrabee, D. *Independent Living Skills Curriculum: Teacher's manual*. Eugene: University of Oregon, 1981.

Thoresen, C.E., & Mahoney, M.J. *Behavioral self-control*. New York: Holt, Rinehart, & Winston, 1974.

Wilcox, B., & Bellamy, G.T. *Design of high school programs for severely handicapped students*. Baltimore: Paul H. Brookes Publishing Co., 1982.

Wimmer, D. Functional learning curricula in the secondary schools. *Exceptional Children*, 1981, *47*, 610–616.

Winshel, J.R., & Ensher, G.L. Educability revisited: Curricula implications for the mentally retarded. *Education and Training of the Mentally Retarded*, 1978, *13*(2), 131–138.

# Chapter 7

# Competitive Employment Education

## A Systems-Analytic
## Approach to Transitional
## Programming for the
## Student with Severe Handicaps

*Frank R. Rusch and Dennis E. Mithaug*

The behavior analytic approach has offered much to the vocational training of severely handicapped individuals. Strategies emanating from this approach have proven successful in teaching, for example, moderately and severely mentally retarded individuals to assemble (Bellamy, Peterson, & Close, 1975; Crosson, 1969; Gold, 1972; Hunter & Bellamy, 1976) and to generalize (Horner & McDonald, 1982) complex tasks and to decrease inappropriate behaviors (Mithaug, 1978; Mithaug & Hanawalt, 1977; Rusch & Close, 1976; Rusch, Close, Hops, & Agosta, 1976). Indeed, a number of texts describe model applications of behavior principles to increase prevocational (Mithaug, 1981a, 1981b) and vocational behavior (Bellamy, Horner, & Inman, 1979; Rusch & Mithaug, 1980; Wehman, 1981; Wehman & McLaughlin, 1980).

Although the behavior analytic approach has assisted in efforts to determine how to teach a particular skill or to change a given behavior, it offers little to suggest *what* to teach. For these guidelines, one must look elsewhere. Traditionally, the developmental model has been utilized, which suggests a sequence of behaviors one might expect if a child were developing normally. Skills or behaviors are taught as they appear in the sequence of normal development. There has been much dissatisfaction with this model, however, leading many to search for more useful and pragmatic approaches. One of the most viable of these takes into account the *social context* in which the individual must ultimately function. This perspective is a dramatic departure from traditional views that focus upon individuals in isolation from their *social environments*. Often referred to as the *criterion of ultimate functioning* (Brown, Nietupski, & Hamre-Nietupski, 1977), this approach searches for answers to the "what to teach" question by examining the behaviors individuals must be able to perform

The authors gratefully acknowledge John L. Gifford, Janis Chadsey-Rusch, and David M. White for their comments on an earlier draft of this chapter.

in settings in which they are ultimately going to be placed (e.g., on the job, in the community). This approach and others like it (Belmore & Brown, 1978; Mithaug, Hagmeier, & Haring, 1977) have opened a new arena for career planning that may prove to be as influential in developing effective educational programs as were the classic studies employing behavior principles to control behaviors of severely handicapped individuals.

Because the social-systems perspective is relatively new and its applications are just beginning to be tested, there is a need to define this approach with respect to vocational training. A set of definitions, implications, and propositions based upon the social-systems perspective has yet to appear in the special education–vocational training literature. Consequently, this chapter introduces two aspects of the social systems perspective: (1) implications of a systems-analytic approach for special education and (2) implications of a systems-analytic approach for competitive employment education. The first part of the chapter addresses current and future roles, role performances, and role expectations for handicapped youth to which special education must respond. In addition, it examines these roles, performances, and expectations as they change throughout the students' life span. Finally, four levels of a systems-analytic approach are introduced. The second part of the chapter expands upon the first by introducing implications for curricula, research, and service. The first implication is that there should be a definition of special education and vocational training based upon the systems-analytic approach through a competitive employment education. The second and third implications regard a framework to develop program content and vocational training approaches. The final implication relates to research directions for competitive employment education.

## SYSTEMS-ANALYTIC
## APPROACH FOR SPECIAL EDUCATION

Brown et al.'s (1977) original formulation of the "criterion of ultimate functioning" for planning programs for a handicapped person postulated the need to carefully analyze behaviors and skills required in *settings* in which that person would ultimately live his or her life. Brown et al. suggested that these behaviors and skills should form the basis for developing educational programs and the instructional environment. This approach raised fundamental questions regarding the nature and importance of targeted settings. All targeted settings share important characteristics. They are foremost, *social settings* in which individuals perform functions or roles in prescribed ways. Targeted settings are, in other words, *social systems* containing "patterns of interhuman behavior which are interdependent in such a way that any change in one pattern is attended by compensatory changes in the others which preserve the general arrangement" (Lundberg, Schrag, Larsen, & Catton, 1968, p. 756). Behavioral skill training typically takes place within a social system comprised of the student and a teacher. The interactions between these two define the parameters of the system. A change in one of the parts results in corresponding change in the other—for example when the teacher ignores undesired behavior and/or praises desired behavior, the student's behavior changes. The relationship between the two illustrates the dynamic and ongoing events of the social system—one person's initiations may increase or decrease reciprocal responses of another person within the social context. These changes in turn affect qualitative behavioral changes. Over time, such interactions take on predictable forms as individuals come to *expect* each other to respond in certain patterns under specified conditions. Gradually, all participants in a setting expect standard behaviors of each other under prescribed conditions. These expectations are the standards that define acceptable and unacceptable behavior.

The social system is a social structure where all participants have *role equipments,* that is, "formal prescriptions or informal expectations specifying the behavior required of the occupants of a given position" (Lundberg et al., 1968, p. 755). Therefore, all participants are expected to engage in *role performances* ("overt action that occurs in a situation governed by normative standards," [Lundberg et al., 1968, p. 755]). These must be consistent with each participant's *position* ("the location of a person or a category of persons within a *set* of persistent interactional relationships with others," [Lundberg et al., 1968, p. 755]) within the system. When training people for a targeted criterion setting, these characteristics dictate the parameter of training.

## Traditional Special Education Perspective

Traditional special education focuses upon a single set of social structures to the exclusion of nearly all others. This, of course, is the classroom. Typically, special educators concentrate efforts on prescribing instructional objectives based upon a review of a student's performance on a variety of diagnostic tests. In classrooms for severely handicapped students, this has produced a variety of problems, including a lack of direction in the planning of longitudinal programs, resulting in effective community placements. In general, this traditional approach does not relate the student's current functioning to the need to adapt to future settings. Rather than viewing the student as someone who will live, work, and recreate in several social contexts over a span of many years, this special education approach concentrates solely upon the severely handicapped individual as a person who is not going anywhere. The role expectations of such persons become embodied in a host of dependent behaviors, most of which involve the receiving of assistance frequently, if not continuously, from those primarily in the roles of teacher, parent, physical therapist, occupational therapist, speech pathologist, nurse, and psychologist. Indeed, while the role relationships of nonhandicapped students may involve similar patterns of receiving assistance, there are peer relations, sibling relations, and occasional adult relations that allow for "giving" and "receiving" within reciprocal relationships. This process of influencing and being influenced through contacts with significant others is a vital component of the socialization process. This reciprocal pattern of action provides the essential foundation for primary socialization, which is "the acquisition of self-consciousness and social skills

through interactions involving the child and his primary groups, including his family, peer groups, and neighborhood" (Lundberg et al., 1968, p. 755). The process gradually shapes the student's behavior and the expectations of others throughout the student's life cycle and culminates as the student becomes a mature adult. But role relationships and expectations for the nonhandicapped student and for the severely handicapped student are often very different. Reciprocal relations available to nonhandicapped students are often unavailable to severely handicapped students.

Social systems including severely handicapped students vary so markedly from those including nonhandicapped students that effective socialization of handicapped students may not occur. Two major problems deriving from the exclusion of handicapped students from normal social systems include: (1) the lack of reciprocal influence and/or environmental control and (2) the lack of role expectations of significant others. Teachers, parents, and others expect the severely handicapped student to be dependent—that is, *acted* upon by others rather than *acting* upon on his or her own. Consequently, this student rarely acquires new roles. Less able to "demand to be heard," as is the case for the newly emerging adult (i.e., the adolescent), the severely handicapped student usually accepts the role assigned to him or her. It is not surprising that these students seem more childlike than adultlike.

This narrow view of instruction, which begins with a diagnostic assessment and prescription of behavioral objectives and ends with the delivery of instruction in accordance with an individualized education program guarantees that students will play the role of dependent receiver of services more efficiently and effectively with each passing year. A traditional special education approach fails to consider that the student's community of significant others is much broader and ultimately more influential than his or her initial group of parents, teachers, and support staff who developed his or her educational program. A contemporary approach must take into account the full range of social systems in which the severely handicapped student may become an actor over the course of his or her life cycle. These social systems might include, for example, the primary family, the elementary classroom, the secondary classroom, the prevocational classroom, the vocational training program, the workplace, the group home, and the social systems connecting each of these systems such as transportation, recreational groups, clubs, religious associations, legal services, and social service agencies.

In summary, the traditional special education perspective, as conceived and practiced in many programs, is inadequate. Its focus upon the severely handicapped student as an object of assistance is too unidirectional and short-sighted to prepare him or her for the independence and community integration that is professed to be so important. To achieve maximal community integration, special educators must consider the full range of social and physical environments that will affect and be affected by the severely handicapped student as he or she moves through the life cycle.

## Contemporary Special Education

The charge of shortsightedness brought against education and training programs for handicapped students has also been leveled against related disciplines, most importantly those providing the research and theoretical bases for special education. Bronfenbrenner (1977) claims that psychology suffered at least as much as special education and maybe even more; he asserts that developmental psychology is "the science of the strange behavior of children in strange situations with strange adults for the briefest possible periods of time" (p. 514). He argues that our understanding of how the human organism grows and develops awaits the acceptance and application of a broader research perspective, one that takes into account the relations between two or more actors, as contrasted with the focus upon a single subject's responses to manipulations by the experimenter. Bronfenbrenner (1977) notes:

Understanding of human development demands going beyond the direct observation of behavior on the part of one or two persons in the same place; it requires examination of multiperson systems of interaction not limited to a single setting and must take into account aspects of the environment beyond the immediate situation containing the subject (p. 514).

Bronfenbrenner (1977) termed this new and challenging perspective the ecology of human development and stated that the field of human development should be the

scientific study of the progressive, mutual accommodation, throughout the life span, between a growing human organism and the changing immediate environments in which it lives, as this process is affected by relations obtained within and between these immediate settings, as well as the larger social contexts, both formal and informal, in which the settings are embedded (p. 514).

The "ecological perspective" goes back prior to 1950 when Kurt Lewin coined the term *ecological psychology*. It has been widely applied to the study and treatment of deviant social behavior (Feagans, 1972; Swap, Prieto, & Harth, 1982). Like Bronfenbrenner, all other "ecologists" believe that patterns of interhuman behavior are interdependent in such a way that any change in one pattern is attended by compensatory changes in the others, and that this general arrangement constitutes a social system.

Bronfenbrenner (1977) described four major social contexts or systems that affect and are affected by the student as he or she develops and progresses through the life cycle. They are the microsystem, the mesosystem, the exosystem, and the macrosystem. Bronfenbrenner (1977) defines the microsystem as the

complex of relations between the developing person and environment in an immediate setting containing that person (e.g., home, school, workplace, etc.). A *setting* is defined as a place with particular *physical features* in which the *participants* engage in particular activities in particular roles (e.g., daughter, parent, teacher, employee, etc.) for particular periods of time. The factors of place, time, physical features, activity participant, and role constitute the elements of a setting (p. 514).

In programs for those with severe handicaps, the microsystem typically is the classroom, and role participants include teachers, teacher's aides, speech pathologists, occupational therapists, physical therapists, psychologists, and nurses. As indicated earlier, the role relations between the teacher and the handicapped student are comparable to that of the experimenter and the subject; the experimenter being the independent variable who manipulates, intervenes, or manages and the subject being the dependent variable who is manipulated, intervened upon, or managed. Bronfenbrenner contended that an ecological perspective that focuses *simultaneously* upon both student and teacher as they interact within a given social context was more appropriate, since interaction patterns best characterize relationships.

Examining adult-child interactions in different social systems, such as in the family or the classroom, illustrates the uniqueness of this approach. Parent-child and teacher-student patterns exhibit differences that at times appear to be understandable and at others almost inexplicable. Although parents and children might be expected to develop unique patterns of responding to each others' needs when resolving such domestic issues as the performance of household chores, going to bed, and engaging in weekend activities, it is often puzzling when the same patterns are not developed for similar problems in other settings. Why, for example, is the classroom teacher successful in getting Fred to eat independently at school when mother cannot achieve comparable success during mealtime at home? Behaviorists typically describe this phenomenon as a failure of the student to generalize (adapt) from one social setting to another. It is equally probable, from an ecological perspective, to suggest that the standards for expected behavior in the home (though, possibly, not the desired behavior) elicit a different pattern of interaction than those governing interactions in the classroom. The shift in perspective from Fred's inability to generalize behavior to the standards of seemingly shared stimuli that elicit a different pattern of adult-child interaction in a different setting is important to note. The implication of this view is that effective intervention requires a change in the rules or standards that govern and control *both* the parent's *and* the child's behaviors as they interact. The ecological per-

spective, while accepting the premise that the adult may influence as well as be influenced by the child's responding, also allows one to view the systematic influences of additional participants such as father and siblings who also contribute to changes or maintenance of observed interaction patterns.

In summary, it is important to underscore how individuals develop, mature, and learn new skills and appropriate behaviors as, for example, the student moves from one setting to another *in the present time.* Bronfenbrenner (1977) describes these sets of relationships as constituting the mesosystem, which is defined as comprising the

> interrelations among major settings containing the developing person at a particular point in his or her life. Thus, for an American 12-year-old, the mesosystem typically encompasses interactions among family, school, and peer groups. For some children, it might also include church, camp, or workplace, although the last would be less common in the United States than in some other societies. In sum, stated succinctly, a mesosystem is a system of microsystems (p. 515).

The concept of mesosystems raises interesting questions about the typical mesosystem for the normally developing child, the way it differs with the severely handicapped child, and the consequences of significantly limiting the severely handicapped child's participation and involvement in alternative social settings. Comparing the mesosystems of an institutionalized severely handicapped student with that of a severely handicapped student mainstreamed into a public school suggests many consequences that result from setting characteristics and that deserve special attention.

Recognizing that the life cycle of a student involves many different microsystems, it becomes apparent that social interactions are multidimensional. Not only do social systems influence the student's development at a given time, they also have the *potential* for future influences *over time.* The child entering adolescence or the adolescent entering adulthood is introduced to new social systems with new life-cycle changes taking place. Analysis of mesosystems over time emphasizes the successive shifts in roles and settings that every person undergoes throughout the life span. An infant and young child undergoes successive role changes through experiencing such events as the

> arrival of a sibling; entering a day care center; the move from preschool to school; getting a new teacher; going to camp; graduation; "dropping out"; finding one's first job; changing jobs; losing a job; marriage; becoming pregnant; having relatives or friends move in (and out again); buying one's first family TV set, car, or home; vacations; travel; moving; divorce; remarriage; changing careers; emigrating; or, to return to the more universal, becoming sick; going to the hospital; getting well again; returning to work; and—the final experience to which there are no exceptions—death (Bronfenbrenner, 1977, p. 525).

Too rarely do special educators consider the role changes that accompany the severely handicapped student's growth and development in community integration. Focusing, instead, upon present levels of dependency, special educators must *anticipate* the significant life-cycle changes that contribute to the increased independence and self-initiative that are necessary to achieve goals. Bronfenbrenner's ecological perspective demands that *future* environments as well as multiple *present* environments be considered in determining the social systems, participants, standards of expected behavior in those settings, and role performances to be learned by students.

In addition to the examination of microsystem influences and how different microsystems contribute jointly to influence different role expectations in the system, Bronfenbrenner (1977) described how the exosystem may indirectly influence individual behavior in a given setting. The exosystem is defined as

> an extension of the mesosystem embracing other special social structures, both formal and informal, that do not themselves contain the developing person but impinge upon or encompass the immediate settings in which that person is found, and thereby influence, delimit, or even determine what goes on there. These structures include the major institutions of the society, both deliberately structured and spontaneously evolving, as they

operate at a concrete local level. They encompass, among other structures, the world of work, the neighborhood, the mass media, agencies of government (local, state, and national), the distribution of goods and services, communication and transportation facilities, and informal social networks (Bronfenbrenner, 1977, p. 515).

The exosystem that needs to be considered in preparing severely handicapped students for community independence includes those institutions involving work and transportation, although others such as social service agencies and informal social networks are important also. There is a need to consider, for example, how general expectations for successful participation in the labor force or for effective mobility within the community actually affect the severely handicapped student's ultimate adjustment. Acknowledging the mesosystem's influence results in considerations such as the impact of high unemployment on the ability of severely handicapped adults to find work and the adjustments in employer-employee relations and/or work settings that can minimize negative influences on severely handicapped persons during major shifts in work-force participation.

Ten years ago, there were few public accommodations that considered the mobility needs of physically handicapped individuals. Today, due largely to passage of Section 504 of the Rehabilitation Act of 1973, modifications of buildings and streets have led to accommodations for wheelchairs, as well as changes in public transportation systems for physically handicapped persons. The exosystem concept suggests that by adapting existing systems, expectations for training should also change. It furthermore suggests an examination of the ability to estimate how much change in an existing structure will lead to significantly increased accessibility. (In the chapter by Janis Chadsey-Rusch in Bruininks and Lakin (1985) the applicability of behavioral measurement techniques to the assessment of such expectations is noted.)

The final conceptual unit in Bronfenbrenner's (1977) ecological perspective takes into account the social-political-ethnic values of the culture that actually dictate the structure and function of social institutions. This cultural system is the basic fabric of national life and, through an ever-evolving series of cultural events, it allows a society to survive by applying its social value system to the problems of daily living. According to Bronfenbrenner (1977) a macrosystem refers to

> the overarching institutional patterns of the culture or subculture, such as the economic, social, educational, legal and political systems, of which micro-, meso-, and exo-systems are the concrete manifestations. Macro-systems are conceived and examined not only in structural terms but as carriers of information and ideology that, both explicitly and implicitly, endow meaning and motivation to particular agencies, social networks, roles, activities, and their interrelations. What place or priority children and those responsible for their care have in such macrosystems is of special importance in determining how a child and his or her caretakers are treated and interact with each other in different types of settings (p. 515).

An excellent example of how our evolving values, ethics, and belief systems affect the nature of our institutions is the passage of Public Law 94-142. For more than a century this country wrestled with problems associated with the care and treatment of handicapped persons. Finally, after recognition of the needs and rights of handicapped persons was stimulated by several wars, major parent movements, civil rights legislation, and numerous court cases, many states passed their own legislation authorizing local educational agencies to provide educational services for handicapped students. In 1975, Congress passed Public Law 94-142, mandating a free and appropriate education for all school-aged handicapped children and young adults. The evolution of our system of values finally reached the ''critical mass'' necessary to affect national legislation, dictating a change in all of our public educational institutions. But, clearly, the passage of that legislation is only a milestone in an evolutionary process. Reviewing the major gains of recent decades accentuates all that is left to be accom-

plished if severely handicapped students are to experience maximum independence and community integration (e.g., changes are needed in the values of employers and employees in a wide variety of work settings, existing attitudes toward severely handicapped students must be analyzed and modified, and further research is needed into the most effective means for providing severely handicapped persons with skills needed to meet the minimal demands of the workplace).

## IMPLICATIONS OF A SYSTEMS-ANALYTIC APPROACH FOR COMPETITIVE EMPLOYMENT EDUCATION

The ecology of human development has much to offer special educators in the search for ways to improve services for severely handicapped students. The central implication of this perspective is simple: programs must be based on an examination of the social contexts in which the student is a participant and of those in which he or she will be a participant. These social contexts include microsystems, mesosystems, exosystems, and macrosystems, as described above and elaborated upon by Bronfenbrenner (1977).

The ecological perspective has several implications for the improvement of a competitive employment education. These implications are the result of sufficient empirical research and are of sufficient contemporary social significance to warrant at least tentative propositions. While special education as it has been applied to those with severe handicaps has produced exciting advances over the past 10 years, in many respects it is still in a primitive state. There is still a pressing need for a unifying theory, for program development models, for vocational training approaches, and even for the identification of the most fundamental questions deserving of expanded and resourceful attention. The remainder of this chapter outlines several implications of the ecological perspective as it is applied to the competitive employment education of students with severe handicaps.

## Broadening Definitions of Special Education and Competitive Employment Education

The ecology of human development suggests the importance of broadening the definition of special education to include the concepts of multiple participants at several levels of the social structure. The authors propose the following definition as a guideline for subsequent discussion of possible applications of the ecological perspective: *Special education is the process of coordinating interaction between developing students and their social and physical environments in order to facilitate adjustment to present and future environments.* Consequently, this definition encompasses the more familiar forms of socialization, such as:

> Primary socialization: the acquisition of self-consciousness and social skills through interaction involving the child and his primary groups; including his family, peer groups, and neighborhood (Lundberg et al., 1968, p. 756); and

> Continuing socialization: the operation of socialization processes during a person's adult years in the acquisition of skills and attitudes required for the performance of marital, occupational, and numerous other adult roles (Lundberg et al., 1968, p. 756).

The broadening of the special education perspective provides the proper context upon which to base a competitive employment education. Rather than delineating the skills and values that may develop as a result of providing competitive employment education, it suggests a comprehensive approach to preparing severely handicapped students for employment, one that takes into account the social contexts that ultimately affect the student's adjustment. Accordingly, the following definition of competitive employment education is introduced here to guide subsequent discussions: *Competitive employment education refers to the systematic arrangement of work-related experiences guided by interactions between developing students and their environment(s) at each of the four successive levels (the micro-*

*system, the mesosystem, the exosystem, and the macrosystem) of the social system.*

Each of the four levels identified in a social system impinges upon the others. The microsystem designates a complex of relations occurring between individuals in immediate settings, such as the father at home, the teacher at school, or the supervisor at work. The mesosystem describes the effects relationships between microsystems have upon the individual (e.g., students are influenced by expectations imposed via interactions among teachers and work supervisors that may sometimes conflict). The exosystem that represents "major institutions of a society, both deliberately structured [e.g., law enforcement practices] and spontaneously evolving [e.g., social networks] as they operate at a concrete local level" (Bronfenbrenner, 1977, p. 515) can influence microsystems directly or indirectly. Lastly, the macrosystem includes overarching formal and informal institutional patterns of a culture and constitutes the blueprints for the other, lower-level systems (e.g., as legislative mandates guide changes in the education system). Since each system's influence reverberates throughout the society, the macrosystem upon the exosystem and the exosystem upon the mesosystem, each of these systems eventually influences relations in a microsystem. These relations are delineated by several factors—such as setting, time, physical features of the environment, activities, participants, and roles—that constitute the immediate environment. Further, these relationships affect the individual throughout his or her life span.

This view of competitive employment education maintains that severely handicapped students grow and change and that growth and change is best aided by considering the present and future ecological environments of each student. Competitive employment education provides students with the opportunity to achieve partial, if not full, participation in their community as they mature. Special education has made major strides in delineating what constitutes comprehensive education, but traditional special education has not been associated with the futures of individuals who mature and leave the formal educational system. *A contemporary special education approach must consider an individual's needs throughout his or her life span.*

## Guiding Propositions for Program Development

A systems-analytic competitive employment education approach is based upon the social contexts in which participants (will) engage in productive and valued work behavior; each of these settings constitutes a microsystem according to Bronfenbrenner (1977). These settings, in turn, define role requirements and role performances that are representative of microsystems. Thus, to reflect the ecological perspective, one must consider settings in which students will be able to work productively.

*Proposition 1: Competitive employment education identifies employment opportunities in the community and is therefore community referenced.* This proposition recognizes that microsystems are the deliberately structured and spontaneously evolving manifestations of a society. These manifestations operate at the local level and comprise a network of occupations that, in turn, determine one's perceived worth to the community. The traditional occupational "choice" for severely handicapped persons is the sheltered workshop. Typically, the sheltered workshop offers subcontract work representative of work generally available within the community. Sheltered workshop employees work at subminimum wages—for example, assembling, packaging, or sorting "widgets." From a rehabilitation perspective this "work" is viewed as therapeutic; from a competitive employment education perspective it is viewed as demeaning and as not contributing to individual growth and development. The fact that handicapped students are educated and eventually work in social systems that do not include nonhandicapped individuals has even more fundamental implications. Because social systems of handicapped students and the associated expectations of others in those systems differ so substantially from those of nonhandicapped persons, there is relatively little opportunity for normal socialization to take place.

Acknowledging this reality and its implications for severely handicapped persons demands that competitive employment education focus upon the development of curricula that are based upon validated, community-referenced survival skills (Rusch, 1979). In recent years, social validation methodology has been expanded and applied to the identification of survival skills believed to be necessary for employment integration (Rusch, 1983). For example, Mithaug and his colleagues (Johnson & Mithaug, 1978; Mithaug & Hagmeier, 1978) identified the role requirements supervisors stated were necessary for entrace into sheltered workshops. More recently, attention has been directed toward the identification of job requisites employers indicate would lead to employment in nonsheltered settings (i.e., competitive employment) (Rusch, Schutz, & Agran, 1982).

Sheltered and nonsheltered work settings share vital characteristics, the most important of which is that they are social settings where individuals perform roles in prescribed ways. For example, employees are expected to complete their work tasks in a manner that results in meeting the prescribed requirements of their positions. The competitive employment education approach focuses upon the requirements of the worker's position.

*Proposition 2: Competitive employment education focuses upon validated, community-referenced survival skills that include the social and vocational work behavior that constitute the role requirements of microsystems.* A competitive employment education approach recommends that students be taught to work in their community as independently as possible. Of necessity, the curriculum of choice for severely handicapped students will reflect community expectations for roles, not the expectations of traditional activities that prepare handicapped students to function in noncommunity (i.e., noncompetitive) sheltered work environments.

Segregating severely handicapped students has resulted in distorted role expectations of significant others (i.e., coworkers) in non-sheltered, competitive employment. Therefore, in addition to roles and role requirements, competitive employment education focuses upon the beliefs and opinions—role expectations—of the community of significant others. As noted above, a social system is a social structure in which each participant has a role requirement and, therefore, in which each participant is *expected* to engage in a role performance consistent with his or her position within that system. Role performances thus eventually take on predictable forms prompted by expectations. These expectations suggest standards that define a range of competence that is acceptable on the job.

*Proposition 3: Competitive employment education considers the expectations of significant others, since these are the standards that define the range of competence in a role. (Significant others* refers to individuals who are knowledgeable in relevant areas [e.g., supervisors] or to individuals who represent the special needs of target employees [e.g., parents].)

Expectations of significant others have been the focus of innovative social validation methodology (Kazdin & Matson, 1981). Two methodological features of social validation include social comparison and subjective evaluation. The *social comparison* method refers to comparison of an individual's behavior before and after instruction with similar behavior of non-handicapped peers such as coworkers (e.g., performance on an assembly line). The expectations of significant others in a microsystem are affirmed when, after training, the *range of competence* of the target individual is indistinguishable from that of nonhandicapped peers. With the method of *subjective evaluation*, the target individual's behavior is evaluated by significant others in order to demonstrate that they view the social system's role expectations as being met.

*Proposition 4: Competitive employment education focuses upon transitions that occur throughout the life span, including changes in role and setting that occur due to growth and development. These transitions are not limited to the early years but recur in various forms throughout life, making competitive employment education longitudinal.* Proposition 4 acknowledges that individuals enter new microsystems throughout their lives and therefore focuses upon preparation for changes in role and setting.

The transitions that occur when children become adolescents and adolescents become young adults require that different educational opportunities be provided to severely handicapped persons. Although instructional procedures may not vary across these time spans, the curriculum content should change throughout one's life. The curriculum should address not only skills needed by severely handicapped students for the roles, role requirements, and role expectations of the immediate microsystem but also community-referenced, survival skills that prepare students for living as independently and as productively as possible in future postschool environments (Brown, Branston, Hamre-Nietupski, Pumpian, Certo, & Gruenewald, 1979).

Just as setting changes throughout the life span of the individual, so do roles. During the early school years, instruction concentrates largely upon future educational, work, domestic, and recreational environments. As the individual grows, the focus shifts away from school environments. During adulthood the emphasis is placed upon the demands of the work setting. As the individual grows older (50–70 years old), recreational and domestic demands take precedence over the demands of the work world.

## Changing Propositions for Training

The goal of special education is to prepare individuals to live, work, and recreate as independently as possible in their present and future community contexts. Consequently, competitive employment education is committed to life-long changes in growth and/or need that result in effective community participation. During the adolescent years a student should be engaged in activities that relate to settings to be encountered as a young adult. As the student matures to young adulthood, he or she typically is engaged in preparation for *actual community participation,* including working, living, and recreating in specific community environments. But not all life changes are related to maturation. Periodically, individuals change residences, jobs, or recreational activities because of events in the life cycle of the individual or "events in the life cycle of others responsible for his or her care and development" (Bronfenbrenner, 1977, p. 526). The following proposition, not confined to the school years, reflects a measure of success based upon individual transitions.

*Proposition 5:* At *different stages of competitive employment education, concern is focused upon different dimensions of prevocational and vocational training.* (Prevocational training emphasizes skill acquisition and stimulus control within and across educational and community settings, while vocational training emphasizes response maintenance within a role through person-person and person-setting adaptation.)

As suggested in the earlier discussion of role differences across microsystems and over time, it is critical to anticipate the role requirements and role expectations of future settings. This is particularly important in preparing students to enter work settings. The terms prevocational and vocational training suggest a sequence of experiences or a socialization process that gradually helps a student progress toward greater integration into the work world. Prevocational training prepares the student for the behavior expectations for work roles that are common to most work settings; vocational training prepares the student for the role requirements within a specific work system (i.e., on the job). Mithaug (1981b) suggested that during prevocational training,

the student learns the support behaviors (interaction and self-help) and the worker behaviors (attendance/endurance, independence, productivity, etc.) required for multiple-targeted vocational programs. During vocational training, the student must apply these abilities and behaviors in order to learn the specific skill and behavior requirements of the job placement (p. 44).

Mithaug et al. (1977) outlined the relation between this anticipation of future roles by suggesting that an analysis of community work settings should take place *before* commencing instruction. Utilizing this paradigm, Mithaug (1981b) defined critical steps to consider in moving the student from one microsystem (e.g., the classroom) to another (e.g., employment in the community). Structuring the transition from one setting to another by preparing a person for the role requirements of the new setting re-creates the age-old problem of developing important skills in the one setting and then transferring them to the target setting. This is especially problematic in prevocational training of students for anticipated roles in the work world, since the two different settings— instructional and community—create cross-situational stimulus features. The problem of training students to respond to these cross-situational stimulus features has been approached through general case programming. General case programming addresses the joint impact of instructional and community-relevant stimuli by defining the instructional universe (e.g., packaging tasks), selecting appropriate examples from that universe (e.g., packaging nuts and bolts), and sequencing the examples to promote generalization of performance from one setting to the next. The next proposition expands upon the general case perspective:

*Proposition 6: Prevocational training is based upon the principle of stimulus control and, consequently, is achieved through the use of general case instructional methodology; a competitive employment education approach considers the joint impact of instructional settings and community-relevant settings, as well as their cross-situational stimulus features.*

The mesosystem is comprised of relations between settings. Few investigations have examined behavior that is acquired by students in one setting (e.g., in the classroom) and that is transferred to settings in which it is expected to be displayed (e.g., in the community). Appreciation for cross-situational display of survival skills is a relatively new area of examination. Bronfenbrenner (1977) defines this focus from an ecologically relevant standpoint.

From a theoretical viewpoint, we may note here a continuity of the traditional research paradigm but not across domains; the restricted two-person system at the level of the individual becomes an analogous person-in-single-context model at the level of settings. If a second setting is introduced the system becomes triadic (so far as the subject is concerned) and thus allows for the possibility of second-order effects, now across settings (p. 523).

This perspective is relevant to the joint impact of instructional- and community-relevant settings. The consideration of interactions between home, school, community, and work suggests that these community-relevant settings contain cross-situational stimulus features that may directly influence the student's behavior. Because of the problematic nature of placement (i.e., the exact placement is uncertain), training must accommodate several potential target employment contexts. However, diverse settings may have similar properties that elicit selective responses from individuals.

General case instructional methodology is based upon the principle of stimulus control, which describes the extent to which antecedent stimuli functionally alter the probability of selected responses (Terrace, 1966). Concepts central to general case programming are stimulus class and response class. A *stimulus class* refers to any group of stimuli that share a common set of stimulus characteristics. For example, when sorting dishes in a kitchen setting, an employee must discriminate between instances of plates, bowls, saucers, and cups. All stimuli that do not fit within the category of "plates" (e.g., bowls, saucers, cups) are outside the stimulus class. A *response class* is defined using similar criteria. "The primary factors determining a class of responses are that all instances of the class produce the same functional effect (i.e., produce the same outcome) and that all members of the class share common topographical characteristics" (Horner, Sprague, & Wilcox, 1982, p. 67). For example, the response class "using a screwdriver to tighten a screw" is defined by a previously loose screw being tight and by the response topography required to achieve this outcome

(i.e., using a screwdriver). General case learning is achieved when a given stimulus class exhibits stimulus control over a given response class (i.e., any member of the stimulus class controls the appropriate member in the response class).

Horner et al. (1982) have suggested six steps in teaching the general case: (1) define the instructional universe by identifying all stimulus situations in which the individual will be expected to respond, (2) define the range of stimulus and response variations that are relevant in the instructional universe by identifying generic responses and generic discriminative stimuli for each of these responses (e.g., given the instructional universe consisting of all table saws, which require 11 matching-specific responses to start them, the generic response might be "activate machine"), (3) select examples from the instructional universe for use in teaching and testing response generalization, (4) sequence the teaching examples in an easy-to-hard format to avoid errors, (5) teach the examples, and (6) test the extent to which general case instruction results in correct responding on untrained stimuli and/or in untrained settings.

The work of R. H. Horner and his colleagues at the University of Oregon (Horner et al., 1982), presents an excellent example of how competitive employment education can consider jointly the mutual impact of instructional- and community-relevant settings (i.e., microsystems). Because the acquisition of survival skills is the goal of prevocational training, it does not fully address the question of skill maintenance in the target situation. Concern for response maintenance gives rise to the next proposition.

*Proposition 7: Since in the work environment concern is centered upon response maintenance, which is enhanced by procedures that promote mutual adaptation between persons and environments, maintenance of survival skills with minimal supervision in the target setting is achieved through the use of stimulus withdrawal methodology. A competitive employment education approach also emphasizes engineering the employment context, including change agents.*

Prevocational and vocational training focus upon students' adaptability and autonomy (Gifford, Rusch, Martin, & White, in press). *Adaptability* refers to the generalization of an individual's use of survival skills in diverse settings; in effect, Proposition 7 complements Proposition 6. Vocational training, however, stresses the goal of autonomy (i.e., maintaining survival skills with minimal supervision). To withdraw supervision requires identification of stimuli responsible for maintenance of survival skills.

One technique that has been used to identify stimuli responsible for skill maintenance is that of stimulus withdrawal (Rusch & Kazdin, 1981). Stimulus withdrawal methodology allows for specification of training components critical to the maintenance of survival skills, thus identifying stimulus components needed to promote maintenance. For example, Rusch, Connis, and Sowers (1979) sequentially withdrew treatment stimuli after assessing the combined effects of praise, tokens, and response cost on increasing an adult's time spent busing tables in a restaurant setting. They initially determined the effects on work output of using prompts and contingent praise; prompts and praise plus tokens; and finally, prompts, praise and tokens plus response cost. Prompts, praise, and tokens plus response cost were shown to differentially increase the percentage of time busing tables. The investigators then turned to maintaining the treatment gains. Therefore, single components of the treatment package were sequentially withdrawn. Initially, a cost-intervention phase was instituted during which the subject received the cost contingency (loss of points) on predetermined, randomly selected days. This phase of the study was followed by a four-step withdrawal of the token economy, including: 1) extending the exchange ratio from twice a day to once a day, 2) eliminating a chalkboard that displayed the points earned, 3) further extending the exchange ratio to once a week, and 4) replacing, with a paycheck, the secondary reinforcers used for exchange of items in a program store. In a final, concluding phase, praise with withdrawn.

Engineering the employment context focuses upon interactions between the trainee and the setting. Development of coworker feedback is illustrative of how a competitive employment education approach can engineer the employment setting. In one example, Rusch, Weithers, Menchetti, and Schultz (1980) involved coworker feedback in order to reduce topic repetition of a moderately mentally retarded worker. The training program was developed in response to indications by coworkers and a supervisor that topic repetitions were a bothersome feature of the handicapped person's work behavior. The results of this study indicated that the handicapped worker's annoying behavior could be significantly reduced via coworker feedback. This illustrates the important effects that peers can have through deliberately applying procedures to decrease undesirable behavior. The reciprocity principle addressed the question of whether the behavior of the subject (i.e., repetitions) was a function of contingencies of reinforcement that were the result of reciprocated and progressively evolving patterns of social interaction. Few studies in the work behavior literature have measured collateral behavior(s) of coworkers as a student's behavior changes and vice versa.

Because each of Bronfenbrenner's (1977) four systems impinges upon the other, competitive employment education requires innovative restructuring of curricula, training practices, and administrative policies and practices that limit individual opportunities for growth and development. The severely handicapped student is heir to a tradition of mandated work requirements and a rehabilitation motif that is primarily social, not economic. The view is widespread that severely handicapped students' work potential is minimal, if it exists at all. Consequently, tradition and practice have created a situation in which unemployment or underemployment is inevitable among those with severe handicaps. The next proposition is aimed at traditional policies, conceptions, and practices focused on severely handicapped students.

*Proposition 8: Competitive employment education advocates innovative restructuring of curricula, training approaches, and administrative policies in ways that depart from prevailing, often debilitating, practices.* Prevailing social systems pose major obstacles to a systems-analytic approach to transitional programming for severely handicapped students. As they are currently structured, social systems limit innovation in the areas of program development and training. These limitations manifest themselves in supporting status-quo administrative policies and practices that are based on a presumption that severely handicapped students have little to offer communities. As a result, advocacy is necessary to counteract the influence of debilitating social systems, particularly the effects of their ideologies.

Traditional curriculum sequences assume children develop normally and that certain performances are characteristic of the early years and certain other performances are characteristic of the older years. As nonhandicapped students mature, they develop more refined and complex motor, social, and cognitive skills. However, because severely handicapped students often possess significant skill deficits, they rarely if ever develop these skills in a typical developmental sequence. Consequently, it is not unusual to find that students who are being instructed via a developmental approach reach a point where they fail to progress. Given a limited number of years in which instruction is formally offered, not to mention the substantial cost to that instruction, an important issue becomes whether to continue to offer instruction based upon normal developmental progress to persons who fail to learn skills as fast, as proficiently, or in the same order as the nonhandicapped persons on whose development the model is based. Competitive employment education rejects the traditional development orientation and emphasizes instead a community-referenced organizational framework for curriculum develop-

ment. Thus, curricula must focus upon the goal of enhancing independence on the job, in the community, and in the home.

Training practices, typically, are constrained by their intended purpose. The vast majority of these practices, prevocational or vocational, do not acknowledge an interactional framework—that is, they rely upon strategies that promote only generalization or only maintenance of learned behaviors from the perspective of the student. A competitive employment education approach recognizes that the goals of prevocational and vocational instruction are met only if the goals of autonomy (i.e., generalization) and adaptability (i.e., maintenance of survival skills) are realized in community settings.

Finally, administrative arrangements, in educational and noneducational contexts, present barriers to competitive employment education. Severely handicapped students are relatively unproductive in programs where instruction and work is based only upon a view of a severely handicapped individual as a service recipient, not a service provider. This would not be the case if curricula and training approaches were geared to work opportunities normally available to nonhandicapped students. Instruction and employment should be based upon the likelihood that severely handicapped students will participate in their community along a partial-to-full participation continuum. Partial participation does not include instruction/employment in segregated settings. Competitive employment education is community-referenced, and participation is considered from this perspective *only*.

## Framing Propositions for Research and Development

Severely handicapped students' achievement of a measure of independence in the world of work is dependent upon complex relations that exist between individuals and environments. The goal of special education should be to facilitate adjustment to present and future environments by coordinating the interaction between developing students and their social and physical environments. Although many nonhandicapped and mildly handicapped students make the transition from school-based, developmentally oriented instruction with minimal support, severely handicapped students require employment-oriented instruction that is based upon a systems-analytic approach. Such an approach recognizes that there are complex, interdependent factors within work environments that are largely unknown and that, therefore, require investigation in their own right. It is important to study these factors.

*Proposition 9: Competitive employment education research focuses upon interdependent elements within the work environment (i.e., the microsystem) and between the work environment and other microsystems (i.e., the mesosystem), including setting, time, physical features, activities, participants, and roles.*

In the United States several research and development efforts are addressing these factors. At present, this research is sufficient to demonstrate the necessity of acknowledging the existence of systems of varying size and magnitude that exist simultaneously, and to suggest the importance of a competitive employment education approach. The concluding proposition indicates the need for research to further investigate the ecology of the world of work in light of larger political and cultural levels that will enhance the competitive employment education approach.

*Proposition 10: Competitive employment education research recognizes the existence of systems of varying size and magnitude that occur simultaneously and that require different levels of analysis (the microsystem, the mesosystem, the exosystem, and the macrosystem). Better recognition of all relevant levels of the environment affecting severely handicapped persons will facilitate a sense of realism and create a better capacity to work at all levels (e.g., classroom, local level, or at the larger political and cultural levels) that are relevant to specific problems.*

## SUMMARY

Traditional special education has not developed its full promise in developing handicapped students' ability to function effectively in natural communities. The traditional perspective has been limited because it focuses only upon the individual student and ignores the social context. A systems-analytic approach has been proposed to improve upon the traditional perspective by addressing the environmental context and by assuming a longitudinal perspective that considers the individual's life span, not just the formative school years. The application of this approach to different aspects of the lives of handicapped persons is discussed in several chapters in this volume.

## REFERENCES

Bellamy, G.T., Horner, R.H., & Inman, D.P. *Vocational habilitation of severely retarded adults: A direct service technology.* Baltimore: University Park Press, 1979.

Bellamy, G.T., Peterson, L., & Close, D. Habilitation of the severely and profoundly retarded: Illustrations of competence. *Education and Training of the Mentally Retarded,* 1975, *10,* 174–187.

Belmore, K., & Brown, L. Job skill inventory strategy for use in a public school vocational training program for severely handicapped potential workers. In: N. Haring & D. Bricker (eds.), *Teaching the severely handicapped,* Vol. 3. Columbus, OH: Special Press, 1978.

Bronfenbrenner, U. Toward an experimental ecology of human development. *American Psychologist,* 1977, *32,* 513–531.

Brown, L., Branston, M.B., Hamre-Nietupski, S., Pumpian, I., Certo, N., & Gruenewald, L. A strategy for developing chronological age appropriate and functional curricular content for severely handicapped adolescents and young adults. *Journal of Special Education,* 1979, *13,* 81–90.

Brown, L., Nietupski, J., & Hamre-Nietupski, S. The criterion of ultimate functioning and public school services for severely handicapped students. In: B. Wilcox, F. Kohl, & T. Vogelsberg (eds.), *The severely and profoundly handicapped child.* Springfield, IL: State Board of Education, 1977.

Bruininks, R.H., & Lakin, K.C. (eds.), *Living and learning in the least restrictive environment.* Baltimore: Paul H. Brookes Publishing Co., 1985.

Crosson, J.E. A technique for programming sheltered workshop environments for training severely retarded workers. *American Journal of Mental Deficiency,* 1969, *73,* 814–818.

Feagans, L. Ecological theory as a model for constructing a theory of emotional disturbance. In: W.C. Rhodes & M.L. Tracy (eds.), *A study of child variance.* Ann Arbor: University of Michigan Press, 1972.

Gifford, J.L., Rusch, F.R., Martin, J.E., & White, D.M. Autonomy and adaptability: A proposed technology for the study of work behavior. In: N.W. Ellis & N.R. Bray (eds.), *International review of research on mental retardation*, Vol. 12. New York: Academic Press, in press.

Gold, M. Stimulus factors in skill training of the retarded on a complex assembly task: Acquisition, transfer, and retention. *American Journal of Mental Deficiency*, 1972, *76*, 517–526.

Horner, R.H., & McDonald, R.S. Comparison of single instance and general case instruction in teaching a generalized vocational skill. *Journal of the Association for the Severely Handicapped*, 1982, *7*, 7–20.

Horner, R.H., Sprague, J., & Wilcox, B. General case programming for community activities. In: B. Wilcox & G.T. Bellamy (eds.), *Design of high school programs for severely handicapped students*. Baltimore: Paul H. Brookes Publishing Co., 1982.

Hunter, J.D., & Bellamy, G.T. Cable harness construction for severely retarded adults: A demonstration of training techniques. *AAESPH Review*, 1976, *1*, 2–13.

Johnson J.L., & Mithaug, D.E. A replication of sheltered workshop entry requirements. *AAESPH Review*, 1978, *3*, 116–122.

Kazdin, A.E., & Matson, J.L. Social validation in mental retardation. *Applied Research in Mental Retardation*, 1981, *2*, 39–54.

Lundberg, G.A., Schrag, C.C., Larsen, O.N., & Catton, W.R. *Sociology* (4th ed.). New York: Harper & Row, 1968.

Mithaug, D.E. Case studies in the management of inappropriate behaviors during prevocational training. *AAESPH Review*, 1978, *3*, 132–144.

Mithaug, D.E. *How to teach prevocational skills to severely handicapped persons*. Lawrence, KS: H & H Enterprises, 1981a.

Mithaug, D.E. *Prevocational training for retarded students*. Springfield, IL: Charles C Thomas, 1981b.

Mithaug, D.E., & Hagmeier, L.D. The development of procedures to assess prevocational competencies of severely handicapped young adults. *AAESPH Review*, 1978, *3*, 94–115.

Mithaug, D.E., Hagmeier, L.D., & Haring, N.G. The relationships between training activities and job placement in vocational education of the severely and profoundly handicapped. *AAESPH Review*, 1977, *2*, 89–109.

Mithaug, D.E., & Hanawalt, D.A. Employing negative

reinforcement to establish and transfer control of a severely retarded child and aggressive nineteen year old girl. *AAESPH Review*, 1977, *2*, 37–49.

Rusch, F.R. Toward the validation of social/vocational survival skills. *Mental Retardation*, 1979, *17*, 143–145.

Rusch, F.R. Competitive vocational training. In: M. Snell (ed.), *Systematic instruction of the moderately and severely handicapped* (2d ed.). Columbus, OH: Charles E. Merrill Publishing Co., 1983.

Rusch, F.R., & Close, D. Overcorrection: A procedural evaluation. *AAESPH Review*, 1976, *1*, 32–45.

Rusch, F., Close, D., Hops, H., & Agosta, J. Overcorrection: Generalization and maintenance. *Journal of Applied Behavior Analysis*, 1976, *9*, 498.

Rusch, F.R., Connis, R.T., & Sowers, J. The modification and maintenance of time spent attending to task using social reinforcement, token reinforcement and response cost in an applied restaurant setting. *Journal of Special Education Technology*, 1979, *2*, 18–26.

Rusch, F.R., & Kazdin, A.E. Toward a methodology of withdrawal designs for the assessment of response maintenance. *Journal of Applied Behavior Analysis*, 1981, *14*, 131–140.

Rusch, F.R., & Mithaug, D.E. *Vocational training for mentally retarded adults: A behavior analytic approach*. Champaign, IL: Research Press, 1980.

Rusch, F.R., Schutz, R.P., & Agran, M. Validating entry level survival skills for service occupations: Implications for curriculum development. *Journal of the Association for the Severely Handicapped*, 1982, *7*, 32–41.

Rusch, F.R., Weithers, J.A., Menchetti, B.M., & Schutz, R.P. Social validation of a program to reduce topic repetition in a non-sheltered setting. *Education and Training of the Mentally Retarded*, 1980, *15*, 208–215.

Swap, S.M., Prieto, A.G., & Harth, R. Ecological perspectives of the emotionally disturbed child. In: R.L. McDowell, G.W. Adamson, & F.H. Wood (eds.), *Teaching emotionally disturbed children*. Boston: Little, Brown & Co., 1982.

Terrace, H.S. Stimulus control. In: W. Honig (ed.), *Operant behavior: Areas of research and application*. New York: Appleton-Century-Crofts, 1966.

Wehman, P. *Competitive employment: New horizons for severely disabled individuals*. Baltimore: Paul H. Brookes Publishing Co., 1981.

Wehman, P., & McLaughlin, P. *Vocational curriculum for developmentally disabled persons*. Baltimore: University Park Press, 1980.

# Chapter 8

# Impact of Federal Programs on Employment of Mentally Retarded Persons

*Ronald W. Conley*

This chapter describes the various ways in which different federal programs, other than the employment programs of the U.S. Department of Labor or the state-federal vocational rehabilitation program, affect the employment of handicapped persons. Given the size and complexity of the federal government and its interactions with state and local governments, this task may appear to be unmanageable. In order to simplify the task, the chapter is organized according to the variables that influence work effort (such as the disincentive effects caused by the loss of benefits if a person accepts gainful work). The effects of the different federal programs on each of these variables are then described. This approach avoids a tedious and disconnected program-by-program recitation. Even so, not all federal programs that have an impact on the employment of disabled persons can be examined here. Primary emphasis is placed on identifying the effects of these programs on mentally retarded persons. However, since these programs usually affect all categories of disabled persons, the broader term *disabled persons* is often used in prefer-

ence to the narrower term *mentally retarded persons*.

## POPULATION AT RISK

There is no generally accepted definition of which people in the population should be counted as mentally retarded persons. This is largely owing to the fact that a distribution of the population by intelligence provides no cutoff point where the population can be logically divided between those who are mentally retarded and those who are not. The problem of identifying who is mentally retarded is further complicated because test measures of intelligence are widely criticized as being unreliable and of dubious validity, since they vary according to cultural background and from test to test (because test takers vary in attitudes, mental alertness, etc.). Another problem especially relevant to this chapter is that persons with the same level of measured intellectual limitation will vary widely in terms of employability, in other types of social adjustment, and in the services they need. These variations

This chapter was written by Dr. Conley in his private capacity. No official support or endorsement by the U.S. Department of Health and Human Services is intended or should be inferred.

can be attributed to differences in emotional stability, types and severities of other mental and physical disabilities, family supports, previous educational experience, and a host of other important factors. Attempts to determine which persons should be numbered among the physically disabled or mentally ill population encounter similar problems.

The problem of defining who should be classified as mentally retarded is usually simplified by counting only persons with significant intellectual limitation who are also unable to carry on activities appropriate for their age and sex. The requirement that these individuals be unable to carry on normal activities is often referred to as the criterion of social competence. The criterion of social competence is used in many other definitions of disability and disabling conditions. Most definitions of disability, for example, require that there be a physical or mental limitation and an inability to carry on appropriate activities. The problem is that a definition that uses the criterion of social competence causes one to lose sight of the fact that there are large numbers of handicapped persons who become socially competent (e.g., employed) and who continue to be socially competent only because of the provision of timely and appropriate services. For example, many intellectually limited people function adequately as adults only because of special education and other services they receive as children and because of vocational services they obtained as adults.

The use of the criterion of social competence causes only about one-third of the persons with IQs below 70 to be counted as mentally retarded (about 1% of the handicapped and non-handicapped population). Many of the persons with IQs below 70 who are not counted as mentally retarded are persons with IQs close to 70 who are usually able to locate work and support themselves. However, these persons (occasionally called the "invisible mentally retarded population") sometimes have deficits in adaptive behavior that are episodic rather than chronic. Events such as unemployment, illness, physical injury, a death in the family, or other misfortune may create a need for services. The services required by the "invisible mentally retarded population" may be different and/or more extensive than the services required for other persons in a similar situation because of added complications caused by the former group's intellectual limitations. If we do not take into account the existence of this group, however, we cannot plan effectively to ensure that their special needs are met. Parallel situations exist among persons with other types of physical and mental limitations.

Although the problem of definition will probably never be resolved, in this chapter, the term *mentally retarded persons* is used to refer to all persons whose intelligence, if measured accurately, would correspond to an IQ of 70 or less. Similarly, the term *disabled persons* is used here to refer to a broad group of people with physical or mental conditions that cause significant functional limitations. This approach is employed because it specifies the full population of persons who need, or who may at some time need, special services because of limited intellect or other physical or mental conditions. Although many, in fact most, of these individuals, as adults, are employed or satisfactorily engaged in other activities at any given time, it is recognized that a small percentage of these satisfactorily performing individuals will require special assistance each year, and that programs must be in place that will provide this assistance when needed. In more general terms, then, this definitional approach is necessary to plan and assess the extent to which programs are meeting the need for services. Definitions of mental retardation and disability that utilize the social competence criterion will not suffice for these purposes.

## EMPLOYMENT OF MENTALLY RETARDED PERSONS

A surprising number of persons assume that mentally retarded persons are unable to work, except possibly in highly sheltered work environments. Often this reflects a failure to understand the enormous diversity that exists among mentally retarded persons and the enormous diversity in skills and abilities required to perform various jobs. Estimates vary, but roughly 88% of the persons with IQs below 70 have IQs between 50 and 70, about 8% have IQs between 25 and 50, and about 4% have IQs below 25 (Conley, 1973). Although at some variance with contemporary diagnostic schema, for the purposes of this chapter, these three groups can be thought of as mildly, moderately, and severely mentally retarded, respectively, in a manner similar to the most commonly used school classifications. The importance of the differences between these groups is made manifest by observing that mildly mentally retarded persons are often able, for example, to read most of what is contained in a newspaper, to use public transportation, and to converse intelligibly; often they are indistinguishable from the remainder of the population. Severely mentally retarded persons, in contrast, are very limited in the above activities, and the presence of severe mental retardation is often quite obvious. Simply put, a mildly mentally retarded person is more similar to a "normal" person than to a person who is severely mentally retarded.

The vocational success of mentally retarded persons is far greater than is generally believed. Several years ago, it was estimated that 87% of noninstitutionalized men identified as mildly mentally retarded while in school (i.e., identified as "educably mentally retarded") were gainfully employed as adults, which at that time was only four percentage points below the norm for all men. In addition, it was estimated that 33% of noninstitutionalized women who were identified as mildly mentally retarded while in school were gainfully employed as adults (Conley, 1973). The employment record for mildly mentally retarded women does not necessarily reflect a work capacity lower than that of mildly mentally retarded men. Mildly mentally retarded women sometimes decide to become full-time homemakers rather than accept the menial jobs that otherwise would be available to them. Moreover, estimates of the earnings of employed

mildly mentally retarded persons were surprisingly high, estimated at 86 percent of the norm for men and 87 percent of the norm for women (Conley, 1973).

These conclusions, amazing to some, were based on the results of 27 follow-up studies, most of which reported substantial lack of employment among mentally retarded persons. This finding, however, was an artifact of how the data were collected and analyzed. Most of the studies were conducted within 1 or 2 years after the mentally retarded individuals left school, when most were still teenagers. Their employment and earnings records were low, but so were the employment and earnings records of most other teenagers. When the data were properly analyzed according to different age and sex groupings, the earnings and employment records of mentally retarded persons were found to rise rapidly as they reached their early twenties. The extremely limited data that were available at that time indicated that few persons with IQs below 50 were employed, and that earnings among those who were employed were very low.

It can, of course, be argued that persons who are able to work and maintain themselves in the community as adults should not be counted as mentally retarded, regardless of how they were classified while attending school. The more important point, however, is that a great many people who are identified as being unable to progress normally in school are able to be independent and self-supporting as adults.

These estimates of vocational success probably understate the vocational potential of mentally retarded persons; almost certainly they understate the vocational potential of persons with IQs below 50. For one thing, the individuals in the samples on which these estimates are based were entering the labor markets before the widespread establishment of educational, vocational, and social service programs for mentally retarded persons. Moreover, in recent years, evidence has been rapidly growing indicating that severely mentally retarded persons (as well as other severely disabled persons) can work on regular jobs if given the opportunity and provided the appropriate services and, in some cases, if given ongoing support (see chapter by Rusch & Mithaug, this volume). Although the data is still largely anecdotal, the large number of successful job placements reported for severely mentally retarded persons is convincing evidence that a large number of severely mentally retarded persons who were formerly thought able to work only in sheltered workshops are capable of substantial, gainful employment.

To understand the reasons for the vocational successes and failures of mentally retarded persons, one must first examine the nature of the requirements for the many different types of jobs that are available. The most important characteristic of the job market is that there are thousands of different types of jobs, each requiring a particular combination of training (vocational and academic), physical strength, dexterity, and other traits. Despite the rapidly evolving technology in our society, there are still, and probably will be for the foreseeable future, many jobs that can use persons with limited intellectual capabilities effectively. In fact, because of the division of labor, severely mentally retarded persons are often able to participate in the assembly of advanced technological products as complicated processes are broken down into simple tasks. In competing for these unskilled jobs, a physically healthy person with limited intellectual capacity might be seen as actually having a slight advantage over his or her more highly skilled counterpart who would be bored and frustrated by such a job, who might be considered overqualified, and who would probably not retain the job long if another became available. Thus, limited intellectual ability is not, in itself, a major barrier to employment for mildly mentally retarded persons or for most persons with IQs below 50.

## CAUSES OF WORK FAILURE

Despite these optimistic conclusions regarding the employment of mentally retarded persons, Conley (1973) also concluded that there was extensive nonemployment among persons with IQs below 50. Even among mildly mentally retarded persons, the level of nonemployment was not insignificant. Given the massive deinstitutionalization that has taken place in recent years, it is probable that the extent of failure to secure and retain work has increased slightly among noninstitutionalized mildly mentally retarded persons in the 10 years since the earlier estimate. In addition, despite the fragmentary evidence that many moderately and severely mentally retarded persons are capable of productive work, it continues to be true that relatively few find substantial employment, although it appears that a large number are employed in sheltered workshops or work activity centers. A recent study conducted by the Denver Research Institute obtained information from 800 board and care facilities in seven states. Of 785 residents in board and care homes for mentally retarded persons (e.g., group homes), only 5.1% were employed on competitive jobs, 25% were not working, and most of the remainder were employed in sheltered workshops or work activity centers (Dittmar, Smith, Bell, Jones, & Manzanares, 1983).

Whether or not a mentally retarded person secures and retains substantial gainful employment depends upon many factors. First, some mentally retarded persons have emotional and physical handicaps that greatly restrict the number of jobs that are within their reach. They are obviously excluded from jobs that require significant ability to reason. But if they have other handicaps, that is, if they are deaf, or blind, or cerebral palsied, they may also be excluded from many of the manual jobs otherwise available. This does not mean that they are barred from every job in the economy, but that the difficulties of being matched with one of the greatly reduced number of jobs that are within their limitations become formidable, particularly if they are not given assistance in locating jobs or support, if needed, in order to perform the job. The prevalence of physically handicapping conditions is greater among mentally retarded persons than among the general population and occurs more often than not among moderately and severely mentally retarded persons. Similarly, the coexistence of mental illness with mental retardation may have devastating effects on employee acceptability and work capacity. Few employers care to employ (mentally retarded) persons who may become belligerent, recalcitrant, or suddenly withdrawn, or who may in other ways disrupt production. In addition, mentally retarded persons who are aged, female, or nonwhite many encounter job discrimination, which will reduce the number of jobs available to them.

Clearly, the attitudes of mentally retarded persons have a major influence on vocational success. Largely because of inexperience, many mentally retarded persons are frightened by the prospect of gainful employment, they may doubt if they can get along with their fellow workers, or they may question their own ability to work. The attitudes of employers, of fellow workers, of the families of mentally retarded persons, and of other persons (such as the operators of board and care homes) may also be a major factor. Coworkers have been known to be reluctant to have mentally retarded persons work beside them. Many prospective employers do not believe that mentally retarded persons can work, and, probably even more to the point, do not want to be bothered.

The greater the level of skills acquired through school, vocational training, on-the-job training, and experience, the greater the likelihood that mentally retarded persons will locate work. Of course, the skills must be needed in the job market. In some cases, mentally retarded persons may be precluded from work not because of a job's requirements but because they have not learned such fundamental attributes as punctuality, proper attire, how to use public transportation, and other skills critical to being a desirable worker.

Obviously, the greater the intellectual limitation, particularly among moderately and severely mentally retarded persons, the fewer the number of jobs that they are able to perform. However, the greater the provision of appropriate supportive services, such as counseling, attendant care, vocational training, assistance in locating work, long-term job support, and orientation to a specific job, the greater the prospects that mentally retarded persons will be able to find and maintain work.

The condition of the national economy also has a major effect on the number of jobs available to mentally retarded persons. When unemployment reaches 8% to 10%, not only is the number of available unskilled jobs greatly reduced, but most employers have no difficulty recruiting able-bodied workers and would have little incentive to employ mentally retarded workers. Finally, whether many mentally retarded persons find work depends upon the luck (or lack of it) of being in the right place at the right time and of knowing the right people.

The above factors often interact so that mentally retarded persons' job choices may be limited by one, two, or even all of these factors. Typically, it requires two or more of these employment impediments to preclude employment for mildly mentally retarded persons, since the intellectual limitations alone do not create overwhelming obstacles to work. It is essential that factors that inhibit employment be explicitly identified in order to formulate appropriate policies for securing jobs for mentally retarded persons.

## PLACEMENT OF SEVERELY MENTALLY RETARDED PERSONS

For a few mentally retarded persons, the number of jobs within their capabilities are so dramatically reduced by the factors just discussed that there is little prospect of employment. For many other mentally retarded persons for whom full competitive employment is not immediately feasible, employment can be made possible by creating a greater or lesser amount of support on a job—support that may be temporary, permanent, or available on an as-needed basis. Most commonly, this is done through sheltered workshops or work activity centers where large numbers of mentally retarded persons can be concentrated under special work conditions and supervision. Another method of providing supported work is to integrate mentally retarded persons into a normal production unit and to modify the work in whatever way is needed—for example, special supervision, periodic counseling, slower work pace, shorter hours, simplification of the job requirements, and so forth (supported work). The advantage of the sheltered workshop or work activity center approach is the ease with which mentally retarded persons can be accepted as clients and provided services. The disadvantages of a sheltered workshop or work activity center are that productivity and hence the earnings of clients are often very low, owing to: 1) the small size of many workshops, which prevents the attainment of economies of scale and efficient production; 2) the concentration of many persons with similar skill limitations in a single work unit with too few skilled workers; 3) the difficulties that sheltered workshops or work activity centers have in obtaining work that provides a variety of job types into which clients with varying work capacities may fit and from which mentally retarded persons can make significant earnings; and 4) the unbusinesslike approach of many sheltered workshops. Unfortunately, there is a tendency to blame the low earnings of workshop employees on their limited work capacity rather than on the inherent inefficiency of the sheltered workshop or work activity center.

Supported work in regular production units has the potential to be far more productive than in sheltered workshops. The employee becomes an integral part of an established and profitable economic activity. Because of the great number and diversity in types of jobs in the general economy, it becomes much more likely that a job that can make the best use of the limited skills of the severely mentally retarded person can be found than would be the case if the job selection were limited to what was available in sheltered workshops. It cannot be emphasized too strongly that, for the most part, the productivity of a worker is much more a function of the efficiency of the productive process and of the value society places on the output, than on the limitations of the worker.

However, supported work in normal production units is obviously much more difficult to initiate and maintain. Jobs must be identified; employers must be convinced that modifying the job is worthwhile; and caseworkers must be prepared to travel extensively among different employment sites and to deal with work environments over which they have limited control.

Despite these difficulties, the placement of severely mentally retarded persons in work sites where persons without disabilities are normally employed (regular production units) and the provision of whatever ongoing support is needed appears to be the next major change under way in the care provided to these individuals. Organizations that specialize in providing these services are springing up throughout the country. Most of the programs that have arisen to date are oriented toward withdrawing the support provided by their programs to mentally retarded workers after workers have adjusted to the job, a process that may take a year or two. New approaches will undoubtedly surface to assist workers who need job support for a longer time, perhaps throughout their lives.

## FEDERAL PROGRAMS PROVIDING SERVICES TO MENTALLY RETARDED PERSONS

Three characteristics of mentally retarded individuals that influence their need for services should be noted. First, their intellectual and physical limitations and sometimes their associated emotional/behavioral problems are lifelong. Second, in some cases, this creates a need for lifelong services (e.g., a supervised community-based residence). In other cases, particularly among mildly mentally retarded persons, the need for services is erratic and unpredictable. A mildly mentally retarded person, for example, may require vocational rehabilitation services and temporary income support after a loss of employment. Finally, some mentally retarded persons will require multiple services—for example, income support, medical and social services, vocational rehabilitation, and/or special supervision.

*The Guide to Federal Resources for the Developmentally Disabled* (Litvin & Russem, 1977) lists 104 programs, including programs for income support, basic and applied research, facilities, and/or housing construction, and planning and coordination. More recently, the White House Working Group on Handicapped Policy (1984) noted that there were over 150 federal programs providing, or funding, services to handicapped persons. These large estimates emphasize the fact that mentally retarded persons are a cross section of the population who are subject to almost all of the problems that may exist elsewhere in the population; in consequence, almost any federal program that assists individuals in some manner is likely to number some mentally retarded persons among its clientele. In general, these programs can be classified under the following headings:

*Income (cash) support.* The primary income support programs serving mentally retarded citizens are the Supplemental Security Income (SSI) Program, the Social Security Disability Insurance (SSDI) Program, the Social Security Childhood Disability Beneficiary Program, and the Food Stamp Program.

*Health care.* Government-funded health services are most commonly provided to mentally retarded persons through Medicare and Medicaid.

*Residential care.* The largest source of federal benefits for residential services for mentally retarded persons is the intermediate care facilities for the mentally retarded (ICFs/MR) component of Medicaid. Other reimbursements derive from social services funds, payments from SSI, and state and local sources.

*Social services.* Social services may be provided to mentally retarded people through the Social Services Block Grant (such as attendant care, recreation activities, counseling). Also available are mental health services—which may be provided through community mental health centers—and protective services—such as provided through the Protection and Advocacy programs funded by the Administration on Developmental Disabilities.

*Rehabilitation and reemployment services.* State-federal vocational rehabilitation programs and the state employment services train mentally retarded persons to perform a wider variety of jobs and assist also in matching them with jobs they can perform. However, other than a few research or demonstration projects, there are no federal programs that fund the ongoing services needed to keep some severely handicapped persons in supported work situations on regular job sites on a long-term basis.

The examples provided in each of these categories are by no means a complete listing of programs providing these services. For example, programs funded by the Veteran's Administration, the Railroad Retirement Board, or federal, state, and local civil service programs have not been listed.

## A BASIC MISCONCEPTION

Some of the more important programs that provide support to mentally retarded persons are founded on the erroneous belief that the population can be neatly divided into those persons who are capable of substantial gainful activity and those who are not. Both the SSI and SSDI programs, for example, define disability as "inability to do any substantial gainful activity by reason of a medically determinable physical or mental impairment which can be expected to result in death or which has lasted or can be expected to last for a continuous period of not less than 12 months" (Social Security Administration, 1982).

Unquestionably, there are cases in which such judgments can be made unambiguously. Usually, however, the issue is far from clear. Although the determination of disability is made on the basis of medical evidence modified by other characteristics of the individual, such as age and education, whether or not a person is actually able to work depends upon the many other variables discussed earlier (e.g., motivation, availability of work, intelligence [even when the person is not diagnosed as mentally retarded], luck). The interactive effect of these variables with physical and mental limitations is not well understood. In fact, not even the extent to which medical conditions limit ability to work is well understood. This is evidenced by the enormous percentage of permanent partial disability cases in workers' compensation that are litigated over the extent of loss of ability to work (Conley & Noble, 1979).

Consequently, a determination that a person is incapable of substantial gainful employment becomes extremely judgmental and subject to considerable error. The judgmental nature of the disability determinations made by the Social Security Administration becomes even more obvious when it is observed that the initial determination is made by a disability determinations unit located in the state vocational rehabilitation program on the basis of forms and medical reports submitted by the Social Security Administration; the applicant is not even seen by the disability determinations unit. It is probable that many persons classified as disabled (including those disabled by mental retardation) could work at some job existing in the economy. However, these jobs are usually hard to find, they often offer little security, some persons may need to endure pain while working, some jobs may require modification, some workers may require extensive vocational training and rehabilitation, and some workers may need ongoing or periodic assistance in order to continue working.

It is appropriate and, from a pragmatic administrative standpoint, necessary to classify persons as disabled for purposes of establishing eligibility for SSI or SSDI if suitable work is unusually difficult to find or maintain. However, it must be stressed that the premises that underlie the eligibility determination as well as the subsequent continuation of benefits may, for reasons described in the next section, substantially reduce the probability that the recipients will seek gainful work or would accept it if the opportunity arose.

## EFFECT OF FEDERAL PROGRAMS ON EMPLOYMENT

Unfortunately, many of the public programs that provide services to mentally retarded clients act in ways that discourage employment. These various impediments to employment are discussed in the following paragraphs.

## Disincentives for Employment

It must be recognized that the present structure of federal programs creates substantial financial disincentives for some mentally retarded persons to accept substantial employment. Most people have two basic, and sometimes conflicting, goals related to employment: to maximize the amount of income they receive and to ensure a secure and consistent source of income. Work disincentives may result from the adverse effects of programs on either of these two basic goals. It should be emphasized that income should be viewed broadly to include not only cash income but also medical care and other services that people receive but for which they do not pay.

Once basic necessities are provided for, it is generally accepted that the lower the reward for working, the less is the incentive to work. Current public programs that ensure that disabled individuals receive the basic necessities of life are structured so as to cause dramatic work disincentives in that they sometimes drastically reduce the improvement in the well-being that disabled persons can achieve by working. In fact, because of the way these programs operate, acceptance of work will sometimes actually cause a decline of income for individuals and a reduction in their standard of living. As will be described here, some public programs are a complicated combination of work disincentives and special provisions designed to reduce these disincentives. In the following discussion, programs that: 1) provide cash support, 2) fund medical care, and 3) provide other services are examined.

## Income Support Programs

The primary federal programs providing income support to mentally retarded persons are the Social Security Disability Insurance Program for disabled adults and the Social Security Childhood Disability Beneficiary Program (jointly designated as the SSDI/CDB program), and the Supplemental Security Income (SSI) program. The SSDI program for adults provides monthly benefits to disabled workers and their spouses and to children who qualify. In order to qualify, a worker must achieve a specified number of quarters of Social Security coverage. A quarter of coverage is credited to a worker if during that quarter the worker pays Social Security taxes on earnings that reach a predetermined level. During 1984 the minimum level of taxable earnings required before a quarter of coverage was granted was slightly less than $400. A worker is eligible to receive SSDI benefits if, at the time he or she becomes disabled, the worker is both fully and currently insured. A worker is fully insured if he or she has at least 1 quarter of coverage for each year elapsing after 1950, or at least 1 quarter for each year after the worker attained age 21 (a minimum of 6 quarters is required), or has 40 quarters of coverage accumulated during his or her lifetime. A worker is currently insured if he or she has 20 quarters of coverage during the 10-year period preceding the onset of the disability, unless the worker is disabled before age 31. In the latter case, coverage is required in at least half of the quarters after reaching age 21 (a minimum of 6 quarters is required). Earnings received from almost all employment in the United States are covered by Social Security, although most federal employees hired prior to 1984 are not covered. Blind workers need only be fully insured to qualify for SSDI. The Childhood Disability Beneficiary Program is somewhat of a misnomer, since it provides a monthly benefit to disabled adults (age 18 or over) whose disability began before age 22—in most cases before the disabled person had a chance to accumulate any quarters of Social Security coverage. To be eligible, the disabled person must be a dependent son or daughter (or eligible grandson or granddaughter) of a retired, deceased, or disabled worker who is eligible (or whose survivors are eligible) for Society Security benefits.

The major purpose of the Supplementary Security Income program is to assure a basic level of cash income to aged or disabled persons who are not adequately covered by Social Security. The program began in 1974 and replaced the state-operated welfare programs for the aged and disabled. The SSI program covers persons who did not accumulate sufficient quarters of coverage to qualify for Social Security. It also will supplement Social Security benefits if they are below the basic level set for SSI beneficiaries. Unlike SSDI, in order to be eligible for SSI, disabled persons must not have assets (other than a home and car) that exceed prescribed amounts. Thus, the SSI program is directed at supporting persons who would otherwise be unable to provide for their basic needs out of either income or assets such as savings accounts, stocks, and bonds.

The potential for erosion of the incentives to work is particularly striking in the SSDI/CDB program. Disabled persons who receive SSDI/CDB retain their eligibility for benefits so long as they are unable to engage in substantial gainful employment (SGA). Under current federal regulations, persons earning over $300 per month are considered to be engaged in SGA (Social Security Administration, 1982), an amount that is substantially less than the minimum wage for persons engaged in full-time work. Major legislation passed in 1980 provided that extraordinary impairment-related work expenses could be deducted from a disabled person's earnings both for purposes of determining initial eligibility and for purposes of subsequently determining if the person is engaged in SGA. Anyone earning above $300 per month either cannot qualify for SSDI/CDB or, if already eligible for benefits, will cease to be eligible after he or she has completed a 9-month trial work period. During this trial work period, the person will not face any reduction of SSDI/CDB benefits, regardless of the level of his or her earnings. The U.S. Department of Health and Human Services has established that any calendar month in which the recipient has earnings of $75 or more must be counted as part of the trial work period, so that a recipient is not able to avoid using up the trial work period by earning less than the SGA level. The trial work period need not be continuous, and only one trial work period is allowed to a beneficiary. In consequence, the trial work period can be used up before the beneficiary begins to work at an SGA level (as happens sometimes to sheltered workshop employees before they are placed on regular jobs). It should be pointed out that the condition for continuing eligibility for SSDI/CDB is not whether earnings are actually over $300, but whether the person is capable of earning over $300 per month. At the end of the trial work period (or at any time that the person is receiving benefits), a determination is made as to whether the beneficiary is capable of earning at an SGA level. If earnings were over $300 during the last month of the trial work period, but it was not believed that earnings would continue to be over $300 per month, then the beneficiary would not be terminated from SSDI/CDB. Similarly, if wages were over $300, but it was believed that they were being subsidized and wages based on actual productivity would be less than $300 per month, then eligibility would continue. On the other hand, if earnings are less than $300 per month, but it is believed that the beneficiary could earn more than this amount, then his or her eligibility for SSDI/CDB would be terminated, even though actual earnings are below the SGA level.

Suppose that a SSDI/CDB recipient accepts employment paying $400 per month after completing a trial work period. The following events occur:

1. The person's disability benefits are terminated. The loss may be substantial and may exceed the person's earnings, since the total family benefit paid to a recipient may exceed $2,000 per month (individual benefits may run as high as $1,000 per month), although most payments are considerably less.
2. In almost all cases, Social Security taxes of 6.13% will have to be paid (more if self-employed), in addition to federal and, possibly, state and local income taxes. These income taxes may be small if the person is the only earner in a household, but if his or her spouse also works, this income must be added to the spouse's income for tax purposes. The federal tax rate alone may be as high as 50%.
3. The person may incur normal work-related expenses, such as transporation costs, clothing costs, and lunches.

In some cases, the reduction in cash income as a consequence of accepting work will be dramatic, conceivably on the order of two-thirds of the SSDI/CDB payment. In most cases, however, the loss will be much less, and in many cases a recipient will increase his or her net cash income by accepting work. The critical point here is that the financial disincentives to accepting jobs paying over $300 per month are sometimes very strong, unless the job pays a high wage—one that is higher than many persons receiving disability benefits can expect to earn. The disincentives to work may be even greater if the person receives cash benefits from other sources that may also be dependent upon continuous inability to work, such as workers' compensation or private disability insurance. Of course, a beneficiary is not necessarily able to avoid being terminated from SSDI/CDB by not working or by earning less than the SGA level, if it can be determined that the person is capable of earning at the SGA level. However, as observed earlier, in the absence of actual earnings, these determinations are judgmental and often controversial.

The disincentive effects are much less dramatic in SSI, partly because the maximum benefits are much lower and partly because of recent legislation. As in the case of SSDI/CDB, the SGA level is $300 per month. Anyone earning in excess of that amount is disqualified from becoming eligible for SSI. Note that in determining initial eligibility for SSI, extraordinary impairment-related work expenses may not be deducted from gross income in determining whether the applicant is engaged in SGA. However, in determining initial eligibility for SSDI/CDB, these expenses are deducted from gross income.

Once a person is on the SSI rolls, then, for purposes of determining the monthly payment to the individual, the first $20 of earned or unearned income and the next $65 of earnings are exempted from consideration; potentially a maximum of $85 of earnings may be earned without penalty, although the amount will be less if there is income from other sources against which the $20 must be offset. Thereafter, benefits are reduced by $1 for every $2 of earnings over the exempted amount.

Beginning January 1, 1984, the basic SSI payment was $314 per month to an eligible individual and $472 per month to an eligible couple. At these levels, all federal SSI payments cease when earnings reach about $713 per month in the case of an individual (if there is no unearned income), and $1,029 per month in the case of an eligible couple. These are the federal break-even points and can be calculated by adding $85 to twice the monthly SSI payment.

Prior to the Social Security Disability Amendments of 1980, an SSI recipient who engaged in substantial gainful work (i.e., who earned over $300 per month) would enter into a trial work period for 9 months, after which he or she would be terminated from SSI. The trial work period operates in the same way as in the SSDI/CDB program. Any month in which earnings exceed $75 must be considered as part of the trial work period. At the end of the trial work period, a judgment is made as to whether the person is capable of working at an SGA level. Consider the case of a single person who obtained employment paying $400 per month and who does not receive a state supplement to the federal SSI payment. If the pre-1981 rules were applied to the benefits and to the SGA level prevailing in 1984, then during the trial work period, the SSI benefit would be about $157 (i.e., $314 − [$400 − $85] ÷ 2]), so that gross income would equal $557. At the end of the trial work period, the single person's SSI benefit would terminate and gross income would be $86 higher than when he or she was on SSI and not working. The net gain would be considerably less, since Social Security taxes; federal, state, and local income taxes; and normal work expenses would have to be paid. The incentive to work is obviously not large and, if work expenses and taxes were taken into account, might well be negative. It should be observed that SSI recipients who return to work are unlikely to be faced with the high marginal income tax rates to which SSDI/CDB recipients conceivably could be subject. This is because SSI is based on family income and, unlike SSDI/CDB, a person with a high earning spouse would not be eligible for SSI. It should also be observed that an eligible couple that began receiving $400 per month in earnings would actually face a reduction in income as a consequence of accepting work.

Another example, using the benefit levels prevailing in 1984, and the benefit determination rules that existed prior to 1981, will make the effect of these rules on work incentives clearer. Consider two SSI recipients, one who accepts a job paying $250 per month and one who accepts a job paying $350 per month. At the end of the trial work period, the higher-paid worker would lose the entire $314 SSI payment and end up with a net increase in gross income of only $36 (i.e., $350 − $314). The lower-paid worker, in contrast, would continue to receive an SSI payment of about $232 per month (i.e., $314 − [$250 − 85] ÷ 2) and end up with a gross income of $482 (i.e., $232 + $250). The lower-earning recipient would end up with $132 more per month (i.e., $482 − $350) than the higher-earning SSI beneficiary. Clearly, a rational SSI recipient would choose the job paying the lesser wages, or perhaps no job at all if he or she were fearful of being judged capable of working at an SGA level.

In an effort to reduce these work disincentives, a special 3-year experiment was authorized in the 1980 Social Security Disability Amendments, beginning on January 1, 1981, which permitted SSI recipients to continue to be paid SSI benefits so long as their gross earnings are below the break-even point (incorporated as Section 1619 [a] of the Social Security Act). In the first example, the individual SSI recipient earning $400 per month would continue to gross $557, which is about $242 more than he or she would receive without working. The net gain would, because of taxes and work expenses, be less and may or may not be sufficient to entice the recipient to accept the discomfort of mental employment. An eligible couple earning $400 per month would have an identical gain in gross income since the SSI benefit would, under these rules, be $314 per month (i.e., $472 − [$350 − $85] ÷ 2) and this, plus $400 in earnings, is about $242 more per month than the basic SSI payment for couples. In the second example, the SSI recipient with earnings of $350 per month would continue to receive an SSI benefit of about $182 per month (i.e., $314 − [$350 − $85] ÷ 2) and total monthly income would be about $532, about $218 more than he or she would receive without working, and about $182 more than he or she would receive under the rules prior to the experiment. Note that break-even points in SSI, the points at which all federal benefits terminate in this special experiment, are two or three times higher than the SGA level, the point at which all SSDI benefits terminate after the trial work period.

The initial authority for this special 3-year demonstration ended on December 31, 1983. In September, 1984, Congress approved an extension of this special demonstration until June 30, 1987. In order to maintain the program during most of 1984, the U.S. Department of Health and Human Services approved a one-year project that continued the demonstration for persons who were eligible for SSI benefits at the beginning of 1984. The examples that follow are based on the special benefit provisions of this special demonstration.

The Social Security Disability Amendments of 1980 provided that any extraordinary impairment-related work expenses were to be deducted from gross earnings before the $1 for $2 reduction of SSI benefits began. (These extraordinary expenses are not taken into account when establishing eligibility for SSI.) Suppose that the previously described hypothetical SSI recipient earning $400 per month incurred $100 per month in extraordinary impairment-related work expenses (e.g., assistance in getting to and from work). The SSI benefit would then rise to about $207 (i.e., $314 − [$400 − $85 − $100] ÷ 2), and gross income would be $607 (calculations based on benefit levels prevailing in 1984). Because extraordinary impairment-related work expenses would be deducted from gross income, the SSI recipient and the SSA, in effect, would split the costs of these expenses; a $2 reduction in gross income results in a $1 rise in SSI benefits.

Blind recipients of SSI are given considerably more favorable treatment since the extraordinary impairment-related work expenses are deducted from what would otherwise be the net deduction in the SSI payment. In the case of an SSI beneficiary earning $400 per month, the reduction in the SSI benefit in the absence of extraordinary impairment-related work ex-

penses would be $157 (i.e., [$400 − $85] ÷ 2). In the case of nonblind SSI recipients with impairment-related work expenses, the reduction in the SSI benefit would be $107 (i.e., [400 − $100 − $85] ÷ 2). If the recipient were blind, however, and had $100 in extraordinary impairment-related work expenses, the reduction in the SSI benefit would be only $57 (i.e., $157 − $100) and the gross income of the blind SSI recipient would be $657 ($400 + $257). In this case, SSA picks up the entire tab for extraordinary impairment-related work expenses.

Slightly over half of the states supplement the federal SSI benefit. At the beginning of 1984, the amount of the supplement varied from $1.70 per month in Oregon to $163 per month in California ($252 in Alaska) for individuals, and from $8.80 per month in Hawaii to $414 in California for couples. In several of these states, the federal break-even point is used as the point at which all benefits, both federal and state, are terminated. In most cases, however, the states continue the $1 reduction for every $2 in earnings, causing the combined federal-state break-even point to be higher than the federal break-even point alone.

Prior to 1980, state supplements to the federal SSI payment increased the amount of the work disincentive by an amount directly proportional to the size of these state supplements, since a reemployed SSI beneficiary would lose, after the trial work period, both the federal benefit and the state supplement. Let us assume that the pre-1981 rules for determining benefits were being utilized in 1984. Then, in the previous example involving an SSI beneficiary who accepts a job paying all $400 per month, if the state supplement were greater than $86 per month, the beneficiary would face a diminution of gross income as the reward for accepting work (since the combined federal and state payments would be greater than $400). If account were taken of taxes and work expenses, a beneficiary earning $400 a month could suffer a loss of net income even if state supplemental payments were lower than $86.

The 1980 amendments, however, greatly reduced the effect of the state SSI supplements on work incentives in most states. For persons earning less than the Federal break-even point, the work disincentives caused by state supplementary payments are totally nullified, since the change in gross income is the same regardless of whether there is a state supplement or not. Consider the example of a beneficiary accepting a job paying $400 a month and living in a state paying a $10 supplement. Prior to obtaining work, he or she received a $324 SSI benefit ($314 federal payment plus a $10 supplement). After obtaining employment, the net SSI benefit is about $167 (i.e., $324 − [$400 − $85] ÷ 2). Gross income is $567, which is $242 more than the person would receive if not working and is identical to the net gain that would be received in the absence of a supplement. It is, of course, the increase (or decrease) in gross income that determines the financial incentive (or disincentive) to work.

If the beneficiary has earnings greater than the federal break-even point but less than the combined federal-state break-even point and resides in a state that continues to reduce the benefit by $1 for every $2 of earnings, then the work disincentive is increased, as compared to the states that do not supplement earnings, by an amount equal to the reduction in the state supplement. If the beneficiary has earnings greater than the combined federal-state break-even point, or lives in a state that terminates all benefits at the federal break-even point and has earnings greater than the federal break-even point, the work disincentives are further increased, since they include the loss of all state supplemental payments as well as the federal payment. Of course, the greater the size of the state supplement, the greater is the importance of these work disincentives.

## Health Care

The primary federal programs providing funding for health care for disabled persons are the Medicare and Medicaid programs. Medicare consists of two separate but coordinated programs: hospital insurance and supplementary insurance. The latter program pays for health services provided by physicians and for outpatient care and services provided by home health agencies. Like private insurance, Medicare has

coinsurance and deductible provisions in determining benefit levels. Persons receiving SSDI/CDB become eligible for Medicare coverage after 2 years of receiving benefits. Medicare, like SSDI, does not utilize an asset test.

Medicaid, like SSI, provides health-care protection to low-income individuals and families who have limited resources. Unlike Medicare, Medicaid usually provides full coverage of medical expenses. It often supplements Medicare when beneficiaries are unable to pay for the portion of the costs of medical care not paid for by Medicare, if their income and assets are within the limits established by the states and the federal government for eligibility for the program. Medicaid also funds health care for persons not eligible for Medicare because they do not qualify for Social Security coverage or because they have not completed the 2-year waiting period required before SSDI recipients become eligible for Medicare if they meet the federal and state criteria for limited income and assets. Persons receiving SSI are automatically eligible for Medicaid in many states. In a few states the standards for Medicaid eligibility are somewhat more restrictive than the federal standards for SSI. However, the vast majority of SSI recipients are eligible for Medicaid.

What happens to Medicare benefits if SSDI/CDB recipients accept substantial work? Prior to 1981, if SSDI/CDB recipients returned to substantial work and became ineligible for cash benefits, eligibility for Medicare also was terminated. The Social Security Disability Amendments of 1980, however, entitled SSDI/CDB beneficiaries who are eligible for Medicare to continue to receive Medicare coverage for 36 months after cash benefits cease. In addition, the 1980 amendments eliminated the 24-month waiting period for Medicare coverage for a former SSDI/CDB recipient who becomes entitled to SSDI/ CDB benefits within a 5-year period after terminating cash benefits.

What happens to Medicaid benefits if SSI recipients accept substantial work? Federal law gives states the option of offering Medicaid coverage to the "working poor," that is, persons whose income is insufficient to pay for adequate medical care. Thus, prior to 1981, in states without a "working poor" program, an SSI recipient who engaged in substantial work and lost his or her entitlement to SSI would also lose Medicaid coverage, while in other states, eligibility for Medicaid would continue for persons who qualified under a "working poor" program.

The 1980 Amendments to the Social Security Act created, in effect, a national "working poor" program for SSI recipients who return to work. Only persons who were on SSI when they obtained employment are eligible for this program (states retain, of course, the option of establishing a "working poor" program). The amendments authorized a 3-year experiment (incorporated as Section 1619 [b] of the Social Security Act) to provide Medicaid coverage to SSI recipients who return to substantial work even if income above the break-even point causes them to stop receiving cash benefits, provided that they meet the following requirements:

1. Continue to have a disabling condition;
2. Would receive SSI benefits if their employment ends (i.e., if they meet the asset test);
3. Would have difficulty maintaining their employment without Medicaid coverage; and
4. Do not have earnings high enough to provide a reasonable equivalent to the SSI benefits, state supplementary payments, and Medicaid benefits that they would have in the absence of employment.

The experiment, as in the case of the SSI experiment, ran from January 1, 1981, through December 31, 1983. As with the SSI experiment, the initial authority for this special 3-year experiment ended on December 31, 1983. It was, however, extended until June 30, 1987 by Congress in September, 1984. The U.S. Department of Health and Human Services maintained this program during the first 8 months of 1984 by means of a one-year demonstration project.

Although not as obvious as the loss of cash benefits, the fear of loss of medical coverage is a major work disincentive, and at times may be even more important than the fear of loss of cash benefits. Medical expenses are unpredictable and often very large. In some instances, annual payments for medical care for a beneficiary will exceed annual cash payments under SSI or SSDI/CDB or anticipated earnings if the beneficiary returns to work. Indeed, Medicaid payments on behalf of disabled beneficiaries are, on the average, almost as high as the basic level of income support to individuals receiving SSI. In fact, during 1982, Medicaid payments to disabled SSI beneficiaries were higher than the basic annual SSI payment to individuals. In addition, some disabled persons have large long-term and even lifelong medical expenses, such as a need to purchase medications to control epileptic seizures. The problem of loss of Medicaid or Medicare is greatly exacerbated because the medical coverage provided by some private employers as employee benefits excludes or restricts coverage for workers with preexisting conditions. In addition, private insurers are sometimes reluctant to offer private policies to workers with preexisting medical conditions. These workers may be excluded from any health coverage at all, or only from coverage for expenses related to their preexisting medical conditions.

The earlier mentioned 1980 amendments were designed to reduce the fear of loss of medical coverage for some SSDI/CDB and SSI beneficiaries who return to employment. Nevertheless, residual disincentive effects remain in the case of SSDI/CDB beneficiaries who are foresighted enough to peer 3 years into the future when their extended eligibility ends, and among SSI beneficiaries who are concerned about whether the experimental extension of Medicaid will continue. Moreover, federal regulations that were developed to implement the Medicaid experiment will continue to create work disincentives for some SSI recipients who contemplate returning to work. Eligibility is restricted to persons whose total income does not exceed the combined total of the break-even point for both the federal SSI and the state supplementary payment and the average expenditure for Medicaid benefits for disabled SSI beneficiaries in the state. If this regulation is rigidly enforced, then obviously, persons living in states with a low state supplement or in states that do not supplement the federal SSI payment are less likely to be covered than persons living in a state with a high supplement. More important, persons with above-average medical expenditures, that is, those most in need of medical coverage and whose prospective earnings exceed the federal/state break-even point plus the average state Medicaid payment to disabled SSI recipients, will still face strong economic disincentives to return to work because of the possible loss of Medicaid benefits.

The ICF/MR program is a special component of the Medicaid program that funds residential care and needed services to mentally retarded persons (and persons with related conditions) who require health-related or rehabilitative care (in other types of Medicaid facilities, only health-related care can be funded). To be eligible for ICF/MR care, a mentally retarded person must be in need of 24-hour-a-day care, and must be in need of, and engaged in, an active treatment program. An active treatment program is one in which there is an individualized written plan of care that sets forth goals and objectives and specifies the experiences and services needed to reach these goals. The ICF/MR program pays all reasonable costs of providing care for mentally retarded persons who qualify. In some cases, these costs are high, over $60,000 per year. These generous funding provisions are alleged to give states an incentive to maintain persons in ICF/MRs where, because of the eligibility requirements, there is little prospect of gainful employment, rather than in less-restrictive group, board and care, or family care homes where financial support is based primarily on the far less generous payments from SSI or SSDI/CDB.

The financial disincentives to moving persons out of ICF/MRs into less-restrictive living arrangements may be somewhat alleviated by the Medicaid Home and Community Based

Services program, passed in 1981, which grants authority to the secretary of the U.S. Department of Health and Human Services to waive existing statutory requirements in order to permit states to finance noninstitutional, nonmedical services for qualified elderly and disabled persons not living in skilled nursing homes or intermediate care facilities who would otherwise require care in Medicaid-certified institutions. These waivers are granted for 3 years and may be renewed.

Two major restrictions were imposed on the waiver authority that sharply limit its impact. First, eligibility is limited to persons who would otherwise be in institutions; and states must at least show that persons receiving services under the waiver could have been placed in institutions by demonstrating unused institutional beds, or proving that they would otherwise have had to build or expand an institution, or showing by some other means that the individuals could have been placed in residential care. Second, the total cost of care under the waiver must not exceed what the total cost of care would have been in the absence of the waiver. In exchange for increased flexibility in the use of funds, states must either hold costs constant or reduce them.

## Social Services

Prior to the passage of the Social Services Block Grant in 1981, social services funded out of Title XX funds (of the Social Security Act) could not, with a few exceptions, be provided to persons in families whose income exceeded 115% of the median income in the state for a comparably sized family unit. In some cases, disabled persons who were receiving social services, such as attendant care, found that they were no longer entitled to these services if they returned to a relatively well-paying job. On the other hand, their earnings were sometimes inadequate to purchase the services they required.

The Social Services Block Grant, enacted in 1981, eliminated federal restrictions on who could be provided social services. However, the states may continue to impose income restrictions, which will create work disincentives.

## Total Financial Disincentives

Although the work disincentives resulting from the individual programs are often substantial, it is their combined effects on the individual—specifically, the anticipated loss of cash benefits, health benefits, and social services—that is relevant to their willingness and/or realistic opportunity to return to paid employment. Although it is not known how many persons on SSI or SSDI/CDB are not working owing to the effects of work disincentives, most people who have worked in these programs can offer anecdotal cases of persons who could work but who cannot afford the loss of benefits that would follow a return to employment.

## EFFECTS OF PROGRAMS ON INCOME SECURITY

The net gain or loss of income that results from returning to work is one aspect of work disincentives. Another critical aspect of work disincentives is the effect on the security of income if beneficiaries of public programs return to substantial work. The job choices of many people are greatly influenced by the security, or lack of it, associated with the prospective job. People will often forego a higher paying, but less secure, job to remain in employment that is protected by union rules, seniority provisions, tenure, civil service, or that is not subject to periodic layoffs.

The employment opportunities available to many persons on SSDI/CDB or SSI are menial, do not pay much more than their disability benefits (and sometimes considerably less), and offer little assurance of long-term employment. Is it unreasonable to expect an individual receiving what appears to be a secure long-term cash benefit and assured medical care to be willing to exchange these benefits for employment that may make him or her better off in the short run, but that may spell financial disaster in the long run? Should highly vulnerable individuals be expected to be greater risk

takers than persons who are far more financially secure?

The Social Security Disability Amendments of 1980 sought to reduce the anxiety of SSI and SSDI/CDB recipients that acceptance of substantial work would put them at risk of having no source of income or health care if they subsequently lost their job. For both the SSDI/CDB and the SSI program, the 1980 amendments provided for a 15-month "reentitlement" period following the 9-month trial work period, during which the disabled beneficiary would automatically become reentitled to disability benefits if the work attempt was not successful. It should be noted that the 15-month reentitlement period will run concurrently with the payment of special cash benefits in the case of SSI beneficiaries who are working at the SGA level or higher so that these persons may use up the reentitlement period while still receiving benefits. Other provisions of the 1980 amendments that would reduce the fear of job insecurity are the extension of Medicare coverage for 36 months for SSDI/CDB beneficiaries after cash benefits cease, the elimination of the second-24-month waiting period for Medicare coverage for persons who become reentitled to SSDI/CDB benefits within 5 years after cash benefits cease, and the 3-year experiment that provides extended Medicaid coverage and special cash benefits to SSI recipients who return to work. As previously noted, these special SSI and Medicaid experiments have been extended.

## Effect on Mentally Retarded Persons

The various work disincentives that have been described apply to all disabled persons who are eligible for, or could be eligible for, benefits from these programs. The number of mentally retarded persons affected is substantial, as indicated by the following statistics:

1. Approximately two-thirds of the Childhood Disability Beneficiary awards made by Social Security are made to mentally retarded persons.
2. In 1982, 2.4% of the disabled workers awarded Social Security disability bene-

fits were diagnosed as mentally retarded (Social Security Administration, unpublished data). This percentage has been rising over time because the number of workers avoiding disability benefits has been falling while the number of mentally retarded workers awarded benefits has been relatively constant.

3. In 1976, 13.2% of the adults and 56.1% of the children (including persons who were blind) awarded SSI benefits were diagnosed as mentally retarded (Social Security Administration, 1980).

If one assumes that the percentage of mentally retarded persons receiving initial awards is about the same as the percentage among all beneficiaries, and that these percentages did not change appreciably between 1976 and 1983 for the SSI program (later data are not available), then, in 1984, an estimated 800,000 benefit checks were distributed to mentally retarded persons by the SSDI/CDB and SSI programs. About 84% of these checks were sent to persons age 18 or over and almost 80% were sent to persons between the ages of 18 and 65 (based on unpublished data provided by the Social Security Administration). This estimate involves some double counting, since some beneficiaries receive both SSI and SSDI/CDB benefits. This is particularly likely among people receiving child disability benefits in that about 38% receive SSI benefits. In the SSDI disability program, the percentage of beneficiaries receiving SSI benefits is about 8%. Assuming that these percentages apply to mentally retarded beneficiaries, it can be estimated that about 100,000 adult mentally retarded persons receive both Social Security and SSI benefits, which would reduce the number of adult mentally retarded persons (18–65 years of age) receiving cash benefits from these two programs to about 500,000.

The true number receiving cash benefits because of mental retardation is almost certainly higher for the following reasons: (1) Some multiply handicapped mentally retarded persons are given a primary diagnosis in a category other than mental retardation; (2) It is probable that there are large numbers of "invisible" mildly mentally retarded persons on SSI or SSDI/CDB who were gainfully employed or functioned as homemakers for a number of years but who later in life may have acquired additional functional limitations enabling them to apply for disability benefits; such limitations, in combination with mild mental retardation, represent substantial impediments to employment; (3) Some mentally retarded persons receiving cash benefits have dependent spouses and/or children, which further increases the number of persons receiving cash benefits because of mental retardation; and (4) Account has not been taken of persons who are awarded disability benefits under other programs such as the federal civil service or the Railroad Retirement Program (both of which have childhood disability beneficiary programs).

## Effect of Structural Disincentives on Work Effort

Recently, Berkowitz (1980) completed an extensive review of the literature on work disincentives. He concluded (not very strongly) that "the findings also point out that for some workers there may be a disincentive effect" (p. 48). He also stated that "all of the evidence points to the fact that there is a group of people on disability rolls, although possibly small in comparison to the total number receiving benefits, who are good candidates for rehabilitation" (p. 68).

It is furthermore noteworthy that the response of SSI beneficiaries to the special experiments in SSI and Medicaid established in the 1980 Social Security Amendments has been limited. At the end of 1982, 2 years after the special provisions went into effect, fewer than 500 SSI beneficiaries were receiving or had received special cash benefits who would not have done so in the absence of these special provisions (i.e., they had earnings above the SGA level but below the federal break-even point). However, almost 5,600 former SSI beneficiaries had retained their eligibility for Medicaid benefits after returning to work and having their cash benefits terminated. These data apparently mean that SSI beneficiaries who returned to work generally had earnings that exceeded the federal break-even point, but that their earnings often fell into the window between the federal break-even point and a higher earnings point, which adds the value of Medicaid and state supplementary benefits to this amount. Although this window varies by state, according to 1984 benefit levels, the amount would be roughly between $8,500 and $13,000 for individuals and between $12,300 and $16,000 for couples. It should be noted that there is no way of determining how many of these beneficiaries receiving special cash benefits and/or Medicaid benefits would have returned to work even if these special benefit provisions had not been established. It should also be noted that the number of persons receiving these special benefits was an infinitesimal percentage of the number of persons receiving SSI; only about 1 in 10,000 SSI beneficiaries obtained special cash benefits. However, the ratio of former SSI beneficiaries who retained their eligibility for Medicaid after they returned to work to the number of persons receiving SSI was over 1 in 1,000.

It would be premature, however, to conclude that persons receiving SSI and SSI/CDB are so effectively screened for the absence of work potential that the great majority are incapable of any level of gainful employment. It is extremely difficult to design research that can accurately measure the extent to which SSI and SSDI/CDB recipients would increase their work effort if the level of cash benefits, or the terms under which they receive them, were changed. Flaws can be detected in most studies. In principle, it would be desirable to compare the work effort of a group of disabled persons under present SSI and SSDI/CDB policies with another group of identical persons under a different set of policies. Unfortunately, two different sets of policies for the same type of persons cannot exist at the same time at a national level. It might be possible, under the SSI program, to compare states with different policies for supplementing the SSI payment. However, it is extremely difficult to identify two perfectly comparable groups of disabled

persons in two different states for comparison purposes, particularly since some persons may not qualify for SSI under the policies of one state but would under the policies of another state. The persons who would have been on SSI if they had lived in a more liberal state are almost impossible to identify.

Moreover, the lack of a large-scale response to the changes in SSI and Medicaid that were designed to enhance the incentives to work may reflect many things other than inability to work. For one thing, there does not appear to have been widespread knowledge of the special provisions for special cash benefits and extended Medicaid eligibility for SSI beneficiaries who return to work. This is particularly important in assessing the impact of these provisions during the initial stages of their operation, particularly if it is believed that among many SSI beneficiaries there is an ingrained fear of losing secure benefits. In extending the SSI and Medicaid experiments (1619 [a] and 1619[b], Congress required the Social Security Administration to establish an outreach program to assure that more people are aware of these special provisions, and to train Social Security Administration personnel to implement these special provisions. In addition, there are other disincentive effects in addition to those already mentioned (e.g., the potential loss of Food Stamps and rent supplements). Moreover, the advent of the Social Security Disability Amendments of 1980 coincided with growing levels of unemployment, which diminished the number of SSI and SSDI/CDB beneficiaries who could locate substantial work.

It is also relevant to ask why it is believed that these work incentives and disincentives may have an impact upon the decisions made by mentally retarded recipients of SSI and SSDI/CDB cash benefits. After all, this discussion has presented a complicated set of laws and regulations that few people understand well, and it can be presumed that few mentally retarded persons understand them at all.

Work disincentives may, however, affect the employment decisions of mentally retarded persons in an indirect way that is as important, and perhaps more so than a direct comparison by them of the gains and disadvantages of accepting employment. Mentally retarded persons, particularly severely mentally retarded individuals, are greatly influenced, if not largely controlled, in their work decisions by a wide variety of persons. In examining whether or not mentally retarded persons avoid work and why, it is important to ask the following types of questions: Will (or should) social workers who have struggled to place a mentally retarded person in a community-based residence counsel him or her to risk losing the secure SSI or SSDI/CDB cash benefit or Medicaid or Medicare entitlement on which his or her placement is based in order to accept work that may provide very little additional income? Will private operators of board and care homes, whose financial solvency is dependent upon a high bed occupancy and assured rent payment, actively encourage their tenants/clients to seek employment with all of its attendant risks? Will relatives who are concerned about their legal or moral obligation, or who may themselves be partly dependent upon the income support payment, be anxious to see a mentally retarded relative relinquish a secure benefit and accept a job?

## Fostering of Dependency

The preceding discussion of work disincentives was based on the premise that some disabled persons receiving cash, medical, and other benefits (or those empowered over them) make decisions about work on the basis of net gain (or loss) and the permanence of this gain or loss. Another important effect of some public programs is that they may promote the development of destructive attitudinal changes, the most important of which is the belief by disabled clients that they cannot work.

It is almost inevitable that some persons become convinced that they are unable to work, given that the basic requirement of eligibility for SSDI/CDB and SSI is an inability to engage in substantial gainful activity due to a medically determinable physical or mental impairment. During the entire time in which applicants are seeking to be declared eligible for SSI

or SSDI/CDB, all of their incentives guide them to maximize the extent of their physical and mental disabilities in order to be declared eligible for program benefits. Other persons seeking to assist the applicants, such as social workers, operators of community residences, the family, the lawyer, and others, will usually support the applicants' efforts to prove that they are unable to work. Efforts to encourage applicants to seek vocational rehabilitation may be met with strong resistance, both from the applicants and from persons advising them. The process of determining whether an applicant is eligible for benefits may last for 2 months to a year, and more. It is little wonder that after the desired goal is finally attained, the recipient of cash benefits, and perhaps his or her friends, relatives, advisors, and social worker, is either convinced of the futility of efforts to obtain work or is frightened at the prospect.

While empirical evidence of the development of such attitudes is scant, it is instructive to note the findings of a report on workers' compensation claimants with permanent partial disability (Ginnold, 1979). Permanent partial disability cases can be divided into two basic categories, those involving scheduled injuries and those involving unscheduled injuries. A scheduled injury is one that is discrete and usually observable, such as the loss of, or the loss of the use of, an arm or a leg, whereby the claimant normally receives a prescribed award based on a workers' compensation schedule. An unscheduled injury, in contrast, is less clearly defined, such as a permanent back injury, and is usually settled by a lengthy litigation process in which the claimant usually seeks to maximize the extent of his or her injury (and therefore also the amount of the subsequent award). Scheduled awards, by their nature, are less subject to manipulation through litigation. This report found that the claimants who received an award based on a scheduled injury were subsequently far more likely to return to work than the claimants who received an award based on an unscheduled injury, even when the comparisons were made among claimants with comparable disability ratings.

In fact, workers' compensation claimants with scheduled injuries suffered no long-term economic loss. It is reasonable to infer that part of the reason for this striking finding was that claimants with scheduled injuries generally had no need to convince themselves and others of the extent of their injuries in order to maximize the size of the award to which they were entitled.

## Problems in Delivery of Services

Many mentally retarded persons (almost all severely mentally retarded persons) require one or more services (income support, health services, vocational services, social services, etc.) in order to enter into and/or maintain gainful employment. There is no shortage of programs offering services. One source (White House Working Group on Handicapped Policy, 1984) has already listed over 150 federal programs providing services or other forms of support to disabled persons. This does not take into account the many other programs financed by state and local governments and private organizations. The multiplicity of programs does not mean, however, that they are always effective in assisting mentally retarded persons toward the goal of employment. In fact, as should be apparent from the preceding discussion, some of these programs provide incentives for mentally retarded persons not to accept substantial employment, even though the federal government usually places a high priority on encouraging employment of disabled persons. Several additional problems can be cited.

First, *mentally retarded persons may not always receive needed services, even when they are available.* The number and complexity of available programs make it difficult for mentally retarded persons to identify and take advantage of them. Often mentally retarded persons are not even aware of the programs or the conditions under which they can become eligible for services. A major role ascribed to the mentally retarded person's case manager, if a case manager exists, is that of directing mentally retarded persons toward needed services and of expediting their acceptance into these

programs. In addition, mentally retarded persons may not always be encouraged to accept, or may not be referred to, services, particularly employment services. A study of board and care homes conducted by the Denver Research Institute reported that few residents of these homes are employed and few receive, or are directed to, available vocational and social services (Dittmar et al., 1983).

Second, *some needed services are not available.* The lack of suitable community-based employment services for mentally retarded persons has often been noted, as has been the absence of resources to develop supported work opportunities in normal work settings and to provide long-term support if needed. There are many reasons for the unavailability of services—for example, limited budgets, the difficulty of extending services to sparsely settled areas, lack of interest in providing such services, lack of knowledge of how to provide services, lack of knowledge of the effectiveness of some services, government inertia, and other reasons. One consequence of a lack of appropriate services is that mentally retarded persons sometimes receive inappropriate services—for example, the highly restrictive care offered in ICFs/MR or the short-term vocational services usually offered by vocational rehabilitation agencies.

Third, *the problems of coordinating available services to achieve prescribed goals, particularly employment goals, are far from being resolved.* There are at least two reasons for these coordination problems. One is that these programs are managed, for the most part, independently of each other. Each has its own set of objectives, priorities, and eligibility conditions and is sometimes unconcerned with the objectives, priorities, and eligibility conditions of other programs. As an example of what can happen when different agencies make decisions about clients, it was recently reported in one state that "some disabled persons have reportedly been denied SSI benefits on the grounds that their disability was not sufficiently severe and yet have been denied VR services because their prognosis for employment was too poor" (Bradley, Allard, Annikis, Billingsley, Liegey, and Cravedi, 1978, p. 53). The inherent difficulties of coordinating programs is further exacerbated because some programs are managed at a federal level (e.g., SSDI/CDB, SSI, and Medicare), some programs are managed at a state level (e.g., vocational rehabilitation and Medicaid), and some are managed at a local level (e.g., some social service programs and some housing programs). Despite the obvious need for close coordination and cooperation among these programs, little such coordination and cooperation exists. As an illustration of the problems that arise, vocational counselors cannot always assure SSDI/CDB or SSI beneficiaries that they can be restored promptly to income support or medical care programs if they accept gainful work and several years later become unemployed.

A second reason for poor coordination is that many programs have limited objectives that, unfortunately, do not always place a high priority on employment. For example, social workers seeking to place mentally retarded persons in secure, community-based residential arrangements may be more concerned about the constancy of a cash flow than the employment of their clients. As another example, the emphasis of the large federally funded income support and health-care programs on identifying and supporting persons unable to engage in substantial gainful activity, rather than on assisting persons in returning to work, has already been described.

Fourth, *effective services are often hindered by rigidity of procedural practices*. For example, it usually takes 60 or more days before persons leaving an institution are declared eligible for SSI benefits, and consequently, needed funds are often not available at the time a resident is ready to be placed in a community-based living arrangement (Bradley et al., 1978).

Fifth, *programs that are not primarily involved with mentally retarded persons often lack the expertise or desire to provide needed services*. In a recent study of SSI and SSDI, it was questioned whether the examiners who determine whether a developmentally disabled person is sufficiently disabled to qualify for cash benefits had an adequate background in developmental disabilities (Bradley et al., 1978). It has also been questioned whether the independent professional review teams for ICFs/MR are sufficiently trained and experienced in mental retardation to certify that a mentally retarded individual is appropriately placed in an ICF/MR.

### Effects of the National Economy

The national economy does not always generate a sufficient number of jobs to hire all mentally retarded persons capable of working. One of the most important ways in which the federal government can stimulate the employment of mentally retarded persons is by creating a strong economy that generates the jobs on which these individuals can be placed. This is true both for regular competitive jobs and for jobs that provide greater or lesser amounts of sheltered work.

As the nation becomes accustomed to higher and higher "normal" rates of unemployment, the issue is bound to be raised as to why an effort should be made to find jobs for mentally retarded persons (or, for that matter, any disabled persons) when persons who do not have physical or mental disabilities are seeking work. The logical answer, of course, is that jobs should be created for both groups. The number of jobs in the economy is not immutably fixed and can be increased through appropriate fiscal and monetary action (although we have not been very successful in recent years, and there remains considerable disagreement as to which fiscal and monetary actions are the appropriate ones). The Full Employment Act of 1946 placed the responsibility for maintaining reasonably full employment on the federal government. Even when this goal is not being achieved, it would be unfair to maintain policies that cause a part of the population that is already highly disadvantaged and discriminated against to bear an unusually large share of the burden of unemployment or to be denied a share of the benefits of an expanding economy until after all able-bodied workers are employed.

The task of providing jobs to all mentally retarded and other severely disabled persons who need them will not be completed for many years and involves fundamental changes in social attitudes, in employment services, and in the structure of jobs (in the case of some severely mentally retarded persons who require supported work). In contrast, high unemployment is usually a cyclical problem that is responded to by federal spending, taxing, and monetary policy. Although national and local economic conditions affect the work opportunities of disabled persons, it would be inappropriate to fail to meet long-term responsibilities to mentally retarded and other disabled Americans because of a failure to fully resolve short-term business-cycle problems. Concerted social efforts are required to assure that employment can be secured and retained by disabled persons.

It is sometimes asserted that our society may someday become so affluent as to render the productivity of mentally retarded and other disabled persons superfluous. If so, why should society be so concerned about their employment? One answer is that there are many reasons to doubt this optimistic forecast. Moreover, we must act on the present, not on the unknown future. And for the present, any increased output should be welcome in a society that restrains social programs because of inadequate resources, that complains bitterly about the level of taxes, and that is still striving vigorously to raise the living standard of the population. But beyond the strict economic reasons for stressing the employment of mentally retarded and other disabled persons is the goal of increasing their participation and integration into the society. Attaining such a goal requires an effort to provide all who wish the opportunity to contribute to the society and its economy the opportunity to do so.

## DIRECTIONS FOR THE FUTURE

Many aspects of current services and programs for mentally retarded persons impede their securing and retaining work. Because working may cause a loss of benefits, the net financial gain may be meager or even negative. The process of establishing eligibility for benefits itself may convince applicants that they are truly incapable of work. Existing programs are often poorly coordinated, they are not oriented toward preparing or encouraging clients to work, and major gaps exist in services. These problems are exacerbated because the jobs available to mentally retarded persons are hard to find, pay little, and provide no assurance of long-term stability. As was observed at the beginning of this chapter, the problems caused by these programs apply, with minor modifications, not only to mentally retarded persons but to all disabled individuals. Resolution of these problems will consequently benefit all disabled Americans.

It will not be easy, but these problems can be resolved. Numerous programs at all levels of government will have to be changed, and detailed analyses and debates will need to be conducted. Many of the changes will have to be evaluated and modified in light of actual experience. The process of modifying programs so that they encourage rather than discourage or impede employment would be greatly expedited if the following three guidelines were employed.

First, programs serving disabled persons should not be based on the misconception that the population can be neatly divided among those who can work and those who either cannot work or whose prospective earnings are inconsequential. The knowledge on which to make these judgments on an irrevocable basis does not exist. Therefore, it would be better to base eligibility for income support and health-care programs on proof of the existence of a medically determinable physical or mental impairment that causes substantial difficulties in obtaining and retaining substantial gainful employment instead of requiring a pejorative judgment that applicants are incapable of engaging in substantial gainful activity.

Second, all programs should explicitly place a high priority on the goal of assisting disabled persons to obtain and to maintain gainful employment. This common goal among programs could be immensely valuable in developing ways to make programs work together to reduce dependency among disabled persons. This would require a major reorientation of the SSDI, SSI, Medicaid, and Medicare programs.

Third, all work performed by disabled persons should be valued by society, even if productivity is low, the job is insecure, or the work is not on a continuous basis. Public programs should not create conditions that discourage disabled persons from accepting such work.

These guidelines would probably lead to identifying a class of individuals who would never be completely severed from existing income support, medical care, and social service programs. It is hoped, however, that services and support would be suspended for long periods at a time and that most of these individuals would not become totally dependent upon public support. However, these programs would be prepared to provide appropriate services, if and when needed. Four points should be noted.

First, the objection will undoubtedly be raised that acceptance of these guidelines could lead to coverage by SSDI/CDB and SSI of a large number of partially disabled persons who are currently employed in unstable or very low-paying jobs, a prospect that could cause the costs of these cash-support programs to rise. On the other hand, it must be emphasized that acceptance of these guidelines will influence some partially disabled persons who are now on SSDI/CDB or SSI to return to partial or total independence, which will cause costs to fall. The net effect of these conflicting influences on costs cannot be predicted.

Second, the implications of the above guidelines are not as radical a departure from current policy as may first appear. The Social Security Disability Amendments of 1980, as already observed, provided extended medical coverage (both Medicaid and Medicare), reentitlement rights (both SSI and SSDI), and special cash benefits (SSI) to beneficiaries who return to work. These are the policy directions in which these guidelines would lead. One type of future policy change that these guidelines would probably instigate would be to modify the benefit structure in SSDI/CDB to allow, as in the case of SSI, for a gradual reduction of benefits

as income rises. The problem, of course, is that applying a $1 reduction in benefits for each $2 rise in earnings would cause, because the benefit levels are much higher than for SSI, the break-even point to be over $20,000 in some cases—an earnings level considerably above the full-time wages of many persons. Some people might find this break-even point too high. Another future policy change would probably be long-term and even lifetime extension of Medicaid or Medicare coverage to persons unable to obtain medical coverage privately or as a work benefit; in these cases, it would be reasonable to require the beneficiaries to pay part (or even all) of the cost of this coverage by requiring premiums based on income, and/or by requiring employers to pay into these funds the amount that they would have spent in health coverage if these employees did not have preexisting conditions. Still another likely policy change would be to revise the current requirement that persons earning over $300 per month cannot become eligible for SSI. Not only is this SGA level low (about 60% of the wages of a full-time worker receiving the minimum wage), but it provides a financial incentive for disabled persons to establish eligibility for SSI before returning to work. After establishing eligibility, the federal break-even point—the point at which all cash benefits end—is far above the SGA level. The same problem would arise in the SSDI/CDB program if the benefit structure is altered so that benefits are reduced gradually as earnings rise. In effect, eligibility for SSI or SSDI/CDB should probably be granted to all handicapped persons whose earning capacity is below the break-even point.

Third, most of the basic components needed to provide appropriate care and services to mentally retarded persons already exist (e.g., unemployment compensation, SSI, SSDI/CDB, social service programs, rent supplements, Food Stamps, Medicare, Medicaid, etc.). What is needed is to close gaps and eliminate overlaps so that these programs operate in a coordinated, efficient, and cost-effective manner.

Fourth, accepting these guidelines and improving existing programs may not be a costly undertaking. In fact, it is conceivable that social costs could decline. As already noted, the effect on costs of offering partial public support to persons not now eligible for cash-assistance programs must be offset against a reduction in the number of persons who are totally dependent upon public support. In addition, improving efficiency and coordination among programs will itself reduce operating costs, and returning persons to paid employment will reduce the demand for services from these programs. Moreover, the nation's annual output should rise as more mentally retarded workers are encouraged to work. Finally, such policies are much more in line with social goals and values that stress the value of employment, the reduction of poverty, and the dignity and self-respect of all citizens.

## REFERENCES

Berkowitz, M. *Work disincentives.* Falls Church, VA: Institute for Information Studies, 1980.

Bradley, V., Allard, M., Annikis, M., Billingsley, K., Liegey, A., & Cravedi, E. *Developmentally disabled persons in the federal income maintenance programs: A critique of issues in SSI and SSDI.* Washington, DC: National Association of State Mental Retardation Program Directors, 1978.

Conley, R.W. *The economics of mental retardation.* Baltimore: Johns Hopkins University Press, 1973.

Conley, R.W., & Noble, J.H. Workers' compensation reform: challenge for the 80's. In: R.W. Conley (ed.), *Research reports of the Interdepartmental Workers' Compensation Task Force,* Vol. 1. Washington, DC: U.S. Government Printing Office, 1979.

Dittmar, N.D., Smith, G.P., Bell, J.C., Jones, C.B.C., & Manzanares, D.L. *Board and care for elderly and mentally disabled populations, Vol. 1: A survey of seven states.* Denver: University of Denver, Denver Research Institute, 1983.

*Federal Register, 47*(69), April 9, 1982.

Ginnold, R.A. A follow-up study of permanent disability cases under Wisconsin workers' compensation. In: R. W. Conley, (ed.), *Research report of the Interdepartmental Workers' Compensation Task Force,* Vol. 6. Washington, DC: U.S. Department of Labor, 1979.

Litvin, M., & Russem, W. (eds.). *The guide to federal resources for the developmentally disabled.* Washington, DC: Federal Programs Information and Assistance Project, 1977.

Social Security Administration. *Social Security bulletin: Annual statistical supplement, 1980.* Washington, DC: U.S. Department of Health and Human Services, Social Security Administration, 1980.

Social Security Administration. *Social security handbook.* Washington, DC: U.S. Department of Health and Human Services, Social Security Administration, 1982.

White House Working Group on Handicapped Policy. *Memorandum for the cabinet council on human resources.* March 29, 1984.

# Part IV

## MANAGING AND ENHANCING INTEGRATION

Integration strategies involve a range of social settings (e.g., educational, residential, recreational) and different types and levels of human interaction. These strategies begin with simple physical proximity, where severely handicapped children and youth attend the same schools and share physical facilities with nonhandicapped students or live in the same neighborhood and share buses, parks and sidewalks with nonhandicapped citizens. But, with concerted and careful efforts, the strategies go beyond mere proximity and promote melding of handicapped and nonhandicapped children and youth into single groups for structured periods of social interaction and even for educational and social activities, where social interaction comes as a natural by-product of membership in an integrated community of handicapped and nonhandicapped persons.

Because this social change requires both an appreciation of many legitimate perspectives and knowledge of the means of successful political and service interventions, a section of this volume is devoted to the subject of managing and enhancing integration. This section includes three chapters on different facets involved in promoting the social integration of severely handicapped individuals through community services, through school programs, and through leisure-recreational pursuits.

In Chapter 9, Lyle Wray and Colleen Wieck draw on their experience as active state-level promoters of community-based services in Minnesota to examine the problems and prospects for improving opportunities of developmentally disabled persons to live in more integrated settings. They discuss the emerging notion of client- or "community-centered" services, which (1) focus on supplementing existing helping networks, such as family and community groups; (2) provide maximum flexibility in service authorization, so that services are truly dictated by individual need; (3) offer a large number and wide range of services that not only meet many different levels of need but that also provide clients with choices; and (4) are as cost-effective as possible. Wray and Wieck conclude that expanded and improved case-management services are the only feasible means to the establishment of such an orientation. They specify a number of ways in which case management should be enlarged and enhanced, and further note related changes that must take place in federal, state, and local government policy to further promote client-centered practices.

In Chapter 10, Luanna H. Meyer and Gloria Shizue Kishi describe the process of integrating severely handicapped students into public schools in Hawaii. Based on extensive interviews with key participants in the process—parents, state education agency and local school personnel, advocacy group administrators and others—they examine the issues and problems involved as well as the strategies and situations that were conducive to their resolution. They present suggestions for similar efforts, including the kinds of assurances that must be made to parents if they

217

are to join in the advocacy for normalized educational experiences for severely handicapped students.

JoAnne W. Putnam, Judy K. Werder, and Stuart J. Schleien, in Chapter 11, examine the leisure and recreational integration of handicapped children and youth. The authors note that integrated leisure/recreational activities have tended to have relatively low priority among community service programs. However, as the importance attributed to leisure/recreational activities in the general population has grown, so has the sense that leisure and recreation opportunities are crucial to the social integration of severely handicapped persons. In this chapter, the authors describe what is known about these programs and the implications of this knowledge for future developments in community-based service programs.

Chapter 9

# Moving Persons with Developmental Disabilities toward Less Restrictive Environments through Case Management

*Lyle Wray and Colleen Wieck*

Over the past 150 years of formal services to persons with developmental disabilities, principles, values, and service models have undergone a number of transformations and cycles (see, for example, Scheerenberger, 1983; Wolfensberger, 1972). Spurred by the availability of federal and state funds, service options have rapidly developed in recent decades and major shifts in service principles have occurred. These principles as applied to individuals with developmental disabilities include: the developmental model—individuals with significant handicapping conditions can grow and develop (Bernstein, Ziarnik, Rudrud, & Czajkowski, 1981; Crosby, 1980); individualization—supports to growth and development are provided most appropriately if they are individualized (Gardner, Long, Nichols, & Iagulli, 1980); community

integration—persons with developmental disabilities should live in and participate as fully as possible in their communities and should not be congregated for services (Flynn & Nitsch, 1980); least restrictive alternative—living, learning, and working should be in the least restrictive alternative that is supportive of an individual's continued growth and development (Turnbull, 1981); criterion of ultimate functioning—tasks selected for teaching in educational, residential, and vocational areas should be firmly linked to the environments in which a person is expected to live, work, and learn in order to ensure relevance and transfer of skills gained (Brown, Nietupski, & Hamre-Nietupski, 1976); community readiness—"readiness" for community placement is most appropriately applied to the service system serving an individual rather than to characteristics of an individual (Loop & Hitzing, 1980); family support priority—children should live with their natural family or if that is not appropriate or possible, in a living arrangement such as an adoptive or foster home that is as close as possible to a natural family (Stark, 1980).

This chapter discusses the case-management process and related themes emerging among service models promoting a continuing movement of persons with developmental disabilities toward less restrictive living, learning, and working arrangements. Remedies for barriers to effective case management and service alternatives are presented using information drawn in part from the state of Minnesota.

## THEMES FROM EMERGING SERVICE MODELS

The outlines of an array of service models supporting less restrictive services are emerging from a number of successful programs in the areas of community-based family support (Allin & Allin, 1982); residential programs using existing housing (State of Kentucky Title XIX Waiver Application, 1982); and vocational programs involving integration of greater numbers of individuals and small groups into community work and training sites (Kessler & Strom, 1983).

These developing services share a number of themes in providing community services to mental health clients, elderly persons, and persons with developmental disabilities. The "social health maintenance organization" approach, for example, assembles a number of service elements to serve elderly persons in the least restrictive setting, and the "community support program" supports long-term clients of the mental health system in community living. These new "community-centered" service models contain a number of common elements that are often interlocked in application.

First, these approaches are designed to *supplement rather than to supplant existing helping networks* such as the family, neighborhood, and community (Sarason, 1972; Skarnulis, 1976). Greater sensitivity is needed

to fill the gap of unmet services based on individual, family, and community strengths and needs, without displacing the informal helping arrangement provided by other residential alternatives.

Second, there is a recognition of the *paramount importance of flexibility in service delivery* both in the intensity of service provided and the type of services offered over the short and long term. Failure to provide one element of a service package for a brief period may lead to a prolonged stay in a more restrictive living, learning, or working arrangement. Flexibility is greatly aided if a case manager has a substantial degree of discretion in organizing funding and service arrangements based upon individual strengths and needs and family and community resources. Avoidance of major capital investment in "bricks and mortar," while investing in the human resources of families and other supportive persons, can avoid the limitations involved in narrow facility-centered approach to service provision.

Third, *the type, intensity, and timing of supports to families and individuals need to be truly individualized.* Often "individualization" has been limited to picking the available service "slot" that the individual most closely fits. In a truly individualized approach, design and implementation of the least restrictive package of supports to that individual are based upon the identified capacities and weaknesses of the individual, family, and community.

Fourth, there is a recognition of the desirability of providing the individual and family with a *choice from the service array* in regard to, for example, who will provide the service. This freedom of choice implies that a variety of service options has been developed or can be developed on reasonably short notice. The individual and family must have these options explained in depth by an informed person; ideally they have also examined the services and talked with prior consumers. Freedom of choice implies that a modified market mechanism will reward efficient providers attuned to consumer needs and eliminate or restructure inefficient providers. Government's role in such a system might be limited to ensuring that such service arrays are available and might not involve a direct role in the production of these services (Kolderie, 1982).

Fifth, there is a common theme of *cost containment* in these service models, in that they make every effort to stretch their dollars. Economic circumstances appear to dictate a choice between, on the one hand, stretching service dollars to meet the needs of more individuals by using less restrictive services based upon existing helping networks and, on the other hand, using more restrictive models to serve fewer people with the same amount of money, controlling costs by systematically excluding persons needing services. A related theme is the principle that prevention or minimization of disabilities is a method of cost containment preferred over the option of employing costly measures at a later point to correct situations that should have been avoided.

Sixth, there is a strong theme that *case management or service coordination is a vital ingredient* for supporting a dispersed family and community-centered array of less restrictive service options. Maintaining quality of living, proper working arrangements, and coherence among various service elements requires skilled brokerage, advocacy, and management, which is best placed at one focal point of accountability.

## DEFINITIONS OF CASE MANAGEMENT

The themes just cited from emerging service models are attuned to individual, family, and community needs and strengths and accentuate the importance of service coordination of case management to service systems. There is, however, little agreement on the scope and definition of case management and upon the functions and activities of persons acting as case managers (National Conference on Social Welfare, 1981). Some activities frequently suggested as elements of case management are:

1. Providing a centralized point of intake;
2. Assisting the client and family in the identification of needs, goals, existing individual and family resources, and supplementary resources;

3. Establishing a team composed of the individual, family members, professionals, and representatives of agencies as needed to meet identified goals;
4. Coordinating team meetings;
5. Developing an individualized service plan (ISP) outlining goals, interventions, responsibilities, timelines, and criteria for evaluation;
6. Distributing the ISP;
7. Arranging support of appropriate community services and informal supports;
8. Objectively monitoring each ISP with an outcome orientation; and
9. Advocating for the client as needed for additional supports (Colorado Department of Institutions, 1980; Krantz, 1980; Lippman, 1975; National Conference on Social Welfare, 1981; North Carolina Department of Human Resources, 1982; Wisconsin Department of Health and Human Services, 1980). Colorado provided a detailed manual of suggestions for implementing case-management services (Colorado, 1980), and the National Conference on Social Welfare (1981) examined case-management services for persons with developmental disabilities from a number of perspectives.

There is a substantial variance in the comprehensiveness and character of the case-management process. Rather than discuss the various lists of proposed functions of case managers (for this, see National Conference on Social Welfare, 1981), it is useful to look broadly at the levels of comprehensiveness proposed for the concept. Ross (1980) outlined three levels of comprehensiveness of case management: (a) minimal, (b) coordination, and (c) comprehensive.

*Minimal*

Outreach
Client assessment
Case planning
Referral to service providers

*Coordination*

Outreach
Client assessment

Case planning
Referral to service providers
Advocacy for client
Direct casework
Developing natural support systems
Reassessment

*Comprehensive*

Outreach
Client assessment
Case planning
Referral to service providers
Advocacy for client
Direct casework
Developing natural support systems
Reassessment
Advocacy for resource development
Monitoring quality
Public education
Crisis intervention

Each element in each category may be varied in the intensity of effort, resources, and competence available at a given time for the functions identified.

A critical component of the case manager's responsibility involves maintaining *interagency linkages*. These linkages may involve local or geographically dispersed elements of services directed toward consumers. Professionals disagree on the issue of whether the case manager providing coordination should be within a direct service agency or independent of a service agency (National Conference on Social Welfare, 1981). Given the claim that the quality of services to clients is directly correlated with interagency connections (Frumpkin, 1978), taking steps to maximize cooperation and coordination is a priority undertaking. Measures to reduce competition for limited resources and interagency conflict can include such actions as an exchange of information between agencies on their perceived roles, policies, and procedures and a clear definition of agency and staff responsibilities (Baumheier, 1979).

Advocates of the use of *generic services* to meet the needs of persons with developmental disabilities strongly support the case-management process (National Conference on Social Welfare, 1981; Yates, 1980). Hersh and

Brown (1977) stated that "specialization" of services is antithetical to the principle of normalization by which means as close to normal as possible are used to attain behaviors as culturally normative as possible (Wolfensberger, 1972). Utilization of generic services is compatible with the basic principle of normalization. Generic services may also ultimately achieve economies of scale and administrative efficiencies and provide less expensive services. Kelly and Menolascino (1975) caution that there may be limits to the use of existing services. Generic service providers may require additional education or training in order for their services—such as medical, educational, recreational, or residential—to adequately address the needs of persons with developmental disabilities. Developing a responsive generic service system may require action on a variety of administrative and policy fronts, including the creation and maintenance of a viable case-management system.

Employing a case-management system both broadens the arena of service providers and the *definition of the client*. Services have typically been said to be directed at the needs of parents of children with developmental disabilities, who have acted as the traditional advocates for their children. In the view of Justice, O'Connor, and Warren (1971) the family is seen as the case manager seeking assistance for a family member. Bertsche and Horejsi (1980) recommended inclusion of the use of family and informal community resources as part of a written individualized service plan. Schodek (1980) noted the potential for conflict between the needs of the client and of the family as the evolution continues from private family advocacy to one based on a broader concept of advocacy. The "client" for services may not be identified easily in these conflicts. Indeed, there may be times when it is unclear whether the individual, another family member, or the community is the client.

## LIMITS OF CASE MANAGEMENT

A number of potential limits to the case-management process are cited in the literature. Morley and Kokaska (1979) suggest that a case manager often has too few contacts to be able to understand and represent the client's needs adequately and may become isolated from client involvement. Skarnulis (1976) stated that a case-management approach can be immobilized through financial restraints and by lack of flexibility. A discretionary fund available for the case manager's use or funding of services through individualized service plans may minimize some of these limitations. The number of clients served by a case manager—the caseload—varies considerably among local units and across states. Gladowski (n.d.) noted that "the data base concerning workloads is at best weak, problematic, and in need of critical scrutiny" (p. 6). A prominent question in the literature on case management concerns the ideal size of caseloads. According to the National Conference on Social Welfare (1981):

> Several states have developed standards which identify a maximum load of around sixty clients per manager. Most felt that a caseload of sixty was deplorably high but admitted that no matter what caseload sizes were, they would probably be regarded as excessive. A minority favored relatively high caseloads, arguing that case managers would thus be forced to rely heavily on other resources, minimizing client dependence on them as individuals....while legislating a specific number may be an important administrative safeguard, fixed ratios neither dictate nor ensure the quality of service, just as time spent on a particular case is not always a fair indicator of effectiveness (p. 11).

*Lack of services to manage* is a critical limit, since case managers are relatively powerless when services are cut back. Local *agency conflicts* in the absence of state-level mandates for service provision and coordination may entangle clients in local disputes over payment responsibilities and jurisdiction. Service programs such as residential and day programs may set *conflicting or incompatible goals* for a client. A delineation of primary, secondary, or limited case-manager roles is necessary to clarify responsibility and accountability, since several agencies are often involved.

Case management itself is easier if the process is well defined and if that *definition* is commonly shared, as it generally has been since passage of Public Law 94-142. *Evaluation of services* by case managers is often tied to completion of forms and reports. Evaluation and monitoring appropriately cover three levels: 1) *individual progress*—to ensure that the programs and providers of service are responsive to individual needs; 2) *program progress*—to guarantee that services improve and meet their organizational objectives; and 3) *system progress*—to ensure that individuals are moving toward independence and toward less restrictive environments that meet their needs for growth and development. *Information availability* provides a limitation. There is great variation in the degree and depth of knowledge about a given individual, about particular services, and about whole service systems among case managers. The *absence of agreements* between agencies also limits case management. Formal and explicit linkages between agencies simplify case management, while ad hoc linkages may be time consuming to develop or may be unavailable. *Limited variety* in case-management models often impedes effectiveness. A realistic and systematic state-level plan for case management should reflect varying needs for and types of case management (e.g., generic case management might be provided to a variety of client groups such as elderly persons in their homes or mental health clients and persons with developmental disabilities in rural areas, with greater specialization in major urban centers; and options might be offered such as training parents to act as case managers for their children).

## CASE MANAGEMENT IN MINNESOTA

Because case-management systems in reality are often very different from what they might be in theory, a brief look at the practices and problems of operating systems is instructive. Case management in Minnesota, the authors' home state, is therefore described. Rule 185, issued in 1981 (12 MCAR 2.185, 1981) was Minnesota's first administrative rule on case-management services. This rule assigns the duties of assessment, planning, and evaluation of services to case managers for persons who are or who may be mentally retarded in all 87 counties of the state. However, the rule is not linked to county case management for clients of the mental health system, elderly persons, or persons with chemical dependency problems. Neither are case-management ratios, required or suggested staff training or competencies, linkages with other types of service provision, or evaluation of case-management processes and client outcomes addressed in the rule.

No formal, comprehensive study of case-management practices has been completed to date in Minnesota. In an unpublished study of 16 of 87 Minnesota counties, the Department of Public Welfare conducted telephone interviews to determine the most frequent problems encountered by case managers of mentally retarded clients. The greatest difficulty in providing services was to clients with behavior management problems or to those with a dual diagnosis of mental retardation and mental illness. Day programs for adults were cited in 13 of 16 counties as the most pressing service need, due to inadequate funding levels. The training most desired by this sample of case managers regarded dealing with behavior problem clients. It should come as little surprise that most clients enter state hospitals in Minnesota for "behavior problems."

It is problematic at this point to make generalizations about the effectiveness of case managers in Minnesota as brokers, advocates, administrators, and providers of services. Indirectly, though, rates of admission to state hospitals and other measures provide informal estimates of the adequacy with which case managers function as "the glue that holds the system together." One measure is that of caseloads for case managers. Although the state of Michigan, for example, has a ratio set by statute of one case manager for every 25 clients, the Minnesota study found the following ratios in Minnesota counties: an average caseload of 47 clients; an average of one case aide for every 171 clients stabilized in community programs; an average of one case manager for 81 adult clients. The two highest caseloads were 280 clients for one case manager with many clients in a state hospital and 380 clients for a case manager responsible for three large community facilities.

Human services in Minnesota are significantly decentralized, with many responsibilities for planning and assuring service provision resting with locally elected county boards. Particularly in rural counties, the social service office of the county functions often as a centralized intake and coordination point, and the case managers employed by the counties act to integrate provision of services. Economic downturns have produced state and local budget cutbacks and have led to increased caseloads in many counties. With real shortages in resources and a paucity of service options, brokerage by a case manager often becomes illusory, with the major outcome being the addition of a person's name to a long waiting list for services. Fragmentary and conflicting responsibilities among county case managers, educators, residential service providers, and health-service providers and planners have yet to be addressed comprehensively across the state. Perhaps the major problem in this regard is the absence of systematic, ongoing evaluation on a regional or state level that could provide a basis by which decision makers could make adjustments in service coordination to improve the integration of persons with developmental disabilities into their home communities.

## FISCAL AND PROGRAMMATIC STEPS TO STRENGTHEN CASE MANAGEMENT

Case management may be viewed as a microcosm of the service system: needs are assessed, planning is undertaken to meet these needs, arrangements are made for services to be delivered, and an evaluation is made of whether services are delivered as planned and whether they are effective in meeting their objectives. Many approaches can be taken to improve the availability, delivery, and effectiveness of services, including: 1) assuring that services are responsive to individual needs rather than being based upon narrowly defined categorical programs, 2) assuring that funding is flexible in addressing individual needs, and 3) assuring that outcomes of services are evaluated on a number of organizational levels and are taken into account in formulating corrective actions.

A number of steps are suggested here to reinforce the case-management process as a tool for enhancing both the individual's movement to less restrictive environments and his or her prospects for financial responsibility. These steps are founded on flexible strategies that are in turn based upon natural helping networks and other alternatives to facility-centered services. Effective case-management services appear to require the following elements: *Well-defined process* + *Clear case responsibility* + *Good information about clients and services* + *Clear interagency agreements* + *Adequate resources.*

Some specific measures that might be taken to achieve such a system are described in the next several paragraphs.

### Needs Assessment in Case Management

Careful analysis of the time and resources required to carry out case-management responsibilities effectively is a first step that should be repeated periodically over time to assure that this pivotal function can be performed at a satisfactory level. A caseload of 25 clients in an urban area may still leave a worker with a very busy schedule time to perform only some of the comprehensive case management functions previously listed. Research might be conducted to compare the effects of a rich case-management ratio and a current average ratio through comparisons of measures such as the recruitment of natural helping networks, rates of institutionalization, and quality of life measures. Such research would be used to begin to identify empirically the impacts of caseloads upon the lives of persons with developmental disabilities.

### Linkages among Agencies: Specialization of Function

Given the diverse service mandates for health, education, and other human services, careful study should be undertaken to determine local roles. It might be appropriate in a given area to designate one agency to take the lead among other agencies in providing case management for persons of particular ages. In such a "chronologically integrated case management" system, for example, community health

personnel could exert leadership in the areas of prenatal and perinatal care with emphasis on high-risk mothers who are young, poor, and malnourished. Following birth, education might assume a major role in parent support and infant development until adulthood, when a local social service agency might assume the lead in the case-management process. Passing case-management leadership along chronologically or dividing areas into zones for which a number of agencies each assume responsibility is an organizational challenge that requires substantial negotiation skills as well as a thorough examination of service mandates, privacy laws, and local characteristics. Strategies both for dealing with "multiple-problem" families and for creating linkages among the various licensing activities, advocacy services, parents, and other groups also need to be addressed. As an example of a strategy based upon this analysis, Nordyke (1982) proposed an approach to improving services to children with handicaps by promoting a coherent response by the service system.

### Dollars Following People, Not Just Programs

"Dichotomous funding" which provides either expensive institutional services or nothing to support families and communities, has not yet been removed from the service system. Further action remains to be taken to reduce the situation in which the only avenue for receiving any service is to enter a facility in which the client often receives more service elements than are originally required, for a longer period of time than actually needed. One step toward improving this situation involves providing case managers with a block of money to fund individualized service plans, rather than relying simply upon a system that funds whole programs to which the case manager seeks admission for an individual. By employing a range of service options, with financial and programmatic accountability mechanisms and intensified interdisciplinary team functioning, such a model could afford the type of flexibility needed to move smoothly to less restrictive living and working arrangements. At present, many individuals may be retained in more restrictive and expensive services than they require because there is no funding base for the more independent and less expensive service alternative. Flexible funding would permit expanded use of family supports such as parent training, in-home assistance, crisis services, and specialized foster care—with little capital investment. Under such an approach, cost containment would be attained by using an array of less expensive, yet appropriate, services rather than by restricting access to a more expensive service.

## Variety of Case-Management Models

Programs supporting elderly persons, persons with developmental disabilities, and mental health clients in the community have a number of similarities in process and delivery. Whether case management and other services for the individuals should be provided by the same or different agencies is worth considering. Parents, siblings, or other interested citizens might be trained to share the role of case manager by monitoring out-of-home placements for quality and by organizing outreach and meetings for parent-to-parent support groups. The choice between specialized case management (e.g., one case manager serving only persons with developmental disabilities) or generic case management (e.g., one case manager serving all persons in need of services in a given area, whether they be elderly persons, mental health clients, or persons with developmental disabilities) is often largely influenced by the realities of client density, geography, and resources. Rural and urban differences in case-management functions should be recognized. For example, case managers in rural areas may more often assume a direct training and support role for parents and individuals with developmental disabilities and their families.

## Federal Support for Case Management

Case management is a relatively invisible service that is, politically, an easy target for budget cuts in times of economic difficulty because facilities do not close, and, beyond case managers, no jobs are lost. One positive occurrence in the recent hard times for human services has been the recognition of the importance of case management in the Medicaid Waiver legislation (Omnibus Reconciliation Act, 1981). The waiver regulations authorize case management as a service that may be funded with Medicaid dollars as part of a community care plan for people who would otherwise be placed in Medicaid-supported facilities. Such support of case management should assist in building a system in which generic services are responsive to individual needs and in which such services maximize the support given to families but minimize the supplanting of natural family and community helping activities by government agencies.

## AGENDA FOR CHANGE: NEXT STEPS IN LESS-RESTRICTIVE SERVICES

Effective case management necessitates a host of appropriate and effective services. Although there has been an increase in the number and availability of the services provided to persons with developmental disabilities, a greater range in types and intensities of services is required to respond flexibly to individual needs. Facilitating the emergence of a variety of new service models that offer less restrictive service potential to persons with developmental disabilities requires actions at a number of levels in both the governmental and private sectors. Both programmatic and fiscal measures need to be addressed, although flexible funding mechanisms that encourage service provision in less restrictive alternatives may be particularly important for states with relatively fully developed, stabilized service systems. It may be an oversimplification to claim that "find a funding source and the services will follow," but it would be unwise to underplay the importance of correcting "perverse" fiscal incentives with positive fiscal incentives for less-restrictive services.

The foundation of any sustained move to a less restrictive service array should be a recomceptualization of program quality that is compatible with continued progress toward community integration and independence of persons with developmental disabilities. Leismer (1983, p. 14) outlined a number of factors to be considered in assuring the quality of living and working arrangements. Program size, staff training, crisis teams, and case management services are among the important factors to be addressed in assuring program quality. There can be no doubt that the move from a facility-centered quality-assurance model to one more attuned to a dispersed service system that supplements existing supports requires more concerted effort.

Turnbull (1981) suggested six steps to be taken to implement the least restrictive alternative services and environment for persons with developmental disabilities. First, an ideology consistent with the least restrictive alternative should be adopted. Second, there needs to be systems-level planning to conceptualize and adopt a full range of program options. Third, the use of generic services, including the availability of specialized support services in the context of generic settings, should be assured. Fourth, there should be fiscal equity between systems so that individual plans for services are developed in a noncoercive atmosphere. Fifth, there should be consumer and professional dialogue and negotiation through advocacy, periodic case review, administrative appeals, due process, ombudsmen, and citizen advocacy programs. Sixth, public awareness and professional development should be expanded to increase understanding of and commitment to the least restrictive alternative.

## GOVERNMENT ROLES IN DEVELOPING LESS-RESTRICTIVE SERVICES

The remainder of this chapter outlines actions at the federal, state, and local levels to facilitate the development of less restrictive services and case-management services for persons with developmental disabilities.

### Actions by the Federal Government

Additional measures need to be taken to afford flexibility in funding alternatives to services for persons with developmental disabilities. Steps such as the Medicaid Waiver legislation (Omnibus Reconciliation Act, 1981) need to be supplemented in the area of vocational rehabilitation to permit restructuring of adult day programs based on new models of service (Kessler & Strom, 1983). In education the mandates of Public Law 94-142 must be maintained. Continued discussion of intergovernmental roles and responsibilities should sort out and retain "national policy issues" such as community integration and education for children with handicapping conditions. Funding streams should be more closely matched to national policy statements favoring community living.

### Actions by the States

The major authority and responsibility within the federal system rests with the states. Despite the expansion of the role of the federal government following the 1930s and World War II, states still set the major direction for human service policy. In Minnesota there are a number of legislative measures that encourage less restrictive services or that remove barriers to these services: prohibition of local zoning discrimination against small group homes, right to least restrictive treatment, case-management rule for persons who are or who may be mentally retarded, and program rules for service provision (Scott & Siuta, 1979). There are, however, a number of obstacles to further progress within the financial system.

Perhaps the most important obstacle is that there are few sources of funds with which to develop less restrictive services. The yearly increase in the cost of the long-term care system is greater than the total financial effort devoted to less restrictive service models to support families and individuals outside of facility services. To remedy this situation, pursuit of a Home and Community-Based Services Waiver under the Medicaid Waiver legislation (Omnibus Reconciliation Act, 1981) is one important incentive for system redesign for many states. However, clearly, conceptualizing an ideal or at least an improved state system is a difficult, yet critical, preliminary step to seeking Title XIX (Medicaid) or any other funding.

Many states encounter numerous problems in taking that first step.

Policy coordination at state levels often neglects assignment of leadership for low-visibility areas such as prevention and early intervention to a particular agency. Furthermore, state legislatures do not regularly perform oversight functions. Although much is known about predictors of infant disability, such as inadequate prenatal nutrition and chemical dependency, full implementation of what is known remains to be accomplished. Although there is recognition of the importance of and a solid base of evidence for the effectiveness of parent training, comparatively little money has been allocated for it. Generally, states invest little in the areas of highest probable payoff.

State government must also face the responsibility and promise of a "new federalism" with increased authority and discretion in trying to achieve a delicate balance between decentralization of service planning and delivery and the maintenance of statewide mandates for service. If local-level government accountability and state mandates for services are diluted, program responsibilities may be abdicated. Yet, if local discretion and flexibility are not possible, it is unlikely that services that are more responsive to individual strengths and needs and to local or regional circumstances will be provided. The mechanisms for setting the balance between local service mandates and funding systems and state responsibilities are frequently complex. Often there are unforeseen consequences of policy choices. Arriving at a functional balance and at a mechanism for its periodic review is critical to a decentralized service system.

The role of the state government in a decentralized system should be in setting broad policy, specifying the range of appropriate living arrangements as well as educational, work, and supportive services that should be made available to persons with developmental disabilities. State government must provide the framework for any necessary changes in services and for reallocation of existing funds following a broad view of costs and benefits. The state's goal should be to adjust the various elements of the service system to perform harmoniously and cost-effectively. An example of such a broad view is: calculating the cost of financing the present institutional and community care systems until the year 2000 and comparing that with the costs and impact on clients of models emphasizing less-restrictive service options with case management in home support services.

To assist in the movement toward less restrictive services, it is critical to examine a program budget for services at a systems level in order to identify aspects of funding or service system organization that may tacitly encourage more restrictive service usage. For example, such a program budget examination might fuel a move toward "prevention rather than repair" by looking at short- and long-range financial impacts of genetic counseling, early intervention, and family support programs (Kolderie, 1982).

State-level leadership is also needed in examining need and implementing innovative service models in areas of particular importance, such as family supports and adult residential and vocational programs, especially for persons with severe handicaps. Such a review should assist both in identifying a range of necessary options for living and working arrangements for persons with developmental disabilities and in setting the parameters for locally controlled human service boards and for family choice. In addition, the state agency should study the adequacy of present case-management arrangements and project future needs for additional resources and/or for state standards in this critical area. The need should be recognized for diverse strategies or organizing case-management services for a number of different target groups in need of services, while taking into account special factors affecting service delivery (e.g., rural and urban differences).

### Actions at the Local Level

Some steps that might be taken at the local level include implementing coordination of services through interagency agreements and case management; performance contracting with service providers; integrating case-management functions where appropriate across various target populations (such as elderly persons, mental health clients, and persons with developmental disabilities); in some cases implementing across traditional jurisdictional lines a consortium approach to meeting needs; and providing case managers with a flexible pool of funds, with instructions on less restrictive service utilization and with a "community development" orientation of using natural helping networks. These steps, in most areas, will require more reasonably sized caseloads and improved training for case-management personnel.

Service providers must also take steps to improve their ability to function in an individual-centered service system. Providers will need to rethink their long-term commitments to physical assets and examine the adequacy of their current management and staffing patterns to meet that challenge. Awareness of "leading-edge programs" and of the implications of these programs for their services should be a high-priority undertaking and must involve all levels of government.

## CONCLUSION

Jean Elder, commissioner of the Administration on Developmental Disabilities of the U.S.

Department of Health and Human Services, characterized the American system of long-term care by stating that "there's nothing systematic about it" and noting the inherent dysfunction of a system that requires people to live away from their families or in institutions that provide more services than they need simply because that is the only way that government will pay for care ("Jean Elder Seeks Solutions, Not Legislation," 1982). Given current knowledge about community integration, special education, and case management, priority should be given to dissemination, implementation, and evaluation of theory, practices, and policies. Much is known about service components, such as prevention of disabilities, early intervention, habilitation, and behavior management, but more attention needs to be paid to the technology of dissemination and to the use of agencies at the federal, state, and local levels to encourage implementing that technology. Much of what must be learned is organizational in nature. As this chapter has stressed, effective models for interagency coordination, for case management, and for planning and providing for all of a community's disabled persons in a integrated fashion have yet to be demonstrated on a broad scale.

## REFERENCES

Allin, R.B., Jr., & Allin, D.W. *The Home Intervention Program: A service delivery program involving intensive home based treatment interventions with mentally retarded/emotionally disturbed individuals and their families.* Chesterfield, VA: Chesterfield Mental Health and Mental Retardation Services, 1982.

Baumheier, E.C. *Interagency linkages in the field of developmental disabilities.* Paper presented at the Interagency Education Conference, American Association on Mental Deficiency, Indianapolis, 1979.

Bernstein, G.S., Ziarnik, J.P., Rudrud, E.H., Czajkowski, L.A. *Behavioral habilitation through proactive programming.* Baltimore: Paul H. Brookes Publishing Co., 1981.

Bertsche, A.V., & Horejsi, C.R. Coordination of client services. *Social Work*, 1980, *25*(2), 94–98.

Brown, L., Nietupski, J., & Hamre-Nietupski, S. The criterion of ultimate functioning. In: M.A. Thomas (ed.), *Hey, don't forget about me.* Reston, VA: Council for Exceptional Children, 1976.

Colorado Department of Institutions. *Case management services for developmentally disabled persons in Colorado: A model and implementation manual.* Denver: Colorado Department of Institutions, 1980.

Crosby, K.G. Implementing the developmental model. In: J.F. Gardner, L. Long, R. Nichols, & D.M. Iagulli (eds.), *Program issues in developmental disabilities.* Baltimore: Paul H. Brookes Publishing Co., 1980.

Flynn, R.J., & Nitsch, K.E. *Normalization, social integration and community services.* Baltimore: University Park Press, 1980.

Frumpkin, M. A practical guide to service system reorganization. *Administration in Social Work*, 1978, *2*, 15–27.

Gardner, J.F., Long, L., Nichols, R., & Iagulli, D.M. (eds.), *Program issues in developmental disabilities: A resource manual for surveyors and reviewers.* Baltimore: Paul H. Brookes Publishing Co., 1980.

Gladowski, G.J. *Allocating human resources: A task analysis.* Unpublished manuscript, Blenheim, Ontario, no date.

Hersh, A., & Brown, G.A. Preparation of mental health personnel for the delivery of mental retardation services. *Community Mental Health Journal*, 1977, *13*(1), 17–23.

Jean Elder seeks solutions, not legislation. (Interview). *APA Monitor*, 1982 (October) p. 27.

Justice, R.S., O'Connor, G., & Warren, N. Problems reported by parents of mentally retarded children—Who helps? *American Journal of Mental Deficiency,* 1971 *75,* 685–691.

Kelly, N.K., & Menolascino, F.J. Physician's awareness and attitudes toward the retarded. *Mental Retardation,* 1975, *13*(6), 10–13.

Kentucky Title XIX Waiver Application. Lexington, KY: State Department for Human Resources, 1982.

Kessler, K., & Strom, B. Vocational education alternatives. *Mental Retardation* (Canada) 1983, *33*(2), 22–27.

Kolderie, T. *Many providers, many producers: A new view of the public service industry.* Minneapolis: University of Minnesota, Hubert H. Humphrey Institute of Public Affairs, 1982.

Krantz, G.C. *Case management: A position statement in the form of a proposed definition.* Paper presented at "Client Focus: Issues in Case Management Conference," Brainerd, MN, April 28, 1980.

Leismer, G. *The Plymouth case: Implementation of a consent decree.* Paper presented at the annual meeting of the American Association on Mental Deficiency, Dallas, May, 1983.

Lippman, L. *Long-term personal program coordination: A report on case management services for developmentally disabled persons.* Submitted to the State of New Jersey Developmental Disabilities Council, April, 1975.

Loop, B., & Hitzing, W. Family resource services and support system for families with handicapped children. Omaha: University of Nebraska Medical Center, Meyer Rehabilitation Institute, April, 1980.

Minnesota Department of Public Welfare. *A survey of selected case managers in Minnesota.* Unpublished manuscript, 1982.

Morley, R.E., & Kokaska, C. Guidance and counseling practices with mentally retarded youth. *Mental Retardation,* 1979, *17*(4), 201–202.

National Conference on Social Welfare. *Final report—Case management: State of the art.* (Grant No. 54-P-71542/3-01.) Submitted to Administration on Developmental Disabilities, U.S. Department of Health and Human Services, April 15, 1981.

Nordyke, N.S. Improving services for young handicapped children through local, interagency collaboration. *Topics in Early Childhood Special Education,* 1982, *2*(1), 63–72.

North Carolina Department of Human Resources. *Developmental disabilities case management system.* Unpublished paper, 1982.

Omnibus Reconciliation Act. Public Law 97-35, 1981.

Ross, C. *Proceedings of the Conference on the Evaluation of Case Management Programs* (March 5–6, 1979). Los Angeles: Volunteers for Services to Older Persons, 1980.

Sarason, S.B. *The creation of settings and the future societies.* San Francisco: Jossey-Bass, 1972.

Scheerenberger, R.C. *A history of mental retardation.* Baltimore: Paul H. Brookes Publishing Co., 1983.

Schodek, K., Liffiton-Chrostowski, N., Adams, B.C., Minihan, P.M., & Yamaguchi, J. The regulation of family involvement in deinstitutionalizaiton. *Social Casework: The Journal of Contemporary Social Work,* 1980, *61*(2), 67–73.

Scott, S., & Siuta, P. *Legal rights of developmentally disabled persons.* Minneapolis: Legal Advocacy for Developmentally Disabled Persons in Minnesota, 1979.

Skarnulis, L. Less restrictive alternatives in residential services. *AAESPH Review,* 1976, *3*(1), 42–84.

Stark, J.A. (ed.). *Family resource systems: The Nebraska Model.* Omaha: Nebraska Governor's Planning Council on Developmental Disabilities and Meyer Children's Rehabilitation Institute, 1980.

Turnbull, H.R., III (ed.), with Ellis, J.W., Boggs, E.M., Brooks, P.O., & Biklen, D.P. *The least restrictive alternative: Principles, and practices.* Washington, DC: American Association on Mental Deficiency, 1981.

12 MCAR 2.185 (Department of Public Welfare Rule 185). County board or human service board responsibilities to individuals who are or who may be mentally retarded. *State Register,* 1981, *5*(33), 1263.

Wisconsin Department of Health and Social Services. *Human services development series: Case management in selected Wisconsin counties.* Madison, WI: Wisconsin Department of Health and Social Services, September, 1980.

Wolfensberger, W. (ed.). *The principle of normalization in human services.* Toronto, Canada: National Institute on Mental Retardation, 1972.

Yates, J. *Model analysis of program services (MAPS).* Boston: Massachusetts Department of Mental Health, 1980.

Chapter 10

# School Integration Strategies

*Luanna H. Meyer and Gloria Shizue Kishi*

P rior to 1975, most severely handicapped students did not attend school with their nonhandicapped peers. If they were provided with any school program, they most likely were transported to a segregated, handicapped-only school serving an entire district or a cooperative of several school districts. Such an arrangement involved traveling long distances by bus or family car to reach a school that was usually far from the student's home and neighborhood, attended only by other handicapped students who were likewise far from home. In other cases, severely handicapped students lived and attended school in an institution. Owing to changes in public awareness and attitudes as well as various state and federal mandates, this situation has changed dramatically during the past few years. Public Law 94-142 ensured a free and appropriate public education for severely handicapped children and youth, in proximity to other school-age students. Of particular relevance to the focus of this chapter, this right to an education is accompanied by the statutory right to associate with nonhandicapped individuals. As Gilhool and Stutman (1978) assert:

There is no cognizable reason under the statutes for handicapped-only centers, certainly not on the scale they now exist. If a child can come to a school at all, even to a self-contained class in a handicapped-only center, he can come to a self-contained class in a normal school. Any teaching technique that can be used in a self-contained class can be used in a regular school building. There are few if any legitimate teaching strategies which require the complete isolation of a child from interaction with other children, and the few such strategies that there may be apply to very few children and for very short periods of time (p. 4).

Nevertheless, as logical and sensible as this may seem, the reality is that in many parts of the country, severely handicapped students continue to be educated apart from and isolated from their nonhandicapped peers. Integration (in the sense intended in this chapter) is not yet the rule in educational services.

Today there is a growing consensus that integration is both proper and overdue. This perspective that all handicapped students—without exception—have a right to receive an education in a neighborhood public school, close to home, and attended by nonhandicapped similar-age peers is represented in position

Preparation of portions of this chapter was supported in part by Contract No. 300-80-0746 awarded to the University of Hawaii and Contract No. 300-82-0363 awarded to the University of Minnesota from the Division of Innovation and Development, Special Education Programs, U.S. Department of Education. The opinions expressed herein do not necessarily reflect the position of policy of the U.S. Department of Education, and no official endorsement should be inferred.

papers (Brown, Branstron, Hamre-Nietupski, Johnson, Wilcox, & Gruenewald, 1979; Sontag, Certo, & Button, 1979), legislative and litigative mandate (*Pennsylvania Association for Retarded Children [PARC] v. Commonwealth of Pennsylvania*, 1982), and increased public acceptance of the right of handicapped persons to participate in the community (Taylor, 1982). The perspective is further supported by empirical evidence that such participation will have a positive impact upon both the quality of services provided to severely handicapped students and their acceptance by nonhandicapped peers (Voeltz, 1980, 1982; Voeltz & Brennan, 1984; Wilcox & Sailor, 1980). Most recently, Certo, Haring, and York (1984) have organized a summary "state-of-the-art" on integration, including coverage of the various issues as well as presentation of a variety of innovative and field-tested models for providing integrated educational services in public schools.

Why, then, do school districts throughout the country continue to serve many severely handicapped students in segregated, handicapped-only schools? One could argue that this partial failure to implement a crucial component of recent legislation does not reflect an unwillingness or refusal to provide services for these pupils. Nor does it imply philosophical rejection of the principles involved—at least not in most cases. Instead, the failure to move severely handicapped students to schools in their own neighborhoods reflects serious difficulties in the ability of systems to accomplish a major and dramatic social and administrative/programmatic shift in existing structures.

It is ironic that given the clear mandate to integrate and the widespread consensus that integrated services offer curricular advantages, there is nevertheless little information available to guide school systems as to how such a reorganization of services can best be effected. How does one prepare children, parents, teachers, administrators, and the "nonhandicapped community" for this integration? One might maintain that successful major systems changes are sufficiently idiosyncratic that attempting to describe significant generalizable change strategies is difficult, if not futile

(Piuma, Halvorsen, Murray, Beckstead, & Sailor, 1983). Yet, it is equally reasonable to contend that even though regional differences will indeed require adaptations to any strategies developed and proven successful elsewhere, the availability of models that have "worked" would greatly facilitate the implementation of regional services. Furthermore, the problems are likely to be similar, such that information on the experiences of districts that have undergone the process will enable others to be prepared in advance for typical difficulties.

This chapter focuses on anticipating common difficulties and describing specific strategies in integrating severely handicapped students into an educational system that formerly served only "typical" and less-handicapped students. Several reports of such systems-change efforts are available and were consulted in the preparation of this summary, particularly to aid in the organization of common problems, issues, and problem-solving strategies. Taylor (1982) has reviewed the experiences of several exemplary integration efforts and articulated a set of implementation recommendations based upon extensive telephone interviews and site visits to 12 such programs located across the country. Wilcox, McDonnell, Rose, and Bellamy (1982) prepared a detailed case study of the experiences of a regular high school that integrated severely handicapped students who had previously attended a handicapped-only school in Eugene, Oregon; their report is based on interviews with various persons involved in the program (e.g., parents, teachers, administrators) and on newspaper accounts that appeared when the integration occurred. Piuma et al. (1983) and Gaylord-Ross and Elkin (1984) present integration strategy recommendations generated by their university-based integration research and development projects that were federally funded; these projects worked extensively with personnel in public schools over a period of several years. Additional reports of similar experiences can be found in Certo et al. (1984).

Such descriptions represent important first steps in assisting educational agencies striving to establish educational services for severely handicapped learners in regular schools. Yet, the information they contain is secondhand, in that the perceptions of how such changes occur and how the process is best facilitated by school districts are reported by primarily university-based professionals who are not, in fact, directly responsible for providing educational services. There can be little doubt that university-based professionals working in the area of servere handicapping conditions have maintained continuous and intimate contact with services and have had a major impact upon defining the nature of quality programs. Still, they are "on the outside, looking in." Valuable data are likely to be unavailable to someone from outside the agency. Another major difficulty is that the data reported generally cover only the integration "episode" (i.e., the series of events that occurred at the time integrated services were being established and shortly thereafter). In contrast, it is likely that both difficulties and solutions to those difficulties evolve over a far longer time period, and that many of those decision points and the strategies utilized to effect them successfully are no longer in evidence once integration is under way.

## THE HAWAII EXPERIENCE

### Background

In the early 1970s, a series of events occurred that stimulated the Department of Education (DOE) in the state of Hawaii to serve all handicapped children in public schools.[1] The events involved two court cases, one involving handicapped children's right to an appropriate education in the public schools, the other involving deinstitutionalization and institutional reform on behalf of mentally retarded persons. The Hawaii Association for Retarded Citizens (HARC) decided to cease providing direct services for school-age youngsters and to adopt instead an advocacy role to encourage the state to provide those services. Hence, the HARC

announced timelines for closing its educational services in various parts of the state. In addition, Public Law 94-142 was in the making, and the DOE was aware that certain changes would soon be mandated by this federal legislation. Several key individuals in state agencies (e.g., the Department of Health, the Department of Education, the University of Hawaii, HARC) who were knowledgeable about and supported the "winds of change" across the country regarding the pattern of services for severely handicapped students provided aggressive personal leadership and arranged also for consultations and extended professional working visits from nationally known "experts" in the relevant disciplines. The consultants shared a public school philosophy and could also provide positive and practical implementation advice on integration. Other factors undoubtedly led to the decision to integrate, making it possible to do so with a commitment to quality services rather than simply out of compliance. But the contributions of these individuals seemed most directly relevant and were frequently cited as precipitating events by the individuals involved in the process of integration. As a consequence, the first classrooms for severely handicapped students were located on regular educational campuses throughout Hawaii's seven school districts beginning in 1977 and were expanded to more than two dozen schools (both elementary and secondary) throughout the state by 1983.

Most of this chapter presents an overview of major issues and problems that arose during this integration experience, along with a summary of strategies found to be effective in accomplishing the transition. The data source for the information discussed here is an oral history: individuals who were principally responsible for and involved in effecting the transition were interviewed for their recollection and perceptions of events at the time. A primary emphasis of the chapter is the concerns of parents of severely handicapped children who participated in the innovative, integrated services,

---

[1]In all states except Hawaii, the local education agency generally determines such policies as reflective of its administrative authority. Although Hawaii's seven regional districts are directly administered by district superintendents, all policies, and (equal) funding patterns are determined by the state Department of Education, and all district superintendents report to the superindendent at the state level.

since these concerns and consequent parent preparation for the move were repeatedly noted by those interviewed as a crucial factor for the ultimate success of integration. In addition, a review of the integration strategies based upon the interview data is offered. Finally, a set of "integration markers" to anticipate difficulties and evaluate integration success is presented based upon work done in Hawaii and currently underway in Minnesota.

**The Interviews**

The authors were active participants during the integration implementation phase (from 1976 onward) and, owing to their professional responsibilities, were involved on a continuous basis with the schools, classrooms, teachers, and students. The authors' familiarity with ongoing services assisted them in identifying and obtaining reports from individuals who were either: 1) directly responsible for the integration decision and/or various implementation components (e.g., administrators, attorneys) or 2) directly affected by and involved in the implementation phase (e.g., parents). An initial list of 37 names of key individuals was generated and then condensed to 18 names as follows:

1. Initial interviews were conducted with a state DOE administrator and the special education administrator from one of the seven districts, both of whom were known to have been extensively involved in the planning and implementation phases. The interview protocol was developed based upon these pilot interviews. At that time those individuals were asked to note other persons who had played important roles in planning and implementing integration.
2. The comprehensive list of potential interviewees was circulated among and discussed with several individuals at the University of Hawaii who had been involved during the planning and implementation phases.
3. The final selection of 18 individuals was identified by the authors as those whose participation had been consistently em-

phasized as known spokespersons either for or against the move and who represented the various "roles" involved in and affected by the move.

Of the list of 18 individuals, one Department of Health administrator (retired at the time of the interviews) maintained that her involvement had been minimal and declined to be interviewed. An additional person was unable to be contacted during the scheduling period.

The 16 individuals who were interviewed had participated in the integration process in the following roles:

1. Attorneys who had participated in litigation in Hawaii on behalf of handicapped individuals
2. Parents of severely handicapped individuals (both children and adults)
3. State DOE special education administrators
4. District DOE special education administrators
5. Regular education principals at the schools that were the first to be integrated
6. Professors at the University of Hawaii who had established and implemented teacher training for severely handicapped persons in cooperation with the DOE (and who supplied the majority of teachers for those integrated sites)
7. Administrators in the state Department of Health (DOH), which provided related services
8. Administrators from the major advocacy organization, HARC
9. Professionals from closely related disciplines who had been actively involved in testimony and consultation throughout this period (e.g., pediatricians)

Some individuals occupied more than one of these roles, some were still in their "position" at the time of the interview, and others had left those positions (e.g., through retirement, promotion).

Table 1 provides an overview of the interviews, including the basic format of each question. This protocol was refined based upon the

Table 1.   Hawaii integration project oral history interview

A.  Planning Phase
    1.   Where were you/What were you doing in 1973–1976?
    2.   When did you first hear of this idea to serve severely multiply handicapped students on regular school campuses? How did you initially get involved in this process?
    3.   Could you describe the existing services for severely multiply handicapped students at that time? Where were they? Who was serving them?
    4.   Who supported/pushed for this move? Was there any one person in particular who you felt was especially responsible for providing the necessary impetus? What did they do?
    5.   Who resisted the efforts? What did they do? How was this handled? What assurances did they receive? Were any compromises made?
    6.   What were some of the concerns/questions regarding the provision of services on public school campuses you had during this time?
    7.   Before the move, what major issues were discussed regarding the decision to serve severely multiply handicapped students on regular campuses? (Were meetings held with various constituents? What did parents, administrators, legislators, press, teachers, university people say?)

B.  Implementation Phase
    1.   When services began in fall 1977, where were you/What were you doing?
    2.   Could you describe the services/programs for severely multiply handicapped students during their first 2 years on regular school campuses?
    3.   What were people's reactions/feelings about these services?
    4.   What were some of the concerns/problems you had to deal with once the programs were in place?

C.  Evaluation Phase
    1.   How do you feel about current services for severely multiply handicapped students on public school campuses? Do you foresee any major changes?
    2.   What/who has contributed to the success of the program? What/who has contributed to the problems of the program?
    3.   Do you feel that anything should have been done differently in the planning phase? In the implementation phase?
    4.   Do you want to make any other comments?

pilot interviews noted previously. Each interview required from $1\frac{1}{2}$ to 2 hours; they were tape-recorded with the full knowledge of those interviewed and assurances that all responses would be confidential (specifically, interviewees were assured that, with the exception of the typist, only the authors would review either tapes or transcripts at any time). Transcripts were typed verbatim from the recordings, checked for accuracy by the author who had done each interview (to correct names, etc.), and sent to the interviewee to review. The interviewee was asked to check for accuracy and also to indicate any material that he or she preferred to delete. No material was deleted by the interviewees.

All interviews were conducted by one or the other of the two authors. The decision as to who would conduct each interview was determined primarily by personal factors such as who was best acquainted with the interviewee and the authors' judgment of who it was felt the

interviewee would prefer to talk with regarding the issues. With one or two exceptions, each person interviewed knew the interviewer well. Candidness of responses was supported by the authors' credibility, which had developed over several years of actively participating in services and training, the fact that neither author had actually been a ''principal player'' during the planning phase, and the high degree of self-disclosure evident in the interviews themselves.

In cases where information was inconsistent across interviews, persons were contacted for clarification. Because 16 individuals were reporting the same events, the reliability of all information provided was easily checked. Although memory is undoubtedly a factor when persons are being asked to recall events that in some instances occurred nearly 10 years previous, there was considerable consistency in the relative emphasis given to various components of the integration process.

## The Findings

The discussion of interview findings focuses upon the three major issues that emerged: planning variables, implementation strategies, and parental concerns. While various other factors were discussed by the interviewees, these areas were consistently emphasized and were common themes across individuals.

*Planning Variables: Preparing for Systems Change*  As alluded to briefly in the introduction, a number of precipitating events assured the establishment of integrated services, while other events greatly facilitated this process:

*Position of Existing Service Providers*  Prior to integration, educational services were provided primarily by a few small private agencies and by HARC. The decision by HARC to cease providing direct services and to function instead as an advocate to promote the development of public school services was viewed as crucial to what followed. This decision was supported by a publicly announced schedule for the actual closing of HARC programs for school-age youngsters and a clear intention to release staff and children. So long as these programs continued to serve children, it was reasoned, the public schools would not be motivated to do so and families and professionals would continue to advocate on behalf of those facilities (private and segregated) with a history of meeting these needs.

The employment status of administrators, teachers, and other personnel working in these nonpublic-school services was always a concern. Some of these individuals had no formal educational training and were unlikely to become qualified for hire by the public educational agency. Most personnel, however, were at least partially qualified, and the provision of extensive training opportunities by the University of Hawaii made it possible for those who wished to do so to "follow their students" into the public schools. Yet throughout this period an attitude of protectiveness and specialization was predominant among many of those who had worked in nonpublic-school settings. These issues are dealt with in detail in the section on parent concerns, and strategies to address them are described in the section on implementation strategies. Briefly, the bias that specialized services could not be provided by a public school and that severely handicapped children would be ignored, if not abused, by their nonhandicapped peers was frequently expressed by special educators and the families of handicapped children.

*Physical and Programmatic Accessibility of Generic Services*  One important programmatic change that occurred in the early 1970s was cited by several respondents: certain "school entry" criteria (e.g., toilet training) were dropped by the DOE. Many of Hawaii's school buildings were already somewhat accessible to handicapped individuals because of a predominant architectural style that favored single-story buildings and wide entrances from rooms onto concrete walkways that traversed the school campus. However, an architect's report commissioned by the DOE early in the 1970s was instrumental in guiding further building modifications and addressing the concerns of budget and facilities management personnel who raised specific cost and design questions. Transportation of handicapped youngsters to schools was a major planning variable that required a solution prior to implementation. This was particularly problematic since Hawaii does not support a comprehensive school-funded bus system for nonhandicapped students; in some areas, students who live too far from school to walk use the public transportation system. Finally, various details regarding funding support for the transition (e.g., for remodeling buildings and classrooms) and each of the service delivery models were thoroughly planned within the various DOE offices prior to integration. Respondents who had played a role within the DOE at that time indicated that, to the extent that they became enthusiastic supporters of the program, their success in addressing the concerns of offices responsible for budget and facilities was a major benchmark for the transition. This was possible because of the architect's report and the availability of reasonable cost estimates provided by outside consultants.

*Advocacy/Legal Climate*  It is difficult to determine, of course, to what extent the two consent decrees noted earlier in this chapter and Public Law 94-142 precipitated the decision to integrate severely handicapped children. These legislative and litigative events clearly supported the provision of quality services by the public schools. Yet, these same legal precedents are evident in many parts of the country where severely handicapped students are still served in handicapped-only settings. As an administrator in the DOE put it:

> Probably the overriding belief was in respect to what we currently call LRE [least restrictive environment]. In fact, these youngsters could receive an appropriate education in a regular school setting with the opportunity to interact and be a part of the future. It was that philosophy and the commitment to that philosophy that ultimately led us to make the decision....The concept of LRE in [PL] 94-142 made it easier to move severely handicapped youngsters from segregated environments to integrated ones, but our philosophy really preceded the law.

Hawaii is an ethnically integrated state and the Hawaiian emphasis upon "ohana" (i.e., that everyone is part of the whole, the family) was frequently cited as an underlying motivator to including severely handicapped children.

Again, the availability of cost estimates and public discussion of these issues was emphasized as well.

*Credibility of Integrated Model*   The issue of credibility is discussed in greater depth in the sections following, but several factors were noted regarding the credibility of the proposed plan: 1) administrators had to be convinced regarding the "rightness" of integration, 2) parents had to be reassured regarding quality program components, 3) conceptual models to guide implementation of the various components were needed (e.g., teaming, preparation of nonhandicapped persons), 4) well-trained personnel to staff the programs were essential, and 5) local expertise and locally relevant program adaptation models greatly facilitated the transition process and implementation phase.

**Implementation Variables: Innovation into Practice**   Across the interviews, five major systems-change strategies emerged as consistent themes in the discussion of issues considered most important during the implementation of integrated services. These factors are not easily characterized as factual information or specific procedures that should be utilized in order to promote the transition to public school services. Instead, they might best be described as interpretations of information and procedures geared to the various individuals and systems (e.g., agencies) being persuaded to do things differently. Seldom is there a consensus on needed innovations or modifications of existing programs for children. Professionals and laypersons have differing opinions on what is best and can generally selectively cite data and arguments to support their position. Thus, a response to these differing opinions is more involved than presenting information favoring integration; it also involves identifying particular attitudes in order to constructively plan for opposition.

*Advance Program Design Preparation* Professionals involved in the integration process at the administrative level repeatedly emphasized how important it was to have some definite notion of what the new program design would look like. Hawaii personnel had extensively communicated with leading professionals in the education of severely handicapped individuals (Lou Brown, Bud Fredericks, Wayne Sailor, to name only three), whose orientation and experiences provided conceptual support for the program. These communications included contracting outside experts to instruct Hawaii personnel and to prepare written position papers and program design descriptions, as well as visits to exemplary programs in other states by key personnel. For example, the principal of the first regular school to include classes for severely multiply handicapped students, that district's special education supervisor, the first teachers in that program, and the state office specialist—all of whom who were instrumental and highly visible in initial implementation—were sent to outstanding programs elsewhere for training and ideas.

Yet, there was a limit on how much advance planning could be done by experts from outside the state. As one program specialist stated:

> I feel they lent their names to our document [the program design] and gave it validity....[Local expertise] did a lot more to legitimize what we had...our program had some of Lou Brown, some of this, some of that...that's the way good pro-

grams are. But I don't think they gave us all the answers. It's just like if we were to go into another state and write something for them. We don't know all their idiosyncracies and their problems. We can write what we think might work from our experience, and that's what they were doing. [The outside experts] with their stature gave weight to the program. Anything that gives weight to the program is fine with me.

One problem that was often cited and that remained years later was the absence of the guidance of a systematic program design that had been successful elsewhere. Both DOE and DOH personnel felt that teaming—the coordination of special education and related services in the classroom—would have benefited greatly from the availability of a conceptual and useful model that might have functioned as a starting point.

On the other hand, many of the administrators interviewed emphasized that planning and generating the initial program design before the fact should be kept in perspective. A state-level administrator felt that one could "plan to death" and never implement and that sooner or later a program must simply begin with a clear message that some problems can only be identified and dealt with as the program evolves. A district administrator agreed:

> The thing was to do it, just to do it! That was the biggest hurdle, because the more you waited, the more obstacles you would face. [You do need] the appropriate facility and qualified staff. I think with those key issues—three actually, you also need a supportive principal—you can start any program at a school.

*Communicating Implementation Timelines* Another factor mentioned frequently by service delivery personnel was that the implementation schedule should be firm, determined in advance, and openly communicated. From the moment the services for severely multiply handicapped students were first proposed, a timetable for full implementation throughout the state was included in program plans. Those individuals who mentioned this issue felt that 2 years from idea to the first demonstration sites was adequate preparation time. They also emphasized the need for rapid system-wide replication of the first demonstration programs on

an equally firm timetable (e.g., within 1 to 2 additional years). A state-level administrator commented:

> One thing I wish we had done more of—and we tried to do as much as we could—was to let everyone know what we were doing. [So] that no one would be surprised. We tried to provide as much lead time as possible for people to know, to become accepting, and to become part of the effort. Everyone of us is at a different stage of development, I guess, at a different stage of understanding, so we certainly need to consider where a person is.

One strategy for such open communication was to appoint various task forces comprised of professionals from throughout the districts and advocates representing each constituency. These task forces, which included persons with different viewpoints, were contracted to propose selected components for the planned programs. One such task force developed Hawaii's individualized education plan (IEP) form and process, while another, smaller group of local special educators from both within and outside the DOE designed Hawaii's first curriculum for severely multiply handicapped students.

*Local Demonstrations of Excellence*    Nearly everyone emphasized the importance of an early model site where others could observe the proposed innovation actually working in a typical school. Crucial components in this first site were a well-trained staff, the provision of full services needed by the students, an enthusiastic regular education principal, and a willingness to serve as a "fishbowl" for the rest of the state for a period of time. A DOH administrator commented that

> once we had the initial success with the model at Kainalu [Elementary School], it was used as a model for the rest of the program, and the people from around the state could see that this worked.

A regular education principal noted the commitment to the least restrictive environment and the excellence of the special education teachers:

> I relied heavily on [the special education teachers'] knowledge, [although] my visit to the University of Oregon gave me the commitment that

there was a place for these youngsters on the regular education campus and there was hope for them, that we could teach them to be more independent. So with that kind of commitment and with highly capable and well-trained teachers from the University of Hawaii, we made an ideal team.

*Anticipating and Accepting Opposition* Whenever an innovation is proposed, the changes implied for the status quo will inevitably stimulate concerns and questions. Proponents of change may not be well prepared to deal constructively with these concerns; they generally prefer that their audience be enthusiastic consumers of the proposed innovation, and they perhaps are inclined to deny problems and to interpret questions as "problems" from the opposition. Several of the persons interviewed suggested that a more positive approach to these questions is not to view this as opposition but as a need for reassurance that the innovations will consider effects upon everyone involved, particularly the children. Concerns should be addressed with specific answers, however, that are backed up with data. For example, when parents express concern that related services will not be available in the public school program, the district should be able to reassure them that a specified number of direct and consultative therapy hours would be available based upon the child's IEP and should, moreover, arrange a visit to a demonstration class where parents can see those services being provided. A HARC administrator stated:

It is important for people who are precipitating changes to be aware and to allow resistance to occur and not see that as opposition. Resistance means that "I'm not certain and the uncertainty is what I can't deal with".... You [must be] be willing to let people resist you and realize that the resistance is not to change but to uncertainty as to what will occur.....If you are willing to allow people to have that [resistance], you will have less opposition over the long run.

This issue is discussed in more detail in the section on parental concerns.

*Assign Key Roles to Persons with Skill and Enthusiasm* This factor may be assumed in attempts to introduce an innovation into a sys-

tem, but it deserves emphasis here. Individuals responsible for convincing other professionals and parents of the model's appropriateness and practicality must be enthusiastically committed to the program design. A HARC administrator added, "What you need is to take a bunch of good people and make them powerful...."

A DOE specialist in the state office saw the unflagging optimism of a regular education principal as crucial to success:

[The principal] was never worried, she knew what the problems would be. She was sure we could handle them, she just went about her business and did it. She dealt with a heck of a lot of things that came up, lots that I don't know about.

The specialist added that another important variable was the fact that those who were unsure and who possibly even opposed the idea within the state office were willing to wait and see rather than present major obstacles. This program specialist further emphasized the need for enthusiastic advocates:

I believe very strongly that difficult concepts like this, controversial concepts like severely multiply handicapped students in the public schools, have got to have a lot of positive reinforcement because there are problems. We know there are going to be problems, so we need all the reinforcement we can get....This is a whole new ball game. We had to create and we were going to take a chance and we were going to be enthusiastic; the name of the game was to convince the district superintendent that he wanted it in his schools. That was it: the big cheerleading act!

*Parent Concerns* Not all parents of severely handicapped children are enthusiastic supporters of the movement of their children to regular public school classrooms. Many parents can recall when their children were excluded from those public schools and they have developed an understandable sense of loyalty to the various special (segregated) schools and programs that willingly filled this gap in services until Public Law 94-142 generated a response from local educational agencies. Parents (and many professionals) may view the provision of services by public school agencies as less desirable than the services they replace. Because the impetus for public school services has often been exclusively litigative and legislative, the commitment to those services is frequently viewed as less strong than that displayed by advocacy groups and private services that existed prior to Public Law 94-142. Concerns of parents and advocates, in such cases, often revolve around a number of critical questions. If the public school agency is merely complying with a legal mandate, does this reflect the same level of caring about the children themselves and their place in society as these same agencies display toward nonhandicapped children? Will severely handicapped children be "left behind" educationally by a system that has its priorities elsewhere? Can a system that is designed primarily to meet the educational needs of nonhandicapped and mildly handicapped children garner the necessary expertise to serve severely handicapped children appropriately? How, in fact, could a grudgingly compliant public school setting, serving primarily regular educational youngsters and having no direct experience in meeting the needs of handicapped students, possibly match the level of commitment and expertise that parents believe is present in the various facilities that have historically welcomed their children?

It is crucial that public school personnel anticipate these worries and appreciate why some parents may resist an agency's good intentions to meet the responsibility to integrate severely handicapped children. In the past, the rationale for students' exclusion from the public schools was extensively and aggressively articulated by both regular and special educators. Thus, it is not surprising that parents may not only continue to adhere to those reasons for serving their children apart from others students but that they are in fact devoted to the places that have traditionally made room for them. By preparing for the anxieties likely to be expressed by families during the planning and implementation process, the transition period can be more comfortable for all involved. The Hawaii experience provides considerable insight into these concerns and suggests effective strategies to address each meaningfully.

*A Fear of the Unknown*    A past executive director of HARC characterized much of the uneasiness expressed by parents as "fear of the unknown." He emphasized that parental resistance to the movement of their children to public schools must be viewed in the context of past failures by the local educational agency to be either willing or able to educate their children:

> At least they knew what HARC was all about; their children had been with us for years. But it wasn't so much the feeling against the DOE as it was the feeling of uncertainty, even though verbally [what they voiced] was mostly, "We know this program, this is something we know, we can physically see it. Moving this program to DOE, we don't know what's going to happen." So it wasn't DOE: It was the uncertainty.

Similarly, an attorney who had been involved for many years in various efforts to improve the quality of services for severely handicapped persons throughout the state commented:

> There has been a vocal group of parents at Waimano [the state institution for mentally retarded persons] who, I think with some justification, are afraid of what happens when their children go out into the community. What they show is that they almost choose not to believe that there are good programs out there. They choose to believe that the only place their children will be safe and in relatively good hands is at Waimano.

When asked why he felt that some parents continued to insist that their children attend school in a private, handicapped-only school years after high-quality public school programs had been established, the attorney again emphasized a reluctance to move to an unknown entity:

> People don't like change. This is universal....there are a number of parents who, maybe some of them justifiably because they know the history of how it has been in the past,...are not aware of the good programs and the amount of money that's gone into the progressive programs that are now going on. So I would say it's largely out of fear....

Ironically, this same preference for an existing program reappeared as apparent resistance to further efforts by the educational agency to keep pace with the advancing state of the art in areas that required change in the integration model once it was implemented. Hawaii's first programs for severely multiply handicapped children were located on elementary school campuses, reflecting a primarily developmental orientation to the students' educational needs that was, in fact, accepted as state of the art in the early to mid-1970s. Professionals in the past emphasized that severely handicapped learners were developmentally young and thus should be offered a curriculum that focused on instruction of skills that would be learned by a normal child at that developmental age, an age that was much younger chronologically than the severely handicapped learners. In Hawaii, as discussion began regarding the need to move adolescent severely handicapped students to chronological age-appropriate secondary campuses within the school districts, many individuals articulated this developmental "data base" for programming. As one parent put it:

What's the kid going to do after the age limit? Because actually they're not really that age anyway, right? Age-wise, mentally, they're not in that age. [Our child] is 10 and she's going to be 11....She's not actually 11, she's about 7.

Hawaii's classes for severely multiply handicapped students were, at the beginning, centralized as well. That is, one or two regular education schools within an entire district had been designated as District Centers. As the movement grew to establish less-centralized placements closer to children's neighborhoods (eventually spreading to nearly 30 schools throughout seven districts), concerns again surfaced regarding the change.

All these years [since the integrated services], we've been pretty well satisfied....we hear bits and pieces from here and there about branching off the kids to their own neighborhood. And I'm thinking, "I don't know if I want to take [my child] out of [her present school]". If it ever came to the point that they'd say, "Well, your child has to go to [the other school closer to my home], you live [in that area], I think I would put up a fight to try and keep her [where she is now]....I wouldn't want to take her from that environment where I'm satisfied and put her some place else where she's going to fall back again. I would rather try to fight and keep her [where she is], because already I know what [that school] has...it's the best place

for her until [she gets so] advanced [that] she [has] to go to another school.

An administrator also noted this resistance to the changes implied and felt confident that the approach that had been used in Hawaii to deal with this resistance had been successful. First, he emphasized the importance of establishing an initial site in an area as an exemplary service, with staff (particularly the principal) who are enthusiastic and committed to the project. Second, he stressed that once this "model" site has been established, it should be utilized as a showcase for professionals, parents and the community to reassure them that the model is a good one. He summarized:

I think one of the things that to me got the severely multiply handicapped program in Hawaii off to a very strong and positive start...is that [the initial] program was put into a community that was more progressive and ready for something new....the selection of the site was critical. But [what] seemed to be unique at the time was that the principal of that school...was just a superb person and principal. That is what I attribute the success of that program [to]. I don't think that the model was as important as was [the principal] in her support of the program....

Once we had the initial success [at the first school site, the site] was used as a model for the rest of the program, and the people from around the state could see that this worked. It wasn't threatening to them and they could see that it got good administrative support at the school level and at the district level and at the state level.

This administrator reported that a similarly committed principal and an "open door" policy was instrumental to success at another public school setting integrating orthopaedically handicapped children for the first time:

He [the principal] arranged for parents to visit the campus, [and for] children and teachers to go from one site to the other so that everyone was familiar with it. I think a lot of it was a fear of....something new, of change. Once he began to address these things in a very calm and sensitive way, it just broke the resistance down tremendously.

*A Sense of Caring* Parents rightly appreciate that the entire staff in a specialized setting has chosen to serve handicapped children. Consequently, the instructors are not only prepared to teach their children, but, presumably, they care about each child's welfare as part of their personal commitment to special education. Theirs is an issue of choice, not of compliance. As the parent of a severely handicapped student attending an integrated public school that had been in place several years explained:

> You walk in the school and you feel so pampered because everybody seems to know you; you're not just another parent coming to school....I think it's not just one individual teacher or one individual person that makes a difference in that program. For that program to work, it's got to be everybody; the whole school has to be involved. At [our school], we have it...from the principal right on down. Everybody's involved in it....they're dedicated....For us [the special education] teacher is special....These people are dedicated to this program, they get satisfaction out of it, just like the parents....Everybody's involved with these kids.

This sentiment favoring personal involvement was a major issue for the families throughout the transition period. The past executive director of HARC emphasized that parents resisted the loss of HARC-sponsored services in many cases for fear that this personal sense of involvement would be lost. He noted that the different levels of parental involvement in different activities are directly reflective of roles parents have traditionally played and feel comfortable with. A comment by a parent supported the view that the parental role would decline as public school agencies began to serve their children and that the needs of those programs would be primarily educational— as opposed to the kinds of personal financial assistance needed by private and parent-organized services:

> The parents [have] to bear in mind, when they send the child to that school [that they must] let the teachers run the programs....the teachers are going to have to set up the program...set the pace. They have to set the goals as to how far that child is going to advance....I have my experiences [with the child] at home. But I figure in school the teachers are more qualified to say, "Your child is able to achieve this much."

A DOE curriculum specialist who had early played a major role in the initial demonstration program characterized the decrease in the parental role and in parent involvement as "normalized":

> I know the ARC [Association for Retarded Citizens] parents were really close because they struggled together and sold sweetbread together and scrounged around....When you go out to public school, a lot of that feeling is gone....I always used to feel bad because we didn't have a strong parent involvement group [in the public school program], and I thought, well, maybe the system is more normalized, that they don't have to run around and sell sweetbread, or be volunteers, and save the school from being torn down.

This perspective was voiced by the HARC administrator as well:

> We have had very little feedback [since the move to public school services], which to me is very positive. It's as if the parents outgrew us, and it was okay.

*Program Quality* The most serious initial parent concerns were focused on how their children would fare in the integrated public school programs. As expressed by a parent who had been active in HARC for many years, the specialized, handicapped-only setting was associated with safety for handicapped youngsters:

> Some parents feel that their main concern is protection. They don't quite understand development. So if they understand protection, that's what they'll be concerned with. To me, development along with a certain amount of protectiveness is the key.

This issue of safety reappeared frequently in reference to kinds of related services that parents and professionals felt were essential program components. There is, of course, a certain logic to the assumption that if public schools were previously unwilling to provide school programs for severely handicapped students, this reflected a social as well as a programmatic rejection. Thus, the handicapped-only settings naturally seemed to "protect" the children from exposure to potentially negative attitudes and behavior both from individuals and from an administrative structure that, in the past, basically preferred that they go elsewhere. We now know that, when properly prepared, regular education campuses can be supportive environments for severely handicapped students (Voeltz, 1984). Administrators must be ready to provide this information to parents and to outline specific plans to prepare each school for integration. *Parents need more than denials from administrators when they express fears that their children will be socially rejected in public school settings.*

The principal of one of the first regular education schools to integrate severely handicapped students also saw program quality concerns as crucial ones for parents:

The parents felt that at the United Cerebral Palsy Center there had been six to nine youngsters, about two teachers, the PT [physical therapist] would be there, the OT [occupational therapist], the speech people. There were so many services, [yet] their [the parents'] understanding of the public school system is mass education....They felt the ancillary services would not be there.

A Department of Health administrator also perceived the availability of ancillary services as a major concern for parents:

They were concerned about the therapy needs and speech, particularly physical therapy...also occupational therapy. And I think medical services. Many of the parents had developed a great deal of dependency on their physicians because their child had so many health needs and that was their only resource. And we did not have nurses out in the programs in DOE...[there] was a concern of what would happen in case of an emergency. It was important to have a plan for what would be done if a child had a severe seizure.

The health issue continued to be a controversial subject for some time, owing at least partially to the efforts of an influential physician who opposed public school placements for severely handicapped children. An administrator in the state DOE commented:

[A continuing question] has been the health needs of these youngsters....I think if I had this to do over again, a group that we would have involved very much from the outset probably would have been pediatricians themselves. I wish we had involved the Hawaii Medical Association in the initial planning....I wish we [had] involved some of the individuals who are raising some of these concerns.

The past director of HARC corroborated parent concerns that the DOE programs would be inadequate:

The overwhelming concern was that DOE could not provide the kind of services that HARC provided. They just could not and would not. They [the parents] were very vehement about that....Their major concern was "Well, I don't think DOE folks know how to handle our kind of kids."

He maintained that although some of these concerns regarding program quality can be addressed at the outset in program design, other concerns cannot be alleviated until after the new program has been given an opportunity to demonstrate results with the children. At some point, everyone involved has to become committed to movement to the community because they are convinced it is the right thing to do. The strategies to do so most effectively, he said, would evolve as the program is conducted.

My viewpoint was that the children missed a lot that was not educational by being isolated. They didn't get an opportunity to be with people....I felt the best way to educate them was to get them out there in the public...the children can handle it....

Mostly [I believed that] we had a responsibility to educate and to give the public the experience of having handicapped folks in "their" program...giving the public an opportunity to be with handicapped people. [The public's] getting the experience and seeing that it's okay to have them out there would be facilitated by us [HARC] giving up the program and letting the public folks handle it. They [handicapped persons] belong to them, they don't belong to us....I think DOE has done an excellent job. There are some individual kids that parents moan and groan about, but DOE has done an excellent job.

As reflected in one parent's statement, parents of handicapped children in Hawaii can be reassured that teachers will be qualified, that ancillary services will be provided, and that the integrated public school setting will offer their child expanded, not fewer, learning and social opportunities.

There are certainly more facilities and activities [at the public school] than the United Cerebral Palsy Program could provide. There's a library that students go to for storytelling, [there are] assemblies, programs in the cafeteria.

Ultimately, however, assurance is not enough, and parents will expect, and have a right to expect, to see actual benefits for their child (i.e., increased social competence and community acceptance). As noted by an attorney who had been active in HARC efforts:

> We are very excited about what has happened to many of the children who have been transferred out [of the institution]. One dramatic example is Ann [the daughter of a prominent ARC activist], who was at Waimano for 14 years, and they thought that was the only place for her. At age 18, Ann was transferred to a group home....In 2 short months, Ann was traveling 10 blocks on her own from the group home to attend church, unaided. She was catching buses to [the vocational workshop]. About 6 months later, her parents testified in the legislature that the transformation was so startling that they couldn't even recognize that this was their daughter.

The parents of a severely multiply handicapped child made several comments regarding the transition to public schools and the community:

> I went to a hearing and this parent was asking that his child stay in an institution and stay at school there—they have a classroom right on the institution grounds....And he made the point that this child is so low functioning that he doesn't really understand the difference between being in an institution versus being out in the community. How do they know that the child doesn't know the difference? That child has been in that one environment, institutionalized, one institution. That's all that child knows, day in and day out. That parent cannot say that that child cannot get back into the community and know the difference unless they [the parents] try it. And [the child is] going to notice...he's going to notice the difference between [eating] in a cafeteria, eating in an institution, or going to McDonald's [Restaurant] and being among different people....(father)
> You put the kid in the public school, and he's going to notice the difference because he's not looking at the same face everyday. He's going to see different faces; there [are] hundreds of different kids there. In due time he's going to notice that there's a difference between being here and being there....My child loves school. I think she's now at the point where she knows she's going there, she's going to see the teacher, she's

going to see her friends. It makes a lot of difference, knowing that she's going and her friends are going to be there. (father)
> And you know what I found out too with Amy now? She's got all these special friends. And I walk to school and when I walk in and they see me with Amy they say, "Are you Amy's mother?" And I said yes and they said, "Oh, you've got such a sweet little daughter and such a good little girl." And I said "Wow, I'm seeing another side of Amy, right?" (mother)

*Summary* Parental concerns regarding the integration of their severely handicapped children into regular public schools can only be understood in the context of past practices. The local education agency is likely to be regarded as an unwilling and inexperienced "Johnny-come-lately" by parents who have had to secure programs for their children through alliances and personal financial support with whatever private and advocacy organizations were willing to provide them. The parents who have been the most active in securing these alternative placements are likely to be the most loyal—personally and programmatically—to their continued existence. Advocates for integration must be in a position to assure parents that:

1. Integrated public school services will be of at least equal quality in comparison to existing special schools. Teachers will be qualified and experienced, related services will be provided in accordance with the child's needs, and facilities, materials, and curricula will reflect appropriate practices for severely handicapped students.

2. Integrated public school programs have a permanent place in the public school system. That is, severely handicapped children have as much right to attend chronological age-appropriate public schools close to home as do nonhandicapped children. Their attendance is not contingent upon the availability of extra funds or extra classrooms, any more than would be the case for a nonhandicapped child. If parents are to wisely "let go" of private and segregated services for their children,

they need reassurances that their children will never again be excluded from the public school system.

3. Severely handicapped students will not be exposed to social rejection and unnecessary risks to safety and health. The nonhandicapped school community must receive some initial preparation for the integration of severely handicapped peers; this preparation can occur simultaneously with the movement of handicapped students to campus and in no way is a condition for integration. At the same time, past errors of overprotectiveness must be avoided; the emphasis should be upon normalized expectations for an educational experience. Just as severely handicapped students have a right to attend school, they have a right to experience the extension of opportunities—as well as the risks associated with those opportunities—afforded by exposure to natural environments and nonhandicapped peers and persons of all ages. This society can and should promise to prepare each child to the best of its ability for full participation in integrated community environments. And it can and should prepare those community settings to function as "congruent" environments (i.e., those that are capable of and willing to meaningfully include severely handicapped persons as participants) (Thurman, 1977).

As community environments become increasingly competent and normalized, support networks, professional special educators, parents, and other constituents of handicapped persons will need to learn how to "let go" of outmoded and overly restrictive services and perspectives. A key administrator in the HARC maintained that, ironically, most of the resistance to the shift in services to the public schools actually came from within the special education network:

> Remember now, for years we provided services that nobody else was willing to provide, so we built our territoriality: "Only we can do this."

Our opposition came from people who thought they knew that things should be a certain way....I noticed that when I got out of the way and involved people, the changes went much more smoothly....

When a mother of a severely multiply handicapped child was asked if she had any advice to parents whose children would be attending an integrated campus for the first time, she responded:

> Give it a try....I've had to talk to one parent because she was holding back. And I kept telling her "the kid has to go." I wouldn't want my child to be in only her type of group. I want her to be with everybody.

This process will also include allowing parents to normalize their involvement on behalf of their children in school and community settings. This is not to say that parents of severely handicapped youngsters would be uninvolved with their child's school program. On the contrary, parents will need assistance in monitoring lifelong planning for their child in particular: teachers come and go, but the parents can provide a longitudinal perspective for their child's skill development goals. But it is unrealistic and may even be inappropriate to expect all families to be "trainers" (see chapter by Turnbull, Brotherson, & Summers, in Bruininks & Lakin, 1985).

## INTEGRATION MARKERS

Public Law 94-142 states that children may be removed from regular education and educated apart from their nonhandicapped peers only when necessary to meet their special education and related services needs. Ironically, what has occurred conflicts with the intent of this directive. Severely handicapped students who are currently receiving all school and community services in handicapped-only settings have already been removed completely from settings and programs where nonhandicapped peers are present. They generally do not share transitions (e.g., movement from class to class, school arrival and departure times), recess periods, or lunch with nonhandicapped peers. Instead, even though they attend a school that also enrolls nonhandicapped peers, handicapped students may remain in their self-contained classroom throughout the day, experiencing only interactions with their handicapped classmates. The teacher who attempts to "integrate" his or her students into situations such as lunch and recess is asked to justify this request with data regarding benefits to the handicapped student, including facilitation of skill acquisition and improved (or at least maintained) adaptive behavior. In contrast, access to mainstreamed environments, activities, and social situations that are noneducational in nature need not be negotiated on behalf of students in regular education. For regular education students, these time periods and activities are generally regarded simply as necessary (children must eat lunch) and socially valuable (recess allows for respite from academic activity, as well as socialization and friendship opportunities). Similar experiences should be available to handicapped students as opportunities that are supplemental to the educational program and reflect the normalization of the social status of handicapped persons.

Table 2 provides a listing of school-based *integration markers* that define this normalization of student status for severely handicapped youngsters. Certain of these markers are determined by administrators and facilities management personnel, such as the proportion of students enrolled at a given school who are severely handicapped persons. Other markers can be shaped by the special education teacher independent of whether or not administratively controlled markers reflect integration (e.g., normalized instructional objectives and intervention strategies). And many of the markers will be influenced by both administrative and instructional personnel, such as schedules and groupings of students.

The Minnesota Consortium Institute for the Education of Severely Handicapped Learners has utilized these integration markers to generate anticipatory problem solving by teachers who are attempting to integrate their students into school and community activities enjoyed by nonhandicapped peers. The Classroom Integration Obstacle Inventory (see Table 3) is used as a worksheet that special education personnel would complete prior to integration efforts in order to anticipate all conceivable difficulties, generate potential solutions to each of those problem areas, and identify priority efforts from among the set of options, based on the information they have provided. Quite simply, since in most cases a teacher's students may not currently have access to any or most of these integrated experiences (the *markers* listed on the Inventory, Table 3), it is possible to identify those activities that have the highest probability of success based upon the problems and response modifications needed to solve each of these as listed by the staff who will be involved in the effort.

As an illustration of this process, Table 4 reflects the information often given by instructional personnel regarding three of the integration markers: use of general facilities (lunchroom), joint activities with regular class (same-age peers), and peer interactions (recess). Based upon the obstacles generated and the possible response modifications to deal with each of these anticipated difficulties, a teacher might decide, for example, that he or she could begin a recess peer interaction program at the beginning of the school year, since there appears to be relatively little "cost" associated with this program and no resistance by staff. Then, because integration into the lunchroom would be greatly facilitated by the availability of nonhandicapped "buddies" and by supportive regular education teachers, and since these markers are likely to be in place once the peer interaction program is under way, this marker could be attempted by midyear. Finally, since any joint activity with a regular classroom is far easier to effect once school personnel have had an opportunity to observe children interacting in social situations (recess and lunchroom) and may also require close coordination between the regular and special education staff, this marker may be postponed until after "easier" arrangements have been successful. Ultimately, of course the

Table 2. School-based integration markers[a]

| Personnel involved | Integration marker | Definition |
|---|---|---|
| Administrative and/or facilities management | • Natural proportion | Percentage of severely handicapped students enrolled at a regular school approximately parallels their percentage in the general population (1%–2%). |
| | • Age range | Students' age range matches age range of nonhandicapped students (e.g., elementary versus secondary schools). |
| | • Classroom location | Location of classroom for severely handicapped students is close to similar-age peers and consistent with instructional facility procedures used in assignment of regular education classrooms. |
| | • Use of general school facilities (restrooms, cafeteria, library, etc.) | Handicapped students share use of general facilities and activities with similar-age nonhandicapped peers and as part of an integrated grouping arrangement reflective of natural proportion. |
| | • Schedules and groupings | Handicapped students follow general school schedule for similar age peers (e.g., arrival, departure, lunch, recess periods) and are variously grouped for different activities (including homogeneous and heterogeneous groups). |
| | • Classroom assignment | Homerooms for all students are integrated (i.e., a severely handicapped student may receive all instruction in a self-contained special education class but begins and ends the day, etc., in a regular fourth grade room if he or she is 9 years old). |
| | • Administration and resource personnel | Special education staff are supervised by general education personnel (principal, etc.) and access general resource personnel (librarian, physical education teacher, etc.) for instructional consultation and direct programming of their students. |
| | • Extracurricular activities | Extracurricular activities are integrated, allowing for involvement of handicapped as well as nonhandicapped students. |
| | • Parent organizations | The Parent-Teacher Association (PTA), etc., is supported as a communication/involvement vehicle for all parents. |
| Classroom teacher | • Use of general school facilities (restrooms, cafeteria, library, etc.) | See above under "Administrative and/or facilities management." |
| | • Schedules and groupings in daily instruction | Daily schedule of handicapped students parallels that of nonhandicapped peers (e.g., recess at elementary level, class changes at secondary level) and grouping arrangements reflect both educational and normalization concerns (including use of heterogeneous groups, both small and large groups, etc.). |
| | • Administration and resource personnel | Special education staff access general education administrative and resource personnel for instructional consultation, including negotiating integration of their students into activities with nonhandicapped peers (e.g., library period integrated with a regular education classroom). |

(continued)

Table 2.   (continued)

| Personnel involved | Integration marker | Definition |
| --- | --- | --- |
| | • Joint class activities with same-age peers | Based upon educational needs and the IEP, special education students are integrated into the regular classroom for selected academic programming (e.g. physical education, story time in first grade, etc.). |
| | • Extracurricular activities | Handicapped students participate in extracurricular activities of interest to the individual (e.g., an after-school sports activity). |
| | • Normalized instructional objectives and intervention strategies | Skills being taught to handicapped students are functional and age-appropriate, and the instructional procedures are consistent with criterion conditions as well as with community standards for regular education students (e.g., corporal punishment guidelines are followed). |
| | • Parent interactions | Parents of severely handicapped students are encouraged to "integrate" themselves into general school parent organizations and events (PTA, etc.). |
| | • Peer/social interactions | Handicapped and nonhandicapped students are prepared and encouraged to interact with one another in social, play, and other available "natural" contexts during the school day (e.g., recess). |
| | • Teacher/staff interactions | Faculty meetings are held jointly rather than separately for regular and special education. Special education staff interact socially, etc., with regular education staff rather than segregating themselves along "categorical" lines. |

[a]These markers represent factors emphasized in various sources as essential components in programs for severely handicapped learners (Brown, Ford, Nisbet, Sweet, Donnellan, & Gruenewald, 1983; Voeltz, Hemphill, Brown, Kishi, Klein, Fruehling, Collie, Levy, & Kube, 1983).

full set of these integration markers must be in evidence if the process of normalizing the social status of our students is to be complete.

## CONCLUSION

This chapter has focused on the integration of severely handicapped students into educational systems that previously served only "typical" students. Two major issues are involved in this integration effort. First, the *physical* integration of severely handicapped students refers simply to whether or not these pupils attend programs located on general education campuses that are also attended by similar-age nonhandicapped peers. There can be varying degrees of physical integration, of course, ranging from attending a self-contained special education classroom for all educational services (enrolling only other severely handicapped pupils) to attending a classroom enrolling primarily nonhandicapped peers for the entire school day. Within this school-based "physical integration," the handicapped students may experience a variety of environments and social interactions as a range of opportunities are presented by the school environments. Alternatively, handicapped students' exposure to these opportunities may be highly restricted even though they attend the same school with their peers. Second, the *social* integration of severely handicapped students refers to whether or not the social status of these children is normalized. Do they share the social environment of the school and participate in the variety of social interactions that parallel those enjoyed by their nonhandicapped peers?

Table 3.   Classroom integration obstacle inventory

| Integration marker | Obstacle to access (specify) | | | | Possible response modification |
|---|---|---|---|---|---|
| | Child's skills and behavior | Staff (spec. ed.) attitudes | "Community" attitudes | Resource distribution | |
| Use of general facilities: | | | | | |
| Lunchroom | | | | | |
| Recess playground | | | | | |
| Restrooms | | | | | |
| Library | | | | | |
| Normalized scheduling of instruction | | | | | |
| Heterogeneous instructional groupings | | | | | |
| Joint activity with regular class (same-age peers) | | | | | |
| Participating in extracurricular events | | | | | |
| Normalization: objectives and instructional procedures | | | | | |
| Parent interactions with general parent organizations | | | | | |
| Peer interactions: recess, etc. | | | | | |
| Teacher/staff interactions | | | | | |

Table 4. Sample completed classroom integration obstacle inventory

| Integration marker | Child skills/behavior | Spec. ed. attitudes | Reg. ed. attitudes | Resource distribution | Possible response modification |
|---|---|---|---|---|---|
| | | Obstacle to access | | | |
| Use of general facilities: | | | | | |
| Lunchroom | Nonambulatory, does not self-feed, and takes over an hour to eat; requires special meal. | Occupational therapy program for eating would be jeopardized/could not be conducted. | Cannot go through lunch room, "help" needed to see that child is okay. | Staff not available on one-to-one basis to go to lunchroom. | Child will bring special meal portion to lunchroom on wheelchair tray, will be pushed to cafeteria and back to room by nonhandicapped "buddy." Most of meal and occupational therapy program would take place in classroom prior to lunch, saving only finger food, drink, etc., for lunchroom. Regular education class would include child at table and buddies taking turns watching out for her. Regular cafeteria staff/teachers, etc., trained for any special needs (e.g., what to do for a seizure). |
| Joint activities with regular class | Child uses communication board not vocal language. | Teacher feels that child will be ignored in regular class. | Regular teacher who might accept child unknown. Principal hesitant to approve idea. | Difficult to schedule training for regular staff and for one-to-one help for child during experience. | Regular education teachers identified through social contact and/or request made at faculty meeting, then trained on communication board to prepare other children and to include child in activity to ensure child is not ignored. Temporary one-to-one available through special program, but faded quickly through more natural "buddy" system in regular class. |
| Peer interactions: Recess | Disruptive and self-stimulatory behaviors are a problem. | Do not know which regular education students could be involved. Not sure what to do with regular students. | Some teachers think interactions are good idea, others think handicapped children do not belong in school. | Teachers have no time to train regular education peers, to answer questions, etc. Recess period not defined for special education kids. | Recess period scheduled to coordinate with similar-age peers. Only those regular education teachers who are interested are "paired" with each special education classroom. Available program used to train students (e.g., The Special Friends Program [Voeltz, Hemphill, Brown, Kishi, Klein, Fruehling, Collie, Levy, & Kube, 1983]), and school counselor contacted to help train children as part of job duties. Staff assured that nonhandicapped peers can accept and deal constructively with problem behaviors if they are told what to do. Rather than attempting to select certain students, regular education students who want to do so are allowed to participate. |

Much of the intervention research in the area of social integration has emphasized the structuring of specific kinds of peer interaction opportunities for students. Many of these are system-dependent, in the sense that the severely handicapped students are otherwise not physically integrated into the school setting, and those interactions that are generated cannot be maintained without an artificial compensation for the absence of a shared environment both during and after school. The primary goal of these efforts appears to be to provide severely handicapped students with a social/peer interaction and, in addition, to develop increased acceptance of individual differences by the nonhandicapped children who participate. In instances where the severely handicapped children attend segregated, handicapped-only schools, peer interaction programs are often structured that consist of visits to the segregated school by selected nonhandicapped students. Such programs are generally referred to as "reverse mainstreaming," and their proponents maintain that this practice adequately compensates for the otherwise restrictive nature of a segregated education environment by the addition of the "only" missing element: interaction with nonhandicapped peers. As should be evident in an examination of the integration markers presented earlier, these artificial arrangements are not an acceptable alternative to the provision of integrated services. Their episodic nature, combined with the learning characteristics of severely handicapped students, makes it unlikely that they involve a significant social learning opportunity either for handicapped or nonhandicapped students. Furthermore, such programs do not parallel the social interactions enjoyed by nonhandicapped peers, they do not allow for extended natural peer interactions by pupils who share environments and activities on a daily basis, and thus they fail to accomplish the goal of normalization.

There is little doubt that efforts to structure significant social and friendship opportunities for severely handicapped children have progressed greatly since such past practices as the annual Christmas party given for institutionalized retarded children. Yet, to the extent that these programs remain artificial, they are episodic in basic design and in the positive effects they might otherwise be expected to produce on the quality of life and social competence of severely handicapped individuals.

## REFERENCES

Brown, L., Branston, M.B., Hamre-Nietupski, S., Johnson, F., Wilcox, B., & Gruenewald, L. A rationale for comprehensive longitudinal interactions between severely handicapped students and nonhandicapped students and other citizens. *AAESPH Review*, 1979, *4*, 3–14.

Brown, L., Ford, A., Nisbet, J., Sweet, M., Donnellan, A., & Gruenewald, L. Opportunities available when severely handicapped students attend chronological age appropriate regular schools. *Journal of The Association for the Severely Handicapped*, 1983, *8*, 16–24.

Bruininks, R.H., & Lakin, K.C. (eds.). *Living and learning in the least restrictive environment*. Baltimore: Paul H. Brookes Publishing Co., 1985.

Certo, N., Haring, N., & York R. (eds.). *Public school integration of severely handicapped students: Rational issues and progressive alternatives*. Baltimore: Paul H. Brookes Publishing Co., 1984.

Gaylord-Ross, R.J., & Pitts-Conway, V. Social behavior development in integrated secondary autistic programs. In: N. Certo, N. Haring, & R. York (eds.). *Public school integration of severely handicapped students: Rational issues and progressive alternatives*. Baltimore: Paul H. Brookes Publishing Co., 1984.

Gilhool, T., & Stutman, E. Integration of severely handicapped students: Toward criteria for implementing and enforcing the integration imperative of P.L. 94-142 and Section 504. In: *LRE: Developing criteria for the evaluation of the least restrictive environment provision*. Philadelphia: Research for Better Schools, 1978.

*Pennsylvania Association for Retarded Children* versus *Commonwealth of Pennsylvania*, Civil Action 71–42 (E.D. Pa. 1982).

Piuma, C., Halvorsen, A., Murray, C., Beckstead, S., & Sailor, W. *Project REACH administrator's manual (PRAM)*. San Francisco: San Francisco State University, 1983.

Sontag, E., Certo, N., & Button, J.E. On a distinction between the education of the severely and profoundly handicapped and a doctrine of limitations. *Exceptional Children*, 1979, *45*, 604–616.

Taylor, S.J. From segregation to integration: Strategies for integrating severely handicapped students in normal school and community settings. *Journal of the Association for the Severely Handicapped*, 1982, *7*, 42–49.

Thurman, S.R. The congruence of behavioral ecologies: A model for special education programming. *Journal of Special Education*, 1977, *11*, 329–333.

Turnbull, A. Parent-professional interactions. In: M.E. Snell (ed.), *Systematic instruction of the moderately and severely retarded* (rev. ed.). Columbus, OH: Charles E. Merrill Publishing Co., 1983.

Voeltz, L.M. Children's attitudes toward handicapped peers. *American Journal of Mental Deficiency*, 1980, *84*, 455–464.

Voeltz, L.M. Effects of structured interactions with severely handicapped peers on children's attitudes. *American Journal of Mental Deficiency*, 1982, *86*, 380–390.

Voeltz, L.M. Program and curriculum innovations to prepare children for integration. In: N. Certo, N. Haring, & R. York (eds.). *Public school integration of severely handicapped students: Rational issues and progressive alternatives*. Baltimore: Paul H. Brookes Publishing Co., 1984.

Voeltz, L.M., & Brennan, J. An analysis of interactions between nonhandicapped and severely handicapped peers using multiple measures. In: J.M. Berg (ed.). *Perspectives and progress in mental retardation, Vol. 1: Social, psychological and educational aspects*. Baltimore: University Park Press, 1984.

Voeltz, L.M., Hemphill, N.J., Brown, S., Kishi, G., Klein, R., Fruehling, R., Collie, J., Levy, G., & Kube, C. *The Special Friends Program: A trainer's manual for integrated school settings* (rev. ed.). Honolulu: University of Hawaii, 1983.

Wilcox, B., McDonnell, J., Rose, H., & Bellamy, G.T. *Integrating adolescents with severe handicaps into the public school system: A case study*. Eugene, OR: University of Oregon, Center on Human Development, 1982.

Wilcox, B., & Sailor, W. Service delivery issues: Integrated educational systems. In: B. Wilcox & R. York (eds.). *Quality education services for the severely handicapped: The federal investment*. Washington, DC: U.S. Department of Education, Office of Special Education, Division of Innovation and Development, 1980.

# Chapter 11

# Leisure and Recreation Services
# for Handicapped Persons

*JoAnne W. Putnam, Judy K. Werder, and Stuart J. Schleien*

P
articipation in leisure and recreation activities is an important aspect of life in American society. When such activities meet the needs of individuals, they promote physical health and conditioning, provide opportunities to develop social relations, and lead to the development of new skills. Unfortunately, leisure services have had relatively low priority in programs for handicapped persons, until recently when some specific leisure and recreation skill-training techniques (Schleien, Kiernan, & Wehman, 1981; Voeltz, Wuerch, & Wilcox, 1982) and leisure curricula (Bender & Valletutti, 1976; Wehman & Schleien, 1981; Wessel, 1976; Wuerch & Voeltz, 1982) were developed. The neglect of relevant programming and services for handicapped persons is particularly unfortunate because appropriate participation in leisure activities is an important aspect in their successful community adjustment (Bell, Schoenrock & Slade, 1975; Cheseldine & Jeffree, 1981; Eyman & Call, 1977; Gollay, 1981; Hill & Bruininks, 1981) and is associated with the development of collateral skills (Newcomer & Morrison, 1974; Schleien, Kiernan, & Wehman, 1981; Strain, Cook, & Apolloni, 1976) and the reduction of maladaptive behaviors (Adkins & Matson, 1980; Flavell, 1973; Schleien, Kiernan, & Wehman, 1981; Voeltz & Wuerch, 1981).

Because society has tended to stigmatize and stereotype handicapped individuals, these individuals often form negative self-concepts of and low expectations for themselves that engender problems beyond those related directly to their handicaps. Fortunately, attitudes are learned and, therefore, are amenable to alteration on the basis of new information and experiences. Indeed, direct and frequent interactions between handicapped individuals and their nonhandicapped peers have been found to stimulate the formation of more positive attitudes (Voeltz & Wuerch, 1981). Leisure and recreational activities also provide handicapped individuals opportunities to experience and demonstrate autonomy and competence, even if in a limited area, and to become more comfortable in interactions with nonhandicapped peers. Participation in community-based leisure and recreational activities offers a natural setting for building competence and improving social interactions.

Unfortunately, a discrepancy exists between what is known about the short- and long-term benefits of participation in leisure activities and the current status of services to persons with handicaps. For handicapped persons to maximally participate in community leisure and recreation activities, specific leisure and recreation skill training in home and school environments and specific provisions by communities to incorporate handicapped persons into recreational activities are necessary. This chapter traces conceptual issues and assumptions in current leisure and recreational services for handicapped persons, types of activities that are available in homes and schools, and obstacles that make participation in community activities difficult for handicapped individuals. The characteristic neglect in providing such services and programming for handicapped persons need not continue. In the last section of the chapter, the authors both review programs designed to normalize the leisure and recreational activities of handicapped persons and provide guidelines for setting up such programs.

It is important to recognize that different handicapped persons have different recreational skill training and programming needs. Individuals may differ markedly in physical abilities, intelligence levels, and sensory characteristics. Certainly, a teenager in a wheelchair has different recreation needs than a visually impaired preschooler. Accordingly, an individualized approach to skill training and programming is required. This chapter focuses primarily on needs of mentally handicapped persons. Although some of the information and ideas presented will generalize to the concerns of all persons with handicaps, the reader is cautioned against overgeneralizing, because of the risk that it may lead to stereotypic and stigmatic thinking.

## CONCEPTUAL ISSUES AND ASSUMPTIONS

The literature on leisure programing for handicapped persons is often confusing because varying and sometimes conflicting conceptualizations of leisure are employed. As the conceptualization of leisure directly influences the degree to which the activities engaged in are or are not considered important, clarification of the term is essential. It is beyond the scope of this chapter to derive such a definition (Murphy, 1981, and Neulinger, 1981, should

be consulted), except insofar as the issues and assumptions underlying leisure programing affect community and educational programing.

## Discretionary Time and Free Time

Sometimes it is easier to think of leisure in terms of what it is not. Leisure is time not spent in work or other required tasks. The latter can include, for example, self-care and domestic or vocational activities, which usually entail shared expectations regarding task responsibilities. During leisure, activities are discretionary, that is, they are based on the individual's choice. Thus, leisure activities are "free to vary on an almost endless basis as a function of choice and performance" (Voeltz et al., 1982, p. 176).

In the past, leisure was equated with free time or with time that was not spent on required activities (Murphy, 1981). If service providers and parents are reluctant to support increased free time for mentally handicapped persons, it may be because of the inordinate amount of time such persons can spend in passive, aimless activity. In fact, a major criticism of institutional care has been the lack of meaningful activity for residents and the excessive periods of "dead time" (Braddock, 1977) (i.e., the periods during which few or no actions are required). At such times, residents tend to engage in inappropriate or counterproductive actions (Ford, Brown, Pumpian, Baumgart, Schroeder, & Loomis, 1981). The absence of programs and services and the lack of variety and quality when programs are available contribute to dead time and are aspects of institutions that clearly are in need of reform (Braddock, 1977).

Researchers also have observed increased frequencies of negative behaviors, such as stereotypic movements (e.g., rocking, head-banging) and nongoal-directed activities in institutionalized mentally retarded persons during free-time periods (Baumeister & Forehand, 1973). Parents and caregivers have reported that mentally handicapped children living at home have an inordinate amount of free time, which often is spent in very passive activities

(Marion, 1979). The critical factor, however, is how free time is used, not the amount that is available. A major assumption in this chapter, therefore, is that the qualitative aspects of leisure time activities should be emphasized.

## Personal Preferences

A view that differs from the conception of leisure as free or spare time is that which sees leisure as periods of individual freedom of choice (Murphy, 1981; Neulinger, 1981; Voeltz et al., 1982). For a person to make meaningful choices and exercise preferences, two minimal requirements must be met: 1) the availability of a reasonable range of leisure activity options, and 2) the individual's possession of the necessary skills to make and communicate leisure preferences. Limited opportunity for personal choices may occur even when individuals have the skills necessary to indicate a preference. Some schools or institutions, for example, may be so regimented that all activities are highly planned, and the possibility of choice is virtually absent (Biklen, 1973). However, when a variety of leisure activity options are available in some situations, the handicapped person may not have the proper training to know how to make a choice. Still another problem is found when residential facilities, materials, or procedures cannot be adapted to allow residents to express preferences and exercise free choice (Wehman, Schleien, & Kiernan, 1980).

## Quality of Life

In addition to freedom of choice, Neulinger (1981) stressed the importance of "quality of life" in evaluations of leisure participation. "Quality becomes the primary concern; the type and nature of the experience, its characteristics, its intensity, its depth, and so on" (Neulinger, 1981, p. 49). *Quality* is an elusive term, of course, which may be why very little qualitative data have been collected on the leisure experiences of persons with handicaps (see, for example, the study by Bell et al., 1975), which is discussed in a later section). Nonetheless, methods of obtaining information from mentally handicapped persons, such as attitude assessment or assessment of personal preferences, are available (Voeltz et al., 1982).

## Normalization

An assumption in this chapter is that leisure services for handicapped persons should be consistent with the principle of normalization. Unfortunately, many genuine efforts to maximize the leisure participation of handicapped persons have not adhered to this principle. To assess consistency with the normalization principle, the leisure activities of handicapped and nonhandicapped persons should be compared.

Special Olympics is an example of a formal recreation event for mentally handicapped persons. Although it has received substantial publicity, the event should be scrutinized in terms of how "normal" it is. Clearly, Special Olympics is a worthwhile activity in many respects, especially in: 1) increasing public awareness of the need for sports programs for mentally handicapped individuals, 2) affording participants the opportunity to experience success, 3) encouraging interaction among handicapped persons and community members, and 4) involving parents (Orelove, Wehman, & Wood, 1982). However, the event also can be criticized for breaching the normalization principle by grouping retarded persons "homogeneously" for training and a single competition. In fact, it is a "segregated imitation" of the genuine Olympic Games and does not foster ongoing social interactions between mentally handicapped and nonhandicapped persons (Voeltz et al., 1982). The inclusion of handicapped persons in community-based recreation activities (e.g., 4-H Club, dances, community swim) is more likely to have greater long-term value for them and to be more consistent with the principle of normalization.

The ultimate aim of leisure skill training is to teach handicapped persons to acquire and use skills in naturally occurring situations. Thus, awareness of an individual's current and future environments, especially integrated community environments, should guide the selection of leisure activity choices (Brown, Branston, Hamre-Nietupski, Pumpian, Certo, & Gruenewald, 1979; Certo, Schleien, & Hunter, 1983).

### Least Restrictive Environment

The least restrictive environment principle should be applied to leisure as well as educational services for handicapped persons. In the past, when leisure services were considered to be a form of therapy for handicapped persons, the services often were delivered in a "therapeutic" milieu, such as in a hospital or rehabilitation center (O'Morrow, 1980). Many mentally handicapped persons still participate in segregated leisure activities in special settings, such as "therapeutic recreation" or "motor rooms" in a school, hospital, or day activity center. Given the adaptations, prosthetic devices, and environmental modifications that presently are available to facilitate handicapped persons' full participation in regular school and community leisure activities (Wehman & Schleien, 1981), there is little justification for limiting their activities to segregated and potentially restrictive environments.

## LEISURE PARTICIPATION IN HOME ENVIRONMENTS

Many investigations into the community adaptation of previously institutionalized handicapped persons have cited these persons' participation in leisure activities and their ability to occupy themselves during unstructured periods as important indications of successful adjustment (Bell et al., 1975; Corcoran & French, 1977; Eyman & Call, 1977; Gollay, 1981; Hill & Bruininks, 1981; Intagliata, Willer, & Wicks, 1981; Scheerenberger & Felsenthal, 1976). The evidence suggests that even though handicapped adults may function successfully in vocational pursuits, they may not adequately adapt to community living because of difficulty both in filling unstructured time (e.g., coffee breaks) in the work setting and in using leisure and recreation services in the community (Birenbaum & Re, 1979; Hill & Bruininks, 1981; Luckey & Shapiro, 1974).

Only minimal information is available on the types of leisure activities in which mentally handicapped persons living in community residences engage and on the major variables that seem to influence leisure participation. In general, this information establishes that living in a community residence does not in itself ensure a normal pattern of leisure activities (Intagliata et al., 1981).

### Active versus Passive Activities

In an investigation on the leisure time activities of residents in community facilities, most of whom were former residents of institutions, Bjaanes and Butler (1974) found that only 3% of the residents' time was spent in active leisure behaviors, as opposed to 22% of their time spent in passive leisure behaviors. Active behaviors were defined as goal-oriented and engaged, such as playing games or dancing, and passive leisure behaviors were defined as nongoal-oriented, such as watching television or staring into space. Leisure activity participation was observed to vary considerably between as well as within the board and care and home care facilities studied. For example, no active leisure behaviors were observed in one board and care facility, whereas active leisure behaviors were exhibited 5.5% of the time in another. According to Bjaanes and Butler (1974), differences in leisure behaviors could not be accounted for simply by the type of location of a facility; variations in the unique environmental climate of each facility were responsible. The investigators also concluded that planning and supervising active leisure activities by caregivers influence how frequently such activities occur.

Cheseldine and Jeffree (1981) surveyed 214 families in Manchester, England, to examine the leisure time activities of mentally handicapped teenagers (average age = 16.1 years). Several teenagers (9.5%) were in residential care, the rest lived at home. Five spare-time activities were most frequently mentioned by parents or guardians: 1) listening to records or tapes, 2) watching TV, 3) shopping (alone or with family), 4) trips in the car with the family, and 5) helping in the house—all activities that are essentially passive or family oriented. Youth clubs for mentally handicapped persons existed in the area, but only 40% of the teenagers in the survey attended them. Transportation was one barrier to participation in the youth clubs. Several teenagers dropped out of the clubs because of the firm desire not to spend their spare time with other mentally handicapped persons. "Indeed, it goes right against the principles of normalization, to provide a special facility for individuals who are mentally handicapped to 'occupy' themselves" (Cheseldine & Jeffree, 1981, p. 52). Cheseldine and Jeffree (1981) cited the following three factors as major barriers to full leisure activity participation:

> Firstly, the attitude of parents who have so fully accepted their role as sole providers of care and recreation that they are unaware of the long-term consequences or "problems" in this area; secondly, it is suggested that the lack of local friendships outside the school environment restricts the development of social activities; thirdly, the lack of basic skills further restricts the choice of activities open to these young people (p. 58).

## Public versus
## Community Residential Facilities

In a comprehensive national study of deinstitutionalization, Hill and Bruininks (1981) compared the leisure activities of mentally retarded persons living in public residential facilities with those living in community residential facilities. Interviews with direct care staff members revealed many similarities; watching television, attending religious services, or going on field trips were equally likely to occur in both types of facilities. Differences were also observed in the amount of time spent and type of participation in leisure activities. Residents of community facilities spent a greater proportion of their time in community-based leisure activities (e.g., shopping or eating out), whereas residents of public facilities were more likely to spend more time participating in typical large-group activities within the facilities (e.g., going for a walk, attending a dance). Residents in community facilities participated in an average of 4.7 categories of leisure ac-

tivity per week, whereas the weekly average was 3.8 for residents of public residential facilities. The latter participated more often in certain types of activities (e.g., going for a walk outdoors, attending a party or dance, or going to a movie or concert). The most frequently cited reasons for lack of participation in active leisure activities were: 1) lack of someone to accompany the resident, 2) lack of access to desired activities, and 3) lack of transportation. Community facility staff members reported that the unavailability of desired leisure activities was the largest single problem (14.9%) for residents.

Ability levels for participation in leisure activities also were assessed by Hill and Bruininks (1981). They found that 77% of the community facility residents and 51.3% of the public facility residents were perceived as capable of spending time outside the boundaries of the facility without direct supervision.

## Community Facilities

Gollay, Freedman, Wyngaarden, and Kurtz (1978) noted that the leisure participation of deinstitutionalized persons differed according to type of residential setting. A greater range of leisure activities was reported in group homes and in semiindependent settings than in natural/adoptive or foster homes.

> Whereas less than two-thirds of the persons living in natural/adoptive homes were allowed to decide how to spend their own money, about three-quarters of those living in group or semiindependent homes were allowed to make such decisions. People living in natural/adoptive or foster homes were much less likely to come and go at will than those living in semiindependent settings (less than 20 percent, compared to 77 percent). Residents in group or semiindependent settings were also more likely to be able to drink alcoholic beverages, to decide when to make appointments, and to go on dates outside the home than were residents in natural/adoptive or foster homes (Gollay et al., 1978, p. 87).

The investigators emphasized that the leisure activities of the persons they studied varied widely and that even within a particular facility some residents regularly and actively

participated in a great variety of leisure activities whereas other residents rarely became
involved. Finding appropriate leisure activities
was reported to be a pervasive problem for the
entire group of formerly institutionalized persons.

Residents of family care homes in Wisconsin tend to use community resources more than
do residents of group or adult homes (Scheerenberger & Felsenthal, 1976). Among the
family care residents, 100% were found to use
stores, 94% used parks/zoos, and 69% used
restaurants, although only 21% used them independently. The investigators suggested that
these residents needed adult escorts because
they tended to live apart from the community
and to lack adequate transportation. Intagliata
et al. (1981) also found that residents of family
care homes in New York had higher rates of
leisure activity participation than did residents
in other types of community facilities. However, Butler and Bjaanes (1977) reported in California a notable lack of involvement of family
care residents in community activities.

One difficulty in comparing the degree of
leisure activity participation among classifications of residences (e.g. group home, family
care) is the variation in the various residential
setting types. Both Intagliata et al. (1981) and
Bjaanes and Butler (1974) suggest that a type
of residence (e.g., family care or group home)
is not a homogeneous class. Taking this factor
into account, Intagliata et al. (1981) compared
residences according to social workers' ratings
of quality (lower and higher quality) rather
than type (e.g., group or family care home).
Quality was judged in terms of the care providers' "encouraging independence," "implementing    treatment    plans,"    supporting
"new behaviors," and so forth. The investigators found that residents of higher-quality
homes were more likely than residents of
lower-quality homes to engage in almost every
type of leisure activity assessed (e.g., going to
restaurants, church, movies). The effects of
location and community characteristics upon
leisure activities of handicapped persons have
not been assessed systematically.

## Longitudinal Perspective

It is probably premature to assess the effect of
the movement from institutions to community
settings on leisure activity participation (Hill &
Bruininks, 1981). Degree and quality of participation must be viewed over time to evaluate
fully what is taking place in community residences. Interestingly, a decline in leisure activity participation (e.g., church, movie, or
Young Men's Christian Association [YMCA]
attendance) following the first 5 months of
placement in the community was found by Bell
et al. (1975) in their longitudinal study of the
community adjustment of formerly institutionalized residents. Birenbaum and Re (1979)
noted a similar tendency in their 4-year longitudinal study of the community adjustment of 63
mentally retarded adults who previously had
resided in three state institutions. Although
these residents continued to participate in sheltered workshops, the time they spent in leisure
activities decreased substantially in terms of
quality and quantity. After 16 to 20 months in
the community, the average number of activities participated in per week was 7.4. This
average dropped to 3.14 after 40–44 months.
A decrease over time (from 3.2 in 1975 to .60
in 1977) in activities led per week by staff
members was also observed. It is important to
note, however, that Bell et al. (1975) did not
necessarily interpret a decrease in community
leisure activity participation as a negative
trend; they suggested that "if going places in
the community is gradually replaced by getting
together with friends, it may be viewed as a
positive trend" (p. 205).

## Family Attitudes

Family attitudes also affect the leisure participation of handicapped persons; Wehman
and Schleien (1981) considered such attitudes a
critical factor. Most investigations of parental
behavior and attitudes toward leisure appear in
the literature on play behavior in infancy and
preschool years; less is known about families
with handicapped adolescents, teenagers, or
young adults (especially for persons formerly

in institutions). The results of two investigations on formerly institutionalized persons illustrate the effect of family attitudes on leisure participation.

Katz and Yekutiel (1974) studied the leisure time problems of 128 graduates of sheltered workshops in Tel Aviv, Tushiyah, and Achikam, Israel. After the investigators collected ideographic data from the graduates' personal files, they interviewed and questioned parents on the leisure and social problems of their sons and daughters, who were either employed, institutionalized, or at home. Findings indicated that most leisure time was spent in essentially passive activities, such as watching television or listening to the radio. A more striking result was that 78% of the sample did not spend any of their leisure time with persons of the opposite sex. Parents perceived the most significant problems in improving their children's use of leisure time to be the absence of suitable friends and the lack of interest in leisure activities. The investigators noted that although parents ranked the lack of appropriate friends as most important, they seemed not to want their sons and daughters to have only mentally handicapped companions or to engage only in segregated group leisure activities. Such attitudes were thought to mitigate against participation. It appears that the parents recognized the importance of integrated activities and were concerned enough with the stigmatizing effects of ''retarded-only'' leisure activities to opt for *no* leisure over segregated group activities.

Gollay et al. (1978), in their study of deinstitutionalized persons, found that severely retarded persons participated in fewer leisure activities and had fewer friends than did mildly or moderately retarded persons, yet families rated the personal adjustment of the severely retarded individuals more positively than did the families of the less retarded persons. In explaining this contradiction, the investigators speculated that the families with severely retarded members may have lowered their expectations in regard to leisure activities and social relations. Cheseldine and Jeffree (1981) suggested that parents often find a *modus vivendi* to deal with the leisure time activities of their children; they seem to learn to cope with little support and thus do not perceive a problem. For example, the parents who were interviewed had very little awareness of the leisure activity options or resources in the communtiy. Bell et al. (1975) observed that parents tend to encourage children's participation in activities that minimize the likelihood of embarrassment (e.g., going to church) rather than promoting engaging in activities that involve strangers in public places.

## Age and Level of Retardation

Gollay et al. (1978) have pointed out that age (or the adult/child distinction) and level of retardation influence the degree of restrictiveness in leisure activity options. The investigators reported that a greater proportion of the adults than children they studied were allowed to participate in leisure activities and make personal decisions. Of course, it is to be expected that age will influence the nature of leisure activity participation for both handicapped and nonhandicapped persons—for example, teenagers are more likely to attend mixed dances and young children are more liable to participate in playground activities.

Severely handicapped persons live in more restrictive environments than do mildly or moderately handicapped persons. One indicator of restrictiveness identified by Gollay and her associates (Gollay et al., 1978) was the degree to which residents have the opportunity to enter and leave their homes by choice. Among the mildly handicapped subjects, 36% were allowed to enter and leave their residences by choice, whereas only 33% of the moderately retarded residents and 20% of the severely retarded residents could do so. Thus, residences for homogeneous groups of severely handicapped persons may tend to prohibit social and leisure activity options. Landesman-Dwyer, Berkson, and Romer (1979) contended that heterogeneous groupings (or, even better, full community integration) may promote more affiliation and sharing of leisure activities than do homogenous groupings by level of retardation. The data in their study on affiliation and friendship in group homes indicate that level of retardation does not appear to determine the amount of social interactions that takes place. One cannot assume that mentally handicapped persons prefer to affiliate with persons at the same level of intelligence, although they often are so grouped.

## COMPARATIVE STUDIES OF HANDICAPPED AND NONHANDICAPPED PERSONS

In order to evaluate the participation of mentally handicapped persons in community leisure activities, a basic understanding must be acquired of how nonhandicapped persons in the same communities occupy their leisure time. Obviously, typical activities will vary according to facilities (e.g., swimming pools, shopping malls) and available activities (e.g., organized clubs), which differ by geographical locale and type of neighborhood (McGregor, 1982). If the participation of mentally handicapped persons in leisure activities were normalized, each person would have the same activity options that nonhandicapped persons have, taking into account individual preferences and skills. It is not known, at this time, if mentally handicapped persons' participation in leisure activities actually departs substantially from the norm. For example, Birenbaum and Re (1979) noted that the participation in leisure/recreation activities of the mentally retarded adults they studied was "not too different from that of those who are not retarded, but are marginally employed or mostly unemployed" (p. 329). Nevertheless, at least two empirical studies reached different conclusions on this issue.

In comparing the recreational activities of 108 mildly mentally handicapped and nonhandicapped students, aged 7–12 years, Matthews (1982) examined the type and frequency of participation for three groups: 1) low socioeconomic status (SES) mentally retarded students, 2) low SES nonretarded students, and 3) middle SES nonretarded persons. Mentally

handicapped students were found to participate significantly more often than nonhandicapped students in informal as opposed to formal, inexpensive to expensive, and accessible to inaccessible activities. There were many similarities in the recreational activities of the three groups, with mentally handicapped students as likely as nonhandicapped students to participate in the same type of activities in the same settings. The only difference linked to mental retardation was that mentally handicapped persons engaged in fewer social activities with each other or in the community. Matthews, contending that the differences in participation between mentally handicapped and nonhandicapped persons have been overemphasized, recommended that future research focus on how mentally handicapped persons and nonhandicapped persons are alike rather than different. Matthews's findings are consistent with the results of a study in which Edgerton (1967) found that the leisure activities of former Pacific State Hospital residents were much like those of peers in their neighborhoods.

Bell et al. (1975) studied 503 adults (age 17 years and over) who had been discharged from state schools for mentally retarded persons in Texas, to ascertain their degree of participation in social and community activities. The group was divided into high IQ (55 or above) and low IQ (below 55) subsets. Questionnaire and interview data were obtained and compared with interview data on a sample of nonhandicapped residents from Lubbock, Texas. Nonhandicapped residents were shown to have higher levels of leisure participation in the community than were mentally retarded residents. Moderately mentally retarded residents participated less frequently in most activities than did mildly retarded residents, except that moderately retarded persons attended church more often. Degree of personal satisfaction in leisure participation was also measured; the results indicated that more former state school residents reported greater problems in finding out what to do with their time and in making friends than did the average citizen. This study is one of the few to consider the qualitative aspects of leisure by obtaining a measure of satisfaction, an aspect often neglected in research on leisure participation.

The finding that mentally handicapped persons participate in the same types of leisure activities with similar frequencies as do other members of communities is not an assurance that their leisure/recreation activity needs are being met or that the manner of participation is typical or desirable. For example, if residents of a group home always went to movies in large, homogeneous groups, the activity would be contrary to the normalization principle. If teenagers attended a puppet show designed for young children, the activity would be considered age inappropriate. Voeltz et al. (1982) developed a checklist for evaluating the appropriateness of leisure time activities and materials in educational contexts, based on the work of Ford et al. (1981). This checklist is applicable to leisure activities in residential or community contexts and is especially useful because it captures qualitative aspects of leisure activities.

## Leisure Skills Training and Programming

Attempts to increase the participation in leisure activities of mentally handicapped persons residing in community facilities are documented in the literature. Johnson and Bailey (1977), for example, showed that access to instruction was a critical factor in increasing the participation of group-home residents in weaving and rug-making activities. High levels of participation were maintained after instruction when the residents had access to these activities. Skills already in the individuals' repertoires were more likely to be used when prizes were awarded, but prizes were not needed to maintain participation levels in rug-making and weaving. The investigators did not collect data in this study on long-term participation in the activities, although they noted that collection of such data is essential for adequately evaluating the effects of instruction. In addition, the investigators were unable to determine whether increased participation in such activities is associated with community adjustment.

A leisure skills program was developed for six moderately mentally retarded adults in a group home setting by Schleien, Kiernan, and Wehman (1981). The training program consisted of a weekly counseling session in leisure time use, reinforcement training, and introduction of new materials. An A-B-A-B reversal design was followed (baseline, instruction/reinforcement, return to baseline, instruction/reinforcement), and behavioral observations were made in the group home. Results indicated that during baseline, few high-quality (HQ) leisure behaviors (e.g., goal-directed recreational and age-appropriate activities) were exhibited by residents. Mostly residents watched television and smoked cigarettes. However, HQ leisure behaviors averaged 60% across the instruction sessions. When the baseline was reinstated, HQ behaviors declined almost to 0%, but with the reinstitution of the intervention program, most residents' inappropriate behaviors were reduced.

## LEISURE/RECREATION PARTICIPATION IN EDUCATIONAL SETTINGS

The influence of the normalization principle has given educators cause to critically evaluate curriculum content and methods of instruction for handicapped children and youth. Traditional educational programs have emphasized the curricular components of cognitive, vocational, and daily living skills to the neglect of leisure/recreation skills. Leisure education, however, was included in Public Law 94-142 as a related service, in response to the long-felt need to provide leisure-skills training for handicapped students. This section reviews the research on training in leisure skills in educational institutions.

## Curriculum Trends

Despite the statutory mandate to include training in leisure/recreation skills in educational programs as a related service, such programs often are given a secondary position in curricular considerations. Traditionally, the designation of "free time" or "recess" at primary age levels and "recreation" at secondary age levels has been the closest approximation to training in leisure skills. Physical education programs may or may not offer skill training in leisure/recreation. Recent trends would establish individualized programs that are community referenced, age appropriate, and based on the preferences of students with suggestions from parents.

*Community-Referenced Programs* Leisure/recreation skills training should facilitate self-initiated, independent skills for current and future settings. Bellamy and Wilcox (1982) have advocated for secondary school programs that focus on the skills needed for participation in local community leisure activities. Environmental inventories can be conducted to assess the leisure areas to which students will have access and to provide the basis for developing locally referenced curriculum content. Environmental inventories also may be useful to ascertain performance demands, natural cues, consequences, and environmental arrangements (Bellamy & Wilcox, 1982; Brown, Branston-McClean, Baumgart, Vincent, Falvey, & Schroeder, 1979; Certo et al., 1983).

*Age-Appropriate Programs* Activities that may be appropriate to the developmental level of mentally handicapped persons may be inappropriate for their chronological age (CA) levels and, thus, may be socially stigmatizing. For instance, large-piece puzzles, building blocks, and dolls are appropriate play materials for younger handicapped students but are age-inappropriate for older handicapped students. Wuerch and Voeltz (1982) have developed a useful leisure curriculum that includes suitable activities for severely handicapped secondary level students. Wehman and Schleien (1981) generated a list of leisure skills in the areas of object manipulation, sports, hobbies, and games that are appropriate for adolescents and adults.

Although leisure skills training usually is associated with secondary programs, instruction in leisure skills can easily be incorporated into curricula beginning in preschool for handicapped as well as nonhandicapped students. The inclusion of play skills is clearly appropriate in curricula for young handicapped children. Researchers generally agree that play is important to the acquisition of social, language, and motor skills, as well as to the enhancement of a positive self-concept (Bills, 1950; Bradtke, Kirkpatric, & Rosenblatt, 1972; Feitelson, 1972; Gunn, 1975).

*Individualized Programs* Leisure activities often are selected by special education teachers on the basis of available facilities, equipment, and schedules. Other and perhaps more important considerations, such as age appropriateness or parental suggestions, tend to be neglected (Hill & Bruininks, 1981; Wehman, 1976b).

Public Law 94-142 mandated a crucial role for parents in the educational program-planning process for handicapped students. Curriculum developers are expected to encourage maximum parental participation in the selection of goals and methods to best meet the needs of such students. The selected objectives for leisure skills, therefore, also should specify the methods of instruction to achieve those skills (Frith, 1980). At the same time, the interests and preferences of students must be recognized (Bellamy & Wilcox, 1982; Voeltz et al., 1982; Wehman & Schleien, 1981). Unfortunately, educators are accustomed to making decisions in the planning process and, consequently, may lack the inclination or skills to honor student preferences. Moreover, in Matthews's (1982) study (discussed earlier in this chapter) a comparison of the recreational preferences of retarded and nonretarded children revealed many similarities between the two groups, suggesting that integrated leisure/ recreation programs are feasible.

Student preferences can be assessed efficiently by teachers by the use of an interest inventory, such as the *Leisure Ethic Scale,* developed by Slivkin and Crandell (1978), which assesses the amount of time a student spends in specific leisure activities. Other measures assess the latency of response to leisure materials or activities. As used by McCall (1974), latency assessment measures the length of elapsed time before a student acts on a variety of presented objects. By gauging latency of response, educators can evaluate the relative attractiveness of and preferences for certain play or leisure materials (Wehman & Schleien, 1981). Although several leisure interest finders are available, Witt and Groom (1979) pointed out that instruments distinguish little among interests, needs, and wants. Interest finders are intended to evaluate enjoyment and voluntary participation, including the measurement of attitudes, personality, drives, and abilities, but they frequently are not used in schools.

Handicapped students frequently cannot identify their interests or recognize their options in leisure time activities (Certo et al., 1983). Thus Voeltz et al. (1982) advocated choice training as part of the educational program for such students. Choice training can be conducted simultaneously with leisure skills training. For example, when students are given the cue for "free time," they can be given the opportunity to choose a leisure activity. In a project that incorporated choice training, the authors reported that after a time the students were spontaneously making activity choices from a range of possibilities. Based on a study of behavior patterns relating to recreation preferences, Granzin and Williams (1978) also conducted training in choice-making behavior by providing maximum exposure to a variety of leisure activities. Developing programs that meet students' preferences may require new methods, increased incentives, and inservice training for teachers. Research into the extent to which expressed leisure interests and activity choices are confounded by situational constraints, learned habits, lack of experience, and availability of resources is sorely needed (Witt & Groom, 1979).

## Methods of Leisure-Skills Training

In order to develop a handicapped student's appropriate leisure-skills repertoire, specific skill-training techniques are often used (Adkins & Matson, 1980; Wehman & Marchant, 1977). Methods of task analysis, data-based instruction, and contingent reinforcement have been employed successfully to teach specific skills like swimming, bowling, and skiing (Bundschuh, Williams, Hollingworth, Gooch, & Shirer, 1972; Seaman, 1973; Sinclair, 1975). Specific skills trained are usu-

ally based upon task analyses of leisure skills practiced by the normal population, as in the *I CAN Program* (Wessel, 1976) and as advocated by Navar (1980).

Many leisure programs include behavior analytic approaches to develop students' repertoires. Wambold and Bailey (1979) used prompting and reinforcement to teach severely retarded children in a classroom the specific skills needed to play with toys. Wehman and Marchant (1977) successfully taught gross motor recreational skills to severely retarded children by using a variety of prompts and contingent reinforcement. Prompts were carried over from verbal to visual to manual guidance and eventually were faded out.

Gains in physical fitness and table game leisure skills were achieved by retarded subjects in two studies reported by Wehman, Renzaglia, Berry, Schultz, & Karon (1978). The data-based training program included three fitness exercises and four table games; it used task analysis and specific instructional directives. The results of the two studies indicated that these mentally retarded individuals could acquire a diverse repertoire of leisure skills in a short time period. Reinforcement sampling, social contingency, modeling, and stimulus fading also are effective methods for training severely handicapped persons in leisure-related skills and for increasing their play behavior repertoires (Ayllon & Azrin, 1968; Wehman, 1977a; Wehman, 1978; Wehman & Rettie, 1975). Other instructional methods, such as counseling, role playing, and self-control, have been shown to be effective in teaching handicapped individuals the components of leisure participation (Gardner & Stamm, 1971; Wehman, 1975; Wehman, 1976a).

*Generalization* Wehman (1977b) argued that however successful instruction in the use of specific toys or materials may be, it does not necessarily generalize to other activities and settings. A number of investigators have proposed skills instruction that will transfer to leisure activity participation in natural community environments (Brown, Branston-McLean, Baumgart, Vincent, Falvey, & Schroeder, 1979; Voeltz et al., 1982). Schleien, Wehman, and Kiernan (1981) promoted generalization by using a seven-step task analysis of motor responses with applied behavior analysis, including a multiple baseline with changing criterion intervention, teaching severely handicapped adults the necessary skills for a dart game. The experimental group not only acquired the dart skills but also generalized them to other appropriate environments. Sedlak, Doyle, and Schloss (1982) examined the ability of severely retarded adolescents to generalize videogame skills to a community setting. The procedures built into the training sequence permitted generalization with a minimal amount of retraining.

## Collateral Skill Development

Leisure/recreation skills training also has yielded unexpected collateral benefits in other areas of educational programming. The areas of language, cognition, and social and motor behavior were shown to benefit from the skills learned in play therapy (Newcomer & Morrison, 1974; Strain et al., 1976). Bates and Renzaglia (1979) designed a multiple baseline study for a profoundly retarded student that included reinforcement contingencies for both language and leisure behaviors. The student acquired new verbal labels while playing a table game.

Another way to promote collateral skill development in severely handicapped youngsters is to cluster skills during instruction. Holvoet, Guess, Mulligan, and Brown (1980) argued that students should not be taught skills in isolation but, rather, in "behavior clusters" that are common to natural environments. This teaching strategy, which is based on the premise that naturally occurring behaviors are rarely present in isolation, supports holistic and stimulus array techniques of training.

Participation in a leisure activity, such as playing videogames, requires that the student learn a number of behaviors that are typically taught simultaneously, often in massed trials. For example, a motor behavior, such as reach and grasp, may be taught for 15 minutes and then instruction in a language behavior, such as

requesting change, may be given for 10 minutes. In skill clusters, various behaviors are taught as a routine. Holvoet et al. (1980) devised specific methods for arranging skills sequentially and functionally into behavior clusters; the techniques seem to be readily applicable to leisure activities and to the enhancement of collateral skills development through leisure activities.

Another useful method for improving the development of collateral skills is illustrated in *Project SELF: Special Education for Leisure Fulfillment* (Schnorr & Bender, 1982). The project is based on the belief that "traditional special education programs have concentrated on teaching basic academics and survival skills with little emphasis placed upon leisure as an integral teaching area" (p. 9). The program was designed to integrate leisure training into the core of an existing special education curriculum. The program spans eight major curricular areas; it makes leisure IEP objectives a high-interest focal point to teach academically oriented objectives. For example, on outings, skills of daily living are practiced while traveling on public transportation systems to locations where the leisure activities will be completed.

A skill area that lends itself naturally to training through leisure activities is social interaction. The development of social skills is an important component of most leisure activities, because participation with others is inherent in many activities. The parallel development of leisure and social skills is based on research into the relationship between participation in recreational activities, such as basketball and dancing, and social acceptance (Eichenbaum & Bednarek, 1964; McDaniel, 1971). Some investigators propose specific group skills training (Holvoet et al., 1980), whereas others encourage skill development while reinforcing independence and integration with age peers in leisure activities (Bellamy & Wilcox, 1982; Brown et al., 1979; Voeltz et al., 1982).

Leisure activities are also a natural medium for enhancing motor behavior. Marini (1978) studied the effects of a physical and recreational program on measures of the perceptual-motor ability of educable retarded children. Students attended a local park and recreation department to participate in bowling, roller skating, ice skating, swimming, and miniature golf, among other leisure activities. Improvement in body perception, balance, locomotor agility, ball throwing, and tracking were evidenced by the students who participated. Physical education, the only curricular area specifically mandated by Public Law 94-142, provides a natural environment for the development of both motor and leisure skills. In fact, the definition of physical education in the federal mandate includes "skills in aquatics, intramurals, and lifetime games and sports" (*Federal Register,* 1977).

## Reducing Inappropriate Behaviors

Leisure activities offer handicapped students positive alternatives to negative or "excess" behaviors. Such behaviors have been found to decrease when individuals are engaged in leisure activities and especially when the activities include a system or reinforcement (Davenport & Berkson, 1963; Lovaas, Freitag, Gold, & Kassorla, 1965). Levy (1944), for example, found that stereotypic behaviors increased when hospitalized children were deprived of toys and were decreased when toys were again made available. Flavell and Cannon's (1976) research on the use of toys by severely mentally handicapped students indicated that behaviors are strongly influenced by toy play and that the students exhibit strong preferences among toys. Data from the time-sampling measurements of the free play of 11 students indicated that the students were idle 65% of the time when they were given the 10 least popular toys but only 25% of the time when the 10 most popular toys were available.

Schleien, Kiernan, and Wehman (1981) conducted a leisure skills training program in a group home for six moderately mentally retarded adults (three males and three females). An inverse relation was found between high-quality (e.g., goal-directed, age-appropriate) leisure behaviors and inappropriate (e.g., ster-

eotypic or age-inappropriate) behaviors. The training program included leisure counseling, reinforcement, and making materials available.

Adkins and Matson (1980) used several experimental conditions to teach the leisure skill of making pot holders to six institutionalized moderately to severely retarded adult females (CA 24–45 years). The design was multiple baseline, consisting of 1) general instructions (informing residents in a group and individually that the classroom and materials were available for use), 2) attention (the trainer discussed the general purpose and benefits of leisure but gave no specific instructions), and 3) specific instructions in pot holder making. Only the third condition increased the appropriate use of leisure time (under this condition the three pairs of subjects spent 50%, 10%, and 17% of their free time making pot holders). Moreover, the learned skills generalized to a follow-up situation in which no training was given for 6 days. A noteworthy side effect of the program was the decrease in aggressive behavior in one student from a frequency of two incidents during baseline to zero during training. Thus, the investigators concluded that leisure skill instruction not only fosters participation in constructive hobbies but also tends to decrease inappropriate behaviors. Age-appropriate and contemporary alternatives to pot holder making certainly are available.

Voeltz and Wuerch (1981) also found increased frequencies of positive behaviors when individuals were systematically trained in leisure activities. Using a multiple baseline design of four leisure activity phases, they measured the effects of leisure instruction on the behaviors of four severely handicapped adolescents (CA 12–14 years) attending a private special education school. Observations were recorded during free-time periods of five appropriate play/affective behaviors (attention, exploration, independent play, smiles, vocalization) and negative/excess behaviors (self-stimulation with materials, self-stimulation without materials, destructiveness). Two students exhibited increased constructive, exploratory, and attending behavior during "down time" as a result of the training. A third student, who was experiencing an overall decline in educational progress, possibly because of increased medications and classroom change, showed no behavioral improvements. A fourth student decreased self-stimulation when using the materials but increased it when she had no objects to manipulate. This student self-stimulated with the play materials, but the acts were perceived by the staff to be an improvement over self-stimulation without materials and "actually a positive indication of interest, enjoyment, and even the beginning of constructive play" (Voeltz & Wuerch, 1981, p. 302). Although the positive effects of leisure skill training on behavior generalized to non-training free time for only two of the four students, Voeltz and Wuerch (1981) viewed the results as offering "cautious" support for associating play training with positive collateral effects.

## LEISURE PARTICIPATION IN COMMUNITY SETTINGS

The responsibility for ensuring appropriate leisure activity participation by mentally handicapped persons does not rest solely with community residential care providers, teachers, and families. When institutionalized persons are moved into community residences following deinstitutionalization and normalization programs, the responsibility for the provision of recreation services shifts from residential institutions to community agencies (Bates & Renzaglia, 1979). Thus the need for a comprehensive community-based service delivery system in leisure/recreation programming for handicapped individuals has been increasingly articulated in the literature (Brown, Branston-McClean, Baumgart, Vincent, Falvey, & Schroeder, 1979; McGregor, 1982).

This chapter has so far been devoted primarily to leisure/recreation activity participation and skill instruction in home and school environments. However, the true test of community integration is the use of acquired skills in community settings.

## Needs Assessment of Community Leisure Services

Schleien, Porter, and Wehman (1979) addressed the topic of community-based leisure services in their survey of community agencies and programs in the state of Virginia. The purpose of the investigation was to assess the roles of various agencies in providing for the leisure needs of developmentally disabled persons. The sample included county and regional parks and recreation departments, special education coordinators of public school systems, community mental health and mental retardation service boards, state hospitals serving mentally ill and mentally retarded persons, and other programs funded by the Virginia Developmental Disabilities Unit. The investigators found that 69% of the agencies offered some form of recreation service to their developmentally disabled clients, but 31% did not, indicating a need for more ongoing (rather than sporadic) recreational services. Among the respondents providing inadequate recreational programs, 66% reported that improvements could be made if professional expertise and appropriate instructional materials were made available. Fifty-eight percent expressed the need for a relevant leisure skills curriculum on which to base programs.

Austin, Peterson, Peccarelli, Binkley, and Laker (1977) distributed questionnaires to municipal park and recreation departments and health care and correctional facilities in the state of Indiana to determine the current status of therapeutic recreation services. Of the 50 responding parks and recreation departments, 80% believed that their agencies should be providing recreation services to special populations. Although 76% of the departments offered some form of therapeutic recreation service, in only two cases (5%) was the individual in charge of the program a therapeutic recreation specialist. The type of assistance most often cited (92%) as necessary to establish a program for special populations was a specially trained staff. The data revealed that existing programs were not extensively developed and that a majority of municipal park and recreation departments were not adequately serving special populations.

Several other studies have been conducted throughout the country to evaluate the status of recreation services for handicapped individuals. Edginton, Compton, Ritchie, and Vederman (1975) and Lancaster (1976) identified the lack of funding, poorly trained professional personnel, and lack of awareness of the need for community/municipal recreation services for special populations as the major factors inhibiting these services.

In addition to inadequately trained recreation professionals, lack of training program materials, lack of funds, and lack of awareness of the need for services, no appropriate recreation service delivery model at the community level has been developed—that is, there is no community-based recreation delivery system addressing the total life and leisure needs of handicapped persons living in communities (Compton & Goldstein, 1976). Thus, although the delivery of therapeutic recreation services and programs is legally mandated and communities have accepted the responsibilities for providing those services, the necessary personnel, methods, and procedures to implement the mandate have not been adequately developed.

## Inhibitors and Facilitators of Leisure Participation

Environmental barriers, long a concern of people who work with handicapped persons, have been brought to the attention of the general public by legislation and consumer advocates. Successful functioning within our society requires the ability to understand, interpret, and act appropriately upon signs, symbols, and communications in the environment. It also requires the ability to influence external forces, to have access to resources, to move about with minimal difficulty, and to assimilate experiences. Handicapped children and adults are greatly hampered in their daily activities by subtle as well as obvious physical barriers.

Often, handicapped persons cannot identify the causes of their frustration and limited participation in normal human activities; it may take a degree of awareness and exposure for them to realize that they are missing something that others have. Availability of transportation to, as well as access into and mobility within recreation areas and facilities, promote or inhibit leisure participation. In addition, the lack of knowledge about and training in the use of recreational services, inaccessibility of services due to physical or geographic impediments, and the presence of architectural barriers inhibit handicapped travelers (Laus, 1977). When handicapped individuals are prevented from traveling independently, they may suffer from boredom and, subsequently, may turn to an inappropriate use of free time that results in minimal community participation (Nippard, 1982). (Nippard, 1982, also provides a list of available agencies [e.g., Society for the Advancement of Travel for the Handicapped], resources, and guides to travel and tourism for handicapped individuals.)

Handicapped children and adults often are excluded from many leisure options because of the limitations imposed by their physical impairments. In general, community recreation programs/services do not provide the degree and types of modifications and adaptations necessary to accommodate such disabilities. To overcome this problem requires not only special equipment and materials, activity space and facilities, and the scheduling of activities, but also the development of suitable rules and regulations and the employment of special instructors. It is important, furthermore, to ascertain what handicapped individuals perceive as barriers to participation in regular recreation programs and facilities and to determine how these can be removed or compensated for.

An important step in the removal of environmental barriers has been federal legislation. The 1968 Architectural Barriers Act, for example, requires any structure built or renovated with public funds to be accessible to handicapped individuals. Strict enforcement of the act is essential, however. In addition, architects, urban planners, and transportation engineers should be made aware of the needs of handicapped persons. Medical technology and engineering can also contribute to increased participation in leisure activities by leading to the design of safe, effective appliances for handicapped persons to facilitate mobility and to correct physical impairments.

MacNeil (1977) identified three major barriers to the delivery of cultural arts opportunities for handicapped persons: the lack of trained personnel to serve disabled persons, architectural barriers, and attitudinal barriers. These obstacles prevent access to various public and private recreation services in the community as well.

Handicapped consumers of goods and services in the community have the right to expect certain levels of service from providers of recreational opportunities. Austin and Powell (1981) identified consumer representation to the service provider, economic feasibility and knowledge of user fees and charges, and an accessible environment as levels of service expected by all consumers. Wolfensberger (1972) recommended that at least one-half of any governing or advisory board consist of consumers representing the special group to be served.

## Leisure Programs
## Fostering Community Involvement

An integrated educational/leisure-time model program emphasizing community involvement was developed at the University of Washington (Thompson & Hannes, 1983) to train local high school and college students to teach deaf-blind children residing at a public residential facility to swim. For 2 hours daily after school the tutors taught specific skills to enable the deaf-blind children to interact normally with non-handicapped persons in "progressively broad environments" (e.g., locker room, gymnasium). The investigators believed that "through the tutors' involvement, their own families, friends, teachers, fellow students, churches, and service organizations are made aware of what deaf-blind children are like" (p. 2). To train the tutors, a multimedia inservice training package was developed to impart information on teaching communication skills, water safety, behavior management, data collection, gross motor skills, and social skills. In

evaluating the effects of training by means of scatter gain scores (these scores take into account behaviors at different age levels, such as, "initiates an interaction with an adult and responds to a single command") Thompson and Hannes (1983) found significant gains in certain skills. Moreover, anecdotal reports by residential and teaching staff were very positive, and student gains in weight, as well as increased alertness and increased social smiling, were observed.

A promising technique for promoting the normalized leisure participation of mentally handicapped adults was offered at the State University of New York's Brockport campus (Corcoran, 1979). The credit-free course, Basic Skills in Independent Living, was supported by state taxes, service organizations, and a student registration fee. The objectives of the program were to teach new leisure and independent living skills and to reinforce the skills gained during school years. In addition, the program sought to provide experiences in the use of skills in public settings. The variety of courses, which were taught by college students and volunteers, included human sexuality, swimming, bowling, judo, pizza making, and public safety. The enrollment included two adults with Down syndrome in the basic skills course. Corcoran (1979) described the two, both 22 years of age, in her anecdotal record:

> It has been hard for Charlie to develop age-appropriate behaviors, but his college student volunteers were not interested in his tantrums. Myra's volunteers quickly learned that Myra was adept at avoiding anything new and a master at manipulating situations to her advantage. Both of these young people have grown and matured in this college setting, and their parents have been quick to capitalize on their more adult behavior. Myra has become a sports fan and watches any gymnastic special she can find on TV—a change from her beloved "soaps." Charlie has learned that he can no longer jump blindly into the pool. He has learned to deal with his own strength and size. He recognizes the responsibility of being in a group of people who are not going to give him special consideration because he is retarded (p. 23).

Salzberg and Langford (1981) designed a "companion" or friendship model program to foster leisure skill development through instruction while providing normalized activities with nonhandicapped peers. The investigators were concerned with the limited opportunities for age-appropriate leisure skills development, noting that community residences often lacked the staff and funds to provide leisure opportunities and vocational rehabilitation services. The investigators also believed that leisure programming is often overly structured and does not foster independence. In the "companion" program, mentally retarded persons were interviewed to determine their leisure interests, past experiences in leisure activities, and leisure skill limitations. Each was then matched with a nonhandicapped volunteer on the basis of mutual leisure preferences. After an orientation session, volunteers were asked to accompany the handicapped "companion" weekly to a mutually agreed upon activity. The investigators reported that friendships developed, participants enjoyed the leisure activities, and handicapped persons learned normative protocols from their companions. Salzberg and Langford (1981) recommended that in setting up "companionships," individuals be carefully matched through preliminary interviews and that orientation and support for volunteers be provided.

## Guidelines for Community Leisure Services for Special Populations

The Leisure Information Studies (1976) insisted that the provision of recreation services to disabled individuals focus on the community in the hope that the majority of institutionalized persons eventually will return to the community. It was noted that, frequently, discharged patients are left stranded between institutionalized recreation programs and community agencies without proper preparation and training to make the necessary adjustment.

Reynolds (1981) summarized the major premise and corollaries of the normalization principle, common misconceptions in its implementation, and the overall concern with normalization as it related to recreation programming. He identified a substantial shift in the roles and orientations of therapeutic recreation specialists and educators and discussed trends that illustrate several new service functions and challenges. The following five trends in leisure programming were described:

1. Large group diversional activities and coordinated special events will be decreased in favor of individualized leisure and educational programming.
2. The medical model will be replaced by more appropriate orientations to leisure services.
3. Behavior techniques can and will be reconciled with the principle of normalization.
4. Recreation and special education personnel will adopt roles as advocates and as community liaisons to ensure the rights of disabled persons to participate in community leisure opportunities.
5. The problem of transfer of training/generalization will be addressed by teachers of leisure skills.

Bates and Renzaglia (1979) discussed a number of areas pertinent to the development and successful conduct of community recreation programs. They were looking for a systematic approach to providing community leisure services for special populations. The areas examined were program planning, assessment, training and skill development, maintenance and generalization of recreational skills, and future research needs.

The National Therapeutic Recreation Society, a branch of the National Recreation and Park Association, approved guidelines and suggested solutions to alleviate identified problems, to be used by public park and recreation agencies in developing community-based recreation programs for special populations (Vaughan & Winslow, 1979). Transportation was identified as the major problem for a special population program in the community. Possible solutions to the problem included car pools, use of federal grant money (e.g., Federal Aid Highway Act of 1973, PL 93-87) available to community recreation and park agencies for the purchase of transportation vehicles, involvement of different service clubs and social service agencies (e.g., American Red Cross, Kiwanis Clubs), and contractual agreements with schools, health agencies, or private organizations.

A project was funded by the U.S. Department of Education, Office of Special Education, to devise a comprehensive inservice education system to promote the development, delivery, and advocacy of leisure services for handicapped persons in New Jersey communities (New Jersey Office on Community Recreation for Handicapped Persons, 1980). A handbook prepared for the administrator of the public recreation agency outlined goals and objectives to guide public agencies wishing to initiate or expand community recreation services for disabled persons.

Certo et al., (1983) presented a concrete strategy or inventory to enable therapeutic recreation specialists and other educators to develop functional, age-appropriate leisure skills instructional content. The investigators believed that this approach, coupled with longitudinal planning, would increase opportunities for severely handicapped individuals to actively participate in normalized leisure activities in integrated community settings. The inventory was divided into three interrelated areas: skill selection and skill/facility description, component skills and adaptations for full/partial participation, and supportive skills.

## SUMMARY

Research on the community adjustment of persons with handicaps, many of whom formerly resided in institutions, indicates that community settings do not ensure the handicapped population adequate or meaningful participation in leisure and recreation activities. Typically, handicapped persons spend the majority of their lives in passive, meaningless activities regardless of where they are housed. Several variables predominate in influencing the quality of leisure activity participation including availability of transportation, caregiver involvement, friends or escorts to accompany individuals, and leisure skills training.

Leisure education should be made an integral part of ongoing educational curricula and should not be perceived as a luxury service. Instruction in leisure skills acquisition should attend to handicapped individuals' chronological ages, personal preferences, and family/community life-styles. The strategies for teaching leisure skills, which are reviewed in this chapter, include behavior analysis and skill training in school, community, and home environments. Of particular importance are procedures that enhance the maintenance and generalization of leisure skills in current and future natural environments.

The responsibility for improving and expanding leisure/recreation programming rests with service providers and families in home, school, and community environments. Maximizing cooperation and coordination among families, schools, public recreation departments, human service agencies, and universities is an important goal that will facilitate leisure/recreation participation across settings. However, if responsibilities are spread too widely among agencies, it is possible that no one organization will make sure they are carried out. Therefore, it is recommended that a lead agency be designated to assume overall programing responsibility. Most likely this assignment would be made on the basis of chronological ages of handicapped persons served. It would be logical, for example, to assign to the schools the burden of responsibility for training leisure/recreation skills to young people (up to age 23) and to give specific social service agencies (e.g., public park and recreation departments) the responsibility for training these skills to adults.

Research documenting the benefits of leisure/recreation activity participation for individuals with handicaps is reviewed in this chapter. It must be emphasized, however, that meaningful participation in leisure/recreation activities is also recognized as a basic human right. The research findings appear promising on the contribution of active leisure activities on enhancing community integration and improving behavior functioning of handicapped persons. Despite limited work in this area, it seems obvious, indeed essential, to upgrade the scope of research and development and of opportunities for constructive leisure participation for handicapped children and adults. With so much focus placed upon education and training, it is important that handicapped persons have sufficient opportunities to express the skills they develop through participation rather than isolation. It is through leisure/recreational activities that many of the ideals implied by the concepts of *normalization* and *least restrictive environment* can best be realized.

## REFERENCES

Adkins, J., & Matson, L. Teaching institutionalized mentally retarded adults socially appropriate leisure skills. *Mental Retardation,* 1980, *18*(5), 249–252.

Austin, D., Peterson, J., Peccarelli, L., Binkley, A., & Laker, M. *Therapeutic recreation in Indiana: Health through recreation.* Bloomington, IN: Department of Recreation and Park Administration, Indiana University, 1977.

Austin, D., & Powell, L. What you need to know to serve special populations. *Parks and Recreation,* 1981, *16,* 40–42.

Ayllon, T., & Azrin, N.H. Reinforcer sampling: A technique for increasing the behavior of mental patients. *Journal of Applied Behavior Analysis,* 1968, *1,* 13–20.

Ball, E., Chasey, W., Hawkins, F., & Verhoven, P. The need for leisure education for handicapped children and youth. *Leisure Today: JOPER,* March, 1976, 29–31.

Bates, P., & Renzaglia, A. Community-based recreation programs. In: P. Wehman (ed.), *Recreation programming for developmentally disabled persons,* 97–125. Baltimore: University Park Press, 1979.

Bates, P., & Wehman, P. Behavior management with the mentally retarded: An empirical analysis of the research. *Mental Retardation,* 1977, *15,*(6), 9–12.

Baumeister, A.A., & Forehand, R. Stereotyped acts. In: N.R. Ellis (ed.), *International review of research in mental retardation.* New York: Academic Press, 1973.

Bell, N.J. Schoenrock, C., & Slade, R. *Leisure activities of previously institutionalized retardates: A comparison with non-retarded community residents.* Paper presented at the Region V American Association on Mental Deficiency Meeting, St. Louis, October, 1975.

Bellamy, G.T., & Wilcox, B. *Secondary education for severely handicapped students: Guidelines for quality services.* Eugene, OR: Center on Human Development, University of Oregon, 1982.

Bender, M., & Valletutti, P.J. *Teaching the moderately and severely handicapped: Curriculum, objectives, strategies, and activities,* Vol. 2. Baltimore: University Park Press, 1976.

Biklen, D., Exclusion. *Peabody Journal of Education,* 1973, *50*(3), 226–234.

Bills, R.E. Nondirective play therapy with retarded readers. *Journal of Consulting Psychology,* 1950, *19,* 140–149.

Birenbaum, A., & Re, M.A. Resettling mentally retarded adults in the community—almost four years later. *American Journal of Mental Deficiency,* 1979, *83,* 323–329.

Bjaanes, A.T., & Butler, E.W. Environmental variation in community care facilities for mentally retarded persons. *American Journal of Mental Deficiency,* 1974, *78*(4), 429–439.

Braddock, D. *Opening closed doors: The deinstitutionalization of disabled individuals.* Reston, VA: Council for Exceptional Children, 1977.

Bradtke, L., Kirkpatric, W., & Rosenblatt, P. Intensive play—a technique for building affective behaviors in profoundly mentally retarded young children. *Education and Training of the Mentally Retarded,* 1972, *7,* 8–13.

Brannan, S.A. Trends and issues in leisure education for the handicapped through community education. In: E. Fairchild & L. Neal (eds.), *Community unity in the community.* Eugene, OR: Center for Leisure Studies, 1975.

Brown, L., Branston, M.B., Hamre-Nietupski, S., Pumpian, I., Certo, N., & Gruenewald, L. A strategy for developing chronological age appropriate and functional curricular content for severely handicapped adolescents and young adults. *Journal of Special Education,* 1979, *13*(1), 81–90.

Brown, L., Branston-McClean, M., Baumgart, D., Vincent, L., Falvey, M., & Schroeder, G. Using the characteristics of current and subsequent least restrictive environments in the development of curricular content for severely handicapped students. *AAESPH Review,* 1979, *4,* 407–424.

Bundschuh, E.L., Williams, S.W., Hollingworth, J., Gooch, S., & Shirer, C. Teaching the retarded to swim. *Mental Retardation,* 1972, *10*(3), 14–17.

Butler, E.W., & Bjaanes, A.T. A typology of community care facilities and differential normalization outcomes. In: P. Mittler (ed.), *Research to practice in mental retardation: Care and intervention.* Baltimore: University Park Press, 1977.

Certo, N., Schleien, S., & Hunter, D. An ecological assessment inventory to facilitate community recreation participation by severely disabled individuals. *Therapeutic Recreation Journal.* 1983, *17,* 29–38.

Cheseldine, S., & Jeffree, D. Mentally handicapped adolescents: Their use of leisure. *Journal of Mental Deficiency Research,* 1981, *25,* 49–59.

Compton, D., & Goldstein, J. *The career education curriculum development project.* Arlington, VA: National Recreation and Park Association, 1976.

Corcoran, E.L. Campus life for retarded citizens. *Education Unlimited,* 1979, *1,* 22–24.

Corcoran, E.L., & French, R.W. Leisure activity for the retarded adult in the community. *Mental Retardation,* 1977, *15*(2), 21–23.

Davenport, R.K., & Berkson, G. Stereotyped movements of mental defectives: II. Effects of novel objects. *American Journal of Mental Deficiency,* 1963, *67,* 879–882.

Edgerton, R.B. *The cloak of competence: Stigma in the lives of the mentally retarded.* Berkeley, CA: University of California Press, 1967.

Edginton, C., Compton, D., Ritchie, A., & Vederman, R. The status of services for special populations in park and recreation departments in the state of Iowa. *Therapeutic Recreation Journal*, 1975, *3*, 109–116.

Eichenbaum, B., & Bednarek, N. Square dancing and social adjustment. *Mental Retardation*, 1964, *2*, 105–109.

Eyman, R.K., & Call, J. Maladaptive behavior and community placement of mentally retarded persons. *American Journal of Mental Deficiency*, 1977, *82*, 137–144.

*Federal Register*, August 23, 1977, 121a.13 *Related Services* 42 (163), Washington, DC.

Feitelson, D. Developing imaginative play in preschool children as a possible approach to fostering creativity. *Early Child Development and Care*, 1972, *1*, 181–195.

Flavell, J.E. Reduction of stereotypes by reinforcement of toy play. *Mental Retardation*, 1973, *11*(4), 21–23.

Flavell, J.E., & Cannon, P.R. Evaluation of entertainment materials for severely retarded persons. *American Journal of Mental Deficiency*, 1976, *81*, 357–361.

Ford, A., Brown, L., Pumpian, I., Baumgart, D., Schroeder, J., & Loomis, R. Strategies for developing individualized recreation/leisure plans for adolescent and young adult severely handicapped students. In: L. Brown, M. Falvey, I. Pumpian, D. Baumgart, J. Nishet, A. Ford, J. Schroeder, & R. Loomis (eds.), *Curricular strategies for teaching severely handicapped students functional skills in school and nonschool environments*. Madison, WI: Madison Metropolitan School District, 1981.

Frith, G.H. Recreation for mildly retarded students: An important component of individualized education plans. *Education and Training of the Mentally Retarded*, 1980, *15*(3), 199–203.

Gardner, W.E., & Stamm, J. Counseling the mentally retarded: A behavioral approach. *Rehabilitation Counseling Bulletin*, 1971, *15*(1), 46–57.

Gollay, E. Some conceptual and methodological issues in studying community adjustment of deinstitutionalized mentally retarded people. In: R.H. Bruininks, C.E. Meyers, B.B. Sigford, & K.C. Lakin (eds.), *Deinstitutionalization and community adjustment of mentally retarded people*. Washington, DC: American Association on Mental Deficiency, 1981.

Gollay, E., Freedman, R., Wyngaarden, M., & Kurtz, N.R. *Coming back: The community experiences of deinstitutionalized mentally retarded people*. Cambridge, MA: Abt Books, 1978.

Granzin, K.L., & Williams, R.H. Patterns of behavioral characteristics as indicants of recreation preferences: A canonical analysis. *Research Quarterly*, 1978, *49*(2), 135–145.

Gunn, S.L. Play as occupation: Implications for the handicapped. *American Journal of Occupational Therapy*, 1975, *29*(4), 222–225.

Hill, B.K., & Bruininks, R.H. *Family, leisure, and social activities of mentally retarded people in residential facilities*. Minneapolis, MN: Developmental Disabilities Project on Residential Services and Community Adjustment, University of Minnesota, 1981.

Holvoet, G., Guess, D., Mulligan, M., & Brown, F. The individualized curriculum sequencing model (II): A teaching strategy for severely handicapped students. *Journal of the Association for the Severely Handicapped*, 1980, *5*(4), 337–351.

Intagliata, J., Willer, B., & Wicks, N. Factors related to the quality of community adjustment in family care homes. In: R.H. Bruininks, C.E. Meyers, B.B. Sigford, & K.C. Lakin (eds.), *Deinstitutionalization and community adjustment of mentally retarded people*. Washington, DC: American Association on Mental Deficiency, 1981.

Johnson, M.S., & Bailey, J.S. The modification of leisure behavior in a half-way house for retarded women. *Journal of Applied Behavior Analysis*, 1977, *10*, 273–282.

Katz, S., & Yekutiel, E. Leisure time problems of mentally retarded graduates of training programs. *Mental Retardation*, 1974, *12*(3), 54–57.

Lancaster, R. Municipal services. *Parks and Recreation*, 1976, *18*, 18–27.

Landesman-Dwyer, S., Berkson, G., & Romer, D. Affiliation and friendship of mentally retarded residents in group homes. *American Journal of Mental Deficiency*, 1979, *83*, 571–580.

Laus, M. *Travel instruction for the handicapped*. Springfield, IL: Charles C Thomas, 1977.

Leisure Information Studies. *A systems model for developing a leisure education program for handicapped children and youth*. Washington, DC: Hawkins & Associates, 1976.

Levy, D.M. On the problem of movement restraint. *American Journal of Orthopsychiatry*, 1944, *14*, 644–671.

Lovaas, O.I., Freitag, G., Gold, V.J., & Kassorla, I.C. Experimental studies in childhood schizophrenia: Analysis of self-destructive behavior. *Journal of Experimental Child Psychology*, 1965, *2*, 67–84.

Luckey, R.E., & Shapiro, I. Recreation: An essential aspect of habilitative planning. *Mental Retardation*, 1974, *12*(5), 33–35.

McCall, R. Exploratory manipulation and play in the human infant. *Monographs of the Society for Research on Child Development*. Chicago: University of Chicago Press, 1974.

McDaniel, C.O. Extra-curricular activities as a factor in social acceptance among EMR students. *Mental Retardation*, 1971, *9*(2), 26–28.

McGregor, G. Leisure and the domains of home, school and community. In: P. Verhoven, S. Schleien, & M. Bender (eds.), *Leisure education and the handicapped individual: An ecological perspective*, 21–41. Washington, DC: Institute for Career and Leisure Development, 1982.

MacNeil, R. Opening minds and entryways at cultural centers. *Parks and Recreation*, 1977, *12*, 41–44.

Marini, D.G. Effects of additional physical and recreational curriculum on selected perceptual-motor abilities of educable mentally retarded children. *Therapeutic Recreation Journal*, 1978, *12*(3), 31–38.

Marion, R.L. Leisure time activities for trainable mentally retarded adolescents. *Teaching Exceptional Children*, 1979, *11*, 158–160.

Matthews, P. Some recreation preferences of the mentally retarded. *Therapeutic Recreation Journal*, 1982, *16*(3), 42–47.

Murphy, J.F. *Concepts of leisure*. Englewood Cliffs, NJ: Prentice-Hall, 1981.

Navar, N. A rationale for leisure skill assessment with handicapped adults. *Therapeutic Recreation Journal*, 1980, *14*(4), 21–28.

Neulinger, J. *To leisure: An introduction*. New York: Allyn & Bacon, 1981.

New Jersey Office on Community Recreation for Handicapped Persons. *A systematic approach to developing and implementing community recreation services for the disabled.* Trenton: Department of Community Affairs, 1980.

Newcomer, B., & Morrison, T.L. Play therapy with institutionalized mentally retarded children. *American Journal of Mental Deficiency,* 1974, *78*(6), 727–733.

Nippard, M. Leisure and the world of travel and tourism. In: P. Verhoven, S. Schleien, C.M. Bender (eds.), *Leisure education and the handicapped individual: An ecological perspective,* 110–120. Washington, DC: Institute for Career and Leisure Development, 1982.

O'Morrow, G.S. *Therapeutic recreation: A helping profession.* Reston, VA: Reston Publishing Co., 1980.

Orelove, F.P., Wehman, P., & Wood, J. An evaluative review of Special Olympics: Implications for community integration. *Education and Training of the Mentally Retarded,* 1982, 325–329.

Reynolds, R. A guideline to leisure skills programming for handicapped individuals. In: P. Wehman & S. Schleien (eds.), *Leisure programs for handicapped persons: Adaptations, techniques, and curriculum,* 1–13. Baltimore: University Park Press, 1981.

Salzberg, C.L., & Langford, C. Community integration of mentally retarded adults through leisure activity. *Mental Retardation,* 1981, *19*(3), 127–131.

Scheerenberger, R.C., & Felsenthal, D. *A study of alternative community placements.* Madison, WI: Research Institute of the Wisconsin Association for Retarded Citizens, 1976.

Schleien, S.J., Kiernan, J., & Wehman, P. Evaluation of an age-appropriate leisure skills program for moderately retarded adults. *Education and Training of the Mentally Retarded,* 1981, *16,* 13–19.

Schleien, S., Porter, J., & Wehman, P. An assessment of the leisure skill needs of developmentally disabled individuals. *Therapeutic Recreation Journal,* 1979, *13,* 16–21.

Schleien, S., Wehman, P., & Kiernan, J. Teaching leisure skills to severely handicapped adults: An age-appropriate darts game. *Journal of Applied Behavior Analysis,* 1981, *14,* 513–519.

Schnorr, J.M., & Bender, M. Project SELF: Special Education for Leisure Fulfillment. *Therapeutic Recreation Journal,* 1982, *16*(3), 9–16.

Seaman, J.A. The effects of a bowling program upon bowling skill number concepts and self-esteem of mentally retarded children. *Dissertation Abstracts International,* 1973, *33*(7-A), 3359–3360.

Sedlak, R., Doyle, M., & Schloss, P. Video games: A training and generalization demonstration with severely retarded adolescents. *Education and Training of the Mentally Retarded,* 1982.

Sinclair, N. Cross country skiing for the mentally retarded. *Challenge,* 1975, *5,* 33–35.

Slivkin, K., American Alliance for Health, Physical Education, Recreation, and Dance, & Crandell, R. *A new leisure ethic scale.* Paper presented at the convention, Kansas City, KS, 1978.

Strain, P.S., Cooke, T., & Apolloni, T. The role of peers in modifying classmates' social behavior: A review. *Journal of Special Education,* 1976, *10*(4), 351–356.

Thompson, M.D., & Hannes, S. *The integrated educa-tional/leisure time model for deaf-blind children and youth: An approach to community involvement,* Seattle: University of Washington, College of Education, 1983.

Vaughn, J., & Winslow, R. *Guidelines for community based recreation programs for special populations.* Alexandria, VA: National Therapeutic Recreation Society, 1979.

Voeltz, L.M., & Wuerch, B.B. Monitoring multiple behavioral effects of leisure activities training upon severely handicapped adolescents. In: L.M. Voeltz, J.A. Apffel, & B.B. Wuerch (eds.), *Leisure activities training for severely handicapped students: Instructional and evaluational strategies.* Honolulu: University of Hawaii, Department of Special Education, 1981.

Voeltz, L.M., Wuerch, B.B., & Wilcox, B. Leisure and recreation: Preparation for independence, integration, and self-fulfillment. In: B. Wilcox & B.T. Bellamy, *Design of high school programs for severely handicapped students.* Baltimore: Paul H. Brookes Publishing Co., 1982.

Wambold, C., & Bailey, R. Improving the leisure-time behaviors of severely/profoundly mentally retarded children through toy play. *AAESPH Review,* 1979, *4*(3), 237–250.

Wehman, P. Establishing play behaviors in mentally retarded youth. *Rehabilitation Literature,* 1975, *36*(8), 238–246.

Wehman, P. A leisure time activities curriculum for the developmentally disabled. *Education and Training of the Mentally Retarded,* 1976a, *11,* 309–313.

Wehman, P. Selection of play materials for the severely handicapped. *Education and Training of the Mentally Retarded,* 1976b, *11*(1), 46–50.

Wehman, P. *Helping the mentally retarded acquire play skills: A behavioral approach.* Springfield, IL: Charles C Thomas, 1977a.

Wehman, P. Research on leisure time and the severely developmentally disabled. *Rehabilitation Literature,* 1977b, *38*(4), 98–105.

Wehman, P. Effects of different environmental conditions on leisure time activity of the severely and profoundly handicapped. *Journal of Special Education,* 1978, *12*(2) 183–193.

Wehman, P., & Marchant, J.A. Developing gross motor recreational skills in children with severe behavioral handicaps. *Therapeutic Recreation Journal,* 1977, *11*(1), 48–54.

Wehman, P., Renzaglia, A., Berry, A., Schultz, R., & Karon, O. Developing a leisure skill repertoire in severely and profoundly handicapped adolescents and adults. *AAESPH Review,* 1978, *3,* 162–172.

Wehman, P., & Rettie, C. Increasing actions on play materials by severely retarded women through social reinforcement. *Therapeutic Recreation Journal,* 1975, *9,* 173–178.

Wehman, P., & Schleien, S. *Leisure programs for handicapped persons: Adaptations, techniques, and curriculum.* Baltimore: University Park Press, 1981.

Wehman, P., Schleien, S., & Kiernan, J. Age appropriate recreation programs for severely handicapped youth and adults. *Journal of the Association for the Severely Handicapped,* 1980, 395–407.

Wessel, J. *I CAN Program.* Northbrook, IL: Hubbard Scientific Co., 1976.

Witt, P., & Groom, R. Dangers and problems associated with current approaches to developing leisure interest finders. *Therapeutic Recreation Journal,* 1979, *13*(1), 19–31.

Wolfensberger, W. *Normalization: The principle of nor-malization in human services.* Toronto: National Institute on Mental Retardation, 1972.

Wuerch, B.B., & Voeltz, L.M. *Longitudinal leisure skills for severely handicapped learners.* Baltimore: Paul H. Brookes Publishing Co., 1982.

# Part V

## ORGANIZATIONAL
## AND FISCAL ISSUES

Throughout this volume reference is made frequently to "service systems." Yet few of the authors employing the term have ventured to define precisely what the term service system means. In its most permissive (and probably most pervasive) use, a *service system* is that amalgam of all services for which members of a particular target population (e.g., severely handicapped children and youth) would be eligible. However, more ideally, and as promoted in this volume, a service system is defined as indeed a system; that is, its components (agencies and people) are interrelated, interdependent, and coordinated to form a unified whole, they are governed by a common overriding principle, and they operate in service of a single purpose.

In the real world, the shape and success of established "systems" have been influenced by the fact that many of their components existed before the recognition of the benefits of service integration. In addition, many of these elements are based on a sense of personal or organizational mission that is stronger than any desire for or sense of the efficacy of purposeful unity. Furthermore, it is frequently the case that these potential system components do not operate on the same principle (e.g., normalization) or have similar conceptions of their purpose or mission. Because of these difficult human and organizational problems, change toward more systematic organization of services is more evolutionary than generative, more administrative than creative.

A number of steps critical to the establishment of a services system can be identified. Among these are: 1) developing a means of obtaining and allocating funding so that programmatic issues rather than financial issues determine clients' placement in the system; 2) establishing a plan for increasing the sense of shared purpose and programmatic direction across individual elements of the system through personnel development procedures; 3) providing active habilitation for clients, including a single set of goals, a unified training program, and standard assessment regardless of the number of different system components with which they have contact; 4) supporting case management that is based on and aggressively promotes the purpose and direction of the system; and 5) establishing a method of systematic and recurrent evaluation of clients, providers, services, and costs across the entire system, with a commitment to use those data for modifying service delivery. The two chapters in this section address some of the means to accomplish these organizational steps toward a working system of services.

In Chapter 12, Travis Thompson and Lyle Wray approach the problem of furthering the integration of severely handicapped persons, a dilemma that service providers and advocates must begin to solve. The approach suggested is an extension of applied behavior analysis, that is, the same basic model used in many effective habilitation programs. Thompson and Wray argue that providers and advocates must work effectively with many different groups of people (e.g., clients, parents, bureaucrats, legislators) at several different organizational levels (e.g., individual, family, local, state and federal) if they are to maximize the integration of handicapped citizens. The authors submit that the contingency manipulation skills of most providers and of many advocates can be readily applied to the policy and organizational impediments to providing appropriate and integrated programs.

Chapter 13, by William C. Copeland and Iver A. Iversen, describes the major fiscal disincentives existing today for deinstitutionalization and for the development of an alternative, community-oriented continuum of care. To counter the notable fiscal incentives that act to maintain severely handicapped persons in the most restrictive levels of care, the authors outline a strategy for coordinating program financing and management of service components so that these components can best accomplish their primary social mission. This "continuum-of-care approach" involves considerable reform and refinancing of present state systems, but the authors detail opportunities available to states to accomplish this. In the long run, they note, if procedures are not taken to establish funding mechanisms that—if not at the federal level, at least at the state level—redirect fiscal incentives toward less restrictive placements, deinstitutionalization will remain a tenuous and decelerated process.

# Chapter 12

# A Behavior Analytic
# Approach to
# Community Integration
# of Persons with
# Developmental Disabilities

*Travis Thompson and Lyle Wray*

Today it is widely believed that all services by congregate care institutions can be provided in local communities and that persons with developmental disabilities are, on balance, better off living, working, and learning in settings integrated into the community. After 20 years of action by the executive, legislative, and judicial branches of government in promoting community integration of persons with developmental disabilities, it is reasonable to ask why so many persons with developmental disabilities remain in large congregate care institutions.

Starting from the assumption that merely closing institutions is not a satisfactory solution, this chapter analyzes variables influencing community integration and addresses major classes of deterrents to community integration. The analysis is drawn from the experimental and applied behavior analysis literature (e.g., Skinner, 1953) and is offered as a framework for planning, implementing, and evaluating measures designed to assure community integration of persons with developmental disabilities. A major purpose is to show how such an analysis applies at different organizational levels in the service system. An account of the variables operating at several levels of organization is provided as the basis for an outline of variables that may be manipulated to achieve community integration. Another purpose of this chapter is to examine features of the behavior analytic knowledge base that may lead to an exploration of specific integration strategies not suggested by other conceptual frameworks. Not discussed, but assumed in the present chapter, are the basic tenets of normalization (Nirje, 1969; Wolfensberger, 1972) and the provision of the least restrictive alternative service, or living, learning, and working arrangement (Turnbull, 1981).

## A FRAMEWORK FOR ANALYSIS, INTERVENTION, AND EVALUATION

Although behavior analysis is widely known to incorporate the most effective set of principles and techniques for delivering services to persons with handicapping conditions in a variety of areas such as self-care (Bensberg, 1965; Haring & Bricker, 1976), residential living (Thompson & Grabowski, 1977), vocational training and placement (Bellamy, Horner, & Inman, 1979), communications (Guess, Sailor, & Baer, 1976), there is a major gulf between services provided to individuals and the translation of these principles into actions that are functional within large organizations or across entire human service systems. Indeed, behavior analysis has been viewed by some as a "bag of tricks" that is best used to deal with single behavioral deficiencies or problems. However, there has been a growing trend of applying behavioral procedures to more complex individual and social problems, with greater attention paid to the context of the planned intervention (e.g., ecological behavior analysis—see Rogers-Warren & Warren, 1977, and chapter by Chadsey-Rusch, in Bruininks & Lakin, 1985). Although incipient solutions are drawn from behavior analysis in waste management (Stokes & Fawcett, 1977), energy conservation (Winett & Nitzel, 1975), health care (Lutzker & Martin, 1981), and remedial or preventive educational programming (Greenwood, Delquadri, Stanley, Sasso, Wharton, & Schulte, 1981; Hall, Delquadri, Breenwood, & Thurstone, 1982), these approaches have not been extended to service systems as a whole for persons with developmental disabilities. Indeed, some applications of behavior analysis principles have bordered on the trivial, with little applicability to complex issues of human services. A number of writers have recognized, however, the potential merits of a behavior analytic strategy for dealing with significant societal issues and have used it to address complex organizations (Gilbert, 1978) and major problems such as population control (Malott, 1974; Zifferblatt & Hendricks, 1974).

The success of behavior analytically trained staff in working with persons with developmental disabilities is owed to the manipulation of proximal variables in the immediate environment of those served. Antecedent stimuli have been controlled carefully (Lovaas & Schreibman, 1971; Sidman & Stoddard, 1967), and responses to be taught have been assiduously broken down into sequences and components (Thompson & Carey, 1980). However, whether these and other variables are manipulated successfully as part of an educational or habilitative plan may not depend upon the proximal environment of the student or client but may, rather, be controlled by variables outside of that situation. The degree to which variables in the client's immediate environment have an opportunity to operate effectively may be determined at higher levels in an organizational framework—in other words, the successful manipulation of variables in a classroom might well depend upon the actions of and support provided by the U.S. Department of Education.

Six levels of social, economic, and political sources of control over variables in an individual's environment are shown schematically in Figure 1. A cardinal assumption of this chapter is that the major reasons community integration has not progressed are not related primarily to factors at the level of the individual's immediate environment; the necessary technology is generally available to deliver services to most students with developmental disabilities in schools, residential, and other community settings. In searching other levels for an explanation to this paradox, it is often not obvious which level within the organizational framework produces the greatest impact in facilitating variables in the individual's immediate environment.

Viewing the six levels of control from a strategic vantage point, it is often wise to first manipulate variables in the target individual's immediate environment and then work upward in the framework to enlist other variables that deter effective action in that individual's environment. If manipulating a variable at a given level fails to activate appropriate processes and events, the strategy calls for moving one step upward in the organizational hierarchy to identify the appropriate controlling events at that level. At some point in this process, altering an

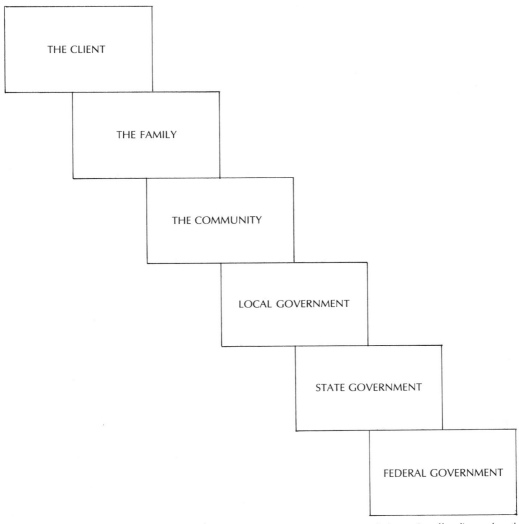

Figure 1.    Levels of social, economic, and political organization having an impact on community integration of handicapped youth.

appropriate controlling variable should, without further assistance, enable the existing variables at each of the lower levels to operate properly to yield the desired outcome. Although many experienced administrators believe that they already know which variables produce the greatest effect, and indeed some may have this expertise, the authors tend to believe that most such administrators too readily assume that they understand an extraordinarily complex network of interacting variables. Empirical evaluation of these assump-

tions for each class of deterrents to community integration is overdue.

*The three-term contingency*, the major conceptual device for a behavior analytic strategy to facilitate community integration of persons with developmental disabilities, was first proposed by B.F. Skinner (1938, 1953). *Put simply, the three terms are: 1) setting events or environmental circumstances, 2) actions, and 3) consequences of actions.* In analyzing organizational behavior, the setting events or environmental circumstances and the consequences following the actions of key agents must be analyzed carefully. This discussion explores the role of situational, agent response, and consequence factors at each level of client impact.

## Assumptions

The reasons many persons with developmental disabilities, particularly with mental retardation, continue to reside in large congregate care facilities or fail to do well in community alternatives can be understood by applying the three-term contingency analysis to: 1) the behavior of persons currently providing services to persons with developmental disabilities, or 2) the behavior of persons potentially influenced by community integration but who are at present affected minimally by persons with developmental disabilities. To increase the likelihood that greater numbers of persons with developmental disabilities will live successfully outside large institutions, reinforcement contingencies must be applied, formally and informally, to the behavior both of persons serving persons with developmental disabilities and of persons now having minimal contact with developmentally disabled individuals.

It is unlikely that any one or two variables will determine the success or failure of community integration. A thorough analysis of current controlling variables incompatible with community integration can result in changes needed to produce necessary organizational changes consistent with community integration. Moreover, persons at various organizational levels can influence the degree to which community integration goals can be met. It is not now known which behaviors of which individuals at which organizational levels offer the greatest potential contribution to realizing community integration goals.

In applying a problem-solving strategy to design organizational and other interventions, emphasis should be placed upon enlisting support of existing behavioral mechanisms rather than upon introducing alien variables into an existing structure. A further assumption of this chapter is that variables should be manipulated

at an organizational level whenever possible such that changing a single three-term contingency will have a widespread impact on relevant variables at lower organizational levels without specific interventions being mounted at those levels.

## THREE-TERM CONTINGENCY ANALYSIS

### The Situation

The environmental circumstances necessary to initiate a sequence of productive actions by an agent comprise the first term of the three-term contingency relationships. Identifiable situations (or stimuli) set the occasion for an action by a key agent in the life of a person with developmental disabilities. For instance, a social worker may receive information from a school program that is inadequate to make a meaningful referral to a residential program. In such a case the school report may show the student in question is labeled as a "behavior problem" or is said to "act out." While such information may affect certain behaviors (or attitudes or predispositions) of the agent, such information does not provide the necessary information for the social worker to take effective action.

A second example of situational variables involves a director of special education in a school district who may be concerned about the lack of student progress through a series of service delivery levels. To sharpen the discriminative power of this situational stimulus (the number of students progressing through service levels per unit of time), the director may develop decision rules based on graphic summaries of student progress, which set the occasion for administrative actions. In a school district in Minnesota, a director of special education found that an average of 7 weeks was required from the time of referral of a possible change in the level of service to the time that action was actually taken. His administrative response was to mandate that all action on referrals for service level change was to be completed within 2 weeks of the date of the referral. As a consequence, there was a vast acceleration in the graduation of students to less-restrictive services within the school district.

A third example of situational variables in the three-term contingency would be the presentation of data to state legislators summarizing the number of persons with developmental disabilities moving from more- to less-restrictive living arrangements. Policy and funding decisions by state legislators should be based upon such information. Too often, however, legislative action is required in the virtual absence of information of this sort.

## Agency Response

At each level of political, social, and economic organization outlined in Figure 1, various people have the opportunity to take actions that may facilitate community integration. In the preceding example, the director of special education services for a school district mandated reducing the time from the date of referral for level of service review by 70%. Frequently, problems of agent response relate to a lack of familiarity with possible actions that can be taken or a lack of skill to take action.

Parents, for example, are presented with seemingly overwhelming responsibilities in connection with the return of their son or daughter to the community from an institution. These responsibilities are ambiguous and frightening, since the parents do not know what to expect from their young adult son or daughter and have no idea how they can help in his or her community integration. If a son or daughter left home at an early age, the parents would likely be familiar with their child's behavioral strengths and weaknesses. In the case of an 18-year-old who has been institutionalized since he or she was very young, however, the parents may not be sure that they have any meaningful role to play in their child's life. Among the repertoires that parents might be helped to learn are advocacy skills for participating in school meetings in relation to the requirements of Public Law 94-142 and in individual program planning meetings at a new residential facility for their son or daughter. Parents who are helped to develop such skills, are provided with relevant responses that they

can make to facilitate successful community integration of their son or daughter, and this may in turn reduce their resistance to having their child returned to the community.

Response deficiencies are commonly presented when social workers are faced with a crisis and a person is about to be removed from a group home because of behavior problems. To increase the probability that effective responses will be made, social workers need to have at their disposal actions that lead to in-home crisis assistance and temporary respite placement for families and others providing residential services. Response deficiencies may arise from a lack of awareness that such options are feasible or because of an inability or unwillingness to expend the necessary effort to find such resources. All too often, few, if any, resources are available until after an institutional placement is made. By giving parents and others help at home, it may be possible to keep in the community a youngster who would otherwise be placed in an institutional setting. If living at home is no longer a viable option even with a range of supports, the social worker should be able to seek alternative placement, such as in a foster home or group home. Finally, as a last resort, the social worker should be capable of taking action to secure short-term placement of an individual in a controlled setting—the most restrictive measure short of institutionalization. These various agent responses, if strengthened, provide options to prevent reinstitutionalization and to facilitate the reintegration into the community of a young man or woman returning from an institution.

## Consequences of Agent Actions

The most common and serious problems associated with integrating mentally retarded individuals into a community revolve around providing adequate consequences consistent with policy objectives. Typically, there are inadequate positive consequences for actions consistent with community integration objectives, and there are few adverse consequences for actions inconsistent with it.

For example, an employer in a fast food restaurant might be reluctant to hire a moderately retarded worker because of feared resistance from other employees. Offsetting consequences could be provided, such as state and federal government tax incentives and productivity subsidies to business to promote hiring of such individuals. In addition, a portion of such tax incentives could be dedicated to salary supplements for nonhandicapped coworkers to assist in the person's successful employment placement.

One of the major impediments to community integration in some states is the political and economic resistance put up by state employees of institutions, who are fearful of losing their jobs. Providing appropriate, meaningful consequences to state hospital employees might be expected to markedly diminish their fears. The state could, for example, provide training for displaced workers to do similar work in community programs and could assure them employment for a specified period during which they would receive the same level of pay for work in community residential, day, or support programs that they received in state hospitals. Since the economic base of many communities in proximity to state hospitals is linked to employment in the state hospital, measures such as identifying substitute employers or providing training for community-based services could diminish the worries of people in the surrounding community who are concerned about income for state hospital employees and the effects that losing that income would have on the community.

In providing incentives consistent with community integration goals, care must be taken to consider the range of currently available responses that various agents have at their disposal and the contingencies of reinforcement associated with each. It is widely known in the literature on behavior analysis that many performances exist in natural settings under concurrent reinforcement schedules. For instance, a worker in a sheltered workshop may be rewarded for the production of assembly items on a token schedule contingent on the number of items produced per unit time. However, the same worker may be concurrently socially rewarded by peers for engaging in a variety of off-task and disturbed behaviors. Social reinforcement for these inappropriate behaviors is often available on a more favorable reinforcement schedule than reinforcement that is contingent on productive work. Depending on the relative parameter values of social reinforcement for maladaptive behavior, and the schedule associated with productive work, a given incentive manipulation may have little effect. Similarly, there are numerous examples in social service systems of attempts to provide incentives to encourage welfare recipients to seek gainful employment rather than continuing dependence on welfare payments. Unfortunately, designers of these programs have often failed or been unable to consider alternative ways in which the welfare recipient can obtain the same reinforcement without having to work, that is, on a much more favorable reinforcement schedule. Hence, it is not surprising that implementing a federal work program may only lead the client to seek county social service agency services instead of applying for work and federal benefits. The literature provides ample guidance in designing ways for using concurrent reinforcement schedules to design incentive systems to increase effective rather than ineffective client outcomes.

## LEVELS OF CLIENT IMPACT

Figure 2 illustrates loci of client impact arranged according to where the client resides, where he or she works or learns, and where the client spends his or her leisure time, as well as the organizational levels at which various agents take actions that have an impact on the client. The result is a matrix of 18 possible combinations of domains of living and of levels of agent action. Events in each cell of this matrix can be subjected to a three-term contingency analysis—that is, the role of the situational stimulus variables, the available agent responses or actions, and the consequences of agent actions that will have an impact on the degree to which variables operating in that cell

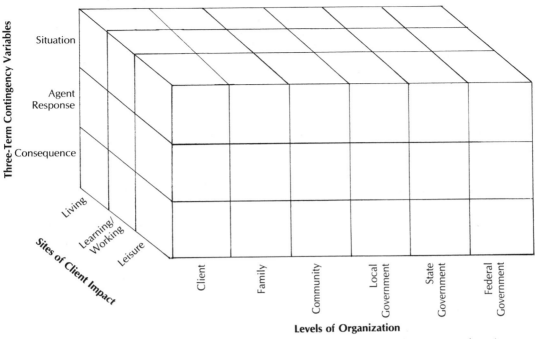

Figure 2. Sites of client impact and levels of organization at which three-term contingency variables operate to determine successfulness of community integration.

facilitate or deter community integration can be specified.

The complexity of the matrix presented in Figure 2 may lead the observer to conclude that the proposed analysis is too onerous to be practical for action. The person with responsibility for managing the analysis of variables in each of these cells—that is, a total of 54 possible classes of locations-domains of living three-term contingency combinations—cannot be the same person directly involved in intervening with the client, family, or school. Because many variables are involved and because it is not known in advance which variables will produce particular outcomes, it is necessary to explore variables at each level for a given client problem. After an initial analysis is performed, it may be possible to weight the contribution of variables at each of the combinations of domains of living and locus of client impact to more effectively allocate resources. Moreover, an effective analysis may make it possible to manipulate variables at higher organizational levels—such as the federal, state, or local gov-

ernment—which will require minimal specific additional intervention at lower organizational levels such as the school, family, or direct client intervention. To facilitate the reader's understanding of the way in which a three-term contingency analysis can be helpful across these domains of living and locations of client impact, an illustrated example is explored here across several cells in this matrix. The reader will then be able to extrapolate similar analyses to the remaining cells.

Karen M. is a fifteen-year-old severely mentally retarded youth who lived at home until she was 7 years old. Because of behavior problems that the family was unable to manage, she was placed in foster care. After living in three successive foster homes, Karen was placed in a state hospital where she resided from the age of eight to fifteen. Because of the development of residential facilities in the community and because of more vigorous action by her county social worker, Karen is now recommended for placement in the community. Although Karen has been labeled "severely retarded," she understands that there are plans for her to be moved from a living unit on the second floor of a ninety-bed building in a large state residential facility. She finds the idea of such a move frightening, and when asked by the social worker whether she wants to move, she indicates great reluctance. Although Karen may receive far fewer rewards and may experience far more aversive events at the state institution than she would in the community, because of her history, Karen finds continued residence in the state institution much less threatening than a move to the community.

A three-term contingency analysis suggests that this recent history, the current stimulus circumstances, and the nature of the reinforcers and punishers associated with changing from one setting to another favor remaining in the state hospital. To help change Karen's perception of such a move, several steps might be taken. Karen might be taken for a one-day visit to a group home in the community near the institution. By spending time with the staff and with other residents of the group home, she may find that there are many reinforcing activities in the group home relative to those in her current residence. She might be assured by her parents that they will visit more often if the group home is near their home. During other visits to the community Karen could be exposed to other rewarding activities that are less available in the institution. Thus, although Karen might initially resist the idea of moving to a community residence, by conducting an analysis of this resistance, it may be possible to assist her in arriving at a different decision concerning her future residence.

Once Karen returns to the community, there may be problems associated with provision of service in the public school program in the local district. The teacher who is available has had experience with children who were mildly retarded and learning disabled, but has had little experience with youngsters with greater handicaps. When the teacher meets Karen for the first time and is confronted with a tantrum, the teacher may decide that Karen does not belong in her classroom in that school. In fact,

the teacher refers Karen to the trainable mentally retarded (TMR) classroom in a consolidated program miles away. That the teacher could refer Karen to a new setting without having thoroughly assessed ways of resolving Karen's resistance to integration suggests that there may be no deterrents to segregating handicapped students and few incentives for integrating handicapped students in that school district.

Since Public Law 94-142, the Education for All Handicapped Children Act, requires that the most appropriate education be provided in the least restrictive environment, Karen's parents can play an important role by bringing an advocate or an attorney to the initial meeting with the teacher to assure that such a referral away from an integrated school is not made. In addition, since the teacher has an inadequate repertoire of responses to make in dealing with Karen's behavior problems, it may be necessary either to obtain assistance from an experienced teacher, or to provide the current teacher released time to receive further relevant training, or to replace the teacher in question with a more appropriate staff member. To make the second option possible, funds must be available at the district level to give the teacher time away from normal classroom duties to attend courses and workshops and to receive direct supervision in the application of appropriate educational procedures for youths with severe handicaps. At the level of the school district, which has control over provision of financial resources to individual schools, funds can be made available contingent on the proportion of students of specified levels of functioning who are integrated into school settings with less handicapped or nonhandicapped peers. Figure 3 shows an example of a formula by which incentives could be provided to a school, contingent on the percentage of students with handicaps in the mild, moderate, and severe range who are integrated by varying degrees with less handicapped or nonhandicapped peers. Although incentives may appear unworkable, it would be relatively easy to provide the necessary incentive to school prin-

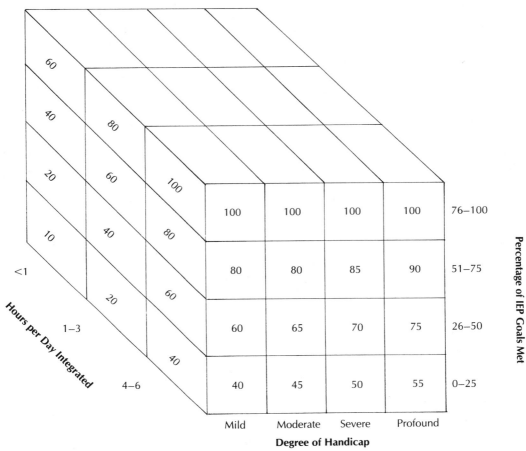

Figure 3. Sample state aid reimbursement formula as a function of degree of student handicap, hours per day of educational integration, and percentage of IEP goals met.

cipals to make efforts to integrate more severely handicapped students within their schools. At present, it is often easier and less costly for a school or district to segregate all students with severe disabilities.

At the level of a state government department of education, data provided by individual districts throughout a state could be summarized and used to mount comparisons of the proportions of students with varying types and degrees of disabilities who spend specified amounts of time within integrated educational activities. In addition, districts would be required to provide data on the proportion of Individual Education Plan (IEP) goals met within particular identified groups of students. It

would be reasonable for a state department of education to make funding and other resource allocation decisions contingent, in part, on progress toward stated objectives. And if a given school district finds that 25% of IEP goals are met, it might be reasonable to set a goal of 40% for a following year.

While there are ways in which districts could manipulate IEP goals to make it easier to reach stated goals—for example by setting goals at an extremely low level—this manipulation could be detected and remedied by periodic monitoring and statewide comparisons among goal systems. Thus although there would probably be some questionable reporting practices, the long-term effect would be improved efforts at integration of students with severe handicaps and the development of more adequate educational programs.

These procedures, from the level of state government to the school district, to the school principal, and to the individual classroom teacher, should have a profound impact on the degree to which Karen is provided with an integrated education that involves effective procedures to meet sound IEP goals. Karen's parents, having been assisted to be more informed and active participants in the IEP planning process, could further assist by monitoring the degree to which reasonable goals are actually set. Finally, federal resources, as ultimately funneled down to school districts, could provide further incentives to provide additional training for teachers such as Karen's and to provide financial incentives in the form of additional support staff contingent upon maintenance of an adequate standard of educational programming for students such as Karen who have severe handicaps.

## A PROBLEM-SOLVING APPROACH TO DETERRENTS TO COMMUNITY INTEGRATION

Zifferblatt and Hendricks (1974) have proposed a seven-step problem-solving approach for addressing complex behavioral systems, which is applicable to the task of assuring community integration of individuals with severe handicaps.

*Step 1: Analyze the problem.* The primary problem is that people are admitted to institutions and tend not to leave them for a long time. While they are there, their quality of life is often seriously wanting (Blatt & Kaplan, 1966). Determining a solution to this problem is predicated on an adequate definition of the problem. An incorrect definition of the problem may lead to entirely nonproductive efforts. For example, from the 1940s to the 1970s it was widely assumed that "the problem" of heroin addiction was that heroin caused physical dependence when the drug was taken repeatedly. Although it is true that heroin causes physical dependence, many other drugs with

high dependence liability cause little or no physical dependence. By defining the problem of heroin addiction in terms of physical dependence, problem solvers were distracted from the more fundamental issue—namely that there are conditions under which various chemicals will and will not serve as powerful rewards or reinforcers that regulate large portions of the user's behavior (see Thompson, 1981). By redefining the question, it has been possible to develop new strategies for treating heroin dependence and to prevent the introduction of new dependence-producing drugs (Thompson & Unna, 1977).

Similarly, the history of attempts to understand the reasons for segregating retarded persons contains numerous tangential and occasionally bogus issues. Not only is it too easy for mentally retarded persons to be admitted to institutions, but there are numerous incentives to keep them there, and there are many deterrents to and few incentives for moving them out of institutions.

*Step 2: Perform a functional analysis of the problem-related behaviors.* Before any intervention is undertaken, it is necessary to perform an interpretive functional analysis. What are the relevant situational stimulus factors (e.g., data) and agent-response factors? Who is reinforcing whom, with what, to what effect, in what situations, and at what variety of levels? Assistance for this analysis needs to be drawn from a variety of disciplines including public administration, organizational psychology, political science, and behavior analysis. The three-term contingency analysis that is typically performed in resolving individual client problems can also be applied more broadly at a given level of organization. Among factors determining actions by a state legislator who serves on a welfare subcommittee that recommends appropriations for state hospitals is the likelihood that the legislator's vote to provide employee incentives in proportion to the percentage of residents who leave the state hospital would influence his or her reelection.

*Step 3: Designate target behaviors or outcomes.* Agents at each level of organization and in each locus of client impact have specific actions that they can take that will influence the degree to which the student or client is effectively integrated into the community. These actions are called *target behaviors,* and each target behavior has associated with it a specific expected outcome. Clients, families, members of the surrounding community, teachers, other school personnel, social workers, administrators, other staff members in local government, officials in state government such as directors of special education, state legislators, the governor, and, finally, federal officials—all have their own target behaviors that are the object of concern within each domain of living.

Our analysis may suggest that a key target behavior of the director of special education for a state department of education is the promulgation of monitoring procedures for school districts. One must ask which discriminative stimuli—that is which setting conditions—and which consequences could be provided for such a government official to increase the likelihood that monitoring procedures will be promulgated. Target behaviors for members of the local community may include visits to a new group home or writing letters to state representatives or county commissioners to comment favorably upon the new group home developed in their neighborhood. The target behavior for a representative of Congress may be a vote on a critical subcommittee bill that will influence funding for special education programs.

As the analysis proceeds higher in the organizational framework, less is likely to be known concerning which behaviors of which agents are most important in producing outcomes. Nonetheless, an experimental approach along with good recordkeeping, should reveal which actions are most effective. By refining the target behaviors one sets as objects of change, it may be possible over a period of years to refine a technology to more adequately define targets at each organizational level.

*Step 4: Formulate behavioral objectives.* The goal of an organizational intervention must be stated in measurable terms, and the agents responsible for carrying out actions must be specified. For instance, a principal in a public school notices that there is a low rate of student progress in self-care skill areas. She hypothesizes that teachers are either collecting no systematic data on student progress or they are not attending to the data they have available to them. Her objective is to double the rate of student progress over a 9-month school year. She implements a new plan by which graphic data of the progress of each student and the average for the class is to be publicly displayed on a bulletin board outside each classroom. In this way, each student's progress is drawn to the teachers' attention daily, and progress toward the objective is immediately apparent to all who might walk by the classroom.

*Step 5: Develop an intervention strategy.* Behavior analysts have been chided for assuming that the same methods that were effective at the individual level will necessarily produce change in broader groups and organizations. This naiveté may have evolved from the myth that positive outcomes of individual clients should serve as major reinforcers for agents acting at higher levels within an organization. Although it may be possible to arrange for client outcomes to become the important and meaningful consequences, this is most often not the case.

The major question concerns the *types* of interventions and levels of interventions required to achieve a given level of community integration (e.g., "no mentally retarded persons shall live in a residential accommodation of over six persons"). Performing a three-term contingency analysis and assigning probable weights to classes of variables in each cell of the matrix shown in Figure 2 provides the information necessary to plan for an effective intervention. A current pressing problem is the determination of priorities in the levels of intervention within the matrix. Several possible priorities exist, including social experimentation strategies involving fostering a variety of approaches to solving problems and transferring technology developed in successful interventions, as well as determining those strategies that produce "ripple effects" (i.e., interventions that with a minimum of effort at one organizational level produce a substantial change in behavior that is widespread and lasting at other levels of possible intervention).

*Step 6: Implement the intervention strategy.* The complexity of intervention strategies and techniques, ranging from setting up parent and child-support groups to altering large-scale government programs, demands a carefully designed system of coordinated management. Methods drawn from operations research and allied areas—for example, latticing and critical-path method—can be very useful (Budde & Menolascino, 1971). In controlling these processes, data and the role of data as stimuli and consequences for decisions are critically important.

*Step 7: Evaluate implementation.* Data must be compared with established behavioral objectives in a timely and ongoing fashion. Behavior analysis is a rich source of technology for data collection and analysis, in that much has been learned about conducting direct measurement of behavior and about setting up behavioral observation systems (Johnston & Pennypacker, 1980). Those data that are to be recorded are determined by the actions that an individual is expected to make at a given level of organization (e.g., parent, teacher, school principal, district special education director, and so on). The frequency of recording and of data review are determined by the sensitivity of the variable in question and the length of time from an agent action until one can expect to see a change in the variable being measured. Recording irrelevant but otherwise interesting data or collecting appropriate data too frequently is counterproductive. Increasing the effort required in data collection without increasing the return from the data jeopardizes the long-term success of such a venture.

In evaluating a child's progress in dressing skills, the child's performance and the degree of assistance provided by the staff might be recorded appropriately several times a day and reviewed for progress weekly. In a classroom, the number of children meeting individual goals on time might be reviewed quarterly. At a school, the number of student goals met per quarter might be measured. At a state department of education, the degree of integration of students with severe handicaps might be reviewed on an annual basis. Decision rules for relating data and agent action are available at the level of the individual student and teacher (White & Liberty, 1976) and are being explored at the level of the classroom and school. Far more attention needs to be paid to the development of decision-making rules for a variety of settings.

## CONCLUSION

Rather than present a detailed agenda for action based upon the matrix presented earlier, the following statements suggest guidelines for moving forward on the complex process of assuring that persons with severe handicaps are integrated into community life.

1. Good intentions are not enough. Critical variables in the three-term contingency must be right for community integration to be fully effected.

2. The reasons that persons with developmental disabilities reside in large congregate care institutions or fail to prosper in the community can be conceptualized by applying the three-term contingency analysis to 1) the behavior of those currently involved in providing services to persons with developmental disabilities; and 2) the behavior of persons who are both potentially influenced by and have the ability to affect the course of deinstitutionalization but who are currently minimally affected by developmentally disabled persons.

3. Reinforcement contingencies applied to the behavior of persons now involved in providing services to persons with developmental disabilities or to the behavior of people currently having minimal contact with such persons but who would influence or be influenced by deinstitutionalization can increase the likelihood that more persons with developmental disabilities will reside successfully outside of institutions.

4. No single or several variables or classes

of variables will determine the success or failure of deinstitutionalization.

5.  A thorough contingency analysis of current controlling variables inconsistent with deinstitutionalization policy can lead to suggestions for manipulating variables to produce system changes more consistent with these policies.

6.  The behavior of persons at various organizational levels affects the degree to which deinstitutionalization goals can be met, but it is not clear on first examination which behaviors of which individuals at which organizational levels contribute most or least to realizing community integration goals.

7.  In designing analyses and interventions, focus should be placed on enlisting behavioral mechanisms and variables that are already operative in settings, rather than relying extensively upon the introduction of alien variables and mechanisms.

8.  Variables should be manipulated at an administrative level such that change of a relevant variable will have widespread impact on other relevant variables at other levels of intervention without specific interventions mounted at those levels.

9.  There may be many ways to achieve the desired community integration outcomes. There is at present little basis for determining which methods are more effective than others and for determining what side effects and costs are to be expected for each. Greater emphasis should be placed on experimental strategies in which various communities pursue alternative data-based tactics and strategies so that ultimately answers to these questions may be obtained.

10. A key element in approving community integration outcomes is the careful design of data management systems at each organizational level, which provide relevant information to decision makers.

11. The objective of such analysis at each organizational level is to develop empirically based educational, habilitative, and service delivery systems based upon knowledge about key variables operating at each organizational level.

## REFERENCES

Bellamy, G.T., Horner, R.H., & Inman, D.P. *Vocational habilitation of severely retarded adults: A direct service technology*. Baltimore: University Park Press, 1979.

Bensberg, G. (ed.). *Teaching the mentally retarded: A handbook for ward personnel*. Atlanta: Southern Regional Education Board, 1965.

Blatt, B., & Kaplan, F. *Christmas in purgatory*. Boston: Allyn & Bacon, 1966.

Bruininks, R.H., & Lakin, K.C. (eds.). *Living and learning in the least restrictive environment*. Baltimore: Paul H. Brookes Publishing Co., 1985.

Budde, J.F., & Menolascino, F.J. Systems technology and retardation: Applications to vocational habilitation. *Mental Retardation, 1971, 9,* 11–16.

Gilbert, T.F. *Human competence: Engineering worthy performance*. New York: McGraw-Hill Book Co., 1978.

Greenwood, G.R., Delquadri, J., Stanley, S., Sasso, G., Wharton, P., & Schulte, D. Allocating opportunity to learn as a basis for academic remediation: A developing model for teaching. In: R. Rutherford & A. Prieto (eds.), *Monograph in behavior disorders*. Reston, VA: Council for Exceptional Children, 1981.

Guess, D., Sailor, W., & Baer, D.M. *Functional speech and language training for the severely handicapped*. Lawrence, KS; H & H Enterprises, 1976.

Hall, R.V., Delquadri, J., Breenwood, C.R., & Thurstone, L. The importance of opportunity to respond in children's academic success. In: E.B. Edgar, N.G. Hanging, J.R. Jenkins, & C.G. Pious (eds.), *Mentally handicapped children: Education and training*. Baltimore: University Park Press, 1982.

Haring, N., & Bricker, D. Overview of comprehensive services for the severely/profoundly handicapped. In: N. Haring & L. Brown (eds.), *Teaching the severely handicapped*, Vol 1. New York: Grune & Stratton, 1976.

Johnston, J.M., & Pennypacker, H.S. *Strategies and tactics of human behavioral research*. Lawrence, KS: Erlbaum Associates, 1980.

Lovaas, O.I., & Schreibman, L. Stimulus overselectivity of autistic children in a two-stimulus situation. *Behavior Research and Therapy, 1971, 9,* 305–310.

Lutzker, J.R., & Martin, J.A. *Behavior change*. Monterey, CA: Brooks/Cole Publishing Co., 1981.

Malott, R.W. A behavioral-systems approach to the design of human services. In: D. Harshbarger & R.F. Maley (eds.), *Behavior analysis and systems analysis: An integrative approach to mental health programs*. Kalamazoo, MI: Behaviordelia, 1974.

Nirje, B. The normalization principle and its human management implications. In: R. Kugel & W. Wolfensberger (eds.), *Changing patterns of residential services for the mentally retarded.* Washington, D.C.: President's Committee on Mental Retardation, 1969.

Rogers-Warren, A., & Warren, S.F. (eds.). *Ecological perspectives in behavior analysis.* Baltimore: University Park Press, 1977.

Sidman, M.R., & Stoddard, L.T. The effectiveness of fading in programming a simultaneous form discrimination for retarded children. *Journal of the Experimental Analysis of Behavior,* 1967, *10,* 3–16.

Skinner, B.F. *The behavior of organisms.* New York: Appelton-Century-Crofts, 1938.

Skinner, B.F. *Science and human behavior.* New York: Macmillan Co., 1953.

Stokes, T.F., & Fawcett, S.B. Evaluating municipal policy: An analysis of a refuse packaging program. *Journal of Applied Behavior Analysis,* 1977, *10,* 391–398.

Thompson, T. Behavioral mechanisms and loci of drug dependence: An overview. In: T. Thompson and C.E. Johanson (eds.), *Behavioral pharmacology of human drug dependence* (NIDA Research Monograph 37). Washington, DC: U.S. Government Printing Office, 1981.

Thompson, T., & Carey, A. Structured normalization: Intellecutal and adaptive behavior changes in a residential setting. *Mental Retardation,* 1980, *18*(4), 193–197.

Thompson, T., & Grabowski, J. (eds.). *Behavior modification of the mentally retarded* (2nd ed.). New York: Oxford University Press, 1977.

Thompson, T., Griffiths, R., & Pickens, R. In: F. Hoffmeister (ed), *Psychic dependence.* Berlin: Springer Verlag, 1973.

Thompson, T., & Unna, K. *Predicting dependence liability of stimulant and depressant drugs.* Baltimore: University Park Press, 1977.

Turnbull, H.R. (ed.). *The least restrictive alternative: Principles and practices.* Washington, DC: American Association on Mental Deficiency, 1981.

White, O.R., & Liberty, K.A. Evaluation and measurement. In: N.G. Haring & R.L. Schiefelbush (eds.), *Teaching special children.* New York: McGraw-Hill Book Co., 1976.

Winett, R.A., & Nitzel, M.T. Behavioral ecology: Contingency management and consumer energy use. *American Journal of Community Psychology,* 1975, *3,* 123–133.

Wolfensberger, W. *Normalization.* Toronto: National Institute on Mental Retardation, 1972.

Zifferblatt, S.M. & Hendricks, C.G. Applied behavioral analysis of societal problems: Population change, a case in point. *American Psychologist,* 1974, *29,* 750–761.

Chapter 13

# Developing
# Financial Incentives for
# Placement in the
# Least Restrictive Alternative

*William C. Copeland and Iver A. Iversen*

Current planning and financing of services for developmentally disabled persons in the United States is fragmented, it tends to keep important parts of the funding for services "invisible" to planners at federal and state levels of government, it promotes fiscal incentives diametrically opposed to program theory and court decisions, and it includes no coherent budget and program strategy. The result is a large, incoherent "nonsystem" of public and private bureaucracies, budgets, and services that is highly resistant to change.

In the arena where change must occur—the state government—there are few instruments available for bringing about massive program reform in a system as large and complex as is the publicly financed developmental disabilities system. This system cost about $15 billion in federal, state, and local tax funds for care and services to about 1.7 million people in 1983. Developing an effective service delivery system requires at least one of the following conditions:

1.  A clear national policy, with financing that supports the policy rhetoric rather than undercuts it;

2.  A large-scale, unrelenting wave of public demand for reform; or
3.  A reform strategy that includes a detailed plan and enough new money to "buy off" or neutralize most of the opposition and to pay for the new initiatives.

A coherent developmental disabilities policy at the national level is a preferred option. However, it is not yet clear that the present or future administrations will support a targeted reform policy and the financing needed to achieve reform. Whatever demands there have been in the past have not been enough to secure reform, and it seems unlikely that a new wave of public pressure is in store. This leaves the third option as the most viable approach at this point. The four sections of this chapter outline various aspects of such a reform strategy.

A focus on the third option implies that it should be possible to reform developmental disabilities programs to meet the requirements of modern program and legal theory, such as the most normalized treatment in the least restrictive environment, while at the same time reducing the total costs. Furthermore, for that option to succeed, the reforms must be instituted in such a way that the reorganized system actually costs less at *each* participating level of government than did the prereform system.

The primary strategy of such reform calls for: first, a rational approach to program design (the continuum of care); second, the means to link this approach to a reasonable set of budget incentives (interagency budgeting); and, third, a management method that employs the budget incentives to advantage in program development (continuum management). (Each of these components is discussed briefly in the paragraphs following.) A family and community-based program of service for developmentally disabled persons can be funded through intertitle transfers of federal funds, client entitlements, and more effective leveraging of state and local revenues. New state or local funds are not needed. Properly managed, the development of a continuum of community resources should achieve a net reduction in total operating costs and in costs to each major fiscal actor.

*The Continuum-of-Care Concept.* In recent years many concepts have evolved to address the general question of how society should provide for its developmentally disabled citizens—prevention (primary, secondary, and tertiary), continuum of care, normalization, deinstitutionalization, communitization, integrated services, community-based services, and various combinations of these concepts. However, there is as yet no unifying theme to satisfactorily replace that of "the institution." This lack is reflected in the diverse array of service systems that have emerged as alternatives to institutions.

In the past, among the competing service systems, only state institutions have enjoyed a stable professional hierarchy, uncomplicated funding, and the confidence of state agencies and legislative bodies, the judiciary, the affected families, and other groups involved in decision-making on behalf of developmentally disabled persons. Despite the many successes of normalization programs over the past decade and the increased public, program, and judicial opinion against institutions, any movement away from institutionalization promises to be slow without the strong backing of elected and appointed officials, legislative leaders, and others in a position to promote change. Such individuals must first be convinced that investments in alternatives to institutionalization are both fiscally attractive and programmatically sound.

The continuum-of-care concept was selected by the authors as best embodying the others and thus may be considered one of the more rational approaches to program design. It calls for housing, care, services, and employment consistent with each client's capabilities. A configuration approaching the full range of options—from total support to independent living—must be available.

*Interagency Budgeting.* Interagency budgeting is a method of tying program design to a reasonable set of budget incentives. A critical element of this strategy is the treatment of all human service budgets as a single budget. This involves ending program fragmentation through initiating budgeting by target group (e.g., aging, developmental disabilities, mental illness, physically handicapped, child welfare). Particularly important is the avoidance of "single-account blindness," in which savings are achieved in one account at greater cost to another or in which truncated pricing is used to hold down one state agency's spending through simultaneous shifts of costs to other state accounts or to county governments and through curtailing of their opportunities for federal reimbursement. This approach also involves using continuum-of-care management as an adjunct to, and as an integral part of, budget management.

Interagency budgeting further involves maximizing client entitlements through integrated eligibility and referral processes. Using such a strategy, intertitle transfers, to the extent permitted by client eligibility for more than one entitlement program, help finance continuum management.

*Continuum Management.* Continuum management requires a strong client orientation and is conducted for programs and clients simultaneously. At the program level, it is best illustrated by example. Using a simplified case of a

Table 1. Alternative long-term care arrangements and associated costs

| Living arrangements | Annual cost for client | Alternative 1 | | Alternative 2 | |
|---|---|---|---|---|---|
| | | Number of clients | Total cost ($ millions) | Number of clients | Total cost ($ millions) |
| Institutions | 40,000 | 2,200 | 88.0 | 1,200 | 48.0 |
| Community ICF/MR[a] | 28,000 | 5,000 | 140.0 | 4,500 | 126.0 |
| Supervised apartment | 18,000 | 0 | 0.0 | 1,500 | 27.0 |
| Total | | | 228.0 | | 201.0 |

Note: See text for further explanation.

[a]ICF/MR, intermediate care facility for the mentally retarded.

midwestern state, Table 1 illustrates two alternatives for the organization of long-term care. Alternative 1 in the table is the present situation. An estimated 1,000 institutionalized developmentally disabled persons would be more appropriately placed in community ICF/MR facilities[1], and 1,500 community ICF/MR residents are ready for at least semi-independent (supervised) apartment living. The move to Alternative 2 can be expected to reduce the total cost of care from approximately $228 million per year to approximately $201 million, with the $27 million in savings distributed to federal ($11.8 million dollars) and state and county ($15.2 million) governments.

At the client level, continuum management calls for options along a continuum of care that are consistent with each client's capabilities. Such options include ICF/MR facilities, non-Medicaid group homes, and other forms of congregate care (e.g., personal care in specialized foster care homes). They also include various forms of assisted and unassisted independent living (such as supervised apartment living) and home support programs.

Client movement along the continuum of care historically has been (and remains in some states) toward the long-term institutional care

end of the continuum. The deinstitutionalization, communitization, service integration, prevention movement, and normalization movement all have evolved to reverse the institutionalization tendency. These trends are documented extensively by Bruininks and Lakin (1985) in their introductory chapter to that volume. Despite the successes of these trends and demonstrations of their cost-effectiveness, there has never been sufficient acknowledgment that they should direct funding strategies. This is particularly disturbing, given the evidence that, with continuum management strategies directing the service system, clients can live at higher levels of independence than before, that all levels of government can enjoy savings from the move to community services, and that there is enough in such savings to provide financing for the program's capital needs.

There are two organizational requirements for implementing interagency budgeting and continuum management. The first is a budget organization capable of treating a large number of budget streams as part of a single, integrated budget for developmentally disabled persons (e.g., a state budget office, a state office for human services, or a multiagency task force

---

[1]ICFs/MR (intermediate care facilities for the mentally retarded) are Title XIX (Medicaid) certified and reimbursed facilities. Most ICF/MR beds are in large state-operated facilities (there were about 99,000 residents in state institutions of more than 150 beds as of June 30, 1982). "Community ICF/MR facilities" are generally smaller and privately operated. As of June 30, 1982, there were approximately 31,600 private ICF/MR residents, of whom about 26,750 were living in facilities of 150 or fewer beds. The federal government's share of allowable Medicaid costs ranges from about half to three-quarters, as determined by the individual state's per capita income.

with some form of budget authority). The second is a program organization capable of coordinating client placements and of budgeting for all program components along the continuum of care—from state institutions down through all of the community programs and into the home.

## CONTINUUM-OF-CARE: DEFINITION AND POLICY OPTIONS

A continuum of care is a set of care opportunities (for a group of persons characterized by similar or identical problems) that are ordered according to their intensity of care, their cost, their restrictiveness of environment, or some other dimension. Such continua can be implicit (developed as a group of fragmented care opportunities that can be described according to the various levels of the continuum) or they can be explicit (organized for programmatic or fiscal purposes—that is, for least restrictive and most appropriate placement, or according to the least cost to one or more of the major fiscal actors).

In most states, the continua of care are implicit. The growth of most continua has been influenced at different times by fiscal history (especially the Social Security Act's Section 1121,[2] Title XIX—ICF/MR statutes, and Title XVI), by program theory (the rise of habilitation approaches and normalization goals), and by court decisions (right to treatment in the least restrictive environment). Most current continua of care for developmentally disabled persons include the following care opportunities, running roughly from most to least restrictive: state institutions, skilled nursing and intermediate care facilities (SNFs and ICFs, respectively), community-based ICF/MR programs, supervised group and apartment living, foster care, semi-independent living and independent living or living at home.

It has been established that the great majority of persons housed at the more-restrictive end of the continuum can also be housed (and served) at the less-restrictive end of the continuum (Hill, Bruininks, & Lakin, 1983; Hill, Bruininks, & Thorsheim, 1982; Lakin, Bruininks, Doth, Hill, & Hauber, 1982) and that once they are moved into that end of the continuum, there is noticeable improvement in function (Close, 1977; Conroy, Efthimiou & Lemanowicz, 1982; Fiorelli & Thurman, 1979; Schroeder & Henes, 1978). It is less well established, but nevertheless strongly asserted, that the more restrictive the program (holding amount of service constant), the more expensive it tends to be (Intagliata, Willer, & Cooley, 1979; Minnesota Department of Public Welfare, 1979; Wieck & Bruininks, 1982).

Given these findings, one wonders why developmentally disabled persons continue to be housed in state institutions and nursing homes in such great numbers (more than 250,000 in 1977 according to Lakin et al., 1982). Some of the reasons can be identified. First is the historic position of the institution. Until recently, the "burden of proof" that institutionalization was not appropriate was on community placement, not on the institutions (i.e., the initial assumption invariably was that a developmentally disabled person was eminently institutionalizable). Beyond this, the institution was well-organized, had an appropriations history, and had an agreed-upon model of "treatment," none of which was available in the community until recently.

A second factor influencing the maintenance of the institutional model has been that the funding of institutions is administratively easy and "clean," requiring only one major federal account—Title XIX (Medicaid)—and one state account; in contrast, the funding of community services requires many accounts and is "messy."

Third, as interpreted by state legislatures, federal funding, especially Medicaid, has tended to encourage (and still encourages) institutional, nonnormalized forms of care, while discouraging the more normalized forms of care in the community. Even when perverse fiscal in-

---

[2] Section 1121 was passed in 1967 as the public-assistance-oriented precursor of the Title XIX legislation of 1974 that created intermediate care facilities for the mentally retarded.

centives might be reorganized to provide incentives for normalized, community care, standard federal and state budget and management practices tend to make that more difficult. However, if there is to be a well-managed, explicit continuum, all incentives must support the most appropriate level of care for each developmentally disabled person in the system; changes must occur in the factors fostering deinstitutionalization described earlier.

## Alternative Approaches

Having defined the strategy, it is important to examine some alternative approaches.

*A Deinstitutionalization Strategy* The main concern of the developmental disabilities service delivery process is the provision of an opportunity for the least restrictive, appropriate level of care. One of the implications of this objective is the transfer of all persons out of institutions for whom such programs are not appropriate. However, merely to deinstitutionalize (i.e., transfer out) can be an error, if the person does not move to a less-restrictive, more-appropriate care program. Such futile movement has happened often in the developmental disabilities area, as evidenced by the large number of persons in nursing homes who were formerly in state institutions and who are receiving little or no active treatment. (See the chapter by Bachrach in Bruininks & Lakin, 1985, for further discussion of this issue.)

*A Communitization Strategy* In providing for developmentally disabled persons, a primary objective is the development of an adequate community network of programs, designed according to the dictates of the normalization metaphor. However, concentration on it alone overlooks those developmentally disabled individuals in institutions and nursing homes and the problem of what may be an inappropriate continuing flow of persons out of the community into nursing homes and institutions. The same problem occurs with an "independent living" strategy, if that strategy is considered in isolation from all the other levels of care and opportunities along the continuum of care.

*A "Continuum-of-Care" Strategy* In the history of the developmental disabilities ser-

vice programs, an implicit continuum of care has emerged, which ranges from more to less restrictive, from more to less normalized, and—in general—from more to less costly. This continuum has three major dimensions: fiscal, programmatic, and managerial.

Because federal funding has been "cleaner" and more adequate for the more-restrictive part of the continuum, fiscal incentives tend to support the more-restrictive forms of care. A major focus of the fiscal policies and practices and each state's developmental disabilities agencies and planning councils should be to reverse these incentives, so that there is more adequate funding from the federal government at the less-restrictive levels of care. If the fiscal strategy concentrates on one level of care only, such budgeting practice typically produces fragmented services, so that decisions about funding each level of care may be entirely opposite to the avowed public policy of the agency.

Along the programmatic dimension, if the embraced goal is the least restrictive appropriate form of care, then only a continuum of care makes sense. If only one form of care predominates in decision making, counterproductive, and, at times, irrational conditions can be created. In Minnesota, for example, the major (and virtually only) systematically supported community form of care has been the ICF/MR program. This system has been revolutionary in its effects. It has, however, been overbuilt, because in the case of a number of persons for whom that form of care is probably inappropriate, the ICF/MR program was the only alternative for them. Other, less-restrictive living options were not available, owing to the fact that there was no full continuum of fiscally healthy levels of residential care.

There are also significant managerial aspects to programs for developmentally disabled persons. There is a constant flow into, through, and out of the system as developmentally disabled persons are identified, as they move through different programs in the system, as they age, as services begin to make a difference in their need for services, as persons leave the public system to live completely independent lives, or as they die. Ensuring that services are adequate and appropriate for a given client at a given time and that there are opportunities to move from one level of care to a more appropriate one, or to move to independent or semi-independent levels of living, or to remain at home for as long as is appropriate with decent support services does not happen unless formal decisions have been made that the available funding for services and subsidies will flow into such supports. Providing appropriate services happens because there is a component in the system to assure that a client is not stopped at a terminal point in residence or services because the interests of a provider in "keeping a client" are more powerful than the interests of the client; it happens also because needs for helping personnel with certain kinds of training have been adequately forseen and because financing for that training has been provided; and it happens because social foresight is exercised, in order to determine how many persons representing each type of need will be the expected responsibility of the public systems.

That is, in order to meet disabled persons' different needs at different times, in order to provide them a variety of services at a number of different locations, and in order for clients, service providers, and financing to mesh as needed, management of the placement and movement of persons and resources is required. This is what is meant by continuum management, which deals with all clients and all levels of care simultaneously. Without provision for such overarching direction and planning, one can only rely on pious hope that everything will turn out all right. As experience teaches, hope is not enough.

While the attempted exercise of wider management vision and control in the continuum of care is never perfect, experience shows that such vision and control can at least help avoid the most egregious errors that have occurred in the past (e.g., overbuilding of one kind of service, nonavailability of other kinds of service that are in greater need, misallocation of finances, inadequate training of needed personnel, or clients "stuck" in forms of service that are supposedly transitional).

## Advantages of the Continuum-of-Care Approach

The continuum-of-care approach to the fiscal, programmatic, and managerial aspects of long-term care has a number of advantages. One primary advantage is that instead of requiring legislation and administration covering all long-term care at once, the approach can operate well from separate legislation for separate target groups of interest. ("Massive" legislative changes tend to be almost impossible to effect in Congress and in state legislatures.) The approach also permits the federal government to deal simultaneously with a number of interest groups having relatively harmonious concerns. (Dealing with all developmental disabilities groups singly, for example, is possible. Dealing with all aging, all mental health, and all mental retardation groups at once is almost impossible.)

As an overall strategy, the continuum-of-care approach forces federal, state, and local governments into total program budgeting. This is important because no level of government knows its own costs or the total costs of any one system. A technical assistance project conducted by the authors in 1980 revealed that mental retardation and related problems cost more than $10 billion per year in public funds—the federal part mainly from the U.S. Department of Health and Human Services (DHHS). At the time this information was a surprise to Secretary Patricia Harris, who believed that the DHHS had only one small $65-million-per-year developmental disabilities program. In California alone, for example, the state budget in 1980 listed mental retardation as costing about $500 million per year in federal and state funds. However, this sum represented only about one-third of the approximately $1.5 billion in federal, state, and local funding being spent for mental retardation/developmental disability services in California. Most of the remainder was (and is) concealed under other account rubrics, such as Supplemental Security Income (SSI), Social Security Disability Insurance (SSDI), state SSI supplement, Medicaid, Medicare, U.S. Department of Housing and

Urban Development (HUD) and local housing authority budgets, Title XX (Social Security Act—Social Services) and its associated state budget, vocational rehabilitation, State Mental Health, Public Law 94-142, and state and local education costs.

The continuum-of-care approach forces states into a posture of integrated placement, case management, financing, and evaluation for each identified target group. It helps to align federal and state policies and programs with currently accepted principles (i.e., least restrictive environment, most normalized appropriate placement, and least costly appropriate behavior on the part of state and local governments in program development and client placement).

In the short term, a continuum-of-care policy saves states money. In the intermediate to long term, it saves all actors money. This short-term gain is precisely the stimulus needed to bring about the massive program changes required at the state and local levels. (About 40 states are responding to these stimuli now). In the long term, because of higher costs of institutional and nursing care—primarily regulation-induced costs—continuum-of-care programs promote deinstitutionalization incentives owing to decreased costs for all actors.

## Funding: "Neatness" and "Messiness"

In general, the more "institutional" the care, the "cleaner" its funding. State institutional care is funded mainly under a single account, Title XIX (Medicaid). As stated earlier, less-restrictive forms of care invariably require multiple accounts, one or more for the residential component and one or more for day programming and other generic services. As a result, multifunded services, even when the money available in the separate accounts is adequate, are difficult to develop and organize. The general rule of service system behavior, therefore, has been, when possible, to organize services only around clean funding.

Table 2 provides an example of the sources of a state's pre-1982 funding. As noted, the farther one moves into the community end of the continuum of care, the more diverse the funding. The need for normalized, separated, community-based services may require a large number of different funding sources.

In early 1981, the authors (and many others) were recommending changes in national policy to make community services administratively cleaner. Among the specific recommendations of the authors were: 1) to put all generic services that are outside the residence (i.e., respite care, transport, social development, work

Table 2.    Sources of state funding prior to 1982

| Level of continuum | Residential room and board and service cost | Service cost outside residence |
| --- | --- | --- |
| Institution | Title XIX | — |
| Community ICF/MR | Title XIX | Title XX, Title XIX (regular medical costs), state grants, county levy, Bureau of Education for the Handicapped (BEH) or local school levy, Vocational Rehabilitation (VR) |
| Supervised living | Supplemental Security Income (SSI), HUD Section 8, Food Stamps, Title XX | Same as for Community ICF/MR |
| Home care | SSI or SSA, State subsidy, Title XIX | Same as for Community ICF/MR |
| Family | Family subsidies from state | Same as for Community ICF/MR |

preparation, infant stimulation, work activity) under Title XIX, and 2) to put all supervised living care under Title XIX (Medicaid). An alternative would to be fund only the habilitation/supervision activities of the staff (about half the budget), while allowing the room and board function to be funded under SSI, HUD, Section 8, and Food Stamps. (The second alternative provides a higher federal matching rate in most states, thus making the increased administrative complexity "worth it" to the state.) To some extent the passage of the Home and Community Based Waiver legislation (now section 1915(c) of the Social Security Act) for Medicaid responds partially to the same types of problems. As part of such waivers, so long as a state meets the "waiver equation" requirements (that services planned under the waiver will cost no more—or will cost less—than the services that would be otherwise planned without a waiver), a much-cleaner set of financing streams can be designed for community financing. The problem with the program is, of course, that states' short-term benefits are limited to the current size of their ICF/MR program. If their program is large, a waiver makes good sense. If, however, the state has only a small program, the fiscal benefits of a waiver are correspondingly smaller.

## Funding: Correcting Perverse Incentives

In order for incentives in a continuum-of-care to promote normalized, community-oriented kinds of care and services, two rules should apply: 1) the more normalized the level of care, the less it should cost, in total; and 2) the more normalized the level of care, the less it should cost each relevant fiscal actor.

Under most current funding arrangements, the first rule nearly always holds, but the second is violated constantly by the "design" of the system. An example of a truncated continuum is given in Table 3, where the levels of care are laid out from least normalized to more normalized.

The continuum in Table 3 is in a state with 50% Medicaid matching, with active treatment in all levels of care, and with separated active treatment in the community ICF/MR and in the supervised living levels. The table reflects a situation that exists in many states, where counties share certain costs (e.g., 10% to 50% of nonfederal Medicaid costs) with the state government. For the state in the example, the incentives for the federal government are ordered as one would want (i.e., cost and restrictiveness are directly related). However, the incentives of the state governments are toward community ICF/MR facilities. The extra-institutional incentives are ordered in exactly the wrong way for the state government. The incentives of the local governments (or counties) are the worst—their fiscal preferences would be the institution first, home care next, and supervised living and the community ICF/MR last.

How can the incentives be made less perverse? Again in 1981, the authors recommended a series of actions that could be taken by the Health Care Financing Administration regarding Medicaid involvement in long-term care for developmentally disabled persons. Among the recommended actions were: 1) an "intergovernmental" provision for state-local matching (specifically, in those states where there is state-local Medicaid sharing for other than state institutions, there should be the same matching formula for state institutions); 2) mandating funding of day activities, workshop activities, and related activities under Medicaid, with that funding physically and admin-

Table 3. Annual cost per client in a "perverse-incentive" continuum (in dollars)

| Level of care | Federal ($) | State ($) | Local ($) | Total ($) |
|---|---|---|---|---|
| Institutions | 18,000 | 18,000 | 0 | 36,000 |
| Community ICF/MR | 11,000 | 5,200 | 11,200 | 28,000 |
| Supervised living | 3,600 | 6,950 | 6,950 | 17,500 |
| Home care support services | 0 | 7,650 | 850 | 8,500 |

Table 4.  Annual cost per client in the "reformed-incentive" continuum (in $)

| Level of care | Federal | State | Local | Total |
|---|---|---|---|---|
| Institution | 18,000 | 9,000 | 9,000 | 36,000 |
| Community ICF/MR | 14,000 | 7,000 | 7,000 | 28,000 |
| Supervised living | 10,550 | 3,475 | 3,475 | 17,500 |
| Home care with family subsidy | 4,250 | 2,125 | 2,125 | 8,500 |

istratively separate from ICF/MR residential care in the community (as was permitted in New York, Massachusetts, and Michigan); and 3) optional funding of personal care staff (now allowed) and rehabilitation staff for the activities specified in the individualized habilitation plan (IHP) of residents in supervised living programs.

With this form of policy action, the fiscal incentives of the continuum displayed in Table 3 would more nearly fit the preferences of the normalization approach, as illustrated in Table 4. In Table 4, the total cost criterion is more nearly met, and the second rule as mentioned earlier (the more normalized the environment, the lower the cost to each actor) is also almost met. This approach furthermore meets the "administrative neatness' criterion in the previous section. Thus, the fiscal incentives criteria for a normalized care-oriented continuum of care would be met.

As it turns out, the Home and Community-Based Waiver can be designed to yield exactly these fiscal results for states with substantial portions of their present program under Title XIX. Thus, for many states both the problems of administrative messiness and perverse fiscal incentives can be solved largely through the Medicaid Waiver.

However, several problems remain. For example, under the waiver, there is still no requirement that the states design, on an intrastate basis, changes in their own incentive structures (this is a special problem in states with strong county governments, where there is a heavy local funding component in the continuum of care). Neither is there any *formal* "quid pro quo" requirement in the negotiation of the waivers, according to which, in return for Medicaid financing of community services under the waiver, there would be a formally

targeted phasedown of state or private institution services, limitation of community ICF/MR expansion and/or requirements on the location in which "community-based" services are provided. These criticisms notwithstanding, the Medicaid Waiver authority is beginning to move states into a wider vision of their developmental disabilities systems and of what they should be accomplishing.

## MAKING A CONTINUUM-OF-CARE STRATEGY WORK AT THE STATE LEVEL

The "natural" incentives of state government agencies are toward separate turfs with separate funding, program design of individual programs without reference to other existing programs, and management of programs without reference to the existence of other programs. When notice is taken, it is usually for turf protection reasons rather than for cooperative reasons. Thus, the "natural" incentives mitigate against any explicit planning, programming, or management of the whole continuum. However, one set of incentives tends to override the fragmentation implicit in the system: the ability of the state to purchase a total continuum of care for significantly less money, in terms of net state costs, than it must pay for the current fragmented system. A continuum budgeting and management approach can be developed to accomplish this objective.

### Unified Budgeting and Planning

The fragmentation of budgets and programs at the federal level communicates itself to the states. As a result, differing elements of the continuum are funded by different agencies at the state and local level, which do not talk to each other. For example, the Community Services Block Grant may be in the department of public welfare, Title XIX in the health department, vocational rehabilitation in the employment services agency, grants for special education in the education agency, and so on. Even within agencies, programs will be in neighboring divisions, which do not talk to each other. (In many states, the mental retardation division, the health licensure division, and the Medicaid division may spend years fruitlessly attempting to get an agreement on a given policy.)

Continuum-of-care strategies recognize the low probability that neighboring agencies, at the same level of authority, would have the capacity to coordinate a major ongoing, multiagency, multiaccount policy. Therefore, an important step in the process is to place the overarching continuum strategy and budget planning at a higher level of authority. Such an authority might be the state budget office, the governor's office, state planning agency, the secretary of human services office, or a permanently staffed interagency task force. Once the strategy is developed in some detail and institutionalized in the appropriations process, however, the operational planning should be done in the responsible line agency.

## Continuum-of-Care
## Organizing: The Tasks

The continuum-of-care approach requires a systems orientation to policy change and implementation. (Such an orientation is discussed in some detail in the chapter by Schalock in Bruininks & Lakin, 1985.) A continuum of care would minimally require the following steps:

1. Defining the levels of care, from the institution to independent living, with both residential and nonresidential components represented;
2. Developing a registry for all programs;
3. Estimating the numbers (by service need) in each level of care; estimating current flow into, through, and out of the system; estimating future effects of demography and epidemiology—both with and without policy change—on number and type of services needed;

4. Estimating the costs of each level of the system, by source of payment, for current conditions, and in the presence of policy changes (e.g., effect of ICF/MR policy on institution costs; effect of nursing home standards enforcement on costs of care for those developmental disability persons in nursing homes; effect of emphasizing a community ICF/MR policy versus an assisted or supervised community living policy);
5. Defining a set of policy options involving the whole continuum and choosing one option for a long-term state plan (e.g., 3 to 7 years);
6. Setting up the financing for the plan (state plan and rule changes, capital and operating plans for the legislature, appropriation requests and program legislation change requests);
7. Setting up an operating plan (numbers and location of programs), long-term transfer planning for institutional and nursing home residents, agreements and operating plans for necessary eligibilities for transferees with SSI, HUD, county and district offices of public welfare, necessary extra appropriations to line agencies, etc.; and
8. Staffing an operating organization to do the planning and the coordination of agencies.

## Role of the State
## Developmental Disabilities Council

Through the federal Developmental Disabilities Assistance and Bill of Rights Act of 1975, states are provided formula grants (based upon population and other factors) to promote more effective planning and services for developmentally disabled persons. This legislation stipulates that each state maintain a planning council comprised of consumers, citizens, and service agency personnel.

Developmental Disabilities Councils in states have several possible missions in supporting the development of a continuum of care. The first is stimulating a continuum-of-care approach, perhaps even paying for the initial planning of the approach until the first legislative appropriation takes over. This is an important role because of the characteristics of state bureaucracies. By nature, appropriations for "planning" in state agencies tend to be for ongoing, narrowly defined incremental tasks. As a result, agency appropriations seldom include money for planning wider policy changes. This makes any "discretionary" money extremely important (the Developmental Disabilities Council funds are discretionary). Indeed, given the way states are organized and behave, the existence of a discretionary dollar for a given task—if that task is well-defined—makes the probability that the task will be attempted relatively high.

Second, a Developmental Disabilities Council can provide for the ongoing measurement of location, costs, and condition of clients in the developmental disabilities continuum of care. Given the existence of a number of operating data systems in the states (SDX for SSI, Title XX, MMIS [Medicaid Management Information System] for Medicaid, R-300 for Vocational Rehabilitation, state special education counts and budgets, etc.), the council's role is not to operate a primary data system but to operate a secondary one, which aggregates the data from the various other systems into its own. This can be done by: 1) assisting current systems to fill in missing data types, 2) assuring that all relevant systems have a cross-system linkage element (e.g., Social Security number) and that issues of confidentiality are resolved, and 3) making financial arrangements for the necessary data processing. At the state level, this would assure that the data are available for ongoing continuum-of-care planning and budgeting. It also assures the council of a continuing role in the development of a deinstitutionalized, normalized, well-funded, well-managed continuum of care.

## COMBINING PROGRAM AND FISCAL STRATEGIES TO REFINANCE AND REFORM A STATE SYSTEM

To develop an ideal budgeting strategy, one should know the full public costs of developmental disabilities for a state: budget alloca-

tions by location, need, and condition of the developmentally disabled persons in the state; the actual costs, by client condition, for each level of care; and the outcome, by client condition, for each level of care. At present, no state comes close to achieving that goal. Nevertheless, effective methods for budget planning still exist.

First, a continuum of care for a state can be defined, even though roughly and incompletely. Second, the full budget can be examined over a large portion of the continuum. For example, the continuum can be defined to be the developmental disabilities residential service system, together with all day programming and other nonresidential services provided to clients receiving residential services. Current costs, unit costs, and revenue sources for each defined level of care in the continuum can be examined. This ignores the costs of providing services to all who are not clients of the residential service system. However, it does allow a close look at the entire residential (and related nonresidential) cost picture. Furthermore, both total and net costs can be analyzed over more than just 1 or 2 years. This is important because significant changes in a state's continuum of care take more than 1 or 2 years. The state must understand its options and the fiscal impacts of each option up to 5 or 6 years into the future. It is also the case that significant changes in the continuum of care have variable effects on funding and funding incentives.

This approach also allows for the examination of alternative strategies, an essential aspect in planning for a continuum of care. Most state plans for developmental disabilities services do not include all relevant budget items and accounts—that is, they do not examine the entire continuum. They also do not evaluate the effects of the plan over a sufficient number of years. And, perhaps most critically, they do not examine enough alternatives. Often only one plan is outlined when a number of policy options should be evaluated regarding impact on: 1) deinstitutionalization and numbers of clients served; 2) speed of phasing down or phasing out certain or all institutions; 3) varying the speed and scope of upgrading residual institutional beds; 4) deinstitutionalizing residents of nursing homes as well as state institutions; 5) alternative resident choice policies (e.g, who is selected first for transfer?); 6) alternative community residence policies; 7) alternative revenue development policies (e.g., should all residential care be covered with Medicaid?); 8) alternative housing development policy in the community (e.g., Should existing housing or new housing be emphasized? Should a state grant and loan policy be developed or should HUD and/or the private market be depended upon?); and 9) the anticipated relationship between the supply of specific community services and the demand for those services by persons living at home (sometimes called the "out-of-the-woodwork" phenomenon).

Depending upon the models and data available, a few or many combinations of policies can be examined through simulation (which may be pencil-and-paper or computerized). Through this process, the fiscal and other effects of following any given set of policies in the deinstitutionalization process can be understood and a specific policy course can be more easily justified and "sold" to the state, whether to the governor, the budget director, or the legislature.

**The Analytic Background**

To understand the problem of reforming and managing a large, complex program area in the public sector, it is important to appreciate that there is a limited set of basic strategies. Potentially, the most powerful is the allocation of large sums of "up-front" money from sources other than a state's general revenue fund (GRF) to be used as incentives for reforming the total program structure. Thus, systems planners must explore ways to "create" the money needed to reform the state's developmental disabilities system and to use the funds in such a way that there is both program reform and long-term cost containment.

The first place some planners look for this money is in federal accounts already accessed by, or potentially available to, the state. However, most states fail to take maximum advantage of all federal funds available, usually because the state's departments (and departmental subdivisions) prepare individual budgets and the legislatures vote on individual program appropriations, without taking into account the interactions among the state and federal accounts. If the entire state human services budget were considered as an investment portfolio, and if both a gross and a net general revenue fund budget were developed, there would be far greater opportunities for maximizing federal reimbursements than now exist. This maximization has been found to be possible whenever five basic conditions of federal and federal-state financing programs exist in a state:

*Service definition.* Although different programs provide different patterns of goods and services to their clients, examination shows that there are considerable numbers of services (counseling, residential services, transportation, etc.) that are the same or similar across programs. Also, the goods received are often the same, or they are complete or partial substitutes for one another (medical care, food, cash, and housing). For example, family planning is identically specified in both Titles XIX and XX of the Social Security Act.

*Overlapping eligibilities.* Although different programs are intended to serve different groups of people, there are significant overlaps among the groups defined as eligible for each program. For example, a person who is on the Food Stamps rolls will be eligible, on the average, for more than two other means-tested programs as well.

*Irregular match of people and services.* Added to the overlaps mentioned above is the fact that neither the service definitions nor the service eligibilities are completely precise. As a result, there is much room for maneuver in deciding which services people need or should receive. There is a wide range of different placements (e.g., home care, group residence, intermediate care facilities, skilled nursing facilities, acute general hospital) that a person can be provided, depending upon who is making the placement decision and what criteria are used.

*Matching ratio differences.* Most of these programs involve some form of federal financing, with a matching ratio of federal and state (or local) funds. Others, which are nonfederal, involve a match between state and county or state and city. Such ratios generally vary between 40% and 100% of the money made available by the higher-level jurisdiction. At the local level, this means that a 40% nonlocal match returns 67¢ for each $1.00 of local money put into the program, a 75% match returns $3.00 for each $1.00, and a 100% match is "free" from a local budget perspective (i.e., requires no state or local funds).

*Open and closed-ended programs.* Most federal programs are closed-ended; that is, there is an appropriations ceiling, and no more than the ceiling can be spent. Title XX (Social Security Act—Social Services) is a closed-end program; $2.7 billion is its current annual spending limit in federal funds. Some of the most important programs in human services, however, are open-ended—for example, Aid to Families with Dependent Children (AFDC), Medicaid, and Supplemental Security Income. Housing and Food Stamps programs, among others, have been "quasi-open-ended" (in that Congress has decided to treat them as if they were open-ended). The open-ended characteristic means that if a person is entitled to receive benefits under the program, he or she must be provided those benefits; there is no ceiling.

A financial reimbursement program for a given target group can be maximized where all five conditions are satisfied. Since the conditions are satisfied in all 50 states, a general example can be provided of how program dollars can be moved across different federal programs to achieve a higher overall federal contribution to a continuum-of-care initiative.

Consider a "worked example" of how the basic principles operate for program sizes of the kind found in the 10 largest states. Table 5 illustrates a current program involving four Social Security Act accounts for children's services: Title XX, Titles XIX and IV-A (considered as one account with, at the beginning, no expenditures), and Title IV-B. Titles XX and IV-B are closed-ended; Title XIX and IV-A are open-ended. The federal matching ratios are 75%, 50%, and 10% federal, respectively. The overall federal match initially is 50%. There is good "communication" between Title XX and Title XIX/IV-A—that is, there are many services provided under Title XX that are similar to, or identical to, services provided under Title IV-A and XIX. Further, many persons eligible for Title XX services are also eligible for Title IV-A and XIX services. There is poor communication between Title XIX/IV-A and Child Welfare Services—little program-service overlap and very little overlap with IV-A eligibility. There is good communication between Title XX and Child Welfare Services. Foster care, adoption, and child protective services, for example, can be provided under either program; and most children eligible for one program are eligible for the other.

Table 6 represents a move of some of the Title XX services (e.g., some health-related services) into Title XIX and some (e.g., day care services) into Title IV-A funding, which results in open-ended match rather than current matching ceiling in Title XX. At the same

Table 5.  Current allocations in a sample state program (in $ millions)

| Source of funds | Title XX | Title XIX/IV-A | Title IV-B (Child Welfare) | Total funding |
|---|---|---|---|---|
| Federal | 240 | 0 | 20 | 260 |
| State | 80 | 0 | 180 | 260 |
| Total | 320 | 0 | 200 | 520 |

Table 6. Move 1: Moving services from Title XX to Titles XIX and IV-A in a sample state program (in $ millions)

| Source of funds | Title XX | Title XIX/IV-A | Title IV-B (Child Welfare) | Total funding |
|---|---|---|---|---|
| Federal | 150 | 60 | 20 | 230 |
| State | 50 | 60 | 180 | 290 |
| Total | 200 | 120 | 200 | 520 |

time, it frees up $120 million in Title XX funding to be used for other services. This move lowers the average federal match—but only temporarily.

In the second move of program dollars, presented in Table 7, Child Welfare Services are placed into the "hole" left in Title XX by the first move, in order to move from the 10/90 match to the 75/25 match. As a result of this move, the total program is still the same, but (compare Tables 5 and 7) the state share has decreased $60 million dollars from current allocations.

At this point only a substitution of federal and state funds has been achieved. If the exercise goes only this far, it not only is sterile (people pay more federal tax, less state tax) but it has not yielded any program reform or service increases in the needed areas. Moving to a reasonable programmatic outcome requires further creative initiatives. Among these might be agreeing with budget officials to reduce net state investment from the original $260 million to $240 million (a savings of $20 million); and agreeing to put the remaining state money saved ($40 million) in move 2 (Table 7) into an $80 million expansion of community-oriented Title XIX and IV-A services to support a deinstitutionalization initiative.

Finally, Table 8 reflects the use of the additional funds for reform (in this particular model, $100 million of new federal money). The net budgeting effect of these moves, which can be seen by comparing Tables 5 and 8, is a program total increase of $80 million, while the state has managed to recoup $20 million for general revenue savings or other areas of need.

The operating premise in such models is that negotiations can occur between the governor's office, the director of the budget, and the legislature, who must agree on a joint utilization of state general fund money for reform and/or improvement in the target group delivery system. In order for this to occur, it is assumed that there is interagency planning and coordination over the whole system of interest. Normally, this practice is rare. However, if such negotiations are made the precursor of large savings and program expansions, they are quite feasible. A number of states have been able to enter into multiyear temporary or permanent arrangements of this sort. Most states could receive an additional 10% to 20% in new federal funding for their entire public human services system if they would systematically rework their human services system over a 3- to 5-year period.

Table 7. Move 2: Moving Child Welfare Services into Title XX in a sample state program (in $ millions)

| Source of funds | Title XX | Title XIX/IV-A | Title IV-B (Child Welfare) | Total funding |
|---|---|---|---|---|
| Federal | 240 | 60 | 20 | 320 |
| State | 80 | 60 | 60 | 200 |
| Total | 320 | 120 | 80 | 520 |

Table 8. Move 3: Allocating savings to a combination of state budget offset and community program expansion in a sample state program (in $ millions)

| Source of funds | Title XX | Title XIX/IV-A | Title IV-B (Child Welfare) | Total funding |
|---|---|---|---|---|
| Federal | 240 | 100 | 20 | 360 |
| State | 80 | 100 | 60 | 240 |
| Total | 320 | 200 | 80 | 600 |

The maximization approach can be applied in a more limited but still powerful way to "rational chunks" of the human services system. The following discussion focuses on an analysis of an individual developmental disabilities system, so as to provide a "worked example" of how the combination of short-term money with long-term system-oriented expenditure controls can result in a system configuration that more nearly resembles the kind of service system that program theorists and practitioners (and the courts) have advocated.

## A "Worked Example" for a Developmental Disabilities System

*Estimating the Current Total Developmental Disabilities Budget for an Exemplary State* The first step in the maximization process is to estimate the total governmental budget in the state for persons with developmental

disabilities (see Table 9). Such a budget, by source of revenue, is needed to understand fully the budgetary and program consequences of state and federal policies and actions. If this full set of costs is not known or is incomplete, the results of state or federal actions may be unpredictable and possibly perverse.

Figures used in Table 9 are similar to, but not identical to, those of several of the larger state governments. It should be noted that the estimates that are discussed do not include any of the voluntary, private, or not-for-profit agency dollars involved in community programs, whether for totally private programs, for subsidizing low reimbursement rates, or for nonpublic capital development. Furthermore, the estimates in Table 9 are based on assumptions that 8% of the state's division of rehabilitation clients would be classified as developmentally disabled; that 16% of the children in foster care

Table 9. Full state developmental disabilities public budget, 1980 (in $ millions)

| Item | Federal | State | Local | Total |
|---|---|---|---|---|
| State hospital | 100.0 | 200.0 | 0 | 300.0 |
| SNF/ICF[a] | 16.8 | 16.8 | 0 | 33.6 |
| Community ICF/MR[b] | 12.5 | 12.5 | 0 | 25.0 |
| Non-Medicaid residential | 5.7 | 16.7 | 0 | 22.4 |
| Division of Rehabilitation | 8.0 | 2.0 | 0 | 10.0 |
| County welfare depts. | 2.4 | 7.1 | 0 | 9.5 |
| Regional centers | 0 | 160.0 | 0 | 160.0 |
| Special education | 90.0 | 180.0 | 200.0 | 470.0 |
| SSI[c] | 110.0 | 30.0 | 30.0 | 170.0 |
| SSDI[d] | 73.5 | 0 | 0 | 73.5 |
| Title XX | 20.01 | 35.0 | 0 | 55.0 |
| Total | 483.91 | 660.1 | 230.0 | 1,329.0 |

Note: See text for explanation of assumptions on which this table is based.

[a]SNF/ICF, skilled nursing facility/intermediate care facility.

[b]ICF/MR, intermediate care facility for the mentally retarded.

[c]SSI, Supplemental Security Income.

[d]SSDI, Social Security Disability Insurance.

Table 10. Public expenditures in 1980 for residential and related services for developmentally disabled persons in the state (in $ millions)

|  | Number of patients | Cost per patient | Federal costs | State costs | Total costs |
|---|---|---|---|---|---|
| Institution | 8,700 | 34,480 | 120.00 | 180.00 | 300.00 |
| SNF/ICF | 2,800 | 12,000 | 16.80 | 16.80 | 33.60 |
| ICF/MR | 1,000 | 25,000 | 12.50 | 12.50 | 25.00 |
| Non-Medicaid | 10,000 | 15,000 | 40.00 | 110.00 | 150.00 |
| Total | 22,500 |  | 189.30 | 319.30 | 508.60 |

institutional placements are classified as developmentally disabled; and that 19% of the individuals receiving Supplementary Security Income (SSI) in the state are classified as developmentally disabled (nationally, 50% of children and 13% of adults receiving SSI are developmentally disabled). The estimates are low since they do not include $30 million to $40 million dollars of housing, Food Stamps, and incidental Medicaid medical expenses.

The first four items in Table 9 consist entirely of out-of-home care (with related day services). The remainder of the items mainly pay for nonresidential services and income maintenance in the community. However, significant portions of these items as well are for out-of-home care.

*Decision-Making within the Residential Care (and Related Services) Budget* It would be useful to analyze alternative sets of policies over the whole budget; but, as yet, not enough is known to do so. Therefore, only a key part of that budget is examined, a part that is largely under state control. The focus on

residential services for persons with developmental disabilities, as a portion of the total $1,329 million budget, illustrates how increased Title XIX and other funds could be used. That portion consists of the first three items of Table 9 ($300 million, $33.6 million, and $25 million, plus $150 million in the non-medical parts of the residential care system).

Tables 10, 11, and 12 represent the 1980 expenditure pattern by category in the model state and two alternative projections for 1985. It should be noted that the unit costs in the institutions and the community ICFs/MR are "bundled" (i.e., they include all supportive services). The unit costs for SNF/ICFs are "unbundled" and thus are probably $2,000 to $3,000 per unit too low. Table 10 presents the current expenditures in the residential-care and related services portion of the developmental disabilities system in 1980. Then, projecting the effects of service changes and inflation on per-client costs over the next 5 years and applying the projected 1985 costs to each of two different residential configurations of patients

Table 11. Alternative I for 1985—current departmental planning (in $ millions)

|  | Number of patients | Cost per patient | Federal costs | State costs | Total costs |
|---|---|---|---|---|---|
| Institution | 8,000 | 60,000 | 240.00 | 240.00 | 480.00 |
| SNF/ICF | 2,200 | 19,320 | 21.25 | 21.25 | 42.50 |
| ICF/MR | 7,800 | 40,000 | 156.00 | 156.00 | 312.00 |
| Non-Medicaid | 7,000 | 24,150 | 108.22 | 60.78 | 169.00 |
| Total | 25,000 |  | 535.47 | 478.93[a] | 1,003.50 |

Note: Alternative I assumes: an inflation rate of 12% per year in state institutions (due to a combination of general inflation plus staff upgrading requirements); a 10% per year inflation rate for all other services; that the state is more aggressive in receiving full state hospital reimbursement in nonmedical residential programs; and that there will be 2,500 more people in the system

[a]$296.92 million general revenue fund in 1980 dollars—a savings of about $22 million over 1980 in 1980 dollars.

Table 12.   Alternative II for 1985—accelerated deinstitutionalization (in $ millions)

|  | Number of patients | Cost per patient | Federal costs | State costs | Total costs |
|---|---|---|---|---|---|
| Institution | 4,000 | 64,000 | 128.00 | 128.00 | 256.00 |
| SNF/ICF[a] | 2,000 | 19,320 | 19.32 | 19.32 | 38.64 |
| ICF/MR | 4,000 | 44,000 | 88.00 | 88.00 | 176.00 |
| Non-Medicaid | 15,000 | 24,150 | 231.84 | 130.41 | 362.25 |
| Total | 25,000 |  | 467.16 | 365.73[a] | 832.89 |

Note: Alternative II assumes: inflation rates the same as in Table 11; that there will be increases in unit cost over Alternative I, due to establishment of new behavior-shaping programs in institutions and in intermediate care facilities for the mentally retarded (ICFs/MR), so that there is much greater use of nonmedical facilities and less use of ICFs/MR; and federal reimbursement and service-population assumptions the same as in Alternative I.

[a]$227.16 million general revenue fund in 1980 dollars—a savings of about $92 million over 1980, in 1980 dollars.

in the continuum of care in 1985, two different sets of fiscal projections are generated.

Alternative I (Table 11) presents a model of the fiscal effects of proceeding under current plans of the state's developmental disabilities department for changes of client location over the next 5 years. This alternative gradually deemphasizes institutional care. Alternative II (Table 12) is a model for reducing net state costs (and at the same time lowering total costs) of developmental disabilities services through use of nonmedical residential alternatives that provide greater budgeting flexibility for providers and that increase continuity and stability for individuals and families receiving services. This alternative rapidly deemphasizes institutional care. Both alternatives assume the state has become more efficient in billing for federal reimbursements.

Court decision and contemporary program theory and research promote the movement of clients from the most restrictive to the least restrictive residential setting. Yet, fiscal decisions have encouraged movement the other way, because current federal-state funding pat-terns, as currently interpreted in state budgeting practice, provide the incentives for institutionalization. Table 12 shows a way to move funding and thus program decisions in the desirable direction.

In reviewing Alternatives I and II (Tables 11 and 12, respectively), several results become apparent. The projected 1985 costs of Alternative II are $170 million less than those of Alternative I. The projected 1985 costs of Alternative II are $58 million less to the federal government than those of Alternative I. Therefore, there is an incentive for federal support for this alternative. Last, the projected 1985 costs of Alternative II are about $112 million less to the state general revenue fund than those of Alternative I. This comparison of the two alternatives is presented in Table 13.

When converted to 1980 constant dollars, the state totals become even more encouraging. The deflated figure for Alternative I is $296 million in state spending. For Alternative II, the deflated figure is $227 million in state funds—a savings of $69 million. When the inflation-adjusted general revenue funding for

Table 13.   Comparison of current and projected costs under alternatives I and II in 1985 for a state's developmental disabilities residential and related care sector (in $ millions)

|  | Federal | State | Total |
|---|---|---|---|
| 1980 | 189.30 | 319.30 | 508.60 |
| 1985 Alternative I | 525.47 | 478.03 | 1,003.50 |
| 1985 Alternative II | 467.16 | 365.73 | 832.89 |

the two alternatives is compared to the 1980 funding of $319.5 million, Alternative II saves $92 million and Alternative I saves $23 million. The most important fiscal result is that the total costs of the developmental disabilities system remain level (when corrected for inflation) under Alternative II, in moving from 1980 to 1985. At the same time, the system is planned to accommodate 11% more people and to accommodate them in a more normalized set of care opportunities. From a fiscal policy perspective, then, as well as from programmatic and legal perspectives, Alternative II should be aggressively pursued by the state. For this to occur, there must be solid interagency coordination and planning with specific targets set out by the budget division, the developmental disabilities department, and the legislature.

## WHAT CAN THE FEDERAL GOVERNMENT DO TO HASTEN NEEDED CONTINUUM-OF-CARE CHANGES?

To this point, this chapter has examined the use of available financing to restructure the continuum of care in program, financing, and management, primarily at the state level. This is reasonable, since the main responsibilities for program and service provision are vested in the state or substate regional levels. Nevertheless, because of its participation in health, income security, and housing services, the federal government is still deeply involved in defining how the developmental disabilities continuum of care works. Therefore, it is important to note areas where the federal government could alter present policies to promote continuum-of-care concepts.

### Shifting the Incentives

In discussions of incentives in human services, the focus is usually on two groups: the consumer of services and the provider of services. This emphasis is most noticeable in the health area, where incentives in the system have been the most perverse, with the largest perceived resulting waste. In this area, the discussion has centered on reform of consumer incentives by using, for example, preferred provider solu-

tions or deductibles and co-insurance provisions, so that the consumer will feel some out-of-pocket pain when benefits are used. This will, presumably, reduce unnecessary usage or redirect demand for care to the most efficient providers. When the discussion deals with providers, it currently centers on giving the key providers, the physicians, the incentive to provide the least, rather than the most, service appropriate to the patient's state. The key instrument for doing this is usually the Health Maintenance Organization (HMO), which accepts a flat capitation payment for each subscriber enrolled. If, for example, too much expensive hospital care is used, the physician suffers economic loss. Thus, the incentive is to use less expensive office and outpatient care.

In human services systems that are heavily publicly funded, however, there is a third important class of incentives, along with those concerned with the consumer and the provider. This class of incentives can be referred to as *system incentives*. Where there is little or no private funding in the care system, these incentives dictate the existence or nonexistence of the provider and the benefits. For example, in Oklahoma, state funding for residential care of mentally retarded persons has been, until recently, almost exclusively reserved to institutions. As a result, there are almost no community services of any kind in the residential area. As another example, in Minnesota, there is strong community funding, but most of it is reserved for community-based ICF/MR programs. Consequently, there are practically no other kinds of residential services for developmentally disabled persons in the state. And in Nebraska, there has been funding for community residential services but no use of federally funded ICFs/MR; as a result, all community services tend to focus on "nonmedical" facilities.

Despite the fact that one might expect some division of residential care into a continuum of large public institutions, community ICF/MF programs, community group homes, foster and personal care, and home care, the actual distribution of public funding has tended to emphasize one or two of these options in each state, even though the distribution of client needs is probably fairly uniform across states.

There are more subtle forms of system incentives in those state systems where most levels of care have funding, but some levels of care are more profitable or administratively easier to deal with. In these cases, the incentives provide differences in emphasis rather than the more stark existence/nonexistence pattern.

Finally, there is a fourth class of incentives for heavily governmentally funded systems of care, like the developmental disabilities system, which might be called *governmental incentives*. Since such systems are funded by governments, the primary actors in their funding have their own preferences that are partly determined by their own status in the governmental system. While these preferences differ among actors, the general ones are: 1) cutting taxes, 2) increasing services, 3) mediating constituency desires for pieces of the pie, 4) obtaining practical, easy, and understandable results before the next election, and 5) appearing to take all of these actions simultaneously.

The usual result of these preferences is to provide across-the-board actions that: 1) evenly distribute benefits or spread the pain (with important exceptions defined by the relative power of the constituency and the technical difficulties of a given area of legislation), 2) focus on the short term, and 3) approach problems in an aggregative fashion (so that "the solution" is big enough to be noticed). Actions that respond to all these political desirabilities (e.g., cutting taxes and increasing services) are elusive. They can seldom be accomplished without instituting a restructuring strategy, major funding area by major funding area, which in itself creates additional political problems. Such strategies require care, persistence, and long-term attention, commodities with no natural reinforcers in the political environment. Therefore, strategies employed must link political desirabilities to the restructuring goal. This can be done only by simultaneously shifting system goals and governmental incentives. Such a strategy would require a look first at the major potential shifts in Medicaid and the Ci-

vilian Health and Medical Program of the Uniformed Services (CHAMPUS) programs at the federal level. The appropriate care and cost-cutting principles of the Medicaid Waiver program must be seen as those of the standard Medicaid program (i.e., Medicaid should support community-based, normalized care), and the same principles should be applied to the CHAMPUS program.

Essentially, today, the over $4 billion spent by Medicaid and CHAMPUS for care of developmentally disabled persons pays for state institutions (ICFs/MR), for large "community" ICFs/MR (facilities with more than 15 beds), for nursing homes (ICF and SNFs) where there is little or no active treatment, and for child welfare institutions that are often more restrictive environments than are needed. Despite the fact that changes in this situation have been recommended by providers and advocates for years, there is still a desperate need for funding rules to be redefined, so that such funding pays for small group homes, semi-independent living in nonmedical facilities and apartments, foster and personal care, home care, and independent living support services, as well as for "unbundled" nonresidential day services. Today, unprecedented opportunities exist to change those rules. If these opportunities are taken to accomplish a desirable reorganization of funding, the system incentives could be altered in powerful ways.

## Providing Improved Knowledge about the True Incentive Structure

Despite the fact that the system incentives with respect to Medicaid and CHAMPUS ineffectively promote appropriate services, a number of implicit system incentives are already in place that, if understood, could go a long way toward moving state legislatures to better support noninstitutional programs in their appropriations. These other system incentives are often only implicit, because they are often not recognized. They are, moreover, not recognized because they are overaggregated in current large, state accounts (e.g., AFDC, Medicaid, Vocational Rehabilitation, Food Stamps, and state housing programs) or because they are not listed as part of the available resources to be used in planning state programs (e.g., Supplemental Security Income, Social Security Disability Income).

When the amounts currently and potentially available for developmentally disabled populations are separated from the overaggregated accounts, and when those funds are budgeted together with the individual accounts specifically appropriated for developmentally disabled persons, a new set of program accounts can be created that reflects greater possibilities and flexibility for program decisions.

If the developmental disabilities continuum is to be managed adequately, it is crucial to understand the true costs of the system to each fiscal source and the expected flows of clients into, through, and out of the system over time. Only with this sort of information can funding bases be simplified and a kind of "quasi-market" orientation (using unified prospective capitation funding such as the HMO-like strategy) be made a realistic goal.

The process of laying the groundwork for the fiscal data needed to comprehend the costs of the system would benefit greatly from increased federal concern and vastly improved federal involvement in collecting data. Much needs to be done in this area, and there are obvious places to begin. For example, Medicaid, which is generally rigidly bound by the early Medicaid Management Information System design, needs numerous and substantial changes if it is to adequately meet the need for data on the Medicaid program and its recipients. Of the changes needed, the most pressing one is to move to a person-orientation in collecting and processing data, so that all costs for all classes of service are easily available for each person in the system each year. In the development disabilities continuum, this would mean that, for each person at each level of the continuum, all Medicaid costs by type of provider would be available. That is, for a person in a community ICF/MR, his or her ICF/MR costs, costs for short-term hospital inpatient stays, outpatient visits, physician charges, OT and PT, drugs, and any other

Medicaid costs would be available. The same would be true for persons in an ICF/MR state institution. With such data systems established for clients of Medicaid programs, both traditional ones and those funded under the waiver, states will be able to create parallel data systems for clients in non-Medicaid facilities, in independent living, and in the home.

Another serious weakness in the existing data system is that at present, SSI and SSDI "target group" information is not available in any systematic way. What states need to know from these two systems is whether a person has (as a primary or secondary diagnosis) a developmental disability diagnosis, a mental-illness-related diagnosis, or a physical diagnosis. Those data, along with type of location and address data, make it possible for a state to match up this information with Medicaid and Medicare data. It is crucial that states be able to merge SSI, SSDI, Medicaid, and Medicare data, if adequate continuum planning is to be done. At present, only Medicaid data are known, and even that is in an overly aggregated way.

There is also a need to break out spending under special education for each developmentally disabled participant in such a way that it can be merged with the Health Care Financing Administration and Social Security information. Similarly, person-oriented data on spending for persons served under the Community Social Services Block Grant should be available.

The programs just mentioned account for more than 75% of federal spending for the developmental disabilities continuum of care (about $4 billion federal dollars were spent in 1979 by the above programs) and about 50% of state and local spending (about $3 billion in 1979). When combined with already-available data on state nursing home and institution care, which has no federal match (about $2 billion in 1979), more than 80% of all public spending for developmentally disabled persons would be accounted for, on a person, level of care, and payment-source basis.

Creating the system of data basic to understanding the work of the system is an essential state function. After major groups are enumerated with respect to other total care costs, there should also be a survey of persons in each state's system using a simple cognitive/behavioral/physical handicap measure. These data should be linked with each person already in a confederated or merged SSI/SSDI/Medicaid/Title XVIII system (along with an estimate of when and where the next move of this person will be or should be). For those not in that system, this should be the entry point to estimating public costs from Vocational Rehabilitation, Public Health, state and local grants, patient payments, family payments, AFDC, AFDC Foster Care, and so forth.

Once a census has been done, future studies could be small-sample-oriented, with periodic updates of name/address/level of care/eligibility data for the census list of those in the public system. The two approaches together would allow for some estimates of flow into, through, and out of the system, where people come from and where they go, and when they enter and exit the system. The key federal assistance here could be that provided through the individual state Developmental Disabilities Councils, keeping the basic continuum-of-care data and providing reports on costs, structure, and flows in the system on a continuing basis, on an interagency, intergovernmental basis, for the state.

With such data and such an approach, legislatures would be freed from the concentration on state institution ICF/MR appropriations versus day activity versus vocational rehabilitation versus home care appropriations, with virtually no knowledge of how the one-half to two-thirds of the funding that the legislature does not appropriate is or could be used in the state system. With a client-oriented data base, the legislature would be able to see both how funding could be packaged at the different levels of the continuum, as well as the relative costs for clients of each kind of condition at each level of care, in such a way as to make legislative appropriations more concentrated on the more-normalized end of the continuum.

This chapter has covered a number of areas critical to the development and management of a continuum-of-care for developmentally disabled persons. Clearly the reform activities described are complex and never easily attained. However, the authors believe that these activities are essential to continued progress in developing a full range of services that can be targeted to the specific needs of developmentally disabled clients. The approaches tendered here are not equally relevant to all states, but all states certainly have much to accomplish in managing and financing a continuum of care.

This chapter has both identified the important needs of developmentally disabled persons for appropriate services and has emphasized that important service and management issues can be resolved. Certainly the experiences of a number of states suggest that change toward more appropriate and cost-effective services is possible. The authors would hope, too, that this discussion might serve to convince persons who have strong convictions about the need for a well-financed and well-managed continuum of care, but who are not themselves in the traditional positions to bring about the changes discussed, that advocacy must be directed at all aspects of the system. Advocacy for normalized services in a state that is totally oriented toward Medicaid funding of long-term care placements will produce limited alternatives. Advocacy of placement in the least restrictive environment in states that have no data on the characteristics and needs of clients in that system and, therefore, no way of planning for facilities that are most appropriate for those clients, has little promise of success.

The concept of a systems approach is a valid one. Advocates, service providers, state agency personnel, legislators, and federal officials must realize the potential for contructive change through this model and act upon that realization. The present system is overly fragmented, overly expensive, and serves too many of its clients inappropriately. Reforming and refinancing the system should be a major goal for all those concerned with the welfare of developmentally disabled persons.

# REFERENCES

Bruininks, R.H., & Lakin, K.C. (eds.). *Living and learning in the least restrictive environment*. Baltimore: Paul H. Brookes Publishing Co., 1985.

Close, D. Community living for severely and profoundly retarded adults: A group home study. *Education and Training of the Mentally Retarded*, 1977, *12*(3), 256–262.

Conroy, J., Efthimiou, J., & Lemanowicz, J. A matched comparison of the developmental growth of institutionalized and deinstitutionalized mentally retarded clients. *American Journal of Mental Deficiency*, 1982, *86*, 581–587.

Fiorelli, J., & Thurman, K. Client behavior in more and less normalized residential settings. *Education and Training of the Mentally Retarded*, 1979, *14*(2), 85–94.

Hill, B.K., Bruininks, R.H., & Lakin, K.C. Characteristics of mentally retarded people in residential facilities. *Health and Social Work*, 1983, *8*(2), 85–95.

Hill, B.K., Bruininks, R.H., Thorsheim, M.J. Deinstitutionalization and foster care for mentally retarded people. *Health and Social Work*, 1982, *7*, 198–205.

Intagliata, J., Willer, B., & Cooley, F. Cost comparison of institutional and community-based alternatives for mentally retarded persons. *Mental Retardation*, 1979, *17*, 154–156.

Lakin, K.C., Bruininks, R.H., Doth, D., Hill, B.K., & Hauber, F.A. *Sourcebook on long-term care for developmentally disabled people*. Minneapolis: University of Minnesota, Department of Educational Psychology, 1982.

Minnesota Department of Public Welfare. *Residential care study*. St. Paul: Minnesota Department of Public Welfare, 1979.

Schroeder, S.R., & Henes, C. Assessment of progress of institutionalized and deinstitutionalized retarded adults: A matched-control comparison. *Mental Retardation*, 1978, *16*, 147–148.

Wieck, C.A., & Bruininks, R.H. *Cost of public and community care for mentally retarded people in the United States*. Minneapolis: University of Minnesota, Department of Educational Psychology, 1981.

Chapter 14

# Challenges to Advocates
# of Social Integration of
# Developmentally Disabled Persons

*K. Charlie Lakin and Robert H. Bruininks*

The chapters of this volume have offered abundant examples of the ways in which programs for developmentally disabled persons fall short of promoting the levels of social integration that they might be achieving. They have also communicated a sense that these shortcomings are increasingly vexing in light of the avowed acceptance by these programs of social and philosophical principles that establish clear reasons for increasing the social integration of developmentally disabled citizens. More important, this book has delineated specific approaches that have been shown to enhance, directly or indirectly, the social participation of this segment of the population. This final chapter reviews several particularly compelling problems that affect the capacity of service systems to provide community-oriented services. This discussion is followed by suggestions of possible steps for advocates to take in approaching some of the challenges ahead in improving current residential, educational, vocational, and support systems.

## IMPEDIMENTS
## TO EFFECTIVE
## INTEGRATION OF SERVICES

It is relatively easy to identify a baker's dozen of obvious, though interrelated and overlapping, impediments affecting the speed and degree to which deinstitutionalization, normalization, and placement in the least restrictive environment are being accomplished. These impediments include the following:

1.  *Significant gaps exist in continua of care in many communities.* Although the number of residential, educational, and habilitation options in communities has grown substantially in recent years, many areas remain ill-prepared to deal with persons of certain levels of disability or who have special behavioral, developmental, or medical needs. Gaps in continua of care create situations of inappropriate levels of supervision, including the inability to move toward less restriction as community living skills are developed, movement of clients away from important relationships and natural supports, and inadequate opportunity to improve the skills and productive capacity of developmentally disabled persons.

2.  *Service systems have insufficient mechanisms for coordinating the activities of their parts.* The decentralization of responsibility for services to developmentally disabled persons has been a major outcome of the deinstitutionalization and

313

least restrictive placement efforts. Coordination of these dispersed centers of service access has become a serious problem. The problem is, in part, organizational, with agencies struggling to maintain well-defined responsibility for specific services and a specific target population; and in part, the problem is managerial, with inadequate mechanisms to coordinate services from the client level through case management services to the state-level operating agencies.

3. *Funding is unevenly and disconsonantly allocated across service options.* Although funding for some service options, particularly the more traditional, tends to be straightforward and frequently relatively ample, less-traditional programs have tended to be built through creative budgeting and substantially fewer total resources. The use of multiple funding sources to initiate and maintain community-based programs has often given the impression, not totally unwarranted, that the programs are less likely to survive over the long-term than are the older institutional or segregated training programs. The generally lower total levels of funding have, of course, established real, although frequently resisted, incentives for maintaining the more traditional models of care.

4. *Crucial complementary services are poorly distributed or unavailable in many communities.* Although, clearly, great improvements have been made in the accessibility of community-based services, frequently the unavailability of critically important benefits undermines the potential utility of other services that are available in the community. For example, the availability of residential programs loses much potential value in the absence of day work or developmental programs, organized recreational opportunities, or other activities to provide a complete and appropriate community-living experience. A primary cause of the

problem has been insufficient coordination among distinct agencies responsible for complementary services. Such problems are particularly evident in areas of low population density, but are also highly visible in many urban areas. Greater efforts must be made to create mechanisms and expectations for securing full complements of the essential elements of a comprehensive service system in areas where one or more services are provided.

5. *Services for natural or adoptive families of developmentally disabled persons to permit and promote the retention of their members at home remain inadequate and often essentially unavailable.* In recent years there has been a marked decrease in the rate at which disabled children and youth leave their natural families for long-term care placement. Both the cost and social implications of this change are substantial. Still, supports to families, whether in the form of respite care, direction services, parent training, counseling, or other services, or through direct subsidies as are now provided by 18 states, are uneven in their extent and availability. Resources invested in family care provide significant benefits to developmentally disabled persons and to the society as a whole and should be a cornerstone to community-oriented programs for developmentally disabled persons. Practices in Scandinavian countries, for example, stress maintenance of developmentally disabled persons in family units as a matter of policy through a variety of fiscal incentives and support services. The organization of such approaches in the United States has occurred on a very limited basis only.

6. *The services designed to move clients into independent or semiindependent residential and/or work roles are in short supply.* Research and demonstration is increasingly showing that the capacity of developmentally disabled persons to exhibit independence and self-determination has been seriously underestimated

until recently. Much of the credit for recognizing this potential goes to parents and professionals who rejected the notion of predetermined developmental limitations and who have striven to teach their family and program members as much as they could of what was necessary to live and work as independently as possible. Perhaps even more of the credit goes to the developmentally disabled individuals who have demonstrated their own will and willingness to work toward the attainment of greater independence and community participation. Semiindependent, supported, and completely independent work and residential programs provide obvious important benefits to their clients, but they also provide significant benefits to the entire services system by reducing the cost of services and by freeing fully supervised residential and work placements for other more severely impaired or less-skilled developmentally disabled persons. Despite their merit in assisting people to achieve their full potential and in obviating stagnation within service systems, the number of such programs remains low. The disincentives to work in government programs cited by Conley in this volume must be altered in order to fully support more integrated employment and living for disabled citizens.

7. *Social, leisure, and recreational programs for developmentally disabled persons remain too low a priority.* Despite increased focus and expenditures within the society as a whole on social, leisure, and recreational activities, it remains hard to find sufficient support for programs offering such services to developmentally disabled persons. In part, this is understandable, given the pressing problem of funding the more visible and costly residential and habilitation programs. On the other hand, the absence of support for such programs overlooks the fact that most developmentally disabled persons live in their natural home and, like many people in natural homes, rely on basic community resources for social, recreational, and leisure activities. Such programs do not need always to be specialized; in fact, in most instances, opportunities that involve nonhandicapped community members are preferable. Services and opportunities should be frequent, they should meet social, leisure, or recreational needs of their clientele at appropriate developmental levels, and they should be free or offered at a reasonable cost to those who can afford them.

8. *The current knowledge base regarding the technology, curriculum, and context of training is not consistently applied.* Recent years have produced truly significant gains in knowledge of how to teach developmentally disabled persons most effectively. Research and demonstration activities have both expanded the specific technology of applying behavioral principles and have greatly enhanced theory and knowledge about effective use of curricula and environments for training developmentally disabled persons. Today, developmentally disabled persons are routinely taught skills and engage in activities that were generally not thought reasonable to expect in past decades. Much of the enhanced contemporary understanding of the capabilities of developmentally disabled persons points to the importance of interrelating the purpose of habilitation (e.g., community participation) with the *context* of instruction (community settings) and with the *curriculum* of instruction (training to perform a specific skill relevant to daily life, like riding the public bus to work). There is a substantial need for bridging the gaps between the levels of the system where knowledge is generated and the levels where, ideally, that knowledge should be reflected in practice.

9. *Minimal standards of professional performance that approximate the state-of-the-art in habilitative programming have*

*not been established.* In the past decade, there has been enormous growth in research related to the performance of the professional and paraprofessional roles in programs serving developmentally disabled persons. This research has led to a knowledge base on demonstrably effective professional practices that is increasingly broad and sophisticated. Unfortunately, the gap between the state-of-the-art and the quotidian "state-of-the-practice" in most programs is wide and may well be growing. There is a need for both uniform minimum standards of individual and organizational performance among community-based services systems and a means for monitoring them.

10. *Evaluation is not a generally expected and commonly performed aspect of professional services.* Human services systems in this country have developed and expanded and, in large measure, have been able to staff themselves only because members of our society have cared about the nature and quality of life of developmentally disabled persons. These systems, founded on sincere caring, often poorly understand and unwillingly accept a need for empirical substantiation of the effects of their activities. Yet, in reality, it is well known that what is accomplished in social programs is often quite different from what was intended. Certainly, the guiding ideals that were the foundation of the establishment of institutions for developmentally disabled people in the 19th century attest to this dilemma. Efforts to provide information about the outcomes of services do not impugn the concern of providers, they demonstrate it; they elevate concern beyond the level of emotional gratification for the providers to a commitment of enhancing demonstrable development and accomplishments of clients. Evaluation must be established as a primary and universal component of service delivery.

11. *Community acceptance of developmentally disabled persons has not yet been fully attained.* There is no question that the acceptance of developmentally disabled persons in the communities where they live and work has undergone significant improvements in the past decade. For example, a recent report of the General Accounting Office (1983) suggests that zoning restrictions to prevent the opening of community-based residential facilities is no longer the problem it once was. Nevertheless, tolerance and acceptance are very different attitudes, and if the former was sufficient to begin the process of integrating developmentally disabled persons into society, the process can approach culmination only through realizing the latter. Continued community education and direct interactions between developmentally disabled persons and their fellow nonhandicapped citizens are critical to this process and must be sustained.

12. *There is still inadequate recognition of formal and informal advocacy and protection activities as a legitimate part of the services system.* Advocacy and protection services are critical elements of service systems for persons with limited or no ability and/or experience in advocating for themselves. The subordinate position of developmentally disabled persons in socially secluded residential and habilitation settings demands that they have access to persons who can represent their interests and services and assure that their rights are acknowledged, whether through formal state advocacy agencies established under the Developmental Disabilities Act, special advocacy–human rights committees in individual residential and habilitation programs, or informal advocates. Increased efforts to build effective advocacy networks among decentralized community-based services systems will be particularly important in providing

adequate protection to developmentally disabled persons as services become increasingly decentralized and dispersed in the future.

13. *The social commitment to research directly related to attaining social integration must be restored.* Over the past few years it has been particularly ironic that while programs of federal and state governments have benefited both in terms of cost and effectiveness from research funded in the previous decade, they have simultaneously reduced their commitment to funding new research. As noted by the National Council on the Handicapped in its August, 1983 report to the president, "A greater, more equitable proportion of resources should be allocated for basic and applied research" (p. 10). Current expenditures for research and evaluation to improve practice represent far less than 1% of the funds expended by service programs (David Braddock, personal communication). With over 100,000 severely/profoundly impaired persons in state institutions and over 250,000 children and youth in segregated schools for handicapped students, there is much left to be done in integrating developmentally disabled persons into their communities, and there is much left to be learned about how such integration can be effectively accomplished. Our society is dependent on more extensive research development and dissemination efforts to guide this process.

## CHALLENGES TO ADVOCATES OF SOCIAL INTEGRATION

Although each of the problems just described is in some ways unique, each is also highly related to the others. They can be linked to four major problem areas that confront the continued development and improvement of contemporary services systems: 1) the elements of service systems are dysjunctive and uncoordi-

nated, 2) funding of service systems is largely dysfunctional and unrelated to the goals of the system or of the larger society, 3) service systems clearly discriminate against their most severely impaired clients, and 4) advocacy for fidelity to standards of high quality is poorly articulated and is disunited. In the following pages, these problems are presented as challenges to those service providers, policy makers, and advocates who would continue the process of integrating developmentally disabled persons and the programs intended to serve them into the general society and its communities.

## The Challenge of Dysjunctive Service Systems

It has long been recognized that people with developmental disabilities have legitimate needs that require the assistance of professionals from a variety of fields. It has also been frequently contended and generally accepted that in order to effectively meet those needs with the limited resources allocated by our society, assistance must be efficiently provided and well coordinated across all sources of assistance. However, continued acknowledgment of these truisms has done little to alter the largely dysjunctive fashion by which services are provided to developmentally disabled persons. In large measure, these services continue to be delivered by self-contained systems that sharply distinguish areas of responsibility and seldom even share common goals for their clients.

If this problem is so widely perceived, why does it persist? In no small measure, of course, the disunion of theoretically linked elements of service provision systems derives from their predominantly bureaucratic structures and the natural tendency toward introversion of social purposes when these become the domain of political organizations. Among the difficulties in stimulating the coordination and integration of the social functions that are the purview of such organizations are: 1) the political protection afforded agencies in maintaining their status of being provider agencies that offer a unique set of services to a recognized legitimate target population, 2) the traditional links between specific disciplinary training and the provision of specific services that greatly impede generic or cross-disciplinary training and flexibility in service delivery, and 3) the lack of unified case-management and client information systems to coordinate the services of different agencies. While these impediments are formidable, there exist both general and specific means to their alleviation.

***Establishing Conditions that Promote Service Integration*** Human services organizations, not unlike other industries, must struggle for their own survival. However, unlike most industries whose struggle is primarily one of productivity and cost-effectiveness and secondarily political, the operation of social services organizations is primarily political and secondarily a matter of productivity and cost-effectiveness. It is the essentially political nature of the human services industry that makes accommodative change so difficult. Although the increased emphasis on evaluation and cost-benefit analysis of recent years may influence some aspects of effectiveness, ultimately the successful and efficient delivery of services hinges on human service agencies being client-centered rather than self-centered. The prevailing service delivery orientation in which the individual is expected to adapt to the provided services rather than vice versa is no longer tenable, given the accomplishments of developmentally disabled persons and their families when homogeneity of need is not presumed.

Reorienting traditional agency-centered service provision involves a number of prerequisite conditions. The first of these is security. Agencies must be able to operate in a context of clear, long-term commitment to maintaining a general level and quality of service for all developmentally disabled persons. A major goal in establishing this context, one that can be shared by advocates and service providers, should be to elicit formal acknowledgment of and commitment to meeting the legitimate needs of developmentally disabled persons by all levels of government. These efforts should include recognition of the quantities and qualities of services that should be the minimum social provision for handicapped persons across age groups and in different domains of daily life (e.g., home, school, work). Such efforts to connect a basic social heritage with a minimal level of service will alleviate much of the extensive diversion of time and talent from service provision to organizational survival at times of crisis such as were caused in the early 1980s by efforts to reduce federal social and educational programs for disabled persons and by recession-induced fiscal crises in many states. Developing such a heritage of assistance to developmentally disabled persons will, of course, demand that advocates and providers reach some consensus of minimal standards responsive to the needs of individuals themselves. The Education for All Handicapped Children Act (Public Law 94-142) has accomplished this to a large extent in special education. Because of the substantial consensus it represented and, to no small extent, inculcated among service consumers, providers, and advocates, when fundamental changes in the rights to education for handicapped children were proposed in the first year of the Reagan administration, there was an unprecedented public protest that quickly caused the unequivocable withdrawal of the proposals.

A recent statement of the National Council on the Handicapped, while having no legal influence on program or policy development, suggests that the goal of developing a unified national policy on services to people with disabilities may indeed be attainable (National Council on the Handicapped, 1983). Among the many pertinent and positive observations in the report are that

> significant social, educational, economic, physical, communication, and transportation barriers prevent a large portion of [disabled] individuals from exercising their basic human rights. Most of them are unable to reach their maximum levels of independence, productivity, and quality of life....This situation is not only morally unacceptable but also impacts negatively the economy and the quality of life of every person in the nation. It must be remedied without delay (p. 1).

Without formal long-term federal commitment to a general level and standard of service provision, it is much less likely that service organizations will become less political and self-protectively oriented in their perspective, particularly in times when budgets for such organizations are being constricted. Like most other individuals and organizations, they will seek to survive first and then serve in ways that are defined by their methods of survival. Irrespective of political views, it is clear that integration and coordination of services to developmentally disabled persons would be substantially enhanced by strong federal commitments to all basic service areas (case management, family support programs, residential services, education/habilitation, and leisure/recreation). Advocates should seek such positive and proactive formal federal commitments as a primary means of developing social and bureaucratic contexts that will enhance the community orientation of services for developmentally disabled persons.

A second important condition for improving integration of services to handicapped citizens is a systemwide, cross-service identification and registration of the needs of handicapped individuals. Under a uniform service management system, the individual can be the focal point of the system, and complete cross-agency records can be maintained on services utilization, program outcomes, client change, and anticipated future needs. Such an approach would greatly improve upon most present systems that are characterized by: 1) needs identification procedures replicated by multiple agencies, and duplicate counting occurring at presumably high, but unknown, rates; 2) client assessment used primarily to confirm eligibility for whatever service each evaluating agency provides; 3) clients often receiving essentially the same services from more than one agency (or worse services with conflicting goals); 4) clients receiving services with no objective evaluation of their impact; 5) provider agencies frequently forming closed systems around sets of clients to whom the agencies continue to provide their services after another agency's services to one or more of their clients would

have been more appropriate; and 6) needs going unmet because each of the individual agencies is responsible for the services it offers, but no one agency has responsibility for needed services that are not offered.

A third important condition for service integration is the organization of service systems around a continuum-of-care concept, with a designated or lead agency charged with responsibility for meeting the overall needs of individuals. In such an orientation, available services are comprehensive and administered around meeting the needs of individuals, and cross-service communication is institutionalized to ensure that service needs are met in a comprehensive and integrated way without undesired duplication. There are four central aspects to organizing and administering such an approach (chapter by Schalock, in Bruininks & Lakin, 1985): 1) system-wide case management (i.e., a single case manager whose role transcends the boundaries of individual service providers), 2) system-wide financing of services (i.e., molding all program budgets into a single fund to permit service decisions to be based primarily on the client and not the funding stream), 3) interagency agreements (i.e., written agreements linking interrelated service agencies to facilitate the development of individualized service packages), and 4) direction services (i.e., programs established to help individuals and agencies identify and secure access to needed services). Wray and Wieck, in this volume, have discussed the case-management component of such an organization; Copeland and Iversen, also in this volume, have described the interagency budgeting process. Volumes by Elder and Magrab (1980) and Magrab and Elder (1979) discuss the establishment of interagency agreements and direction services.

Another prerequisite for an integrated services system is a commitment that, to the maximum extent possible, services provided to severely handicapped persons should be generic in nature. Such an approach establishes a hierarchical preference that, when feasible, first those services already provided in the community for the entire populace (e.g., public buses) are used, second those services required for persons with general needs (e.g., special bus service for mobility-impaired persons) are used, and only finally are specifically targeted services (e.g., a sheltered workshop van) used. Such an approach reinforces the commitment of integrated systems to provide services that deal with needs of people, not with categories of people; it also conserves limited resources to create specialized services where existing agencies cannot meet the needs of clients, even through modifications of existing services. Finally, it encourages the use of program resources in training clients in the skills necessary to use community resources, which tends, eventually, to augment their independence, rather than using these same resources to actually provide services, which tends to maintain a level of dependence. This strategy is frequently resisted out of fear that lowered visibility of specialized services will result in decreased support for handicapped persons. Although this concern is real, it is not well founded. Community-oriented training programs, through their effects on clients' skills and the greater efficiency they achieve in the use of both generic and specialized programs, have provided a visibility for services to developmentally disabled persons that is far greater than ever before. Integrated services will not lead to diminished public support, particularly if what is publicized is the ultimate impact of resources on the lives and abilities of the system's clients. Obviously, increased use of generic services requires that some of the resources no longer utilized in specialized services be diverted into case management and training in the use of community services to further increase the access to community resources and opportunities.

Another condition necessary for an integrated services system is a mechanism to coordinate information about programs, treatment plans, services, and relevant personal, medical, and diagnostic information to those developing plans of habilitation and service delivery. Such information includes evaluation information not only on the abilities and deficiencies of service recipients but also on the

effectiveness of the programs that are available to serve them. Client input and client case studies, as well as objective evaluation data, should be seen as essential information in determining agency capabilities for the purposes of allocating resources within the system.

***Reinforcing the Key Elements of an Integrated Services System*** The cornerstone of an integrated services system must eventually be the establishment of a multiagency case-management system. Case-management systems must be developed so that case managers will have the ability and authority to structure and coordinate transdisciplinary services packages across primary areas of community life, such as education, working/training, leisure/social, residential, health, and recreation. At present, case-management services are generally inadequately organized and funded to authorize needed services or to properly support integration of available services. To support the importance of case management, it can be pointed out that not only has case management been included as a specifically authorized service under the Medicaid Home and Community-Based Services Waiver of 1981, it has been the most frequently (almost universally) requested service by states seeking such a waiver (Greenberg, Schmitz, & Lakin, 1983). However, it is yet to be seen whether this service will evolve into one with sufficient expertise and power to effectively realize its potential. Unfortunately, in a number of states, case managers, despite their unique perspective with respect to services needed by and available to clients of the system, do little more than assure that services are not abusive of clients or of the regulations governing their provision.

Reinforcing the key elements of services systems also involves support to and an appreciation of the worth of natural or quasi-natural service providers (e.g., natural and foster families, neighbors) and of generic service providers (e.g., bus drivers, local recreation agency personnel). Documented failures of professionals to adequately value the importance of these natural providers are common. For example, a report by Freeman (1978) of a pilot program to assess the effectiveness of foster family care as an alternative placement to public institutions showed that the children in foster care gained in both intelligence test scores and in social-emotional behavior. Yet, despite these positive changes, foster parents and the agency supporting them were frustrated in their efforts to work with public school systems. According to Freeman:

> The agency had great difficulty working with the public schools. Some school districts resent foster homes for retarded children. Any agency that wants to keep retarded children in the community has to find ways to help school districts increase their commitment to these special resources (p. 20).

An integrated services system requires leadership at all levels of the system that communicates that the only accepted agenda is improving services and developing opportunities for effective collaboration among agencies, clients, and families. In a study of 30 service integration projects, Gans and Horton (1975) noted generally low but variable levels of coordination among service agencies. Three factors in their analyses, supportive climate, clarity of mission and objectives, and leadership, emerged as the primary facilitators of integrated services:

> Services integration has a better chance of occurring when the sociopolitical leadership in a locality wants it to happen; when integration is high priority objective...; when the project director aggressively pursues coordination and has good contacts with important actors in the process; and when service providers have strong incentives to cooperate.
> Conversely, services integration is less likely to occur...when the local leadership opposes change; when the integrator is so burdened by service delivery responsibilities and internal operations that he has no time to pursue coordination; when the project fails to define its mission as the development of integrative linkages; when service providers actively protect the status quo, jealously guarding their prerogatives, and when the project is poorly administered (p. 6).

Much greater emphasis and pressure must be forthcoming from united advocacy networks as well as from individuals in order that the authorities of federal, state, and local agencies reflect leadership of the former type described by Gans and Horton rather than the latter type. For too long, advocacy has overlooked the importance of human service agency leadership, an oversight that largely accounts for the significant variance both in the quality of different services nationwide and of the same types of services from state-to-state and county-to-county.

Finally, an integrated services system operates from a shared sense of its purpose that overrides the individual goals of its constituent providers. In the area of services to developmentally disabled persons, that shared sense of purpose should include: 1) primary prevention of disabilities and secondary prevention of unnecessarily debilitating effects of disability through institutionalization and other forms of segregation or absence of early identification and intervention programs; 2) access to one's own community, including both physical access through structural modifications and assistive devices, and social access through opening normal social institutions and experiences to handicapped persons; and 3) creation of incentives for the individual clients and service providers to move toward independence and integration in work, school, residence, and other activities. Such a system is committed to providing to clients and families support and assistance in determining their own needs, in evaluating alternatives, and in exercising personal choice in determining the best solutions to meeting their needs within limited available resources. It values the resources that families and communities expend on behalf of their handicapped members, but even more, the level, surety, and naturalness of their commitment. Integrated services implies incentives attached to choices that generally favor family support over family supplantation, community-based or socially integrated services over institutional or segregated services, generic services over specialized services, less-professionalized over more-professionalized services, temporary services over long-term services, less-intensive over more-intensive services, and habilitation in natural settings with natural reinforcement over habilitation in contrived settings with contrived reinforcement. In other words, an integrated services system derives from a view of the community itself as a major component of the total system. While such an outline of an integrated services system may be idealized to some extent, there has been considerable evidence that movement in this direction is both attainable and can reasonably be expected.

## The Challenge of Dysfunctional Funding Approaches

In addition to currently existing organizational problems, service integration is also impeded by the fact that resources are seldom equitably distributed across an idealized continuum of services. Two problems are readily evident in contemporary service system resource allocations. First, in general, higher levels of funding are available for the most institutionalized services, and, second, higher levels of stability and commitment to funding are associated with institutionalized services.

### Greater Commitment to the Lesser Good

The disparity of funding at different levels of service intensity frequently encourages placement decisions to be based to some extent—often to a large extent—on the amount of non-reimbursable costs that will befall the placement agency given its different placement alternatives. This situation is particularly susceptible to negative effects along continua of care where different levels of authority (federal, state, local governments, families) are responsible for different proportional and total contributions to the cost of care. Frequently, placement agencies find that decisions to place persons in a particular type of program bring with them substantially different costs to the agency's governing body than do other types of placements. Obviously, this often creates a tacit pressure (that often becomes explicit to the individuals actually involved) to authorize less-costly services to the placement agency, even when those services may not be the most appropriate for the client or when the combined cost to all contributors of the less-desirable services is actually greater. For example, in states where placement decisions are made by county social workers, there is often a bias toward placement in a residential facility funded primarily by state and federal Medicaid funds rather than a foster home because, although foster care might be more appropriate and entail considerably less total cost, it often requires more extensive county contributions. Similarly, state special education financing is often structured so that it is cheaper for districts to send a child to a residential setting than to meet the needs of that child in his or her home district.

Furthermore, because multigovernment funding tends to be controlled by bureaucratic considerations, it is often more visibly structured according to auditable units and required procedures than human needs. For example, in schools, large amounts of the local district's most important and most expensive resource, personnel time, may be spent confirming handicapped students' membership in educationally irrelevant diagnostic groups in order to secure state and federal funds. Among residential care systems, Medicaid agencies spend millions of dollars annually to monitor whether Title XIX institutional standards are being met, with much less frequent, if any, consideration of whether the required client assessment data indicate that such placements are appropriate or habilitatively beneficial to the persons placed in them. Fortunately, in both government and professional circles, there are those who are beginning to articulate that the so-called entitlements that are converted into comprehensive services ought to entitle persons to the best contemporary applications of those services. For example, it is reasonable to question the merit of extensive cosmetic certification processes that are required by Medicaid agencies in approving institutions as meeting Medicaid standards of care, while judges examining one of the same institutions found that in 1977, at a cost to state and federal Medicaid programs of $60 per day, "residents of Pennhurst [State School and Hospital] have not received, and are not receiving, minimally adequate habilitation. Furthermore, on the basis of the record, we find that minimally adequate habilitation cannot be provided in an institution such as Pennhurst" (*Halderman v. Pennhurst State*

*School and Hospital*, 1977, p. 1295). While the state of Pennsylvania has agreed to close Pennhurst by July 1, 1986, dozens of other institutions will maintain Medicaid certification and reimbursement with no evidence that they are providing a service of any greater benefit and in the midst of growing evidence that their activities are of substantially less benefit than are those of the available alternatives (chapter by Rotegard, Bruininks, Holman, & Lakin in Bruininks & Lakin, 1985).

The lack of application of systematic evaluation to questions of the appropriateness and effectiveness of care has by default created a system where payment for services is directly linked to the extensiveness of care, in many instances creating incentives to make "more placement" than needed, at least to the point where the costs of the more-intensive services to the placement agency approach its costs for less-intensive services. Good examples of this principle in operation can be found among the 35,000 mildly and moderately retarded persons in Intermediate Care Facilities for the Mentally Retarded (ICFs/MR) (Medicaid) certified beds on June 30, 1982, who, for the most part, do not need the level of care required in ICF/MR facilities but, by being placed there, have had half or more (50% to 77%, depending on the state) of their cost of care covered by the federal government. In the absence of a Medicaid-reimbursed placement, state and local governments would contribute the total cost of care minus the individual's much-more-modest Supplemental Security Income (SSI) payment and any private contribution. However, although federal policies have contributed to this problem, Copeland and Iversen (in this volume) have demonstrated how unnecessary it is for states to have their long-term care decisions dictated by funding streams rather than client-centered assessment procedures.

### Weaker Commitments to Greater Good

The integrity of a service system is negatively affected not only by heterogeneity of fiscal support for different levels and types of service, but also by real or perceived differences in the stability of funding for different levels and types of services. Such differences are commonly recognized. For example, most state institutions operate with a long history of state commitment to their operation, which predated the massive funding that became available in the 1970s through Medicaid's ICF/MR program. On the other hand, many community-based facilities rely on the federal SSI and Social Security Disability Income (SSDI) programs, special state and county appropriations, Food Stamps, private donations, family support, and whatever other sources can be lumped together. Although this process can often provide reasonably adequate resources for the programs, it also tends to portray such programs as makeshift and not well protected from the whims of political actors at many levels of government. Many parents express concern that although this new system may promise a temporary improvement in their children's living arrangement, over the long run it appears to provide little assurance of continuous care. When state and county governments link all programs under a single funding arrangement with a commitment that the system will be treated as a whole, regardless of what reimbursements are collected for which facilities and services—that is, when they demonstrate direction by a goal rather than a reimbursement stream—these concerns are somewhat alleviated. Furthermore, once state leadership becomes committed to a more humanistic purpose than maximizing the share of costs borne by someone else, creative methods can be found to fund them (Copeland & Iversen, in this volume).

Deinstitutionalization of severely handicapped persons has been hindered by a lack of supply of community alternatives. In some states, this has been compounded by moratoria on certificates-of-need for new Medicaid-reimbursed facilities. Such moratoria, in the absence of other constructive efforts to provide adequate placements, has locked thousands of potential beneficiaries out of community-based services. Those affected are persons whose cost of care to state governments would have been less in the community if the federal government's Medicaid share were available, but whose care in community-based programs in

the absence of Medicaid is seen as prohib-
itively expensive. The Medicaid Home and
Community-Based Services Waiver program
offers new alternatives in such situations to
build continua of care that incorporate extra-
institutional services for severely handicapped
as well mildly and moderately handicapped
persons. Under this waiver, states have flexibility under approved plans to transfer Medicaid funds within existing Medicaid allotments
from institutional to community services.
However, the generally lower level of willingness to fund community-based services as opposed to institutional services is even visible
under the Medicaid Waiver. While Medicaid
reimbursements were made available in this
legislation for deinstitutionalized clients up to
the cost of their institutional care, a number of
the earliest applications for waivers specified
that community-based care actually would
have to be substantially lower (15%–25%) before being authorized (e.g., Kansas, Utah,
West Virginia). Unfortunately, the Health
Care Financing Administration, the administrative agency for Medicaid, adopted these
doubtfully appropriate standards as its own in
screening later waiver applications. Putting attempts to maximize cost savings above the responsibility to provide the most appropriate
care possible, given the resources that are
available, should be openly recognized as unacceptable. Even as fiscal policy, such practice
shows a narrow-minded attempt to maximize
short-term gains, and at the long-term cost of
retaining greater numbers of people in more
costly institutional settings at considerable
probable detriment to their development.

Even when funding appears adequate for the
continuum of a specific type of service (e.g.,
residential), services needed to support that
continuum are often not available. A contemporary example is the frequent absence of day
activity, vocational, or prevocational positions
for handicapped adults that in many areas preclude clients' placements in available noninstitutional settings or remaining with their
families. Federal and state government funds
(generally half or more federal) are spent rather
lavishly on largely custodial institutional care

(well over $30,000 per client per year on the
average), while the needed day training programs that offer promise of permitting, maintaining, or increasing community integration
are funded far less generously (usually by a
different level of government). Too frequently,
for want of funds to support community-based
programs that are at the forefront of contemporary practice, much more money is spent on
less-desirable programs, and often for no better
reason than that the money "comes from
somewhere else." Of course, taxpayers know
where the money comes from, and the time is
overdue for advocates and service providers
alike to begin to widen the discussion of dysfunctional funding policies across county,
state, and federal agencies to the general
public.

## The Challenge of Discrimination Against the Most Severely Impaired Population

When services are viewed across a continuum
from highly integrated to highly segregated, it
can be seen that there has been clear discrimination against those clients who have the most
severe handicapping conditions. For example,
despite the fact that thousands of severely and
profoundly retarded persons are demonstrating
daily their adaptability to community-based
placements (or more realistically, the mutual
adaptation of residents and their care providers), the vast majority of severely and profoundly retarded persons in long-term care remain in state institutions (Center for
Residential and Community Services, 1983).
In the meantime, most mildly and moderately
retarded individuals in long-term care have
been placed in private, vastly more communi-
ty-integrated group residences. The educational experiences of severely and profoundly
retarded children and youth in long-term care
settings show the same patterns of discrimination. Lakin, Hill, Hauber, and Bruininks
(1982) found among school-age children and
youth (3–17 years old) in a 1979 national sample from both public and private facilities that
19% of the severely/profoundly retarded potential students had no daytime training activity
whatsoever (including homebound education),

despite the promise of Public Law 94-142 that they should. This finding compared with 2% of the sample of mildly/moderately retarded school-age children and youth.

It seems predictable today that in as much as the previous decade brought greatly increased allocations of funds for programs for severely handicapped persons, the next decade must bring redistribution of those funds to better support and stimulate the social goals that are espoused, but still unrealized, for developmentally disabled persons. There have been visible efforts in this direction with regard to Medicaid funding of long-term care in the area of supporting community-based services. Under the 1981 Medicaid Home and Community-Based Services Waiver program, funds once utilized to provide institutional care to severely handicapped children and adults are now available for community-based residential and related services. However, conservative operationalization of the cost-saving mechanisms in this legislation are reducing its applicability to tens of thousands of the most severely impaired institution residents whose levels of disability require community-based services packages that are nearly equal to the cost of their institutional programs. Not only are such interpretations fundamentally out of line with general expectations for this legislation by Congress and by those who advocated its passage, but they are another blatant example of a national willingness to abrogate standards of equal treatment when the subjects of that treatment are severely and profoundly developmentally disabled persons. Similar unfortunate examples of conservative interpretation of the "related services" provisions of Public Law 94-142 can also be cited as showing how fragile are the promises of "equal protection under the law" to developmentally disabled persons and how constant must be the vigilance and advocacy on their behalf.

In response to the need to formally establish a national commitment to developing community-oriented services for the predominantly severely/profoundly impaired populations of state and private institutions, legislation submitted to Congress in November, 1983, pro-

vided that Medicaid funding would slowly be withdrawn from supporting institutional placements (facilities of 16 or more residents) for developmentally impaired persons over a 10- to 15-year period. While such proactive legislation is more difficult to obtain support for than value-neutral legislation like the Medicaid Waiver authority, which was actually submitted to Congress as a cost-cutting measure, though widely supported for its programmatic merits, advocates increasingly recognize the need for fiscal as well as philosophical provocations for change in the treatment of developmentally disabled persons. The realization that state governments must become more conscious of funding alternatives in facing growing human services budgets in a period of decreasing philosophical and real-dollar financial commitments from the federal government has led to increased recognition of the power of available federal (and state) dollars to induce positive change. Such realizations illustrate even more clearly the importance of demanding that funding mechanisms create incentives for the kinds of services that are most beneficial to their target populations, particularly when such arguments can be made on the grounds of cost benefit as well as humanistic and constitutional values. In pursuing programmatic goals through political means, it is equally important not to promote incentives that are narrowly focused (e.g., that support the general development of community-based residential care without concurrent inducements to develop a full range of levels of care) or that are so widely focused that political viability is lost. To some extent, the aforementioned legislation to limit the size of facilities authorized for Medicaid reimbursements faces an uncertain future because, in addition to its provisions with respect to residential care, it proposes to authorize new services and wider eligibility criteria in ways that would substantially increase the number of developmentally disabled Medicaid beneficiaries. Furthermore, in the pursuit of significant change, it must be remembered, particularly in the process of rhetorical advocacy, which often provokes simplicity, that the wholesale changes brought about on the conviction that everyone will benefit from a certain program generally have a short-lived acceptability (e.g., the smaller regional institutions that were built in lieu of new state institutions in the 1950s and 1960s and the large group homes and segregated, categorical special education settings that were opened in the 1970s).

Community-based service systems have less experience in serving severely and profoundly handicapped persons than might be desired. There are excellent examples of high-quality community-based services, but the assumption that most community service systems are currently prepared to meet the challenges of increased integration of the most severely impaired developmentally disabled persons is overly optimistic. Therefore, there is a great susceptibility to the common human and bureaucratic tendency of applying old solutions to new problems in developing the "new" programs and policies that will support the integration of developmentally disabled persons into their own society (e.g., the use of large group home models or segregated classes in local schools originally developed for mildly/ moderately handicapped persons in community settings for severely/profoundly handicapped persons). Care must be exercised that placement in settings meeting superficial conditions of being community-based does not become an end in itself. And although it is vital to recognize that much of the knowledge needed to develop effective community-based programs and the policies to stimulate and sustain them is available and awaits application, it is also important for advocates and professionals to disperse this knowledge, to develop and monitor standards for its applications, and to recognize and pursue the need to continually develop new knowledge on the impacts of programs and policies focused on the development and integration of severely and profoundly impaired persons in community settings.

## The Challenge of Disunity in Advocacy for High-Quality Services

Changes in word and, to a lesser degree, deed (i.e., practice) in the last two decades have favored organizational models and treatment strategies based upon principles of integration. Despite such changes, the agenda is far from complete for fully achieving the synthesis of thought and action. Research findings on residential services, in particular, demonstrate that the majority of severely handicapped persons living under supervision outside the natural or adopted family still remain in rather large, isolated care settings. The situation in education, although seemingly better, still includes extensive use of settings and educational approaches for developmentally disabled children and youth that segregate them from nonhandicapped persons and from normal circumstances of childhood. Furthermore, when the appearance of physical integration is accomplished, it is all too often accompanied by social and psychological isolation through natural physical barriers, absence of contact with nonhandicapped members of the community, social rejection, or even neglect. If, as has been noted, policy surfaces in its implementation, it is obvious that much remains to be accomplished in deinstitutionalization, in placement in the least restrictive setting, and in normalization. Flynn and Nitsch (1980) recently commented on this situation with respect to the adoption of the normalization principle in human service programs.

> Perhaps the greatest challenges facing normalization is the "theory-practice gap." This principle has been met with widespread intellectual, judicial, and legislative approval on the one hand. On the other, implementation has frequently been sporadic and superficial, and, indeed, in many jurisdictions it can be said to have scarcely begun (p. 3).

Accepting the proposition that policy is exemplified in its implementation suggests the importance of better understanding how policies are generally implemented when designing strategies for narrowing the gap between desired practices and the application of public policy. However, the study of the implementation of public policies is a relatively new research focus. Regrettably, the initiation and defense of policies to implement ideological principles—such as normalization, deinstitutionalization, and social integration—receive far less attention than discussion of the ideals themselves.

Improving the implementation of programs to increase the social integration of developmentally disabled persons represents a considerable challenge in the years ahead. Assuring continued public support for this effort requires the awareness that by nature, planned change is "deliberate effort...to create a modification in the structure and process of a social system such that it requires members of that system to relearn how they perform their roles" (Zaltman & Duncan, 1977, p. 10). The recognition that much is left to be relearned is a helpful first step in improving the adoption of new ideas and practices. But it is not enough.

What is missing from current advocacy activities is a clear, coherent, and unified strategy for facilitating the adoption of deinstitutionalization and mainstreaming as a framework for practice at all levels, not merely in the articulation of broad principles and policies. Zaltman and Duncan (1977) have described four general strategies for promoting adoption of change and innovations: a) reeducation or rational empirical strategies, b) facilitative strategies, c) persuasive strategies, and d) power strategies. To protect past gains while modifying and improving upon complex public policies undoubtedly requires the combining of methods. It also requires that each method be applied judiciously and, to the maximum extent possible, concertedly. Above all, it is important to recognize that each strategy brings about a qualitatively different result in addition to the more visible quantitative effects. Evidence of this point has been visible in recent years as numerous programs for developmentally disabled persons were eyed for reductions in funding and/or regulatory assurances under the Reagan administration. One case in point relates to the administration's plan, announced in its first months in office, to repeal provisions of Public Law 94-142 and to roll its authorizations, along with many other programs, into a block grant of compounded federal education grants to states. Advocates who opposed such changes could have taken several potential actions in response to this proposal, but, iron-

ically, the more persuasive styles of action available to them were virtually neutralized by lack of useful evaluation data in special education outcomes. In the final analysis, they had only three viable choices: 1) to battle in concert over any change whatsoever in the law (power), 2) to accept the proposition that certain modifications in the law could be beneficial and work through their negotiation with the administration (facilitative), or 3) to accept the block grant program, attempting to influence the distribution and utilization of those funds on the state and local levels through the use of one or more of the rational approaches that led to the original passage of the federal legislation. Given the disunity of advocates for handicapped children, the wide differences in opinion they represented, and the immediacy and severity of the challenge, it is not surprising, and probably fortuitous, that advocates accepted the importance of uniting to reject any changes whatsoever in Public Law 94-142. Although this approach was remarkably successful, producing hitherto unheard of amounts of mail to members of Congress, it did nothing to reform special education and may have actually distanced the day when advantageous reform might be attained.

Another example with a different outcome was the Medicaid Waiver program, approved in 1981, which permits Medicaid funds to provide community services to aged or handicapped persons who, in the absence of those services, would require institutional services of greater or equal cost. This program represents the culmination of work by advocates who developed the empirical substantiation of both the benefits of such programs in terms of client independence and cost savings and the conditions under which the waivered services could be viably provided and, finally, who successfully diagnosed the political context to find a workable means of selling the program.

Through careful analysis of services that are unavailable or inadequate and of specific impediments to delivering those services, efforts can be devised that provide information to potential change agents, that create and strengthen incentives and reinforcements for improved program practices, and that solidify the networks of those who urge improved program design and facilitative, administrative, and regulatory practices. Persons interested in the quality of educational and human services programs have made too little use of system analytical tools to facilitate the implementation of policies that promote responsiveness to standards of good contemporary practice. The value of such strategies lies in their clarification of agreed-upon goals and objectives, in their identification of barriers to the realization of these goals and objectives, in their development of coordinated approaches to overcome such barriers, and in their establishment of knowledge and data bases that can flexibly respond to the exigencies and vagaries of political decision making.

Effective advocacy in the remainder of this century will be a very different process than it was in the 1960s and 1970s. In the earlier period, program development was more often predicated solely on the identification of need. In the future, program development or, more realistically, program modifications will require demonstration that proposed programs respond cost-effectively to that need. This will require a less polemical and more analytical advocacy. In the face of occasional threats to important programs for developmentally disabled persons, rallies to save these programs will probably muster more than enough power for immediate success. The real battle in the near future, however, is to develop ways to redistribute the resources of existing programs to meet the standards that can reasonably be expected of them. Accomplishing this will require even more in-depth understanding of the system of services in its many layers and often conflicting purposes.

The foundation for improving services must be based upon several requirements, not the least of which is developing a broader consensus and renewed commitment to the ideas and standards of state-of-the-art practices. Little constructive change can likely occur without such consensus as an alternative to the strident forms of polarization that have often been witnessed among contending groups in recent years. But consensus of purpose is not sufficient to sustain true reform in our service programs. Such reform will also require greater analytical sophistication; greater appreciation of the perspectives of all the constituents of the system, from clients and their families, to direct service providers, to agency administrators, to politicians; it will require better anticipation of future issues and of the information and experiences that will be relevant to them; and it will require a willingness to think beyond the circle of agencies, types of services, and political alliances that have traditionally dominated action focused on developmentally disabled persons.

As funding levels stabilize, conflicting interests surface. Those who continue to advocate for accelerated social integration for developmentally disabled persons can expect to find more ready allies in persons who advocate similar perspectives for aged, physically handicapped, and mentally ill persons than they will among those who press for moderation in deinstitutionalization efforts. To pursue those alliances and, even preferably, to ensure that they produce unified definitions of issues and concerted actions, will be critical to the future of services for developmentally disabled persons in community settings. But, finally, advocates must be ready and able to separate what they know from what they suspect, what they feel from what is true. There is much to learn in bringing about the successful physical, social, and productive integration of the over 125,000 severely/profoundly impaired developmentally disabled persons in large isolated residential settings, of the over 250,000 children and youth who attend school in settings that provide no contact with nonhandicapped peers, of the tens of thousands of day activity and sheltered work center employees who should be working in real job settings, of the hundreds of thousands of developmentally disabled persons living at home with inadequate social, leisure, and recreation activities. In advocating for the integration of these persons into community living, spokespersons must accept responsibility for continuing to learn more about how such integration can be accomplished successfully.

# REFERENCES

Bruininks, R.H., & Lakin, K.C. (eds.). *Living and learning in the least restrictive environment*. Baltimore: Paul H. Brookes Publishing Co., 1985.

Center for Residential and Community Services. *1982 national census of residential facilities: Summary report*. Minneapolis: University of Minnesota, Department of Educational Psychology, 1983.

*Education for All Handicapped Children Act of 1975*, 20 U.S.C. 1401.

Elder, J.O., & Magrab, P.R. (eds.). *Coordinating services to handicapped children: A handbook for interagency collaboration*. Baltimore: Paul H. Brookes Publishing Co., 1980.

Flynn, R.J., & Nitsch, K.E. (eds.). *Normalization, social integration, and community services*. Baltimore: University Park Press, 1980.

Freeman, H. Foster care for mentally retarded children: Can it work? *Child Welfare*, 1978, *57*, 113–121.

Gans, S.P., & Horton, G.T. *Integration of human services: The state and municipal levels*. New York: Praeger Publishers, 1975.

General Accounting Office. *An analysis of zoning and other problems affecting the establishment of group homes for the mentally disabled* (GAO/HRD-83-14). Washington, DC: General Accounting Office, 1983.

Greenberg, J.N., Schmitz, M., & Lakin, K.C. *An analysis of state responses to the home and community-based waiver program (Section 2176)*. Washington, D.C.: National Governors Association, 1983.

*Halderman v. Pennhurst State School and Hospital*, 446, F. Supp. 1295. (E.D.Pa. 1977).

Lakin, K.C. *Demographic studies of residential facilities for the mentally retarded: An historical review of methodologies and findings*. Minneapolis: University of Minnesota, Department of Educational Psychology, 1979.

Lakin, K.C., Hill, B.K., Hauber, F.A., & Bruininks, R.H. Changes in age at first admission to residential care of mentally retarded people. *Mental Retardation*, 1982, *20*(5), 216–219.

Magrab, P.R., & Elder, J.O. (eds.). *Planning for services to handicapped persons: Community, education, health*. Baltimore: Paul H. Brookes Publishing Co., 1979.

National Council on the Handicapped. *National policy for persons with disabilities*. Washington, D.C.: National Council on the Handicapped, 1983.

Zaltman, G., & Duncan, R. *Strategies for planned change*. New York: John Wiley & Sons, 1977.

# Index

AAMD Adaptive Behavior Scale, school edition, 79

Acquisition building stage, 63
  illustrations of, 65

Adaptation
  enhancing instruction for, 29–71
  instructional design for, 41–60
  response in severely handicapped persons, 66

Adaptive behavior, *see* Behavior(s), adaptive

Adaptive Behavior Inventory for Children, 79

Adaptive social development, 120–121

Agencies, linkages in case management and, 225

Antecedent events, *see* Events, antecedent

Arrangement of behaviors and events
  to accelerate learning, 50–53
  changing, to reinforce increasingly fluent responding, 52
  as a criterion for best performance, 52
  two-banded, to provide more powerful reinforcers, 52

Assessment
  of adaptive behavior, 73–104
    *see also,* Behavior(s), adaptive
  intervention strategies and, 27–158
    *see also,* Behavior(s), adaptive; Behavior(s), problem; Education, early
  of problem behaviors, 105–128
    *see also,* Behavior(s), problem

Assistance
  decreasing, 57
  in the form of error-correction events used subsequent to incorrect or no-responses, 58
  increasing, 57

Autistic children, language intervention with, 153

Balthazar Scales of Adaptive Behavior for the Profoundly and Severely Mentally Retarded, 80

Behavior(s)
  adaptive
    administration procedures for measuring, 83
    assessing and training, 73–104

content areas of instruments assessing, 90–91, 165
content of scales measuring, 92–94
criterion for evaluating research on the training of, 94–95
deficiencies in, at various age levels, 74
diagnosis and placement, 72
findings from the evaluation of research on the training of, 95–98
population description as a purpose for measuring, 78
program evaluation and management as a purpose for measuring, 77
program planning as a purpose of scales measuring, 72
purposes of assessing, 76–78
recommendations from the evaluation of research on the training of, 98
reliability of scales measuring, 84
review of selected scales measuring, 78–83
structure of, 74–76
technical considerations in assessing, 84–92
training, 94

analysis
  as approach to community integration, 277–290
  as a framework for intervention and evaluation, 277–278
  three-term contingency of, as a conceptual device for facilitating community integration, 279–280
  *see also* Community integration

arrangement of, to accelerate learning, 50–53

classification schema for environmental-social impact, 113

consequating incorrect, 57

instructional planning and, 34–35

management, *see* Management of behavior

problem
  assessment of, 110–114
  characteristics of strategies for managing, 116–121
  destructive, 113

Behavior(s)—*continued*
    11 most cited, 113–114
    establishing priorities for, 115
    extended effects of, 107–108
    maladaptive, 113
    management of, 105–128
    response to, 108–110
    reducing inappropriate, for leisure/recreational
        educational participation, 265
    target, in unsuccessful instruction, 62
Behavioral programming for behavior manage-
    ment, 118
    characteristics of applied research on, 118
*Brown v. Board of Education,* 9
Bureaucratic contexts of integrated service deliv-
    ery, 20–23


Caregiver-child interactions in early education,
    130–133
    need for improving, 131
Case management
    definitions of, 221–222
    federal support for, 226
    frequently suggested elements of, 221
    funding people, not programs, 225–226
    limits of, 222–223
    linkages among agencies, 225
    in Minnesota, 223–224
    moving toward least restrictive environment
        through, 219–230
    needs assessment in, 225
    steps to strengthen
        fiscal, 224–226
        programmatic, 224–226
    themes from emerging service models, 220–221
    three levels of comprehensiveness, 221–222
    variety of models for, 226
Center-based intervention study, 144
Cerebral palsy, intervention with children with,
    145–147
    effects of physiotherapy on reflexes, 147
    three approaches to treatment, 145
    vestibular stimulation and, 146
    visual-motor training program and, 145
Client impact on community integration, 282–286
Communitization strategy as continuum-of-care
    alternative, 295–296
Community integration
    behavior analytic approach to, 277–290
    extended effects of behavior problems as deter-
        rents to, 107–108
    guidelines for, 288–289
    initial placement in public residential facilities
        as a factor affecting, 106–107
    levels of client impact determining success of,
        282–286
    levels of organization having an impact on, 279

    problem-solving approach to deterrents of,
        286–288
    problems affecting, 106
    *see also* Behavior, analysis; Integration; Social
        integration
Community-referenced programs for lei-
    sure/recreational activities, 262
Community residential facilities, 257
    leisure activity and, 257
    longitudinal perspective on, 258
Competence, Greenspan's model of personal, 76
Competitive employment education, 177–193
    broadening definitions of special education and,
        184–185
    changing propositions for training and,
        186–190
    contemporary special education, 180–183
    framing propositions for research and develop-
        ment and, 190–191
    guiding propositions for program development
        and, 185–186
    implications of the ecological perspective ap-
        plied to, 184
    implications of systems-analytic approach for,
        183–191
    role equipments in, 178
    systems-analytic approach for special education
        and, 178–179
    target settings in, 178
    traditional special educational perspective and,
        179–180
Content of instruction, 17–19
Context(s)
    bureaucratic, of integrated service delivery,
        20–23
    of instruction, 19–20
Continuum-of-care
    advantages of, 296–297
    alternative approaches to, 295–296
    definition of, 294–299
    developing fiscal strategies for state system,
        301–308
        analytic background of, 302–305
        current allocations in sample state program,
            303
        irregular match of people and services in,
            302–303
        open- and closed-ended programs, 303
        overlapping eligibilities, 302
        service definition and, 302
    federal government responsibility for change
        and, 308
        improved knowledge, 309–312
        shifting incentives, 308–309
    funding of
        accounting of, 297–298
        correcting perverse incentives, 298–299
    making it work at state level, 299–301

organizing, 300
role of state developmental disabilities council, 300–301
unified budgeting and planning, 299–300
policy options for, 294–299
sources of state funding prior to 1982, 297
strategy, 295–296
Conversational method of learning, 172–173
Curriculum and instruction, 18

Deinstitutionalization
definition of, 4
problems in establishing uniform connotation of, 5
quantitative support for effectiveness of, 105
in residential services programs, 73
strategy as continuum-of-care alternative, 295–296
Delivery of services, problems in, 212–213
Dependency, fostering of, 211–212
Design instruction, 41–60
Development, adaptive social, 120–121
Developmental training programs for behavior management
future implications of, 124–125
present status of, 124
Developmentally disabled individuals
behavior analytic approach to community integration and, 277–290
challenges to advocates of social integration of, 313–329
effectiveness of stimulation program and, 140
intervention and, 140–145
moving toward less restrictive environments, 219–230
philosophical principles underlying services for, 12–13
social goals for services to, 4–6
social integration of, 3–25
system for, working example of, 305–308
Disincentives
effects of structural, on work effort, 209–211
fostering of dependency and, 211–212
total financial, 208
Down syndrome
efficacy findings involving children with, 135–140
language stimulation and, 135–138
importance of early transactions between mother and child with, 131
knowledge of karyotype in research, 152
negative outcomes for some intervention programs, 139
Drugs
management of behavior through, 116–118
need for monitoring of, 117
psychotropic, potential effects of, on behavior acquisition, 117

EDGE project, *see* Expanding Developmental Growth Through Education project
Education
competitive employment, 177–193
early
caregiver-child interactions in, 130–133
establishing efficacy of, 133–135
establishing need for, 130–133
implications for policy and research improvements, 154–156
pre-experimental designs, 134
quasi-experimental designs using control group employed in studies of, 134
services to aid parents in, 154–155
as a strategy for producing less restrictive environments, 129–158
validity checklist for, 133
right to, 9–10
standards of effective, 16–17
Educational integration, reimbursement formula and, 285
Educational settings
leisure/recreational participation in, 261–266
collateral skill development in, 264
community-referenced programs in, 262
curriculum trends in, 261–262
generalization and, 263
individualized programs and, 262
methods of training for, 263
reducing inappropriate behaviors as a result of, 266
Efficacy findings
in children with severe handicaps, 140–151
in Down syndrome children, 135–140
Efficiency in programs for behavior management, 121
Employment
competitive education for, *see* Competitive employment education
federal impact on, for mentally retarded persons, 193–216
Environment(s)
auditory, in enrichment program for children with language handicap, 148
enrichment of, to reduce problem behaviors, 123
factors affecting behavioral problems, 121–134
physical and social, as aspects of the environmental design for managing problem behaviors, 122
removal of aversive characteristics in, 122
as seen from a behavioral perspective, 122
Environmental selection in response to behavior problems, 108–109
Events
antecedent, 43–50
enhancing stimulus characteristics, 46–50
examples of necessary and synthetic, 44

Events—*continued*
fading and, 48
fluency building, 48
setting, instructional design for, 42–43
subsequent, 53–60
reinforcers and, 53–57
Exosystem in contemporary special education, 182
Expanding Developmental Growth through Education project (EDGE), 136
External validity requirements for research in early education, 155


Facility, size and structure of, as potentials for adaptation to community settings, 123
Fading in antecedent events, 48
Family attitudes toward leisure for handicapped persons, 258–259
Federal programs
basic misconception concerning, 199–200
causes of work failure, 196–197
classifications of programs serving mentally retarded persons, 199
directions for the future, 214–216
disincentives for employment, 200
effects of, on employment, 200
health care and, 205–207
impact of, on employment of mentally retarded persons, 193–216
income support programs, 200–202
placement of severely mentally retarded persons in, 197–198
problem of defining population at risk and, 193–194
as providers of services to mentally retarded persons, 198–199
Federal support for case management, 226
Financial disincentives, social services and, 208
Financial incentive
for placement in least restrictive alternative, 291–312
continuum-of-care concept as a, 292
continuum management and, 292–292
long-term care arrangements and, 293
Fiscal issues, 275–329
Fluency in antecedent events, 48
Fluency building stage, 63
illustrations of, 65
Food, overuse of, as reinforcer, 55


*Garrity v. Galen,* 8
Generalization
current approaches to programming for, 168–171
deduction and, 169
definition of, 167
effective teaching for, independent living and, 167–171

enhancing instruction for, 29–71
functional skills for, 168
historical perspective on, 167–168
induction and, 168
instructional design for, 41–60
response in severely handicapped persons, 66
self-management strategies as an approach to training for, 169–170
training in criterion environment as an approach to training for, 169
Goals of services for developmentally disabled persons, 4–6
Government roles in developing less restrictive services, 227–229
Greenspan's model of personal competence, 76
Group structure
intervention addressing effect of, 149–151
Grouping arrangements as intervention agents, 149


Habilitation, right to, 10–12
Handicapped individuals
moving toward competitive employment education for, 177–193
services for
leisure/recreational, 253–274
*see also* Community integration; Education; Service(s)
severely, efficacy findings in children who are, 140–151
Hawaii experience
accessibility of generic services as a planning variable in, 236
advance program design preparation for integration in, 237
anticipating and accepting opposition concerning, 239
assigning key roles to persons to introduce, 239
background of, 233–234
communicating timelines for implementing, 238
credibility of integrated model as a planning variable for, 237
innovation into practice as an implementation variable in, 237
interviews with those involved in the integration process of, 234–245
legal climate as a planning variable in, 236–237
local demonstrations of excellence as an implementation variable in, 238–239
planning variables as a major issue in, 236–237
program quality as a parental concern in, 242–244
summary of parental concerns in, 244–245
Health care, federal programs and, 205–207
Home environments, leisure participation and, 256


Implications of early education findings for policy and research improvements, 154–156

Income security, effects of federal programs on,
    208–214
  mentally retarded persons and, 208–209
Independent living
  adult skills development program for, 174
  available curriculum materials designed for,
      171–173
    analysis of, 171–172
    conversational method and rehearsal as, 172
    in vivo training as, 173
  desirable program characteristics of, 162–164
    functional content of, 162–163
    generalization of skill as, 163
    independent performance as, 163
    normalized service settings as, 163
    program-related assessment as, 163
  effective teaching for generalization and mainte-
      nance in, 167–171
  normalized instructional program for transition
      to, 173–174
  problems experienced by mildly retarded per-
      sons in transition to, 161
  program-related assessment and, 164–167
    approaches to, 164–166
    content of, 164
    stages of decision making within, 166
    use of information on, 166–167
  programming transition to, for retarded persons,
      161–175
  reasons for difficulty in transition to, 162
Institutionalization, common definition of, 5
Instruction
  content of, 17–19
  context of, 19–20
  enhancing
    for adaptation, 29–77
    for generalization, 29–71
    for maintenance, 29–71
  measuring pupil performance in planning for,
      41
  remediating plans for unsuccessful, 62–65
  sequencing, methods for, 37–41
  technology and, 18
Instructional aims, establishing functional, 35–36
Instructional design
  for adaptation, 41–60
  for generalization, 41–60
  for maintenance, 41–60
Instructional planning, 34–41
  establishing functional aims and, 35–37
  measuring pupil performance and, 41
  methods of remediating, 64
  selecting behaviors and, 34–35
  sequencing instruction and, 37–41
Integration
  enhancing, 217–275
  growing consensus concerning, 231
  managing of, 217–275
  resistance to, 232

social, of developmentally disabled persons,
    3–25
  strategies for, 217
    Hawaii experience as a, see Hawaii
        experience
    markers for, 245–248
    obstacle inventory for classroom, 249
    physical, 248
    Public Law 94-142 and, 245
    sample obstacle inventory for classroom, 250
    school, 231–252
    social, 248
  see also Community integration; Social
      integration
Interagency budgeting and least restrictive alter-
    native, 292
Internal validity requirements for studies in early
    education, 155
Intervention
  and assessment strategies, 27–158
  cerebral palsied children and, 145–147
  early
    summary of studies supporting, 153–154
    support for, 153
  evaluation of specific practices of, as research
      goal, 155
  group structure effects and, 149–151
  in non–Down syndrome severely handicapped
      persons, 153
  severe language handicap in children and, 147–
      149
  short-term effects of, on language of autistic
      children, 153
  in unsuccessful learning, 62–65
Inventory for Client and Agency Planning, 80

Knowledge base for integrated services, 14–16

Language handicap, intervention with children
    with, 147–149
Language quotients in hearing-impaired children,
    153
Language stimulation studies in Down syndrome
    children, 135–138
Learning, observational
  facilitation of, 60
  self-control techniques and, 60–62
  shaping and, 32
Learning process, 30–34
  antecedent stimuli and, 32
  schedules of reinforcement and, 31
  shaping new behaviors and, 32
  subsequent stimuli and, 30–31
Least restrictive alternative, 13–14
  financial incentives for placement in, 291–312
  long-term care arrangements and associated
      costs of, 293

Least restrictive environment
  categories of service system function based on,
    15
  early education as strategy for production of,
    129–158
  as ideological concept, 73
  leisure services for handicapped persons and,
    256
  moving persons with developmental disabilities
    toward, 219–230
Least restrictive placement, provision for in PL
    94-142, 10
Leisure/recreation participation
  in community settings, 266–270
    facilitators of, 267
    inhibitors of, 267
    needs assessment for, 266–267
    programs fostering, 268–269
  comparative studies of handicapped and non-
    handicapped persons, for evaluation of,
    260–261
  in educational settings, 261–266
    age-appropriate programs as curriculum
      trends in, 262
    collateral skill development in, 264–265
    community-referenced programs as curricu-
      lum trends in, 262
    generalization as a method of leisure-skills
      training in, 263–264
    individualized programs as curriculum trends
      in, 262–263
    reducing inappropriate behavior in, 265
  in home environments, 256–260
    active versus passive activities and, 256–257
    age of retardation and, 259–260
    family attitudes and, 258–259
    level of retardation and, 259–260
    public versus community residential facilities
      and, 257
Leisure/recreation services for handicapped per-
    sons, 253–274
  conceptual issues and assumptions of, 254–256
    discretionary time as a, 254–255
    free time as a, 254–255
    normalization as a, 255–256
    personal preferences as a, 255
    quality of life as a, 255
  guidelines for special populations, 269–270
Less restrictive environment, agenda for change in
    services for, 227
Less restrictive services
  actions by federal government, 227–228
  actions by local level government, 228–229
  government roles in developing, 227–229

Macrosystem in contemporary special education,
    182

Mainstreaming, 73
  as perspective for examining group structure,
    150
  see also Integration
Maintenance
  current approaches to programming for, 168–
    171
  deduction and, 169
  definition of, 167
  effective teaching for, independent living and,
    167–171
  enhancing instruction for, 29–71
  functional skills for, 168
  induction and, 168
  instructional design for, 41
  response of severely handicapped persons, 66
  self-management strategies as an approach to
    programming for, 169–170
  training in criterion environment as an approach
    to programming for, 169
Management
  of behavior
    behavioral programming and, 118
    characteristics of strategies for, 116
    through drugs, 116–118
    environmental factors and, 121–124
    present status of developmental training pro-
      grams for, 124–125
    program efficiency and, 121
    punishment strategies for, 118–121
  of problem behavior, see Behavior(s), problem
Mental training in Down syndrome children, 138
Mesosystem in contemporary special education,
    181
Monitoring behavioral changes as a goal in early
    education research, 155

National economy, effects of, on mentally re-
    tarded persons, 213–214
Neurodevelopmental treatment approach in Down
    syndrome, 138
Nondiscrimination in placement practices, 7–9
Noninstitutionalization
  advocates of, 6–7
  deinstitutionalization versus, 6
Normalization, 12–13
  categories of service system function based on,
    15
  definition of, 105
  as ideological concept, 73
  as key concept in Wolfensberger's definition,
    105
  leisure services for handicapped persons and,
    255–256
Nurturing attention in intervention programs, 143

Object permanence intervention efforts, 141–142
Organizational issues, 275–329

Parents, benefits of early education for, 154–155
Peer influences as intervention agents, 149–151
*Pennsylvania Association for Retarded Citizens,*
    *(PARC) v. Commonwealth of Pennsylva-*
    *nia,* 10
Performance, measuring pupil, 41
Philosophy of integrated services for developmen-
    tally disabled persons, 12–13
Physiotherapy, effects of, on cerebral palsied
    children, 147
Piaget's theory of cognitive development, 136
Placement in least restrictive alternative, financial
    incentives for, 291–312
Planning, instructional, 34–41
Portage Curriculum Guide, 142–143
Pre-experimental designs, 134
Premature babies, degree of stimulation and later
    performance scores, 132
Preparation, vocational, and employment,
    159–216
Problem behaviors, assessment and management
    of, 105–128
Program efficiency in behavior management, 121
Programming for transition to independent living
    for retarded persons, 161–175
Project EDGE, *see* Expanding Developmental
    Growth Through Education project, 136
Public Law 94-142, 245
Public residential facilities
    leisure activity and, 257
    placement and, 105–106
    readmission to, 107
Punishment strategies for behavior management,
    118–121
    arranged, 120
    guidelines for, 119–120
    possible negative side effects of, 119
    practical implications of, 119
Pupil, measuring his or her performance, 41

Quality of life and leisure services for handi-
    capped persons, 255
Quasi-experimental designs
    time series, 134
    using controls, 134

Recreation services for handicapped persons,
    253–274
Reimbursement formula as a function of degree of
    student handicap, 285
Reinforcement
    performance and, 52
    schedules of, in learning process, 31
Reinforcer(s)
    distribution of instructional trials to preserve
        power of, 56
    hidden, 56

implementing a token system to obtain, 54
overuse of food and drink and, 55
programming events as, 54
programming an instruction trial as, 54
reprogramming of proven, 54
select, events available to same-age peers and, 54
selection of, from variety of available events, 55
subsequent events as, 53–57
survey events in nontraining setting that serve
    as, 53–54
variable ratio and, 56
Reliability in assessment of adaptive behavior,
    84–92
Reliability data in manuals of selected adaptive
    behavior scales, 86
Remediating plans for unsuccessful instruction,
    62–65
Research goals stemming from early education
    findings, 155
Response cost technique, 59
Response from severely handicapped persons, 66
Retarded persons
    effects of national economy on, 213–214
    effects of federal program on income security
        of, 208–209
    impact of federal programs on employment of,
        193–216
    and independent living, *see* Independent living
    problems of delivery of services to, 212–213
    programming transition to independent living
        for, 161–175
Right to education, 9–10
Right to habilitation, 10–12
Role equipments in systems-analytic approach to
    special education, 178
Role performances in systems-analytic approach to
    special education, 178

Scales of Independent Behavior, 80
School integration strategies, 231–252
Security, effects of federal programs on income,
    208–214
Self-control techniques, observational learning
    and, 60–62
Sequencing instruction, 37–41
    methods of, 38
Service(s)
    direct, categories of system function and, 15
    indirect, categories of system function and, 15
    integrated
        bureaucratic contexts of, 20–23
        knowledge base for, 14–16
        philosophical principles underlying, 12–13
    problems in delivery of, 212–213
    social
        federal programs and, 207–208
        goals for developmentally disabled persons,
            4–6

Service delivery system, conditions for, 291
Service models, themes emerging from 220–221
Service systems, critical steps in establishment of, 275
Setting events, instructional design and, 42–43
Shaping behaviors, learning process and, 32
Social development, adaptive, 120–121
Social goals for services to developmentally disabled persons, 4–6
Social integration
    challenges to advocates of, 317–329
    of developmentally disabled persons, 3–25
    discrimination against severely impaired population as a challenge to, 324–326
    disunity in advocacy for high-quality services as a challenge to, 326–329
    dysfunctional funding approaches as challenge to greater commitment to lesser good and, 322–323
    weaker commitments to greater good and, 322–323
    dysjunctive service systems as a challenge to, 317
        conditions that promote service integration and, 318–320
        reinforcing key elements of integrated service system and, 320–322
    impediments to, 313–317
    see also Community integration; Integration
Social network, impact of experimental program on, 155
Social and Prevocational Information Battery, 81
Social services
    federal programs and, 207–208
    total financial disincentives and, 208
Social systems
    effects of handicapped students' exclusion from, 179
    in systems-analytic approach to special education, 178
Special education
    contemporary, 179–180
        ecological perspective of, 180–181
        traditional perspectives of, 179–180
Staff training in response to behavior problems, 108
Standards of effective education and training, 16–17
Standards for Services for Mentally Retarded and Other Developmentally Disabled Individuals, 122
Stimulation program effectiveness in children with developmental disability, 140
Stimuli
    antecedent, learning process and, 32
    enhancing characteristics in antecedent events as, 46–50
    learning process and, 30–31

Strategies for school integration, 231–252
Strategy for producing least restrictive environments through early education, 129–158
Student, systems-analytic approach to transitional programming for handicapped, 177–193
Systems-analytic approach
    to competitive employment, 183–191
    to transitional programming for student with handicap(s), 177–193

TARC Assessment System, 82
Target behavior in unsuccessful learning, 62–65
Technology, instruction and, 18
Tests for Everyday Living, 82
Three-term contingency analysis
    agency response, as a term in, 281
    assumptions of, 280
    as conceptual device for community integration, 279–280
    consequences of agent actions, as a term in, 281–282
    levels of organization of, 283
    sites of client impact and, 283
    situation of, 280–281
Training
    of adaptive behaviors, 73–104
    standards of effective, 16–17
Transition
    bleak picture for mildly retarded persons, 161
    to independent living for retarded persons, 161–175
Transitional programming toward competitive employment, 177–193
True experimental designs, 134

Validity
    in assessment of adaptive behavior, 85–92
    checklist of threats to, in early education program evaluation, 133
    external, requirement in early education research, 155
    information from manuals of selected adaptive behavior scales, 88
    internal, requirements for early education, 155
Variable ratio reinforcers, 56
Vestibular stimulation as intervention method in cerebral palsy, 146
Vineland Adaptive Behavior Scales, 82
Vocational preparation and employment, 159–216

Weller-Strawser Scales of Adaptive Behavior, 82
Work effort, effect of structural disincentives on, 209–211